CANADIAN EDITION

VISUALIZING
THE LIFESPAN

VISUALIZING
THE LIFESPAN

CANADIAN EDITION

Jennifer L. Tanner, Ph.D.
Rutgers University

Amy Eva Alberts Warren, Ph.D.
Institute for Applied Research in Youth Development, Tufts University

Daniel Bellack, Ph.D.
Trident Technical College

Colleen MacQuarrie, Ph.D.
University of Prince Edward Island

WILEY

Credits

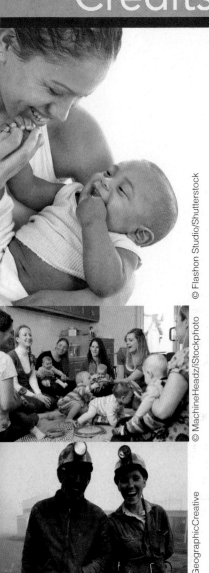

VICE PRESIDENT AND DIRECTOR: George Hoffman
DIRECTOR: Veronica Visentin
SENIOR MANAGER, LEARNING DESIGN AND CONTENT DEVELOPMENT: Karen Staudinger
PRODUCT DESIGNER: Wendy Ashenberg
DEVELOPMENTAL EDITOR: Gail Brown
EDITORIAL ASSISTANT: Ethan Lipson
SENIOR MARKETING MANAGER: Patty Maher
SENIOR CONTENT MANAGER: Dorothy Sinclair
PRODUCTION EDITOR: Meaghan MacDonald
MEDIA SPECIALIST: Jane Lee Kaddu
COVER DESIGNER: Joanna Vieira
PHOTO EDITOR: Alicia South
TYPESETTER: codeMantra
PRINTER: Quad/Graphics Versailles

TOP IMAGE: © Nisian Hughes/Getty Images, Inc.; Bottom images (from left to right): © Marc Romanelli/
Getty Images, Inc.; © Simon Punter/Getty Images, Inc.; © Alison Wright/Getty Images, Inc.;
© Jose Luis Pelaez Inc/Getty Images, Inc.

Library and Archives Canada Cataloguing in Publication

Tanner, Jennifer Lynn, author

Visualizing the lifespan / Jennifer L. Tanner, Ph.D. (Rutgers University), Amy Eva Alberts Warren, Ph.D. (Institute for Applied Research in Youth Development, Tufts University), Daniel Bellack, Ph.D. (Trident Technical College), Colleen MacQuarrie, Ph.D. (University of Prince Edward Island). – Canadian edition.

Includes bibliographical references and index. Issued in print and electronic formats.
ISBN 978-1-119-33539-9 (looseleaf).–ISBN 978-1-119-33544-3 (epub)

1. Developmental psychology–Textbooks. I. Warren, Amy Eva Alberts, author II. Bellack, Daniel, author III. MacQuarrie, Colleen, author IV. Title.

BF713.T35 2016   155   C2016-905806-9
                                                         C2016-905807-7

Printed in the United States of America
20 19 18 17 QVS 1 2 3 4

Why *Visualizing the Lifespan?*

Visualizing the Lifespan, Canadian Edition is a comprehensive textbook, covering the standard developmental content expected by college and university professors while incorporating contemporary theories, research, and critiques. In addition to offering students an array of photos, illustrations, graphs, and pedagogical features that deeply and broadly explore the lifespan, ***Visualizing the Lifespan***, Canadian Edition also: (1) considers the intricate interrelations among the various domains of development; (2) presents perspectives on development from around the world, emphasizing the essential connection between culture and development; (3) includes application of content to other fields including education, nursing, social work, and public policy; and (4) considers challenges that can arise over the course of the lifespan, ranging from psychopathologies to growing up in poverty.

A Visual Presentation

The lifespan texts currently available provide a good survey of the major concepts of development. Many of the leading texts today, however, are traditional, highly descriptive texts that are somewhat encyclopedic in length and style. They present the basics of lifespan development topic by topic in a standard pedagogical format. Although these texts are often handsomely illustrated, they do not fully exploit the importance of a visual presentation of lifespan concepts in relation to the visual learning style of today's students. Indeed, they typically use images for purely decorative purposes—as placeholders on which the eye can rest among dense text—rather than employing photos and illustrations as powerful explanatory tools.

Visualizing the Lifespan, Canadian Edition uses visual material to tell the absorbing story of development in an in-depth, clear manner, while relying less on straight text than do other textbooks. Lifespan development is a visually exciting topic and thus lends itself naturally to a visual-learning treatment. Photos are a core resource for this book, providing images that are not only excellent but also *new and different* from those seen repeatedly in standard texts. These images engage students and aid in their application and elaborative understanding of the material. In addition, because the people captured in the photos hail from around the world and throughout all aspects of society, ***Visualizing the Lifespan***, Canadian Edition presents a more diverse and realistic representation of our society than is found in many textbooks.

Combinations of photos, line art, computer-generated images, and numbered steps can convey processes faster and more powerfully than can thousands of words. Using this approach, ***Visualizing the Lifespan***, Canadian Edition conveys complex material with clarity. This book and its ancillaries take full advantage of the power of visual learning to convey the fascinating human story that is the lifespan.

A Succinct and Comprehensive Approach

Visualizing the Lifespan, Canadian Edition is designed to be comprehensive, accurate, up-to-date, and pedagogically robust, all while going a few steps further by enhancing student comprehension and retention through the use of explanatory and organizational visuals; by appealing not only to psychology majors but also to students from other fields such as education or health professions through the choice of content and perspectives of features; and by providing a uniquely contextualized approach that depicts diversity across gender, race, income level, ethnicity, and nationality. Importantly, it includes and examines Canadian research, data, and relevant examples to put material into context from a Canadian perspective. All of this information is packed into a text of 600 pages—brief compared with other textbooks.

A visual text is no less rigorous than a traditional text. For example, this text:

- offers a rich array of in-text visuals, learning tools, and active learning experiences that make developmental psychology concepts easier to understand for all students.

- discusses and visually depicts developmental research techniques while actively encouraging students to consider both the benefits and challenges inherent in conducting research across the lifespan.

- explains physical development using a proximodistal and cephalocaudal organization, following this organizational structure throughout the lifespan.

- evaluates the relationship between scientific theory, research, and practical application.

- emphasizes the need for critical thinking in assessing explanations of developmental concepts and the validity of research.

Accordingly, *Visualizing the Lifespan*, Canadian Edition aims to keep students turning the pages, engaging with the content, and remembering what they have learned, all while presenting the research rigor; current, relevant content; and breadth of coverage.

Organization

Visualizing the Lifespan, Canadian Edition is organized both chronologically and by domain. Across the length of the textbook, the lifespan is explained, described, and analyzed using a chronological structure. Within this structure, the chapters are divided into three basic domains: (1) physical; (2) cognitive; and (3) psychosocial. Throughout the presentation of the lifespan and across the domains, five themes appear:

1. Emphasis on how the domains are inextricably interrelated.

2. Focus on the relationship between culture and development through both observational comparison and examination of underlying processes.

3. Discussion of how critical thinking makes it easier to remember, understand, and apply information, combined with features that actively stimulate critical thought.

4. Presentation of how various normative and non-normative events affect individuals and their contexts.

5. Consideration of the role health professionals and educators play as forces of change and intervention throughout development.

Teaching and Learning Environment

WileyPlus Learning Space   WileyPLUS Learning Space

What is *WileyPLUS Learning Space*? It's a place where students can learn, collaborate, and grow. Through a personalized experience, students create their own study guide while they interact with course content and work on learning activities.

WileyPLUS Learning Space provides a dynamic e-textbook for your course—giving you tools to quickly organize learning activities, manage student collaboration, and customize your course so that you have full control over content as well as the amount of interactivity among students.

Instructors can:

- assign activities and add their own materials.

- guide students through what's important in the e-textbook by easily assigning specific content.

- set up and monitor collaborative learning groups.

- assess student engagement.

- benefit from a sophisticated set of reporting and diagnostic tools that give greater insight into class activity.

Learn more at www.wileypluslearningspace.com. If you have questions, please contact your Wiley representative.

Wiley's Real Development   REAL 🐒🚶🚶 Development

Human development does not take place in isolation. It happens in larger familial, interpersonal, and cultural contexts. Capturing these powerful dynamics in a lifespan development course was a challenge—until now.

Wiley's **Real Development** is an innovative multimedia product that uses authentic video capturing moments from four real families, allowing students to view the pivotal stages of development within larger interpersonal and cultural contexts. In each **Real Development** activity, created by Nicole Barnes, Ph.D. of Montclair State University and Christine J. Hatchard, Psy.D. of Monmouth University, students analyze and evaluate concepts—demonstrated in a variety of naturalistic and professional settings—through assessment activities grounded in real-world applications. Through this active engagement with visual media, pictures, and artifacts, students will gain a deeper understanding of developmental theories and concepts.

Real Development also includes a filterable topic-based library with dozens of selections by Shawn Guiling of Southeast Missouri State University and Nicole Reiber of Coastal Carolina Community College. It includes observational footage and interviews to help further illustrate key concepts central to the understanding of human development in today's world. The result is an authentic media experience that prompts students to apply and interact with the course material in ways that will be meaningful in their personal and professional lives.

Acknowledgements

Reviewers of *Visualizing the Lifespan*, Canadian Edition

Thank you to the following reviewers for their invaluable and insightful feedback:

Daniel Beliciu, *University of Windsor*
Philip Burge, *Humber College*
Tara Carpenter, *University of British Columbia*
Mary Close, *Canadore College*
Sue Davis-Mendelow, *Humber College*
Carlo Alberto Grandi, *University of Windsor*
Bob Heller, *Athabasca University*
Louise Jarrold, *Dawson College*
Nancy Ogden, *Mount Royal University*
Luigi Pasto, *John Abbott College*

Verna Raab, *Mount Royal University*
Saôde Savary, *University Canada West*
Joel St. Pierre, *Mohawk College*
Natalie Stelmach, *George Brown College*
Veronica Stinson, *Saint Mary's University*

Thank you also to the following for all their contributions to materials associated with this title:

Tara Carpenter, *University of British Columbia*: *Instructor's Manual*
Kim Robinson, *Saint Mary's University*: *PowerPoint Lecture Slides and Test Bank*

Special Thanks

I thank first the editors and staff from the Canadian Wiley offices, who made this project an enjoyable and informative adventure in publishing. I owe a debt of gratitude to my colleagues, peers, community, and family for providing me with the passion and the inspiration to create teachable moments and researchable questions. Growing up in a rural Canadian province grounded me in the recognition of how the individual is both shaped by and shapes their world. Adapting this text to a Canadian context at this time of strengthening voices from marginalized groups has been an honour, which I hope is reflected in this text. The work would not have been possible without the assistance of Emily Rutledge and Angele DesRoches, who devoted many hours of research to supply me with an endless stream of current Canadian scholarship for every chapter. It is my hope this text is able to reflect the diversity and the breadth of scholarship on development across the lifespan in a way that acknowledges Canadian identities and struggles within a global context. Finally, I wish to thank you, the reader, for your interest and your passion that you bring to this scholarship.

Colleen MacQuarrie
Charlottetown, PEI
October 2016

About the Authors

Jennifer L. Tanner, Ph.D. (The Pennsylvania State University, Human Development and Family Studies, 2001), was most recently a Visiting Assistant Research Professor at The Institute for Health, Health Care Policy and Aging Research at Rutgers University in New Brunswick, New Jersey.

Dr. Tanner is an applied developmental psychologist. Her research has been published in peer-reviewed journals, books, and handbooks and presented in professional forums. Dr. Tanner's research program takes a multidisciplinary approach to developing theory of normal, abnormal, and optimal development from adolescence to young adulthood, roughly ages 12 to 35. Complementing theory design, her empirical work takes advantage of cutting-edge methodologies to examine ways in which different pathways taken from adolescence through emerging and young adulthood are associated with diverse experiences and outcomes (such as mental health, health, and functioning). She is dedicated to translating her work and the work of others to inform programs, policies, and services that seek to enhance and optimize development and adjustment during the transition to adulthood.

Dr. Tanner balances her research pursuits with teaching, consulting, advising, and writing for a wide variety of audiences. Dr. Tanner is Co-Founder of the Society for Research on Emerging Adulthood, established in 2003. She serves on numerous editorial and governing boards and professional committees. She conducts workshops as trainings on mental health in emerging adulthood, and educates and consults as a Certified Family Life Educator (National Council on Family Relations) and for family court as a Certified Parent Coordinator.

Amy Eva Alberts Warren, Ph.D., is an applied developmental scientist and practitioner. Her work has been published in peer-reviewed journals, books, advanced textbooks, encyclopedias, and professional handbooks, and presented at academic conferences in the United States and abroad. She is co-editor of *Thriving and Spirituality Among Youth* (Wiley, 2012) and *Current Directions in Developmental Psychology* (Prentice Hall, 2004).

Dr. Warren is currently a Research Associate at the Institute for Applied Research in Youth Development, Tufts University. Her research and writing centres on the development of love and compassion toward the whole of humanity—what is known as great love-compassion—and, in particular, on the formative effects of childbirth and early child care practices on such development. Dr. Warren also supports families throughout the child-bearing years and beyond as an infant and child development specialist, Certified Postpartum Doula (DONA International), and Certified Lactation Counselor (Academy of Lactation Policy and Practice). She lives with her husband, daughter, and son near Boston, Massachusetts.

Daniel R. Bellack, Ph.D., has spent the majority of his 30+-year career in the classroom working with students. His doctorate is in cognitive developmental psychology from the University of Kentucky, and he earned his Bachelor's degree in psychology from the University of Florida. For the last 23 years he has been department chair and then coordinator of psychology courses for the Department of Behavioral and Social Sciences at Trident Technical College. He also serves as visiting professor of psychology at the Citadel Graduate College in Charleston, South Carolina. Prior to his current position, he was visiting professor at the College of Charleston, associate professor at Lexington Community College, and visiting professor at Berea College in Berea, Kentucky. His professional and academic focus has always been on facilitating the learning process in every aspect of education. He has been an invited presenter at the National Institute for the Teaching of Psychology as well as the Foundation for Critical Thinking. He is a member of the American Psychological Society, the South Carolina Psychological Association, and Fellow of the Foundation for Critical Thinking. His areas of research have focused on pedagogy in the classroom and the use and assessment of critical thinking learning activities. He has served as a consultant for several introductory and developmental psychology texts.

Courtesy D. Bellack

Colleen MacQuarrie, Ph.D., is Associate Professor and Graduate Faculty at the University of Prince Edward Island, where she is a dedicated teacher and researcher. Her program of research is directed toward better understanding the multi-faceted nature of health and wellness across the lifespan and within diverse community settings and contexts. Dr. MacQuarrie has been working with population health interventions to better understand how environments support individuals' and families' health. Her varied research examines a range of content areas, from individual to policy-level foci, including the examination of change processes for health behaviours as well as transitions following diagnosis of specific diseases or other transitional moments in a person's life/health experience. Her doctoral research with community members and their families living with Alzheimer's type dementia helped to advance clinical and applied initiatives for dementia care. Her current work with a local seniors care facility is examining various facets of impact for an intergenerational program on both seniors and children as well as staff members for the facilities. Active in anti-violence initiatives for more than 30 years, Dr. MacQuarrie conducts research with survivors of abuse across the lifespan that informs her passion and scholarship for social justice issues. Her research has examined the impacts of specific health policies concerning abortion access in PEI and the value and implications of using a reproductive justice lens to inform policy. Most recently she has been working with local First Nations communities on collaborative action projects to promote mental wellness. Thematically her research program can be conceptualized within a liberatory psychological framework as developmental health with a critical feminist/social justice lens.

Brief Contents

Contents

© MachineHeadz/iStockphoto

Francis Leroy, Biocosmos/Photo Researchers

Peter Dazeley/Getty Images

Jeff McIntoch/The Canadian Press

© Hero Images/Corbis

© Bob Thomas/iStockphoto

Joel Sartore/National Geographic Creative

© Michael Freeman/Corbis

© epa european pressphoto agency b.v./Alamy

BSIP/Science Source

© Blend Images/Shutterstock

© DragonImages/iStockphoto

Ariel Skelley/Blend Images/Corbis

© Dennis McDonald/ Photo Edit

Bill Bachmann/The Image Works

© microgen/iStockphoto

© The Star-Ledger/Ed Murray/TheImage Works

CANADIAN EDITION

VISUALIZING

THE LIFESPAN

Understanding Human Development: Theories and Approaches

For all 18 years of John's life, he has joined his family on the last Sunday in June for an annual reunion. This year he brought his sweetheart—a first! When he posted a photo of the two of them at his reunion on his Facebook page, he laughed at the teasing comments added by his relatives. John posted more reunion photos, including one of three generations—his grandparents, his sister, and her two daughters—and another photo of the young nieces and nephews he adores. Later, when he looked at photos from all 18 reunions, he couldn't decide if he was more impressed with how much he had stayed the same or how much he had changed.

It's not surprising that John is intrigued by his own development. As he approaches the transition to adulthood, it makes sense that he wants to know more about his past to make decisions about his future. We all do.

In the following pages, we start our exploration of how people grow and mature from conception through death. The concepts and theories presented in this chapter will lay the foundation for your own understanding of lifespan human development. As you progress through this text, stage by stage, chapter by chapter, be prepared to be in awe of the potential we are all born with to grow and change throughout our lives.

Hill Street Studios/Blend Images/Getty Images

CHAPTER OUTLINE

CHAPTER PLANNER ✔

❑ Study the picture and read the opening story.

❑ Scan the Learning Objectives in each section:
   p. 4 ❑   p. 12 ❑   p. 26 ❑

❑ Read the text and study all visuals. Answer any questions.

Analyze key features

❑ Process Diagram, p. 27

❑ What a Developmentalist Sees, p. 30

❑ Development InSight, p. 33

❑ Stop: Answer the Concept Checks before you go on:
   p. 11 ❑   p. 25 ❑   p. 35 ❑

End of chapter

❑ Review the Summary and Key Terms.

❑ Answer the Critical and Creative Thinking Questions.

❑ Answer *What is happening in this picture?*

❑ Complete the Self-Test and check your answers.

3

What Is Lifespan Human Development?

LEARNING OBJECTIVES

1. **Define** lifespan human development.
2. **Describe** how the developmental perspective has been used to study lifespan human development over the past century.
3. **Summarize** the key issues that concern lifespan developmentalists.

What is human development? • Figure 1.1

What exactly do we mean when we say we are studying human development?

▼ **a**. Sometimes when we discuss human development we are talking about growth—increase in size. For example, this illustration shows expected fetal growth throughout a normal pregnancy.

Fetal growth from 8–40 weeks

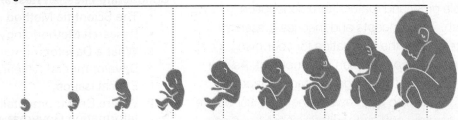

8 weeks	12 weeks	16 weeks	20 weeks	24 weeks	28 weeks	32 weeks	36 weeks	40 weeks
Embryo	Fetus							

▼ **b**. Human development may also be used to refer to maturation, the process of becoming increasingly complex. The human brain matures at a rapid pace throughout pregnancy and infancy.

Brain development

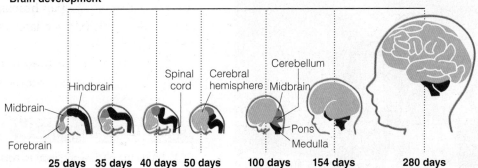

25 days   35 days   40 days   50 days   100 days   154 days   280 days

▼ **c**. Human development may also refer to the fulfillment or achievement of human potential. Indicators of human development include, but are not limited to, mental and physical health. Since 1990, the United Nations has ranked world nations from high to low on conditions known to promote human development. In 2013, Canada ranked eighth out of the 187 countries evaluated on the Human Development Index (United Nations Development Programme, 2014).

Components of the Human Development Index
The HDI—three dimensions and four indicators

Think Critically How is individual human development influenced by the context in which people live?

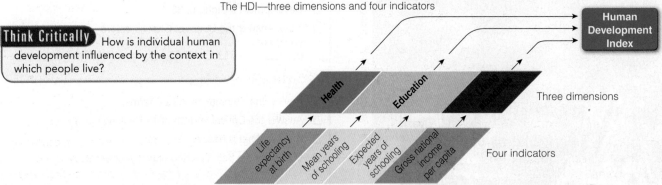

Source: HDRO (Human Development Report Office)

P retend for a moment that you are writing for the student newspaper and your assignment is to describe a new course: *Lifespan Human Development*. How would you explain the basic idea of the course? **Lifespan human development** is the growth and maturation of individuals from conception through death. **Developmental scholarship** is the professional field devoted to the study of lifespan human development (**Figure 1.1**).

Being the thorough school newspaper reporter you are, you recognize that students will want to know the benefits of taking a course in lifespan human development. As described in **Figure 1.2**, you would want to help students understand that **developmental scholars** advance our understanding of change and constancy in the **cognitive**, **physical**, and **socio-emotional domains of development** across the lifespan. **Applied developmental scholars** study the way human development shapes and is shaped by the contexts we live in—families, schools, communities, countries—to describe, explain, and optimize human development. Knowing that students are preparing for the school-to-work transition, you might help students understand that many of them are or aspire to be applied **developmentalists**— even though few jobs carry this title. For example, school teachers are applied developmentalists because they draw heavily on developmental scholarship to design and deliver effective practices. Last, you would certainly want to let students know that understanding lifespan human development will help them gain insight into their own lives and better understand others throughout their lives.

The Developmental Perspective

People have always been interested in understanding how and why people change. Centuries ago, the unknowns about human development were primarily the concern of the great philosophers. Based on their observations of young and old, philosophers debated opposing views about the underlying forces shaping the maturation of children into adults. By the 1800s, scientific study replaced debate as the primary method used to describe and explain human development. In 1859, Charles Darwin published *On the Origin of the Species*, in which he introduced the evolutionary perspective. To this day, Darwin's **evolutionary theory** continues to influence our understanding of lifespan human development, as we'll see later in this chapter.

By the turn of the twentieth century, scientists had adopted the **developmental perspective** to study the way infants and young children matured and gained new skills and abilities. These were the first studies that laid the foundation for what came to be known as the field of **developmental psychology**, also sometimes referred to as child psychology because the vast majority of developmental studies focused on the very young. That changed when G. Stanley Hall published *Adolescence* (1904), a two-volume set filling over 1,000 pages of findings from his studies of growth and maturation through the teen years. Hall's work triggered an explosion of research on adolescent

---

lifespan human development The growth and maturation of the human from conception through death.

developmental scholarship A multidisciplinary field of scholarship concerned with describing change and constancy in growth and maturation throughout the lifespan.

developmental scholar Someone specializing in the study of development in order to advance what is known about developmental processes and experiences.

cognitive domain of development The domain that includes the underlying mental functions, such as thinking, memory, attention, and perception.

physical domain of development The domain that includes the biological systems that make up a human being, including the nervous, skeletal, and muscular systems.

socio-emotional domain of development The domain that includes the social, cultural, and emotional components of development, such as the family, society, schools, and other social institutions.

applied developmental scholar Someone specializing in the study of how human development shapes and is shaped by the environment in order to describe, explain, and optimize human development.

developmentalist A scholar of development who uses their knowledge for research or applied purposes.

evolutionary theory The assumption that specific human traits and behaviours develop over the lifespan and are maintained throughout history because those characteristics are adaptive for survival.

developmental perspective The approach and basic set of assumptions that guide the scientific study of growth and maturation across the human lifespan.

developmental psychology The subfield of psychology concerned with studying and understanding human growth and maturation.

Developmental specialists at work • Figure 1.2

Professionals in a variety of settings use developmental scholarship to help, care for, manage, and educate people. Developmental approaches help us understand people of all ages. For example, developmental specialists provide us with useful information about the way older adults communicate their needs.

Think Critically Thinking about your future plans, how will understanding lifespan human development be relevant to your personal, career, and family goals?

Occupations with the most predicted job growth

Professions	% increase 2010–2020
Personal care aides	70.5
Home health aides	69.4
Medical secretaries	41.3
Medical assistants	30.9
Registered nurses	26.0
Physicians and surgeons	24.4
Receptionists and information clerks	23.7
Licensed practical and licensed vocational nurses	22.4

Fuse/Getty Images

development. Over the years, research on adolescent development has helped us gain insight into why teens behave and think the way they do and has helped us find new ways to support adolescent health and development. By the 1960s, adolescence had been clearly distinguished from childhood and had inspired a new branch of pediatrics, adolescent medicine (Alderman, Rieder, & Cohen, 2003). Such specialists conduct research focusing on the unique developmental aspects of adolescents; one such example is the way adolescent sleep patterns are different from childhood sleep patterns. Adolescent specialists apply developmental concepts to provide teens with health care tailored to meet their distinct needs; for example, helping parents and teens understand puberty, sexuality, substance use, and even body piercing.

During the last decades of the twentieth century, developmental specialists came to recognize the need for information about adult development and aging. Compared with our accumulated knowledge about development through adolescence, we know much less about the adult years. Despite knowing less, what we do know is rapidly expanding. In just the past few decades, exciting new findings in developmental research have demonstrated great potential and capacity for change after adolescence. These findings challenge the popular myth that aging is all downhill.

Most recently, developmental scholarship has turned attention toward transitions into adulthood. Dramatic global, social, and economic shifts have led to significant changes in the way young people become adults in the twenty-first century. Compared with their parents, for example, young Canadians generally spend more time in school, join the full-time labour market at a later age, remain residents of the family home for longer periods of time, and postpone significant events like childbearing (Clark, 2007). Developmentalists studying the late teens through the 20s are debating whether **emerging adulthood** represents a new and distinct **life stage**. Is emerging adulthood a process of ongoing

emerging adulthood The developmental stage between adolescence and adulthood during which individuals are searching for a sense of identity and maturity.

life stage A period of time with a beginning and an end within which distinct developmental changes occur.

culture The beliefs, customs, arts, and so on, of a particular society, group, and place.

individual change occurring in concert with environmental factors (Arnett, Kloep, Hendry, & Tanner, 2011) or is it a generational response to socio-economic changes (Moos, 2014)? Despite these conceptual differences, researchers generally agree that, in industrialized societies, it is taking young people longer to reach the independence and stability associated with adulthood. What these changes mean in the lives of young people is interpreted in a variety of ways. Some relate how these years are exciting and filled with possibilities (Arnett, 2000, 2004). Others portray the experiences as a stage of crisis (Robbins & Wilner, 2001). Others examine the diversity of how the opportunities and challenges associated with emerging adulthood are distributed throughout different cultures (Silva, 2013). These various ideas about what has happened to the transition to adulthood over the past few decades is a good reminder that we have much more to learn about the way lifespan human development is influenced by **culture** and history.

Get ready to learn much more about lifespan human development. We expect that you will be surprised by the many different ways developmental approaches inform and influence our everyday lives. Modern-day developmental inquiry has such widespread impact because it brings together many disciplines and professions, embraces the complexities of human development, and draws on many theoretical perspectives in response to the key issues of human development.

Key Issues of Human Development

If you were an observer at John's family reunion, what type of interactions might grab your attention? You might find yourself wondering, *why does John's grandmother look so happy compared with her anxious sister?* Or, you might wonder, *why are the children of John's uncle Roger all so obviously talented at music?* When seeking explanations for human development, five overarching issues guide developmental pursuits.

Nature and nurture When we hear about a shocking behaviour or an exceptional achievement, we often ask, *what made that person do that?* We might wonder whether people are genetically influenced to do what they do

or whether their behaviour is best predicted by their life experiences. Developmentalists sometimes use the word **nature** to imply that a behaviour can be explained by genetic and biological traits. On the other hand, if a behaviour is believed to be an outcome of **nurture** effects, then they would be saying the environment, such as the family or peer group, is causing behaviour.

nature The hereditary influences that are passed from the genes of biological parents to their offspring.

nurture The environmental influences that have an impact on development, including social, geographic, and economic factors.

Not too long ago, developmental psychologists were engaged in a nature *versus* nurture debate. Some believed that nature casts a stronger effect on development, whereas others argued that nurture is more influential. Today there is no longer a nature versus nurture debate because there is no escaping the fact that both influences are *always* involved in *all* behaviour—one influence never exists independent of the other. As you examine **Figure 1.3**, take a second to think about it. Can we develop if we have only nature or only nurture to influence how we become who we are?

When studying the influences of nature and nurture, developmental specialists no longer ask the question, *what causes people to develop this way, nature or nurture?* Instead, they now agree that all theories of development must reflect the fused influences of nature and nurture (e.g., Hebb, 1949; Anastasi, 1958). So now, developmental scientists study a new question, *how do nature and nurture interact to influence human development?*

This idea about the fusion of nature and nurture sets the stage for some other key themes of lifespan human development. The next one we look at is continuity and discontinuity.

developmental continuity A characteristic or feature of an individual that stays the same as a person matures through the lifespan.

Continuity and discontinuity

One issue at the forefront of developmental scholarship is the question of whether individual development is best explained by **developmental continuity** or **discontinuity**. In other words, *does a person change or stay the same over the lifespan?* Knowing the answer

developmental discontinuity A characteristic or feature of an individual that changes as a person matures through the lifespan.

The fused influences of nature and nurture • Figure 1.3

Look at these three images. Which photo most accurately captures sources that influence the expression of behaviour in this young child?

▼ **a.** Without genes, this little girl would not exist. Nature is an essential influence on our behaviour and development.

▼ **b.** But genes do not exist in a vacuum; they depend on the context for their expression. This little girl could not enjoy making bubbles without a context that supports it.

▼ **c.** So we can conclude that nature and nurture are always completely involved in all behaviour.

Courtesy Amy Warren

Courtesy Amy Warren

Courtesy Amy Warren

to this question helps us predict and explain human development (**Figure 1.4**).

Developmental stability and instability In some cases, developmental researchers are interested in knowing how individuals change or stay the same compared with others. This is often the case when the goal is to describe average change over a period of development and when we want to assess whether an individual is developing in expected ways. To do this, developmentalists study rank order across the developmental period of interest (**Figure 1.5**). If rank order remains the same, this demonstrates **developmental stability**—everyone is developing at the same rate. **Developmental instability**, in contrast, suggests that individuals are changing in different ways compared with one another.

developmental stability A person is developing at the same rate as their peers.

developmental instability A person is developing at a different rate than their peers.

Normative and non-normative events Developmental scholars recognize the influence of both normative and non-normative events on individual development across the lifespan. **Normative events** are those that happen to most of the people in a population. Some normative events happen during a particular period of life, such as graduating from high school at age 17 or 18, getting married in one's 20s or 30s, and often retiring in one's 60s or 70s. Developmental scientists call these incidents *normative age-graded events*. Events can also occur that affect everyone in a particular generation, such as the Great Depression in the 1930s, the Montreal Massacre in 1989, or more recently the Occupy movement's reactions to global economic and cultural shifts, and the Syrian refugee crisis. Developmental scientists call such occurrences *normative history-graded events* (Fisher, Lerner, & Casas, 2004).

Incidents that are experienced by relatively few people, such as the loss of a limb, are considered **non-normative events**

normative event An incident that matches the sequential and historical events shared by the majority of people.

non-normative event An incident that does not happen to everyone or that happens at a different time than typically experienced by others.

Developmental continuity and discontinuity • Figure 1.4 _____

Young children often participate in activities their parents expect them to enjoy. When children go to school, their worlds expand. They have many new experiences and learn about new activities from friends.

▼ **a.** This photo shows a little girl dancing when she was 3 years old.

Courtesy Jennifer Tanner

▼ **b.** Here she is at 8 after she had been dancing for 5 years. What does the developmental continuity in her love of dance tell us? Perhaps dance helps her regulate her body. Or perhaps her consistent preference for this activity reflects a need for intense, demanding experiences. This example demonstrates how studies of developmental continuity and discontinuity can help us learn more about how and why people change across the lifespan.

Courtesy Jennifer Tanner

Think Critically If you were asked to replace the second photograph in this example to illustrate developmental discontinuity, what would the little girl be doing?

(Fisher et al., 2004). Examples of both normative and non-normative events can be seen in **Figure 1.6**. It is important to understand that non-normative events can be positive, such as winning the lottery. Non-normative events can also be negative: think poverty, disease, disability, maltreatment, and traumatic stress. But regardless of the emotions they elicit, they typically have a significant impact on the course of one's development.

gender A social construction of expectations that a given culture associates with a person's biological sex.

race A way of categorizing humans that typically focuses on physical traits.

Socio-cultural variation Development does not occur in a bubble. Socio-cultural factors, including **gender**, **race**, **ethnicity**, **socio-economic status (SES)**, and culture, inevitably affect the way we see ourselves and the ways we interact with the world.

Socio-cultural variables have been found to have long-lasting impacts on who we are, what we believe, and why we do what we do. Looking back on our opening story, think about how John's life might be different if John were a girl, for example, or, if most of his family lived in another country and only he, his parents, and his siblings had immigrated to Canada. Because each socio-cultural factor affects development in unique ways at various points in the lifespan, we will be returning to these diversity variables throughout the text (Eshun & Gurung, 2009). We will especially consider culture.

Culture is the beliefs, values, and social practices that influence

ethnicity A specific set of physical, cultural, regional, or national characteristics that identifies and differentiates one person or group from others.

socio-economic status (SES) The combination of a person's education, occupation, and income.

Developmental stability and instability • Figure 1.5

First-time parents Olga and Christa couldn't stop wondering why their son remained the smallest in his playgroup. Why didn't he ever catch up? The pediatrician helped them understand. Staying at the 25th percentile on his growth chart, he was growing at the same rate as his peers.

WHO GROWTH CHARTS FOR CANADA

👤 BOYS

2 TO 19 YEARS: BOYS
Height-for-age and Weight-for-age percentiles

NAME: _____
DOB: _____ RECORD# _____

AGE (YEARS)

MOTHER'S HEIGHT _____
FATHER'S HEIGHT _____

DATE	AGE	HEIGHT	WEEIGHT	COMMENTS

HEIGHT

WEIGHT

BOYS

97
85
50
15
3

WHO recommends BMI as the best measure after age 10 due to variable age of puberty
Tracking weight alone is not advised.

Think Critically If Olga and Christa had seen developmental instability on Christopher's growth chart, what might that have looked like?

SOURCE: The main chart is based on World Health Organization (WHO) Child Growth Standards (2005) and WHO Reference (2007) adapted for Canada by Canadian Paediatric Society, Canadian Paediatric Endocrine Group (CPEG), College of Family Physicians of Canada, Community Health Nurses of Canada and Dietitians of Canada. The weight-for-age 10 to 19 years section was developed by CPEG based on data from the US National Center for Health Statistics using the same procedures as the WHO growth charts.
©Dietitians of Canada, 2014. Chart may be reproduces in its entirety (i.e., no changes) for non-commercial purposes only. www.whogrowthcharts.ca

Normative and non-normative events • Figure 1.6

Normative and non-normative events like those shown here occur throughout our lifespans.

a. Normative events
First days of school are almost universal rites of passage during childhood.

Pamela Moore/iStockphoto.com

b. Non-normative events
Being removed from one's home due to a mortgage foreclosure is a rare event.

Erik Lesser/ZUMA Press/Corbis

Ask Yourself

1. If the child in photo **a** was a child actress playing the role of a Grade 3 student, this child getting an acting contract would be an example of a _____ event.
2. If photo **b** depicted the cleaning of the family garage, this would be an example of a _____ event.

what we do, yet operate below our level of awareness. We cannot separate culture from who we are and why we do what we do. Culture influences what we eat, how we dress, how we speak, and what we think. Because culture and development are inextricably linked, our study of human development would be too narrow if we did not consider the artifacts, customs, beliefs, and points of view from cultures other than our own (Greenfield, 2002). A key consideration in Canada is not only the diverse cultural experiences of First Nations peoples that enrich their lifespan development but also the context of national policies and practices designed to eradicate Aboriginal cultures. This was recently tragically outlined in the Truth and Reconciliation Commission of Canada findings, released in 2015 (Truth and Reconciliation Commission of Canada, 2015). Such issues of culture and discrimination have serious developmental implications across the lifespan and they will be considered throughout this text.

As culture evolves, so too does our understanding of the way human lives develop across the lifespan. In the next section, you will learn how the developmental lens has evolved to reflect cultural change.

CONCEPT CHECK   STOP

1. **What** is lifespan human development?
2. **How** has the developmental perspective been used over the past century to guide the study of lifespan human development?
3. **What** are the five key issues of lifespan human development?

Theoretical Perspectives on Development

LEARNING OBJECTIVES

1. **State** the assumptions of psychodynamic theories.
2. **Explain** key mechanisms described in theories of cognitive development.
3. **Describe** how developmental metatheories are different from developmental theories.

The developmental perspective never wavers—the focus is always on change. Over the years, however, the developmental perspective has transformed to reflect new knowledge about human development. Advances in the way we understand development across the lifespan occur when new theories are introduced and when scientific studies reveal new findings about growth and maturation.

Theoretical Approaches

eclectic Drawing on a broad range of ideas and perspectives from various sources.

As we move through this section, you will learn about various theoretical approaches that have, each at its own point in history, contributed elements to an increasingly **eclectic**, twenty-first-century approach to developmental scholarship. We'll see that the variety of approaches has led scholars to suggest that what is and is not *development* is determined by the developmental scientist's lens.

As you read about the major theories that have contributed to the developmental perspective, think critically and actively evaluate them. Just because they are considered classics in the field does not mean that they are immune to serious critiques. You may also find yourself wanting to take some information from one theory, combine it with information in another theory, and create some kind of hybrid. That's great; in fact, many developmental scholars do exactly that when they attempt to explain complex behaviours and the way they change over the lifespan. If we think of the various theories of development as tools in a toolkit, each may be one more wrench that helps us unpack the complexities of human development.

Psychodynamic Perspectives

The psychodynamic perspective stresses the significance of early life experiences in shaping and determining adult personality and behaviour. For this reason, the psychodynamic perspective is inherently developmental. There are now hundreds of psychodynamic theories. Sigmund Freud and his student Erik Erikson introduced the first psychodynamic theories and the idea that human growth and maturation through the lifespan are organized and driven by progression through a set of universal, developmental stages.

Sigmund Freud's psychoanalytic theory Most people have heard of Sigmund Freud. And, although many would argue that Freud's ideas have been discredited and are irrelevant in the twenty-first century, others would counter that it would be impossible to completely disentangle Freudian theory from our most current ideas about lifespan human development. Think about that last argument you had with your friend, your partner, or your parent. *Why did you get so angry? So frustrated?* If you don't know, maybe you're not fully aware of the reasons you got so mad. Developmentalists who have integrated psychodynamic theory into their eclectic approach would wonder what childhood experiences influence the expression of anger in adulthood.

Freud believed that we are unaware of a good deal of the interactions among the different parts of our personalities. Most of the mind is **unconscious**, a hidden reservoir of conflicts, urges, and longings that don't usually reach our **conscious** awareness (Freud, 1915). One of the main jobs of our unconscious is to reduce anxiety, which results from conflicts among the desires of different parts of our personalities and the demands of our environments. One key source of anxiety that was especially prominent during the Victorian era when Freud developed his theory is the clash between the desires of our inborn **libido** (a person's desire for life energy translated as sexual activity) and the rules and values of society.

Freudian theory is inherently developmental. Freud not only emphasized the significance of early life experiences, but also believed these early experiences determined adult personality, with very little potential

id One of three components of the mind according to Freud; the id represents instincts.

ego One of three components of the mind according to Freud; the ego is the part of the mind that deals with reality and mediates between the id instincts and superego morals.

superego One of three components of the mind according to Freud; the superego represents the internalized rules for socially appropriate behaviour.

psychoanalysis A treatment method introduced by Sigmund Freud to relieve mental distress by freeing conflicts from the unconscious, bringing them into conscious awareness so they can be resolved.

stage theory A theory that rests on the assumption that development is discontinuous, with new features of development emerging at each distinct stage.

psychosexual development A Freudian theory in which maturation of personality and sexuality occur as children experience the concentration of libidinal energy from specific body areas.

for developmental change in adulthood. According to Freud, parent–child relationships influence early personality organization. These relational experiences influence the development of all the components of the mind— the **id**, **ego**, **superego**—and the way personality develops through the teen years (Freud, 1949). **Figure 1.7** shows how the three components of the mind are organized and visually explains how early experiences remain powerfully influential, albeit out of our awareness. When development goes awry, Freud (1974) proposed **psychoanalysis** as a technique for helping adults resolve their unresolved childhood conflicts.

Freud proposed the first **stage theory** of human development. **Figure 1.8** illustrates Freud's theory of **psychosexual development**, the process through which maturation of personality and sexuality co-occur. Psychosexual maturation, according to Freud, involves the transfer of **libidinal energy** from one part of the body to another through five stages until an individual reaches full maturation. At each life stage, the individual makes progress in ability to function more independently until reaching full sexual maturity, at which point the individual is able to care for self, reproduce and have children, and care for dependents.

As you may have come to conclude, Freud had a lot to say about human development. When introduced over a century ago, his work influenced the thinking of the general public and professionals and would do so for decades to come. Freud also made a

significant impact on the field through his training of many students and emerging professionals. One of his students, Erik Erikson, made well-known adaptations to Freud's ideas and ways of thinking about development and also made significant contributions of his own to further our understanding of lifespan human development.

libidinal energy The vital energy that brings life through sexual behaviour.

Erik Erikson's psychosocial theory Erik Erikson, a proponent of **neo-Freudian theory**, rejected Freud's strong emphasis on biology, retained Freud's view of life stages, and promoted a conceptual view of development as an outcome of the interaction between an individual's biological maturation and the social context in which a person develops. Erikson also retained the Freudian notion that later development builds on early development. Given that Erikson rejected the idea that human development is driven purely by biology, it may not be surprising that he did not view sexual

neo-Freudian theory A theory that has been influenced by Freud's work but extends and critiques his ideas.

The id, ego, and superego • Figure 1.7

The personality develops in three phases. The newborn is all id, born to survive. The ego develops around age 3, in response to the child learning to control the id by requesting rather than demanding. Around 6, the superego uses morals of society to control the id when the ego fails.

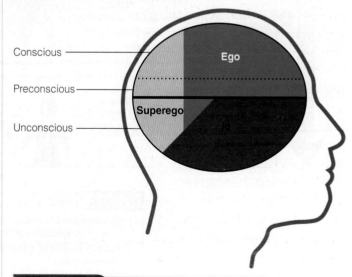

Think Critically Why did you come to class today? How might your id, ego, or superego have influenced your thoughts and behaviours?

Freud's five psychosexual stages of development • Figure 1.8

Freud identified five developmental stages, each named after the part of the body where libidinal energy concentrates throughout development (Freud, 1949). As a result of mastering biological maturation and learning to behave according to society's rules, Freud theorized that a different part of our personality arises during each stage.

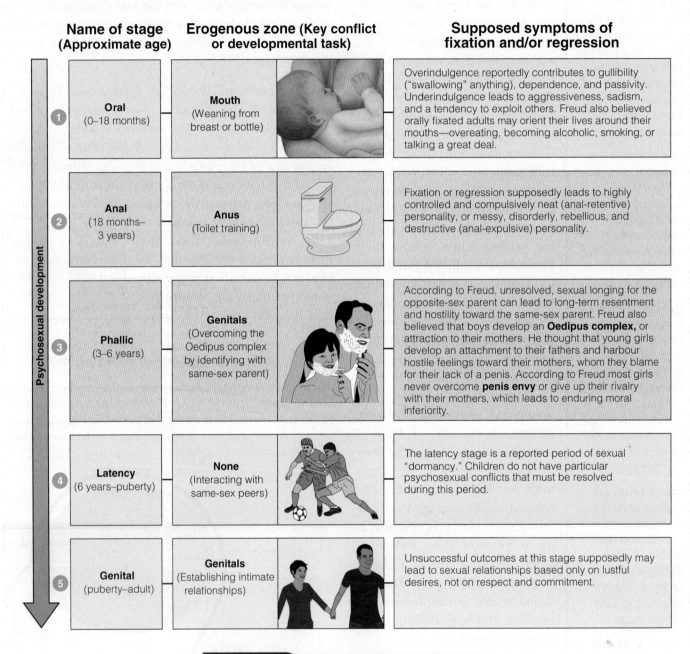

Name of stage (Approximate age)	Erogenous zone (Key conflict or developmental task)		Supposed symptoms of fixation and/or regression
1 Oral (0–18 months)	Mouth (Weaning from breast or bottle)		Overindulgence reportedly contributes to gullibility ("swallowing" anything), dependence, and passivity. Underindulgence leads to aggressiveness, sadism, and a tendency to exploit others. Freud also believed orally fixated adults may orient their lives around their mouths—overeating, becoming alcoholic, smoking, or talking a great deal.
2 Anal (18 months–3 years)	Anus (Toilet training)		Fixation or regression supposedly leads to highly controlled and compulsively neat (anal-retentive) personality, or messy, disorderly, rebellious, and destructive (anal-expulsive) personality.
3 Phallic (3–6 years)	Genitals (Overcoming the Oedipus complex by identifying with same-sex parent)		According to Freud, unresolved, sexual longing for the opposite-sex parent can lead to long-term resentment and hostility toward the same-sex parent. Freud also believed that boys develop an **Oedipus complex,** or attraction to their mothers. He thought that young girls develop an attachment to their fathers and harbour hostile feelings toward their mothers, whom they blame for their lack of a penis. According to Freud most girls never overcome **penis envy** or give up their rivalry with their mothers, which leads to enduring moral inferiority.
4 Latency (6 years–puberty)	None (Interacting with same-sex peers)		The latency stage is a reported period of sexual "dormancy." Children do not have particular psychosexual conflicts that must be resolved during this period.
5 Genital (puberty–adult)	Genitals (Establishing intimate relationships)		Unsuccessful outcomes at this stage supposedly may lead to sexual relationships based only on lustful desires, not on respect and commitment.

Psychosexual development

Think Critically 1. What does Freud's model of psychosexual development imply about the age at which an individual reaches full maturity?
2. Does this model make sense in today's world? Why or why not?

ego identity The goal of development in Erikson's psychosocial theory where a sense of oneself as a distinct and continuous entity is achieved.

maturity as the final stage of development. Rather, as illustrated in **Figure 1.9**, Erikson outlined eight stages of development from birth through death (Erikson, 1950). The goal of development, according to Erikson, is to establish what is known as **ego identity**, the sense of oneself as a distinct, continuous entity. Resolution of each stage-specific task makes a distinct contribution to an integrated, coherent sense of self. We will have more to say about each of these stages as we move throughout the text.

Cognitive Perspectives

As we've learned, psychodynamic theories provide us with a framework for understanding personality development across the lifespan. Cognitive theories focus on how our thinking, or *cognition*, develops. Two major theorists have influenced our understanding of the development of thought: Jean Piaget and Lev Vygotsky. Both theorists focused primarily on patterns of cognitive development in childhood. Although each stresses different underlying processes, Piaget and Vygotsky both emphasized the impact that children have on their own development.

Jean Piaget's theory of cognitive development

Few psychologists have had as great an impact on understanding the minds of children as Jean Piaget. In his work, published in numerous books and scientific articles, he presents details on concepts such as logic, morality, language, play, perception, and the continuous evolution of the human desire for knowledge (Gruber & Vonèche, 1977).

Piaget assumed that our thinking develops in ways that meet the demands of our environment, in order to

Erikson's psychosocial stage theory • Figure 1.9

According to Erikson, at each stage, we face a new challenge that requires us to balance and integrate the demands of biology and society. Meeting the challenge of each stage results in the gain of a specific strength that contributes to overall psychosocial development. Failure to resolve a challenge at a particular stage doesn't mean that a person will never gain that skill, but it is more difficult to gain a skill in later stages.

Think Critically 1. If you were designing an after-school program for high school students struggling to meet the developmental challenges of their life stage, what "developmental task" would be the goal of your program?
2. Who should you involve in the group? Their parents? Peers?
3. What would you hope the students would develop?

Stage	Age	Psychosocial issue	Relational focus	Central question How can I...	Associated virtue
Infancy	0–1	TRUST— mistrust	Mother and other caregiver(s)	Be secure?	Hope: Trust and optimism
Early childhood	2–3	AUTONOMY— doubt, shame	Parents	Be independent?	Will: Use & exercise freedom and self-restraint
Childhood (play)	4–6	INITIATIVE— guilt	Basic family	Be powerful?	Purpose and direction: Ability to initiate own activities; pursue goals
Childhood (school)	7–12	INDUSTRY— inferiority	Neighbourhood; school	Be good?	Competence in intellectual, social, and physical skills
Adolescence	13–19	IDENTITY— role confusion	Peer groups	Fit into the adult world? Who am I?	Fidelity and an integrated image of oneself as a unique person
Young adulthood	19–35	INTIMACY— isolation	Partners in friendship; the other	Love?	Love: Mutuality, finding and losing self in the other; career commitments
Adulthood	35–55	GENERATIVITY— stagnation	Divided labour and shared household	Fashion a "gift"?	Care: Solicitude, guidance, and teaching a new generation
Maturity	55+	EGO INTEGRITY— despair	"Humankind"	Receive a "gift"?	Wisdom: Sense of fulfillment and satisfaction with one's life

schema An organized pattern of thinking that guides our experience in the world.

equilibrium A state of cognitive balance.

assimilation A process to expand a schema by adding information.

accommodation A process to create a new schema in response to information.

improve our chances of surviving in that particular environment (Piaget, 1952). One of Piaget's most significant contributions was his understanding of the way our thoughts influence our behaviour. He introduced the term **schema** to describe the way a person's perception develops, and in turn, how that perception shapes their interpretations and life experiences. Piaget suggested that we strive for a state of cognitive balance, or **equilibrium**, in which our schemas meet the needs of our environments. Sometimes, however, we find that our schemas don't match our environments, and we are in an uncomfortable cognitive state of disequilibrium. When that happens, we can change schemas through the processes of **assimilation**, adding new information to existing schemas, and **accommodation**, creating new schemas.

Consider this example of a child's development of a schema. Two-year-old Henry has a schema for *dog* because he has lived with his family's black and white pet dog, Jones, since birth. When he goes to a farm for the first time, Henry sees an animal he has never seen before—a cow. The cow is black and white and covered in fur, just like Jones. Because Henry has never seen a cow, he uses his schema for "black and white animal" and he attempts to assimilate this experience with others he has had in the past. He points his finger at the cow and says, "Jones!" His parents tell Henry, "No, that is not Jones. That is a cow, not a dog. See how big she is? See her swishing tail? Listen to the cow say, 'Moo.'" Henry's parents are helping him develop a new schema for cow. Henry must now change his schema for animals to accommodate a new category, *cow*.

Piaget studied children in a unique way. He took special interest in understanding the *wrong* answers children gave on logical thinking tests. Children's wrong answers provided Piaget with insight into the cognitive abilities that they had not yet developed. This led him to outline a four-stage theory of cognitive development, described in **Table 1.1**. Piaget's model of intellectual development from infancy through adulthood assumes that cognitive development evolves from a simple foundation to increasing complexity, and that early development affects later development. As a stage theory, it also assumes that we all move through the same stages, in the same order.

Piaget based his theory on the idea that we all construct our own knowledge through our interactions with the world around us. Thus, he argued, children must be allowed to explore their environments (Piaget, 1951, 1952), an idea that has strongly influenced early childhood education in Canada. Similarly, Russian developmental psychologist Lev Vygotsky's theory of cognitive development influenced the Russian educational system. Later, it significantly influenced Western psychology and education as well (Newman & Holzman, 1997).

Lev Vygotsky's theory of cognitive development

Unlike Piaget, Vygotsky emphasized the role of sociocultural interactions in his theory of cognitive development. He believed that children's interactions with others are the catalysts of development. In contrast to Piaget, who believed all of us progress through the same stages of development in much the same order, Vygotsky viewed a child's unique social world as the main influence on cognitive change. He believed that a child's historical, political, and societal contexts, as well as the immediate influences of family and friends, shape the development of a child's thinking.

According to Vygotsky, of particular importance to children's cognitive development are particular types of interactions between a child and a more experienced person, such as a parent, teacher, or older child. In these interactions, the more experienced person guides a child's learning through activities that are difficult for the child to learn, but not so difficult that the child is overwhelmed with frustration. In such **guided participation** (Rogoff, 2003), a "teacher" not only instructs, but also shares in the learning process. For optimal cognitive change, the teacher **scaffolds** the student's learning by encouraging the learner to work in his or her **zone of proximal development (ZPD)** (del Río & Álvarez, 2007). As learners progress,

guided participation A process in which a more experienced teacher becomes an interactive guide, helping a younger or less experienced person do tasks that they could not complete independently.

scaffold The process of assisting a less experienced individual through complex tasks by providing supports, which may be verbal or physical.

zone of proximal development (ZPD) Vygotsky's term for the range of tasks that a person cannot accomplish independently but that can be done with the assistance of a person with more experience or more advanced cognitive ability.

Piaget's four stages of cognitive development   Table 1.1

Sensorimotor stage (birth to age 2)

Limits
- Beginning of stage lacks object permanence (understanding that things continue to exist even when not seen, heard, or felt)

Abilities
- Uses senses and motor skills to explore and develop cognitively

Example
- Children at this stage like to play with their food

The Copyright Group/SuperStock

Preoperational stage (ages 2 to 7)

Limits
- Cannot perform "operations" (lacks reversibility)
- Intuitive thinking versus logical reasoning
- Egocentric thinking (inability to consider another's point of view)
- Animistic thinking (believing all things are living)

Abilities
- Has significant language and thinks symbolically

Example
- Children at this stage often believe the moon follows them

Igor Demchenkov/iStockphoto

Concrete operational stage (ages 7 to 11)

Limits
- Cannot think abstractly and hypothetically
- Thinking tied to concrete, tangible objects and events

Abilities
- Can perform "operations" on concrete objects
- Understands conservation (realizing that changes in shape or appearance can be reversed)
- Less egocentric
- Can think logically about concrete objects and events

Example
- Children at this stage begin to question the existence of Santa

Hill Street Studios/Blend Images/Getty Images

Formal operational stage (age 11 and over)

Limits
- Adolescent egocentrism at the beginning of this stage, with related problems of the personal fable and imaginary audience

Abilities
- Can think abstractly and hypothetically

Example
- Children at this stage show great concern for physical appearance

Roy Melnychuk/Taxi/Getty Images

Carpenter, S., & Huffman, K. (2012). *Visualizing psychology* (3rd ed). Hoboken, NJ: John Wiley & Sons.

teachers use new strategies, gradually removing their scaffolding of tasks the learner can now do alone.

This won't be the last time you hear about the ZPD and Vygotsky. You will learn much more about these ideas throughout the chapters on development through childhood. Now we turn our attention to a non-stage theory of cognitive development—information-processing theory.

Information-processing theory The information-processing view of cognitive development takes a quantitative approach, focusing on gradual, cumulative changes instead of stages. It seeks to describe various types of cognitive changes that occur throughout childhood, including development of memory, attention, and language. Information-processing theorists compare the mind's functioning to the functioning of a computer, as depicted in **Figure 1.10** (Siegler, 2009).

Information-processing theorists believe that our various cognitive processes interact and influence one another. For example, increases in memory, or storage, abilities may be related to other cognitive skills, such as language use.

Space does not permit a full discussion of the information-processing model in this chapter, but we will return to it throughout the text when we discuss cognitive development at various stages through the lifespan. For now we turn our attention away from the mind and consider what can be readily observed: behaviour.

Behavioural Perspectives and Social Learning

Beginning early in the twentieth century, many psychologists believed that the inner workings of the mind were ambiguous and too difficult to measure (Zuriff, 1985). For this reason, behaviourism and its focus on studying readily observable and quantifiable behaviours gained popularity.

Classical conditioning Early in the twentieth century, Russian physiologist Ivan Pavlov was studying the digestive systems of dogs. He noticed that the dogs in his studies would start to salivate near feeding times, but before food was placed in their cages. Pavlov concluded that the dogs had associated the people who delivered the food with the food itself. When these individuals appeared, the dogs would salivate, even if no food was in sight. Pavlov's work earned him the 1904 Nobel Prize and introduced

Information-processing theory • Figure 1.10 ⎯⎯⎯⎯⎯⎯⎯⎯⎯⎯⎯⎯⎯⎯⎯⎯⎯⎯⎯⎯⎯⎯⎯⎯⎯

Information-processing theorists use the computer as a metaphor for human cognition.

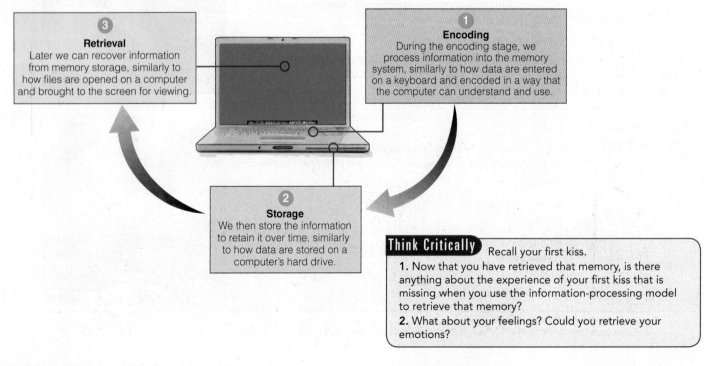

3 Retrieval
Later we can recover information from memory storage, similarly to how files are opened on a computer and brought to the screen for viewing.

1 Encoding
During the encoding stage, we process information into the memory system, similarly to how data are entered on a keyboard and encoded in a way that the computer can understand and use.

2 Storage
We then store the information to retain it over time, similarly to how data are stored on a computer's hard drive.

Think Critically Recall your first kiss.
1. Now that you have retrieved that memory, is there anything about the experience of your first kiss that is missing when you use the information-processing model to retrieve that memory?
2. What about your feelings? Could you retrieve your emotions?

classical conditioning A type of learning that occurs when an original stimulus acquires a capacity to evoke a response that was originally evoked by a different stimulus.

unconditioned stimulus (US) Something that reliably produces a naturally occurring reaction.

unconditioned response (UR) A reaction that is reliably produced by an unconditioned stimulus.

the world to the idea of **classical conditioning** (Pavlov, 1927).

Classical conditioning takes advantage of naturally occurring relationships between a stimulus and a response. For example, dogs salivate when they smell food. The food is called an **unconditioned stimulus (US)** because it triggers an unlearned response, and salivating to the food is an **unconditioned response (UR)** because it is an instinctive response. To demonstrate classical conditioning with dogs, Pavlov paired food with a ringing bell, which was a **neutral stimulus (NS)** that elicited no response initially. The result: he produced an association between the bell and the food. After many pairings of the bell with the food, the dogs salivated in response to the bell alone. The bell was no longer a neutral stimulus; it had become a **conditioned stimulus (CS)**. Salivating in response to the bell is a **conditioned response (CR)**.

Early in the twentieth century, behaviourist John Watson (1878–1958) studied how classical conditioning

could be applied to humans. In a classic study, Watson and Rosalie Rayner (1920) worked with an 11-month-old boy known as Little Albert. In a series of experiments, they changed his response to a white lab rat (**Figure 1.11**). Although studies such as this help us understand how we can become classically conditioned, we'll learn later in this chapter that Watson and Rayner's experiments with Little Albert would not be considered ethically acceptable today.

Two key concepts related to the classical conditioning process are *generalization* and *discrimination*. Generalization occurs when the same response is elicited by a variety of different stimuli. For example, you generalize when you answer your mobile phone regardless of which ring tone it sounds. Discrimination is the opposite of generalization; it occurs when different stimuli elicit different responses (Brandon, Vogel, & Wagner, 2000). For example, when you stop at a red light and go at a green light, you are discriminating between the two. Can you think of other examples of generalization and discrimination in your everyday life?

neutral stimulus (NS) A stimulus that does not elicit a natural reaction.

conditioned stimulus (CS) A previously neutral stimulus that reliably produces a response after conditioning.

conditioned response (CR) A response that is reliably produced by a conditioned stimulus.

Increasing or decreasing behaviours • Figure 1.11

At first Albert was fond of the rat (a neutral stimulus/NS) and played with him each day. Watson then began making a loud, frightening sound (an unconditioned stimulus/US) whenever Albert saw the rat. Soon Albert associated the loud sound with the rat, which had become a conditioned stimulus (CS), and was afraid of the rat (a conditioned response/CR) even when no sound was present.

Think Critically Describe how an unhealthy habit such as smoking may be the result of classical conditioning.

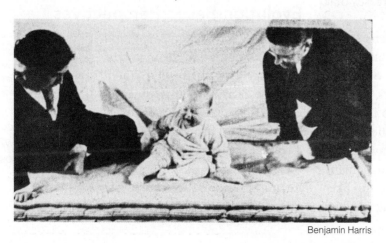

Benjamin Harris

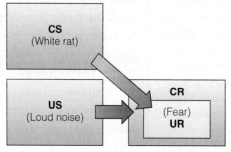

CS (White rat)

US (Loud noise)

CR (Fear) UR

Operant conditioning In addition to conducting the classic study with Little Albert, Watson founded a school of thought called **behaviourism**. This perspective maintains that science should study *only* observable behaviours. Behaviourists believe, for example, that the unconscious is not an appropriate subject of scientific study (Hergenhahn, 2005; Watson, 1930). An important contribution of behaviourism is the concept of **operant conditioning**, originally developed by B. F. Skinner, a prominent behaviourist.

Unlike classical conditioning, which happens passively, operant conditioning focuses on what happens after organisms perform actions in their environments. Skinner built upon E. L. Thorndike's **law of effect**. This law states that behaviour that is followed by a positive outcome tends to be repeated, whereas behaviour that is followed by a negative outcome tends not to be repeated (Thorndike, 1927). For example, if a behaviour such as hand-raising in class is *reinforced* with attention or high grades, a student is more likely to raise his or her hand in the future. On the other hand, if a behaviour such as hitting a classmate is punished, a student should be *less* likely to hit a classmate again. There are both negative and positive forms of reinforcement and punishment (Skinner, 1963). In operant conditioning, the term *positive* means that something is added to a situation, and *negative* implies that something is withheld or taken away. In each case, reinforcement always increases the likelihood of a behaviour reoccurring and punishment always decreases that likelihood.

Although punishment theoretically decreases the likelihood that a behaviour will occur, in actuality it tends to work only for behaviours that occur in the same context and/or when the person doing the punishing is present. In simpler terms, punishment probably won't decrease the likelihood that you will engage in a behaviour when you think you will not be caught. Thus, psychologists largely agree that it is more effective to *extinguish* unwanted behaviours by ignoring them than to use punishment (Nemeroff & Karoly, 1991). For example, a teacher might not respond when a student fidgets in his or her seat, but might give the student a sticker or other small reward when the student is sitting still.

Operant conditioning explains simple associations between a cause and behaviour, but one drawback is that this concept over-focuses on the individual and neglects the influence the social world has on learning. The final behavioural perspective we will discuss—social learning theory—makes social context and the observation of others its main focus.

Social learning Social learning results from observation and imitation. From this perspective, all the rules of learning through reinforcement and punishment are applied. In addition, behavioural change can result from observing the reinforcement and punishment of another person rather than receiving consequences oneself. For example, if Amira sees her friend, Jessica, receive a reward for sharing her candy with a friend, the probability of Amira's sharing her own candy increases. The most notable proponent of this perspective is Canadian-born Albert Bandura, who conducted a series of unique studies demonstrating the power of social learning through the media (Bandura, 1965; Paignon, Desrichard, & Bollon, 2004). We will consider his work in more detail in later chapters.

As you can see, the environment is a frequent subject in theories of development. It is also an essential component of evolution-based perspectives, as we'll see next.

Evolution-Based Perspectives

Charles Darwin's theory of **natural selection** holds that the members of a species who are best suited to their own particular environments will be the ones most likely to survive and produce offspring. Two major theories use this basic biological theory as a foundation for understanding human psychology (Darwin, 1927).

---

behaviourism
A theoretical perspective on learning that assumes human development occurs as a result of experiences shaping behaviours.

operant conditioning A learning process through which the likelihood of a specific behaviour is increased or decreased through positive or negative reinforcement.

law of effect As asserted by E. L. Thorndike, the law that behaviour that is followed by a positive outcome tends to be repeated and behaviour that is followed by a negative outcome tends not to be repeated.

natural selection The Darwinian idea that the members of a species who are best suited to their own particular environments will be the ones most likely to survive and produce offspring.

Evolutionary psychology The best-known proponent of contemporary evolutionary psychology is David Buss (Buss, 1995, 2004; Buss & Barnes, 1986). He believes that evolutionary principles help us understand not only the origin of human physical features but also the workings of the human mind (Buss, 2004). He and other evolutionary psychologists believe that we behave and think as we do because these qualities are *adaptive*: they helped our ancestors survive in their environments (Buss, 2004).

Evolutionary psychologists have examined the adaptive functions of a range of human behaviour, from how we perceive stimuli (Pinker, 1997) to how we select our mates (Miller, 2000). The research described in **Figure 1.12** points out the underlying assumption of evolutionary psychology: even though the context of our world changes, how might we be influenced by the process of survival?

The ethological perspective The **ethological perspective** relies heavily on evolution. Ethologists study animal behaviours, particularly those that promote survival. One of the

ethological perspective A theory that assumes that human development is an outcome of individual experiences in the social environment that provide information about which behaviours should be adopted to increase chances of survival.

imprinting Learning at a particular age or stage that is rapid and independent of the consequences of behaviour.

comparative psychology The scientific study of the behaviour and mental process of non-human animals.

most influential ethologists was Austrian zoologist and animal psychologist Konrad Lorenz (Lorenz, 1950, 1965, 1981), who was awarded the Nobel Prize in medicine in 1973 (Archer, 1992). One of the most interesting concepts emerging from Lorenz's work is **imprinting**, as shown in **Figure 1.13**. Ethologists suggest that patterns such as imprinting provide evidence that living things are born with "prewired" features that guide survival. It is thought, therefore, that similar instincts may underlie some human development (Lorenz, 1965).

Modern developmental work continues to draw on some principles of ethology, primarily through its influence on biology and **comparative psychology**, which involves the study of the development of behaviour and mental processes of non-human animals (Archer, 1992). Evolutionary theories, in much the same way as psychodynamic, cognitive, and behavioural theories, have made significant contributions to our increasingly eclectic approach to understanding lifespan human development.

Evolutionary research • Figure 1.12

Researchers study physical attractiveness because it predicts mate selection. Buss and Barnes (1986) posed the question, "What would you look for in an ideal mate?" to 100 undergraduates. They discovered that, as shown here, males ranked physical attractiveness significantly higher than females did, whereas females ranked being a college graduate and good earning capacity significantly higher than males did.

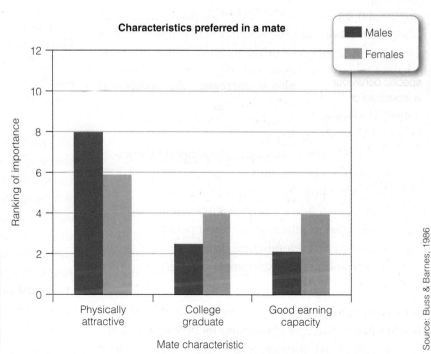

Source: Buss & Barnes, 1986

Think Critically 1. Why might young males and females place value on different characteristics when selecting a potential mate?
2. How might actual experience differ from these hypothetical ideals?
3. How might homosexual attraction be studied in this perspective?

Imprinting • Figure 1.13

Ethologist Konrad Lorenz believed that animals are born with certain instinctual behaviours that foster survival (Lorenz, 1981). For example, birds are born with an instinct to imprint the first thing they see and to follow it. Because the first thing they see usually is their mother, the key provider of food and protection, imprinting increases their chances of surviving. In a dramatic example of imprinting, Lorenz made himself the first object seen by a gaggle of geese, so they followed him everywhere (Lorenz, 1950, 1965, 1981).

Put It Together *Review the section on the ethological perspective and answer the following question: Is imprinting a feature of early or late lifespan human development?*

Nina Leen/Time & Life Pictures/Getty Images

Developmental Systems Theory

Currently, cutting-edge developmental scholarship is guided by **developmental systems theory**. Developmental systems theory is a **metatheory**, an eclectic view that integrates developmental theories across a variety of disciplines, including biology, psychology, evolution, and sociology, as well as others. Because metatheories help scientists analyze, interpret, and organize theories, some refer to metatheories as theories about theories. Developmental systems theory integrates the fundamental assumptions from multiple developmental theories with research from an array of fields, such as biology, genetics, and psychology. Developmental systems theory is organized around four basic assumptions (Overton, 2006):

1. Human development occurs throughout the lifespan from birth through death.
2. Human development shapes and is shaped by interactions between people and the contexts in which they live, including family and community.
3. Lifespan human development is not static across time, but varies in different historical periods.
4. Normal human development is diverse: there is great normal variation in the way people change across the lifespan.

   Developmental systems theories have significantly influenced developmental scholarship by shifting researchers' and theorists' focuses away from stage models, rejecting the notion that we have completely matured when we reach adulthood, and appreciating person-in-context interactions. Despite the complexity of developmental systems theory, it makes a lot of common sense. Embracing the many factors that shape and are shaped by lifespan human development, we are learning how to more effectively prevent developmental disturbances and promote healthy adjustments. In this section, we'll introduce you to two of the more influential developmental systems theories. Throughout the rest of the text, we'll refer to both of them to help you understand the behaviour and research we describe.

Lifespan developmental psychology

Paul Baltes (1987) was the first to contribute a lifespan theory of human development based on studies primarily of adult development rather than child development. The six features of Baltes' theory of **lifespan developmental psychology** provide us with a framework for understanding how individuals develop throughout the lifespan (**Figure 1.14**).

developmental systems theory A metatheory that draws from and integrates many theories, sources, and research studies related to human development.

metatheory A theory where the focus is the integration of multiple theories.

lifespan developmental psychology The systematic study of how and why human beings change, or stay the same, over the course of their entire life.

Lifespan developmental psychology • Figure 1.14

According to Baltes, lifespan human development is multidirectional and involves both gains and losses; plasticity is the rule over stability; development is influenced by historical and social contexts; and human development is multidisciplinary in nature. His model has guided researchers' study of trajectories of development over time. For example, our levels of creativity might change, increasing or decreasing across our lifespans, and be affected by the era or location in which we live, the people in our social networks, or our physical health.

Think Critically What is gained and what is lost as you move closer to your personal goals and make the transition from student to worker?

Characteristic lifespan development is...	Explanation	
Multidirectional	A young adult may return to live with his parents after receiving his first job. Moving back home may represent a gain in financial independence if he saves money to buy a home.	 Michael Blann/Getty Images
Full of gains and losses	Development at every age involves both gain and loss. It is incorrect to say that childhood is a time of gains while later adulthood is a time of losses. As a child gains height, she can access higher shelves and playground equipment. She loses nearness to the ground, which reduces her focus on the ground, grass, insects, and flowers.	 Courtesy Jennifer Tanner
Contextualized	Moving away from one's family before starting a family of one's own is influenced by a culture's value for independence versus interdependence in adulthood.	
Historically embedded	Women may achieve more in mathematics and the natural sciences than their mothers did because of changes in social norms, expectations, and messaging.	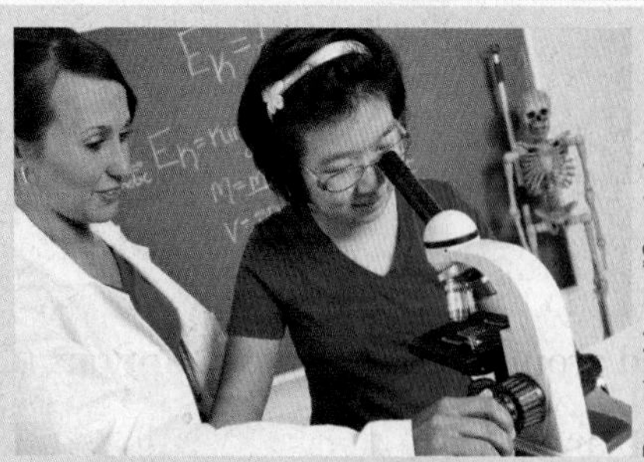 Pamela Moore/iStockphoto
Plastic	A person who was not a high school or a college athlete may become a master swimmer in his or her 50s.	 Pamela Moore/iStockphoto
Multidisciplinary	The study of lifespan human development requires us to learn from multiple disciplines, including psychology, to learn about the relative influence of income, genetics, and culture on development from conception through birth.	

Baltes was particularly interested in understanding how development continues through adulthood. As a developmental scientist working in the 1970s, Baltes was interested in understanding pathways to successful, even optimal, adult development. This led him to study wisdom. Together he and his colleagues conducted dozens of studies exploring the research question, *what makes older people wise?* (Baltes & Staudinger, 1993; Baltes & Smith, 2008). These studies led to the identification of specific factors that predict increases in knowledge and good judgement throughout adulthood (**Figure 1.15**).

Baltes's theory highlights the role context plays in developmental systems theory—a theme that is spotlighted even more directly in Urie Bronfenbrenner's

ecological systems model A theoretical approach to the study of human development that emphasizes five environmental systems that influence individual development and assumes that individuals shape the contexts in which they develop.

ecological systems model (Bronfenbrenner, 1979), as we'll see next.

Ecological systems model Bronfenbrenner believed that development cannot be adequately studied by focusing on the individual alone. In his **ecological systems model**, each person is at the centre of an overlapping set of environmental contexts, as shown in **Figure 1.16**.

Bronfenbrenner points out that not only do these various contexts influence us, but we also simultaneously influence them. Our physical, cognitive, and socio-emotional qualities interact intimately with these systems throughout our development. These interactions enhance or disrupt the systems, resulting in either positive or negative developmental outcomes (Bronfenbrenner, 1979).

The development of wisdom • Figure 1.15

Baltes and colleagues identified factors that contribute to the development of wisdom in adults (Baltes & Staudinger, 2000). Bringing together findings from many studies, Baltes was able to conclude that wisdom-related knowledge is more than intelligence or personality. Wisdom is the result of an accumulation of life experiences and knowledge.

Ask Yourself

1. Which factors contribute the most to wisdom in adulthood?
2. Which factors contribute very little?
3. Which one contributes none at all?

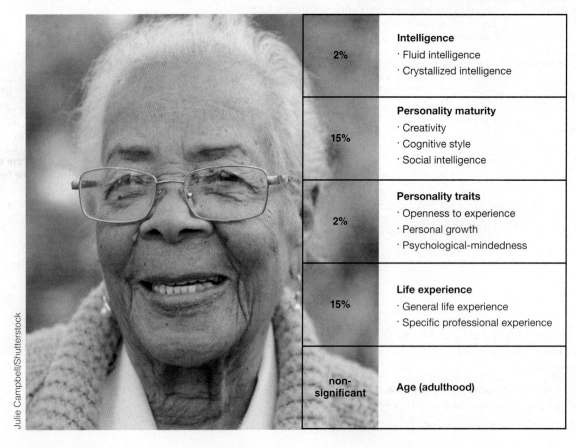

2%	**Intelligence** · Fluid intelligence · Crystallized intelligence
15%	**Personality maturity** · Creativity · Cognitive style · Social intelligence
2%	**Personality traits** · Openness to experience · Personal growth · Psychological-mindedness
15%	**Life experience** · General life experience · Specific professional experience
non-significant	**Age (adulthood)**

Julie Campbell/Shutterstock

The ecological systems model • Figure 1.16

Here's one example of how each system in Bronfenbrenner's ecological systems model might influence the vocabulary development of an 8-year-old named Harry.

Phi2/iStockphoto

Bronfenbrenner's ecological systems	Influence on 8-year-old Harry
Microsystem A system that contains the most direct influences on a child's development, including the home, neighbourhood, church, and school.	Harry's parents and teachers affect Harry's vocabulary.
Mesosystem The relationships among microsystems.	Harry's vocabulary expands when his parents (one microsystem) borrow books for him from the well-stocked public library (another microsystem).
Exosystem A system that contains institutions and organizations that have indirect influence on a child's development but no direct contact with the child.	Harry's city indirectly affects his vocabulary by funding high-quality schools and libraries.
Macrosystem The highest-level system, which includes the socio-cultural forces, societal values, and traditions that have indirect effects on all the other systems influencing a child's life.	The society in which Harry lives values quality education, which supports his vocabulary development.
Chronosystem The effect of the passage of time on both a child's development and the evolving complexity of the other systems influencing the child.	Harry learns words such as "computer" that did not exist in other eras.

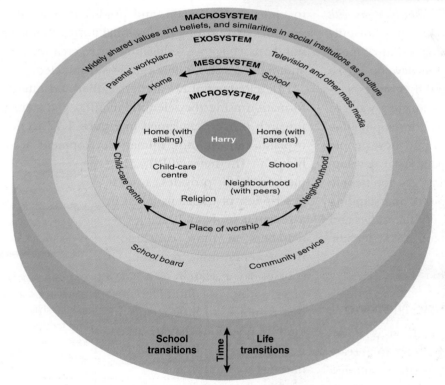

Think Critically Harry's grandfather was making the argument that this terrible economy is ruining Harry's childhood.
1. Using Bronfenbrenner's model, why can you argue that the economy is not directly responsible for ruining Harry's childhood?
2. How might the economy indirectly be affecting Harry's childhood?

CONCEPT CHECK STOP

1. **What** do psychodynamic theories of development assume about stages of development?

2. **How** is Piaget's theory of cognitive development different from other theories of cognitive development?

3. **How** are metatheories different from theories of development?

As developmental theories have moved toward embracing the complexity of lifespan human development, developmental scientists have had the opportunity to study more complex scientific questions. Regardless of how advanced our theories and questions get, however, the scientific method guides the work of developmental scientists, who use a wide range of methods to collect and organize developmental data.

Conducting Lifespan Research

LEARNING OBJECTIVES

1. **Identify** the stages of the scientific method.
2. **Identify** three research methods used to collect observations for scientific study.
3. **Compare** and **contrast** the advantages of various developmental research designs.
4. **Discuss** ethical issues related to research.

How do babies show they have learned? How are children affected by screen time? What happens with our cognitive processes as we age? It's not only developmentalists who want to know more about how and why people change and develop across the lifespan. People want to understand themselves, parents want to understand their kids, managers want to know how to support their employees' development—we all want to know more about why and how people change and develop across the lifespan. What developmental researchers do know is this: answers don't come easily or simply. Understanding comes from scientific studies and the accumulation of systematic research.

> **scientific community** A group of people who sustain the production of scientific knowledge through collective attitudes, rules, and conventions.
>
> **scientific method** The specific procedure researchers use to ask and explore scientific questions in a way that makes connections between observations and leads to understanding.

The Scientific Method

The scientific method is an attitude toward how to create knowledge. It is the **scientific community**'s agreement about a set of approaches concerning ideas, rules, and techniques for generating understanding about our world. Within the scientific method there are intriguing differences in the approach to science; however, there tend to be general agreements about a way of looking at the world to understand, explain, and predict it. Scientific communities share strong professional norms about rigorous standards, diligence, ethical integrity, creativity, honesty, and openness about how a study is conducted.

Developmental researchers gather and interpret information using the scientific method and steps in the research process explained in **Figure 1.17** to describe, explain, and optimize human development across the lifespan (Lerner, 2012). The method both provides a clear description of the steps taken in a research study and enables researchers to draw conclusions that generate more research. Of course, all research also takes place within a cultural context that is subject to influencing the kinds of questions that are asked, how they are explored, and how findings are interpreted.

Developmental researchers use the **scientific method** to de-**scribe**, **explain**, and **optimize** human development across the lifespan (Lerner, 2012).

The scientific method is a valuable tool for guiding developmental research and generating

> **describe** A goal of developmental scholarship in which careful observations of behaviour are made and recorded.
>
> **explain** A goal of developmental scholarship that focuses on identifying the underlying causes of behaviour.
>
> **optimize** A goal of developmental scholarship that applies current information to future possibilities in the service of enhancing development.

The scientific method • Figure 1.17

Seven Steps in Research Process and Theory Development

The scientific method is an organized method of moving from observation to understanding. The process usually involves back-and forth-movement between the steps, depending upon the research methodology used.

Step 1
Select topic

Cycle continues

Step 7
Mobilze knowledge

Step 2
Focus question

zhang bo/iStockphoto

Step 6
Interpret data

Step 3
Design study

Step 5
Analyze data

Step 4
Collect data

Think Critically The digital age has brought with it an increasingly rapid flow of information through methods such as Internet publishing, email, and blogging. Generate a research question you could pose to examine any potential impacts these changes may have on the mental health of young people. Think through the scientific method. How would you collect data? How would you make meaningful conclusions and what next questions might you want to answer?

---

empirical study
A systematic study of human behaviour and development using methodological observations, which can be analyzed quantitatively or qualitatively.

anecdotal evidence
Non-systematic observations, including personal experiences. Has the potential to inspire interesting research questions.

credible findings. Findings from **empirical studies** help us avoid drawing on personal experience or **anecdotal evidence** to make sense of people's behaviour. This helps us avoid the serious negative consequences of making misassumptions about human development, as illustrated in **Figure 1.18**. Collectively, research findings accumulate and are integrated into existing **theories** or are reorganized into new ones. Theories are used to generate new research questions about development, which can lead us to increasingly complex ways of understanding ourselves and others.

The scientific method is the standard framework for conducting empirical research not only in developmental scholarship, but in all scientific disciplines. Sharing

common principles and rules for conducting authentic and trustworthy research is the key to inter-disciplinary collaboration. In the next section, you will learn about the wide variety of theoretical perspectives used to study lifespan human development.

Research Methodology

For more than a century, science has had two distinctive approaches, which could be roughly divided between basic and applied purposes. **Basic research** tends to advance general knowledge, whereas **applied research** attempts to solve specific or immediate problems with a direct, practical application. Regardless of the use of the research, scientists gather information from multiple

theory A coherent set of statements that explains an observation or set of observations in relation to one another.

basic research
Research designed to create fundamental knowledge about the world.

applied research
Research designed to examine specific contexts to solve a concrete problem or address policy; it has a direct and practical purpose.

Sugar and hyperactivity • Figure 1.18

When people make conclusions based on anecdotal information, misassumptions can be made. For example, sugar causes hyperactivity in children, *right*? Wrong. Scientific evidence suggests there is no scientifically established link between eating sugar and hyperactivity in children (Williams, 2013). Genetics explain between 71 and 90 percent of the differences in hyperactivity that we see among children. Yet, one quarter of parents and adolescents believe that sugar causes hyperactivity (Bussing, Zima, Mason, Meyer, White, & Garvan, 2012).

Think Critically If hyperactivity in early childhood is a risk factor for the development of problems later in childhood and adolescence, how might the sugar myth influence the type of treatments and interventions available to children with hyperactivity?

Development pathways in boys' disruptive and delinquent behaviour

Age

Adolescence ← Delinquency (arrest)

← Association with deviant peers

← Covert or concealing conduct problems

← Academic problems

← Poor peer relationships

← Withdrawal

← Overt conduct problems/ aggressiveness

← Hyperactivity

Preschool

← Difficult temperament

0

---

sources using a variety of techniques. Developmental researchers are no different, turning to **quantitative** and **qualitative data** to answer questions. Quantitative techniques include experiments, surveys, and existing statistics. Qualitative approaches include interviews with individuals or groups, field research, historical-comparative research, and interpretive analysis. Researchers combine these various techniques in innovative ways depending upon the purposes of the research. Research purposes may be exploratory, descriptive, or explanatory.

quantitative data Information in the form of numbers.

qualitative data Information in the form of words, pictures, sounds, visual images, or objects.

exploratory research An examination into an area in which a researcher wants to develop initial ideas and more focused research questions.

Exploratory research Exploratory research creates a new understanding or portrayal of an area of study so that more focused research can be conducted. It is often the first stage of research requiring creative, flexible, and open approaches to the area of study and a willingness to embrace conjectures. It can be used to determine the feasibility of conducting further research as well as to develop techniques for locating future empirical material.

Descriptive research Researchers would typically build from an exploratory study to design a descriptive one as part of their research process. **Descriptive research** methods focus on observing, rather than explaining, behaviour. The goal of descriptive research is to describe the phenomenon of interest from as many perspectives as possible in as much detail as possible. Descriptive research designs are especially appropriate when a new social phenomenon is observed. Three key types of descriptive designs are used in studying the lifespan: naturalistic observations, case studies, and surveys. We describe these designs in **Figure 1.19**. In all types of

descriptive research Research methods used to observe, record, and describe behaviour and environments; it is not for making cause–effect explanations.

Descriptive research designs • Figure 1.19

Developmentalists primarily use descriptive research designs when they are exploring new ideas or conditions.

a. Naturalistic observation

In naturalistic observation, developmental scientists observe behaviour in real-world settings, such as children interacting with one another at the park or in a laboratory setting, such this classroom where the observer is hidden from view. The researcher does not control variables or become involved in any way. One form of naturalistic observation is *ethnography*, in which a researcher, often a participant–observer, analyzes the underlying *ethos* or nature of a society.

Jeffrey Greenberg/Photo Researchers

b. Case study

In a case study, researchers gather information on one or a small number of individuals. For example, they might study the spoken vocabulary of a toddler, as shown here. Although case studies often uncover detailed, nuanced information, findings from case studies cannot be generalized to the population as a whole, due to the small number of participants.

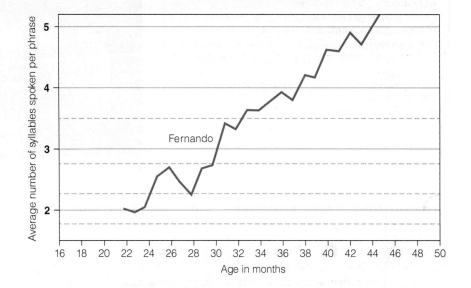

Fernando

(y-axis: Average number of syllables spoken per phrase; x-axis: Age in months, 16 to 50)

Ask Yourself

Match the type of research with the example of research provided.
a. naturalistic observation
b. case study
c. survey

1. Heng interviewed Lenore about her experiences adopting three children.
2. Research assistants Nevaeh and Pierre called 200 people via telephone. Each person answered 13 questions about their parenting practices.
3. Blake observed parents shopping at the grocery store and took notes about parent–child interactions.

operational definition A definition that uses words that are quantitative, in order to allow some form of measurement.

quantitative research, including descriptive studies, scientists use **operational definitions** to state concepts in clear and measurable terms.

As the term suggests, descriptive research methods offer rich, detailed descriptions of developmental phenomena. These designs cannot, however, explain *why* people think or act the way they do. Researchers often build on the findings from descriptive research with more precise types of research, such as correlational research.

Correlational research aims to uncover the strength of a relationship between two or more variables. Some correlations are positive, meaning that both variables change in the same direction, whereas others are negative, meaning that one variable increases as the other decreases, as

WHAT A DEVELOPMENTALIST SEES
Correlations

Today, if you walked into a coffee shop, you wouldn't be surprised to see a twenty-something serving specialty coffee drinks. It is likely that you associate young age with working as a barista (**Figure a**). A developmentalist is likely to see a number of additional factors that explain how age is or is not associated with seeking employment as a barista. A developmentalist recognizes that the barista position allows an employee to work part-

time and younger age is associated with "desire to work part-time" (**Figure b**). Older people are more likely to report they have "never worked as a barista" in their twenties (**Figure c**). Last, developmentalists are likely to conclude that there is no developmental reason why young people "desire to make coffee for others" compared with older people (**Figure d**).

Ask Yourself

Describe the type of correlation expressed in each statement:
1. The statistical association between "number of days worked (lifetime)" and age.
2. The statistical relationship between the number of careers a person may pursue in her future and age.
3. The correlation between distance (in kilometres) to work and age.

a.

James Steidl/Shutterstock

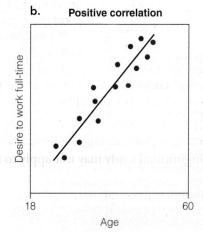

b. **Positive correlation**

Desire to work full-time / Age (18 – 60)

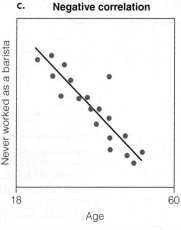

c. **Negative correlation**

Never worked as a barista / Age (18 – 60)

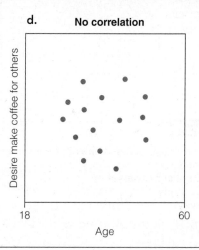

d. **No correlation**

Desire make coffee for others / Age (18 – 60)

shown in *What a Developmentalist Sees* (Thompson, Diamond, McWilliam, Snyder, & Snyder, 2005).

Although correlational research methods can help us predict behaviour, and therefore understand it more deeply than descriptive methods allow, correlational research does not allow us to draw conclusions about the causes of behaviour. For example, children's difficulties in paying attention for long periods at age 4 may be positively correlated to the amount of TV that they view per week, yet we cannot say that watching TV *causes* attention

problems. A **third variable** is a variable that may be responsible for the correlation between the other two variables of interest. For example, 4-year-old Dennis may have a physiological problem that causes him both to have difficulty paying attention *and* to watch more television. To draw conclusions about causation, researchers

third variable A confounding variable influencing the correlation between variables, or a variable having an unintended impact on the relationship between the independent and dependent variables.

independent variable (IV) The variable controlled by the experimenter to observe the impact it has on the behaviour of interest.

dependent variable (DV) The variable measured by the experimenter to observe the effects of the independent variable.

experimental group The group or groups that receive the manipulation of the independent variable, which is often called the *treatment*.

control group The group or groups that provide comparison for the experimental group and do not receive manipulation of the independent variable.

must use the experimental method (Febbraro, 2006; Thompson et al., 2005), described next.

Experiments In an experiment, researchers control the variables of interest and compare their effects. This control allows them to make causal statements about the variables of interest. Experimenters manipulate an **independent variable (IV)** so that they can see how it affects the **dependent variable (DV)**, the variable that is being measured. Independent variables come in a variety of forms, depending on the focus of research. In developmental research, often the independent variable is age (Hager & Hasselhorn, 1995). In order to control independent variables, research participants are assigned to at least two groups. Participants in an **experimental group** are exposed to the independent variable. After exposure, the experimental group is compared with the **control group**. Because the control group does not experience exposure to the independent variable, any differences between the two groups are explained by exposure to the independent variable. **Figure 1.20** presents an example of an experiment.

When conducting an experiment, precision and specificity in variables are essential, in order to rule out as many alternative explanations for the conclusions as possible. Similar precision is needed when a researcher employs developmental research designs (Becker, Roberts, & Voelmeck, 2003).

Developmental Research Designs

A major focus in developmental research is change over time, and developmentalists have devised different research designs to help them study changes that occur with time or age. For example, we may be interested in determining changes in drivers' reaction times between the ages of 50 and 80. We could conduct a study using

cross-sectional design that compares a group of drivers who are currently 50 with a group of drivers who are currently 80. Such a study might take a few months to complete. Or we could carry out a study using **longitudinal design**, testing a group of 50-year-olds repeatedly over the course of 30 years until they are 80. Why would we do the latter if it will take three decades to complete? We could also use **cross-sequential design**, combining elements of both approaches. **Figure 1.21** shows the advantages and disadvantages of each of these strategies.

One challenge that developmental researchers face is the problem of **cohort effects**. Cohort effects result from the fact that certain historical events affect people born in one period of history differently than those born in another period. For example, if we were testing 50-year-olds and 20-year-olds on their mathematics knowledge, educational methods might have changed since the first cohort went to school, so that any conclusions we drew about mathematics ability would be *confounded* with schooling practices. Longitudinal research helps to address the problem of cohort effects. However, the findings from one longitudinal study may not apply to future cohorts of people.

Like all researchers, developmental researchers must follow clear ethical guidelines when designing a research study.

cross-sectional design Research in which different age groups are compared simultaneously.

longitudinal design Research in which one group of subjects is followed for an extended period.

cross-sequential design Research in which an experimenter combines the benefits of both cross-sectional and longitudinal designs by adding a new group of subjects at progressive intervals.

cohort effect The unique impact a given historical era has on people living during that period as compared with people living during a different historical period.

Ethical Issues

All researchers, whether in biology, psychology, or various other fields, must follow ethical practices when conducting research. For psychologists, the Canadian Psychological Association (CPA) has created and maintained the *Canadian Code of Ethics for Psychologists* (CPA, 2000), a code of ethical standards to help protect study participants as well as the integrity of the research. In

Experimental design • Figure 1.20

Here is an example of one experiment that could be conducted to study the effects of watching violence on TV.

1. The experimenter begins by identifying the hypothesis.

2. In order to avoid sample bias, the experimenter randomly assigns participants to two different groups.

3. Having at least two groups allows the performance of one group to be compared to that of another.

4. The experimental group watches violent programs while the control group watches non-violent programs. The amount of violent TV watched is the independent variable (IV).

5. The experimenter then counts how many times the child hits, kicks, or punches a large plastic doll. The number of aggressive acts is the dependent variable (DV).

6. The experimenter relates differences in aggressive behaviour (DV) to the amount of violent television watched (IV).

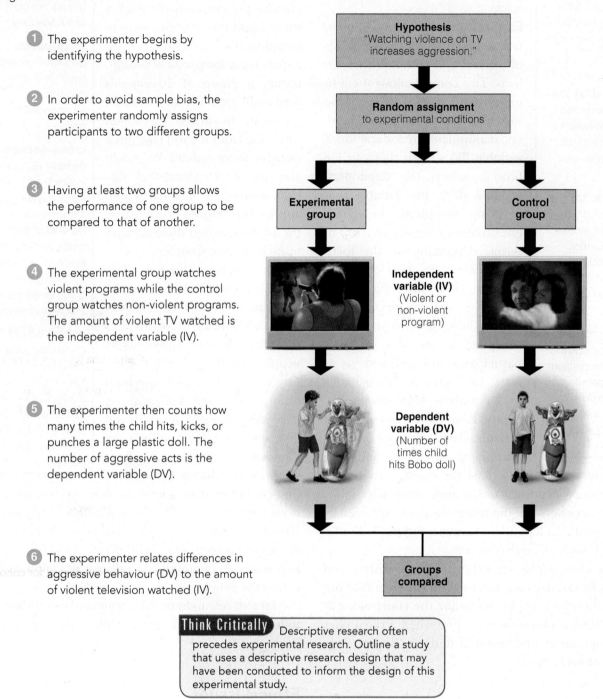

Hypothesis
"Watching violence on TV increases aggression."

Random assignment
to experimental conditions

Experimental group

Control group

Independent variable (IV)
(Violent or non-violent program)

Dependent variable (DV)
(Number of times child hits Bobo doll)

Groups compared

Think Critically Descriptive research often precedes experimental research. Outline a study that uses a descriptive research design that may have been conducted to inform the design of this experimental study.

addition, *The Tri-Council Policy Statement: Ethical Conduct for Research Involving Humans* (TCPS; Government of Canada: Panel on Research Ethics, 2015) governs all research involving humans that is funded by any of the three federal research agencies: the Canadian Institutes of Health Research, the Natural Sciences and Engineering Research Council, and the Social Sciences and Humanities Research Council. Further, as shown in *Where Developmentalists Click*, Aboriginal cultures in Canada have innovated additional safeguards for ethical research in their communities. Key ethical considerations in conducting developmental research include avoidance of harm,

When designing a research study, researchers consider the advantages and disadvantages of each design.

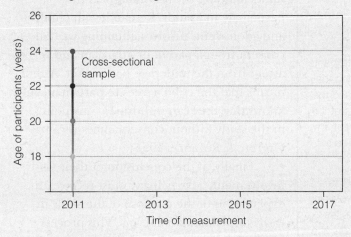

a. Cross-sectional design

A cross-sectional design compares participants of various ages at one point in time.

Advantage: Can collect data quickly

Disadvantage: Differences among groups may reflect factors other than age

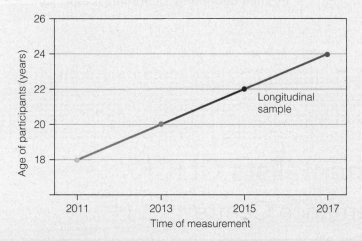

b. Longitudinal design

A longitudinal design follows the same participants, measuring them at several different points in time.

Advantage: Helps determine whether changes are related to development

Disadvantages: Takes a lot of time to complete; some participants may drop out of study in non-random ways that affect the results

c. Cross-sequential design

Cross-sequential design combines cross-sectional and longitudinal methods to compare participants of various ages at the same point in time and follow these same participants, collecting data from them at multiple points in time.

Advantages: Can collect data quickly; can control for cohort effects

Disadvantage: Participants may still drop out of the study in non-random ways that affect the results

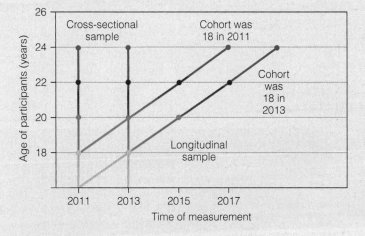

Ask Yourself

Which type of developmental design is used in each example below?

1. Researchers collect and compare average self-esteem from data collected during the first week of school from students in grades 1 through 8.
2. Researchers measure self-esteem of students in Grade 1 and then decide to measure them again during the first week of school for the next eight years to compare change in self-esteem.
3. Researchers decide to follow students in grades 1 through 8 for four years, measuring their self-esteem the first week of school each year.

confidentiality, informed consent and assent, and debriefing (Fry & Irwin, 2009). The TCPS asserts the following:

- Researchers must take into consideration the possibility of any physical or psychological harm to participants, especially when working with children who may not know or be able to express what is in their own best interest. For example, in studies of attachment in which parent–child separation occurs, moments of child distress are common. Following ethical guidelines, researchers must work to reduce the distress as much as possible and must ensure that participants are aware of their right to withdraw at any point during a study (Fry & Irwin, 2009).
- **Confidentiality** involves keeping records of the study and the identity

confidentiality The responsibility of researchers to keep private the identity and data of all research participants.

informed consent The process of requesting that research participants assert in writing that they understand the study, know that they can withdraw at any time, and agree to participate.

debriefing The process of explaining the true purposes and hypotheses of a study.

of the participants private. If a researcher is conducting intelligence testing, for example, leaking the scores could be highly detrimental to participants (Millstein, 2000).

- **Informed consent** is an adult's understanding of and willingness to participate in a study. Research with children and adolescents involves obtaining written consent from a parent or guardian and verbal assent from the underage participant. Assent means that the child agrees to participate and knows that they can withdraw at any point in the study without consequences (Franzi, Orgren, & Rozance, 1994).
- Finally, at the conclusion of their study involvement, a participant must receive an explanation of the purpose of the study in easily understandable terms. This process is called **debriefing**. Debriefing is especially

Where Developmentalists CLICK

First Nations Information Governance Centre

The First Nations Information Governance Centre (http://fnigc.ca) is an important development because it provides a dedicated centre for the *First Nations Regional Longitudinal Health Survey* that houses an abundance of information, research, training, data collection, analysis, and dissemination services for First Nations at the community, regional, and national levels.

important if participants were initially told that a study was investigating a different phenomenon than what was actually being investigated—a practice called *deception*. Deception can be used only when participants' knowledge of the real interest would affect the study results (Scott & White, 2005).

Ethics protect research participants, with the goal that no harm is done to people during the pursuit of knowledge intended to help people. Ethical Canadian research with Aboriginal peoples has become more possible with the inclusion of a new chapter in the TCPS. Chapter 9 of this policy manual emphasizes the need for equitable partnerships and provides safeguards specific to First Nations, Inuit, and Métis people. It is considered innovative because it starts to address the historic biases in approaches that have not generally reflected or benefited Aboriginal peoples or communities, and it will continue to be revised with ongoing input from Aboriginal communities and scholars. See *Where Developmentalists Click*, which features the First Nations Information Governance Centre.

CONCEPT CHECK

1. **How** does the scientific method guide developmental scholarship?
2. **What** is the difference between basic and applied research?
3. **How** do quantitative and qualitative data differ?
4. **What** are the differences among descriptive research, correlational research, and experiments?
5. **What** are the advantages and disadvantages of different developmental research designs?
6. **What** are the ethical codes of conduct related to study of the lifespan?

Summary

1 What Is Lifespan Human Development? 4

- **Lifespan human development** is the growth and maturation of individuals from conception through death. **Lifespan developmental psychology** is the systematic study of how and why human beings change, or stay the same, over the course of their entire life.

- **Developmental psychology** is the subfield of psychology concerned with studying and understanding **life stages** from infancy, to **emerging adulthood**, to adulthood.

- **Developmental scholarship** is the multidisciplinary field using a **developmental perspective**: the approach and basic set of assumptions that guide the systematic study of growth and maturation across the human lifespan in order to study development.

- **Developmental scholars** study **physical**, **cognitive**, and **socio-emotional development** across the lifespan to better understand and help support healthy growth and maturation.

- An **applied developmental scholar** is someone specializing in the study of how human development shapes and is shaped by context in order to describe, explain, and optimize human development.

- Key issues in the study and application of developmental scholarship include, but are not limited to **nature–nurture**, **developmental stability–instability**, **normative–non-normative events**. and **developmental continuity** (as shown in the figure) and **discontinuity**.

Developmental continuity and discontinuity • Figure 1.4

- Socio-cultural factors, including **gender**, **race**, **ethnicity**, **socio-economic status (SES)**, and **culture**, influence and are influenced by human development.

Theoretical Perspectives on Development 12

- Developmental scholars are part of a **scientific community**, and use an **eclectic** range of ideas from many sources. They follow the steps of the **scientific method** to **describe**, **explain**, and **optimize** human development across the lifespan. The **scientific method** is a common language used by scientists from all scientific disciplines. Similar to other kinds of scientists, developmentalists use **empirical studies** and **anecdotal evidence** to support their **theories**.

- Sigmund Freud proposed a **stage theory** of **psychosexual development** that focused on the transfer of **libidinal energy** through five stages of development until the individual reaches full sexual maturity. Freud identified three parts of the mind: **id**, **ego**, and **superego**. He developed **psychoanalysis** as a treatment method wherein **unconscious** conflicts could be pushed into the **conscious** mind, thereby freeing them. Erik Erikson diverged from Freud's emphasis on sexual development and **libido** and proposed an eight-stage **neo-Freudian** theory of psychosocial development and the concept of **ego identity**, which matures as a function of the resolution of psychosocial tasks.

- Piaget's stage theory of cognitive development suggests that children develop mentally through **assimilation** and **accommodation** of their mental **schemas** as they seek **equilibrium** in the face of new information. Vygotsky believed that socio-cultural interactions, such as **guided participation** and **scaffolds** that take place in a child's **zone of proximal development**, are essential to cognitive development. Information-processing theories take a quantitative approach, viewing changes in memory, attention, and language as occurring gradually rather than in stages.

- **Classical conditioning** focuses on learning that takes place when we associate stimuli with one another. Pavlov's experiments in classical conditioning demonstrate the interaction of **unconditioned stimuli** (US), **unconditioned responses** (UR), **neutral stimuli** (NS), **conditioned stimuli** (CS), and **conditioned responses** (CR).

- **Operant conditioning** involves learning from the consequences of our behaviour. The **law of effect** states that behaviour that brings rewarding, reinforcing consequences is likely to be repeated. Social learning theory focuses on learning by observing others, in person or through the media.

- **Behaviourism** maintains that science should study *only* observable behaviours. The **evolutionary theory** applies the principles of evolution, including survival of the fittest and **natural selection**, to human behaviour. Similarly, the **ethological perspective** focuses on the survival behaviours of animals, such as **imprinting**. Modern developmental work continues to draw on some principles of ethology, primarily through its influence on biology and **comparative psychology**.

- **Developmental systems theory** is a **metatheory**, integrating many theories, sources, and research studies related to human development. Lifespan researcher Paul Baltes proposed that the laws of lifespan human development include the following: lifespan development is multidirectional, involves both gains and losses, involves plasticity, is historically embedded, is context-dependent, and is multidisciplinary. Baltes' study of the development of wisdom is one example of this approach, as shown in the figure.

The development of wisdom • Figure 1.15

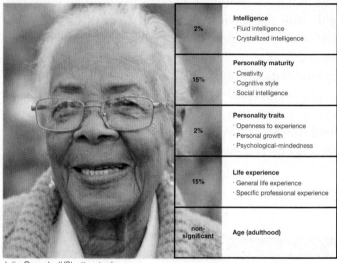

Julie Campbell/Shutterstock

- Bronfenbrenner's **ecological systems model** proposes that we are influenced by various levels of our environment: microsystems, mesosystems, exosystems, macrosystems, and chronosystems.

Conducting Lifespan Research 26

- Science has two distinctive research approaches, which can be roughly divided between basic and applied purposes. **Basic research** tends to advance general knowledge, whereas **applied research** attempts to solve specific problems with practical application. Regardless of the approach, developmentalists gather information from convergent sources using **quantitative** and **qualitative** techniques to answer questions.

- **Exploratory research** creates a new understanding of an area of study so that more focused research can be conducted. It can be used to determine the feasibility of conducting further research as well as for developing techniques for locating future empirical material. Researchers would typically build a descriptive study from exploratory research.

- **Descriptive research** focuses on observing rather than explaining. Descriptive methods include naturalistic observation, case studies, and surveys. Scientists use **operational definitions** to state concepts in clear and measurable terms. Correlational research describes relationships between two or more variables. It allows researchers to make predictions, but they cannot use the findings to explain the causes of behaviour due to **third variables** and other possible explanations.

- Experiments allow researchers to determine the causes of behaviour. They expose an **experimental group** of participants to manipulations of an **independent variable**; a **control group** of similar participants is not exposed to that variable. The experimenters measure the effects of their manipulations on a **dependent variable**.

- Researchers can compare different groups over different periods of time using **cross-sectional design**, **longitudinal design**, and **cross-sequential design**, as shown in the chart in the figure. To avoid **cohort effects** related to

historical timeframes, researchers can use **longitudinal** or **cross-sequential** designs.

- Ethical research requires avoidance of harm, **confidentiality**, **informed consent** and assent, and **debriefing**.

Developmental research designs • Figure 1.21

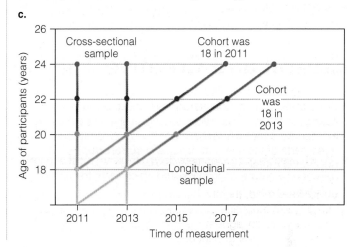

c.

Key Terms

- accommodation 16
- anecdotal evidence 27
- applied developmental scholar 5
- applied research 27
- assimilation 16
- basic research 27
- behaviourism 20
- chronosystem 25
- classical conditioning 19
- cognitive domain of development 5
- cohort effect 31
- comparative psychology 21
- conditioned response (CR) 19
- conditioned stimulus (CS) 19
- confidentiality 34
- conscious 12
- control group 31
- cross-sectional design 31
- cross-sequential design 31
- culture 7
- debriefing 34
- dependent variable (DV) 31
- describe 26
- descriptive research 28
- developmental continuity 7
- developmental discontinuity 7

- developmental instability 8
- developmental perspective 5
- developmental psychology 5
- developmental scholar 5
- developmental scholarship 5
- developmental stability 8
- developmental systems theory 22
- developmentalist 5
- eclectic 12
- ecological systems model 24
- ego 13
- ego identity 15
- emerging adulthood 6
- empirical study 27
- equilibrium 16
- ethnicity 9
- ethological perspective 21
- evolutionary theory 5
- exosystem 25
- experimental group 31
- explain 26
- exploratory research 28
- gender 9
- guided participation 16
- id 13
- imprinting 21

- independent variable (IV) 31
- informed consent 34
- law of effect 20
- libidinal energy 13
- libido 12
- life stage 6
- lifespan developmental psychology 22
- lifespan human development 5
- longitudinal design 31
- macrosystem 25
- mesosystem 25
- metatheory 22
- microsystem 25
- natural selection 20
- nature 7
- neo-Freudian theory 13
- neutral stimulus (NS) 19
- non-normative event 8
- normative event 8
- nurture 7
- operant conditioning 20
- operational definition 29
- optimize 26
- physical domain of development 5
- psychoanalysis 13
- psychosexual development 13

Critical and Creative Thinking Questions

1. Which theory of development appeals most to you? If you favour an eclectic orientation, which elements of each theory would you combine? Why?

2. Which aspects of development do you think are most strongly affected by nature, or genetics, and which seem to be most influenced by nurture?

3. What are some examples of continuity and discontinuity that you have seen in your own development or in the development of people you know?

4. What examples have you seen or experienced demonstrating that development is multidirectional, plastic, or full of gains and losses across the lifespan?

5. Describe your current microsystems, mesosystems, exosystem, macrosystem, and chronosystem. If possible, compare them with a person in a different segment of the lifespan.

What is happening in this picture?

Shichi-Go-San, or 7-5-3, festivals are celebrated throughout Japan every November 15th, honouring the healthy growth and development of children. The tradition recognizes these ages because at 3, children have learned language to communicate with others; at 5, children have learned wisdom; and at 7, a strong tooth grows. This marker of health at age 7 indicates that a child has grown healthy and strong and acknowledges and appreciates the fact that the child has avoided various dangers and diseases during his or her most dependent years.

Think Critically How does this traditional celebration of the child map onto what you have learned about lifespan human development in Chapter 1?

Brytta/iStockphoto

Self-Test

(Check your answers in Appendix A.)

1. All of the following are TRUE about developmental scholarship EXCEPT that developmental scholarship _____.

   a. is a scientific discipline concerned with studying change throughout the human lifespan

   b. is different from developmental psychology

   c. is informed by a single theory

   d. relies on the scientific method

2. What kind of event is this little boy experiencing in this picture of his first day of school?

   a. non-normative

   b. cognitive

   c. normative

   d. continuous

Pamela Moore/iStockphoto.com

3. Dr. Horvath studies how children are affected when their parents experience marital discord and divorce. Dr. Horvath is interested primarily in which domain of development?

   a. physical

   b. cognitive

   c. socio-emotional

   d. multidirectional

4. A researcher wants to be able to know which children are most likely to be aggressive at age 5 given their level of aggression at age 2. Which goal of psychology is this researcher focusing on the most?

   a. prediction

   b. optimization

   c. preventive intervention

   d. explanation

5. Konrad Lorenz used which approach to studying development?

   a. ethological

   b. psychoanalytic

   c. cognitive

   d. behavioural

6. This graph of boys' growth trajectory illustrates _____.

   a. developmental continuity

   b. developmental discontinuity

   c. developmental stability

   d. developmental instability

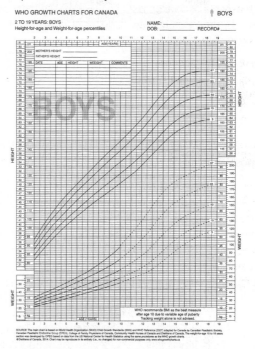

7. The first step in the scientific method is to _____.

   a. publish results

   b. review literature

   c. develop a theory

   d. draw conclusions

Seven Steps in Research Process and Theory Development

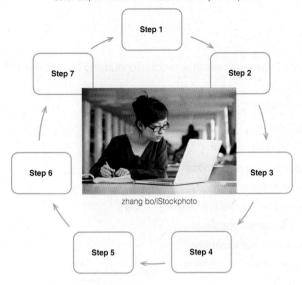

Step 1
Step 2
Step 3
Step 4
Step 5
Step 6
Step 7

zhang bo/iStockphoto

8. Descriptive research methods include _____.

a. case studies

b. naturalistic observation

c. surveys

d. all of these

9. Which of the following correlations is shown in this graph?

a. a positive correlation between the number of days children spend in school and their reading test scores

b. a negative correlation between the number of days children spend in school and their reading test scores

c. a causal relationship between the number of days children spend in school and their reading test scores

d. a predictive relationship between reading test scores and the number of days children spend in school

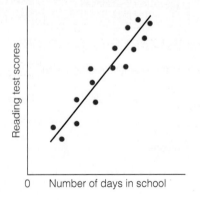

Reading test scores

0   Number of days in school

10. Delvin is conducting an experiment. He assigns participants to drink 1, 3, or 6 energy drinks every day for a month and then measures changes in their weight. In this experiment, change in weight is the _____.

a. dependent variable

b. operational variable

c. control variable

d. independent variable

11. Which developmental research design is depicted in this figure?

a. cross-sectional

b. longitudinal

c. correlational

d. cross-sequential

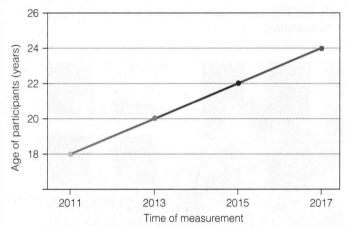

Age of participants (years)

Time of measurement

2011   2013   2015   2017

12. Rajiv is 10 years old and Philippe is 60 years old. It would be difficult to directly compare their cognitive abilities in childhood because _____ may have caused them to have different experiences, such as Rajiv getting better schooling and nutrition.

a. cross-sequential effects

b. experimental effects

c. cohort effects

d. control effects

13. According to Erikson, the crisis of basic trust versus mistrust occurs during what Freud described as the _____ stage of personality development.

a. oral

b. anal

c. genital

d. phallic

14. Jean Piaget's theory suggests that children try to achieve cognitive equilibrium, or balance, through the processes of _____.

a. consciousness and unconsciousness

b. assimilation and accommodation

c. discrimination and generalization

d. reinforcement and punishment

15. The ring closest to Harry, representing his immediate context, is his _____.

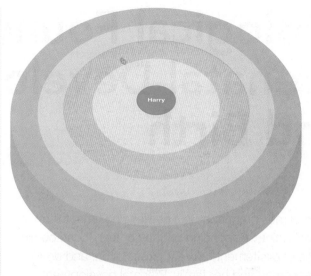

a. exosystem

b. macrosystem

c. microsystem

d. mesosystem

THE PLANNER ✓

Review your Chapter Planner in the chapter opener and check off your completed work.

2 Biological Foundations, Prenatal Development, and Birth

Sometimes pregnancy is a challenging time, full of uncertainty. Depending on the context, it can be nine months of excitement, anxiety, expectation, and doubts for the woman and her family. Prenatal development happens inside the woman's body as the embryo changes to fetus and becomes viable to exist apart from the mother. For the expectant parents a birth can be a much-anticipated one, yet it will be a life-altering experience. They have spent months preparing, perhaps learning about pregnancy and birth processes, maybe taking childbirth classes and planning for their ideal birth scenario. The baby's arrival may unfold in the way they expect, or it may include unexpected elements, and interventions such as induction or a Caesarean section.

But, for now, the fetus is still tucked deep within the folds of the uterine wall, encased in amniotic fluid that fills with the flavours of the foods the mother eats. The uterine world is filled with the sounds of the mother's digestion,

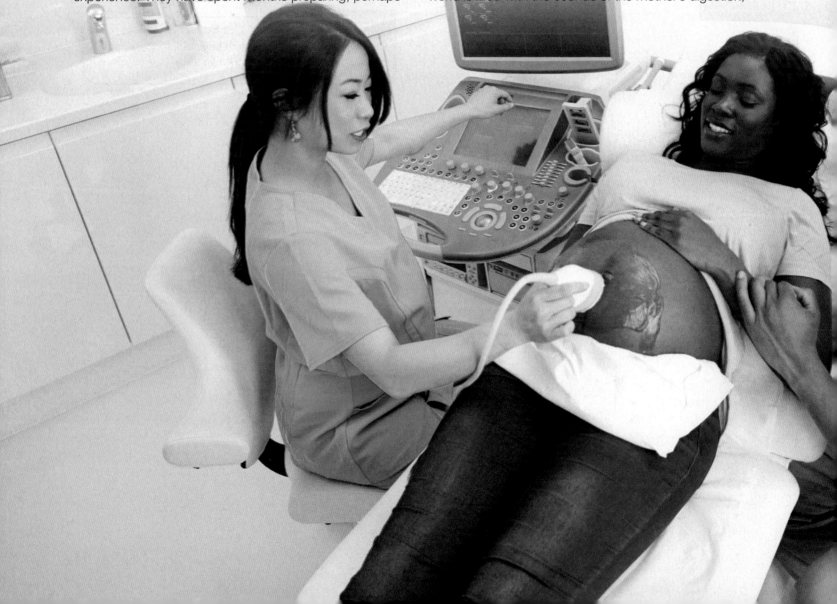

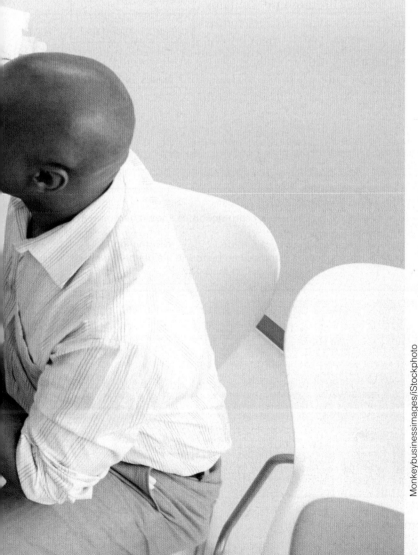

heartbeat, and voice. The baby will prefer these familiar sounds and be soothed by them after birth (see Fifer, 2002). In this chapter we will follow the prenatal journey from conception through viability and birth. We will discuss topics ranging from substances that may harm developing fetuses to the behavioural assessment of newborns. Before we begin this journey, we must first consider the biological foundations of prenatal development and birth that are universal among all humans.

Monkeybusinessimages/iStockphoto

CHAPTER OUTLINE

CHAPTER PLANNER ✓

- ❑ Study the picture and read the opening story.
- ❑ Scan the Learning Objectives in each section:
  p. 44 ❑   p. 47 ❑   p. 62 ❑   p. 70 ❑
- ❑ Read the text and study all visuals. Answer any questions.

Analyze key features

- ❑ Process Diagram, p. 45 ❑   p. 64 ❑
- ❑ Development InSight, p. 52
- ❑ What a Developmentalist Sees, p. 71
- ❑ Stop: Answer the Concept Checks before you go on:
  p. 46 ❑   p. 62 ❑   p. 70 ❑   p. 74 ❑

End of chapter

- ❑ Review the Summary and Key Terms.
- ❑ Answer the Critical and Creative Thinking Questions.
- ❑ Answer *What is happening in this picture?*
- ❑ Complete the Self-Test and check your answers.

Genetics and Heredity

LEARNING OBJECTIVES

1. **Explain** how genes work.
2. **Discuss** the difference between phenotype and genotype.

Take a walk around your campus and observe the people you pass. Some are tall, some have blue eyes, some have dark skin, and some have thin lips. Hundreds of combinations of physical traits pass you each day. Yet, despite our uniqueness, all humans have some qualities in common. What are the origins of these similarities and differences? And how are they transmitted from one generation to the next? These questions lie at the heart of genetics, the study of heredity and of the incredible variation of inherited characteristics that we see all around us.

Nature's influence on individual variation in human development has been changing for millions of years—continuously adapting to a changing environment. At the most fundamental level, nature shapes the expression of individual differences through **genes**.

> **gene** A microscopic structure made of thousands of links of chemical particles that combine to construct all the parts of a living being.

What Is a Gene?

To understand genes, you must understand cells. Cells from various parts of our body look different from one another, but they share the same structure. At the centre of each cell lies a dark centre, the nucleus. Inside the nucleus of every cell, except sperm and ova, you will find 46 chromosomes, arranged in 23 pairs, as shown in **Figure 2.1**. Biologists call the first 22 chromosome pairs **autosomes** and the 23rd pair the **sex chromosome**, where females have XX chromosomes and males have XY.

Each chromosome contains molecules called *deoxyribonucleic acid* or **DNA**. DNA is made up of four chemical bases called *adenine (A)*, *guanine (G)*, *thymine (T)*, and *cytosine (C)*. These four bases have a key quality: A always pairs with T, while G always pairs with C.

> **autosome** Any one of the 22 pairs of chromosomes shared by both males and females.
>
> **sex chromosome** The 23rd chromosome pair, containing the genes that determine biological sex characteristics of females (XX) and males (XY).
>
> **DNA** Deoxyribonucleic acid, the fundamental chemical of all genes that guide the construction of cells.

Human chromosomes • Figure 2.1

Each cell in our body (except for the ova of females and the sperm of males) contains 23 pairs of chromosomes that are numbered from 1 to 23 based on size. One member of each chromosome pair comes from the mother and one from the father. Each of these pairs holds the genes that determine the composition and functions of the body. The arrangement of chromosomes by size is called a *karyotype*.

> **Ask Yourself**
> 1. The first 22 pairs of chromosomes shown here are called _____.
> 2. The final pair is called the _____ chromosome.
> 3. These chromosomes can be found inside the _____ of every cell in the body.

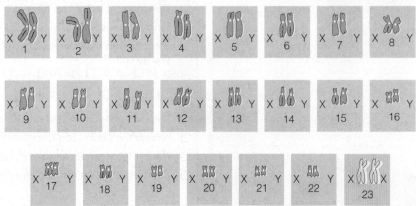

The building blocks of biological inheritance • Figure 2.2

At the moment of conception, a sperm and an ovum each contribute 23 chromosomes, for a total of 46.

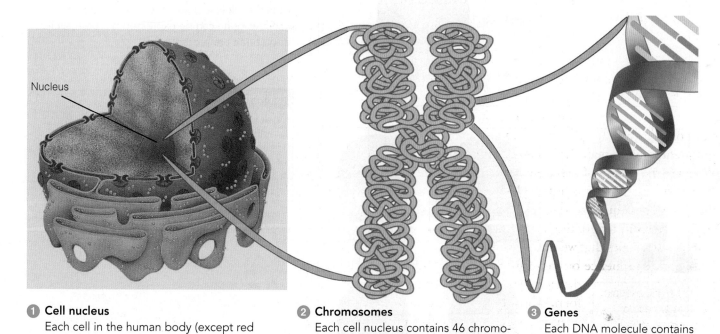

Nucleus

1 **Cell nucleus**
Each cell in the human body (except red blood cells) contains a nucleus.

2 **Chromosomes**
Each cell nucleus contains 46 chromosomes, which are threadlike molecules of DNA (deoxyribonucleic acid).

3 **Genes**
Each DNA molecule contains thousands of genes, which are the most basic units of heredity.

Ask Yourself

The most basic building blocks of heredity are _____.

As **Figure 2.2** illustrates, the nucleus of a cell contains chromosomes, which carry DNA. Genes on each chromosome are arranged in a particular sequence.

The specific place of a gene on a chromosome is called a **locus**. If you know the gene on one side of the helix, you can predict the other side. For example, if the gene is TCACGGT on one side of the DNA strand, it must be AGTGCCA on the other side, inasmuch as A always pairs with T and C with G. As cells divide, the DNA separates and then recombines with its partner to form a copy of the same cell.

locus The specific place on a chromosome where a gene is located.

Genetic Transmission

Now that you have a basic understanding of genes, let's look at how genetic information moves from parents to children. At conception, the sperm and the ova each contribute half of the new organism's genetic material. An individual's **genotype** determines the genetic potential and limitations of an individual, or the traits that genetically distinguish the individual from any other. It is made up of one set of chromosomes from our mother and one set from our father. Each genotype can result in a variety of

genotype An individual's collection of genes.

How genotypes are expressed • Figure 2.3

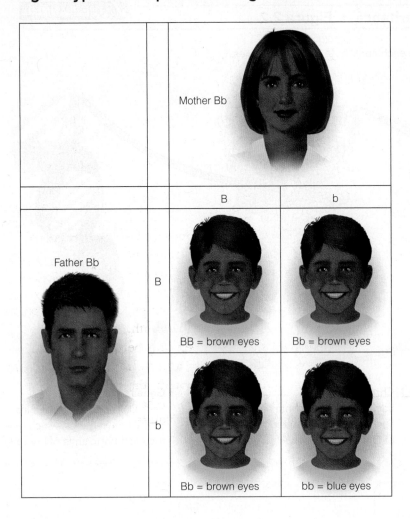

Mother Bb

Father Bb

	B	b
B	BB = brown eyes	Bb = brown eyes
b	Bb = brown eyes	bb = blue eyes

Eye colour provides an example of the combination of dominant and recessive genes. An allele for brown eyes (B in this figure) is dominant over an allele for blue eyes (b). The phenotype is expressed when the allele is dominant. The only way a recessive gene can be expressed is if both alleles for that trait are recessive (bb).

Ask Yourself

1. A child whose genotype includes one B allele and one b allele would have _____ eyes.
2. What if both of the mother's alleles were for brown eyes (BB) and both of the father's alleles were for blue eyes (bb)? Would it be possible for their child to have blue eyes?

---

phenotype
The observable characteristics of an individual.

allele Normative variation between genes.

dominant The quality of an allele that influences the expression of a trait.

recessive An allele that can only influence the expression of a trait in the absence of a dominant allele.

characteristics depending on the genes' interaction with the environment. The observable characteristics of an individual that result from this gene–environment interplay are called the **phenotype** (Deeb, Mason, Lee, & Hughes, 2007; Mayer, 1953). A multitude of phenotypes can result from the same genotype.

In addition to environmental interactions, variations in genes also help to determine a person's unique phenotype. Biologists use the term **allele** to describe any normative variation between

genes. If a person inherits two alleles that are in competition with one another, only one allele will influence the individual's phenotype (**Figure 2.3**). The expressed allele is called **dominant**, whereas the other allele, which has no observable effect on the person's phenotype, is termed **recessive**. With this biological foundation in mind, we begin our exploration of the lifespan at the very moment a genotype becomes a phenotype: the moment of conception.

CONCEPT CHECK STOP

1. **What** is the main function of a gene?
2. **How** is it possible for one genotype to result in numerous phenotypes?

Prenatal Development

LEARNING OBJECTIVES

1. **Describe** the process of conception.
2. **Discuss** key changes during the three stages of prenatal development.
3. **Differentiate** between critical and sensitive periods.
4. **Explain** the role of teratogens and genetic abnormalities in birth defects.
5. **List** the most common prenatal tests used within the medical model of care.
6. **Name** a critical task during the transition to parenthood.

S top for a moment and think about how you came into being. The multicelled, complex organism that you are today began through the union of just two solitary cells. Over the course of approximately 40 weeks, these two cells transformed into a complete organism. How does this happen?

Reproductive Anatomy and the Process of Conception

Conception is one of nature's most awe-inspiring processes. Before conception can occur, the **gametes**, **ovum**, and **sperm cells** have to form. Ova (eggs) develop within the female's ovaries located on either side of the uterus (**Figure 2.4a**). During a female's reproductive years, except when she is pregnant, the ovaries undergo cyclic changes known as the *menstrual cycle*. These changes, which typically occur every month, cause an ovum to ripen and be expelled by the ovaries, a process called **ovulation**. Although the ovaries contain hundreds of thousands of ova, only about 400–450

> **gamete** A male or female cell that contains 23 chromosomes in their singular form.
>
> **ovum** A female gamete containing 22 autosomes and 1 sex (X) chromosome.
>
> **sperm cell** A male gamete containing 22 autosomes and 1 sex (X or Y) chromosome.
>
> **ovulation** The typically monthly process that causes an ovum to ripen and be expelled by the ovaries.

Female and male reproductive anatomy • Figure 2.4

The ovum and sperm cells have different origins and go on very different journeys prior to conception.

a. Female reproductive anatomy

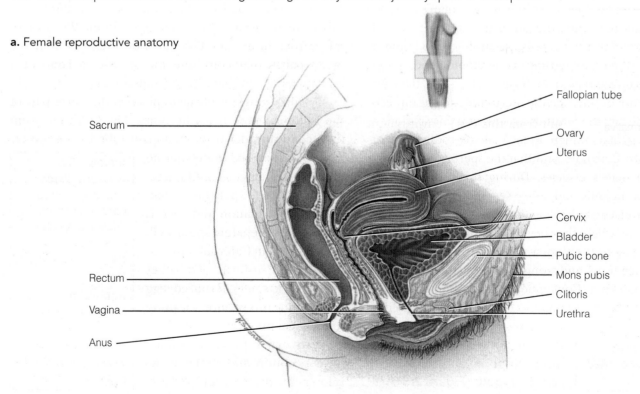

Sacrum

Rectum

Vagina

Anus

Fallopian tube

Ovary

Uterus

Cervix

Bladder

Pubic bone

Mons pubis

Clitoris

Urethra

b. Male reproductive anatomy

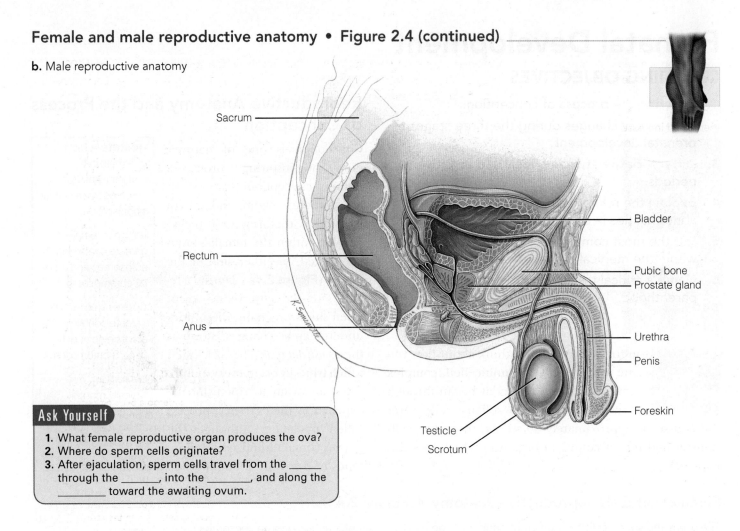

Sacrum

Rectum

Anus

Bladder

Pubic bone

Prostate gland

Urethra

Penis

Foreskin

Testicle

Scrotum

Ask Yourself

1. What female reproductive organ produces the ova?
2. Where do sperm cells originate?
3. After ejaculation, sperm cells travel from the _____ through the _____, into the _____, and along the _____ toward the awaiting ovum.

ova mature and are expelled during a woman's lifespan. After leaving the ovary, the ovum travels along the Fallopian tube toward the uterus. Meanwhile, the lining of the uterus (the endometrium) is developing and getting ready to receive and nourish the fertilized ovum. If fertilization does not occur, then the uterus will shed its unneeded lining during the monthly process of menstruation.

Turning for a moment to the male reproductive anatomy (**Figure 2.4b**), we find that the sperm cells develop within the male's testicles. During sexual intercourse, semen (sperm cells and other secretions that enhance fertility) is ejaculated through the urethra into the female's vagina, where they begin their journey. The sperm must travel from the vagina through the cervical opening, into the uterus, and along the Fallopian tubes toward the awaiting ovum. Conception occurs when one of the millions of sperm cells released by the male manages to penetrate the tough shell of the female's ovum to form a fertilized egg called a **zygote** (**Figure 2.5**).

zygote A fertilized ovum, in which the male and female gametes have united in one cell.

At conception, the genetic material from the father, carried in 23 chromosomes, merges with the 23 chromosomes from the mother. There are now 46 chromosomes—or 23 pairs—that constitute the genetic makeup of a human being (Batshaw, 2007; Goldschmidt, 1952).

Fertilization typically takes place in the outer part of the Fallopian tube near the ovary. The fertilized ovum then continues down the Fallopian tube to the uterus, where it will embed in the uterine lining several days later. On occasion, a woman expels more than one egg at ovulation and each is fertilized by a separate sperm cell, which results in fraternal twins (or triplets, and so forth). On other occasions a single fertilized egg divides into two or more, leading to identical multiples.

Two major processes underlie conception and prenatal development: **meiosis** and **mitosis**

meiosis The process by which cells containing 23 pairs of chromosomes divide into daughter cells containing one half of each chromosome pair.

mitosis The process by which cells create an exact copy of themselves, including all 23 pairs of chromosomes.

The moment of conception • Figure 2.5

Conception is marked by the joining of (typically) one ovum and one sperm cell. During conception, only a small fraction of 100 million or more sperm introduced into the vagina actually make it through the cervix and uterus to the ovum in the Fallopian tubes. Prostaglandins present in the semen also help produce cervical changes that aid in the sperm's journey through the uterus. If the female has an orgasm, she releases oxytocin, which creates pleasurable muscle contractions that facilitate the movement of the sperm and increase the chances of sperm contacting the ovum.

Francis Leroy, Biocosmos/Photo Researchers

a. Many sperm surround the ovum (egg) in the Fallopian tube.

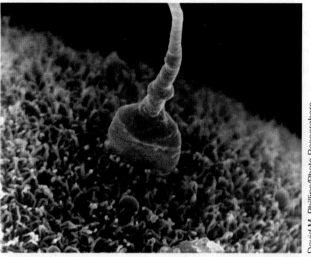

David M. Phillips/Photo Researchers

b. Once sperm reach the ovum, they undergo a 5- to 6-hour process of capacitation, which enables them to be selected by the ovum. They retain this ability for 24 to 72 hours. The ovum selects a sperm with tiny outgrowths called *microvilli*. Once the ovum encircles it, the sperm then secretes enzymes, which allow it to merge with the ovum. The internal membranes of the two cells, ovum and sperm, fuse and within seconds the egg produces a 30-second electric shock on its surface, which dislodges any sperm trying to attach to it. Next the ovum creates a hard outer protein coat to prevent more than one sperm being selected. In the rare event that two sperm enter, the product is not viable and is expelled in the next menstrual cycle. The merged ovum and sperm cells form a fertilized egg called a zygote.

morula A post-zygote collection of connected cells that continue to divide before forming a more complicated structure.

blastocyst A collection of cells arranged as a layer surrounding a central cavity containing fluid, into which an inner cell mass protrudes.

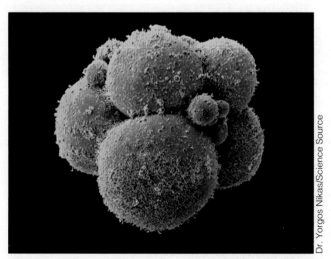

Dr. Yorgos Nikas/Science Source

c. Within 30 hours the zygote splits in two and through the process of cell division a **morula** forms. Over the next 3 or 4 days, the cells in the morula continue to divide as it moves down the Fallopian tube and enters the uterus.

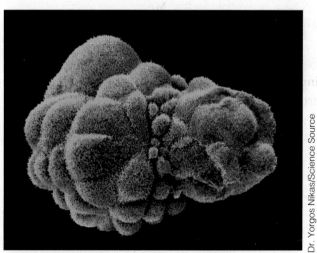

Dr. Yorgos Nikas/Science Source

d. Around 6 days after conception, the morula has transformed into an arrangement of cells called a **blastocyst**, which has a central cavity containing fluid and an inner cell mass. It is the blastocyst that may implant in the wall of the uterus and further develop into an embryo. In some women the implantation may be accompanied by bleeding, which may be confused with a light menstrual period and lead to a miscalculation of the pregnancy timeline.

Think Critically What does the moment of conception look like in the case of fraternal twins?

(**Figure 2.6**). Gametes, which we just discussed, form through meiosis. Mitosis occurs after conception, as the zygote rapidly divides and the DNA within the nucleus of each cell splits and replicates. Mitosis is a vital process during prenatal development (Batshaw, 2007).

As you can see, the process of conception is quite complex, and it is therefore no surprise that not everyone who wants to conceive is able to. Assisted reproductive technologies (ART) are a category of procedures designed to create the opportunity for a pregnancy. Women may use such technologies regardless of their sexual orientation or partnership status. Research indicates the value of ART for single women and lesbian couples alike (Fiske & Weston, 2014), as well as the estimated one in eight heterosexual couples experiencing infertility (Health Canada, 2015). People with genetic anomalies that can interfere with the viability of the fetus or other longer-acting genetic disorders can also benefit from ART.

The Assisted Human Reproduction Act (2004) provides national ethical oversight that prohibits human cloning or commerce in the products for conception and human reproduction. Clinical practice guidelines and standards provide professional oversight through the Society of Obstetricians and Gynaecologists of Canada, The Royal College of Physicians and Surgeons of Canada, and the Canadian Fertility and Andrology Society. Health care is a provincial jurisdiction, which results in uneven public policies governing ART eligibility for public funding. Add the burden of time and travel to the cost of the procedures and you have extensive barriers to access depending on where you live in Canada (Dunn, Stafinski, & Menon, 2014).

In vitro fertilization is one ART procedure in which eggs are removed from the ovaries, exposed to semen for fertilization, then inserted into the uterus for implantation. Data from the most recent analyses of the Canadian Assisted Reproductive Technologies Registry indicate the chances of live birth following a procedure vary markedly by age: 41 percent for women under 35 years, 30 percent for women aged 35–39, and 14 percent for women 40 years and over (CARTR PLUS, 2015).

Best practices in Canada recommend that every ART procedure be prefaced by a discussion of fetal outcomes and a routine ultrasound for congenital structural

The processes of meiosis and mitosis • Figure 2.6

In meiosis a parent cell divides, creating daughter cells that have only one half of the original 23 chromosome pairs. Sperm and ovum cells are formed through meiosis. Mitosis, on the other hand, occurs when the cell replicates itself, creating an exact copy. This process governs the formation of the multicellular organism that becomes the embryo and ultimately the newborn.

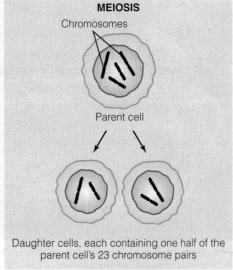

MEIOSIS

Chromosomes

Parent cell

Daughter cells, each containing one half of the parent cell's 23 chromosome pairs

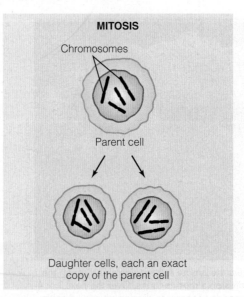

MITOSIS

Chromosomes

Parent cell

Daughter cells, each an exact copy of the parent cell

Ask Yourself

Chronologically, the process of _____ occurs before the process of _____.

abnormalities between 18 and 22 weeks (Okun & Sierra, 2014). Canada has one of the highest rates for multiple pregnancy using ART (Cook, Collins, Buckett, Racowsky, Hughes, & Jarvi, 2011), which prompted interventions to reduce the rate from 32 percent in 2009 to 13.3 percent in 2014 (CARTR PLUS, 2015).

Stages of Prenatal Development

Prenatal development is generally divided into three unique stages, as shown in **Figure 2.7**.

The germinal stage The zygote becomes a multicellular organism called a blastocyst through the process of mitosis. The entire blastocyst is about the same size as the zygote, but it contains hundreds of cells. As the blastocyst travels, it is nourished by secretions in the Fallopian tube and uterus. Eventually, the blastocyst begins to differentiate into two types of cells: a shell-like outer structure that will become the fetal support system and a multicellular centre that will become the embryo.

A great number of fertilized eggs do not result in live births. It is estimated that 30 to 50 percent of zygotes are lost before the woman even knows she is pregnant, and about one in five known pregnancies ends in miscarriage (Tortora & Nielsen, 2009).

The embryonic stage Unlike the germinal stage, when only two types of cells were present, the cells of an embryo rapidly differentiate for their specific purposes. Differentiation generally occurs in two characteristic ways. The first is in a **cephalocaudal pattern**, in which differentiation occurs from the head through the base of the spine. The second is a **proximodistal pattern**, in which the embryo differentiates from the spine through the limbs. Thus, an embryo's brain forms before its feet and its internal organs form (through a process called organogenesis; Muotri, 2009) before its limbs (Blanco, Martinez-Padilla, Dávila, Serrano, & Viñuela, 2003). Because these same patterns guide postnatal development, we will discuss them in greater detail in Chapter 3.

In addition to the embryo itself, a support system for the embryo forms during the embryonic period. The amniotic sac, containing clear amniotic fluid, takes shape around the embryo to protect the developing organism from shocks and abrupt temperature changes. A thick organ called the placenta forms along the uterine wall. The placenta does the work that will eventually be taken over after birth by the baby's lungs, digestive system, liver, and excretory organs. It allows nutrients to pass from the mother's blood to the embryo, but it keeps the blood of mother and embryo separate. The embryo connects to the placenta through the umbilical cord, a vein-filled cord that serves as the embryo's lifeline (Lamb, Bornstein, & Teti, 2002).

By the end of the embryonic stage, the embryo has features that resemble arms, legs, hands, and fingers, along with differentiated facial features, including eyelids (Tortora & Nielsen, 2009). In contrast to the focus on differentiation during the embryonic period, the next period of prenatal development is a time of rapid growth.

The fetal stage The fetal stage is characterized by rapid growth of all the body's physical systems following the cephalocaudal and proximodistal patterns we just discussed. The fetus grows from a little over 2.5 cm to an average of about 50 cm long and about 3.4 kg by birth. In addition to growing larger, fetuses become increasingly viable and functional as birth approaches. Shortly into the fetal stage, urination, swallowing, and some reflexes appear.

Because organ differentiation occurs before the fetal stage, the fetus is less vulnerable to outside influences than are blastocysts or embryos. These varying periods of vulnerability are called *critical* or *sensitive periods*.

Sensitive and Critical Periods

During the lifespan, periods of time exist when humans are most responsive to certain types of stimulation, when plasticity, or the potential to change, is high.

---

miscarriage An abrupt stop in the development of the pregnancy and subsequent delivery of the embryo or non-viable fetus before the 20th week of pregnancy.

cephalocaudal pattern A pattern of physical growth that proceeds from the head down through the long axis of the body.

proximodistal pattern A pattern of physical growth that proceeds from the centre of the body through the appendages.

organogenesis The early development and differentiation of the internal organs such as the lungs, heart, and gastrointestinal systems.

placenta A short-lived, multifunctional organ that passes nutrients from the mother's blood to the embryo.

umbilical cord A vein-filled cord that connects the embryo to the placenta.

plasticity The potential for systematic change within a person.

Development InSight

The stages of prenatal development • Figure 2.7

The germinal stage, the embryonic stage, and the fetal stage are the three stages of prenatal development (Zoldosova & Prokop, 2007).

a. Germinal stage— 0–2 weeks postconception

The single-celled zygote becomes a multicelled blastocyst as it travels down the Fallopian tube. The germinal stage ends when the blastocyst implants in the thick, nutrient-heavy lining of the uterus, called the *endometrium*.

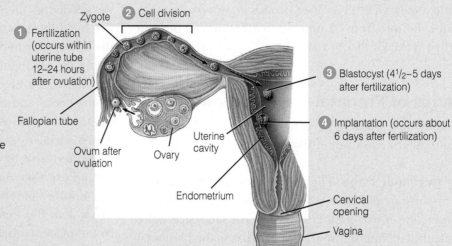

Zygote

2 Cell division

1 Fertilization (occurs within uterine tube 12–24 hours after ovulation)

Fallopian tube

Ovum after ovulation

Ovary

Uterine cavity

Endometrium

3 Blastocyst ($4^1/_2$–5 days after fertilization)

4 Implantation (occurs about 6 days after fertilization)

Cervical opening

Vagina

b. Embryonic stage—2–8 weeks post-conception

During this period, organs, as well as the support system for the developing organism, begin to develop. This is a critical time in prenatal development because organ formation can be highly vulnerable to outside influences.

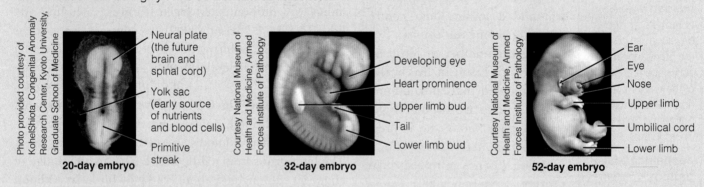

Photo provided courtesy of KohelShiota, Congenital Anomaly Research Center, Kyoto University, Graduate School of Medicine

Neural plate (the future brain and spinal cord)

Yolk sac (early source of nutrients and blood cells)

Primitive streak

20-day embryo

Courtesy National Museum of Health and Medicine, Armed Forces Institute of Pathology

Developing eye

Heart prominence

Upper limb bud

Tail

Lower limb bud

32-day embryo

Courtesy National Museum of Health and Medicine, Armed Forces Institute of Pathology

Ear

Eye

Nose

Upper limb

Umbilical cord

Lower limb

52-day embryo

c. Fetal stage—8 weeks post-conception to birth (approximately 38 weeks post-conception)

The fetal stage is a time of rapid growth and increasing functionality. The fetus also becomes increasingly active, with mothers first feeling fetal movements, called *quickening*, around the four-month mark (Lamb, Bornstein, & Teti, 2002). Historically, this was an important point in gestation, leaving women a greater freedom of action to terminate suspected pregnancies prior to quickening (Mohr, 1978).

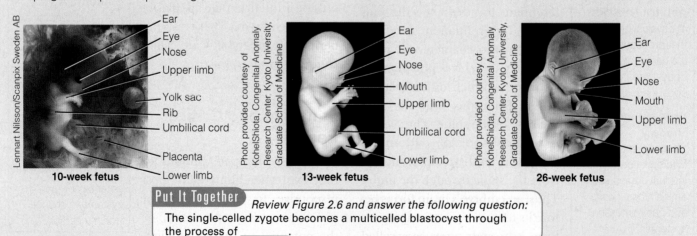

Lennart Nilsson/Scanpix Sweden AB

Ear

Eye

Nose

Upper limb

Yolk sac

Rib

Umbilical cord

Placenta

Lower limb

10-week fetus

Photo provided courtesy of KohelShiota, Congenital Anomaly Research Center Kyoto University, Graduate School of Medicine

Ear

Eye

Nose

Mouth

Upper limb

Umbilical cord

Lower limb

13-week fetus

Photo provided courtesy of KohelShiota, Congenital Anomaly Research Center, Kyoto University, Graduate School of Medicine

Ear

Eye

Nose

Mouth

Upper limb

Lower limb

26-week fetus

Put It Together

Review Figure 2.6 and answer the following question: The single-celled zygote becomes a multicelled blastocyst through the process of _____.

These periods of time, known as **sensitive periods**, have to do with the potential of environmental influences—both positive and negative ones—to affect development (MacDonald, 1985; Thomas & Johnson, 2008). For example, normal visual experiences early in life are essential for the development of normal vision (see Lewis & Maurer, 2005, for a review). Children deprived of normative developmental experiences, for example, in the case of infants born with blinding cataracts, may never achieve normal vision even after corrective interventions. This is because sensitive periods dictate the brain development responsible for functions such as sight.

Different from a sensitive period, a **critical period** is conceptualized as a finite window of opportunity for a given feature of development to emerge. If that feature does not develop normally during its critical period of development, it will never have a second chance, no matter how strong the environmental influences. However, we know that even the most vulnerable periods

> **sensitive period**
> An interval of heightened plasticity, when environmental influences are most efficient at affecting an organism's development.
>
> **critical period**
> A finite window of opportunity for development, outside of which environmental influences are said to have no effect.

allow for some flexibility in both the quality and timing of environmental influences (Nelson, 1999).

The general rule is that plasticity is present throughout the lifespan. This is why there are many more sensitive periods than critical periods. Researchers are still not certain why sensitive periods occur when they do. What they do know is that sensitive periods are pervasive, and that those occurring soon after birth significantly influence potential for expected development (Thomas & Johnson, 2008). For example, during the first two years of life, babies appear to have sensitive periods in all of their sensory systems, including vision (as previously noted) and hearing (**Figure 2.8**; Huttenlocker, 2002). There appear to be sensitive periods for language and motor skills development, as well as infant attachment to a primary caregiver (Sullivan & Holman, 2010; Varin, Crugnola, Molina, & Ripamonti, 1996). Prenatally, sensitive periods are times when the brain and organs are most sensitive to harmful environmental agents called *teratogens*.

Teratogens

Drugs, disease, foods, and other environmental influences on the mother can alter prenatal development.

An example of sensitive periods • Figure 2.8

The concept of sensitive periods is illustrated well by changes in the brain from conception to 2 years of age. The more synapses that are being created, the more vulnerable the brain is to environmental influences. As shown here, the prefrontal cortex has the earliest sensitive period, followed by the brain systems involved in vision and hearing. Similar sensitive periods in other systems, including the organs, are believed to occur during prenatal development.

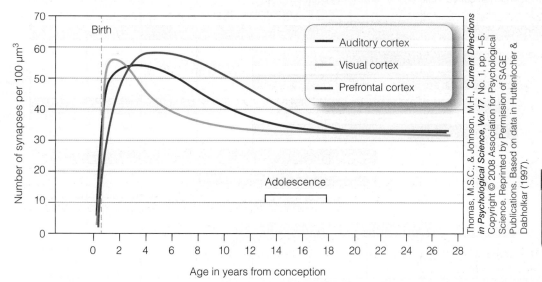

Thomas, M.S.C., & Johnson, M.H., *Current Directions in Psychological Science, Vol. 17*, No. 1, pp. 1–5. Copyright © 2008 Association for Psychological Science. Reprinted by Permission of SAGE Publications. Based on data in Huttenlocker & Dabholkar (1997).

Ask Yourself

Can vision and hearing develop outside of the sensitive period depicted here?

teratogen An environmental agent that can adversely affect prenatal development and can have long-lasting effects on subsequent development.

Potentially harmful environmental agents are called teratogens, a term derived from the Greek word for monster. The study of environmental agents that cause birth defects is therefore called **teratology**.

Although scientists have been able to examine the specific effects of teratogens through animal research, many unanswered questions remain. Some studies (e.g., Woehrmann, Volland, Tuch, Bode, & Hübel, 2005) suggest that teratogens may affect neurons as they travel from undifferentiated tissue to their final locations during prenatal development.

Wilson's six principles of teratogenic effects Much remains unknown about teratogenic effects. However, fundamental principles outlined decades ago provide a framework for understanding how adverse influences undermine prenatal development (Wilson, 1973; Kalter, 2003). These six principles continue to guide our understanding of teratogenic effects.

Principle 1: Susceptibility to teratogens partly depends on the genetic makeup of the developing organism. The way the genes interact with environmental agents determines the effect of a specific agent.

Principle 2: Timing of exposure is crucial to how teratogens affect development. In general, the embryonic period is an especially vulnerable time, as shown in **Figure 2.9**.

Vulnerability to teratogens during prenatal development • Figure 2.9

The point at which a specific teratogen appears makes all the difference in how it affects prenatal development. As shown here in PURPLE, major abnormalities tend to occur when teratogen exposure takes place prior to about 8 weeks of development, and there is no vulnerability to teratogens prior to the third week. However, the severity of effects at any point during prenatal development varies depending on the bodily system being affected and the teratogen itself.

Think Critically Given what we know about teratogen exposure during early pregnancy, what actions might a policy-maker take to foster optimal prenatal development?

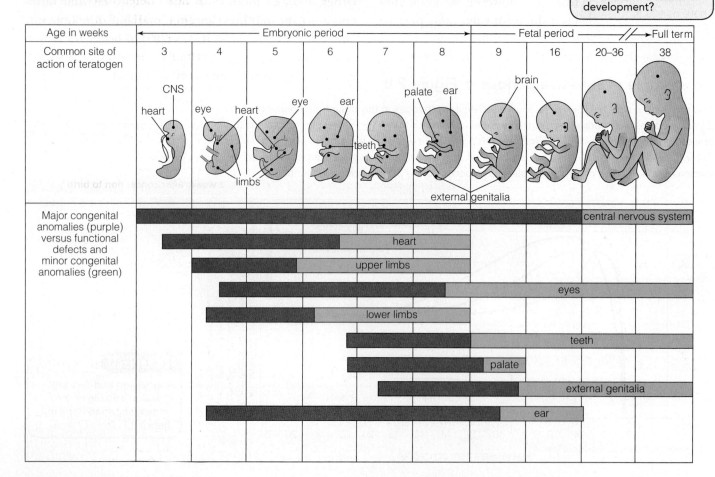

neural tube In the developing embryo, the precursor to the central nervous system.

For example, essential development of the central nervous system (CNS), including the formation of the **neural tube** that will become the brain and spinal cord, occurs before the woman typically even knows she is pregnant. Thus, exposure to teratogens that affect the CNS can be particularly problematic early in development.

Principle 3: Dose or amount may play a role in how teratogens affect developing organisms. For example, it is known that greater prenatal exposure to alcohol relates to increased effects. In addition, some substances cause greater harm in combination than they would alone.

Principle 4: The level and severity of the effect of a teratogen depend on the interaction of many factors, including genetic makeup, timing, and what is occurring in the developmental process.

Principle 5: There are four manifestations of deviant development due to teratogen exposure: growth retardation, functional defect, malformation, and death.

Principle 6: The overall effect of teratogen exposure operates in a dose: response relationship. The greater the adverse exposure, the greater the deviation from normal, healthy development.

Common teratogens The most commonly discussed teratogens and their possible effects are listed in **Table 2.1**. Building on our previous discussion of sensitive periods,

we note the period during prenatal development when these teratogens are most likely to have an effect.

Alcohol is the leading teratogen worldwide and no amount is safe to consume during pregnancy, according to the Royal College of Obstetricians and Gynaecologists (2016). The Public Health Agency of Canada (2012) advises that "there is no safe amount or safe time to drink alcohol during pregnancy." Fetal alcohol spectrum disorders (FASD), which result from a mother's consumption of alcohol, can range from low body weight to poor memory and intellectual disabilities (Wedding et al., 2007). Some common physical characteristics are shown in **Figure 2.10**.

There are some prenatal issues, such as those due to genetic or chromosomal aberrations, that may not be preventable through behavioural change. However, given the potential harms of teratogens, pregnancy may influence a woman to change her behaviour—for example, by giving up wine or cigarettes during pregnancy. Mounting evidence from human and animal research indicates that paternal preconception exposure to certain chemical agents, environmental toxins, or radioactivity can affect fetal genetic mutations (Brinkworth, 2000; Trasler & Doerksen, 1999) and that heart defects are associated with paternal smoking (Deng et al., 2013). Unfortunately, while much more research is needed to better influence men's preconception behaviours, research with sperm cells has not had the same level of interest.

Major teratogens and their effects   Table 2.1

Teratogen	Possible Effects	Sensitive Period
Alcohol	Fetal alcohol syndrome	2 weeks after conception to birth
Smoking	Low birth weight	Embryonic stage
Marijuana	CNS damage; stunted growth	Embryonic stage
Cocaine; crack	Behavioural issues; prematurity	2 weeks after conception to birth
Methamphetamine	Prematurity; inhibited fetal growth	2 weeks after conception to birth
Heroin	Addiction; behaviour problems	2 weeks after conception to birth
Maternal diseases: measles (rubella); herpes; HIV	Disease; CNS implications	Embryonic stage
Tranquilizers	Low birth weight	2 weeks after conception to birth
Chemical agents: pollution; lead paint	Genetic abnormalities	2 weeks after conception to birth
Radiation	Mental retardation	2 weeks after conception to birth
Prescription drugs: Thalidomide	Limb and organ defects	27–40 days after conception

The features of fetal alcohol syndrome • Figure 2.10

Alcohol use during pregnancy may lead to a variety of physiological effects. "Discriminating features" uniquely describe fetal alcohol syndrome in an individual, whereas "associated features" are more commonly observed in individuals with fetal alcohol syndrome than in individuals who do not have fetal alcohol syndrome.

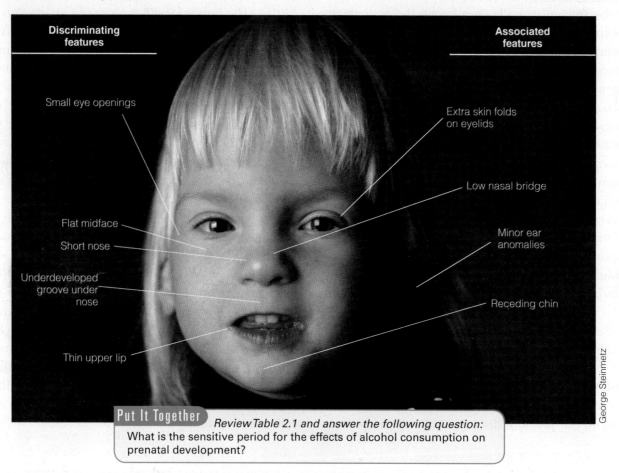

Discriminating features

Small eye openings

Flat midface

Short nose

Underdeveloped groove under nose

Thin upper lip

Associated features

Extra skin folds on eyelids

Low nasal bridge

Minor ear anomalies

Receding chin

George Steinmetz

Put It Together *Review Table 2.1 and answer the following question:* What is the sensitive period for the effects of alcohol consumption on prenatal development?

Genetic and Chromosomal Abnormalities

During the processes of meiosis and mitosis, chromosomes divide and recombine as gametes are formed and

> **mutation** An abnormality that occurs during genetic transmission and that may affect the entire chromosome or specific genes.

the embryo develops. Errors, or **mutations**, can occur during either of these processes. These errors can have negative effects on the developing organism.

Two major categories of abnormalities can occur during genetic transmission. Chromosomal abnormalities produce greater effects than genetic abnormalities, because an entire chromosome is involved.

Chromosomal abnormalities Chromosomal abnormalities generally have to do with having either too many or too few chromosomes (Omoto & Lurquin, 2004). These errors typically occur during meiosis. As we discussed earlier, meiosis is the process by which the gametes form. Occasionally during this process, the chromosomes do not divide adequately, resulting in an egg or a sperm with an incorrect number of chromosomes. When a zygote is formed from such a gamete, the zygote will also have too many or too few chromosomes.

In about half of the cases of chromosomal abnormalities, a spontaneous miscarriage occurs (Omoto & Lurquin, 2004). In the remaining cases, fetuses with an incorrect number of chromosomes make it to full term

Disorders resulting from chromosomal abnormalities   Table 2.2

Disorder	Cause	Effect
Trisomy 21 (Down syndrome)	Three chromosomes instead of two on the 21st pair	Rounded face, an extra fold over the eyelids, intellectual disability, cardiovascular system abnormalities
XXX (Triple X syndrome)	Extra X chromosome (in females)	In girls; low mean birth weight, small head circumference, delayed language development, lower IQ
XYY (Jacob's syndrome)	Extra Y chromosome (in males)	In boys; increased growth velocity in earliest childhood with a final height higher than average; increased risk of learning disabilities
Turner syndrome	Only one sex chromosome: an X; affects females only	Short stature, webbed neck, ovaries that do not function, learning disorders
Klinefelter's syndrome	Two or more X chromosomes alongside a Y chromosome; affects males only	Underdeveloped genitalia and average or low-average IQ

of about 40 weeks gestation. This outcome is most likely when the abnormality occurs on the smaller chromosomes, such as the sex chromosomes. Infants with chromosomal abnormalities experience a variety of effects. **Table 2.2** presents five common disorders resulting from an incorrect number of chromosomes. The most common of these is Trisomy 21, also known as Down syndrome (Baty, Carey, & McMahon, 2005), in which there is an extra chromosome on the 21st pair.

On each chromosome, thousands of genes create the proteins and enzymes responsible for every part of our body. As we will now see, sometimes these genes themselves form incorrectly, resulting in a variety of outcomes.

Genetic issues Every time a cell divides, the entire DNA chain of that cell must be copied. Sometimes during this replication process a DNA base is omitted or copied incorrectly. If the gap is small enough, nothing negative happens. If numerous base deletions occur, however, the gene is significantly changed (Omoto & Lurquin, 2004). In these cases, notable defects can result, as we learn in *Where Developmentalists Click.*

Not all genetic defects result in observable outcomes. For example, chromosome 12 contains a gene responsible for breaking down the amino acid phenylalanine, a substance found in many foods, such as pop. When this gene is damaged or absent, the disease phenylketonuria (PKU) can result, in which a person is unable to process phenylalanine (Swarts, 2009). PKU occurs only if both parents transmit the defective gene.

If a child receives the trait from the father but not the mother, there is no impact on the child at all because PKU is an **autosomal recessive trait** rather than an **autosomal dominant trait**.

Other genetic disorders are sex-linked; that is, they involve the **sex-linked gene**. Defective sex-linked genes are usually carried on the X chromosome. Because the male child gets only one X, if his mother is a carrier of a defective sex-linked gene he will automatically get the disorder because his Y chromosome acts like a recessive gene. In order for a daughter to get the disorder, however, both the mother and the father must be carriers of the defective gene on their X chromosomes, in which case the father will already be exhibiting the symptoms of the disorder. An example of a sex-linked disorder is colour-blindness, a disorder controlled by a gene on the X chromosome. Because it is sex-linked, 7 percent of men in the population have colour-blindness, but only 0.4 percent of women do (Dudek, 2009).

The leading cause of inherited developmental delay is the result of a weakened section on the X chromosome and, as such, it is known as Fragile X syndrome; usually it is diagnosed as a child demonstrates developmental

> **autosomal recessive trait**
> A trait that requires the presence of both paternal and maternal genes for the phenotype to be expressed.
>
> **autosomal dominant trait**
> A trait that requires the presence of only one parental gene for the phenotype to be expressed.
>
> **sex-linked gene**
> A gene located on one of the sex chromosomes (X or Y).

Where Developmentalists CLICK

Genetic Counselling

The Online Mendelian Inheritance in Man database, a site sponsored by the National Institutes of Health (an agency of the U.S. Department of Health and Human Services), compiles all known disorders that have some type of genetic cause. Typically used

by physicians and other helping professionals concerned with genetic disorders, the site provides information on the human genome, as well as links to other genetics resources.

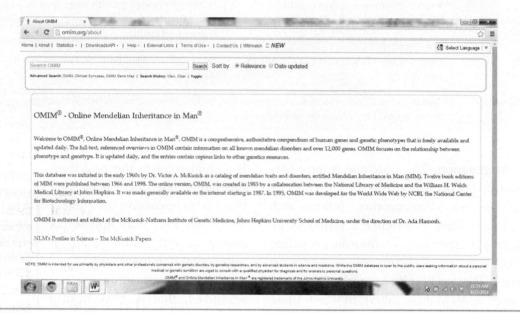

delays, but it is also marked clinically by long, narrow facial features with protruding chin and large ears and enlarged testes. The rate of occurrence in the population ranges markedly from about 1/1250 to 1/4000 in males and 1/2000 to 1/8000 in females (Sherman, 1991; Turner, Robinson, Laing, Purvis-Smith, 1986; Turner, Webb, Wake, Robinson, 1996). Fascinating regional variations in Canada show an extremely high estimate with as many as 1/259 females from Quebec being carriers (Rousseau et al,) and a phenomenal absence of carriers within the Nova Scotia founding population (Beresford et al., 2000).

A variety of prenatal tests have been developed over the last three or four decades. These technologies are used to detect the various teratogenic effects, chromosomal abnormalities, and genetic issues discussed previously.

Prenatal Care and Monitoring

It is very important for pregnant women to be monitored and checked by trained medical professionals throughout the various stages of pregnancy. This is called *prenatal care*

or *maternity care*. Two general models of maternity care exist in Canada, as well as in many other countries around the world: the **midwifery model of care** and the **medical model of care** (Canadian Institute for Health Information, 2004). The midwifery model of care views pregnancy and birth as normal, inherently healthy life processes (Midwifery Task Force, 2008). Therefore, this model of care involves (1) monitoring the physical, psychological, and social well-being of the mother throughout pregnancy and birth; (2) providing individualized education and prenatal care, as well as continuous support during labour and birth; (3) minimizing technological interventions; and (4) identifying and referring women who require obstetrical attention. The midwifery model has been

> **midwifery model of care** A woman-centred model of maternity care based on the idea that pregnancy and birth are normal, inherently healthy life processes.
>
> **medical model of care** A comparatively new model of maternity care guided by the belief that pregnancy and birth are potentially dangerous life processes that must be medically managed.

Caesarean surgery A medical intervention in which the abdomen is cut and the fetus(es) removed.

shown to greatly reduce the incidence of birth injury, trauma, and **Caesarean surgery**, commonly called a *C-section*, in which the mother's abdomen is cut and the fetus (or fetuses) removed (Midwifery Task Force, 2008).

The medical model of maternity care is comparatively new, having emerged on the world scene just two centuries ago (Gaskin, 2003). Nevertheless, it has been dominant in Canada, and throughout North America, since the early 1900s (Mitchinson, 2002). The medical model of care views pregnancy and childbirth as potentially dangerous conditions that make medical intervention necessary in all cases (Berg, Ólafsdóttir, & Lundgren, 2012).

In both models of care, in order to ensure the health and safety of mother and baby, certain prenatal tests are considered essential. At various visits, different tests are performed to monitor the health of both the mother and the developing fetus. For example, urine is checked for excess sugar and protein; blood pressure is taken because high blood pressure is one of the most common medical problems in pregnancy; fundal height is measured (**Figure 2.11**); and ankles are felt for extreme swelling, which can be a sign of a more serious problem.

A variety of optional prenatal tests have been developed over the last three or four decades (**Figure 2.12**). Obstetric **ultrasound**—the use of high-frequency sound waves to visualize the embryo or fetus within the mother's uterus—was introduced shortly after a large study showed an increase in cancer among children who were X-rayed in utero (Stewart, Webb, Giles, & Hewitt, 1956). Unlike the case with an X-ray, there is no ionizing radiation exposure with ultrasound. By 1980, obstetric ultrasound was routine in many countries. In Canada, experts recommend that all expectant women have at least one ultrasound, ideally between the 18th and 22nd week of pregnancy. Additional ultrasounds may be requested if deemed necessary by a health care professional (Society of Obstetricians and Gynaecologists of Canada, 2015). The Canadian Medical Association has accredited 13 diagnostic ultrasound technology programs to train technicians, or ultrasonographers, in Canada (Secretariat of Health Professions Regulatory Advisory Council, 2013). Health Canada regulates ultrasound technology through the Medical Devices Regulations of the Food and Drugs Act and the Radiation Emitting Devices Act (Health Canada, 2006).

Although obstetric ultrasounds are considered safe, and there is no standard **informed consent** process, the Society of Obstetricians and Gynaecologists

ultrasound The use of high-frequency sound waves to visualize the embryo or fetus within the uterus.

informed consent In a clinical context, the process of explaining the purpose of a procedure, outlining the benefits and risks associated with it, and requesting the patient's signature to verify they understand and agree to participate.

Measuring fundal height • Figure 2.11

Measured in centimetres, fundal height is the distance from the top of the uterus to the pubic bone. After the first 12 weeks of pregnancy, it is common for fundal height to match the number of weeks of pregnancy.

Think Critically What might the fundal height tell doctors and midwives about the health of the fetus?

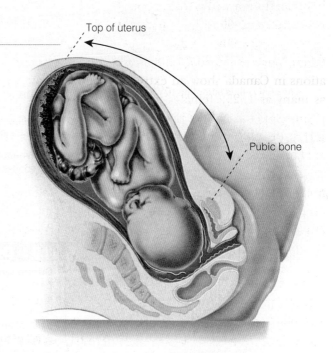

Top of uterus

Pubic bone

Common prenatal tests • Figure 2.12

Ultrasound, amniocentesis, and chorionic villus sampling are three common prenatal tests. Although originally envisioned for use only with high-risk populations of women, these technologies have since become widespread within the medical model of maternity care. Most provincial health insurance plans cover the cost of diagnostic screening, leading many women to undergo these tests.

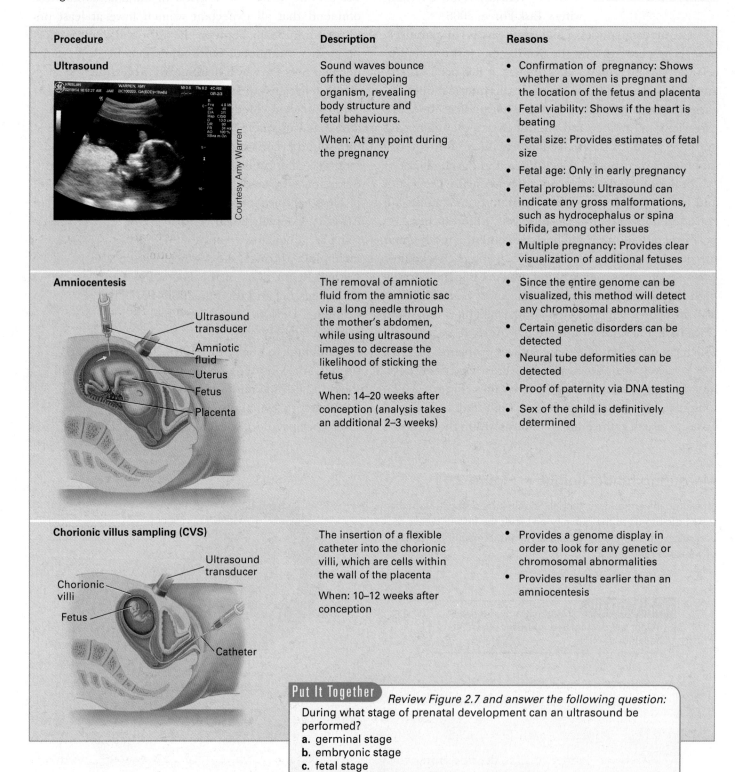

Procedure	Description	Reasons
Ultrasound	Sound waves bounce off the developing organism, revealing body structure and fetal behaviours. When: At any point during the pregnancy	• Confirmation of pregnancy: Shows whether a women is pregnant and the location of the fetus and placenta • Fetal viability: Shows if the heart is beating • Fetal size: Provides estimates of fetal size • Fetal age: Only in early pregnancy • Fetal problems: Ultrasound can indicate any gross malformations, such as hydrocephalus or spina bifida, among other issues • Multiple pregnancy: Provides clear visualization of additional fetuses
Amniocentesis	The removal of amniotic fluid from the amniotic sac via a long needle through the mother's abdomen, while using ultrasound images to decrease the likelihood of sticking the fetus When: 14–20 weeks after conception (analysis takes an additional 2–3 weeks)	• Since the entire genome can be visualized, this method will detect any chromosomal abnormalities • Certain genetic disorders can be detected • Neural tube deformities can be detected • Proof of paternity via DNA testing • Sex of the child is definitively determined
Chorionic villus sampling (CVS)	The insertion of a flexible catheter into the chorionic villi, which are cells within the wall of the placenta When: 10–12 weeks after conception	• Provides a genome display in order to look for any genetic or chromosomal abnormalities • Provides results earlier than an amniocentesis

PUT IT TOGETHER *Review Figure 2.7 and answer the following question:*
During what stage of prenatal development can an ultrasound be performed?
a. germinal stage
b. embryonic stage
c. fetal stage
d. all of the above

of Canada (2015) recommend that ultrasounds not be used for non-medical purposes. This is partially because, although there are no known short-term effects of obstetric ultrasound on human development, researchers do not yet know if there are any long-term effects. Notably, routine ultrasound scans during pregnancy do not seem to improve neonatal outcomes more than if scans are used only when medically indicated (for a review, see Belizán & Cafferata, 2011).

amniocentesis
The process of removing fluid from the amniotic sac of a pregnant woman and surveying the genome under a microscope.

chorionic villus sampling (CVS)
The process of obtaining a tissue sample from the villi of the chorion, which forms the fetal part of the placenta.

If a more detailed assessment of the fetus is required, medical professionals may suggest **amniocentesis** or **chorionic villus sampling (CVS)**—testing a biopsy of chorionic villus cells (placental tissue) for chromosomal abnormalities. The main risk of both procedures is miscarriage. In Canada, the risk of complications after amniocentesis, including miscarriage, is reported at 0.5 to 1 percent. The risk of complications following CVS is slightly higher, at 1 to 2 percent (Government of Canada, 2013). Within the medical model, amniocentesis is routinely offered to pregnant women over 35. At this age, the probability of having a baby with a chromosomal abnormality is about the same as or greater than the likelihood that the test will cause miscarriage or injury to the fetus. Women undergoing amniocentesis and their partners report feelings of uncertainty, tension, and anxiety about fetal injury (Kukulu et al., 2006). Raised levels of anxiety and other difficult feelings typically recede when no abnormalities are detected (Marteau, Johnston, Shaw, Michie, Kidd, & New, 1989).

We have been discussing the ways in which soon-to-be mothers and fathers monitor pregnancy in preparation for labour and birth. Pregnancy is also a time when preparations are made for parenthood.

The Transition to Parenthood

"What am I concerned about? That life will be over! Let's see. . . . I'm concerned that I won't be able to stay as active as I always have been and that we'll get on one another's nerves because we'll all be home together more." (McHale, Talbot, & Kazali, 2007, p. 56)

—Orlando's reflections on the upcoming birth of his first child

"I'll be the primary caregiver during the day, but when he gets home, he'll take over. . . . I think he'll be a very involved dad because his father wasn't. . . . I want us to be really together and involved as a group so the baby will respond to both of us." (McHale et al., 2007, p. 56)

—Cynthia, Orlando's wife

"During pregnancy, expectant parents begin to imagine family life and to construct expectations about life after birth (McHale et al., 2007). At the forefront of their minds is whether they will be good and effective mothers or fathers (Biehle & Mickelson, 2011). *Do I have the knowledge and skills needed to be an effective parent? Will my co-parent and I work well together and will we be a positive influence on our child's development and behaviour?* How parents think about future parenthood has a lot to do with how future parenthood plays out. Parents who anticipate problems after the baby comes may be primed to respond negatively to the normative challenges of new parenthood (McHale & Rotman, 2007). At three months postpartum (after birth), parents with pessimistic outlooks show lower levels of co-operation and warmth (McHale, Kazali, Rotman, Talbot, Carleton, & Lieberson, 2004).

"On the other hand, parents who feel prepared for parenthood report lower levels of stress and higher levels of self-esteem (**Figure 2.13**; Delmore-Ko, Pancer, Hunsberger, & Pratt, 2000). The relationship between parents-to-be is also of prime importance. A critical task of the transition to parenthood is the development of a strong **co-parenting** relationship. Are parents supportive (warm and co-operative) or undermining (hostile and competitive) of one another?

co-parenting
The extent to which parents are supportive of one another's parenting.

Do they agree about different aspects of parenting (for example, do they have shared expectations about their children's behaviour)? Are they satisfied with the division of child care? These questions have to do with co-parenting, and their answers help us predict who will have a smoother transition to parenthood (McHale & Rotman, 2007).

The realities governing prenatal expectations of parenthood are situationally located and historically embedded. Couples who have planned a pregnancy, for example, may have a more romanticized view of parenthood when compared with couples continuing with an unplanned pregnancy (Bouchard, Boudreau, &

Prenatal expectations of parenthood • Figure 2.13

Mothers' expectations of parenthood can be organized into three categories, as depicted in this pie chart (Delmore-Ko et al., 2000). A little less than one third of mothers self-report feeling prepared for parenthood, whereas one third of mothers self-report feeling fearful and a little more than one third self-report feeling satisfied and unconcerned (complacent). Women who report feeling prepared for parenthood demonstrate better postpartum adjustment compared with mothers in the other groups. In the Western world, current ideal child-rearing practices tend to necessitate intensive resource investment (Hays, 2006). Women experiencing pregnancy from a context of disadvantage—such as young women, single women, and women marginalized by economic factors—may find feelings of preparedness difficult to achieve and maintain (Neiterman, 2013). In short, perceptions of parental preparedness are highly influenced by the context in which a pregnancy occurs.

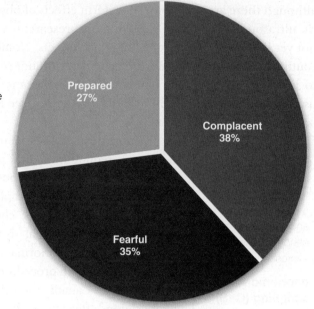

Think Critically 1. If you are a parent, which of the three categories best described your prenatal expectations of parenthood?
2. If you are not a parent, in what category might you expect to fall?

Hébert, 2006). Contemporary constructions of motherhood and fatherhood, as well as perceptions of one's ability to perform these roles, also influence individual expectations (Rizzo, Shiffrin, & Liss, 2013; Wall & Arnold, 2007).

Co-parenting is also tied to young children's socio-emotional health (e.g., Brown, Schoppe-Sullivan, Mangelsdorf, & Neff, 2010; Karreman, van Tuijl, van Aken, & Deković, 2008). In fact, co-parenting is a better explanation of the variation in children's socio-emotional health than the parent–child relationship or the couple relationship (Karreman et al., 2008). We turn now to a pivotal moment in the transition to parenthood—labour and birth.

CONCEPT CHECK ⬣STOP

1. **Where** does fertilization take place?
2. **Why** is the developing organism more vulnerable during the embryonic period than other periods of prenatal development?
3. **When** during the lifespan is plasticity particularly high?
4. **How** do teratogens differ from genetic abnormalities?
5. **What** are the differences between the midwifery and medical models of care?
6. **Why** is the co-parenting relationship important?

Labour and Birth

LEARNING OBJECTIVES

1. **Describe** the four stages of labour.
2. **Discuss** the different types of maternity care providers.
3. **Name** some common obstetrical interventions and their associated risks.

The human body performs many miraculous functions, and perhaps none is greater than the work the mind and body do together in the process of birthing an infant. The changes in the human body during pregnancy, in preparation for childbirth, involve each and every physiological system. Indeed, unless you have seen a baby born, it may seem like an impossible feat. And yet it is a normal, everyday occurrence. Let's look at how it happens.

Stages of Labour

cervix A powerful ring of muscles that keeps the uterus tightly shut during pregnancy but then thins and opens during labour.

The **cervix**, a powerful ring of muscles at the lower end of the uterus, keeps the uterus tightly shut throughout pregnancy (Gaskin, 2002). The cervix must be strong considering that, by the end of pregnancy, it has approximately 7 kg of baby, placenta, and fluid pressing against it—more in the case of multiple pregnancies. A plug of thick mucus seals the cervix during pregnancy. In the hours before labour begins, the blood-tinged mucus plug is discharged, known as **bloody show**. Labour begins with the onset of rhythmic uterine contractions that thin (efface) and open (dilate) the cervix, moving it out of the way of the descending baby. These contractions also push the baby, and eventually the placenta, through the dilated cervix and out of the vagina. Labour and birth proceed in four stages, as explained and depicted in **Figure 2.14**.

bloody show A plug of thick, blood-tinged mucus that is discharged from the cervix shortly before labour begins.

Hormones play an essential role in the various functions of labour and birth described in Figure 2.14. The complex interplay of hormones such as prostaglandins, oxytocin, adrenaline, and endorphins stimulate the regulation and timing of uterine contractions and the various maternal and infant responses (emotions and actions) that are essential to the newborn's survival (Gaskin, 2002). Prostaglandins soften and thin the cervix in preparation for labour. Oxytocin stimulates uterine contractions, and later, when the baby passes through the vaginal canal, oxytocin levels suddenly increase and stimulate bonding between mother and newborn. Whereas oxytocin accelerates birth, adrenaline—associated with the fight-or-flight response—can stall it. Finally, endorphins alter pain perception and give us a feeling of pleasure. Endorphins increase when we exert ourselves and, especially, when we feel loved and supported and not frightened (Gaskin, 2002). In other words, mothers who feel afraid and unsupported during labour and birth tend to secrete hormones that delay or impede birth, whereas mothers who feel unafraid and supported tend to secrete hormones that make labour and birth easier, less painful, and sometimes even pleasurable (**Figure 2.15**).

Labour and birth serve as a striking example of the powerful connection between mind (emotions) and body (hormones) that is, in fact, present throughout the lifespan. Given this connection, some women opt to have professional, continuous labour support, such as that provided by a **birth doula** (**Figure 2.16**). A birth doula is a specially trained birth companion who provides emotional, physical, and informational support during labour, birth, and the immediate postpartum. In other words, birth doulas focus on the non-clinical aspects of care during childbirth. Their support has been shown to improve certain clinical outcomes (for a review, see Hodnett, Gates, Hofmeyr, Sakala, & Weston, 2011). For example, labouring women supported by birth doulas are 28 percent less likely to have a Caesarean section, 31 percent less likely to use drugs that speed up labour, and 9 percent less likely to use pain medication (Hodnett et al., 2011). Birth doulas also strengthen emotional ties between mother and newborn, enhance breastfeeding, and increase women's self-esteem and satisfaction with the birth experience (Langer, Campero, Garcia, & Reynoso, 1998; Martin, Landry, Steelman, Kennell, & McGrath, 1998).

birth doula A specially trained birth companion, who provides physical, emotional, and informational support during labour, birth, and the immediate postpartum.

Given good clinical and non-clinical maternity care, maternal death is a rare occurrence, so rare that it is measured by the number of deaths per 100,000 live births. In 2013, the **maternal mortality rate (MMR)** in Canada was 11 deaths per 100,000 live births (World Health Organization, United Nations Children's Fund, United Nations Population Fund, & The World Bank, 2014). However, the 2013 MMR represents an 81 percent increase since 1990, when the MMR was 6 deaths per 100,000. These data are particularly concerning when we consider that the world MMR is steadily decreasing, down from 400 (in 1990) to 210 (in 2013) deaths per 100,000 live births. In Canada, total health spending for maternity care accounts for approximately 1 of every 10 dollars spent by hospitals on in-patient care (Canadian Institutes of Health Information, 2006). Despite significant spending, the Canadian MMR is higher than that of at least 28 other countries. Clearly, high health care spending is not the only factor affecting MMR; the United States spends more money per capita for maternity care than any other country yet its MMR increased from 12 deaths per 100,000 live births

maternal mortality rate (MMR) The number of maternal deaths per 100,000 live births.

PROCESS DIAGRAM

The process of labour and birth can be divided into four stages.

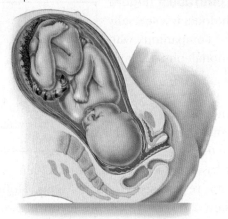

1 Dilation

The period of labour when the cervix is opening is known as the first stage of labour. Women and all mammals often feel a strong desire to move during this stage of labour, as this is the time when the baby must be twisted and turned into the most advantageous position to move through the birth canal (Gaskin, 2002).

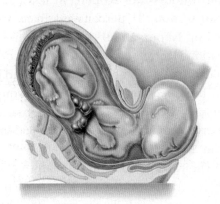

2 Descent and birth

Once the cervix is fully effaced and dilated to approximately 10 cm, the second or pushing stage of labour begins, ending with the birth of the baby. During this stage, chest and abdominal muscles contract along with the uterus, pushing the baby down the birth canal (Gaskin, 2002). Like the woman's pelvis, the baby's skull is made of separate bones linked together by flexible ligaments, enabling temporary moulding for easier passage.

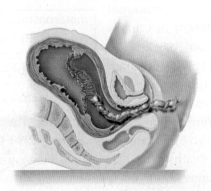

3 Delivery of placenta

The third stage of labour begins with the baby's body fully emerged and ends with the expulsion of the placenta. Immediately after the baby is born, placing the baby skin-to-skin on the mother's chest helps to regulate the baby's body temperature and facilitate early bonding and breastfeeding (Charpak et al., 2005), Public Health Agency of Canada, 2009). Allowing the baby, regardless of vaginal or caesarean birth, to remain without interruption for at least 1 to 2 hours has benefits for both mother and infant. The critical period for the skin-to-skin benefits is up to 2 hours after birth, with the strongest effects showing with immediate, uninterrupted skin-to-skin contact in the first hour (Dumas, 2014).

Courtesy Erin Tierney Stone

4 The postpartum period

The fourth stage of labour is the postpartum period, lasting approximately six weeks following childbirth (Gaskin, 2002). During this time, the woman's body adjusts to motherhood and reassumes a non pregnant state.

Ask Yourself

What stage of labour ends with the birth of the baby?

The story of Aoife's birth as told by her mother and father • Figure 2.15

Dan: Amy woke me up with the infamous, "I think things are happening." I went into coach mode and tried to keep her calm and relaxed in order to conserve energy for the task that lay before us.

Amy: I paced the house, sometimes walking away from Dan midsentence to focus. The sensations were completely manageable, as long as I kept moving! After talking with the midwife on the phone, Dan said that we should get ready to go to the birth centre. I threw on a black maternity dress and made my way out to the car, dropping down on all fours—by the back door, in the yard, next to the car—to handle each contraction.

Dan: We arrived at the birth centre. The midwives checked Amy, and she was 100 percent effaced and fully dilated! Amy's water broke almost immediately, like the security of being at the birthplace allowed her to stop resisting the progress of the labour. Her whole demeanour changed, and she became calm and determined.

Amy: Dan rubbed my back while I laboured on all fours in the tub, giving me sips of water between contractions, and offering words of encouragement. One of my contractions in the tub peaked twice before subsiding. "That was a hard one," he said. He was so tuned into my body, he knew what had happened without my saying a word. The midwives were a calm, quiet presence. Their faith in our ability to birth our daughter was palpable. To them, birth was an everyday occurrence, the most normal and healthy thing in the world.

In front of Dan and the midwives, I could be completely and honestly me. I was stripped of all pretense, operating directly from my core. And in this unadorned state, I was powerful. I roared with the rushes of energy, my vocalizations matching their intensity. I reminded myself that this incredible power I felt, these powerful waves of energy, was MY power. It wasn't separate from me, something being done to me, it WAS me. Merging with and taking ownership of that power allowed me to surrender to it. If the power was mine, then there was nothing to fear. I felt proud to show Dan my strength as I gave birth to our daughter.

Dan: Aoife went from crowning to fully out in one push. She shot past my waiting hands and into the water like a baby torpedo. We sat together for some time in the tub just staring at each other and taking in the magic of the moment.

Amy: Giving birth to Aoife was everything. It was natural and honest; it was wet and wild; it was intimate and sensual; it was at times even pleasurable, a delicious and long-awaited release; and it left in its wake many lasting gifts. It left me with a strong sense of my power and endurance as a woman and a mother. It showed me that I can stay centred and calm, open and loving, when things get hard. It revealed the strength of my relationship with Dan, that we'll remain kind and patient with each other even in the thick of parenting. And it filled me with an infinite love and respect for our daughter, for her inherent wisdom and potential. She knew how to be born and she showed me that I knew how to give birth, that I, too, have inherent wisdom as a mother.

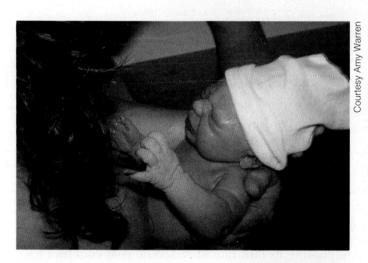

Courtesy Amy Warren

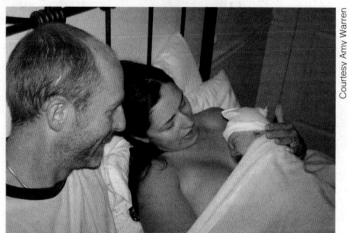

Courtesy Amy Warren

Think Critically How might a woman's experiences giving birth affect her development as a mother?

Birth doulas • Figure 2.16

Birth doula Alexis Topham provides physical, emotional, and informational support as she strokes this labouring woman's arm and guides the supportive efforts of the father-to-be.

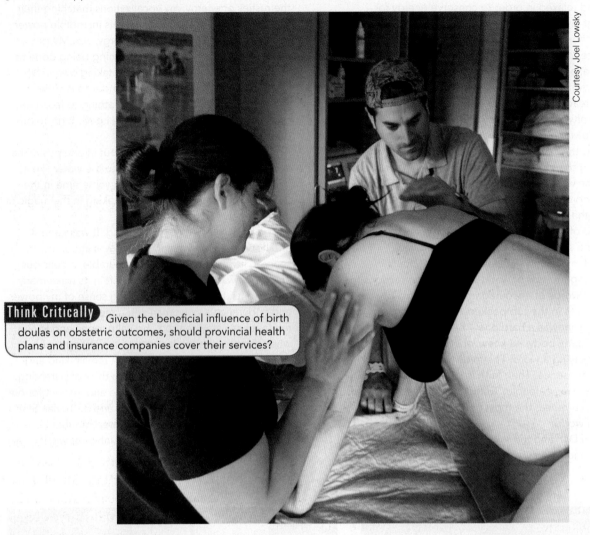

Think Critically Given the beneficial influence of birth doulas on obstetric outcomes, should provincial health plans and insurance companies cover their services?

Courtesy Joel Lowsky

in 1990 to 28 deaths per 100,000 live births in 2013 (World Health Organization et. al, 2014).

infant mortality rate (IMR) The number of infant deaths occurring in the first year of life per 1,000 live births.

The **infant mortality rate (IMR)**, the number of infant deaths occurring in the first year of life (per 1,000 live births), is a measure used by governments and health agencies as an indicator of the health of a nation. In 2013, Canada's IMR resulted in a ranking of 21st when compared with other developed countries (UNICEF, 2013). However, given the differences in data collection and reporting, research suggests that some caution should be exercised when interpreting these international rankings (Joseph et al., 2012). In Canada, IMR steadily decreased between 1990 and 2015, with an average

reduction of 2.1 (per 1,000 live births) each decade, such that there were 7 deaths (per 1,000 live births) in 1990 and 5 deaths (per 1,000 live births) in 2000; it remained there until 2015, when it fell again to 4 (per 1,000 live births; The World Bank, 2015) (**Figure 2.17**). Nonetheless, Canada is outperformed on this important measure by other industrialized nations and did not meet the 2015 Millennium Development Goal of 3 (per 1,000 live births; You, Hug, Ejdemyr, & Beise, 2015). That Canada does not seem able to improve its IMR rate while several peer countries have done so indicates a need for further investigation to better understand these international differences. Some have suggested that Canada's rise in preterm births, low birth weight babies, and multiple births should be considered as a factor in the IMR (Bohnert, 2013).

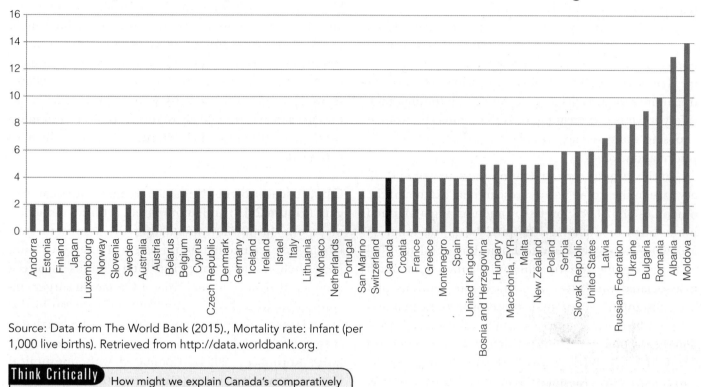

Source: Data from The World Bank (2015)., Mortality rate: Infant (per 1,000 live births). Retrieved from http://data.worldbank.org.

Think Critically How might we explain Canada's comparatively higher infant mortality rate relative to other countries?

Childbirth Variations

Although the stages of labour just described are a universal feature of normal childbirth, a number of important variations exist. One of the greatest influences on childbirth variations is the type of maternity care and birth setting.

Maternity care and birth setting As noted previously, the midwifery model of care and the medical model of care represent two general ways of thinking about and managing labour and birth (Rothman, 1982). We can think about these models as the poles of a continuum, along which various maternity care providers fall. In Canada, maternity care is provided by midwives, family doctors, and obstetricians.

Most midwives adhere to the midwifery model of care, and so they specialize in normal pregnancy and birth, and identify and refer the small percentage of births that require obstetrical attention (Gaskin, 2002). Midwifery care is associated with a decrease in **epidurals**, **episiotomies**,

epidurals A local anaesthetic injected into the lower back to numb labour pain.

episiotomies A surgical cut in the muscles that surround the vagina in order to enlarge the vaginal opening.

and Caesarean surgeries (Hatem, Sandall, Devane, Soltani, & Gates, 2009; Johnson & Daviss, 2005).

In Canada, the number of midwives declined in the 1990s as a result of regulating processes, before stabilizing and then rising sharply with the introduction of Bachelor of Midwifery graduates to the labour market in the early 2000s (Service Canada, 2014). Midwifery is regulated in Canada by provincial and territorial authorities; some provinces and territories recognize and regulate midwifery and some do not. In all regulated provinces and territories, midwives must be registered with the regulatory authority in order to legally offer birthing services (Canadian Association of Midwives, 2015). Registered midwives are primary care providers; they provide the complete course of low-risk prenatal, intrapartum (during the act of birth), and postnatal care, including physical examinations, screening and diagnostic tests, the assessment of risk and abnormal conditions, and the conduct of normal vaginal deliveries. Depending on the specific provincial regulations, midwives may work in collaboration with other health professionals and attend births in hospitals, private homes, or birthing centres—such as the one where Aoife was born (Figure 2.15). Coverage of midwifery care through the Canadian public health system also varies among provinces (Canadian Institute for Health Information, 2004).

Most births in Canada occur in the hospital setting. In 2007, 1.2 percent of births occurred in a private home, and only 0.8 percent occurred at a birthing centre (Public Health Agency of Canada, 2009). However, as the number of jurisdictions regulating and funding midwifery services is increasing, so is the number of women choosing these services (Canadian Institute for Health Information, 2004).

In the largest study to date on the safety of midwifery care in the home setting, researchers examined the outcomes of 529,688 low-risk women having a planned home birth or a planned hospital birth (de Jonge et al., 2009). Midwife-attended home birth and hospital birth are equally safe. In addition, planned home birth is associated with rates of medical interventions that are substantially lower than those of low-risk planned hospital birth (Janssen et al., 2009; Johnson & Daviss, 2005). Despite mounting evidence of the safety of planned home birth for low-risk women (e.g., Leslie & Romano, 2007; Lindgren, Radestad, Christensson, & Hildingsson, 2008; Macfarlane, McCandlish, & Campbell, 2000;), birth setting remains a controversial issue in Canada (Public Health Agency of Canada, 2009). In a policy statement, the Society of Obstetricians and Gynaecologists of Canada acknowledged the importance of maternal and familial choice regarding birth setting, but asserted that women should understand any identified limitations of care at their planned birth setting (Executive Committee of the Society of Obstetricians and Gynaecologists of Canada, 2003).

In Canada, most expectant women receive some level of care from their family physician before, during, and/or after childbirth. However, the number of family physicians attending births has been in decline since the mid-1990s (Canadian Institute for Health Information, 2004). Almost 70 percent of Canadian women report that their primary birth attendant was an obstetrician/gynaecologist, while only 15 percent report their family doctor as their birth attendant (Public Health Agency of Canada, 2009). Studies indicate that family doctors tend to have lower rates of obstetrical intervention than obstetricians (e.g., Hueston, Applegate, Mansfield, King, & McClaflin, 1995).

Obstetricians are medical doctors who specialize in the detection and treatment of pathology during pregnancy, labour, and birth. Accordingly, in most countries around the world, obstetricians care for only high-risk birthing women (Gaskin, 2003). However, across Canada and the United States, obstetricians care for both high-risk women and healthy, low-risk women, and so interventions suitable for high-risk women are often applied to all women (Public Health Agency of Canada, 2009). As we learned earlier, low-risk women in the care of an obstetrician are more likely to undergo obstetrical intervention, another type of childbirth variation to which we turn next.

Obstetrical interventions Sometimes Caesarean surgery (**Figure 2.18**) and, more rarely, artificial induction of labour (artificially stimulating the uterus to start labour) may be needed for the safety of mother or baby. Nevertheless, these obstetrical interventions involve a number of risks. Maternal risks of Caesarean surgery include infection, chronic pain, future Caesarean births, and placental complications resulting in hemorrhage, hysterectomy and, occasionally, death (Guise et al., 2010; Koroukian, 2004). Compared with nonsurgical birth, elective Caesareans (Caesareans that are not medically necessary) increase the chance of maternal death by nearly three times (Chez & Stark, 1998). Risks to babies include accidental laceration and respiratory distress (Hansen, Wisborg, Uldbjerg, & Henriksen, 2007; Liston, Allen, O'Connell, & Jangaard, 2008; Smith, Hernandez, & Wax, 1997). Caesareans may also affect future pregnancies by increasing preterm birth and associated morbidity and mortality (Galyean, Lagrew, Bush, & Kurtzman, 2009; Kennare, Tucker, Heard, & Chan, 2007; Osborne, Ecker, Gauvreau, & Lieberman, 2012; Yang et al., 2007).

Some experts are concerned that Caesarean surgery is performed too frequently. In Canada the Caesarean rate has been on the rise, from approximately 17% of all births in 1995 to nearly 27% in 2010 (Born, Konkin, Tepper, & Okun, 2014). In 2011, Caesarean sections were performed in 28 percent of all hospital births (Public Health Agency of Canada, 2013). The U.S. Caesarean rate has also been on the rise. Reasons for this increase range from greater use of **electronic fetal monitoring (EFM)** and artificial induction of labour, which we describe next, to maternal choice and legal

> **electronic fetal monitoring (EFM)**
> A technology for monitoring the heart rate of a fetus with electrodes attached to the mother's abdomen or placed internally on the scalp of the fetus.

A Caesarean delivery • Figure 2.18

During a Caesarean delivery, a surgical incision is made in the abdominal wall. Notice how various layers of anatomy must be moved in order to remove the fetus.

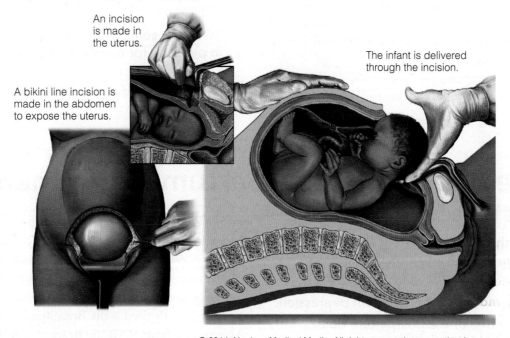

An incision is made in the uterus.

A bikini line incision is made in the abdomen to expose the uterus.

The infant is delivered through the incision.

Put It Together *Review Figure 2.14 and answer the following question:* How might a Caesarean delivery affect the four stages of labour?

pressures, such as physicians' concerns about malpractice lawsuits (Murthy, Grobman, Lee, & Hall, 2007; Williams, 2008).

Continuous EFM became routine in the hospital setting based on the assumption that it would make labour safer for the baby. In addition, it cuts costs by enabling one person to simultaneously monitor multiple labouring women. However, research has shown that continuous EFM can falsely signal fetal distress, leading to an emergency Caesarean surgery (Thacker, Stroup, & Chang, 2006). Furthermore, routine use of EFM has not reduced infant deaths. Unnecessary Caesareans are less likely to occur when the baby's heartbeat is intermittently monitored with a fetoscope (a type of stethoscope used to listen to fetal heart tones).

Another way that medical professionals may intervene during childbirth is by inducing labour; that is, artificially starting or augmenting (speeding up) labour. Some medical reasons for induction are maternal hypertension (high blood pressure) and diabetes (Gaskin, 2003). The most common medical methods include breaking the water bag that surrounds the baby and various chemical methods, such as Pitocin. Pitocin is a synthetic version of oxytocin, a naturally occurring hormone that stimulates uterine contractions, as we discussed previously. It is given intravenously at a dose that far exceeds the level of oxytocin naturally secreted by the woman's body in early labour. Pitocin induction is more likely than spontaneous labour to result in fetal distress from abnormally strong and lengthy contractions and, thus, in Caesarean delivery.

All forms of induction tend to bring on stronger, longer, and more painful contractions, leading women to seek pain medication (Caughey et al., 2009). Chemical induction can also lead to uterine rupture, prematurity (discussed in the next section), and increased postpartum blood loss (Kayani & Alfirevic, 2005; Sheiner, Sarid, Levy, Seidman, & Hallak, 2005). Although uterine rupture is a rare outcome of induction, it is far rarer in spontaneous labours.

As with Caesarean delivery, artificial induction rates are on the rise. The rate of induction in Canada increased steadily from 12.9 percent in the early 1990s before peaking at 23.7 percent in the early 2000s. Canada's induction rate has since remained steady at approximately 21 percent (Leduc, Biringer, Lee, & Dy, 2013). Today, in developed countries like the United States, up to 25 percent of all full-term births are artificially induced (World Health Organization, 2011).

CONCEPT CHECK 🛑 STOP

1. **What** role do hormones play in the four stages of labour?
2. **What** are some of the issues and considerations in planning for a midwife assisted birth in Canada?
3. **Why** are Canadian Caesarean rates on the rise?

The Newborn and Postpartum Adjustment

LEARNING OBJECTIVES

1. **Discuss** methods of assessment that can be used with newborns.
2. **List** the causes and risks of low birth weight.
3. **Name** the symptoms of postpartum depression.
4. **Describe** the role of the postpartum doula.

The moments immediately following birth are a time of heightened sensitivity for mother and newborn. Changing hormone levels in the mother's bloodstream prepare her physically and emotionally for the task of mothering a newborn (Gaskin, 2002). In turn, labour and birth stimulate a state of quiet alertness that makes a newborn especially well-suited to gazing into their mother's eyes and suckling at her breast. Close proximity between mother and newborn, skin-to-skin contact, and suckling during this sensitive period of development have long-term benefits (Bystrova et al., 2009; Moore, Anderson, Bergman, & Dowswell, 2012). Accordingly, medical assessment of healthy newborns may be done in the mother's arms, so as not to disturb this important bonding time.

anaesthesiologist Virginia Apgar for this very reason, as discussed in *What a Developmentalist Sees.*

During their first few days, newborns may also experience several other types of assessments. One of the most frequently used is the Brazelton Neonatal Behavioral Assessment Scale (NBAS; Brazelton & Nugent, 1995). Dr. T. Berry Brazelton started using this scale in the 1970s as a way to measure both physical and social responses from birth to about two months. The NBAS focuses on the baby's (1) ability to regulate his or her breathing, (2) ability to control body movement, (3) levels of arousal from fully awake to sleep, and (4) social interaction with parents and others. As we see in **Figure 2.19**, the purpose of the NBAS is to help parents understand their baby's patterns and abilities. This understanding will hopefully foster positive parent–child relationships based on appropriate knowledge and expectations. Such understanding may be particularly useful for parents of low-birth-weight infants, who may follow a different developmental trajectory from typical newborns (Ohgi et al., 2002).

Medical and Behavioural Assessment of Newborns

Apgar scale
A scoring system that assesses the health of newborns based on five key areas: activity and muscle tone, heart rate, reflexes, skin colour, and respiration.

Right after a birth, care providers must quickly and accurately judge the condition of the newborn to determine whether or not medical intervention is needed. The **Apgar scale** was introduced in 1952 by

Low-Birth-Weight (LBW) and Very Low-Birth-Weight (VLBW) Infants

Although most babies today are born at a normal birth weight, typically in the range of 2.5 to 4.5 kg, many Canadian babies are born at a **low birth weight (LBW)** (Canadian Institute for Health Information, 2006). LBW infants may be further categorized as

low birth weight (LBW) A birth weight of less than 2,500 g.

WHAT A DEVELOPMENTALIST SEES
Neonatal Assessment Using the Apgar Scale

Developmental specialists like neonatal pediatricians and midwives perform the Apgar test on newborns. Apgar scores are calculated at one minute and five minutes after the baby is born. Medical care providers examine five key indicators of health, summarized with the acronym APGAR, and then add together the five scores to produce a total between 0 and 10.

Seventy-five percent of newborns receive a 7 or higher (Lamb et al., 2002), indicating they are not in danger. Newborns who score 3 or under, however, need immediate medical attention.

Score	Appearance	Pulse	Grimace (reflex)	Activity	Respiration
0	Blue or pale membranes	Absent	No response	Limp	Absent
1	Pink body, blue legs/arms[a] (fingernails, membranes)	Slow	Grimace	Some movement	Irregular breathing
2	Pink all over (fingernails, membranes)	Rapid	Cry	Actively moving	Strong cry

[a] Babies often have lighter skin than their parents at birth, so this scale can be used with many ethnicities where possible.

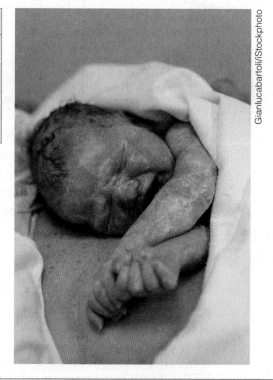

Gianlucabartoli/iStockphoto

Think Critically
1. What would the Apgar score most likely be for this baby?
2. What additional information would you need to collect to be able to fully determine this baby's Apgar score?

Neonatal Behavioral Assessment Scale (NBAS) • Figure 2.19

The NBAS examiner rings a bell next to a sleeping newborn to see how she responds. The newborn pictured here is not awakened by the ringing bell. Newborns who can tune out such stimulation conserve energy for development.

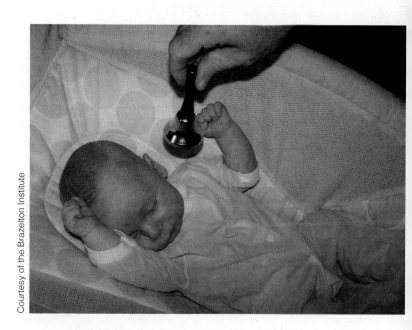

Courtesy of the Brazelton Institute

Think Critically
1. How might an infant's NBAS score inform parenting?
2. If the newborn did wake in response to noise (or light, or touch), what advice might the NBAS examiner give to parents?

either **preterm** or **small for gestational age (SGA)** if they have reached full gestation, approximately 38–42 weeks, but still have low birth weight. The U.S. Centers for Disease Control and Prevention also uses the category of **very low birth weight (VLBW)** to differentiate an even more serious condition (see **Figure 2.20**).

LBW has been linked to teratogens, including maternal smoking and alcohol use. Research suggests that smoking, in particular, may influence the migration of neurons during the embryonic period, causing delays in various organ systems. These delays may affect the length and weight of the newborn (Huijbregts et al., 2006). Other potential causes, including genetics and age of the mother, have also been considered (Pesonen et al., 2008). Age of the mother,

> **preterm** An infant born earlier than the full gestational period, usually less than 37 weeks.
>
> **small for gestational age (SGA)** A birth weight of less than 2.5 kg for an infant with a gestational age that is normal (37+ weeks).
>
> **very low birth weight (VLBW)** A birth weight of less than 1,500 g.

however, appears to be less of a factor than racial background. According to some research, African American mothers have a higher chance of having LBW infants than Caucasian or Asian mothers (Covelli, 2006). The overrepresentation of African American mothers in lower socio-economic groups makes this race–LBW correlation unclear. Is the relationship caused by economic issues, such as decreased access to prenatal care and lower-quality nutrition, or is it due to physical conditions, such as a higher overall rate of high blood pressure among African American populations? (See Kuzawa & Sweet, 2009, for a review.)

Serious problems are associated with both LBW and VLBW (Pesonen et al., 2008) and are the leading cause of infant mortality (McCormick, 1985). The most immediate threats to the survival of LBW babies are cardiovascular and respiratory distress. Later in life, LBW infants appear to be different from their average-birth-weight counterparts in both health and non-physical domains (Pesonen et al., 2008). In particular, LBW children are at risk for later cognitive, emotional, and social functioning deficits (Kajantie, 2006). Early intervention programs have been

Newborn weight and gestational age • Figure 2.20

The newborn on the right weighs 3,400 g, a typical weight for a full-term infant. The newborn in the middle was also born full term but is low birth weight and small for gestational age at 1,900 g. The newborn on the left is very low birth weight at 1,200 g. He was born nine weeks before his due date.

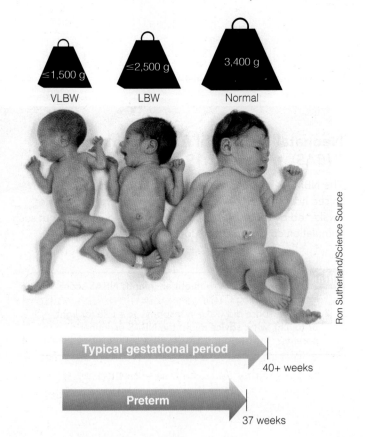

Ron Sutherland/Science Source

Ask Yourself

1. Though small for gestational age, the newborn pictured in the middle was born sometime after _____ weeks.
2. Born nine weeks before his due date, the newborn on the left is considered _____.

successful in improving the developmental outcomes of LBW children (Bono & Sheinberg, 2009).

As you can imagine, parents of LBW and VLBW infants face special challenges after birth. However, all parents undergo a period of adjustment after the birth of a baby, as we discuss next.

Postpartum Adjustment

The postpartum (after birth) period is a time of physical and emotional adjustment. The mother's reproductive organs return to a non-pregnant state, typically within six weeks. Parents assume new roles and experience big changes in daily schedules and sleep. The research on parental postpartum adjustment ranges from dealing with these everyday challenges to tackling more severe psychological issues such as **postpartum depression (PPD)** (Dennis, 2004).

> **postpartum depression (PPD)** Clinical depressive symptoms such as apathy, sadness, and detachment associated with late pregnancy and the period of time following the birth of an infant.

Postpartum depression The appearance of depressive symptoms among women during and after pregnancy has been extensively studied (DaCosta, Larouche, Dritsa, & Bender, 2000; Vliegen & Luyten, 2009). The symptoms are similar to a major clinical depression and include, but are not limited to, withdrawal, a sense of deep sadness, lack of communication, emotional distress, periods of crying, and a sense of detachment (Blatt & Shahar, 2004). The postpartum period has also been associated with increased anxiety, insomnia, irritability, agitation, and other psychological issues (Beck & Indman, 2005; Besser & Priel, 2003; Heron et al., 2004; Vliegen & Luyten, 2009). These symptoms are not limited to the mother. Fathers also experience postpartum depression (Serhan, Ege, Ayrancı, & Kosgeroglu, 2013), though most research focuses on maternal issues (Vliegen & Luyten, 2009).

The causes of PPD and anxiety have also been examined. As in most of the psychology research, definitive conclusions have not been reached. This is particularly true with postpartum psychological issues (Robertson, Grace, Wallington, & Stewart, 2004). Studies reveal that certain personality traits, such as self-criticism, are correlated with postpartum depression and anxiety (Vliegen & Luyten, 2009).

Theory and research have also focused on the various factors that may protect women from postpartum depression. Breastfeeding appears to play an important protective role (e.g., Gallup, Pipitone, Carrone, & Leadholm, 2010; Kendall-Tackett, 2007). As we know, stress is a powerful risk factor for depression (Kendall-Tackett, 2007). Breastfeeding decreases stress and promotes calmness (Groër, Davis, & Hemphill, 2002). In a study of mothers who were both breast- and bottle-feeding, researchers measured stress levels right before and right after both types of feeding (Mezzacappa & Katkin, 2002). They found that breastfeeding decreased negative mood, whereas bottle-feeding decreased positive mood.

Another important factor in the prevalence of postpartum depression is the amount of social support that mothers receive after birth. As we learn in this final section, the services provided by an experienced **postpartum doula** can ease and enhance the transition following the birth of a baby, and reduce the likelihood of postpartum depression (MacArthur et al., 2002).

> **postpartum doula** A specially trained advisor and helper who provides physical, emotional, and informational support to women and their families during the postpartum period.

Postpartum doulas In traditional societies, new mothers and families receive emotional, physical, and informational support from close family members who themselves were previously exposed to birth, breastfeeding, infants, and children (Placksin, 2000). Women in these societies, who are expected to nurture only themselves and their babies for a period of time following birth (known as the *lying-in period*), have superior outcomes in postpartum adjustment (Kruckman, 1992; see also Placksin, 2000) (**Figure 2.21**). Such support is less common in modern societies, where new parents often live a great distance from their immediate families. Postpartum doulas, lactation consultants, and other community resources like Visiting Mom volunteer programs seek to fill the gaps in our customary postpartum practices, enabling the mother's recovery from pregnancy and birth, as well as promoting her ability to bond with her new baby.

The postpartum doula's role is to provide reliable and factual information, nonjudgmental emotional support, and hands-on assistance with family adjustment (Kelleher, 2008). Postpartum doulas are trained to support families in such matters as breastfeeding, postpartum adjustment, and bonding and attachment. As such, they

The lying-in period • Figure 2.21

The lying-in period—a circumscribed period of time for postpartum women and their babies to rest and recover from birth—is seen in a variety of customs and traditions around the world. For example, *la cuarentena* refers to the *cuarenta días* (40 days) of recovery for Mexican women after the birth of a child (Waugh, 2011). During this time, family and friends care for the postpartum woman so that she can rest and bond with her new baby.

Stephen Chiang/Getty Images

Think Critically Why might the lying-in period of traditional societies lead to better postpartum adjustment outcomes?

meet the practical, educational, and psychosocial needs of postpartum families and thereby complement the medical support provided by health care professionals such as doctors, midwives, and nurses.

Research has shown that women who feel supported and cared for around the time of birth have greater breastfeeding success, more self-confidence, and less postpartum depression (Cutrona & Troutman, 1986; Deshpande & Gazmararian, 2000; MacArthur et al., 2002). Parents also benefit from receiving education about newborn development, feeding, and soothing (Terry, Mayocchi, & Hynes, 1996).

As you can see, the postpartum period can be a sensitive time, as the family must adjust to meet the needs of a new member. Every family's postpartum adjustment is unique. Some families find a comfortable new rhythm within weeks. Others experience a slower adjustment process. Although numerous factors influence this process, ample social support appears to be one of the most important in postpartum adjustment. As we will see in the chapters that follow, social support is an important factor throughout the lifespan.

CONCEPT CHECK	STOP

1. **How** do medical and behavioural assessments of the newborn differ?
2. **What** is the difference between preterm and small for gestational age?
3. **What** factors have been shown to protect women from postpartum depression?
4. **Why** are postpartum doulas needed in modern societies?

THE PLANNER

Summary

1 Genetics and Heredity 44

- Although cells throughout the body differ, the nucleus of each contains 23 pairs of chromosomes: 22 pairs of **autosomes** and 1 pair of **sex chromosomes**. A chromosome is made up of **DNA**, and a gene is a sequence

of DNA at a particular **locus** on the chromosome, as depicted in Figure 2.2.

- A person's **genotype** is his or her combination of **genes**, microscopic structures made of thousands of links of chemical particles that combine to construct all the parts of a living being. The person's **phenotype** is the observable physical or behavioural expression of his or her genotype. When a person inherits different **alleles** of a particular gene, the **dominant** allele will influence his or her phenotype, and the **recessive** allele will not, although it can be passed along to the person's children.

The building blocks of biological inheritance • Figure 2.2

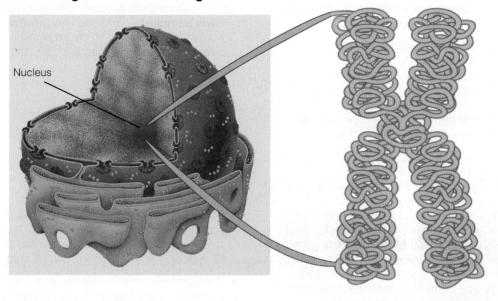

Nucleus

The processes of meiosis and mitosis • Figure 2.6

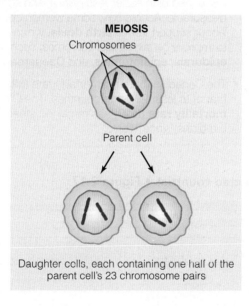

MEIOSIS

Chromosomes

Parent cell

Daughter cells, each containing one half of the parent cell's 23 chromosome pairs

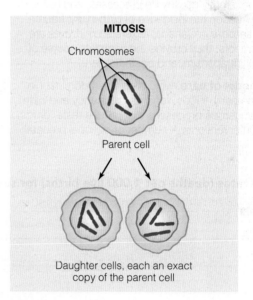

MITOSIS

Chromosomes

Parent cell

Daughter cells, each an exact copy of the parent cell

2 Prenatal Development 47

- **Ovulation** causes an ovum to ripen and be expelled by the ovaries. Conception unites two **gametes**—a **sperm cell** and a mature **ovum**—to form a fertilized egg, or **zygote**, that contains 23 pairs of chromosomes, half contributed by the mother and half by the father. Within 30 hours the zygote splits in two and through the process of cell division a **morula** forms. Gametes are formed through the cell-division process of **meiosis**. After conception, the zygote grows through the process of **mitosis** (see the portion of Figure 2.6 reproduced below). Many fertilized eggs do not result in live births—30 to 50 percent of zygotes are lost before a woman even knows she is pregnant, and one in five known pregnancies ends in **miscarriage**.

- Prenatal development is divided into the germinal, embryonic, and fetal stages. In the germinal stage, the **blastocyst** travels through the Fallopian tubes and begins to differentiate into two types of cell. During the embryonic stage, the embryo forms three layers of cells. The inner layer will undergo **organogenesis** to form the body's internal organs. Support structures, including the amniotic sac, **placenta**, and **umbilical cord**, also form during the embryonic stage. During the fetal stage, all physical systems grow rapidly and become more functional as birth approaches. Growth occurs in two ways—in a

cephalocaudal pattern (from the head through the base of the spine) and in a **proximodistal pattern** (from the centre of the body through the appendages).

- During **sensitive periods** of development, environmental influences are most efficient at affecting an organism's development, and so **plasticity**, or the potential to change, is high. The environment can still bring about changes outside of sensitive periods, but it is more difficult to do so. In contrast, **critical periods** are conceptualized as finite windows of opportunity for the environment to affect development, outside of which the environment has no influence.

- The timing of and the amount of exposure to **teratogens**, as well as genetic makeup, determine the potential for damage to a developing zygote, embryo, or fetus. **Neural tube** formation is at risk when there is exposure to teratogens in the embryo's early development. **Mutations** during meiosis or mitosis can lead to chromosomal abnormalities, such as Down syndrome. Genetic disorders can result from **autosomal recessive traits** or **autosomal dominant traits**, or from mutations in **sex-linked genes**.

- The **midwifery model of care** conceptualizes pregnancy and birth as normal, inherently healthy life processes, and has been shown to greatly reduce the incidence of birth injury, trauma, and Caesarean section. In Canada, registered midwives are primary care providers; they provide the complete course of low-risk prenatal, intrapartum, and postnatal care.

- The **medical model of care**, which has been dominant in Canada since the early 1900s, regards pregnancy and birth as potentially dangerous processes that require tests, drugs, and obstetrical interventions. A number of optional prenatal tests have gained popularity within the medical model of care, including **ultrasound**, **amniocentesis**, and **chorionic villus sampling**. In order to give **informed consent**, women must be given ample information about these procedures—their benefits and their risks.

3 Labour and Birth 62

- **Bloody show** signals that labour will soon begin. Uterine contractions signal the onset of labour. Labour proceeds in four stages: (1) dilating of the **cervix**, (2) pushing, (3) expulsion of the placenta, and (4) postpartum.

- Hormones play an essential role in labour and birth. Labouring women who feel afraid and unsupported tend to secrete hormones that delay or impede birth, while women who feel unafraid and supported tend to secrete hormones that make labour and birth easier, less painful, and sometimes even pleasurable. Accordingly, some women opt to have continuous labour support from a **birth doula**, which has been shown to improve certain clinical outcomes, such as a decrease in **epidurals**, **episiotomies**, and **Caesarean surgery**.

- The Canadian maternal mortality rate (MMR) is higher than that of at least 28 other countries. The Canadian **infant mortality rate (IMR)** has remained steady at 5 (per 1,000 live births) since 1997.

Infant mortality rates (deaths per 1,000 live births) for selected countries • Figure 2.17

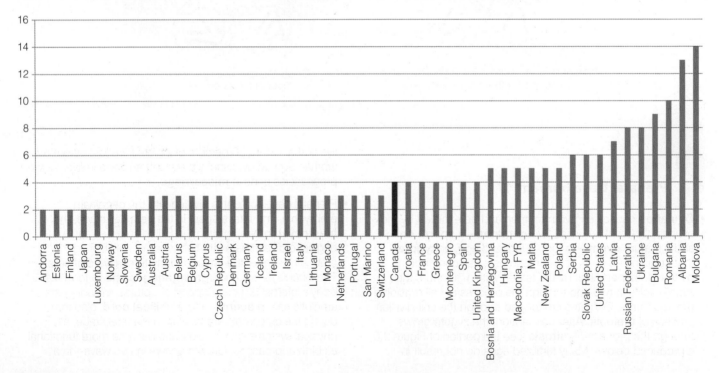

- Maternity care is provided by midwives, family doctors, and obstetricians. A very small minority of women (1.2 percent in 2007) give birth at home, though planned home birth is just as safe as planned hospital birth for low-risk women and is associated with lower rates of medical interventions.

- The rate of Caesarean surgery in Canada (28 percent in 2011) is on the rise due to factors such as greater use of **electronic fetal monitoring (EFM)**, artificial induction of labour, and maternal choice. Artificial induction rates (21 percent in 2013) are also on the rise.

- **Low birth weight (LBW)** is a leading cause of infant mortality and is related to several serious physical problems among babies who survive. **Very low birth weight (VLBW)** puts newborns at even greater risk. Babies may have low birth weights because they are born **preterm** or because they are **small for gestational age (SGA)**.

- All family members face major changes after the birth of a baby. Parents, especially mothers, are at risk of **postpartum depression**, and other psychological problems. Breastfeeding and ample social support, such as the support provided by a **postpartum doula**, reduce the likelihood of postpartum depression. Developing a strong **co-parenting** relationship can also reduce the stress of the transition.

4 The Newborn and Postpartum Adjustment 70

- Newborn health is assessed using tests such as the **Apgar scale** or the Brazelton Neonatal Behavioral Assessment Scale (NBAS).

What a Developmentalist Sees: Neonatal Assessment Using the Apgar Scale

Score	Appearance	Pulse	Grimace (reflex)	Activity	Respiration
0	Blue or pale membranes	Absent	No response	Limp	Absent
1	Pink body, blue legs/arms[a] (fingernails, membranes)	Slow	Grimace	Some movement	Irregular breathing
2	Pink all over (fingernails, membranes)	Rapid	Cry	Actively moving	Strong cry

[a] Babies often have lighter skin than their parents at birth, so this scale can be used with many ethnicities where possible.

Key Terms

- allele 46
- amniocentesis 61
- Apgar scale 70
- autosomal dominant trait 57
- autosomal recessive trait 57
- autosome 44
- birth doula 63
- blastocyst 49
- bloody show 63
- Caesarean surgery 59
- cephalocaudal pattern 51

- cervix 63
- chorionic villus sampling (CVS) 61
- co-parenting 61
- critical period 53
- DNA 44
- dominant 46
- electronic fetal monitoring (EFM) 68
- epidurals 67
- episiotomies 67
- gamete 47
- gene 44

- genotype 45
- infant mortality rate (IMR) 66
- informed consent 59
- locus 45
- low birth weight (LBW) 70
- maternal mortality rate (MMR) 63
- medical model of care 58
- midwifery model of care 58
- meiosis 48
- miscarriage 51
- mitosis 48

Critical and Creative Thinking Questions

1. What advice concerning teratogens would you give to a friend or family member who is pregnant or considering getting pregnant?

2. Would you seek genetic testing and counselling before having a child (or did you, if you are already a parent)? What factors would influence such a decision?

3. What would be your ideal birthing scenario? Consider prenatal testing, maternity care provider and model of care, setting, attendants, use of medications, and other interventions.

4. What factors do you think might contribute to the high rates of Caesarean deliveries in Canada and around the world? Are these rates positive or negative for infant and maternal outcomes? Why do you think so?

What is happening in this picture?

> **Think Critically**
>
> **1.** What tests might this baby and her parents have undergone before conception and birth?
> **2.** What was the most likely setting and scenario for the baby's birth?
> **3.** If the parents were friends of yours, what advice would you give them about how to avoid or cope with symptoms of postpartum anxiety and depression?

ERproductions Ltd/Blend Images/Getty Images

REAL  Development

Biological Foundations, Prenatal Development, and Birth

In these video activities, you will help expectant mothers answer questions about genetics, prenatal development, and birth.

In the first activity, you help Adeline Gray predict the likelihood that her new baby sister will have blonde hair like her mom, Julianne. Using the genetic diagram provided, you will determine the possible alleles for hair colour. Assume that Matt, who has brown hair, carries the recessive gene for blonde hair (Bb) and that Julianne carries two recessive genes for blonde hair (bb).

In the next activity, you will observe two expectant mothers, Julianne and Erica, as they engage in routine activities.

You will help them decide whether or not it is safe to participate in each activity, given the status of their pregnancies. In an accompanying activity, you will sit in on their physician visits and help them identify risk factors they may be facing.

In the last set of activities, you will observe Julianne meeting with a doula to learn about birth plan options and then observe and respond post-birth as the health, behavioural states, and reflexes of baby Olivia are measured using the Apgar scale.

John Wiley & Sons, Inc.

WileyPLUS Go to WileyPLUS to complete the REAL Development activity.

03.01

Self-Test

(Check your answers in Appendix A.)

1. What are these?

   a. genes

   b. chromosomes

   c. cytosines

   d. cells

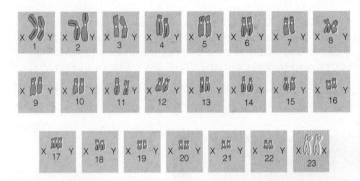

2. Mikhail inherits one green-eyed allele of an eye-colour gene and one blue-eyed allele. His blue eyes are his _____.

   a. genotype

   b. recessive allele

   c. recessive trait

   d. phenotype

3. Conception unites a sperm cell with _____.

   a. a blastocyst

   b. an ovum

   c. a zygote

   d. an embryo

4. Organogenesis, the formation of organs, happens during which prenatal period?

   a. fetal

   b. germinal

   c. embryonic

   d. teratogenic

5. A period of time when the organism is especially responsive to environmental influences is called a _____.

   a. critical period

   b. fetal period

   c. germinal period

   d. sensitive period

6. This fertilized egg is growing through the process of _____.

   a. meiosis

   b. mitosis

   c. myelination

   d. migration

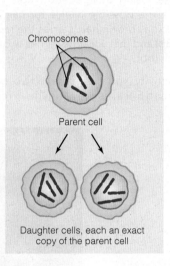

7. Which of the following determines the effect that a teratogen will have?

   a. the timing of exposure

   b. the dosage or amount of teratogen

   c. the genetic makeup of the embryo or fetus

   d. all of these

8. A disorder caused by a defective gene on the X chromosome is called _____.

   a. a sex-linked disorder

   b. an autosomal recessive disorder

   c. an autosomal dominant disorder

   d. a chromosomal disorder

9. The _____ model of maternity care has been shown to greatly reduce the incidence of birth injury, trauma, and Caesarean surgery.

   a. medical

   b. obstetrical

   c. midwifery

   d. professional

10. What stage of labour is shown here?

    a. first

    b. second

    c. third

    d. fourth

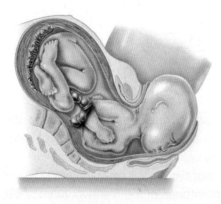

11. When women feel frightened during labour and birth, they are more likely to secrete hormones, such as _____, that _____ birth.

    a. oxytocin; augment

    b. adrenaline; decelerate

    c. endorphins; stall

    d. adrenaline; accelerate

12. This surgical procedure is called _____.

    a. inducing labour

    b. chorionic villus sampling

    c. amniocentesis

    d. Caesarean delivery

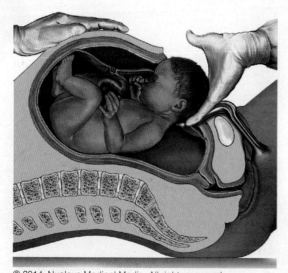

13. An assessment of a newborn's health, conducted one and five minutes after birth, is called the _____.

    a. Apgar scale

    b. Brazelton Neonatal Assessment Scale

    c. Caesarean Infant Rating Scale

    d. Depression and Postpartum Adjustment Scale

14. Compared with normal birth-weight infants, very low-birth-weight (VLBW) infants may be more likely to experience _____.

    a. deficits in emotional functioning

    b. respiratory distress as newborns

    c. cognitive deficits

    d. all of these

15. Factors that may protect women from postpartum depression include _____.

    a. breastfeeding

    b. ample social support

    c. postpartum doulas

    d. all of these

THE PLANNER

Review your Chapter Planner in the chapter opener and check off your completed work.

Physical and Cognitive Development in Infancy: The First Two Years

Nine-month-old Simone has just learned how to pull herself up. Although this may seem like a simple physical act, it actually represents much more. For her parents, the feat serves as a reminder of how fast their little girl is growing up. For researchers, it marks the successful interplay between complex muscular, skeletal, perceptual, and cognitive systems. And for Simone herself, it symbolizes a brand-new way of seeing and exploring the world.

In this chapter, we will examine the physical and cognitive milestones of the first two years of life. We will explore how infants' bodies and brains grow, as well as

the types of motor and language skills they develop. We will consider how infants come to sense and interpret the world around them, and what kinds of health care, nutrition, and sleep support their optimal development. Through it all, we will come to appreciate the always important family context in which infants develop.

JGI/Tom Grill/Blend Images/Corbis

CHAPTER PLANNER ✓

- ❑ Study the picture and read the opening story.
- ❑ Scan the Learning Objectives in each section:
  p. 84 ❑   p. 94 ❑   p. 101 ❑
- ❑ Read the text and study all figures and visuals. Answer any questions.

Analyze key features

- ❑ Development InSight, p. 93
- ❑ Process Diagram, p. 96
- ❑ Challenges in Development, p. 114
- ❑ What a Developmentalist Sees, p. 115
- ❑ Stop: Answer the Concept Checks before you go on:
  p. 92 ❑   p. 101 ❑   p. 117 ❑

End of chapter

- ❑ Review the Summary and Key Terms.
- ❑ Answer the Critical and Creative Thinking Questions.
- ❑ Answer *What is happening in this picture?*
- ❑ Complete the Self-Test and check your answers.

Physical Development

LEARNING OBJECTIVES

1. **Differentiate** between the cephalocaudal and proximodistal growth patterns.
2. **Discuss** brain development in infancy and the process of making synaptic connections.
3. **Identify** the key differences between fine and gross motor changes.

In just two years, infants change from wholly dependent, reflexive beings into walking, talking individuals. Their entire bodies also change right before our eyes as they stretch taller and grow wider. If we stop to think about it, when else in the lifespan do two years signify so much?

Growth Patterns

At birth, the average Canadian infant weighs about 3,400 g and is about 48 cm long (Statistics Canada, 2007) but over the next two years will triple in body weight and will grow approximately 30 cm—almost doubling in height (Canadian Pediatric Endocrine Group, 2014). Pause to think about this: in just two years, the infant's weight has more than tripled and height has almost doubled. Imagine what we would look like if this rate of growth continued after infancy. By age 20 years we would be as tall as the 800-year-old trees in Cathedral Grove on Vancouver Island, standing well over 75 m (Wonders, 2009)! Perhaps this phenomenal growth of a baby was part of the inspiration for creation of a French Canadian lumberjack folk hero, Big Joe Mufferaw, the giant of the Ottawa Valley.

Fortunately, our rate of growth significantly slows, and not just after the infancy period ends. Although there is little variation in size at birth, individual differences in height and weight have clearly emerged by age 2 (Fogel, 2009). These variations are influenced by genes, culture, socio-economic status, nutrition, and socialization. In fact, weight and height gains occur most rapidly in the first six months after birth and begin to slow after that point (Fogel, 2009). This growth does not occur randomly. Instead, as described in Chapter 2, it is characterized by two major growth processes that begin during the prenatal period: the **cephalocaudal** and **proximodistal** patterns (**Figure 3.1**).

cephalocaudal
The cephalocaudal pattern is the tendency for growth and development to proceed from the head downward.

proximodistal
The proximodistal pattern is the tendency for growth and development to occur from the inside of the body outward.

The cephalocaudal and proximodistal patterns of growth • Figure 3.1

Two patterns guide our physical growth and development.

a. Cephalocaudal growth
The cephalocaudal pattern is the tendency for growth and development to proceed from the head downward.

b. Proximodistal growth
The proximodistal pattern is the tendency for growth and development to occur from the inside of the body outward.

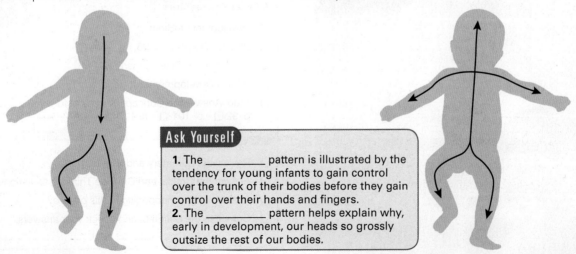

Ask Yourself

1. The _____ pattern is illustrated by the tendency for young infants to gain control over the trunk of their bodies before they gain control over their hands and fingers.
2. The _____ pattern helps explain why, early in development, our heads so grossly outsize the rest of our bodies.

These growth patterns characterize physical development throughout the lifespan, so they are helpful for predicting the course of development. We will follow their lead throughout this textbook. In each chapter on physical development, we will begin our discussion with the inner systems and with the head. We will work outward and downward to describe the various physical systems, how they develop, and how they are ultimately interconnected. We begin this approach with a discussion of the nervous system.

The Nervous System

As illustrated in **Figure 3.2**, the nervous system consists of two parts: the central nervous system (CNS) and the peripheral nervous system (PNS). We will consider each in turn.

The central nervous system (CNS) During the first two years of life, the brain develops at an incredible rate.

Given the cephalocaudal growth pattern, this fact should not be too surprising. The **cerebral cortex**, the uppermost part of the brain, is also the centre of our most sophisticated abilities. It is responsible for thought, perception, language production, and motor function; it is what makes humans human. Such sophistication takes time to develop, so a tremendous amount of brain growth occurs after birth—most of it during infancy.

The brain's primary job during these early years of the lifespan is to make and strengthen connections between brain cells or **neurons**. A connection is made when the **axon** of one neuron sends a message—an electrical

cerebral cortex The uppermost part of the brain and the centre largely responsible for complex brain functions.

neuron A brain or nerve cell that serves as the basic building block of the nervous system.

axon A nerve fibre that typically sends electrical impulses away from the neuron's cell body.

The nervous system • Figure 3.2

The CNS is the control centre of the body. It comprises the brain and the spinal cord. The PNS connects the CNS to the internal organs, bones, and muscles.

Ask Yourself
Does the CNS or PNS control spontaneous breathing?

Nervous system
Consists of the brain and all other neurons that extend throughout the body

Central nervous system

Peripheral nervous system

Central nervous system (CNS)
Directs mental and basic life processes

Peripheral nervous system (PNS)
Carries information to and from the central nervous system

Spinal cord
Sends information to and from the brain and PNS and controls reflexes

Brain
Directs mental processes and maintains basic life functions

Somatic nervous system (SNS) (voluntary)
Controls voluntary muscles, conveys sensory information to the CNS, and sends motor messages to muscles

Autonomic nervous system (ANS) (involuntary)
Controls involuntary basic life functions, such as heartbeat and response to stress

dendrite A branching structure arising from the cell body that typically receives electrical impulses from the axons of neighbouring neurons.

impulse—that is received by the **dendrite** of another neuron (**Figure 3.3**). The space between neurons, across which messages are sent and received, is called a **synapse**. Synaptic connections become increasingly complex as

infants grow, and more are made than the brain will ultimately need. The synapses that are used infrequently are discarded, and the remaining ones become a permanent part of the brain. Maturing neurons and synapses help an infant

synapse The space between adjoining neurons, across which electrical impulses are sent from the axon of one neuron to the dendrite of another.

Maturing neurons and synapses • Figure 3.3

By the end of infancy, we have about twice as many synapses as we will eventually have in adulthood (Gopnik, Meltzoff, & Kuhl, 1999).

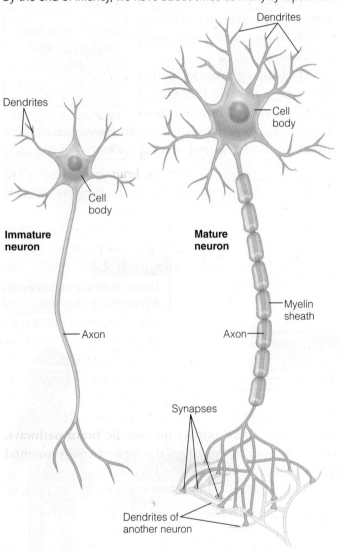

Dendrites

Dendrites

Cell body

Cell body

Immature neuron

Mature neuron

Myelin sheath

Axon

Axon

Synapses

Dendrites of another neuron

a. As the neuron matures, synaptic connections become more complex and the axon becomes increasingly insulated with myelin.

Think Critically An infant's experiences stimulate the development of synapses and help determine the ones that are eventually made permanent. What advice would you give to parents who, for example, want to raise a loving and compassionate child?

At birth　**1 month**　**3 months**　**15 months**　**24 months**

b. Synaptic connections increase over the course of infancy, from about 2,500 synapses per neuron at birth to over 10,000 at age 2 (Gopnik et al., 1999).

Gopnik, Meltzoff, & Kuhl, 1999

develop increasingly advanced motor skills—from crawling, to pulling up, to walking.

myelination The process through which the axon of a neuron is coated with a fatty tissue, which serves as insulation and enhances speed of firing.

One key brain process during these early years is **myelination**, in which the axons of neurons become increasingly insulated with a fatty tissue called myelin (Zöller et al., 2008). Myelin allows electrical impulses to travel more rapidly, making better coordination and faster reaction speed possible. The infant who has learned to reach for and grab an object and the toddler who can now kick a moving ball are examples of myelination at play. In fact, all of the infant's and toddler's developing behaviours and abilities are made possible by myelination.

How does the brain decide which synapses to keep and which to discard? It appears that this selection is a result of the infant's interaction with the environment.

synaptic pruning The process by which the brain removes unused synapses through redirecting nutrition, cell injury, and cell death.

Synaptic connections that are activated repeatedly, such as those involved in walking, become strengthened. Infrequently used connections, on the other hand, are discarded through a process called **synaptic pruning** (Chechik, Meilijson, & Ruppin, 1998). During infancy, however, the brain's primary task is to make synaptic connections.

This process of overproducing and then, eventually, pruning synapses makes humans highly flexible. The human brain changes and adapts itself to the challenges necessary for survival in any given environment by sculpting out a network of the millions of available neural options. Thus, different cultural contexts present diverse environmental challenges, resulting in unique patterns of synaptic connections. We saw in the preceding chapter that this potential for systematic change within the individual is termed

plasticity Changes in the brain resulting from our interactions with the environment; influenced by age-related change.

plasticity. Although brain plasticity exists throughout the lifespan, it becomes less prominent with increasing age (Baltes, Lindenberger, & Staudinger, 2006). The central role of plasticity early in the lifespan has led to an ongoing debate about the value of early experience in shaping the brain, as we will see (Lidzba & Staudt, 2008).

Early experience and brain development Researchers have identified two types of processes related to early experience and brain development (Greenough & Black, 1999). **Experience-expectant processes** are shared by all members of the human species and depend on environmental stimulation to occur at a particular point in development. For example, in order for normal visual and auditory development to occur, one must receive light and sound stimuli. If an infant is deprived of light, for example, the part of the brain involved with vision will not develop fully (Haith, 1986). This supports the idea that the internal structure of the brain is predisposed to receive certain types of stimuli (Norcia, Sampath, Hou, & Pettet, 2005).

experience-expectant process Brain development that occurs based on environmental experiences that all members of the species typically encounter.

experience-dependent process Brain development that occurs based on unique environmental stimuli shared only by individuals in particular environmental circumstances.

On the other hand, **experience-dependent processes** also exist. These processes are unique to specific environments (Sengpiel & Kind, 2002). For example, it has been found that repeated exposure to the sounds of a particular language helps a child create those sounds. As they get older, however, children's ability to make the sounds of languages other than their own decreases or disappears. For example, without having been exposed to English as a child, it is nearly impossible for an adult Mandarin Chinese speaker to make the *th* sound in English. In this case, early environment is having an impact on specific brain pathways, causing variations based on the type of environmental stimulation received (Huttenlocker, 2002).

Given that both experience-expectant and experience-dependent processes exist, the relationship between early experience and brain development is a complex one (Johnson, 2000). We know that neurons need to be stimulated in order to develop new connections, so many parents play classical music for their children in hopes that early exposure will increase their child's intelligence, spatial ability, and music appreciation (Huttenlocker, 2002; Rauscher, Shaw, & Ky, 1995). Unfortunately, there is little evidence that this Mozart effect has merit—other than, of course, getting parents and children to listen to some interesting music, and perhaps soothing some infants to sleep (McKelvie & Low, 2002).

Sleep and early brain development Much brain development occurs during an infant's sleep. During the first three months after birth, newborns sleep between 10 and 19 hours a day (**Figure 3.4**). As any new parent will tell you, though, this sleep is not continuous, and it is equally distributed across the day and night (Jenni & Carskadon, 2012). Infants wake frequently for a variety of reasons, including hunger, discomfort, and most notably, immature brain development (Joseph, 1999; Rivkees, 2003).

The brainstem is largely responsible for infants' sleep–wake cycles, so the patterns we see and how they change early in life have much to do with babies' immature central nervous systems (Anders, 1975; Steriade & McCarley, 1990). How can this knowledge of early brain development help us think about infant sleep? If frequent night wakings happen because of immature brain development, then does it make sense to "train" an infant to sleep, as health professionals often recommend (Douglas & Hill, 2013)?

One recent review found that, despite the popularity of behavioural treatments for infant sleep, these interventions do not improve outcomes for mothers and

Sleep patterns in infancy • Figure 3.4

Infants show remarkable changes in their sleep during the first two years of life. As shown in this graph, newborns spend a good deal of time sleeping, not seeming to care whether it is day or night.

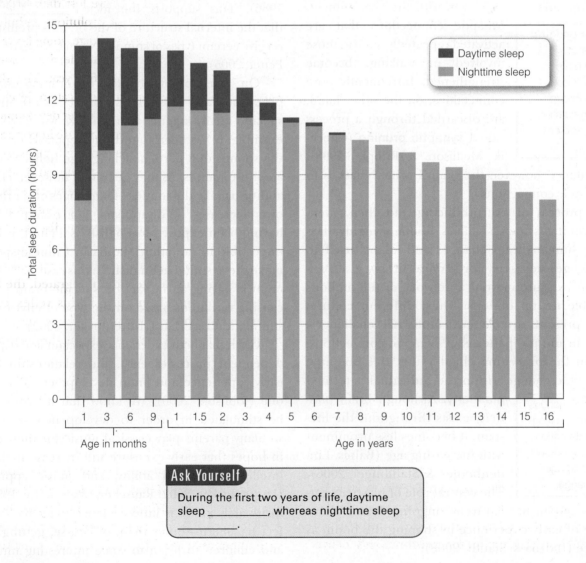

Ask Yourself

During the first two years of life, daytime sleep _____, whereas nighttime sleep _____.

infants during the first six months of life (Douglas & Hill, 2013). Contrary to popular belief, early sleep training does not decrease infant crying, prevent sleep and behavioural problems in later childhood, or protect mothers from postpartum depression. There may also be some unintended consequences of sleep training, such as worsened maternal anxiety, premature weaning from breastfeeding, and, if infants are required to sleep in a separate room from their parent, an increased risk of sudden infant death syndrome (SIDS) (Douglas & Hill, 2013; McKenna & Gettler, 2010), which we will discuss later in this chapter. Thankfully, as infants' brains mature, sleep needs decrease and become more in tune with the rising and setting of the sun.

Sleep can be divided into two primary categories: **rapid-eye-movement (REM) sleep** and **non–rapid-eye-movement (NREM) sleep**. REM sleep tends to be a deeper kind of sleep and helps us to feel most rested. Newborns spend up to 50 percent of the time they are asleep in REM sleep. By the end of the first two years, REM time makes up only about 20 to 25 percent of sleep (Carskadon & Dement, 2011). Why do newborns need so much REM sleep? Many scholars believe that REM sleep aids in learning and memory consolidation. Another theory posits that the high neural activity of REM sleep provides the internal stimulation required for synaptic connections to form (McNamara, 2004).

> **rapid-eye-movement (REM) sleep** A sleep state during which rapid and random eye movements, intense and irregular brain-wave activity, and dreaming occur.
>
> **non–rapid-eye-movement (NREM) sleep** A sleep state during which rapid-eye-movement and dreaming do not occur, and brain-wave activity is slow and regular.

More research is needed to determine what exactly is going on in infant brains during REM sleep. Organizations such as the National Sleep Foundation are investigating these issues (National Sleep Foundation, 2011). Developmentalists have a better understanding of changes in the peripheral nervous system, the topic to which we now turn.

The peripheral nervous system (PNS) The peripheral nervous system (PNS) connects the body to the central nervous system (CNS) through a highway of neural networks. It delivers environmental stimuli to the CNS via sensory neurons, takes information from the CNS to the skeletal muscles via motor neurons, and delivers information to and from organs such as the stomach, lungs, and heart. During the first two years of life, the PNS becomes more complex and adaptive. Of particular interest to developmental scientists is the development—and disappearance—of reflexes (Merkulov, Zavalishin, & Merkulova, 2009).

The simplest and quickest neural pathway is a **reflex**. Reflexes are quick because they involve few neurons: a sensory neuron (stimulated by a particular type of sensory signal) and a motor neuron (leading to a rapid motor response). There are a variety of **newborn reflexes**, as shown in **Table 3.1**. These newborn reflexes serve as indicators of healthy nervous system development (Brazelton & Nugent, 1995). Some reflexes are necessary for survival, whereas others have lost their original function through the process of evolution. Although most newborn reflexes disappear with age, some become incorporated into usable skills. For example, the grasping reflex becomes voluntary early in the first year. The absence of certain newborn reflexes could indicate a developmental problem. This is why doctors and other developmental specialists check for them and why they are important overall.

> **reflex** An involuntary response to a stimulus.
>
> **newborn reflex** An inborn automatic response to stimuli, which may disappear before the end of the first year of life.

Reflexes provide a behavioural measure of the development of the nervous system, and so they are often incorporated into newborn assessments, such as the Brazelton Neonatal Behavioral Assessment Scale (NBAS; Brazelton & Nugent, 1995), discussed in Chapter 2. For example, the Babinski reflex is associated with incomplete myelination. As the spinal cord and brain become myelinated and integrated, the Babinski reflex disappears. Therefore, if this reflex continues to appear in the second year, we can suspect delays in myelination and abnormal spine–brain integration (Schott & Rossor, 2003).

We now turn to parts of the body that are connected to the CNS via the PNS: the bones and muscles.

The Skeletal System

At some point you may have learned that the human body contains 206 bones (Gray, 2008). At birth, though, there are approximately 270 bones in the human body. Why the difference? As we grow, a number of smaller bones, such as bones in the spinal column, fuse together.

Newborn reflexes Table 3.1

Reflex

Plantar grasp

Appears: 28 weeks gestation

Integration: 9 months

Testing: With infant lying down, head midline, legs extended, apply firm pressure to ball of foot.

Expect: Flexing of all of the toes

Significance: This reflex is referred to as the readiness test because its integration corresponds with readiness to walk.

Voisin/Phanie/The Image Works

Babinski (plantar response)

Appears: Birth to 12–18 months

Integration: After walking

Testing: Stimulate the outside of the foot

Expect: Extension of big toe, fanning out of other toes

Significance: Failure to integrate the Babinski reflex interferes with walking and indicates neurological abnormality.

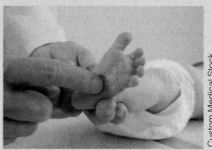

Custom Medical Stock Photo/Alamy

Moro

Appears: 28 weeks gestation

Integration: Between 5 and 6 months

Testing: Supporting the head and neck with one hand, lower the infant halfway to a lying-down position; allow the head and neck to drop into the other hand.

Expect: Shoulders pull back. Fingers, elbows, and wrists extend.

Significance: Asymmetry in this reflex may indicate injury to peripheral nerves in upper extremities.

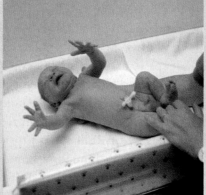

Picture Partners/Alamy

Palmar grasp

Appears: 10 weeks gestation

Integration: 4–6 months

Testing: With infant lying on back, with head at midline and arms and hands free, place adult finger in palm of infant's hand.

Expect: Infant's fingers flex around the finger.

Significance: Following full development of grasp, infant begins reaching for objects to grasp.

Corbis/Age Fotostock

Newborn reflexes Table 3.1 *(Continued)*

Reflex

Rooting and sucking

Appears: 28 weeks gestation

Integration: 3 months

Testing: With infant lying down on back, with head in midline and hands on chest, stroke infant from lips to cheek.

Expect: Infant turns head with mouth open toward finger and attempts to suck on finger.

Significance: Absence of this reflex indicates neurological impairment.

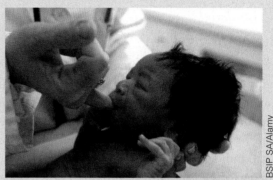

BSIP SA/Alamy

Stepping or walking

Appears: 37 weeks gestation

Integration: 2 months

Testing: Support standing infant with feet touching a hard surface; tilt infant forward to accommodate any stepping.

Expect: Alternating, rhythmical, coordinated steps

Significance: Absence of this reflex is a possible indicator of disease or prenatal drug (e.g., opiate) exposure.

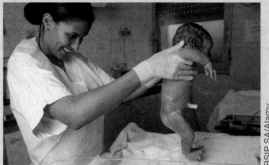

BSIP SA/Alamy

Crawling

Appears: At birth

Integration: 3–4 months

Testing: Put infant on abdomen.

Expect: Infant pulls legs underneath abdomen and pushes forward.

Significance: This reflex is essential for voluntary crawling behaviour.

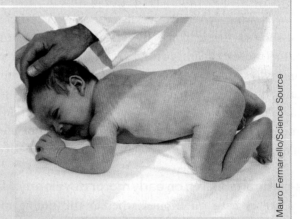

Mauro Fermariello/Science Source

Tonic neck

Appears: At birth

Integration: 6–7 months

Testing: While the infant is lying on its back, the infant's head is turned to one side.

Expect: The arms will briefly come into the "fencer's position" on the side to which the head is turned: the infant's arm will momentarily straighten and the other arm will flex in at the elbow toward the infant's body.

Significance: This helps the infant explore one side of its environment at a time by coordinating sensing on the same side.

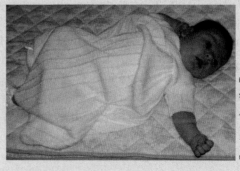

Courtesty Jennifer Tanner

As infants become more mobile, bones experience greater impacts. Just think of the difference between a lying newborn and a hopping toddler. These impacts aid in the development of both bones and muscles.

The Muscular System

When discussing muscle development, developmentalists focus mainly on the skeletal muscles that enable an infant to manipulate the world. The key ingredient in muscles that affects their flexibility and strength is muscle fibre. During the first two years, muscle fibre becomes more differentiated and innervated. These changes allow the muscles to perform more specific and finely tuned behavioural operations (Harris et al., 2005).

> **gross motor skills**
> A motor skill that relies on large muscles, such as those in the legs and arms.
>
> **fine motor skills**
> A motor skill that relies on small muscles, such as those in the fingers.

Motor skill development in infancy Researchers categorize motor movements based on the types of muscles involved in an activity and the degree of specificity of the task. Skills that use the large muscle groups, such as those in the legs and arms, are called **gross motor skills**. Skills that use the smaller muscle groups, such as those in the fingers and the eyes, are called **fine motor skills**. Most newborn movements are involuntary responses to sensory stimulation. By the end of infancy, however, they have developed an array of gross and fine motor skills, as depicted in **Figure 3.5**. Such development is largely due to improving integration of the muscular and nervous systems.

Cross-cultural research on early motor development

Some scholars have questioned whether the timing of motor skill development is the same around the world (e.g., Geber, 1958). Cross-cultural studies conducted in the 1950s through the 1970s found that African children sat independently, stood up, and walked earlier than U.S. infants (e.g., Geber, 1958; Kilbride, Robbins, & Kilbride, 1970). These findings led researchers to examine the comparative role of genes and experience in the timing of motor development (Figure 3.5) (Adolph, Karasik, & Tamis-LeMonda, 2009).

In investigating the timing of motor development around the world, researchers have considered how parents in various cultures handle infants. Infants are carried for much of the day in several traditional cultures around the world, such as India, Bali, Namibia, Vietnam, and Canada's North where Inuit mothers use an amautik. (**Figure 3.6**) (Fearn, 2006; Guerts, 2005). Inuit mothers use an amautik. In other parts of Canada and other Western cultures, parents tend to encourage babies to move around on their own. Researchers continue to ponder whether cultural differences like these affect infants' muscle growth and development.

Although this cultural question is intriguing, contemporary researchers tend to de-emphasize the earlier findings. First of all, many of the original cross-cultural studies employed poor research methodologies. Second, recent studies have failed to fully replicate the original findings (Adolph et al., 2009). Finally, the timing of motor development may not be as important an issue as was once thought. Developmentalists note that children in all cultures eventually learn to walk, run, and play with the same level of enthusiasm and skill.

Regardless of culture, **posture** is the integrating process that connects and provides a foundation for all gross motor activities

> **posture** The way a person holds his or her body as a whole.

(Metcalfe et al., 2005). Infants have no voluntary postural control at birth. With age, however, they learn to coordinate arms and legs and gain an understanding of where their body is in space. As attention shifts from self to external objects during the sensorimotor period, which we will explore in the next section, these physical developments increasingly enable infants to explore their world (Piaget, 1977).

CONCEPT CHECK 🛑 STOP

1. **What** are some examples of how physical development follows cephalocaudal and proximodistal growth patterns?

2. **What** role does early experience play in brain development?

3. **How** do infants' motor skills change from birth to age 2?

Although the exact timing of motor development varies greatly from one infant to another, these charts present a basic time frame for gross and fine motor skill development (WHO Multicentre Growth Reference Study Group & de Onis, 2006).

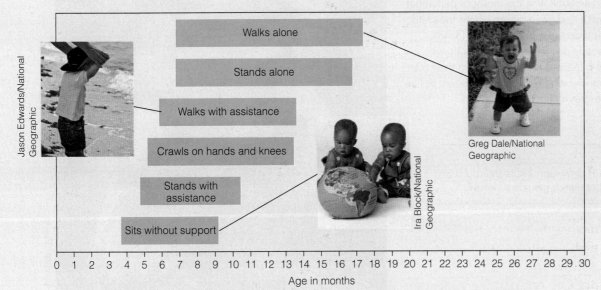

Walks alone

Stands alone

Walks with assistance

Crawls on hands and knees

Stands with assistance

Sits without support

Jason Edwards/National Geographic

Greg Dale/National Geographic

Ira Block/National Geographic

0 1 2 3 4 5 6 7 8 9 10 11 12 13 14 15 16 17 18 19 20 21 22 23 24 25 26 27 28 29 30
Age in months

a. Gross motor milestones
Notice the substantial overlap in timing of these gross motor milestones. Some babies are walking, while others of the same age have just learned to sit without support.

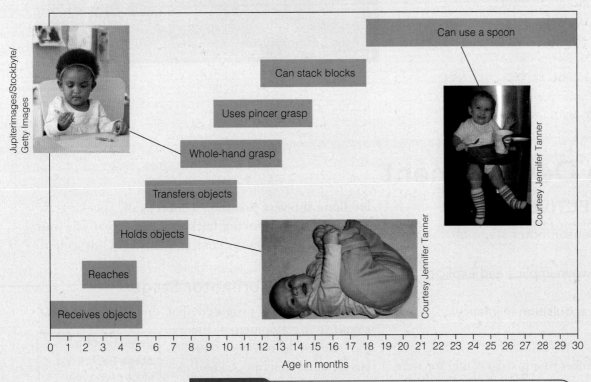

Can use a spoon

Can stack blocks

Uses pincer grasp

Whole-hand grasp

Transfers objects

Holds objects

Reaches

Receives objects

Jupiterimages/Stockbyte/ Getty Images

Courtesy Jennifer Tanner

Courtesy Jennifer Tanner

0 1 2 3 4 5 6 7 8 9 10 11 12 13 14 15 16 17 18 19 20 21 22 23 24 25 26 27 28 29 30
Age in months

b. Fine motor milestones
Similarly, the timing of fine motor milestones varies considerably among individuals. An infant's ability to manipulate objects with his or her hands reflects maturation of the central nervous system.

Ask Yourself

1. With respect to gross motor development, by 9 months almost all infants are able to _____.

2. With respect to fine motor skill development, by 9 months almost all infants have most recently mastered the ability to _____. _____.

Infant carrying and early motor development • Figure 3.6

In investigating the timing of motor development around the world, researchers have considered how parents in various cultures handle infants. Infants are carried for much of the day in several traditional cultures around the world, such as India, Bali, Namibia, Vietnam, and Canada's North (Fearn, 2006; Guerts, 2005). Inuit mothers use an amautik. It is the mother's parka that is worn by women in Nunavut and has a pouch where the child fits snugly as they are carried on their mother's back (Fearn, 2006). In other parts of Canada and other Western cultures, parents tend to encourage babies to move around on their own. Researchers continue to ponder whether cultural differences like these affect infants' muscle growth and development.

Ask Yourself

What type of motor development is the focus of the cross-cultural research described here?

Jeff McIntoch/The Canadian Press

Cognitive Development

LEARNING OBJECTIVES

1. **Discuss** Piaget's sensorimotor stage of development.
2. **Differentiate** between implicit and explicit memory in infancy.
3. **Explain** language acquisition in infancy.

D o you remember your first day of life? You were lying there in your mother's arms, wondering who would hold you next. As adults went on with their lives around you, you contemplated your hunger, your warmth, and your rapidly filling diaper.

Wait. This does not ring any bells? Of course it does not. Who can remember any of their life in infancy,

let alone the very first day? Theoretically speaking, we know you were thinking back then. But what was your thought like? That is the central question of this section.

Piaget's Sensorimotor Stage

In Chapter 1, we proposed that the most influential cognitive developmental theory was that of Jean Piaget (1977). His detailed descriptions and explanations laid the foundation for our understanding of children's thinking. When studying infancy, we focus primarily on the **sensorimotor stage** of Piaget's theory.

> **sensorimotor stage** Piaget's first stage of cognitive development, in which infants develop from reflex-driven organisms to more complex and symbolic thinkers.

According to Piaget, the goal of the sensorimotor stage is to develop from a reflexive organism to a more complex and symbolic thinker. As in all of Piaget's theory, the key processes that drive the change from one substage to the next are assimilation and accommodation. These processes underlie the ongoing development of mental structures called **schemes**.

> **schemes** Mental structures that help us organize and process information.
>
> **object permanence** The understanding that an object continues to exist even when it is not immediately present or visible.

Piaget divided the sensorimotor period into six substages, shown in **Figure 3.7**. As is clear in these substages, Piaget believed that infants develop a concept of objects that goes beyond immediate sensory contact. He called this specific understanding **object permanence**. As illustrated by Piaget's observations of his daughter, Jacqueline, children show an understanding of object permanence when they search for a hidden toy:

I take the potato and put it in the box while Jacqueline watches. I place the box under the rug. As soon as I remove my empty hand Jacqueline looks under the rug, finds and grasps the box, opens it and takes the potato out of it (Piaget, 1977, p. 266).

In order to have object permanence, Jacqueline must be able to mentally represent the object for which she searches. Once she has representational ability, she can search for an object that is outside her visual awareness.

Piaget noticed that, although infants begin to search for a toy at around 8 months, their understanding remains vulnerable. For example, if an object is repeatedly hidden in one spot and then hidden elsewhere, infants may become confused (**Figure 3.8**).

> **A-not-B error** A mistake made by children in Piaget's sensorimotor stage as they search for a hidden object in a location where it has been repeatedly placed but is no longer hidden.

Piaget called this the **A-not-B error** because the infant is looking in hiding place A when the object is actually in hiding place B.

Interestingly, both object permanence and understanding of the A-not-B error may be accomplished at younger ages than Piaget thought. Piaget relied on reaching behaviour (such as infants reaching with their arms) to study infants. When looking (or visual) behaviour is used to test object permanence, infants as young as 3.5 months seem to understand the concept (Baillargeon, 1994). Likewise, the A-not-B error disappears sooner if we observe which cloth infants look at—rather than which cloth they reach toward.

These findings underscore an important distinction between competence and performance. If infants are not able to perform a particular task, this does not necessarily mean that they lack the competence to understand the task. If the task was presented differently, they might perform well and show their true competence (Baillargeon, 1995). Following the principle of proximodistal development, infants control looking (visual) behaviour earlier in life than they do movement of the limbs and hands. Accordingly, testing infants through "looking" behaviour rather than "reaching" behaviour gives us the best sense of what babies really understand. These newer findings obtained through infants' looking behaviour would have surprised Piaget greatly. Similarly, Carolyn Rovee-Collier's (2008) research yielded surprising evidence of the early development of memories.

Memory

What is your first memory? When did it take place? Most people recall something from when they were 2 or 3 years old, at the very earliest. So what is happening during infancy?

Long-term memory in infancy Because we have no scientific evidence that conscious representation of information occurs, and infants cannot talk, the study of infant memory is a challenge. In a creative attempt to solve this problem, Carolyn Rovee-Collier developed a memory task that makes use of a crib mobile (**Figure 3.9**; Rovee-Collier & Cuevas, 2008).

Prior to Rovee-Collier's research, it was believed that infants could not form long-term memories until at least 1 year of age. Clearly, her work has shown otherwise. Nevertheless, long-term memory skills in infancy are highly context-dependent, especially through 6 months of age. For example, infants who are trained to kick the mobile in one room usually fail to kick when the mobile is shown to them in a different room (Rovee-Collier & Cuevas, 2008). Some researchers have questioned what exactly is being remembered (Mandler, 2004).

> **implicit memory** Repetition of a behaviour, such as a leg movement to make an object move, that occurs automatically and without apparent conscious effort.

Memory researchers suggest that there are two types of memory: implicit and explicit. **Implicit memory** occurs automatically

The sensorimotor period • Figure 3.7

✔ THE PLANNER

Piaget divided the sensorimotor period into six substages. Although we indicate age ranges associated with each of the substages, Piaget emphasized that the sequence of the substages is more important than the age of the infant (Piaget, 1977).

 Goldmund Lukic/Getty Images

 Sozaijiten/Datacraft/Getty Images

 Marc Oeder/STOCK4B/Getty Images

 Dorling Kindersley/Getty Images

 Roderick Chen/First Light/Corbis

 Harrison Eastwood/Getty Images

Substage 1: Reflexes (birth to 1 month)
According to Piaget, cognitive schemes during the first substage consist of passive reflexes such as sucking and grasping. Over the first month, this passive quality gradually changes and babies show more intentional and complex ways of interacting with their environments.

Substage 2: Habits and repetition (1–4 months)
Infants refine their schemes by performing formerly reflexive actions, such as grasping, in the absence of any stimulus. Piaget called these actions *habits*. When these habits are repeated, he called them primary circular reactions.

Substage 3: Actions with objects (4–8 months)
Attention begins to shift from self to external objects. Infants might use a newly developed grasping behaviour to pick up a rattle and, if it makes an interesting sound, they might continue to shake it. Piaget called this repetition of a behaviour a secondary circular reaction.

Substage 4: Coordination of schemes and intentional behaviour (8–12 months)
Senses are becoming more coordinated and schemes are working together. Infants show signs of intentional behaviour. Now they expect a noise when they bang a toy.

Substage 5: Using objects in novel ways (12–18 months)
Toddlers begin to use objects in new ways. For example, drum sticks can be used to hit the table to produce new sounds. Piaget called these types of behaviours tertiary circular reactions.

Substage 6: Symbolic thought (18–24 months)
Toddlers develop the ability to internalize sensory stimuli. Now they can think about a favourite toy even if it is not present.

Infant age →

Ask Yourself

Tertiary circular reactions are characteristic of which substage?

and is not in conscious awareness. The infants in Rovee-Collier's study demonstrate this type of memory. They appear to automatically remember muscle movements and environmental cues with no clear conscious effort. **Explicit memory**, on the other hand, is of the conscious type, in which infants demonstrate awareness of a memory. The best illustration of this type of memory is imitation (Carver, 2007).

Imitation requires that an infant internalize an observed behaviour and then produce it. One research team reported that 2- and 3-week-old infants have the ability to imitate facial expressions (Meltzoff & Moore, 1977). These infants, however, were engaging in immediate imitation. What about imitating an action after a delay and not in the presence of a model? This ability is called **deferred imitation**. It seems to emerge around 6 to 7 months and steadily improves during the second year (Bauer, 2008; Carver, 2007). As we will see, attentional skills aid in this and other forms of remembering.

explicit memory
Repetition of a behaviour that shows a clear, observable, conscious effort to recall an event, such as when an infant imitates at a later time a behaviour seen earlier.

deferred imitation
The ability of 6- to 7-month-old infants to imitate an action after a delay and not in the presence of a model.

a.

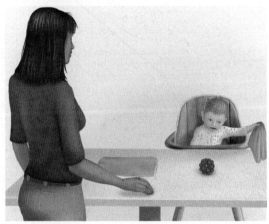

The A-not-B error • Figure 3.8

In an extended test of object permanence, an object is repeatedly hidden under cloth A. Each time, the infant (8 months or older) finds it correctly **(a)**. But when the researcher suddenly switches the hidden object to cloth B right in front of the child's eyes, infants under 18 months still tend to look under cloth A first **(b)**.

Put It Together *Review Figure 3.7 and answer the following questions:*
1. During what substage of the sensorimotor period do infants typically STOP making the A-not-B error?
2. What cognitive ability enables object permanence?

b.

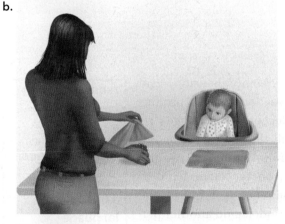

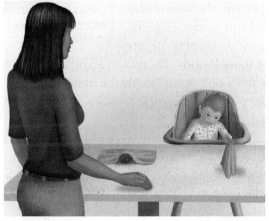

Attention, habituation, and dishabituation In order to remember objects, infants must concentrate on them. Thus when researchers investigate memory, they are usually also interested in attention (Posner & Rothbart, 2007). Attention increases with age and appears to be actively driven (Courage & Richards, 2008). That is, infants and children pay attention to what they think will be interesting, rather than passively attending to any stimulus in their environment (Anderson & Hanson, 2009).

One quality that makes an object interesting may be how familiar or novel it is. You may have noticed that perfume or aftershave smells strongest when you first put it on. This occurs because over time you experience **habituation**, or decreased responding to a continuously present stimulus. If you came across someone else who is wearing a different perfume or aftershave, though, you would immediately notice it: their scent is new and creates **dishabituation**, or increased responding. The way researchers use habituation–dishabituation in research is explained in **Figure 3.10** (Jeffrey & Cohen, 1971).

> **habituation** Decreased responding to a stimulus that occurs because of continuous presentation of the stimulus.
>
> **dishabituation** Increased responding to a stimulus, usually because it is novel.

Given that both attention and memory abilities improve with age, it should not come as a surprise that habituation also occurs more quickly with age. In addition, the more complex the stimulus, the longer it takes same-age infants to habituate to it. These findings imply that information processing underlies habituation and dishabituation (Lamb, Bornstein, & Teti, 2002). Speed of habituation in infancy has been found to be correlated with later IQ (Kavšek, 2004). In other words, the faster infants

Rovee-Collier's memory research • Figure 3.9

Rovee-Collier designed a paradigm for studying long-term memory in infancy.

a. Researchers begin by measuring how often the baby kicks in the absence of any interventions (the *baseline*). In the *training phase*, researchers tie a ribbon to the baby's leg, so that kicking moves a mobile overhead. The baby quickly begins to kick much more than he or she did before training. During *testing*, hours or days later, the mobile is still visible, but kicking no longer makes it move. The baby's kicking tells researchers that he or she is trying to get the response from the mobile that he or she remembers.

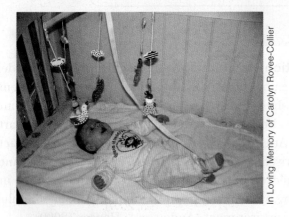

In Loving Memory of Carolyn Rovee-Collier

Think Critically Developing methods to study memory in infancy is no small feat. Can you think of another way to test long-term memory in infancy?

b. The maximum amount of time that babies can remember the task increases with age. This rise is quite smooth and continuous, even when the infants switch to a train task that is similar to the mobile task but better suited for the skills of older infants.

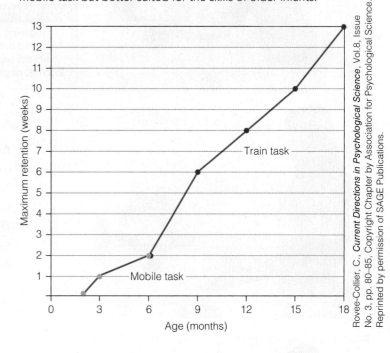

Rovee-Collier, C., *Current Directions in Psychological Science*, Vol.8, Issue No. 3, pp. 80–85, Copyright Chapter by Association for Psychological Science. Reprinted by permission of SAGE Publications.

---

habituate to stimuli relative to peers, the higher they are likely to score on intelligence tests as children. Of course, making the transition from habituation–dishabituation tests to intelligence tests requires a qualitative leap: the ability to use language.

Language Development

Picture yourself in a room, sitting in a chair, looking at a curtain. Behind the curtain are five 6-month-old infants from various countries. Each infant is making sounds. Your job is to identify which infant comes from which country. Will you succeed? It may be tempting to think you will, but sorry, you probably will not. In fact, although people speak different languages around the world, the process of early language development is virtually universal.

Early language development: Description Infants always understand more words than they can produce (Owens, 1996). This is the difference between **receptive**

language (comprehension) and **expressive language** (production). Receptive language requires only the ability to hear and process information. Expressive language, on the other hand, is quite complex. It requires the ability to understand another person's perspective, the motor ability to control and produce sounds, and cognitive awareness of the meaning of those sounds. Therefore, an infant who is unable to say the word "juice" might be able to point to a bottle of juice when that word is spoken (Ross & Weinberg, 2006).

Although the timing of language milestones can vary greatly, the sequence is virtually universal. Developmental scientists have developed norms for both receptive and expressive language, as shown in **Table 3.2**. Note how receptive language precedes expressive language.

receptive language Language that an infant understands but may not be able to produce.

expressive language Language that an infant can produce.

Research using habituation–dishabituation • Figure 3.10

In a habituation task, researchers first obtain a baseline by recording an infant's level of responding in the absence of any stimulus. The measured response might be looking behaviour, heart rate, or sucking behaviour, for example.

Ask Yourself

1. What perceptual ability does dishabituation in this example imply?
2. What cognitive ability does this example of dishabituation imply?

a. Habituation

The researcher then records responses when the infant is presented with a stimulus, such as the visual pattern shown here. Over time the infant will habituate to, or become bored with, this pattern. When this happens, the infant will stop paying attention and return to baseline levels of responding.

b. Dishabituation

During dishabituation, the old stimulus is replaced with a novel one such as the one shown here. If the infant shows an increased response, we can infer that he or she has discriminated the new stimulus from the old one (Sirois & Mareschal, 2004). This method offers insight into perceptual and cognitive abilities. In order to show dishabituation to the orange checkerboard, the infant in this example needed two abilities: (1) perception that the orange checkerboard was different from the black checkerboard and (2) memory of what the black checkerboard looked like in order to compare it to the orange checkerboard (Bremner, Bryant, Mareschal, & Volein, 2007).

Language milestones in infancy **Table 3.2**		
During this age range infants typically begin to...	**Show these signs of receptive language:**	**Show these signs of expressive language:**
1 to 4 months of age	• Respond to voices • Make sounds when spoken to	• Make one-syllable sounds • Coo
4 to 7 months of age		• Babble • Produce a variety of syllables
7 to 10 months of age	• Know when words begin and end • Comprehend gestures	• Repeat two syllables in a row (e.g., "mama")
10 to 13 months of age	• Respond to some commands • Understand simple words	• Say first word
13 to 16 months of age		• Say more than five words
16 to 19 months of age	• Understand "do not"	
19 to 22 months of age	• Understand a question • Repeat simple things others say	• Say two words in combination
22 to 25 months of age	• Understand "in" and "under"	• Say first sentence

The sequence for expressive language is as follows:

Crying: Crying communicates a variety of emotional states, especially when alternative forms of communication are not available (Rottenberg, Bylsma, & Vingerhoets, 2008). For this reason, crying is most common in infancy, though it punctuates the entire lifespan. Infant crying has been conceptualized as a part of an interactive and communicative system—the cry signals to the parent the existence of a need, and the parent responds by meeting the need (Ainsworth, Blehar, Waters, & Wall, 1978; Bowlby, 1988; Papoušek & Papoušek, 1990). When parents do not respond or respond inappropriately, infants suffer a number of physiological and interpersonal consequences (Tronick & Weinberg, 1997; see also Porter, 2007).

Cooing: At about 1 to 2 months, babies begin to make a gurgling sound that is described as a coo. This sound comes from the back of the throat and generally occurs in response to some pleasurable activity or interaction (Masataka, 1995).

> **babbling** The repeated creation of meaningless sounds that typically consist of one syllable.
>
> **holophrase** One-word utterances that express a complete thought or phrase.

Babbling: At approximately 6 to 8 months, babies begin to incorporate consonants into their communication. They start making **babbling** sounds such as *ma, ba, da,* and *pa,* because those are the easiest consonants to produce. It is at this stage that parents often repeat the sounds made by their babies, adding their own cultural inflection. Thus, the influence of cultural sounds begins to have an impact on the development of expressive language (Fasolo, Majorano, & D'Odorico, 2008).

First words: Although babies sound as if they are creating meaningful words when babbling, they are not. At approximately 10 to 12 months (though with much variation in this time frame), babies begin to understand that *ma* represents mother. And these first words are soon spoken in a variety of ways, each way encapsulating a different complete thought. *Ma* (said softly) and *Ma!* (said loudly) and *Ma?* (said with a playful smile) are all examples of a **holophrase**, one-word utterances that express a complete thought or phrase. Not coincidentally, by the way, *ma* is the word for mother in more than 50 languages.

Telegraphic speech: Around the time that their first words emerge, babies accompany the words with physical gestures in **telegraphic speech**. These gestures add meaning to the words. Different gestures used with the same words may have different meanings. Phrases such as *daddy go!* accompanied by extended arms may mean *daddy take me with you.* The same phrase without that gesture may mean *where is daddy?* Thus, these same one- to two-word phrases telegraph different meanings when accompanied with different gestures (Sheehan, Namy, & Mills, 2007).

Using gestures to direct the attention of others and, in turn, following the line of vision and/or pointing gestures of others represents an important developmental milestone of infancy known as **joint attention** (Adamson, 1995). It is not surprising that this type of early communication greatly contributes to the early acquisition of language (Carpenter, Nagell, & Tomasello, 1998; Mundy et al., 2007). The rudiments of joint attention emerge around 3 months of age (D'Entremont, Hains, & Muir, 1997; Hood, Willen, & Driver, 1998). By 6 to 10 months of age, the associated behaviours are observable (Brooks & Meltzoff, 2005).

> **telegraphic speech** The creation of short phrases that convey meaning but lack some of the parts of speech that are necessary for a full and complete sentence.
>
> **joint attention** The ability to direct the attention of a social partner to objects or events and, in turn, follow their attention-directing gestures, such as head-turning and pointing.

By their first birthday, most infants can produce between 10 and 50 words. By age 2, their vocabularies consist of about 200 words (Tan & Schafer, 2005). Most of these gains come after 18 months, during which a vocabulary spurt is said to take place. At all points, of course, the number of words they understand is even higher.

Between the first and second birthdays, language development begins to accelerate. Not only does vocabulary increase, but a baby's ability to use language in different contexts becomes more complex. The explanation for why language develops so quickly is controversial. The controversy builds from the relative emphasis of nature and nurture in divergent perspectives (Kauschke & Hofmeister, 2002).

Early language development: An explanation How can a newborn be plunked down in any society and, without being explicitly taught, pick up that society's complex language skills within just two years? This task is so difficult that many linguistic theorists believe we have an innate ability to learn language. Most notably, Noam Chomsky proposed that humans have an inborn **language acquisition device (LAD)**, which helps us learn the rules of language. The LAD is not a physical part of the brain, but rather a theoretical structure (Chomsky, 2007). It is notable, though, that two physical parts of the brain *are* involved in the comprehension and production of speech: Wernicke's and Broca's areas, respectively.

If language is entirely innate, why do we see differences in the ages at which language milestones are reached, particularly across different economic and family contexts (Hart & Risley, 1995)? As with all developmental processes, nature and nurture together influence language development. Indeed, adults and even young children automatically change their language when speaking to an infant, using high-pitched, simple language called **infant-directed speech**. Use of this speech may help the infant learn language (Trainor & Desjardins, 2002).

> **language acquisition device (LAD)** The name given by Noam Chomsky to a theoretical structure possessed by all humans that prewires us to learn language and grammar rules.
>
> **infant-directed speech** A way of speaking to infants that is higher in pitch, simpler, and more repetitive than speech directed at adults or children. It seems to be used automatically when in the presence of an infant.

Proponents of the **interactionist approach**, which stresses the role of socialization in language learning, also point to a number of other findings. For instance, studies have found that the amount and type of speech that parents direct toward their infants are correlated with the child's rate of language acquisition. In addition, differences in vocabulary size have been found to relate to parent–infant communication (Brent & Siskind, 2001; Robb, Richert, & Wartella, 2009). Finally, the vocabulary spurt may be related to increased communication by the parents, changes in the brain, and increasing social and cognitive abilities (Bloom, 1993).

> **interactionist approach** A view of language learning that stresses the role of socialization.

Language plays an important role throughout infancy. As you will see in the next section, it is a vital part of the relationship between the physical and cognitive systems.

CONCEPT CHECK 🛑 STOP

1. **How** does thinking evolve during infancy, according to Piaget?
2. **What** can infants remember?
3. **What** do theorists and researchers believe about how we learn language?

All the Systems Working Together

LEARNING OBJECTIVES

1. **Describe** the development of the five senses during infancy.
2. **Explain** how infants perceive depth and pain.
3. **Discuss** the MMR vaccination controversy.
4. **List** the benefits of breastfeeding for mother and child.
5. **Discuss** what is known about sudden infant death syndrome (SIDS).

We have just explored some of the key aspects of physical and cognitive development during the first two years of the lifespan. Interactions between these developmental domains produce various changes, most notably in sensation, perception, health, nutrition, and sleep.

Sensation

Parents, health professionals, and developmentalists all share an interest in infants' sensory capacities. What can a baby see at birth? Does a child's hearing get better with age? How does touch affect an infant's experiences in the world? These questions have both practical and theoretical importance, making them a target of early and ongoing research.

In this section, we will explore **sensation**, the physical reception of stimulation. There are five general receptor sites (retina of the eye, cochlea in the ear, olfactory membrane in the nose, taste buds, and skin), which receive different sources of stimulation (light, sound, chemical contact, temperature change, and pressure). Developmental scientists distinguish sensation from **perception**, the active interpretation of incoming stimulation. We begin by exploring the senses one by one.

> **sensation**
> Physical reception of stimulation.
>
> **perception**
> Interpretation of stimulation that occurs in the higher processing centres of the brain.

Vision The newborn's visual acuity (the ability to see clearly) is estimated to range from 20/120 to 20/240 (Aslin & Lathrop, 2008; Hamer & Mirabella, 1990). In other words, a newborn must be 20 feet (about 6 m) from an object to see what a normal adult can see at 120 to 240 feet (36.5 to 73 m). No wonder we naturally pull young infants close when we want to interact with them.

During the first month, a newborn's focal length (the distance at which things can be clearly seen) is about 18 to 30 cm. Not coincidentally, this is the distance between nursing newborns and their mothers' faces. By about 2 months, focal length and acuity have improved (Aslin & Lathrop, 2008; Hamer & Mirabella, 1990). By 1 year of age, infants can see like adults (Snowden, Thompson, & Troscianko, 2006).

Researchers have gathered this acuity information using a research technique called the visual preference paradigm. Robert Fantz (1963) developed this paradigm with the creation of a looking chamber.

Fantz realized that if infants can see a difference between two items, they will look longer at one of them. If, on the other hand, infants can detect no difference, they will not show a preference. Based on this observation, Fantz first inserted a grey card into the looking chamber beside a card containing vertical lines. He determined whether the infant perceived the lines by the infant's preference or lack of one. Fantz then made the lined card progressively denser. Eventually the infant stopped showing a preference. At this point, Fantz assumed that the infant perceived the lined card to be grey. Based on this experiment, Fantz obtained a rough estimate of acuity (Fantz, Ordy, & Udelf, 1962).

To understand why newborns have poor visual acuity, let us imagine for a moment a newborn boy trying to see his father's face. As he looks at his father, the very small muscles of his eyes (called **ciliary muscles**) work to move each eyeball and change the shape of each eye's lens. These muscular changes aim to focus an image of the father on the retina. From there, the optic nerve transports the information to the brain's occipital lobe. It is here that visual processing of the image actually takes place. In newborns, however, two primary issues affect the process: the ciliary muscles are not mature, and the vision centre in the brain is not fully developed (Snowden et al., 2006). Thus, the newborn boy can make out his father's face, but not all that clearly, especially if he is more than about 30 cm away.

With regard to colour vision, infants as young as 2 weeks old can discriminate between colours, though not nearly as well as adults can (Snowden et al., 2006). By about 4 months, though, infants appear to have fully developed colour perception (Okamura, Kanazawa, & Yamaguchi, 2007). Why the delay? It's because the neurons in the retina that respond to colour, called **cones**, are still developing in the months after birth.

> **ciliary muscles**
> The small muscles of the eye that work to move each eyeball and change the shape of each eye's lens.
>
> **cones** Neurons in the retina that respond to colour.

Finally, an infant's ability to scan the environment also changes over the first few months. Immediately after birth, newborns prefer to look at the contours of faces and objects, suggesting that they find areas with the most contrast interesting. With age, however, infants begin to look at the interior features of objects. This is clearly an adaptive change, because most information in the world, especially in faces, comes from the interior, not the edges (Haith, Bergman, & Moore, 1977; Salapatek, 1975).

Hearing When do humans begin to hear? At birth? At 1 week or 1 month? How about even before they are born? If you answered the latter, you are right. Three to four months before birth, the ear is fully formed and functional (Lecanuet, 1996). Inside the womb, the baby hears an only slightly muffled version of all the sounds outside the mother, along with the various internal sounds of the mother's body, such as heartbeat or digestion. After birth, these sounds—such as the mother's heartbeat and voice, and music played prenatally—are preferred by and soothing to babies (DeCasper & Fifer, 1980; Sai, 2005; Woodward, Fresen, Harrison, & Coley, 1996).

The development of hearing Table 3.3	
Age	**Typical Abilities**
Birth to 3 months	• Startles to loud sounds • Quiets or smiles when spoken to • Seems to recognize your voice and quiets if crying • Increases or decreases sucking behaviour in response to sound
4 to 6 months	• Moves eyes in direction of sounds • Responds to changes in tone of your voice • Notices toys that make sounds • Pays attention to music
7 months to 1 year	• Enjoys games like peek-a-boo and pat-a-cake • Turns and looks in direction of sounds • Listens when spoken to • Recognizes words for common items like "cup," "shoe," "book," or "juice" • Begins to respond to requests (e.g., "Come here" or "Want more?")

Infants respond reflexively to soft stimuli and other simple auditory signals (Lasky & Williams, 2005). Their hearing improves dramatically between 4 and 7 months of age. By this point, they turn their heads in response to sounds and appear able to localize the source of the sound (Krumm, Huffman, Dick, & Klich, 2008). Although there are variations in the normal development of hearing, in general, sensory development proceeds in a similar fashion for all infants who have normal hearing. **Table 3.3** presents a typical sequence of hearing milestones during the first year.

While most infants born in Canada experience normal hearing, each year approximately 4 per 1,000 babies born have some degree of hearing loss or will develop early progressive childhood hearing loss (Canadian Hearing Society, 2010). Early detection can significantly improve options for treatment and can lower the impact of hearing loss on the development of speech (Françozo, Fernandes, Lima, & Rossi, 2007). One organization that focuses on hearing issues is the Canadian Hearing Society (www.chs.ca), as presented in *Where Developmentalists Click.*

Smell, taste, and touch At birth, infants are not adapted to the outside physical environment, but rather to the mother's body (McKenna, 2009). And so it is her familiar smell, taste, and touch that help newborns feel secure and have their physical needs met in an optimal way.

Babies are born with fairly acute smell capabilities. In fact, it is babies' sense of smell that helps them find and latch on to their mothers' breast for the first time (Varendi, Porter, & Winberg, 1994). This is a wonderful example of our smart biological design and of the interrelatedness of smell, taste, and touch—the mother's areola secretes a substance that smells very similar to the familiar and comforting smell of amniotic fluid. Newborns are drawn to this smell and, when placed skin-to-skin between their mothers' breasts after birth, they will use the smell to locate the nipple and begin suckling.

As early as 1 week of age, infants will turn their heads away from smells that they do not like (Yonas, Arterberry, & Craton, 1993). They also exhibit positive emotional responses to sweet smells like fruit and negative reactions to bitter smells like that of rotten eggs (Engen, Lipsitt, Lewis, & Kaye, 1963). In general, infants appear to prefer a familiar scent over an unfamiliar one (MacFarlane, 1975).

Babies also have well-developed taste abilities at birth. Even during the very first day of life, we can observe different facial expressions when babies are given different tastes (**Figure 3.11**).

Finally, touch, the sense that develops earliest in the fetus, is well developed by birth (Heller, 1997). The newborn's face, which is chock-full of nerves, is especially sensitive to touch, ready to be stroked by the mother's fingertips. Newborns and infants thrive on this type of loving touch. The more they get of it, the more they grow (Field, 2002). So touch in the form of massage has been used with preterm and low-birth-weight babies to promote growth and development (Vickers, Ohlsson, Lacy, & Horsley, 2004).

Continuous physical touch is the expectation of the human newborn and infant, as humans are a carrying species (Lozoff & Brittenham, 1979) (**Figure 3.12**). Two important characteristics distinguish carrying species from nesting species: breast-milk composition and the frequency of feedings. The breast milk of carrying species is relatively low in fat and protein, suggesting that frequent feedings and continuous physical contact are the norm. Nesting species, on the other hand, are adapted for intermittent feedings because their breast milk is relatively high in fat and protein. Because human infants, like the young of other carrying species, are adapted for continuous touch, we find that infant care practices such as babywearing and co-sleeping (discussed later in this section) are associated with various physiological and psychological benefits (e.g., Blair, Heron, & Fleming,

Where Developmentalists CLICK

The Canadian Hearing Society

Unique in North America, the Canadian Hearing Society (www.chs.ca) is a charitable agency that has been a key leader for over 60 years in the provision of services, products, and information to promote diversity and remove communications barriers related to hearing. The CHS not only advances hearing health, but also promotes equity for people who are culturally deaf, oral deaf, deafened, and hard of hearing. It offers a complete roster of essential services for children, including one-on-one language development for deaf and hard-of-hearing children, using play as the medium of learning; baby monitors; and other supports

for parenting. It has a comprehensive set of resources for adults, such as sign language interpreting and instruction, employment consulting, speech reading training, hearing testing, hearing aids, and counselling, and a complete range of communication devices that assist and augment communication, including text telephones (TTYs) and signalling devices. Click on the Programs and Services Tab to locate details of what is available for accessibility, hearing clinics, counselling, education, and employment services and follow links to connect to helpful resources and regional supports throughout Canada.

2010; Hunziker & Barr, 1986; Keller & Goldberg, 2004; Mosko, Richard, McKenna, Drummond, & Mukai, 1997; Richard & Mosko, 2004).

You may notice the next time you pick up a baby that he or she will immediately reach out to touch you. This exploratory behaviour serves as a major modality for the acquisition of information during the first months of life (Kellman & Banks, 1998).

Perception

As we discussed earlier, it is not easy to study infants' abilities. Researchers are arguably at their most creative when

designing studies to test infant perception. Some of the first studies of infant perception had to do with depth perception.

Depth perception The **visual cliff** method is used to examine the development of depth perception (**Figure 3.13**; Gibson & Walk, 1960). Five- to six-month-old infants stop crawling at the drop-off, and so it is assumed that depth perception emerges around that time (Yonas &

> **visual cliff**
> A method used to examine infant depth perception using a patterned floor and a pane of Plexiglas over a deep drop. When infants willingly crawl over the Plexiglas, it is assumed they do not perceive the depth.

Taste preferences at birth • Figure 3.11

This newborn is tasting sweet, sour, and bitter fluids. Like most babies, he appears to prefer sweet tastes (Crook, 1978). Not coincidentally, breast milk is very sweet.

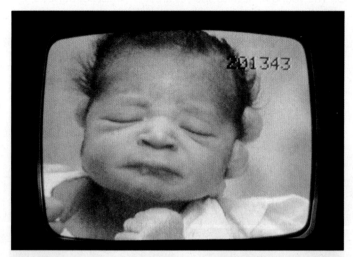
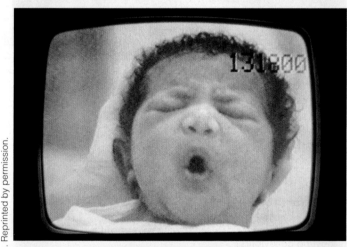
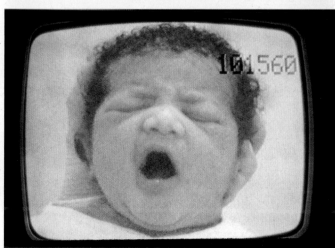

Think Critically How might taste preferences benefit us early in life?

Granrud, 2006). Notably, infants who had been crawling for a while were less likely to cross the Plexiglas than were infants who were new to crawling. This difference suggests that experience plays a role in the development of depth perception.

Notably, other research has reported depth perception at earlier ages (e.g., Campos, Bertanthal, & Kermoian, 1992). These findings raise the question of whether children may be aware of depth at a young age but do not become fearful until they are older.

As infants develop independent mobility, they discover new things about their environment and themselves. This observation led researchers to question the relationship between perceptual and motor systems (Reed, 1982). Developmentalists continue to explore the idea that perceptual and motor systems develop interdependently, or are functionally related, and influence each other throughout the course of development. Such interdependence between perception and action is referred to as perception–action coupling, and this concept underlies a great deal of current research and theory on the development of perceptual and motor systems in infancy (Hubbard, Hertenstein, & Witherington, 2000). What do you think the functional relationships might be between perception and locomotion and spatial skills?

Pain perception The amount of pain an infant experiences has been a controversial issue among scientists and doctors. Practices such as circumcision have operated under two assumptions: that an infant does not experience severe pain, and that cases of minor pain will not be remembered over time (Owens & Todt, 1984). After a review of the literature, researchers have concluded that there is enough evidence to infer that infants experience pain (Anand & Hickey, 1987). In addition, there may be negative behavioural consequences resulting from early pain experiences. Breastfeeding, which we discuss in greater detail later in this section, has been shown to be a potent painkiller in healthy newborns. In a study of newborns undergoing heel lance and blood collection—a painful hospital procedure—breastfeeding during the procedure reduced crying by 91 percent, compared with the control infants who received the standard hospital care during the procedure of being swaddled in their bassinets (Gray, Miller, Philipp, & Blass, 2002).

At times, though, pain is inflicted in the course of seeking to protect the infant, as in the case of infant immunizations.

Carrying species versus nesting species • Figure 3.12

Terrestrial (land) mammals can be divided into two categories: those with extensive physical contact between mother and infant (carrying species), and those with intermittent contact (nesting species) (Lozoff & Brittenham, 1979).

a. The young of carrying species are carried by, hibernate with, or follow the mother. Both monkeys and humans are carrying species. ▼

b. The young of nesting species are left in nests or burrows, while the mother is absent for extended periods of time. Birds are an example of a nesting species. ▼

◀ **c.** In Canada and in other industrialized nations, the pattern of carrying seen throughout most of human history has been replaced by one that resembles nesting. This shift has inspired research on the role of continuous touch in infant development and maternal sensitivity (e.g., Anisfeld, Casper, Nozyce, & Cunningham, 1990).

Think Critically What are the likely effects on infant development of a carrying species adopting nesting behaviours?

Health and Well-Being

Few measures in preventive medicine are as effective against infectious diseases as routine immunization. In Canada, publicly funded immunization schedules vary across provinces and territories. However, during the first two years of life, the average Canadian infant will receive vaccines for approximately 14 different illnesses. As a result of regular vaccinations, Canada has completely or nearly eliminated a variety of illnesses, including polio, diphtheria, and smallpox

vaccine
A substance that is usually injected into a person to improve immunity against a particular disease.

The visual cliff • Figure 3.13

The visual cliff research paradigm uses a checkerboard floor and a pane of Plexiglas over a deep drop. Parents call to their babies from the end of the "deep" side and encourage them to crawl across. When infants willingly crawl over the Plexiglas, we assume that they do not perceive the depth.

Plexiglas only

Shallow side

Floor as seen through the Plexiglas

Ask Yourself

What do we assume when infants refuse to crawl over the Plexiglas?

(Public Health Agency of Canada, 2014b). A loss of public confidence in vaccines can reduce the number of people who receive immunizations, resulting in the reappearance of vaccine-preventable diseases. **Vaccine hesitancy** is defined by the Public Health Agency of Canada as "a refusal or delay in immunization schedules due to concerns about immunization" (2013). Vaccine hesitancy may have played a role in the outbreak of measles in Quebec and Western Ontario in 2015 (Public Health Agency of Canada, 2015). Of late, there has been intense interest in understanding why people are unwilling to receive vaccines and how to best address those concerns (Public Health Agency of Canada, 2013).

> **vaccine hesitancy**
> A refusal or a delay in immunization participation caused by concerns about vaccines.

Vaccine hesitancy is not only a concern in Canada. The measles, mumps, and rubella (MMR) vaccination, which is typically given around age 1, became a matter of much controversy after a 1998 study, published in *The Lancet*, claimed to link the MMR vaccine to autism (Wakefield et al., 1998). Evidence has recently established that the lead researcher falsified the data (Deer, 2009) and no other researchers have been able to establish a link.

Unfortunately, the damage has already been done. In England, where *The Lancet* is published, MMR vaccination rates fell from 92 percent before the study's publication to under 80 percent afterwards. Consequently, measles rates skyrocketed, from 56 cases in 1998 to 1,348 in 2008, contributing to at least two deaths (Deer, 2009). The case of the MMR vaccine controversy speaks to the importance of ethics and accountability in research.

Most vaccinations happen during well-baby checkups. During a well-baby checkup, a medical practitioner may check the baby's head to assess how well the bones of the skull are fusing, test reflexes, and assess the baby's gross and fine motor skills.

Nutrition

Optimal infant and young child feeding practices are among the most effective interventions for improving child health (World Health Organization, 2009b). Inadequate **nutrition** is associated with at least 35 percent of child deaths. Those who do survive may

> **nutrition** The process of consuming carbohydrates, fats, proteins, and other elements in the form of calories, to obtain energy and regulate body functions.

find that the lack of proper nutrition prevents them from reaching their full developmental potential.

exclusive
breastfeeding When infants receive only breast milk, whether from the breast or expressed, and no other liquids or solids including water.

on-demand breastfeeding
Nursing a baby whenever the baby shows signs of hunger during the day and night, such as by crying or rooting, rather than according to a set schedule.

complementary feeding The process of consuming other foods and liquids, along with breast milk, to meet the nutritional requirements of infants after 6 months of age.

According to the World Health Organization (WHO), optimal nutrition means **exclusive** and **on-demand breastfeeding** for the first six months of life, followed by the introduction of **complementary feeding** (solid foods) along with continued, on-demand breastfeeding for a minimum of two years (WHO, 2009a; see also Kent et al., 2006; Kramer & Kakuma, 2012). The Canadian Paediatric Society (Critch, 2014), in alignment with Health Canada (2014), takes a similar position to the WHO, stating that "breast milk is the optimal food for infants, and breastfeeding may continue for up to two years and beyond." And yet, globally, only 35 percent of infants under 6 months of age are breastfed exclusively (WHO 2009a). In Canada, the figure is only 26 percent (Gionet, 2013).

Breastfeeding Breast milk contains all the nutrients—fat, carbohydrates, proteins, vitamins, minerals, and water—that an infant needs during the first six months of life (Lawrence & Lawrence, 2005; Riordan, 2010; WHO, 2009b). It also contains a number of factors that prevent infection and that aid digestion and nutrient absorption. These qualities of breast milk cannot be replicated in infant formula. It is also impossible to replicate the dynamic nature of breast milk—its composition is always changing within a feeding, throughout the day, and over the course of lactation, adapting itself to the changing needs of the growing infant (Hartmann & Prosser, 1984).

Colostrum is the special yellowish, sticky breast milk that is secreted during the first two to three days after

colostrum The yellowish, sticky breast milk that is secreted during the first two to three days after birth.

birth (Lawrence & Lawrence, 2005). Though produced in small amounts, it is full of white cells and antibodies perfectly suited for newborns. Breast milk increases in amount between two

and four days after birth, at which point the milk is said to have *come in*. But it is not until two weeks postpartum that the milk may be called *mature*. The first two weeks of breastfeeding are considered a sensitive period for establishing milk production; a look at the hormones behind breastfeeding explains why.

Two maternal hormones directly affect breastfeeding: prolactin and oxytocin. As we see in **Figure 3.14**, when a baby nurses at the breast, the stimulated nipple sends a message to the brain. The brain responds by secreting prolactin for milk production and oxytocin for milk ejection. During those first sensitive weeks of breastfeeding, the more the baby suckles and stimulates the nipple, the more prolactin is secreted, and the more milk is produced. The idiom "use it or lose it" applies perfectly to this sensitive period of breastfeeding. If the nipples are not sufficiently stimulated, then breast milk dries up. Although prolactin is always necessary for milk production, after the first few weeks the amount of milk produced is not so closely tied to the amount of prolactin secreted.

Breastfeeding offers both child and mother short-term and long-term benefits (León-Cava, Lutter, Ross, & Martin, 2002). The benefits of breastfeeding in developing countries are especially profound. Infants who are not breastfed are 10 times more likely to die in the months following birth than those who are breastfed (Bahl et al., 2005). Diarrhea and pneumonia, which occur more frequently and with greater severity in formula-fed infants, cause many of these deaths (Bachrach, Schwarz, & Bachrach, 2003; De Zoysa, Rea, & Martines, 1991). Yet even in developed nations, formula-fed infants are at risk for a variety of acute and chronic disorders, such as **otitis media**, meningitis, urinary tract infections, type 1 diabetes, and childhood leukemia (Duncan et al., 1993; Kwan, Buffler, Abrams,

otitis media
Infection of the middle ear and a common cause of earaches.

& Kiley, 2004; Mårild, Hansson, Jodal, Odén, & Svedberg, 2004; Sadauskaite-Kuehne, Ludvigsson, Padaiga, Jasinskiene, & Samuelsson, 2004; Silfverdal, Bodin, & Olcén, 1999). Because breastfeeding helps children build strong immune systems, formula-fed children are more likely to suffer from diseases with an immunological basis, such as asthma, celiac disease, and Crohn's disease (Akobeng, Ramanan, Buchan, & Heller, 2006; Gdalevich, Mimouni, & Mimouni, 2001; Klement, Cohen, Boxman, Joseph, & Reif, 2004).

Studies have also pointed to the protective role of breastfeeding against obesity in later childhood and

The hormones behind milk production • Figure 3.14

The prolactin level is highest about 30 minutes into the feeding, so its most important effect is to produce milk for the next feed. Because oxytocin is secreted more quickly than prolactin, it helps make the milk that is already in the breast flow for the current feed.

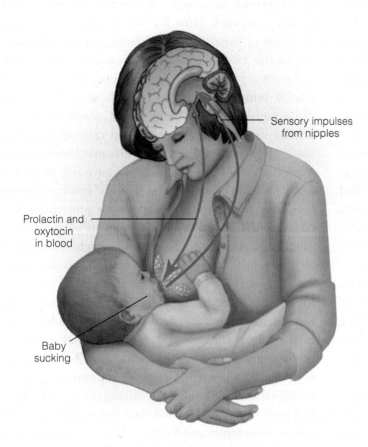

Sensory impulses from nipples

Prolactin and oxytocin in blood

Baby sucking

Think Critically

Given what you have learned about the hormones behind milk production, what advice would you give to a new breastfeeding mother?

adolescence. The relationship appears to be dose dependent: The longer children are breastfed, the lower the risk of obesity (Burke et al., 2005; Harder, Bergmann, Kallischnigg, & Plagemann, 2005). Prolonged and exclusive breastfeeding reduces the risk of sudden infant death syndrome (SIDS), which we discuss later in this section (Ip et al., 2007). Breastfeeding also protects against cardiovascular illnesses in later life, such as high blood pressure and problematic blood cholesterol levels (Martin, Gunnell, & Davey Smith, 2005; Owen, Whincup, Odoki, Gilg, & Cook, 2002).

Although many studies have concentrated on the physical benefits of breastfeeding, there are also demonstrated cognitive benefits. One team of researchers conducted a meta-analysis of 20 studies and found that, compared with formula-fed children, breastfed children scored significantly higher on tests of cognitive function (Anderson, Johnstone, & Remley, 1999). For those children who were born with low birth weight (see Chapter 2), the advantages of breastfeeding were even more pronounced. As with obesity, this relationship between breastfeeding and intelligence is dose dependent. That is, longer breastfeeding duration is associated with greater intelligence in late childhood and in adulthood (Daniels & Adair, 2005; Mortensen, Michaelsen, Sanders, & Reinisch, 2002).

And what are the benefits for breastfeeding mothers? In the short term, breastfeeding immediately after birth may reduce the risk of postpartum hemorrhage (bleeding). Exclusive breastfeeding for six months postpartum can delay the return of fertility and of the menstrual cycle, called **lactational amenorrhea** (World Health Organization Task Force on Methods for the Natural

lactational amenorrhea Natural postpartum infertility that occurs when a woman is breastfeeding and her menstrual cycle has not yet returned.

Regulation of Fertility, 1999). Longer spacing between births is associated with better health outcomes for both mother and child (Norton, 2005). Breastfeeding women also return to their pre-pregnancy weight more quickly than non-breastfeeding women (Dewey, Cohen, Brown, & Rivera, 2001). Later in life, women who breastfed their children will have lower rates of breast cancer and ovarian cancer compared to women who birthed and did not breastfeed (and the risk lowers further with longer breastfeeding; Collaborative Group on Hormonal Factors in Breast Cancer, 2002; Robenblatt & Thomas, 1993; Stuebe, Willet, Xue, & Michels, 2009).

Given the significant health and developmental benefits of breastfeeding, and the fact that many of the benefits are dose dependent, Health Canada recommends that breastfeeding continue for two years or more—along with introducing age-appropriate solid foods (Public Health Agency of Canada, 2014a). The American Academy of Pediatrics has reported that there is no scientific evidence of psychological or developmental harm from breastfeeding into the third year of life or longer (AAP, 2005). In Canada, where only a small minority of infants are still breastfeeding at 12 months, two years or more might sound like a long time (Health Canada, 2012). However, according to anthropological data, the natural age of weaning for humans is between 2.5 and 7 years of age (Dettwyler, 1995).

When given accurate information and ample support, virtually all mothers can breastfeed. Nevertheless, there are a small number of health conditions that may warrant temporary or permanent avoidance of breastfeeding, including maternal HIV infection; severe maternal illness, such as sepsis; and the taking of certain maternal medications, such as chemotherapy drugs (WHO, 2009a, 2010). Infant conditions that warrant the use of breast-milk substitutes include galactosemia (which affects the processing of galactose, a type of sugar) and maple syrup urine disease (which affects the ability to process certain amino acids). Breast milk is the best feeding option for **preterm** infants

preterm An infant born before 32 weeks gestation.

very low-birth-weight Infants born weighing less than 1,500 g.

(infants born before 32 weeks' gestation) and **very low-birth-weight** infants (infants born weighing less than 1,500 g), though these newborns may require complementary feeding for a limited period.

Breast-milk substitutes Manufacturers of infant formula have a history of promoting and marketing their goods in ways that make breastfeeding and artificial feeding seem like comparable methods (WHO, 1981, 2009b). Such marketing campaigns can undermine health workers' and mothers' own confidence in breast milk, leading to widespread use of breast-milk substitutes and, in turn, less than optimal health outcomes. How has the culture shifted around the issue of breastfeeding? Historically, in colonial Canada in the 1850s, long-term breastfeeding was originally common across class and ethnic lines. Nathoo and Ostry (2009) demonstrate that industrialization slowly changed the pattern of infant feeding in Canada. However, improper storage brought increased rates of tuberculosis, scarlet fever, diphtheria, typhoid, and cholera in infants from the use of tainted milk and gave rise to pure milk depots as part of a maternal feminist reform movement. Increased scientific knowledge and a general acceptance of germ theory bolstered the feminists' claims about the need for pure milk. For approximately 40 years, from 1920 onward, breastfeeding continued to decline to almost non-existent levels. A confluence of cultural factors contributed to this demise, not the least of which was the medicalization of birthing. The increase in hospital births meant women in the hospital did not have ready access to their babies to practise on-demand breastfeeding. As well, formula was often given at the first sign of difficulty. Simultaneously, during this period the medical profession also became embedded in the creation of patent baby foods and formulas through research on the role of vitamins and supplements. As the various baby formulas were being developed, they were also being aggressively marketed. In a famous example, in the 1930s Canada's Dionne quintuplets became the "spokesbabies" for Carnation formula despite the fact that they had actually been fed donated breast milk in infancy. Adding to this aura of modern infant technology was the improvement in refrigeration, which removed some of the dangers of bottle-feeding. There was also a shift away from traditional lay knowledge about breastfeeding passed along through women's networks and multigenerational families.

In a fascinating turn of events, breastfeeding became repopularized during the 1960s for some women and continues to gain in practice today, nearly 50 years later. Most scholars credit the women's movement and related natural childbirth movement, as well as international concerns about formula feeding, as the central forces for change. The La Leche League formed to disseminate previously lost breastfeeding information to mothers wishing an alternative experience. Hospitals began allowing "rooming-in," where the baby would spend increased amounts of time with the mother in her room, thus making breastfeeding a viable option. As rates of breastfeeding increased in affluent cultures, formula manufacturers shifted their attention to more impoverished parts of the world; the concomitant increased infant mortality there focused attention on the content of formula and the advertising tactics of the manufacturing companies. Concerned women and men participated in a worldwide boycott of Nestlé, a main producer of formula. The "Anytime, Anywhere" campaign by Health Canada was devised to bolster breastfeeding, to desexualize the breast and make public breastfeeding more acceptable.

In 1981, the World Health Assembly (WHA) adopted the **International Code of Marketing of Breast-milk Substitutes** to improve the health and nutrition of infants and young children (WHO, 1981) (**Figure 3.15**). The code is designed to regulate the marketing of breast-milk substitutes, bottles, and pacifiers. It does not seek to ban these products, but rather to control promotional campaigns that may influence families to use breast-milk substitutes when they are not needed.

> **International Code of Marketing of Breast-milk Substitutes** A code adopted by the World Health Assembly to improve the health of infants and children.

The International Code of Marketing of Breast-milk Substitutes • Figure 3.15

This map shows the widespread adoption of the International Code as of April 2011. Countries have used some innovative strategies for implementing the code. In Iran, formula is available only by prescription (UNICEF, 2012). In India, containers of infant formula have a warning label, like the ones we see on cigarette packs.

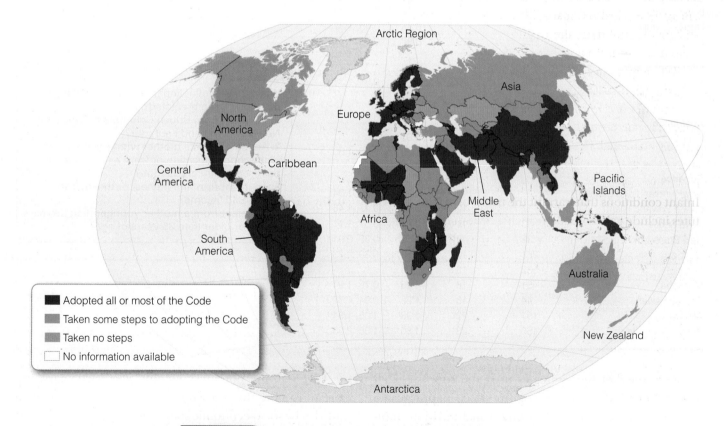

- ■ Adopted all or most of the Code
- ■ Taken some steps to adopting the Code
- ■ Taken no steps
- □ No information available

Ask Yourself

What has been the Canadian response to the International Code?

	Estimated number who had baby excluding mothers still exclusively breastfeeding '000	Breastfed exclusively at least 6 months		
		Prev-alence %	Adjusted odds ratio	95% confidence interval
Total	1,319	17	...	...
Age group			1.05*§	1.04, 1.07
<25	140	8†	...	...
25–29	323	15†	...	...
30–34	421	18	...	...
35+	435	21†	...	...
Marital status				
Married	1,140	18†	1.09	0.82, 1.44
Not married†	179	14†	1.00	...
Education				
Less than secondary graduation†	131	11†	1.00	...
Secondary graduation	260	15	1.14	0.76, 1.71
Some postsecondary	99	15	1.26	0.78, 2.04
Postsecondary graduation	815	19†	1.46*	1.00, 2.12
Household income				
Lowest‡	145	13†	1.00	...
Lowest–middle	278	18	1.18	0.81, 1.71
Upper–middle	435	16	0.95	0.65, 1.37
Highest	360	19	0.96	0.66, 1.42
Immigrant status				
Immigrant	293	20†	1.07	0.84, 1.37
Non-immigrant†	1,016	16†	1.00	...
Residence				
Rural‡	235	13†	1.00	...
Urban	1,083	18†	1.29*	1.03, 1.60
Province				
Newfoundland and Labrador	22	9†E2	0.54	0.28, 1.04
Prince Edwand Island	7	12E2	0.74	0.37, 1.46
Nova Scotia	43	14E1	0.91	0.57, 1.47
New Brunswick	32	8†E1	0.52*	0.30, 0.91
Québec	281	10†	0.53*	0.39, 0.73
Ontario‡	532	18	1.00	...
Manitoba	51	18	1.23	0.79, 1.91
Saskatchewan	44	18	1.29	0.94, 1.77
Alberta	151	22†	1.38*	1.05, 1.81
British Columbia	156	28†	1.80*	1.38, 2.33

Source: Statistics Canada, *Health Reports*, Vol. 16, No. 2, Catalogue no. 82-003-XIE

Data source: *2003 Canadian Community Health Survey (CCHS)*

Note: *Based on 6,802 women who had a baby in previous five years, including those who did not breastfeed, but excluding those still breastfeeding exclusively at the time of CCHS interview. "Missing" categories for education, household income, and immigrant status were included in model to maximize sample size, but prevalences and odds ratios are not shown. Because of rounding, detail may not add to total.*
† *Significantly different from value for total (p < 0.05)*
‡ *Reference category*
§ *Treated as continuous variable*
* *Significantly different from reference category (p < 0.05)*
E1 *Coefficient of variation 16.6% to 25.0%*
E2 *Coefficient of variation 25.1% to 33.3%*
Not applicable

Ask Yourself

Which of the following infants is least likely to have ever been breastfed?
1. An infant from British Columbia or from Newfoundland and Labrador?
2. An infant from a mother with less than high school education or from a mother with post-secondary graduation?
3. An infant from the highest or the lowest household income?
4. An infant from a mother younger than 25 years of age or older than 35 years of age?

Regardless of the strategies used the countries that have adopted the code recognize that inappropriate feeding practices can lead to infant malnutrition, morbidity, and mortality across all segments of the population. In the next section, we take a closer look at the issue of malnutrition.

Given all the potential benefits, it is particularly important to note that breastfeeding rates vary by province and also by socio-economic status level (**Figure 3.16**) and to consider the potential long-term outcomes of this disparity (Sullivan, 2008). Education alone is a very poor strategy to promote breastfeeding because there are so many structural barriers to breastfeeding—including such issues as maternity leave, breastfeeding at work, understaffed hospitals, and the need for more breast-milk banks. Breast-milk banks are places where breastfeeding mothers can donate their extra milk for the benefit of other babies. Cultural, socio-economic, and educational elements affect the decision, in addition to the mother's personal preferences, needs, and milk production. Regardless of choice, though, the baby will be nourished. Unfortunately, this cannot be said of all infants.

What do you think are the social, cultural, and economic factors that contribute to these differences? Because it is free, there are obvious economic benefits to breastfeeding. Women with lower incomes, however, are less likely to breastfeed. Why? Part of the explanation may lie in the workplace. Low socio-economic status (SES) mothers tend to work in settings that do not support breastfeeding. Middle- and higher-SES mothers, on the other hand, are often provided with rooms in which they can pump milk privately or are given breaks for pumping (Rabin, 2006). What else do you think is contributing to differences?

malnutrition
A deficiency of one or more key nutrients, such as proteins, vitamins, or minerals, that has a significant impact on energy and the function of bodily systems.

protein-energy malnutrition (PEM) A type of malnutrition in which insufficient food intake results in a significant lack of protein and calories.

Malnutrition Malnutrition is a deficiency of nourishment to the body. The most common cause of malnutrition is **protein-energy malnutrition (PEM)**. PEM occurs when there is a lack of food and/or a dietary imbalance. Two of the more common types of PEM are kwashiorkor and marasmus, discussed further in *Challenges in Development*. Both of these forms of malnutrition are found primarily in nations with significant poverty and extreme food deficiencies (Kar, Rao, & Chandramouli, 2008). Malnutrition in Canada is more often an outcome of poor nutrition, including vitamin and mineral deficiencies, rather than extreme food deprivation. Despite Canada's wealthy status, just over 19 percent of Canadian children live in poverty. It is important to note that income insecurity is not randomly distributed among Canadians: 40 percent of Canada's indigenous children live in poverty (Campaign 2000, 2015). **Figure 3.17** shows changes in child poverty rates in the provinces and territories in 2013.

As you will see in the next section, optimal nutrition during infancy has implications for infant sleep. On-demand breastfeeding calls for close sensory

2013 Child poverty rates in the provinces and territories • Figure 3.17

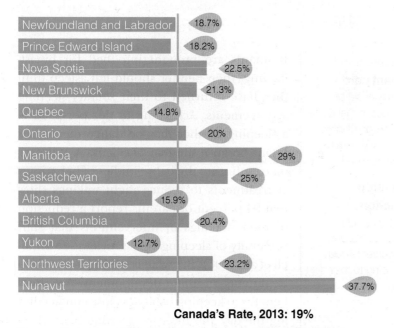

Canada's Rate, 2013: 19%

Source: Campaign 2000, *2015 Report Card on Child and Family Poverty in Canada*, p. 4, Chart 3. Data from Statistics Canada. Accessed at http://campaign2000.ca/report-cards/national.

Ask Yourself
What factors might contribute to the discrepancies in poverty throughout Canada?

CHALLENGES IN DEVELOPMENT
Malnutrition

Malnutrition indirectly contributes to at least one third of deaths of children under age 5 (WHO, 2012b). Kwashiorkor is characterized by a swollen belly, whereas marasmus, shown here, is associated with an emaciated appearance.

Malnutrition is considered a global public health challenge because human development in any country requires well-nourished populations who can learn new skills and contribute to their communities.

Child malnutrition undermines healthy physical growth and development, which, in turn, contributes to the cycle of poverty by impeding individuals' abilities to become productive, responsible members of society.

The highest mean rate of malnutrition is found in South Asia (57 per 100 children) and the smallest mean rate is found in Europe (1 per 100 children) (El-Ghannam, 2003).

Child malnutrition is associated with the same risk factors in all regions of the world:

- illiteracy
- unemployment
- poverty
- high fertility rate

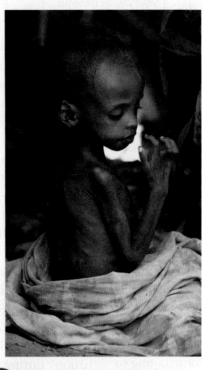

Per-Anders Pettersson/Getty Images

Think Critically If you were to write a brief description of this child's life, what exosystem, macrosystem, and microsystem risks contributed to this case of malnutrition?

- large family size
- low food consumption
- high maternal mortality rate
- large population per physician
- high child mortality

Six global targets have been identified to reduce the burden of malnutrition in children (United Nations Children's Fund, World Health Organization, The World Bank, 2012):

1.–3. Reduce rates of (1) stunting (inadequate growth due to poor nutrition), (2) child wasting (significantly low weight-height ratio), and (3) overweight (due to poor diet).

4. Treat anemia in women of reproductive age because it is a known risk factor for nutritional insufficiency during pregnancy.

5. Recognize and respond to low birth weight as a risk factor for malnutrition in the earliest months of life.

6. Encourage exclusive breastfeeding.

---

mother–infant contact during the day and night (Ball & Klingaman, 2007).

Sleep

There is an ongoing debate in Western industrialized countries about where infants should sleep and how nighttime feedings should occur (Ball & Klingaman, 2007). The dominant Western **medical model of infant care** states that infants should sleep separately from their mothers and that night wakings should be treated with a variety of behavioural interventions, such as **graduated extinction** or "controlled crying" (Ferber, 2006; Ramos & Youngclarke, 2006; for a review, see Mindell, Kuhn, Lewin, Meltzer, & Sadeh, 2006).

medical model of infant care
A dominant set of assumptions that guide the provision of infant care in the Western part of the world.

graduated extinction
A variety of sleep-training techniques, where parents delay responding to their infants' cries for specified intervals of time, and then respond only in a limited and prescribed way.

If infants are brought into bed for breastfeeding, then neither should fall asleep until they have returned to their solitary sleeping arrangements. According to this perspective, a sleeping mother may be dangerous to her infant because she may accidentally roll over on or suffocate the baby. Studies of behavioural treatments to reduce night wakings show that 94 percent of parents report a reduction in night wakings in interventions that shift proximity of sleeping (for a review, see Mindell et al., 2006). But what is the impact of these treatments on infant development? Are there benefits to keeping babies in close contact during the day and night? A growing body of research about infant sleep and feeding patterns suggests that infants are biologically designed to sleep in close proximity to their mothers and that there are important benefits to this ancient and still widespread practice (for a review, see McKenna, Ball, & Gettler, 2007).

Co-sleeping A look at our evolutionary past reveals the normality and the necessity of mother–infant **co-sleeping** (McKenna et al., 2007; Worthman, 2008). Born the most neurologically immature of all primates, human infants would have been vulnerable to predators when sleeping alone (Konner, 1981). The easy digestibility of breast milk requiring frequent nighttime feedings would

co-sleeping A variety of shared sleeping arrangements, where infant and caregiver sleep within sensory range of one another (on the same or separate surfaces), thereby permitting each to detect and respond to the cues of the other.

bedsharing A specific instance of co-sleeping, where infant and caregiver sleep together in the same adult bed.

have also encouraged co-sleeping, especially **bedsharing**, throughout our human evolution (McKenna et al., 2007). Today, co-sleeping remains a cross-cultural, species-wide, and physiologically normal practice. Only in a few cultures (typically Western, industrialized societies) do infants sleep outside the context of their breastfeeding mothers.

Researchers in anthropology and evolutionary medicine have argued that there is a potential mismatch between the conditions under which human biology evolved and contemporary Western lifestyles (Trevathan, Smith, & McKenna, 2008). For

WHAT A DEVELOPMENTALIST SEES

Safe Co-sleeping

The Canadian Paediatric Society maintains that the safest place for a child to sleep during the first year of life is in a crib that meets the Canadian government's safety standards. However, the Canadian Paediatric Society does distinguish between *bedsharing* (where an infant shares a sleeping surface with another person) and *co-sleeping* (where an infant is in arm's reach, but not on the same sleeping surface). An infant sleeping in a bedside bassinet is one example of co-sleeping. The Canadian Paediatric Society recommends co-sleeping for the first six months of life in order to support breastfeeding and reduce sudden infant death syndrome. Safe co-sleeping requires a firm sleep surface, the placement of infants on their backs, and the presence of a committed caregiver. Risk factors include loose bedding, exposure to cigarette smoke, and any type of makeshift bed (Cyr & Canadian Paediatric Society, 2012).

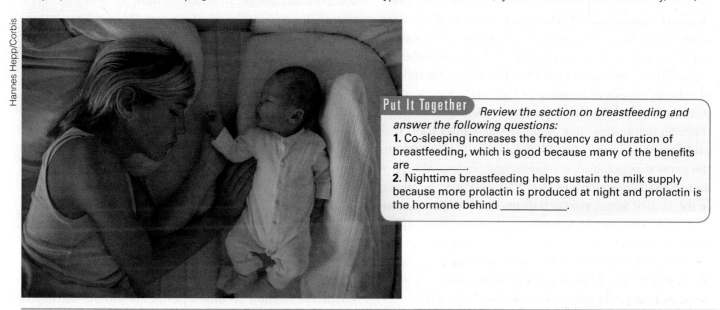

Hannes Hepp/Corbis

Put It Together *Review the section on breastfeeding and answer the following questions:*
1. Co-sleeping increases the frequency and duration of breastfeeding, which is good because many of the benefits are _____.
2. Nighttime breastfeeding helps sustain the milk supply because more prolactin is produced at night and prolactin is the hormone behind _____.

example, formula feeding, infant schedules, delayed responses to crying, and the like are thought to clash with the evolved needs and natural inclinations of infants and their caregivers (e.g., Hrdy, 1999; McKenna & McDade, 2005). What are the effects on health of such a mismatch? Research has shown that these modern parenting practices (in the grand scheme of our evolutionary history) are associated with negative developmental outcomes, such as gastrointestinal infection, dehydration, failure to thrive, and **attachment** issues (Aney, 1998; Howie, Forsyth, Ogston, Clark, & Florey, 1990; Sroufe, 1995). As depicted in this chapter's *What a Developmentalist Sees*, development and well-being are enhanced when mothers meet their infants' evolved needs for physical and emotional closeness at night.

> **attachment** An enduring emotional bond that connects two people across time and space.

In cultures where mothers and infants routinely breastfeed and co-sleep, we find the lowest rates of sudden infant death syndrome (SIDS), the topic we turn to next (Nelson et al., 2001; Watanabe et al., 1994).

Sudden infant death syndrome (SIDS) Sudden infant death syndrome (SIDS) is the leading cause of death for Canadian infants after congenital malformations, deaths associated with pregnancy and birthing complications, and fatalities attributed to prematurity and low birth weight (Statistics Canada, 2012). Also known as "crib death" or "cot death," SIDS strikes 1 in every 3,000 babies. A seemingly healthy infant falls asleep in his or her crib, stroller, car seat, or parents' arms, and never awakens. No signs of suffering are associated with the death (Sender, 2005). Aboriginals in Canada appear to be more at risk: sadly, First Nations communities in Canada face a rate of SIDS at least three times higher among their infants. And studies show that while the death rate from SIDS has fallen since 1980 in the general population, it remains high among Aboriginals in Canada (Assembly of First Nations, 2008). Similarly, in the United States, research shows African-American infants and American-Indian/Alaska Native infants die of SIDS at two to three times the rate of white infants (National Institute of Child Health and Human Development, 2010). The highest rates of SIDS occur in infants between 2 and 3 months of age (Mayo Clinic, 2011).

> **sudden infant death syndrome (SIDS)** The sudden and unexplained death, usually during sleep, of a seemingly healthy infant younger than 1 year of age.

Although we do not yet understand the causes of SIDS, certain risk factors have been identified. The most important modifiable risk factors for SIDS are infants sleeping in the prone position (stomach-lying) and maternal smoking during pregnancy (Public Health Agency of Canada, 2012). Accordingly, the National Institute of Child Health and Human Development created the "Safe to Sleep" campaign—formerly known as the "Back to Sleep" campaign—to educate parents about ways of reducing SIDS, such as laying infants to sleep on their backs (**Figure 3.18**). The overall trend for SIDS in Canada has been downward; associated mortality declined from 1.0 per 1,000 live births in 1981 to 0.3 per 1,000 live births in 2009. The decrease in SIDS may be explained by an increase in two major protective behaviours: infants being placed on their backs to sleep and infants being breastfed. A decrease in maternal smoking during pregnancy may be playing a role as well. The Safe Sleep campaigns conducted by Health Canada, the Public Health Agency of Canada, the Canadian Paediatric Society, as well as other organizations may have also contributed to the decline. A recent analysis done by the Public Health Agency of Canada ruled out changes in reporting practices as the explanation for the SIDS decline (Public Health Agency of Canada, 2014c).

SIDS is greatly reduced by breastfeeding (Vennemann et al., 2009). A higher risk of SIDS has been found in infants who sleep in a hot room or among excessive blankets and pillows (Mayo Clinic, 2011; Richardson, Yiallourou, Trinder, Walker, & Horne, 2006). Other risk factors include premature birth, low birth-weight, and exposure to second-hand smoke. In addition, most SIDS deaths occur during the colder months of the year (Mayo Clinic, 2011).

The rate of SIDS varies by culture. In Japan, and in other parts of the world where mother–infant breastfeeding and co-sleeping are the cultural norm, SIDS is either absent or substantially less prevalent (Nelson et al., 2001; Watanabe et al., 1994). The supine (back-lying) infant sleep position, the one promoted by the Safe to Sleep campaign, is universally chosen by breastfeeding, co-sleeping mothers (Richard, Mosko, & McKenna, 1998). This makes sense, if you think about it—infants sleeping next to their mothers on their stomachs would have a harder time initiating and receiving a breastfeed (McKenna & McDade, 2005). So back sleeping evolved along with both breastfeeding and mother–infant co-sleeping. Only after the separation of mother and infant for eating and sleeping did the prone position become a possibility—to the detriment

Back sleeping and the rate of SIDS • Figure 3.18

Since the Safe to Sleep (originally known as the Back to Sleep) campaign began in 1994, there has been a dramatic increase in the percentage of infants placed on their backs to sleep. In turn, the rate of SIDS has dropped by more than 50 percent. Although it may not be causal, the relationship is intriguing. What other factors might be contributing to the drop in SIDS?

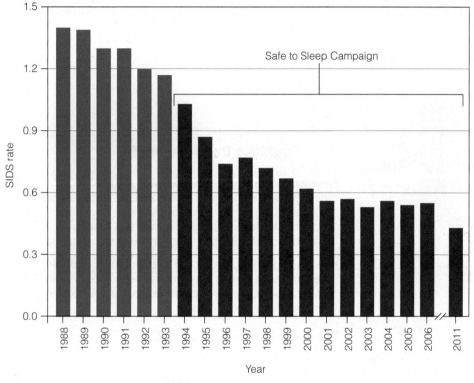

 Think Critically How might the rate of SIDS be affected by the recent adoption of nesting behaviours?

Source:

of many Western babies. Thankfully, with the help of the Safe to Sleep campaign, there is increasing awareness of the dangers of the prone infant sleep position.

Taken together, the first two years of life are a busy time in terms of physical growth, language learning, development of sensation and perception, and the ability to think. The rapidity of the changes that take place during these two years, in fact, are far greater than during any other stage of life. As we will see in the next chapter, socio-emotional development in infancy proceeds just as rapidly, and is just as complex, as physical and cognitive development.

CONCEPT CHECK STOP

1. **How** do newborns experience the world around them?
2. **Why** is it difficult to study depth perception and pain perception in infants?
3. **What** does a well-baby checkup typically entail?
4. **What** is optimal infant nutrition according to the World Health Organization (WHO)?
5. **Where** are infants biologically safer to sleep?

Summary

1 Physical Development 84

- By the end of infancy, children weigh an average of three and a half times their birth weight and are nearly twice as tall as they were at birth. This phenomenal growth during the first two years follows a cephalocaudal pattern and a proximodistal pattern, as shown in the diagram in the figure.

The cephalocaudal and proximodistal patterns of growth • Figure 3.1

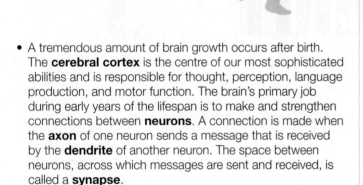

- A tremendous amount of brain growth occurs after birth. The **cerebral cortex** is the centre of our most sophisticated abilities and is responsible for thought, perception, language production, and motor function. The brain's primary job during early years of the lifespan is to make and strengthen connections between **neurons**. A connection is made when the **axon** of one neuron sends a message that is received by the **dendrite** of another neuron. The space between neurons, across which messages are sent and received, is called a **synapse**.

- During infancy, the neurons of the brain become increasingly **myelinated** and develop many new synapses. Later, **synaptic pruning** removes unused synapses. Both **experience-expectant processes** and **experience-dependent processes** seem to guide brain **plasticity**. Infants' brains develop during their sleep; newborns spend up to 50 percent of the time they are asleep in **rapid-eye-movement (REM) sleep**, which is distinguished from **non–rapid-eye-movement (NREM) sleep.**

- The simplest and quickest neural pathway is a **reflex**. Some **newborn reflexes** are important to survival, whereas others seem to have no purpose. Some reflexes, including those that disappear as the nervous system develops, can be used to determine the health of a baby's nervous system.

- Some small bones fuse together during infancy. Bone changes, along with differentiation and innervation of muscles, allow infants to develop **gross motor skills**, such as sitting and walking, and **fine motor skills**, including grasping

objects. Cultural differences in the age at which the infant takes his or her first steps suggest that a baby's experiences may influence the timing of motor-skill development. **Posture** is the integrating process that connects and provides a foundation for all gross motor activities.

2 Cognitive Development 94

- Piaget formulated the **sensorimotor stage** of cognitive development in infancy. The sensorimotor stage includes six substages: (1) reflexes, (2) habits and repetition, (3) actions with objects, (4) coordination of **schemes** and intentional behaviour, (5) use of objects in novel ways, and (6) symbolic thought.

- According to Piaget, children's development of **object permanence** means they can mentally represent, or think about, objects that are not immediately visible to them, as represented in these diagrams.

The A-not-B error • Figure 3.8

a.

b.

- Rovee-Collier's experiments with infants showed that they can develop long-term **implicit memories** at much earlier ages than previous researchers believed they did. Babies begin to show **explicit memory**, by **deferred imitation**, at about 6 to 7 months. Using **habituation** and **dishabituation** methods, researchers have found that babies who habituate faster are likely to have higher IQ scores later in life than infants who process stimuli more slowly.

- **Receptive language** develops faster than **expressive language**. Babies around the world follow a similar sequence in learning to talk. They proceed from crying to cooing, then to **babbling**, and then to first words, or **holophrases**, around age 1. First words are often accompanied by gestures evidencing **joint attention**, and combined into **telegraphic speech**.

- Many theorists believe that we have an inborn capacity for learning the rules of language, an ability Chomsky called a **language acquisition device (LAD)**. Experience also plays a role, as demonstrated by the relationship of **infant-directed speech** and other factors to variations in the timing of children's language milestones. An **interactionist approach** to language learning stresses the role of socialization.

3 All the Systems Working Together 101

- **Sensation** is the automatic reception of physical stimuli from the environment. **Perception** is the interpretation of those stimuli.

- An infant's **ciliary muscles** are not mature, resulting in limited visual acuity and ability to scan the environment. The neurons in the retina that respond to colour, called **cones**, are also still developing in the months after birth. However, vision improves quickly over the first few months of life. The senses of hearing, smell, touch, and taste, as shown in the photos in the figure, are well developed in most babies by the time they are born.

- Developmental researchers use the visual preference paradigm to study visual acuity.

- Some researchers using a **visual cliff** suggest that crawling may contribute to infants' ability to perceive depth. Researchers are in greater agreement that infants can perceive pain and may show later behavioural consequences as a result of early painful experiences. One of the most common painful experiences for Canadian infants is immunizations, which can prevent outbreaks of many deadly diseases if enough children are **vaccinated**.

- According to the World Health Organization (WHO), optimal infant **nutrition** means **exclusive** and **on-demand breastfeeding** for the first six months of life. This is true for **preterm** and **very low-birth-weight** infants as well. **Colostrum** is the special yellowish, sticky breast milk that is secreted during the first two to three days after birth and that is perfectly suited to meet the needs of a newborn. After six months, WHO recommends the introduction of **complementary feeding** along with continued on-demand

Taste preferences at birth • Figure 3.11

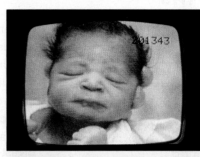

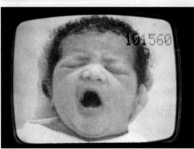

From: "Differential Facial Responses to Four Basic Tastes in Newborns" by D. Rosenstein and H. Oster, 1988, Child Development, 59, pp. 1561–1563. © 1988 The Society for Research in Child Development, Inc. Reprinted by permission.

breastfeeding for a minimum of two years. Breastfeeding offers both child and mother short-term and long-term physical and cognitive benefits, and many of these benefits, such as **lactational amenorrhea**, are dose dependent (more breastfeeding is more beneficial). Although virtually all mothers can breastfeed, there are a small number of health conditions that warrant the use of **breast-milk substitutes**.

- Infants fed breast-milk substitutes are at risk for a variety of acute and chronic disorders, such as **otitis media**. The **International Code of Marketing of Breast-milk Substitutes** (WHO, 1981, 2013) was designed to regulate promotional campaigns that may influence families to use breast-milk substitutes when they are not needed. As of April 2011, 84 countries had adopted legislation enacting all or many of the code's provisions. Canada has taken few steps to implement the code.

- Shortages of nutrients can cause various forms of **malnutrition**, including **protein-energy malnutrition (PEM)**.

- Contrary to the **medical model of infant care** and associated interventions, such as **graduated extinction**, which may interfere with **attachment** development, infants are biologically designed to sleep in close proximity to their mothers, such as in **co-sleeping** and **bedsharing**. When done safely, there are many benefits to this practice. One benefit is lower rates of **sudden infant death syndrome (SIDS)**.

Key Terms

- A-not-B error 95
- attachment 116
- axon 85
- babbling 100
- bedsharing 115
- cephalocaudal 84
- cerebral cortex 85
- ciliary muscles 102
- colostrum 108
- complementary feeding 108
- cones 102
- co-sleeping 115
- deferred imitation 96
- dendrite 86
- dishabituation 97
- exclusive breastfeeding 108
- experience-dependent process 87
- experience-expectant process 87
- explicit memory 96
- expressive language 98
- fine motor skills 92
- graduated extinction 114

- gross motor skills 92
- habituation 97
- holophrase 100
- implicit memory 95
- infant-directed speech 101
- interactionist approach 101
- International Code of Marketing of Breast-milk Substitutes 111
- joint attention 100
- lactational amenorrhea 109
- language acquisition device (LAD) 101
- malnutrition 113
- medical model of infant care 114
- myelination 87
- neuron 85
- newborn reflex 89
- non–rapid-eye-movement (NREM) sleep 89
- nutrition 107
- object permanence 95
- on-demand breastfeeding 108
- otitis media 108

- perception 102
- plasticity 87
- posture 92
- preterm 110
- protein-energy malnutrition (PEM) 113
- proximodistal 84
- rapid-eye-movement (REM) sleep 89
- receptive language 98
- reflex 89
- schemes 95
- sensation 102
- sensorimotor stage 94
- sudden infant death syndrome (SIDS) 116
- synapse 86
- synaptic pruning 87
- telegraphic speech 100
- vaccine 106
- vaccine hesitancy 107
- very low-birth-weight 110
- visual cliff 104

Critical and Creative Thinking Questions

1. Name some additional examples of behaviours or abilities, besides those mentioned in the chapter, that seem to you to be experience-expectant and experience-dependent processes.

2. Which of the patterns of growth and development seem to be evident in the progressions of development of fine and gross motor skills listed in this chapter?

3. If you were a health professional, how would you respond to parents who expressed concern about the safety of immunizations?

4. Would you (or did you) breastfeed your baby or want your partner to breastfeed? Why or why not? What are some public policy steps that could be taken to make breastfeeding more popular?

5. Speak to someone or something using infant-directed speech, then analyze your speech. What specific characteristics do you think are most helpful for infants who are trying to learn their language?

What is happening in this picture?

This 1-year-old is reaping the many physical and cognitive benefits of breastfeeding.

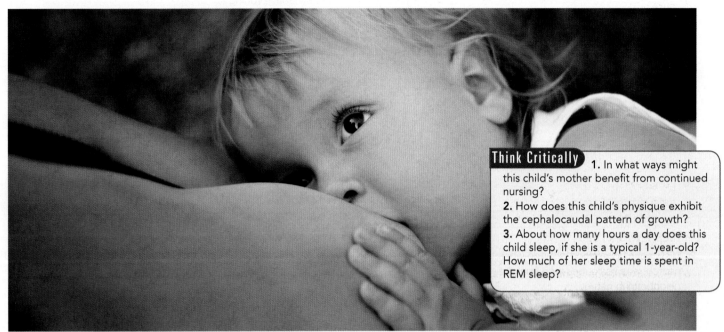

Think Critically
1. In what ways might this child's mother benefit from continued nursing?
2. How does this child's physique exhibit the cephalocaudal pattern of growth?
3. About how many hours a day does this child sleep, if she is a typical 1-year-old? How much of her sleep time is spent in REM sleep?

Katsiaryna Drobysheva/Shutterstock

REAL Development

Physical Development and Health in Infancy and Toddlerhood

In these video activities, you will observe babies' and toddlers' physical development and health.

Tia Wagner is considering enrolling her son, Brandon, in a "Mommy and Me" class that uses both structured and unstructured play to help children with motor development during the first two years. Your task is to observe the children to discern whether or not they are developing at normal rates. You will then report your observations to Tia in order to help her make this decision.

In the next activity, you have been asked to visit Julianne and baby Olivia as part of your field experience as a psychology major. Olivia is now 4 months old. You will observe her and assess her cognitive development.

John Wiley & Sons, Inc.

WileyPLUS Go to WileyPLUS to complete the REAL Development activity.

03.01

Self-Test

(Check your answers in Appendix A.)

1. Which pattern of growth is depicted in this illustration?

a. proximodistal

b. bottom to top

c. cephalocaudal

d. sensorimotor

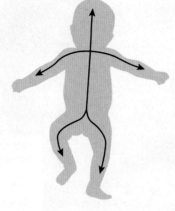

2. A synaptic connection is made when the _____ of one neuron *receives* a message from the _____ of a neighbouring neuron.

a. axon; dendrite

b. dendrite; axon

c. cell body; dendrite

d. dendrite; myelin

3. Simone, the baby described at the beginning of this chapter, has just learned to pull herself to a standing position. Her accomplishment is an example of ____.

a. a fine motor skill

b. a gross motor skill

c. a primitive reflex

d. innervation pruning

4. The process by which unused connections among brain neurons are discarded is called _____.

a. myelination

b. synaptic pruning

c. experience dependency

d. experience expectancy

5. Which of the following describes the sleep of babies, compared with that of adults?

a. Babies sleep more in the daytime.

b. Babies sleep for shorter chunks of time.

c. Babies spend a bigger portion of their sleep in REM sleep.

d. All of these describe babies' sleep.

6. What cognitive milestone is this baby demonstrating?

a. object permanence

b. primitive reflex

c. circular reaction

d. habituation

7. When a baby learns to kick a mobile in one room, but does not transfer the ability to kick a mobile in another room, this is an example of _____ memory in infancy.

a. explicit

b. implicit

c. context-dependent

d. optimal

8. What do the results of research using habituation and dishabituation suggest about babies' cognitive abilities?

a. Babies may never reach some of the milestones that Piaget described.

b. Most babies do not reach cognitive milestones until later ages than Piaget believed they did.

c. Babies may actually have key cognitive milestones at much earlier ages than Piaget believed they did.

d. Waiting until babies can use motor skills to demonstrate cognitive abilities is the most accurate way to measure those abilities.

9. Which of the following is evidence of the role of socialization, or the environment, in language learning?

a. the relationship of amount of parent speech to infant speaking

b. joint attention

c. infant-directed speech

d. all of these

10. Which sense develops earliest in the fetus and is well developed at birth?

a. hearing

b. smell and taste

c. touch

d. vision

11. Which of an infant's abilities is this apparatus used to test?

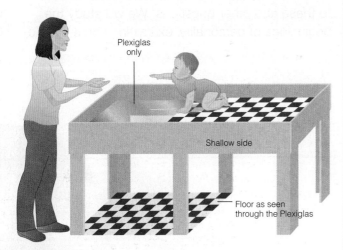

Plexiglas only

Shallow side

Floor as seen through the Plexiglas

a. depth perception

b. colour perception

c. visual acuity

d. all of these

12. What two maternal hormones are responsible for milk production and ejection?

a. prolactin and oxytocin

b. estrogen and oxytocin

c. prolactin and estrogen

d. adrenaline and prostaglandins

13. What are the goals of the International Code of Marketing of Breast-milk Substitutes?

a. to ban breast-milk substitutes, bottles, and pacifiers

b. to promote the marketing of breast-milk substitutes

c. to regulate the marketing of breast-milk substitutes

d. all of these

14. The benefits of safe co-sleeping include _____.

a. more infant sleep

b. more maternal sleep

c. less infant crying

d. all of these

15. One measure that has helped to reduce Canadian infant deaths from SIDS is to put babies to sleep on their _____.

a. stomach

b. left side

c. right side

d. back

THE PLANNER ✓

Review your Chapter Planner in the chapter opener and check off your completed work.

Socio-emotional Development in Infancy: The First Two Years

Marie Arsenault is getting ready to take her 9-month-old son Michel to the park. The weather is so cool that Michel is bundled up, yet his eyes dart around, inspecting his surroundings. He looks up at his mother and smiles. Marie looks back and says "Michel va au parc aujourd'hui" ("Michel is going to the park today").

What emotions does Michel experience as his mother bends down and pulls a blanket tight around him? How does Michel's play reflect his social influences? What types of social influences will Michel experience?

In this chapter, we will explore the answers to these and other questions. We will study the beginnings of personality, examining some classic

theoretical perspectives. We will then describe the influence of the social world, including the formation of attachment and the complexities of early infant–parent bonding. Finally, we will discuss early emotions and the sequence of events typically observed during the first two years of life. First, we turn to the development of personality.

CHAPTER PLANNER ✓

- ❏ Study the picture and read the opening story.
- ❏ Scan the Learning Objectives in each section:
  p. 126 ❏   p. 131 ❏   p. 141 ❏
- ❏ Read the text and study all visuals. Answer any questions.

Analyze key features

- ❏ Process Diagram, p. 132
- ❏ What a Developmentalist Sees, p. 135
- ❏ Challenges in Development, p. 136
- ❏ Development InSight, p. 142
- ❏ Stop: Answer the Concept Checks before you go on:
  p. 131 ❏   p. 140 ❏   p. 144 ❏

End of chapter

- ❏ Review the Summary and Key Terms.
- ❏ Answer *What is happening in this picture?*
- ❏ Answer the Critical and Creative Thinking Questions.
- ❏ Complete the Self-Test and check your answers.

Personality Development

LEARNING OBJECTIVES

1. **Discuss** early personality development from the psychodynamic perspective.

2. **Explain** the concept of temperament and its role in the development of personality.

3. **Explain** the temperamental differences between sociable and shy infants and toddlers.

4. **Describe** the concept of goodness of fit.

How does an infant's personality develop? What are the underlying causes of this development? In earlier chapters we considered the impact of nature and nurture. Now we will look at psychological approaches to personality development.

The Psychodynamic Perspective

Theorists have offered a number of different perspectives about early personality development. We begin by revisiting the psychodynamic perspective of Sigmund Freud and Erik Erikson.

Freud's oral and anal stages Freud believed individuals are passive agents whose personalities are driven by unconscious conflict between the biology of survival and societal rules and regulations (Freud, 1915). As we discussed in Chapter 1, Freud asserted that the libido, a force of sexual energy, moved around the body in a predetermined manner dictated by functions related to survival. During the first two years, Freud segmented development into two basic stages, according to where libidinal energy is focused, which is called the erogenous zone: first the oral stage and then the anal stage (Freud, 1920) (**Figure 4.1**).

Freud's oral and anal stages • Figure 4.1

Here we see examples of how infant behaviour can match Freud's oral and anal stages. According to Freud, an infant derives gratification from stimulating the region where the libido is centred, as the children in these photos are doing.

a. Freud believed that the libido is centred in the mouth during the oral stage, creating a desire for oral stimulation. A baby satisfies this desire by nursing or putting other objects, such as toys or a thumb, into the mouth.

b. As time goes on, the libido eventually migrates to the anal area, signalling the beginning of the anal stage. Freud focused on toilet training, which normatively takes place in toddlerhood. He believed that toilet training triggers personality development as the infant masters the challenge of delaying immediate gratification of the desire for bowel movements.

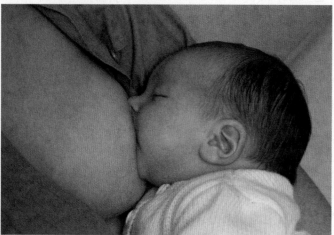

Jennie Woodcock; Reflections Photolibrary/CORBIS

Think Critically What advice would you give to parents for supporting their children through the oral and anal stages?

Peter Dazeley/Getty Images

Adult outcomes of infant fixations, according to Freud • Figure 4.2

Freud believed that certain problem behaviours in adulthood could be explained by early-life fixations.

a. Freud suggested issues such as overeating, alcoholism, smoking, sarcasm, and talking too much might develop from fixations developed during the oral stage of development.

b. Freud also believed fixation in the anal stage could result in one of two paths: an anal-retentive personality, which means being overly neat, orderly, and controlled; or an anal-expulsive personality, which means being messy, highly emotionally expressive, and undercontrolled.

Think Critically Can you think of other adult problem behaviours that, from Freud's perspective, could be explained by oral fixation or anal fixation?

Coka/Shutterstock

Jessica Miller/Getty Images

The part of the personality—or psychic structure—that emerges during the oral stage is called the *id*. As we discussed in Chapter 1, the id has no boundaries or limits, and gratification must happen immediately. Thus, when a baby is hungry, regardless of what time it is and what the parent is doing, the baby insists on being fed. The oral stage, like many of Freud's ideas, has been controversial (Cioffi, 1998; Dunn & Dougherty, 2005). In spite of this controversy, anyone who observes infants can readily see that they are indeed preoccupied with putting things in their mouths (Freud, 1914).

Freud believed the anal stage—and toilet training in particular—initiated a new personality component called the *ego*. You may recall from Chapter 1 that this part of the personality works to control the id and impulsive bodily functions such as bowel movements. Thus, as a toddler develops a sense of control over its bowels, the ego emerges as a significant part of the toddler's personality. The emergence of the ego and its role in controlling the id was one of Freud's continuing life themes (Freud, 1915).

According to Freud, events during the oral and anal stages could lead to later personality issues. In particular, if a specific erogenous zone is either overstimulated or understimulated, the child can become fixated, or stuck, in that stage. Freud asserted that **oral fixations** and **anal fixations** could result in a variety of adult personality outcomes, as we explore in **Figure 4.2**. Notably, though, Freud fails to specify what constitutes too much or too little gratification.

Freud's view of the early years has come under critical attack for reasons including being too sexually based and not being testable (Lothane, 1999). Yet Freud's influence in theoretical and counselling circles remains. Erikson's psychodynamic perspective takes a psychosocial approach in dealing with personality and has met with less criticism than Freud's theories.

oral fixation A return to the oral stage in later life, shown through habits such as smoking or gum chewing, as a result of too much or too little gratification during the oral stage.

anal fixation A return to the anal stage in later life, shown through obsessive personality issues, as a result of too much or too little gratification during the anal stage.

Erikson's stages of trust versus mistrust and autonomy versus shame and doubt Erikson emphasized social interaction and de-emphasized sex, though he did not discount Freud's ideas completely (Hoare, 2005). Erikson believed early development was acutely influenced

trust versus mistrust stage
Erikson's first stage of psychosocial development is resolved when the individual develops a sense of trust in the environment to meet his or her needs.

by an infant's social context. During the initial **trust versus mistrust stage** of psychosocial development, infants' primary task is to develop a sense of trust in their caregivers, in themselves, and in the world around them (Erikson, 1950). When caregivers respond to babies' needs appropriately, consistently, and competently, over time babies come to expect and trust that their needs will be met by the environment; each trust-building experience further confirms this expectation.

Erikson also suggests that if a baby's cries are met with inconsistent or inappropriate responses (for example, responding to a baby's daytime cries but ignoring his or her nighttime cries, as in the case of *graduated extinction*; see Chapter 3), the baby might come to mistrust the caregiver. According to Erikson (1950), early patterns of trust or mistrust influence how the next stage progresses and help guide later developments. For example, he asserted that a basic sense of trust underlies the child's developing sense of identity, "of being 'all right,' of being oneself, and of becoming what other people trust one will become" (Erikson, 1950, p. 249).

autonomy versus shame and doubt stage
Erikson's second stage of psychosocial development, during which the toddler begins to understand self-control through key accomplishments.

During the **autonomy versus shame and doubt stage**, toddlers undergo a transformation based on physical and cognitive changes. Just as in Freud's theory, the central issue here is toilet training, but this stage also includes mastery of the environment in general. Erikson believed that toddlers who developed trust during the previous stage will be more comfortable attempting to control their bowel movements because they are confident that their caregivers will understand and respond caringly to mistakes and accidents. Mistrusting toddlers who are already insecure about their environments can feel shame and doubt when they have toilet-training accidents. However, Erikson also believed that this stage provides opportunities for a mistrusting child to develop autonomy, or for a trusting child to fail to do so, especially if the child's environmental context changes. Thus, choices to move toward people for guidance facilitate a sense of independence, whereas choices to move away result in feelings of

easy temperament
The temperament of a child who is generally cheerful and adaptable and has regular patterns of eating and sleeping.

shame and doubt (Erikson, 1950). Poorly resolved psychosocial development in infancy and childhood has the potential to influence adult beliefs about self and others. A sense of mistrust is associated with beliefs that others will lie, hurt, manipulate, or take advantage of them. Internalized shame is associated with believing one is defective, flawed, unwanted, and unlovable (Thimm, 2011).

Although Freud and Erikson bring interesting perspectives to personality development during infancy and toddlerhood, some theorists have challenged the idea of unconscious conflict (Schafer, 1976). Instead, they prefer to focus on underlying dimensions of personality that can be observed and measured.

Temperament

temperament
Biologically based individual differences in how one responds to the environment that influence emotions, physical activity level, and attention.

Researchers used to think **temperament** was stable and unchanging across the lifespan. Infants who react strongly and negatively to their environments are sure to grow into adults who do the same. In recent years, these early views have been replaced by a more dynamic understanding of temperament, one that allows for developmental change across the lifespan. First we turn to one of the earliest studies of temperament.

The New York Longitudinal Study In the early 1960s, Alexander Thomas, Stella Chess, and their colleagues were concerned with individual differences in our primary reaction patterns, or the way babies tend to react to situations and events in their lives. As part of their **New York Longitudinal Study (NYLS)**, these researchers carried out extensive interviews with parents about their infants' behaviours across different contexts (Thomas, Chess, Birch, Hertzig, & Korn, 1963). They then sorted the parents' behavioural descriptions into nine categories, which became known as the NYLS temperament dimensions. Mary Rothbart revised the original list of nine NYLS dimensions of temperament to focus on just three dimensions, summarized in **Table 4.1**.

Three patterns—temperament categories—emerged from the NYLS nine dimensions of behaviour: easy, difficult, and slow to warm up:

- A child with an **easy temperament** adapts readily to new experiences, is generally cheerful, and has regular patterns of eating and sleeping.

Dimensions of infant temperament Table 4.1	
NYLS Dimensions	**Rothbart's Dimensions**
Adaptability Does the child adjust well to novelty?	**Negative affectivity** Fear, frustration, sadness, discomfort, soothability (how quickly a child can recover from extreme distress, excitement, or general arousal)
Quality of mood Does the child tend to be happy or sad?	
Distractibility Does the child shift attention easily whenever an interesting item appears?	
Attention span/persistence Does the child like to stay on one activity for a long time or not?	**Extraversion/surgency** Low shyness, high-intensity pleasure (pleasure experienced from activities involving high intensity or novelty), smiling and laughter, activity level, impulsivity, positive anticipation (excitement for anticipated pleasurable activities), affiliation (desire for closeness with others)
Rhythmicity Is there a rhythm to the child's sleeping, eating, and eliminating?	
Activity level Is the child highly physically active?	**Effortful control** Inhibitory control (the ability to plan future action and to suppress inappropriate responses), attention control, low-intensity pleasure (pleasure experienced from simple activities involving low intensity, complexity, or novelty), perceptual sensitivity (perceptual awareness of slight or low-intensity stimulation in the environment)
Threshold of responsiveness Does the child respond to all stimuli, or just to powerful stimuli?	
Approach/withdrawal Does the child want to go toward new situations or avoid them?	
Intensity of reactions Are the child's emotional expressions strong or muted?	

Based on Thomas, Chess, Birch, Hertzig, & Korn, 1963, and Rothbart, 2007.

difficult temperament The temperament of a child who is generally fussy, does not respond well to new situations, and has irregular patterns of eating and sleeping.

slow-to-warm-up temperament The temperament of a child with low activity level who adjusts to new situations over time.

- A child with a **difficult temperament** does not respond well to new experiences or people, is fussy and irritable, and has irregular patterns of eating and sleeping.

- A **slow-to-warm-up temperament** is characterized by low activity level and initial withdrawal from new experiences and people, gradually adjusting over time.

Thomas and Chess determined that 65 percent of the children in their sample could clearly be placed in one of the categories. The remaining 35 percent demonstrated behaviours that were impossible to correlate, because they did not fit into any of the three categories. What impact do you think this last 35 percent of unclassifiable children has on Thomas and Chess's hypothesis? Although the influence of the NYLS continues, other researchers have refined the definition of temperament and approached it from a slightly different perspective.

Rothbart's perspective on temperament Mary Rothbart and her colleagues (Rothbart, 2007; Rothbart

& Bates, 2006; Rothbart & Sheese, 2007) go beyond the descriptive dimensions outlined in the NYLS. They suggest that temperament has underlying neurological influences (Posner, Rothbart, & Sheese, 2007) that affect infants' ability to mediate and control their behaviour and behavioural responses to environmental stimulation. Rothbart believes that differences in their brains explain why some babies are at ease and approachable, whereas others are more fearful and avoidant.

As shown in Table 4.1, Rothbart (2007) identified three broad dimensions: **negative affectivity**, **extraversion/surgency**, and **effortful control**. These dimensions of temperament can be seen in newborns and can even be measured during the fetal stage before birth.

Sociable versus shy infants and toddlers The behavioural dimension of approach and withdrawal (see Table 4.1) is one of the most popular topics in temperament research (Schwartz,

negative affectivity A dimension of infant temperament having to do with fear, frustration, sadness, discomfort, and soothability.

extraversion/ surgency A dimension of infant temperament defined by low shyness, high-intensity pleasure, smiling and laughter, activity level, impulsivity, positive anticipation, and affiliation.

effortful control A dimension of infant temperament indicated by inhibitory control, attention control, low-intensity pleasure, and perceptual sensitivity.

The approach–withdrawal dimension of temperament • Figure 4.3

Toddlers who fall on the very ends of the approach–withdrawal continuum are uninhibited (sociable) and inhibited (shy), respectively (Kagan, Reznick, Clarke, Snidman, & Garcia-Coll, 1984). Toddlers with uninhibited temperaments readily approach new people, objects, and situations, whereas inhibited toddlers are more cautious of novelty.

Put It Together *Review Table 4.1 and answer the following question:* In Rothbart's dimensions of infant temperament, the approach–withdrawal dimension falls under the broader dimension of ____.

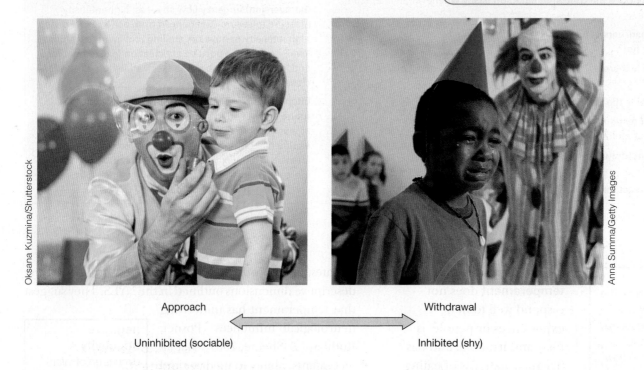

Approach   Withdrawal

Uninhibited (sociable)   Inhibited (shy)

Wright, Shin, Kagan, & Rauch, 2003). As depicted in **Figure 4.3**, this dimension involves an infant's or toddler's response to unfamiliar people, objects, and situations. Rothbart and her colleagues view temperament as governed by biological forces. Temperament begins as a generalized physiological level of arousal and slowly becomes integrated into an infant's adaptation to the world. Jerome Kagan and his colleagues (Schwartz et al., 2003) also considered the physiological features of temperament in their research on uninhibited (sociable) versus inhibited (shy) infants and toddlers. They found that children's behavioural differences in approach and withdrawal are accompanied by physiological differences in heart rate, pupil dilation, vocal cord tension, and cortisol levels (Kagan, Reznick, & Snidman, 1987).

Other research suggests differing responses to novelty in the **amygdala**—the part of the brain that mediates emotional arousal—are responsible for these behavioural and physiological differences in temperament. One group of researchers studied adults who had been

amygdala The part of the brain that mediates emotion.

identified as either uninhibited or inhibited at age 2 (Schwartz et al., 2003). Using functional magnetic resonance imaging (fMRI), the researchers found differences between the two groups of adults in arousal of the amygdala when the participants were shown novel and familiar faces: compared with uninhibited adults, inhibited adults had a stronger amygdala response to novel versus familiar faces.

This research suggests that some biological tendencies don't change dramatically as we grow out of infancy. They stick with us throughout our lives. But researchers also noticed not every shy toddler grows up to be a socially withdrawn adult. This observation led temperament researchers to consider environmental influences and to develop a concept known as goodness of fit. **Goodness of fit** is the relationship between an infant's predispositions to behave a certain way and their parents' tendencies to respond (Chess & Thomas, 1986). This interplay between child and parental constitutions

goodness of fit The relationship between environmental forces and predisposed temperamental behaviour.

mediates the infant's future emotional attachments and outcomes.

For example, some babies react with a lot of distress to situations that do not seem to bother other babies. Goodness of fit is most likely to occur in these cases if parents respond calmly and find ways to arrange the environment to avoid sudden changes, loud noises, or other situations that trigger their babies' outbursts. In other cases, however, parents are not able to adapt their expectations for a quiet, calm baby to match their highly reactive babies. If parents are unable to adjust their responses to match the child's temperament, less-than-optimal development may result (Jagiellowicz, Aron, & Aron, 2016; Thomas & Chess, 1977; Shaw & Feldman, 1997).

| CONCEPT CHECK | |

1. **What** are the central issues facing infants and toddlers according to the psychodynamic perspective?

2. **What** behaviours are associated with each of the three temperament categories: easy, difficult, and slow to warm up?

3. **What** physiological differences are there between sociable infants and toddlers and shy ones?

4. **What** does goodness of fit tell us about the relationship between nature and nurture?

Social Influences

LEARNING OBJECTIVES

1. **Describe** the stages of attachment during infancy and toddlerhood.

2. **Understand** the origins and outcomes of individual differences in attachment security.

3. **Differentiate** between sex and gender differences in early development.

As we are learning in this chapter, infants and toddlers develop in the context of relationships. It is in these close relationships with parents and other caregivers that infants begin to establish early patterns for relating to others throughout life.

Attachment

The next time you have a chance, observe the way an infant stares at his or her parents. It is obvious that an important connection is forming. This connection is called **attachment**. Primary attachment figures are typically parents, though other reliable and enduring caregivers can become attachment figures as well. For more than four decades, developmentalists have approached the study of early parent–child relationships from the perspective of attachment theory (Ainsworth, 1973; Bowlby, 1969/1982, 1973, 1980; see also Thompson, 2006).

From an evolutionary perspective, attachment relationships are believed to have evolved for the sake of infant survival and development. Keeping caregivers physically close would have kept infants safe and enabled them to learn what it means to be a member of their social group. Parents also offer infants and toddlers the security they need for confident exploration and mastery of their world (Ainsworth, 1973). These important people also contribute to infants' and toddlers' **self-regulation** in times of stress (Horton, Riddell, Flora, Moran, & Pederson, 2015). It is not surprising, then, that sustained separation from

attachment An enduring emotional bond that connects two people across time and space.

self-regulation The ability to deliberately change one's behaviour and emotion.

Bowlby's attachment theory • Figure 4.4

Bowlby believed the four-phase sequence of attachment shown here could be observed across many cultures (see Bretherton, 1985, for a review).

JGI/Tom Grill/Getty Images

BURGER/phanie/Phanie Sarl/Corbis

1 Birth to about 12 weeks: pre-attachment
Infants and toddlers seem predisposed to social stimulation and will smile or stare when they hear human sounds.

2 About 3 to 6 months: beginning of attachment
Infants appear to recognize primary caregivers and prefer to be around them. They may, as shown here, begin to have separation anxiety.

TIME

attachment figures is disruptive to normal development (Bowlby, 1973, 1980).

Several social-cognitive advances during infancy enable attachment to emerge (Thompson, 2006). Babies develop recognition of their parents' characteristics, such as face, voice, and smell. They become able to form increasing expectations about parents' behaviour. Also, as we'll see later in this chapter, babies develop increasing awareness of themselves as separate people from their parents. As children become more cognitively sophisticated, their attachment relationships also become more complex and dynamic (Crittenden, 2000).

British psychiatrist John Bowlby was one of the first scientists to examine the complex nature of attachment (Bowlby, 1958, 1959, 1969/1982, 1973). Bowlby's **attachment theory** is shown in **Figure 4.4**. Bowlby's work was influenced by Jean Piaget's theory (Bretherton, 1992), specifically by Piaget's concept of object permanence (Piaget, 1951). You may also notice that Bowlby's work is consistent with Erikson's trust versus mistrust stage of psychosocial development discussed previously.

> **attachment theory** The perspective that the process of social, emotional, and cognitive development occurs in the context of caregiver–infant attachment.

Peter Dazeley/Getty Images

Gladskikh Tatiana/Shutterstock

③ 6 to 8 months until early childhood: clear attachment
Infants and toddlers initiate closeness to primary caregivers and often express emotional distress when separated. They may show stranger anxiety.

④ Preschool years onward: goal-directed attachment
Children become increasingly aware that their parents are significant sources of safety, security, and love. Bowlby suggested that attachment patterns become more and more clearly defined throughout life (Bowlby, 1973).

Think Critically What would Bowlby have said about the attachment of children who are adopted after their first birthday, versus being immediately placed with an adoptive family?

Bowlby identified two key developments that indicate a baby's growing attachment to caregivers. During the beginning of the attachment phase, infants begin to show signs of discomfort when separated from primary caregivers, which Bowlby called **separation anxiety** (Bowlby, 1959). This anxiety becomes even more evident in the clear attachment phase. Bowlby viewed separation anxiety as evidence of object permanence, occurring because the infant has the capacity to think about the caregiver even when the caregiver is not present. After infants have developed clear attachments, they may also show emotional distress in the presence of a stranger, a development Bowlby referred to as **stranger anxiety**.

separation anxiety A set of seeking and distress behaviours that occur when the primary caregiver is removed from the immediate environment of the infant/child.

stranger anxiety Distressed avoidance of a novel individual.

Behaviourist and other perspectives on attachment Bowlby's work explains the attachment process from an adaptive and ethological perspective; others have taken different approaches, often examining the feeding process. Behavioural theorists focused on feeding as reinforcing; attachment was the result of positive

Harlow's research on attachment • Figure 4.5

Harlow's work demonstrated that the terry-cloth mothers were a significantly greater source of comfort than the food-providing mothers. His work suggests that attachment is a basic need and necessary for survival.

Martin Roger/Getty Images

Think Critically Why might attachment, like food, be necessary for survival?

reinforcement associated with feeding (Sears, Maccoby, & Levin, 1957). This controversy was made even more interesting by the work of Harry Harlow (Harlow, 1961; Harlow & Zimmermann, 1958), who used an ethological perspective.

In a series of classic studies, Harlow placed infant monkeys in a cage with two artificial mother surrogates.

One surrogate was a cold, metal monkey that had the ability to provide food. The other surrogate had no food but was made of terry-cloth and provided fuzzy contact comfort (**Figure 4.5**). The infant monkeys spent significantly more time with the terry-cloth surrogates even though these surrogates did not provide any food. Harlow concluded that attachment is an inborn developmental process necessary for survival, and not merely the result of reinforcement (Harlow, 1961). Why, then, do we see so many individual differences in attachment?

Individual differences in attachment security In contrast to Harlow's work, which focused on the universal nature of attachment, the lifelong work of Mary Ainsworth (1963, 1967, 1968, 1989) focused on individual differences in attachment. Ainsworth created a laboratory procedure through which researchers could reliably observe and categorize **attachment behaviours**. This procedure, which she called the **Strange Situation**, is shown in **Figure 4.6** (see Ainsworth, Blehar, Waters, & Wall, 1978, for details).

> **attachment behaviour** A behaviour that promotes proximity or contact, such as approaching, following, and clinging, in the older infant and toddler.
>
> **Strange Situation** A means of categorizing attachment styles, consisting of a series of episodes in which a mother and her child are observed together, separated, and reunited in the presence of a stranger.

The Strange Situation • Figure 4.6

The Strange Situation is actually a series of different episodes. Researchers carefully note the baby's reactions during each episode, especially the ones during which the parent leaves and returns.

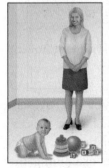

1. The baby plays while the mother is nearby.

2. A stranger enters the room, speaks to the mother, and approaches the child.

3. The mother leaves and the stranger stays in the room with an unhappy baby.

4. The mother returns and the stranger leaves.

5. The baby is reunited with the mother.

Put It Together *Review Figure 4.4 and answer the following question:* If the toddler becomes distressed and tries to avoid the stranger in the Strange Situation, we might say the toddler is showing _____, which emerges during the _____ phase according to Bowlby's attachment theory.

WHAT A DEVELOPMENTALIST SEES
Attachment Styles and Associated Behaviour

If you saw a toddler cry and cling to a parent as they left, you might call the child needy or clingy. By contrast, if you saw a child who seemed unaffected by a brief separation from a parent (**Figure a**), you might think the child was admirably independent. In fact, the opposite may be true. Researchers assign an attachment classification based on infants' behaviours when reunited with their caregivers after brief separations (**Figure b**; Ainsworth et al., 1978). Securely attached children become distressed when their caregiver departs, but then are happy when the caregiver returns and actively seek them out. However, when toddlers avoid or delay greeting their caregiver after separation, developmentalists interpret this behaviour as an indication of insecure–avoidant attachment.

B. BOISSONNET/BSIP/AgeFotostock

a.

Ask Yourself

When children remain in sight of caregivers but feel comfortable exploring new parts of the room, we would predict that the child has _____ attachment.

Infant's or toddler's behaviour		
	With caregiver in room	When caregiver departs	When caregiver returns
Secure attachment	Explores happily, but glances back at caregiver	Cries, but can be comforted	Happy, goes to caregiver
Insecure–avoidant attachment	Explores far away from caregiver	Keeps playing, does not notice	Avoids or delays greeting caregiver
Insecure–resistant attachment	Clings to caregiver instead of playing	*Very* upset, unable to be soothed	Angry at caregiver, hits or pushes away

b.

The Strange Situation procedure is designed to elicit attachment behaviours by creating conditions of increasing stress. Of particular interest to researchers is the infants' behaviour when reunited with their caregivers after brief separations, as shown in *What a Developmentalist Sees*.

Based on her research using the Strange Situation, Ainsworth suggested there are three basic styles of attachment. **Secure attachment** is demonstrated when infants treat their primary caregivers as a secure base throughout the procedure. Securely attached infants show distress when separated from their caregiver and joy when reunited.

There are also patterns of insecure attachment. Infants and toddlers with **insecure–avoidant attachment** show little distress at separation, and avoid or delay contact when the caregiver returns (Michiels, Grietens, Onghena, & Kuppens, 2008). On the other hand, infants and toddlers with **insecure–resistant attachment** are very distressed by separation and continue to cry and express anger at the caregiver when he or she returns (Ainsworth, 1963, 1967, 1968, 1989; Lickliter, 2008).

secure attachment An attachment style characterized by flexible proximity between parent and infant and positive reunion behaviour.

insecure–avoidant attachment A type of insecure attachment in which infants show little or no distress upon separation and avoidant behaviour such as running from the parent upon reunion.

insecure–resistant attachment A type of insecure attachment in which infants show very high distress when separated and mixed reactions when reunited.

CHALLENGES IN DEVELOPMENT
Failure to Thrive

An infant with failure to thrive has obvious weight loss, or is not growing or gaining weight at a healthy pace, and is showing signs of malnutrition. **Failure to thrive (FTT)** is a disturbing condition in which a baby ceases growing and loses the desire to take in food. In industrialized countries, approximately 3 to 10 percent of infants develop FTT (Keen, 2008; Stephens, Gentry, Michener, & Kendall, 2008).

Failure to thrive is a controversial diagnosis. One reason is that babies who suffered birth complications can show the same symptoms of losing or failing to gain weight (Stephens et al., 2008).

Another reason for controversy involves uncertainty regarding the causes of failure to thrive (Olsen, Skovgaard, Weile, & Jørgensen, 2007; Taylor & Daniel, 1999). Clear-cut risk factors for

FTT have not been identified yet (Olsen et al., 2007). Historically, cases of FTT were categorized based on their origin: organic (such as disease) or nonorganic (such as parental neglect). It has been found, however, that almost all cases of FTT have some organic, or biological, roots and are not the fault of the parenting. Therefore, researchers tend not to categorize FTT any more (Stephens et al., 2008; Keen, 2008), but they are still unsure of the exact causes.

Researchers have firmly established, however, that FTT correlates with a number of developmental issues in later life, including lower-than-average weight and height (Black, Dubowitz, Krishnakumar, & Starr, 2007; Rudolf & Logan, 2005). Therefore, early intervention in the form of high-calorie feedings or, in severe cases, hospitalization, is critically important.

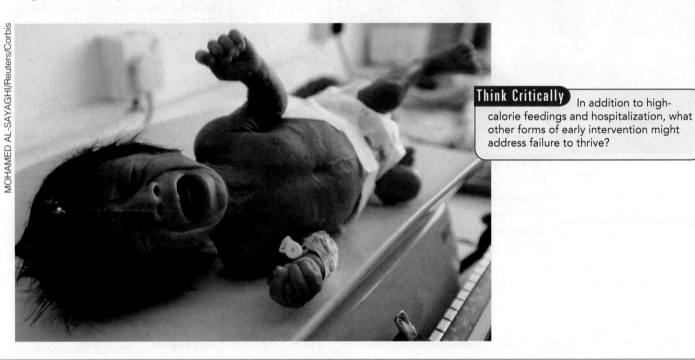

MOHAMED AL-SAYAGHI/Reuters/Corbis

Think Critically In addition to high-calorie feedings and hospitalization, what other forms of early intervention might address failure to thrive?

---

disorganized/ disoriented attachment A type of insecure attachment characterized by inconsistent behaviour upon separation and reunion that shows no clear pattern.

Since Ainsworth's original studies, researchers have identified a third type of insecure attachment called **disorganized/disoriented attachment** (Main & Solomon, 1990). Infants and toddlers with this type of attachment relationship seem confused, fearful, and inconsistent in the Strange Situation. For example, these children may combine avoiding behaviours with proximity-seeking behaviours. Children with disorganized/disoriented

attachment are more likely than those in other groups to have suffered some form of maltreatment. In extreme cases, these children may even develop failure to thrive, a condition discussed in *Challenges in Development* (Main & Solomon, 1990; Ward, Kessler, & Altman, 1993).

As **Figure 4.7** shows, nearly two-thirds of typically developing middle-class infants and toddlers are classified as securely attached (Thompson, 2006). This proportion is consistently smaller in lower socio-economic status families and among parents seeking therapy (van IJzendoorn, Schuengel, & Bakermans-Kranenburg, 1999). What else affects attachment security?

Distribution of attachment groups • Figure 4.7

The percentages in this pie chart are typical for non-clinical middle-class samples (Thompson, 2006). Around 62 percent of infants and toddlers are judged to be secure. The remaining 38 percent fall into one of the insecure or disorganized groups.

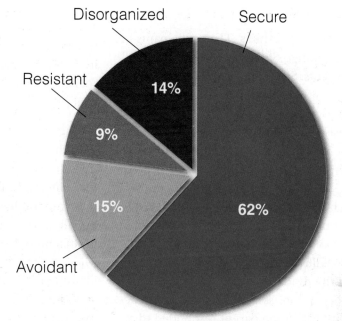

Think Critically Why might researchers find a higher proportion of insecure infants and toddlers among lower-income and clinical samples?

The basis of attachment security Researchers have discovered a number of potential variables affecting attachment security. Certain psychological attributes, such as sociability and extraversion, are higher in mothers of securely attached children (NICHD Early Child Care Research Network, 1997). These mothers also tend to be lower on measures of depression, neuroticism, and anxiety. A mother's insightfulness about her infant's internal states and motives is also positively associated with attachment security (Oppenheim & Koren-Karie, 2002). Beyond the caregiver–infant relationship, marital satisfaction has been found to predict attachment security (see Thompson, 2006, for a review). Couples experiencing marital conflict may have a harder time responding sensitively to their infant's cues. Indeed, all of the variables we've mentioned so far have implications for caregiver sensitivity.

According to attachment theorists, caregiver sensitivity is the central factor in the development of attachment security (Thompson, 2006). A sensitive caregiver is one who (1) consistently attends to the infant's cues, (2) accurately interprets their meaning, and (3) promptly responds appropriately to enhance the infant's trust in the caregiver (Ainsworth et al., 1978). This perfect attunement between infant and caregiver, where interactions are reciprocal and mutually rewarding, is called **synchrony** (Isabella, Belsky, & von Eye, 1989).

In the context of sensitive caregiving, infants develop an **internal working model (IWM)** of their caregiver as available, responsive, and reliable (Thompson, 2006). This IWM, as a set of beliefs and expectations about attachment relationships, will serve as a guide and an interpretive filter for all future relationships (Bretherton & Munholland, 1999). Attachment theory posits that IWMs influence conceptions of self, particularly those having to do with how lovable one is (Thompson, 2006).

The link between caregiver sensitivity and secure attachment has been borne out in the literature (Belsky, 1999; Milijkovitch, Moss, Bernier, Pascuzzo, & Sander, 2015; NICHD Early Child Care Research Network, 2001; see also De Wolff & van IJzendoorn, 1997, for a meta-analysis), in both biological families and cases of adoption (Beijersbergen, Juffer, Bakermans-Kranenburg, & van IJzendoorn, 2012). Synchronous interactions predict attachment

synchrony The reciprocal and mutually rewarding qualities of an infant–caregiver attachment relationship.

internal working model (IWM) A set of beliefs and expectations about attachment relationships based on the infant's experience of sensitive or insensitive caregiving.

security, whereas asynchronous interactions—those characterized by "onesided, unresponsive, or intrusive behavioral exchanges" (Isabella & Belsky, 1991, p. 376)—predict insecurity (Isabella et al., 1989). This link is stronger for mothers than it is for fathers.

Attachment security and fathers The participants in Ainsworth's original Strange Situation research were all mothers and their infants. Since the late 1970s, when this work was published, fathers have become increasingly involved in parenting.

Research suggests that fathers have slightly different patterns of attachment than do mothers and that child sex is associated with this difference. In one study, researchers used the Strange Situation to examine attachment security in 1-year-olds by observing 87 parent/infant pairs, or dyads, representing different gender compositions: father/son, father/daughter, mother/son, and mother/daughter (Schoppe-Sullivan et al., 2006). Researchers examined videos of the dyads looking for specific behaviours that indicated parental sensitivity, such as the accuracy and speed with which the parent responded to an infant need. Fathers and mothers showed the same level of sensitivity to sons, but fathers were less sensitive than mothers to daughters. In turn, mothers were more sensitive to daughters than to sons. Schoppe-Sullivan et al. (2006) also identified the attachment style in each dyad using Ainsworth's classifications. For all dyads, caregiver sensitivity was correlated with attachment security.

Daycare and attachment Separation from attachment figures appears to cause stress in infants and toddlers (Gunnar & Brodersen, 1992). As more and more families use daycare, researchers have intensified their study of the association between non-parental child care and various child outcomes, including attachment. Looking at the brief separations involved in the Strange Situation, researchers found that infants who are securely attached show lower levels of the stress hormone cortisol than do infants who are insecurely attached (Spangler & Schieche, 1998; see also Ahnert, Gunnar, Lamb, & Barthel, 2004). However, we know nothing about the stress levels of securely and insecurely attached babies who are experiencing prolonged and multiple separations, such as those experienced by babies in daycare.

Regular non-parental child care does not appear to increase the likelihood of insecure attachment. However, extended and poor-quality care can negatively affect infant attachment relationships when the relationships are problematic in the first place (NICHD Early Child Care Network, 1997). In general, how infants and toddlers respond to separation depends on the characteristics of the separation environment, in particular on the presence of sensitive and responsive substitute caregivers (Bowlby, 1973; Gunnar & Brodersen, 1992). How parents handle the transition to daycare also matters for attachment security. Securely attached infants remain so when their mothers spend more time adapting them to the daycare (Ahnert et al., 2004).

Lifespan across cultures: Patterns of infant attachment John Bowlby's attachment theory views infant-caregiver attachment as a universal phenomenon that emerged through human evolution in order to protect vulnerable infants (Bowlby, 1969/1982). Researchers all around the world have studied the universality of attachment theory. These studies seek to understand whether the patterns of security and insecurity originally identified in U.S. samples are present elsewhere. And, as **Figure 4.8** shows, the distribution of secure versus insecure attachment among infants is roughly the same across diverse cultures (e.g., Jin, Jacobvitz, Hazen, & Jung, 2012; see also Nakagawa, Lamb, & Miyaki, 1992; Sagi & Lewkowicz, 1987; van IJzendoorn & Kroonenberg, 1988).

However, infants classified as insecure vary in terms of the extent to which they are placed in the avoidant and resistant groups. For example, in Japan, Israel, and Indonesia, insecure infants tend to be classified as resistant (Miyake, Chen, & Campos, 1985; Takahashi, 1986; van IJzendoorn & Sagi-Schwartz, 2008; Zevalkink, Riksen-Walraven, & Van Lieshout, 1999), whereas in Germany, insecure infants are more often classified as avoidant (Grossmann, Grossmann, Huber, & Wartner, 1981). Researchers point to cultural differences in caregiving as a potential explanation, though few have actually examined whether such cultural differences are tied to attachment group distributions (Jin et al., 2012).

When researchers zero in on a given national group, such as Japanese, Israeli, German, and American, they also find substantial variability in attachment patterns *within* nationalities (Thompson, 2006). These findings suggest that cultures are not uniform influences on the development of attachment security, and that shared values and practices are adapted differently by different families.

Attachment in infancy and socio-emotional outcomes Secure attachment in infancy is associated with a host of socio-emotional outcomes. Perhaps the

Distribution of secure versus insecure infants across diverse cultures • Figure 4.8

Across cultures, the majority of non-stressed and non-clinical infants are classified as securely attached (Jin et al., 2012; van IJzendoorn & Kroonenberg, 1988). Parents in most countries prefer the behaviour of securely attached children, though they may differ in their reasons for this preference (Harwood, Miller, & Irizarry, 1995).

Think Critically How do you think culture affects the different reasons that parents give for their preference for securely attached children?

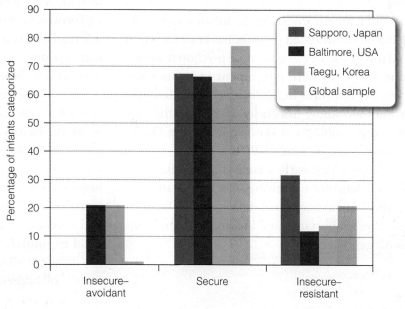

most obvious outcome of early secure attachment is a more harmonious parent–child relationship later on (e.g., Frankel & Bates, 1990). Secure infants tend to have more harmonious relationships with their caregivers in the second year; however, findings are mixed after that, suggesting that there are other important mediating factors in long-term harmony. As **Figure 4.9** shows, one factor might be children's continuing experiences of sensitive caregiving (see Thompson, 2006, for a review).

Attachment security may also benefit children's other close relationships, such as with peers and close friends (Schneider, Atkinson, & Tardif, 2001). Even with unfamiliar adults, we find that secure infants

are subsequently more sociable than insecure infants (Thompson & Lamb, 1983).

Researchers have also examined associations between attachment security and personality development (see Thompson, 2006, for a review). For example, one team of researchers studied personality characteristics in a sample of participants over nearly three decades of their lives, from infancy to age 28 (Sroufe, Egeland, Carlson, & Collins, 2005). Participants who were categorized via the Strange Situation as securely attached at 12 and 18 months were more likely than those categorized as insecure to exhibit a variety of personality dimensions throughout childhood and adolescence,

Attachment, sensitivity, and subsequent functioning • Figure 4.9

Researchers Jay Belsky and Pasco Fearon (2002) assessed children's attachment when the children were 15 months old, maternal sensitivity when they were 2 years old, and a variety of cognitive outcomes at 3 years. Children who were securely attached in infancy and continued to receive sensitive care scored highest on cognitive outcomes at age 3. Those who were insecurely attached and experienced subsequent insensitive care scored lowest.

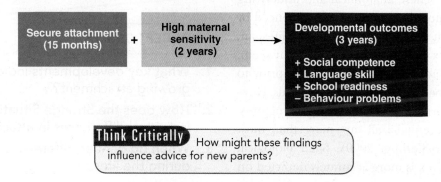

Think Critically How might these findings influence advice for new parents?

including emotional health, self-confidence, and social competence.

In turn, attachment insecurity in infancy, especially the disorganized/disoriented pattern, has been shown to be a risk factor in the development of psychopathology. In the same study, insecure attachment in infancy was linked to anxiety disorders in adolescence (Sroufe et al., 2005). In another study, insecurity at 24 months predicted behaviour problems at age 3 (McCartney, Owen, Booth, Clarke-Stewart, & Vandell, 2004).

It would appear that early secure attachment, along with continued sensitive caregiving, is a significant predictor of positive socio-emotional development. We turn next to another important and lifelong influence on development: gender.

Gender

The influence of **gender** begins quite early in life. Both biological and social factors related to gender interact in predictable and not so predictable ways to affect development. Gender will be a recurring theme and the centre of much discussion throughout this text. Our discussions will focus on both similarities and differences between people that are attributed to gender and or sex. First, we need to clarify some terms.

In this text, when we speak of **gender differences**, we are referring to cognitive and behavioural differences in children due to both biological predispositions and social influences. Whereas gender and therefore gender differences are behavioural and social, **sex differences** are biologically based. These anatomical and underlying biochemical and hormonal differences are influenced by genetics and emerge at various times during the lifespan. However, biological sex is not as concrete as it may seem. A person's sex is generally assigned at birth, or prior to birth, based on the appearance of the outer genitals. However, chromosomes, hormones, the internal sex structures, gonads, and external genitalia all vary more than most people realize (Fausto-Sterling, 2000). Such biological variation suggests that sex is more accurately depicted on a spectrum than it is in a male–female binary. Despite this fact, the notion of a sex binary has heavily influenced how we construct the world—including language. So, while you will read about many male–female, girl–boy, men–women comparisons, keep in mind that there is often more variance within these groupings than between them (Hyde, 2005). Nonetheless, during the first two years, differences attributed to sex and gender are just beginning to emerge, as are the factors that influence them.

After birth, prenatal exposures interact with social forces, resulting in myriad socio-emotional differences between boys and girls during the lifespan. As early as the fetal period, differences can be observed between males and females. Some sex differences are influenced by prenatal exposures. For example, maternal stress exposure has different effects on neurodevelopment in utero, predictive of higher risk for disorders such as autism and schizophrenia in males over females, not only early in the lifespan but later in the lifespan as well (Bale, 2011; Dunn, Morgan, Bale, 2011).

Males weigh more and are more active than females, and these activity-level differences continue throughout childhood (Almi, Ball, & Wheeler, 2001). Boys are more likely to die in childbirth and are more vulnerable to early illness than are girls.

Girls appear to be more emotionally expressive than boys (Fabes & Martin, 1991), and these differences also begin quite early. One of the reasons girls appear more emotionally expressive may be that they tend to be more attentive to social cues, look more at animate objects, and exhibit more eye contact than do boys (Lutchmaya, Baron-Cohen, & Raggatt, 2002). Some believe that these differences may be due to a neurological readiness for facial recognition that emerges earlier in females than males (Hampson, van Anders, & Mullin, 2006). Do these differences continue into childhood and adulthood? Clearly, sex and gender differences will be an ongoing area of discussion as we explore the lifespan.

gender A social construction of expectations that a given culture associates with a person's biological sex.

gender differences Cognitive and behavioural differences associated with gender.

sex differences Biologically based differences between sexes.

CONCEPT CHECK 🛑

1. **What** key developments indicate an infant's growing attachment?

2. **How** does the Strange Situation reveal individual differences in attachment security?

3. **When** do gender differences first emerge during the lifespan?

Emotional Development

LEARNING OBJECTIVES

1. **Distinguish** between primary and secondary emotions.

2. **Explain** what social referencing is and how it develops.

3. **Describe** the development of self-awareness and how researchers have investigated this topic.

E motion is the language of the infant. It is the only way that infants can communicate in their world (Emde, 1998, p. 1236). We know that emotions affect attachment and are involved in most social interactions. What are the first emotions, and how do we understand an infant's emotional state?

Early Emotions

When we think about the development of emotions, we have to consider what actually defines *emotion*. There are both physical and cognitive associations with emotional states, but when we study early emotions we have to rely on our knowledge of what emotions look like to determine their presence.

Are we born with emotions? Most researchers agree that emotion is present at birth (Brazelton, Kolowski, & Main, 1974; Izard, Huebner, Risser, & Dougherty, 1980; Pawluski, Lieblich, & Galea, 2009). Early emotions are observed by the first cry after birth, followed by varied states of interest and distaste (Emde, 1998). Later, infants' facial expressions, such as the **social smile**, enable us to make some inferences about what they are feeling.

Emotions that are present early in life and, as such, are most likely innate, are called basic or **primary emotions**. Theorists debate, however, exactly which emotions to include in this category (Lamb, Bornstein, & Teti, 2002). What they tend to agree on, however, is that emotions can be identified based on facial expressions. **Figure 4.10** illustrates how some commonly agreed-upon primary emotions are displayed on the face.

Emotions are a form of early communication, motivation, and adaptation. As **Figure 4.11** shows, emotions become more complex as an infant develops, based on both inherited predispositions and contextual factors.

> **social smile** In infancy, the first facial expression of pleasure, enabled by neurophysiological maturation and an increasing readiness for social interactions with caregivers.
>
> **primary emotion** An emotion that is present early in life and is most likely innate.

How can we tell what an infant is feeling? • Figure 4.10

Emotion researchers propose that we can accurately identify infant emotions based on movements in their faces. Of the five primary emotions—sadness, surprise, fear, joy, and anger—which two are pictured here (Lamb et al., 2002)?

Think Critically What is happening in each region of the face (eyebrows, eyes, mouth) to signal the emotion to you?

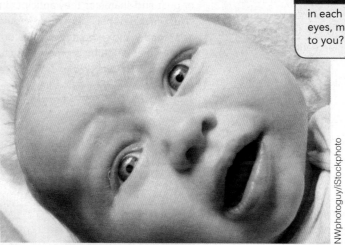

There are several transitions or phases in emotional development during the first 2 years of life (Emde, 1998).

Universal Images Group/Getty Images

Flashon Studio/Shutterstock

a. From birth: Infants express basic emotions

Infants express instinctive, general positive or negative emotions in response to environmental situations or states of need, such as hunger. Caregivers' responses set up patterns of interaction that, in turn, influence later development (Brazelton, 1976; Epps & Jackson, 2000).

c. About 6 months: Memory aids emotions

Infants' developing memories let them enjoy new games such as peek-a-boo, shown here. Their early understanding of the shared meaning of emotions makes games more fun if caregivers join in. Memory also contributes to separation anxiety at about this time.

Spencer Grant/PhotoEdit

b. At 2–3 months: Awakening sociability leads to emotion complexity

Increasing readiness for social interactions with caregivers promotes the emergence of the social smile, the infant's first facial expression of pleasure (Wörmann, Holodynski, Kärtner, & Keller, 2012). Infants at this age make more eye contact and sounds of satisfaction. These expressions foster closeness with caretakers, enhancing attachment and provoking more social interaction, which spirals into more infant expressiveness. Reciprocity emerges, in which infant and caregiver influence one another's emotions (Sroufe, 2000). These social events lead to increased emotion complexity and cognitive ability (Emde, 1998).

TIM LAMAN/National Geographic Creative

d. From about 9–20 months: Physical and cognitive development enable the emergence of secondary emotions

As infants develop the ability to stand and then walk, they begin to display pride, an early secondary emotion.

e. End of second year: Emotional awareness explodes

By about 22 months, toddlers are aware of rules and morality. Awareness of the past, present, and future lets them experience abstract emotions, such as disappointment if expectations are not met, or guilt and shame as they anticipate punishment for breaking rules (Wu, Ulrick, Looper, Tiernan, & Angulo-Barroso, 2008). Emotions such as empathy and sympathy also become more evident, though some believe that empathy is present much sooner than this (Campos, Campos, & Barrett, 1989).

Design Pics/Misty Bedwell/Getty Images

Think Critically What role does memory play in the development of emotions?

One key emotional milestone is the appearance of separation anxiety by 6 months of age. As described earlier in this chapter, infants develop separation anxiety when they are able to notice parental absence and are attached enough to find that absence unpleasant. Separation anxiety requires a more complex memory system and the beginning of a shared understanding of the meaning of emotions than earlier stages of emotion.

> **secondary emotion** An emotion that emerges with the help of certain cognitive and social developments.
>
> **guilt** A painful feeling of regret that arises when one causes, anticipates causing, or is associated with a negative act that violates one's moral standards.
>
> **empathy** An emotional response to another's emotional state that is similar to what the other person is feeling or might be expected to feel.

Another key milestone is the development of **secondary emotions**, such as pride, **guilt**, shame, and **empathy**. Unlike primary emotions that appear early in life, secondary emotions cannot appear without certain cognitive and social developments, such as an understanding of self (Lewis, 2000). Secondary emotions serve a different type of purpose from the earlier cries for food or proximity. For example, a toddler who accidentally breaks a dish displays emotional expressions related to disappointment and anticipated consequences. These secondary emotions play an important role in socio-emotional development across the lifespan.

Taken together, early emotional development evolves from and is intimately connected to the social world, a point that is particularly obvious when we look at how infants react to the emotions of their closest social partners: their parents (Hawley, 2003).

Social Referencing and Self-Awareness

As infants begin to understand the communicative power of their emotions, they begin to also understand that others' emotions hold meaning. This ability to read another's emotional state provides valuable information to a developing infant.

Social referencing Between 6 and 12 months of age, infants become increasingly social and interactive with their caregivers and others (Campos & Sternberg, 1981). When situations arise that are ambiguous or cause distress, such as a sudden loud noise, the developing connection between infants/toddlers and their caregiver is evident: The infant typically looks to a primary caregiver's facial cues and/or vocal cues to help make decisions about how to respond (Campos & Sternberg, 1981; Mumme, Fernald, & Herrera, 1996). Developmentalists call this looking behaviour **social referencing**.

> **social referencing** Using a caregiver's emotional cues to help understand an uncertain or ambiguous event or stimulus.

Social referencing is significant for at least two reasons. First, it means that infants are good at reading the emotional cues of others and using this information to guide their own responses to events. Second, social referencing is the beginning of a lifelong process and feature of social development: using others' emotional signals to understand what is meaningful within one's society. So why do infants and toddlers engage in social referencing? There are two theories that attempt to answer this question (Walden & Kim, 2005). One theory, the attachment perspective, suggests that infants look to their primary caregivers for emotional support and anxiety reduction (Ainsworth, 1992). The other, the social referencing hypothesis, suggests that infants look at their caregiver in an effort to understand the social situation and to reduce ambiguity (Baldwin & Moses, 1996). The classic study described in **Figure 4.12** provides support for this second theory (by Hornik, Risenhoover, & Gunnar, 1987).

Parents seem to be very much aware of their infants' and toddlers' social referencing behaviour, and use their emotional cues to send various messages (Thompson, 2006). A parent's furrowed brow and stern voice may be used to instill caution in their toddler who is reaching for a breakable vase. Later, when that child encounters an energetic puppy, the parent may deliberately offer a broad smile with the intention of providing reassurance.

Social referencing is an important way that infants and toddlers learn about their world. We know that infants are curious about their world and are constantly making decisions about what information is relevant and what is not. This process becomes even more important when they begin to develop an understanding of themselves.

Self-awareness When do infants begin to develop an awareness of self? Piaget suggested that, during the first months of life, infants are undifferentiated from their surrounding environment, that a baby probably is not aware of his or her "own existence as a separate entity" (Gruber & Vonèche, 1977, p. 200). Thus, Piaget believed we have

Social referencing • Figure 4.12

One team of researchers asked mothers of 12-month-old infants to show positive, neutral, or negative reactions when novel toys were presented to their children (Hornik et al., 1987). Infants stayed away from toys when their mothers showed a negative, disgusted reaction. This is maybe one subtle way adults communicate gender norms to young children. If the child, pictured below, had picked up a doll, how would adults respond and how would this influence the child?

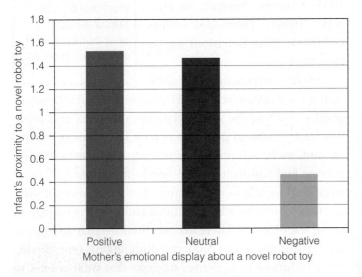

Pavel L Photo and Video/Shutterstock

Think Critically What facial emotion about the robot did this child's mother most likely display?

no early awareness of ourselves as separate beings, though Piaget's theory does allow for a slowly evolving differentiation during the first year of life (Piaget, 1927).

Other researchers are less certain about the lack of differentiation at birth and believe infants are born with predisposed behaviours that foster self-awareness (Stern, 1984). Most researchers suggest that true **self-awareness** does not exist until 14–18 months, when language and cognitive complexity allow such things as self-labelling or embarrassment (Rochat & Striano, 2002), but some believe it arises earlier.

self-awareness
The ability to recognize oneself as a separate being.

Investigating the question of when exactly self-awareness emerges presents a daunting research task. What kinds of behaviour are infants capable of producing to evidence self-awareness? One of the more interesting approaches to this question involves having babies look into a mirror (Amsterdam, 1972; Bertenthal & Fisher, 1978; Lewis & Brooks-Gunn, 1979). Researchers

discretely put rouge on an infant's nose or cheek and then sit the baby down in front of a mirror. The researchers watch to see whether the infant touches the rouge mark. Doing so is a behavioural indication of recognition or self-awareness (Schulman & Kaplowitz, 1977).

As we mentioned earlier in this chapter, babies' increasing awareness of themselves as separate people from their parents is an essential step in the development of their attachment relationships. These key relationships continue to play a critical role in early childhood and beyond.

CONCEPT CHECK STOP

1. **What** are some examples of primary and secondary emotions?

2. **What** function does social referencing serve?

3. **What** infant behaviours indicate emerging self-awareness?

Summary

1 Personality Development 126

- Freud suggested that personality develops in a series of stages. The id is the dominant part of personality during the oral stage. Later, during toilet training in the anal stage, the ego emerges as the conscious part of personality that controls the id. Events during either stage can have lifelong effects on personality, leading to either **anal fixations** or **oral fixations**, such as smoking, shown in the photo in the figure.

Adult outcomes of infant fixations, according to Freud • Figure 4.2

- Erikson proposed that infants' primary task is to develop a sense of trust in their environment. The **trust versus mistrust stage** is resolved when infants' needs are met appropriately, consistently, and competently. Toddlers then enter the **autonomy versus shame and doubt stage**, when they try to learn to master themselves and their environments.

- **Temperament** is biologically based individual differences in how one responds to the environment. Early researchers classified infants as having **easy**, **difficult**, or **slow-to-warm-up temperaments**. Rothbart has suggested that biological and brain processes influence infants' patterns of **negative affectivity**, **extraversion/ surgency**, and **effortful control**.

- Behaviourally uninhibited (sociable) infants readily approach new people, objects, and situations. Behaviourally inhibited (shy) infants withdraw from novel stimuli. The **amygdala** is thought to be responsible for these behavioural and physiological differences in temperament. The concept of **goodness of fit** is the match between these behavioural and physiological—temperamental—differences and the responsiveness of the infant's environment.

2 Social Influences 131

- John Bowlby's **attachment theory** suggested that **attachment** proceeds in four phases: pre-attachment from birth until about 12 weeks of age; beginning of attachment from 3 to 6 months, during which infants develop **separation anxiety**, as illustrated by the photo in this figure; clear attachment from about 6 to 8 months until early childhood, when infants show **stranger anxiety**; and goal-directed attachment beginning during the preschool years. Research by Harlow and others suggested that attachment is an inborn process.

Bowlby's attachment theory • Figure 4.4

- Researchers use the **Strange Situation** to classify different types of **attachment behaviours**: **secure attachment** and two types of insecure attachment, **insecure–avoidant attachment** and **insecure–resistant attachment**. A third type of insecure attachment, **disorganized/disoriented attachment**, was identified by later research.

- The mothers of secure infants tend to score higher on measures of sociability, extraversion, and insightfulness. In turn, these mothers score lower on depression, neuroticism, and anxiety. According to attachment theorists, caregiver sensitivity is the central factor in the development of attachment security. Caregiver sensitivity underlies the perfect attunement between infant and caregiver known as **synchrony**. Secure infants develop an **internal working model (IWM)** of their caregiver as available, responsive, and reliable.

- Researchers employed the Strange Situation in non-Western nations and found similar patterns of security and insecurity as seen in U.S. samples. Parents in most countries prefer the behaviour of securely attached children, although they may differ in their reasons for this preference.

- Attachment security may benefit children's relationships with parents, peers, and even unfamiliar adults. Attachment figures contribute to infants' and toddlers' **self-regulation** in times of stress. Attachment security continues to influence emotional health, self-confidence, and social competence as a child develops.

- **Gender** is socially based while sex is biologically based. **Gender differences** are related to both biological and social influences, whereas **sex differences** are strictly biological. Sex differences occur even before birth, and gender differences are observable from birth. However, there is often more variance within these groups than between them.

3 Emotional Development 141

- Infants are born with basic or **primary emotions**, including distress, happiness, interest, disgust, and anger. These early emotions help babies communicate and form attachments with their caregivers. **Secondary emotions**, such as pride, **guilt**, shame, and **empathy**, appear only after certain cognitive and social advances have taken place.

- The **social smile** emerges at about 2 to 3 months of age. Infants' developing memories contribute to separation anxiety but also allow them to start enjoying peek-a-boo games, as illustrated in the photo in the figure. Feelings of pride emerge when infants learn to walk and are related to a developing sense of self. Guilt and shame emerge just before 2 years of age.

Emotional development • Figure 4.11

Spencer Grant/PhotoEdit

- Between about 6 and 12 months of age, infants rely on **social referencing** to help them decide how to respond to distressing or confusing situations. Although some research suggests that self-recognition occurs as early as 6 months, most researchers agree that babies are fully aware of themselves as separate beings from others by about 14–18 months. Their **self-awareness** allows them to experience new emotions, such as self-labelling and embarrassment.

Key Terms

- amygdala 130
- anal fixation 127
- attachment 131
- attachment behaviour 134
- attachment theory 132
- autonomy versus shame and doubt stage 128
- difficult temperament 129
- disorganized/disoriented attachment 136
- easy temperament 128
- effortful control 129
- empathy 143
- extraversion/surgency 129

- failure to thrive (FTT) 136
- gender 140
- gender differences 140
- goodness of fit 130
- guilt 143
- insecure–avoidant attachment 135
- insecure–resistant attachment 135
- internal working model (IWM) 137
- negative affectivity 129
- New York Longitudinal Study (NYLS) 128
- oral fixation 127
- primary emotion 141
- secondary emotion 143

- secure attachment 135
- self-awareness 144
- self-regulation 131
- separation anxiety 133
- sex differences 140
- slow-to-warm-up temperament 129
- social referencing 143
- social smile 141
- Strange Situation 134
- stranger anxiety 133
- synchrony 137
- temperament 128
- trust versus mistrust stage 128

Critical and Creative Thinking Questions

1. Based on Erikson's psychosocial stage theory, what advice would you give parents about toilet training their children?

2. If you were the parent or caregiver of an infant high in negative affectivity who tends to be fearful and easily frustrated, how might you need to adapt the child's environment, including your own behaviour, to increase goodness of fit for that child's temperament?

3. In this chapter we talked about the concept of goodness of fit as it relates to temperament. How does goodness of fit relate to the development of attachment?

4. How would you characterize your own early attachment experiences? How do they affect you today?

5. How might social referencing be related to the formation of attachments between infants and caregivers?

What is happening in this picture?

This toddler is meeting his infant brother for the first time and relying on his father for guidance about how to respond to this novel situation.

Courtesy Charity Robey

Think Critically
1. How might this toddler be engaging in social referencing?
2. What is the toddler likely to do if his father seems tense?
3. What should the father do if he wants the toddler to interact with the newborn in a gentle and calm way?

REAL Development

Socio-emotional Development in Infancy: The First Two Years

In this video activity, you will observe the socio-emotional development of a group of toddlers. Tia Wagner is considering enrolling her son Brandon in a "Mommy and Me" class that uses both structured and unstructured play for specific age groups. As you know, children's social skills change in various ways during the first two years. Your task is to observe the class and the children's social skills to assess how the class activities influence these skills. You will then share your observations with Tia so that she can make a decision.

John Wiley & Sons, Inc.

WileyPLUS Go to WileyPLUS to complete the REAL Development activity.

03.01

Self-Test

(Check your answers in Appendix A.)

1. Erikson believed that for toddlers to develop a sense of mastery over their environments, parents should _____.

    a. avoid giving toddlers any choices

    b. avoid praising toddlers too much

    c. respond with care to the toddler's mistakes

    d. respond randomly to the toddler's requests

2. Baby Juana sleeps and eats on a regular schedule, smiles a lot, and seems to enjoy new people and places. Chess and Thomas would have characterized Juana's temperament as _____.

    a. difficult

    b. easy

    c. disorganized

    d. slow to warm up

3. Based on their explanations, identify the three temperament dimensions of Thomas and Chess.

Temperament dimension	Explanation
_____	Does the child tend to be happy or sad?
_____	Is the child highly physically active?
_____	Are the child's emotional expressions strong or muted?

    a. threshold of responsiveness; intensity of reactions; quality of mood

    b. quality of mood; activity level; intensity of reactions

    c. approach/withdrawal; rhythmicity; distractibility

    d. adaptability; attention span/persistence; threshold of responsiveness

4. Which of the temperament characteristics defined by Mary Rothbart is this child displaying?

Anna Summa/Getty Images

    a. high negative affectivity

    b. high extraversion/surgency

    c. high regularity

    d. high effortful control

5. A child who clings to a well-known caregiver and refuses to engage a new person is experiencing _____.

    a. self-conscious emotions

    b. separation anxiety

    c. stranger anxiety

    d. self-recognition

6. Harry Harlow concluded from his experiments with infant monkeys that attachment is _____.

    a. an inborn process needed for survival

    b. a result of oral stimulation that happens during feeding

    c. learned through the principles of reinforcement

    d. unlikely to be found in any species except humans

7. Children who become angry with their caregiver when reunited during the Strange Situation typically have _____ attachment.

a. insecure–avoidant

b. disorganized/disoriented

c. insecure–resistant

d. secure

8. Infants suffering from failure to thrive may experience _____ later in life.

a. lower-than-average weight

b. higher-than-average weight

c. greater-than-average height

d. all of the above

9. Attachment researchers have shown _____.

a. that fathers and mothers have slightly different patterns of responsiveness to their children

b. that disorganized/disoriented attachment is associated with failure to thrive

c. that, across cultures, the majority of non-stressed and non-clinical infants have been found to be securely attached

d. all of the above

10. Sex differences are clear _____ differences between males and females, whereas gender differences also involve differences related to _____ influences.

a. biological; social

b. behavioural; cognitive

c. biological; behavioural

d. social; biological

11. Some researchers believe that because girls have earlier neurological readiness for facial recognition they are more likely than boys to _____.

a. be emotionally expressive

b. contract early illnesses

c. be physically active

d. do all of these

12. Which primary emotion is this baby showing?

a. joy

b. interest

c. pride

d. surprise

Flashon Studio/Shutterstock

13. Which of the following results from infants' social smiling?

a. enhanced social interactions

b. closeness with caretakers

c. influence on caregivers' emotions

d. all of these

14. Feelings of pride typically emerge around the time toddlers begin to _____.

a. talk

b. walk

c. toilet train

d. play peek-a-boo

15. The classic research depicted in this chart provides support for _____.

a. the attachment perspective

b. the social referencing hypothesis

c. the self-awareness hypothesis

d. emotional awareness

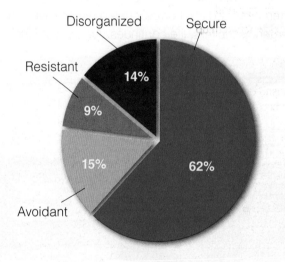

THE PLANNER ✓

Review your Chapter Planner in the chapter opener and check off your completed work.

Physical and Cognitive Development in Early Childhood: Two to Six Years

In 2016, a massive wildfire forced more than 80,000 people to flee Fort McMurray, Alberta (Cotter, 2016). The 2015 wildfire season forced the evacuation of more than 7,500 First Nations people from their Saskatchewan homes; during the 2011 forest fire season in Northern Alberta, whole neighbourhoods in Slave Lake were destroyed (CBC News, July 4, 2015; Wingrove, September 4, 2011). For evacuated families living in emergency shelters, life continues. Adults continue to work, focus on rebuilding their community, care for the elderly, and tend to their daily lives, and children—although affected by the natural disaster—continue to do what children around the world do: play!

Is their play mere folly? Or are they instead doing their most important job? According to neo-Freudian psychologist Alfred Adler, these children are working as hard as their parents. "Play is a child's work," he said, "and this is not a trivial pursuit."

In this chapter, we will examine two domains that are vital to and vitally dependent on play: the physical and cognitive systems. During our journey we will study changes in the nervous, skeletal, and muscular systems; explore the cognitive perspectives of Piaget and Vygotsky and the information-processing model; and discuss the development of language. Throughout, we will see why kids work hard at play wherever they live, whether in a quiet suburban home or in a land perpetually threatened by natural disasters.

Cole Burston/AFP/Getty Images

CHAPTER PLANNER ✔

- ❏ Study the picture and read the opening story.
- ❏ Scan the Learning Objectives in each section:
  p. 152 ❏ p. 157 ❏ p. 169 ❏
- ❏ Read the text and study all visuals. Answer any questions.

Analyze key features

- ❏ Development InSight, p. 159
- ❏ Process Diagram, p. 162
- ❏ Challenges in Development, p. 181
- ❏ What a Developmentalist Sees, p. 182
- ❏ Stop: Answer the Concept Checks before you go on:
  p. 157 ❏ p. 169 ❏ p. 183 ❏

End of chapter

- ❏ Review the Summary and Key Terms.
- ❏ Answer the Critical and Creative Thinking Questions.
- ❏ Answer *What is happening in this picture?*
- ❏ Complete the Self-Test and check your answers.

151

Physical Development

LEARNING OBJECTIVES

1. **Identify** how the brain develops during the early-childhood period.

2. **Describe** the key processes of skeletal growth.

3. **Explain** how gross-motor and fine-motor skills become more refined during the preschool years.

I f you were able to visit your infant cousin only once every six months, would you notice changes in her weight and height? Absolutely. But if you kept up the same rate of visitation during your cousin's preschool years, would her growth be as obvious to you? Probably not. What would be obvious, though, is differences in the shape of her body. As shown in **Figure 5.1**, during the preschool years children appear slimmer as their "baby fat" melts away and they "stretch out."

Growth rates during early childhood • Figure 5.1

On growth charts, the steeper the line, the more rapidly growth is occurring. As can be seen here, increases in height and weight slow down dramatically during the early-childhood years compared with the rapid growth during infancy. Between the ages of 2 and 6, the average child in Canada gains about 2.7 kg and 5 to 8 cm each year (Shields, 2008). Much individual variability exists in growth rates due to heredity, socio-economic status, nutrition, ethnicity, and culture.

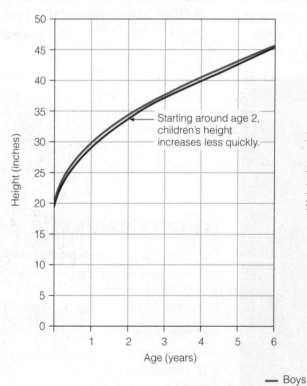

Starting around age 2, children's height increases less quickly.

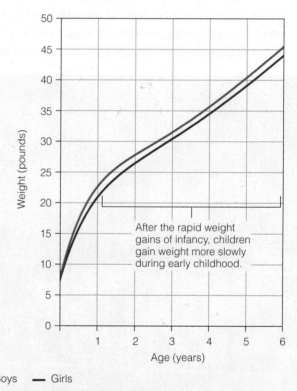

After the rapid weight gains of infancy, children gain weight more slowly during early childhood.

— Boys   — Girls

Think Critically What might a developmental pediatrician say to the parent of a 3-year-old who wants to know why his child's height and weight do not match the lines on the charts?

Frank and Helena/Cultura RF/Getty Images

The Nervous System

Just as children's growth rate slows during the preschool years, so too does their rate of brain maturation. In Chapter 3, we introduced the process of **synaptic pruning**. By the beginning of early childhood, this process is taking place more slowly than it did during infancy. Even so, pruning continues to some degree throughout the lifespan (Seeman, 1999), and our brains undergo dramatic changes throughout childhood (Lenroot & Giedd, 2006).

> **synaptic pruning** The elimination of synaptic connections in order to increase efficiency.

Between 2 and 6 years of age, the brain gains 20 to 25 percent of its adult weight (Kolb & Whishaw, 2011) or around 300 g, roughly equivalent to the weight of a banana. Just think what adding the weight of a mere banana means for increased brain function and more complex behaviours compared with infancy. However, as we'll see in this chapter, growth rates vary tremendously from child to child. In fact, the brain volumes of normally functioning children at the same age can differ by as much as 50 percent because one child's brain is growing faster than another's.

Gains children make in brain weight and size during this period arise mainly from increased numbers of connections and from the continuing process of **myelination**, or the coating of neurons with myelin, both of which we discussed in Chapter 3. Dendritic growth results in more complex connections among neurons. These connections, or **synapses**, make possible more complex movement and thinking, which are evident in the increasingly advanced ways in which children walk, run, and negotiate their worlds (Nelson & Bloom, 1997). Meanwhile, increased myelination allows neurons to communicate at a more rapid pace (**Figure 5.2**) (Howard, 2006). Thanks to

> **myelination** The coating of neurons with myelin.
>
> **synapses** The connections among neurons.

Myelination of the cerebellum • Figure 5.2

The children in these photos are demonstrating a great deal of coordination. What makes their actions possible? In large part, myelination—in particular, myelination of the neurons that link the cerebral cortex to the cerebellum, an area near the brain stem that is vital for balance and fine muscle movements. As these neurons become increasingly myelinated during the preschool years, children become more coordinated while running, climbing, and jumping (Paus et al., 1999).

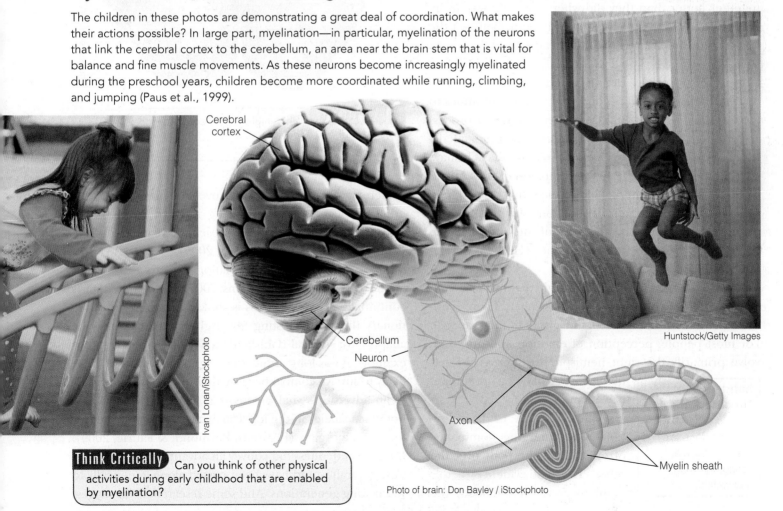

Cerebral cortex

Cerebellum

Neuron

Axon

Myelin sheath

Ivan Lonan/iStockphoto

Huntstock/Getty Images

Photo of brain: Don Bayley / iStockphoto

Think Critically Can you think of other physical activities during early childhood that are enabled by myelination?

myelination, a preschooler can think faster than he or she could as an infant. Preschoolers can also react more quickly and have better hand–eye coordination than they did as babies (Paus et al., 1999; see also Nelson, Thomas, & de Haan, 2006).

At any point during development, deviations in brain maturation are the product of an ongoing, complex interaction between genetic and environmental factors

toxin A harmful substance that causes adverse effects.

lead poisoning An environmental factor that interacts with genes to produce cognitive deficits in children.

(Karmiloff-Smith et al., 2004; Paus, 2010). Exposure to **toxins** or poisonous substances during early childhood illustrates this complex interaction. For example, as we learn later in this chapter, **lead poisoning** is an environmental factor that interacts with genes to produce cognitive deficits in children.

During early childhood, myelination of the corpus callosum, shown in **Figure 5.3**, allows the two hemispheres of a child's brain to communicate and work together better than they did when the child was an infant (Cook, 1986). Improved coordination between the two sides of the brain is helpful because, in the midst of

lateralization The process by which the right and left hemispheres of the brain take on specific functions.

all its pruning, myelination, and dendritic growth, during early childhood the brain continues to undergo **lateralization**, a process that begins during prenatal development (Kolb & Whishaw, 2011). Lateralization is the differentiation of the left and right hemispheres of the brain such that each hemisphere takes on specialized functions. In other words, during lateralization the two sides of the brain become increasingly different from each other (Hopkins & Cantalupo, 2008; McManus, 2002).

In the physical domain, the right hemisphere controls the left side of the body and vice versa. There is evidence of lateralization in cognitive functioning, as well. For most people, perception of emotion appears to involve primarily the right hemisphere, whereas the left

handedness The preference for using one hand over the other for basic activities such as eating, throwing, and writing.

hemisphere plays a dominant role in language.

One outcome of lateralization is an emerging dominance of one side of the body over the other. The first evidence of this dominance is **handedness**, the

The corpus callosum • Figure 5.3

During the preschool years, the corpus callosum, a thick band of nerve fibres that connects the hemispheres of the brain, grows and becomes increasingly myelinated. This enables the two sides of the brain to work together better. As a result, children move with increasing coordination and speed.

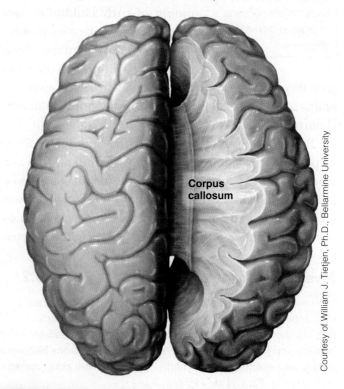

Corpus callosum

Courtesy of William J. Tietjen, Ph.D., Bellarmine University

Think Critically What might we expect to see in early childhood if the corpus callosum was not well myelinated?

preference for using one hand over the other. This preference typically emerges during infancy and becomes well established during the preschool years (Halpern, Güntürkün, Hopkins, & Rogers, 2005).

Most of the world's population appears to be right-handed (Annett, 2002; Hopkins, 2007). Developmentalists continually debate why this is so. Most support an evolutionary theory, suggesting that right-handedness may be adaptive for survival (Ghirlanda & Vallortigara, 2004). For example, it was long argued that right-handers were more likely to survive combat because their weapons were closer to an adversary's vital organs (e.g., the heart). Similarly, holding a shield on the left arm, while fighting, protected those same organs (Llaurens, Raymond, & Faurie, 2009). If right-handedness did convey an advantage to our ancestors, the trait would have been passed along genetically to succeeding generations. And some researchers do suggest that genetic inheritance is a possible factor in handedness (e.g., Carter-Saltzman, 1980; McManus & Bryden, 1992). They point out that the percentage of left-handed people is consistently about 8 percent across cultures (McManus, 1991). However, research on twins shows that genetics alone cannot explain handedness. For example, one study found that 20 to 30 percent of identical twins have an opposite-handed twin, despite their identical genetic makeup (McGee & Cozad, 1980). Based on these and other studies, developmental scientists now argue that children's handedness is not genetically predetermined, but rather results from a complex interaction of genetic and environmental/cultural influences (Güntürkün, 2005; Hellige, 1993; Leconte and Fagard, 2004).

In addition to the causes of handedness, developmentalists have been interested in the various implications of handedness. For example, handedness has long been associated with language dominance. As noted earlier, language processing is centred in the left hemisphere of the brain for most people (Knecht, Deppe et al., 2000). This seems especially true of right-handers. One study found that only 4 percent of strong right-handers processed language primarily in their right hemispheres (Knecht, Dräger et al., 2000). Given that left-handed neurological patients are more likely to process language in the right hemisphere, developmental scientists have wondered whether handedness could be a sign of pathology. To explore this possibility, one research team looked at the relationship between handedness and language dominance among healthy individuals and found the same tendency for left-handers to have right-hemisphere language dominance (Knecht, Dräger et al., 2000). Twenty-seven percent of strong left-handers processed language predominantly with their right hemispheres. They concluded that the link between handedness and language dominance is a natural phenomenon and simply evidence of our brains' individual differences.

In the past, left-handers were also thought to be more susceptible to developmental delays and immune deficiencies, as well as other behavioural and physiological anomalies, including substance abuse, migraine headaches, and disrupted sleep patterns (Coren & Halpern, 1991; Geschwind & Behan, 1982). However, more recent research has challenged this position by finding no significant differences between left- and right-handers (Leconte & Fagard, 2006).

We now turn to a matter of considerably less debate: how bones develop during early childhood.

The Skeletal System

ossificat[…]
process thr[…]
which cartila[…]
becomes b[…]

During the preschool years, the most obvious changes in the skeletal system involve the length, width, and hardness of bones. The process of **ossification**, through which cartilage turns into bone, occurs from infancy through adolescence. The study of this process can aid in determining a child's skeletal age (the degree of maturation of the child's bones) and in predicting a child's eventual height: The more cartilage that remains, the taller the child can still be expected to grow.

The length and width of bones and the sequence of ossification vary greatly from one child to another, even between siblings. These variations arise from both genetic and environmental influences (Tortora & Nielsen, 2009). Environmental influences include nutrition, physical stimulation, overeating, and food choices; deficiencies in any of these can negatively affect bone growth (Jacoangeli et al., 2002). For healthy bone growth, the World Health Organization recommends adequate calcium intake, exposure to sunshine (and supplementation when needed) to increase Vitamin D, and consumption of a variety of fruits and vegetables (World Health Organization/Food and Agriculture Organization, 2003). Following these recommendations benefits young children and individuals at all ages (Prentice et al., 2006).

Children whose diets are deficient in key nutrients may develop skeletal disorders, such as stunting, also known as chronic growth retardation (Prentice et al., 2006). Stunting affects more than the bones; it is linked to delayed cognitive development and poor educational attainment. Growth retardation in childhood is also associated with physical problems later in life. Skeletal growth stunting in early childhood is a risk factor for girls who, decades later, are at increased risk for obstructed labour, which is a common cause of maternal and infant mortality in developing countries.

Although stunting in early childhood appears to be decreasing globally, it remains a major public health problem. Global estimates in 2010 suggested that 171 million, or more than one in four, preschool children met clinical criteria for growth stunting, with the highest rates in south-central Asian countries, where over a third of preschoolers suffer stunting, and east African countries, where rates top 45 percent (de Onis, Blössner, & Borghi, 2012). International nutrition efforts are expected to decrease the global percentage somewhat, to just over one in five children in 2020. Even in North America and many nations in western Europe, where stunting appears to have been largely eradicated (Prentice et al., 2006), some children may be at risk for less severe nutritional deficiencies that can compromise the growth of their bones. As we discuss later in the chapter, diet is a central factor in children's health.

As the skeletal system changes, so do the muscles of the body. These muscles become stronger, thicker, and more complex.

The Muscular System

During the early-childhood years, children's muscles develop slowly and steadily (Tortora & Nielsen, 2009). The most obvious evidence of muscle change is displayed through improvements in children's gross-motor and fine-motor skills. We first encountered these skills in Chapter 3, when we noted that fine-motor skills are controlled by small muscles, such as the muscles of the hands and fingers, and we explained how large muscles power gross-motor skills.

The major gross-motor and fine-motor milestones of early childhood can be seen in **Table 5.1**. Gross-motor changes result largely from improved body stability, enhanced muscle complexity and growth, and myelination of the central nervous system. Brain and muscle maturation also underlies much fine-motor development.

Along with the physical changes that children experience during the preschool years, children also make great strides in their cognitive development. We consider this domain, including language development, in the next section.

Gross-motor and fine-motor milestones in early childhood   Table 5.1

Children vary greatly in the timing and cultural expression of these milestones (Adolph & Berger, 2006). For example, children in some places may not typically wear shoes with laces.

By the age listed, most children can . . .	Fine-Motor Skills		Gross-Motor Skills	
2 years	• place simple shapes into corresponding holes • draw lines	Oleksii Khmyz/iStockphoto	• jump using both feet • go up and down steps • throw a small ball • kick a large ball • run	Heather Perry/NG Image Collection
3 years	• hold a crayon properly (with the fingers) • build large towers with blocks	Rich Reid/NG Image Collection	• throw and catch more efficiently • stand on one foot • jump over an object	Tim Laman/NG Image Collection
4 years	• use a pencil or pen • begin to use scissors • copy geometric shapes such as a circle or square • draw recognizable human forms • button shirts	Marilyn Nieves/iStockphoto	• skip • climb ladders • hop on one foot • change direction quickly while running	Ariel Skelley/Corbis
5 years	• print first name • tie shoes • write numbers	Stacy Gold/NG Image Collection	• ride a bicycle with training wheels • jump almost a metre forward • climb in precarious places	Peter Cade/Getty Images

1. **How** does myelination help children become more coordinated?

2. **How** might environmental factors affect skeletal growth?

3. **How** do gross- and fine-motor skills change from infancy to early childhood?

Cognitive Development

LEARNING OBJECTIVES

1. **Explain** the features of children's thinking during Piaget's preoperational period.

2. **Summarize** Vygotsky's ideas about children's cognitive development.

3. **Describe** the areas of focus of the information-processing theory in early childhood.

4. **List** key changes in language development that occur during early childhood.

Developmentalists have proposed a variety of theories to explain how children think. In this section we'll consider three of those theories: Piaget's cognitive theory, Vygotsky's socio-cultural theory, and the information-processing model of cognition. We will also consider young children's remarkable explosion of language skills.

Piaget's Preoperational Stage

In Chapter 3, we discussed the foundation of Piaget's theory of cognitive development. On that "ground floor" level of sensorimotor thought, infants use assimilation and accommodation to construct a mental representation of their world. By the end of the sensorimotor stage,

object permanence The ability of an infant to think about things that are not present.

preoperational stage Piaget's second stage of cognitive development, in which the child begins to think symbolically; that is, with words.

babies have developed **object permanence**, the ability to think about things that are not present (Piaget, 1962).

In Piaget's second, **preoperational stage**, the preschool child begins to use language to make sense of the world. Although children use increasingly varied and complex vocabulary, Piaget believed that their perception of the world is still centred on immediate events. In other words,

to preschoolers, everything is happening in the moment. No wonder that when they want something, they want it now. Piaget also suggested that young children tend to overlook the sequential steps in getting from point A to point B, which is why they are famous for saying, "Are we there yet? Are we there yet?" We'll see later that some developmentalists disagree with Piaget's ideas (e.g., Carey, 1985; Gelman & Kremer, 1991). First, let's explore Piaget's theory in more detail.

The symbolic function substage Piaget separated the preoperational stage into two substages: (1) **symbolic function**, stretching from about age 2 to age 4, and (2) **intuitive thought**, from about age 4 to age 7 (Gruber & Vonèche, 1977). As the preoperational period begins, children actively demonstrate their ability to think symbolically (**Figure 5.4**) (Piaget, 1962). One form of symbolic substitution is language. We use words to refer to objects, feelings, beliefs, and intentions. Later in the chapter we will see that there is an incredible increase in vocabulary during the preschool years.

symbolic function The first substage of the preoperational period, during which the ability to use language gives children a new way of thinking about the world.

intuitive thought The second substage of preoperational thinking, during which children want to know how and why.

An example of symbolic thinking • Figure 5.4

Children who can think symbolically understand that one object can stand for another.

Dan Bellack

Ask Yourself

According to Piaget, would this little girl have thought to try to "play" a box when she was an infant?

Piaget believed that, although preschoolers' ability to think in symbols emerges early in the preoperational stage, their cognitive processing remains limited in a number of ways. As we consider these limitations, keep in mind that cognitive abilities do not turn on and off like a television. Instead, they gradually emerge, gain significance, and then decline as the child interacts with the world and develops more complex thought (Gruber & Vonèche, 1977; Piaget, 1962).

One feature of children's preoperational thinking is **centration**. The best way to understand centration is to imagine being focused on one "thing" and one "thing" alone. Everything else ceases to exist. What is this "thing" that preschoolers focus on? It can be nearly anything. It may be one point of view, a particular feeling, or a favourite toy. Piaget made children's understanding of physical objects famous with his tests of **conservation**, the understanding that changes in appearance do not change the physical properties of objects. Preoperational children typically fail to understand conservation, as we see in **Figure 5.5** (Markovits, 1993; McCune-Nicolich, 1981; Piaget, 1962).

centration A quality of thinking in which a person focuses on one aspect or dimension of an object while disregarding any other dimension.

conservation The understanding that key physical properties of an object remain constant even if the appearance of the object changes.

Children often centre on a single point of view to the exclusion of others. Which perspective do you think they typically choose? If you have had any interactions with preschoolers, your answer probably came without hesitation: their own. Piaget called this inability to think from other points of view **egocentrism**. Not to be confused with egotism, egocentrism has nothing to do with being selfish or self-indulgent. Many preschoolers are actually quite empathic. Rather, egocentric thinking informs the lens through which preoperational children view the world: all events happen exactly as they are experienced through their own eyes (**Figure 5.6**) (Piaget, 1954). Preoperational children believe that what they see, you see; what they hear, you hear; and what they feel, you feel. No wonder they seem irritated when they have to tell you they are hungry!

egocentrism A cognitive quality in which one is centred in one's own frame of reference.

animism An egocentric belief that all inanimate objects have qualities associated with humans.

Another feature of preoperational thought that Piaget pointed out is **animism**, the belief that inanimate objects have human qualities (**Figure 5.7**). This feature gives rise to some of the more endearing aspects of a preschooler's behaviour. Thanks to animism, preoperational children live in a world where sponges can sing, letters

The three mountains task • Figure 5.6

Piaget used the three mountains task to study egocentrism. The child shown in this illustration would be asked, "What does the doll see?" Children in the preoperational stage would be very likely to describe the mountains as they see them, from their own perspective, rather than from the doll's perspective.

Think Critically How might egocentrism be beneficial or adaptive during early childhood?

Development InSight

If you have an opportunity to spend time with children in the preoperational or concrete operational stages, try some of the following experiments, which developmentalists use to test Piaget's various forms of conservation. Since preoperational children tend to centre on one aspect of each of these tasks, they usually fail to conserve. Keep in mind that their "failure" is developmentally normal, so be careful not to make the children you test feel bad about their answers.

Type of conservation task (average age at which concept is grasped)	Your task as experimenter	Child is asked...
Length (ages 6–7)	**Step 1** Centre two sticks of equal length. Child agrees that they are of equal length. **Step 2** Move one stick.	**Step 3** "Which stick is longer?" Preoperational child will say that one of the sticks is longer. Child in concrete stage will say that they are both the same length.
Substance amount (ages 6–7)	**Step 1** Centre two identical clay balls. Child acknowledges that the two have equal amounts of clay. **Step 2** Flatten one of the balls.	**Step 3** "Do the two pieces have the same amount of clay?" Preoperational child will say that the flat piece has more clay. Child in concrete stage will say that the two pieces have the same amount of clay.
Liquid volume (ages 6–7)	**Step 1** Present two identical glasses with liquid at the same level. Child agrees that liquid is at the same height in both glasses. **Step 2** Pour the liquid from one of the short, wide glasses into the tall, thin one.	**Step 3** "Do the two glasses have the same amount of liquid?" Preoperational child will say that the tall, thin glass has more liquid. Child in concrete stage will say that the two glasses have the same amount of liquid.
Area (ages 6–7)	**Step 1** Centre two identical sheets of cardboard with wooden blocks placed on them in identical positions. Child acknowledges that the same amount of space is left open on each piece of cardboard. **Step 2** Scatter the blocks on one piece of the cardboard.	**Step 3** "Do the two pieces of cardboard have the same amount of open spaces?" Preoperational child will say that the cardboard with scattered blocks has less open space. Child in concrete stage will say that both pieces have the same amount of open space.

From Carpenter & Huffman, *Visualizing Psycholoy*, 1st Edition. Copyright © 2008 by John Wiley & Sons, Inc. Reprinted by permission of John Wiley & Sons, Inc.

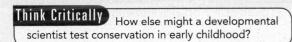

Think Critically How else might a developmental scientist test conservation in early childhood?

An example of animism • Figure 5.7

Is this statue alive? Because of animism, these girls just might think that statues can talk, think, and interact. They certainly seem to hope so!

Think Critically What other examples of animism have you seen displayed by young children? Explain.

Stacy Gold/NG Image Collection

can dance, and stuffed animals can carry on whole conversations. If you were to ask young Fernando where a cup or dish went, he might say, "It walked away." Coupling animism with egocentrism, preschoolers tend to think that everything has the same thoughts and feelings that they do, regardless of whether or not those objects are human. As a result, preoperational children experience a highly subjective—albeit interesting—world.

Irreversibility is another cognitive feature of early childhood that can limit children's understanding of objects and events. Irreversibility is the belief that no procedure can be undone (**Figure 5.8**). Once a ball of clay has been rolled into a hot dog, for example, preoperational children believe that it cannot possibly be turned back into the original ball of clay. According to Piaget, preoperational children's world is linear and only moves forward (Piaget & Inhelder, 1975). Processes move forward, never backward: If a stuffed cat is dressed in clothes, it can never be a naked cat again.

> **irreversibility** The belief of preoperational thinkers that objects and events, once changed, can never return to their original form.

The intuitive thought substage According to Piaget, the intuitive thought substage is characterized by the desire to know how things work and where things come from. Because of this desire, 4- to 7-year-old children tend to ask a lot of "why" questions. At the same time, however, children often arrive at their own explanations of events based on purely intuitive ideas, hence the substage's name. For example, if we ask little Élise where clouds come from, she may be quick to tell us that they come from smoke that has drifted up to the sky. Élise may seem sure of this explanation, but she has no logical cause-and-effect thinking to back up her assertion (Kelemen, 2004).

Reversibility in action • Figure 5.8

Do these children realize that letting the air out of these balloons will cause them to return to their original shape? Since they are in the preoperational stage, probably not. Irreversibility prevents a child from understanding the concepts of cause and effect and how objects and events in the world are connected to one another.

Think Critically Can you think of other examples of preschoolers' belief in irreversibility?

Steve Raymer/NG Image Collection

One common explanation that preoperational children use is human interference. In their world, if you want to know about the cause of any natural event or object, you can look to a human's actions. Piaget called this type of thinking **artificialism** (Piaget & Inhelder, 1975). *Why do rivers flow? Because a man pushes them. Why are trees green? Because a woman painted them that way.* Preoperational children's desire for explanations sets the stage for the next stage of thought, the concrete operational stage, which you'll learn about later, in school-aged children.

artificialism The belief that all objects and events are affected by human influences.

Criticisms of Piaget's theory Although many of Piaget's preoperational concepts match informal observations of children, his views have not gone unchallenged. As with the sensorimotor stage, probably the most frequently cited criticism of this stage is that Piaget underestimated children's cognitive abilities (see Birney & Sternberg, 2011, for a review). For example, research has demonstrated that children as young as age 3 are able to distinguish between animate and inanimate objects (Carey, 1985). Other developmental scientists have found that children as young as age 4 understand that certain events in the world exist independently of human influence (Gelman & Kremer, 1991). By simplifying the questions and making the tasks more "child friendly," we can observe fewer egocentric responses at earlier ages than Piaget thought possible. One study that did this demonstrated evidence of conservation abilities earlier than Piaget believed they appeared (Gelman, 1969).

Piaget's stages and non-Western cultures Piaget's research has also been criticized for its narrow focus on cognitive development of children raised in the United States (Rogoff, 1990). In response, cross-cultural studies did find evidence of Piaget's stages in non-Western cultures (Dasen, 1972). However, there is a lack of evidence that Piaget's stages of cognitive development are universal across all cultures. There is variation, for example, in the ages at which children develop conservation in thinking (e.g., Za'rour, 1971; see also Modgil, Modgil, & Brown, 2006). Although Piaget believed that there are only minor social influences on how we develop thought (Piaget, 1962), such cross-cultural research provides strong evidence that our social environment does shape our understanding of the world. One theory that embraces this very idea is Vygotsky's (1978) cognitive theory.

Vygotsky's Theory of Cognitive Development

In contrast to Piaget, who believed that cognitive development simply unfolds from within, Russian psychologist Lev Vygotsky believed that a child's social world facilitates the development of his or her thinking (Vygotsky, 1978). Social interactions facilitate cognitive development by shaping the **zone of proximal development (ZPD)**, which is shown in **Figure 5.9**. According to Vygotsky, the ZPD is the range of optimal learning for children. In the ZPD, children learn tasks that they cannot yet do alone but are able to complete with guidance from an adult or a more experienced peer. This process of assistance is called **scaffolding**; it supports new behaviour similar to the way a scaffold holds up unfinished construction on a building. As the child becomes more practised at a task, helpers can gradually decrease the level of assistance they provide, just as workers take down a scaffold from a building one piece at a time. Scaffolding is a form of **guided participation** in which the more experienced person serves as a "cognitive guide" for the young child (Rogoff, 1990).

Vygotsky also emphasized the importance of language for cognitive development. He believed that language drives the internalization of cognitive rules and thinking. In particular, Vygotsky believed that when children talk to themselves, a process he called **private speech**, they perform better cognitively (**Figure 5.10**). Think about when you were learning a new task, such as driving. The first few times you drove, you may have found it helpful to talk yourself through the process: *turn the key, step on the brake, shift into reverse,* and so on. Similarly, young children tend to talk themselves

zone of proximal development (ZPD) Vygotsky's term for the range of tasks that a person cannot accomplish independently but that can be done with the assistance of a person with more experience or more advanced cognitive ability.

scaffolding The process of assisting a less experienced individual through complex tasks by providing supports, which may be verbal or physical.

guided participation A process in which a more experienced teacher becomes an interactive guide, helping a younger or less experienced person do tasks that he or she could not complete independently.

private speech A language process in which children talk to themselves as they attempt to perform a task or solve a problem.

Moving through the zone of proximal development • Figure 5.9

Before the Zone of Proximal Development: The child attempts a task but finds it too difficult to do alone.

In the Zone of Proximal Development: An adult or more-experienced peer helps the child with the task, a process called scaffolding. Here the mother provides a *verbal scaffold*, talking the child through shirt buttoning. During the child's first attempts at buttoning her shirt, the mother may have used a *physical scaffold*, perhaps moving the child's fingers in the right motions.

After the Zone of Proximal Development: With practice, the child can now accomplish the task on her own.

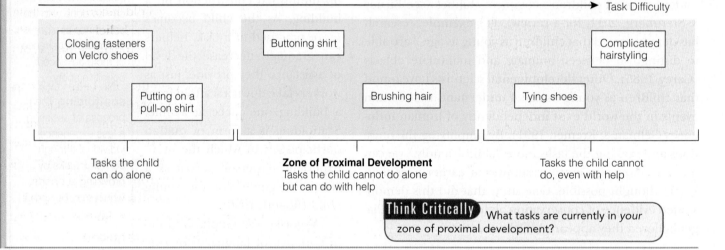

Task Difficulty →

Closing fasteners on Velcro shoes

Putting on a pull-on shirt

Buttoning shirt

Brushing hair

Complicated hairstyling

Tying shoes

Tasks the child can do alone

Zone of Proximal Development
Tasks the child cannot do alone but can do with help

Tasks the child cannot do, even with help

Think Critically What tasks are currently in *your* zone of proximal development?

---

through difficult tasks. With time, children learn to regulate and internalize this private speech, no longer needing to speak before acting.

Piaget and Vygotsky disagreed about the meaning of private speech. Piaget believed that such language during early childhood is egocentric and immature. He described a **collective monologue** that children sometimes demonstrate when in groups. In this situation, children all talk out loud at once without intending to communicate anything to one another (Piaget, 1926a).

One team of researchers found early support for Piaget's notion of egocentric speech (Krauss & Glucksberg,

> **collective monologue**
> Piaget's term for the egocentric private talk that sometimes occurs in a group of children.

1969). They told one 4-year-old (Child A) that he would need to guide another 4-year-old (Child B) through the process of putting illustrated coins in order. The catch was that the children would be unable to see each other and would have to rely on language to get the task done. When the illustrations were simple (e.g., "Pick up the one with the cat on it"), there was no problem. When the illustration on the coin was ambiguous, however, Child A would often say, "Pick up this one," even though Child A could not show Child B which coin was "this one." Child B would respond, "This one?" to which Child A would say "Yes, that one." Since neither of them could see what the other had, the researchers concluded that egocentric speech was demonstrated. Both children believed that the other saw the world from his point of view.

Private speech • Figure 5.10

What is this child saying? Is he simply keeping himself company, or is his private speech more meaningful? Vygotsky believed the latter, suggesting that private speech aids in problem solving and improves performance of tasks.

Matt Carr/Getty Images

Despite this evidence, there is more support for Vygotsky's claim that language helps to support cognitive development (e.g., Berk, 1986; Gaskill & Díaz, 1991). In one study, Vygotsky (1962) put normal-hearing 4-year-olds in a room with deaf children who could not speak. If childhood speech is egocentric, the normal-hearing children should have engaged in a collective monologue. Instead, Vygotsky found that the normal-hearing children spoke less when they knew that the other children could not hear them. Thus, he concluded that children's speech reflects a rich social process rather than simply the egocentricity of preoperational thought.

Whereas Vygotsky thought that social interaction is essential for cognitive development, our next theory focuses on cognitive changes that happen regardless of context.

Information-Processing Perspective

As we discussed in Chapter 1, the information-processing perspective uses the analogy of the mind as a computer (Siegler, 2003). In this chapter, we will focus on three key changes.

Theory of mind As children begin to think about where their thoughts come from, they wonder whether other people also have thoughts. Developmentalists have called this the emergence of a **theory of mind**. Developing theory of mind indicates that a child is learning that other people have wishes and desires of their own. Theory of mind research reveals details about children's developing understanding of beliefs, desires, and emotions of self and others (Harris, 2006). It is impossible to lie without some degree of a theory of mind. This explains why 3-year-olds will often "tattle" on themselves for spilling paint or harassing the family cat even if there are no witnesses. They assume that mom and dad already know what they have done.

> **theory of mind**
> The ability to understand that others have mental states and that their thoughts and knowledge differ from one's own.

One indicator of an emerging theory of mind is the understanding that others can hold incorrect, or false, beliefs. Developmentalists use false-belief tasks like the one shown in **Figure 5.11** to study the development of a theory of mind (Astington, 2001).

A review of studies that used the false-belief task confirmed that a shift in children's performance takes place between 3 and 5 years of age. At 30 months, children were incorrect more than 80 percent of the time, whereas, by 56 months, they were correct about 75 percent of the time (Wellman, Cross & Watson, 2001).

To understand the relationships between themselves and others—an ability known as social cognition—children need to be able not only to take the perspective of another person, but also to consider multiple intersecting perspectives (Harris, 2006). Theory-of-mind researchers use the second-order false-belief task to test this ability (Perner & Wimmer, 1985). They ask children what one person would believe about the beliefs of another person. For example, one research team told children a story in which one person did not know that a second person knew about an object's unexpected change in location. Using the same children from Figure 5.11, the researchers might ask, "Let's ask Sally where Anne thinks the ball is. What will Sally say that Anne thinks?" By around 6 to 7 years of age, most children were able to correctly identify the first person's mistaken belief about the second person's belief (Perner & Wimmer, 1985).

Theory-of-mind research supports the view that young children are less egocentric than Piaget believed they were. In fact, abnormally delayed development of

This is Sally. This is Anne.

Sally has a basket. Anne has a box.

Sally has a ball. She puts the ball into her basket.

Sally goes out for a walk.

Anne takes the ball out of the basket and puts it into the box.

Now Sally comes back. She wants to play with her ball.

Where will Sally look for her ball?

A false-belief task • Figure 5.11

This classic false-belief task enables developmental scientists to study theory of mind in children (Wimmer & Perner, 1983). One little girl (Sally) puts a ball in a basket and then leaves. Another girl, Anne, takes the ball out of the basket and puts it in a box. When Sally returns to play with the ball, where will she look? When 3-year-olds were asked the question, they said that Sally would look in the box. When 4-year-olds were shown the task, they chose the basket. Thus, as children grow older, they appear to understand that others can have beliefs that differ from their own.

theory of mind in childhood may indicate problems in a child's development. For example, children with autism typically do poorly on false-belief tasks, and one researcher believes that inability to understand a theory of mind is a central feature of autism (Baron-Cohen, 1995).

Cross-cultural studies of theory of mind Scholars have argued that the theory of mind is a universal human phenomenon (e.g., Fodor, 1987). Indeed, cross-cultural studies have shown that false beliefs are understood by children living in vastly different cultural settings. For example, at approximately 5 years of age children living in Canada, India, Thailand, Peru, and Samoa were found to understand that people can hold false beliefs (Callaghan et al., 2005). Even though children in some cultures, including the Mofu of northern Cameroon and Tolai from Papua New Guinea, come to understand others' false beliefs later, around 7 years of age, development of theory of mind does appear to be a cross-cultural phenomenon (Vinden, 1999).

Attention Children also improve their ability to direct their attention during the early-childhood years. When presented with a problem like the one shown in **Figure 5.12**, preschool children tend to focus on the most noticeable, or salient, features of the task. Often the salient features are not the ones that would be most helpful in solving the problem. With increasing age, children come to understand that salience is not nearly as important as relevance. They begin to attend appropriately, and their performance on problem-solving tasks improves (Sinson & Wetherick, 1972).

Memory Memory abilities improve during early childhood, too. Preschoolers of all ages are quite good at *recognizing* information that they have seen before. However, younger preschoolers do not do as well as older ones at *recall*—remembering without any cues (Schneider & Pressley, 1997).

Problem solving in early childhood • Figure 5.12

Can you find a jar of honey, a pie, a loaf of bread, and a man's face hidden in this drawing? What did you pay attention to when answering this question? Most likely you looked around carefully at all the tiny elements of the drawing. Preschool children, on the other hand, tend to focus on the most obvious features, such as the woman and the hanging laundry, and fail to solve the problem.

Think Critically Why might it be beneficial or adaptive for young children to focus on the most salient features around them?

Look and Learn/The Bridgeman Art Library

Criticisms of information processing The information-processing perspective seeks to answer some of the fundamental development questions: *How do children represent and process information? How do these representations influence their behaviours? How does this process change across development?* However, information processing theory has been criticized for being too simplistic, for reducing the richness of human cognitive development down to a few underlying mechanisms, such as memory and attention, that can be generalized across time and place (Munakata, 2006). Many cognitive psychologists have countered this simplistic approach by devising theories that can explain individual differences in cognitive development (e.g., Feldman, 1994; Fischer & Bidell, 2006).

As all of these cognitive changes are happening in early childhood, language is also becoming more complex. As they move through early childhood, young children are increasingly able to use words to describe what and how they think about things. In this way, language facilitates children's knowledge of their thought process, even as expanding cognitive capacities, such as memory, contribute to their language development.

Language Development

Early childhood is a time of significant language development, as shown in **Table 5.2**. As children learn new words and rules, they often first use them quite literally. This sets the stage for some creative—and funny—uses of language. For example, when a kindergarten class was learning about marine life, one little girl asked her teacher if electric eels need to be plugged in. Such humorous misunderstandings are understandable, given the intersection of cognitive development coupled with the enormous task of learning an entire language.

How does language develop? Children experience such rapid expansion of their vocabulary during early childhood that developmentalists have a name for the period of most rapid acceleration—a **vocabulary spurt** or **naming explosion** (Li, Zhao, & MacWhinney, 2007). Children go from being able to speak about 500 to 600 words as 2-year-olds to saying over 12,000 words when they start school (MacWhinney, 2002). From infancy, children understand

> **vocabulary spurt** or **naming explosion** The rapid expansion of vocabulary that children experience during early childhood.

Cognitive Development **165**

Language development during early childhood   Table 5.2

Although psychologists have compiled general time frames for language milestones, normal language development can vary greatly from one child to another.

Age	Most children this age . . .
18–30 months	• can understand 100–2,000 words, including many nouns and some verbs • use strategies, such as saying only the first or the accented syllable of a word, to simplify pronunciation • may have difficulty pronouncing some sounds, such as *l* or *r* sounds • use telegraphic sentences (see Chapter 3) and start to ask questions • learn plurals and verbs, but may overgeneralize language rules
30–36 months	• learn new words almost every day • can say up to 1,000 words • combine two or three words • can use the past tense • make exclamations • use possessive • start to observe turn-taking and other rules of conversation • use plurals
3–4 years	• pronounce words more clearly • can say over 1,000 words • use *wh-* questions (*who, what, where, when*) • learn conjunctions, adverbs, and articles • use complete sentences of three to five words
4–5 years	• can understand 3,000 to 10,000 words • can use sentences of 5 to 20 words • can use sentences with dependent clauses and tag questions, such as "aren't we?"
5–6 years	• speak nearly as clearly as most adults • understand about 20,000 words and speak about 2,500–5,000 • can use sentences of any length • can use complex grammar, including passive voice and subjunctive tense • can retell the plots of stories • begin learning to read

more words than they can say. Receptive language skill (the ability to understand words) always precedes expressive language skill (the ability to use words to express ourselves), regardless of the language being learned (Reznick & Goldfield, 1992; Caselli et al., 1995).

During the preschool years, children are also learning grammar, the rules for using words and forming sentences. As they learn the rules of grammar, they often **overgeneralize** them. You might have heard a young child say something like, "I sitted on the bus," or "We runned home." These mistakes occur because the child

> **overgeneralization** Applying the rules of grammar to cases in which they do not apply.
>
> **noun bias** The suggestion that children use nouns more frequently than other parts of speech.

has begun to learn how to use the past tense of verbs but does not yet understand that there are exceptions to grammar rules. By the time school begins, most of these overgeneralizations have disappeared.

Some developmental scientists have reported a **noun bias** in early language development (Goldfield, 2000). They suggest that, since nouns are more easily understood than verbs or adjectives, children use them more frequently and earlier than other parts of speech. Other researchers have challenged this idea. They point out that English-speaking children may have a noun bias, but children around the world do not necessarily follow this pattern. For example, young Mandarin Chinese speakers tend to use verbs more often than nouns (Lee & Naigles, 2005).

One challenge that all new speakers face, regardless of their native language, is how to use language socially. This ability is called **pragmatics**. One example of pragmatics is shown when children speak to peers, as opposed to adults (**Figure 5.13**; Nelson, 2006). Egocentric children tend to have poor pragmatics. Imagine how hard it would be to communicate socially if you thought everyone saw the world exactly as you do. As egocentrism declines and the child gains theory of mind, use of pragmatics improves. Around age 5, children's word choices show greater sensitivity to the fact that others see the world from their own perspectives, and they provide information more clearly and thoroughly (Nelson, 2006).

Explaining language development Given that children need to learn words, grammar rules, *and* the social use of language all in a short time frame, an obvious question developmentalists ask is, How do they do it? One answer may be **categorization**. According

> **pragmatics** The social use of communication.
>
> **categorization** The process of forming a cognitive compartment, or grouping, based on specific properties.

Pragmatics of speech in action • Figure 5.13

Children understand pragmatics at a young age, speaking more politely to adults than to peers.

Think Critically Why is egocentrism related to poor pragmatics?

to Gopnik and Meltzoff (1992), the ability to form categories is one of the fundamental building blocks of language development. Children's earliest categorizations are very broad and draw on physical features they can observe. Features of first categories reflect what we know about young children's reliance on what they can see and understand about the world because they have yet to develop a sense of the internal world of self and others (Oats & Grayson, 2004). For example, once children learn a word such as "dog", they are likely to use the category "dog" to classify all four-legged animals. Children's categories tend to become more abstract at the same time as the vocabulary spurt takes place. This correlation has led developmental scientists to believe that categorization drives early language development (e.g., Gopnik & Meltzoff, 1992).

fast mapping A process by which a child can relate unknown words to known words, thus rapidly expanding vocabulary.

Another process that may explain the rapidity of word learning is **fast mapping**, a process in which children use categories and context as a basis for understanding the meaning of a new word (Carey & Bartlett, 1978), as shown in **Figure 5.14**. Fast mapping is thought to have both biological and cognitive components.

Social and cross-cultural language development

Fast mapping offers a biological explanation of language development based on the work of the famous linguist Noam Chomsky (1965, 1966, 1986). As we discussed in Chapter 3, Chomsky believed that humans have an innate mechanism for processing words, which he called a **language acquisition device (LAD)**. Children internalize the meanings of novel words because they are biologically "prewired" to do so. However, Chomsky has been criticized for his nativist perspective; that is, for his

language acquisition device (LAD) A term coined by linguist Noam Chomsky to describe the innate mechanism for processing words that he believed humans had.

Fast mapping in the real world • Figure 5.14

Even though this little boy has never heard the word "dragonfly" before, he instantly knows what it means. There is nothing else over the water, so a dragonfly must be the flying insect Mom is pointing to. This is an example of fast mapping; he has used his knowledge of word order and syntax to make sense of the unknown word (Lee & Naigles, 2005).

Think Critically Can you think of a time when you used fast mapping to relate unknown words to known words?

Richard Drury/Getty Images

focus on a few innate rules as a universal basis of language development (e.g., Fischer & Bidell, 2006; Horowitz, 2000). Critics argue that Chomsky's theory does not account for the variations found among human languages (Fischer & Bidell, 2006). Everyday communication skills are highly variable across cultures, so how can it be that one's context has no bearing on language development? Such criticisms inspired developmental scientists to consider social influences on fast mapping.

Michael Tomasello (1999, 2003), for example, has proposed a **functional language** approach. He suggests that the "need to understand and explain things motivated language acquisition." That is, children learn language because they have to. They live in a social world in which they hear words, produce words, and are forced to create meaning based on the context in which the words are used. Research showing that the more parents communicate, the bigger their children's receptive and expressive vocabularies tend to be supports the functional language view (Blackwell, 2005). Children whose parents use a lot of words "have to" learn a lot of words.

> **functional language** The idea that language acquisition is a "need-based" process in which children construct meaning out of a need to understand what others are saying and to be understood.

The multilingual environment Canada is a bilingual nation of English and French; however, only the province of New Brunswick is officially bilingual. The vast majority of Canadians, 98 percent, speak at least one of the two official languages; English is the first language for close to 75 percent of the country, while French is the first language for approximately 23 percent of Canadians. In their homes, 17.5 percent of the Canadian population speak more than one language; 11.5 percent report speaking both English and a language other than French (Statistics Canada, 2012). Children who speak more than one language tend to understand words more quickly and have larger vocabularies than their monolingual counterparts (Baker, 2011; Bates, Dale, & Thal, 1995). Bilingualism appears to have some cognitive advantages.

Whether monolingual or multilingual, children have much to learn about language during the early-childhood years: what words mean, how to properly put words together into sentences, and how to use language for social purposes. As we will see in Chapter 6, all three play a role in healthy socio-emotional development.

CONCEPT CHECK

1. **What** are the major hallmarks of symbolic and intuitive thought?
2. **How** could parents use Vygotsky's zone of proximal development to help teach their children new skills?
3. **How** is theory of mind related to Piaget's theory?
4. **What** is involved in the process of "fast mapping"?

All the Systems Working Together

LEARNING OBJECTIVES

1. **Describe** the different types of young children's play.
2. **List** several of the best practices of early-childhood education.
3. **Identify** the effects of childhood overweight and obesity.
4. **Describe** ways to prevent unintentional injuries of young children.
5. **Explain** how lead poisoning affects children's cognitive and physical development.

Although the physical and cognitive systems we just studied appear to have their own, independent developmental sequences, these systems are in fact interdependent. In addition, development of the physical and cognitive systems co-occur with socio-emotional changes. We can observe this interconnectivity by exploring children's play, early-childhood education, and three common health and safety concerns of early childhood: obesity, unintentional injury, and lead poisoning.

Play

Every child has the right to play. The United Nations has even declared that this is so (Hodgkin & Newell, 2007; United Nations Convention on the Rights of the Child, 2007). Obviously, UN resolutions cannot guarantee that every child has opportunities to explore, create, and interact with the world. For this reason, the Canadian Coalition for the Rights of Children has provided leadership in implementing the UN resolution. In its research paper, "Children's Right to Rest, Play, Recreation, Culture and the Arts", the barriers to free play experienced by many young Canadians are described (**Figure 5.15**).

Barriers to free play • Figure 5.15

Think Critically What are some ways to overcome these barriers to free play?

Inti St Clair/Getty Images

a. "Free" time is decreasing for many children due in part to economic requirements for working families and a shift in public policy toward "early education" that fosters parents turning to structured activities and lessons over free play time, not just for school-aged children, but also for preschoolers.

Lapina/Shutterstock

b. Statistics show that children spend an alarming number of hours watching screens of one type or another.

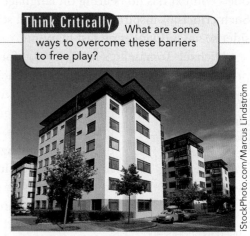
iStockPhoto.com/Marcus Lindström

c. More green space provision for children should be considered by architects, developers, landscape and interior designers, planners, health professionals, teachers, early learning and care providers, coaches, and recreationists.

iStockphoto.com/RiniSlok

d. Increasingly, more children live in cities than in rural settings; however, traffic and land-use patterns have both restricted and diminished the natural play territory of childhood. Open space is reduced, due to competition for urban land and commercial priorities for its use. The built environment, such as town squares and shopping malls, does not always anticipate, plan for, or even permit children playing. Traffic is a serious and increasing hazard in many communities.

Arcaid Images / Alamy Stock Photo

e. Ninety-six percent of major municipalities surveyed in Canada have policies that hinder or limit children's physical activity and recreation, such as bylaws that prohibit skateboarding or road hockey.

Volodymyr Kyrylyuk/Shutterstock

Amy Cicconi / Stockimo / Alamy Stock Photo

f. A national trend of closing schools in both rural and urban settings, due to low enrolments and/or a need to reduce costs, means children are being faced with excessive commutes, and closed schools mean even less access to a vital, community-based resource for play, recreation, sports, and the arts.

g. Fear of abduction and abuse has become one of the threats to children's free play, particularly outdoor play.

Sources: Canadian Coalition for the Rights of Children, 2011, "Children's Right to Rest, Play, Recreation, Culture and the Arts"; Statistics Canada, National Longitudinal Survey of Children and Youth, 1998–1999 and 2002–2003; Health Behaviour in School-Aged Children, World Health Organization Collaborative Cross-National Study, 2005–2006 Survey Report, retrieved from www.hbsc.org/membership/countries/canada.html.

These barriers have evolved along with a rapidly shifting Canadian society (Canadian Coalition for the Rights of Children, 2011). How might the barriers be addressed and how might professionals working on behalf of children be included in design projects? For the barriers, think about how various levels of the community and government might be engaged to create better environments for play.

Why is play so important? And how does it change over time? To answer these questions, we first need to define play. Although play may sound like a simple concept, developmentalists continue to disagree about what child's play is and what it isn't (Jenvey & Jenvey, 2002). Since a consensus has not yet been reached, we will present two competing views of childhood play—one view suggests that play serves social functions and another view emphasizes cognitive functions of play.

In a classic study, researcher Mildred Parten observed children and noted that their age affected the way they played with others (Parten, 1932). Parten described four types of play, categorized by social function, which she believed developed sequentially: **non-social play**, **parallel play**, **associative play**, and **co-operative play**. These are explained in **Figure 5.16**.

Parten's research provided a clear categorization scheme, but other researchers have expressed some criticisms. One concern is that older children actually engage in all of Parten's categories, rather than participating solely in co-operative play (see Scarlett, Naudeau, Slonius-Pasternak, & Ponte, 2005, for a review). In addition, some developmentalists argue that play is better categorized by its cognitive functions than by the social functions that Parten described (Rubin, Fein, & Vandenberg, 1983).

The major cognitive classification of play follows Piaget's theory of cognitive development (Piaget, 1951). This classification, described in **Figure 5.17**, defines four types of play: **functional play**, **constructive play**, **symbolic play**, and games with rules. These types of play parallel Piaget's sensorimotor, preoperational, and concrete operational stages, with constructive and symbolic play often emerging at the same time.

Regardless of the categorization scheme they favour, developmental scholars and educators agree that play has many benefits. Through play, children have the opportunity to simultaneously practise their physical, cognitive, and socio-emotional skills, such as in the case of **rough-and-tumble play** (**Figure 5.18**). Play also serves to release energy, whether mental or physical. It allows children to be creative and imaginative while increasing muscle flexibility, cognitive abilities, and emotional maturity (Ginsburg, 2007). Finally, play facilitates many core personality strengths, including competence, confidence, and resilience (Piaget, 1926b; McArdle, 2001).

Play has been found to be particularly effective when children have no specific adult supervision (see Elkind, 2007). This "undirected play" gives children the opportunity to engage in sharing, negotiation, leadership, and conflict resolution (Barnett, 1990; Hurwitz, 2003). Internationally renowned child psychologist David Elkind has contributed greatly to our understanding of how unscheduled, imaginative play supports both academic and social success. For example, playing with blocks, an opportunity to develop fine-motor skills needed for things like handwriting, also involves concepts such as sameness and difference that underpin mathematics (Elkind, 2007). In turn, through self-initiated dramatic play, children learn social skills, such as co-operation and mutual respect, which are needed for classroom learning. In the context of play, we can see how the various systems—physical, cognitive, and socio-emotional—interact in the service of development.

Undirected play often mimics the adult interactions that children observe. Ideally, those interactions are

non-social play
Non-interactive play in which a child focuses on either an object or a toy and appears unconnected to others, or acts as an onlooker, watching others play without joining in.

parallel play A form of play in which children appear to be together but are not interacting with one another.

associative play A form of play in which children interact and share materials but do not work together toward the same goal.

co-operative play A form of play in which children interact to work toward a common goal.

functional play
A form of play that involves repetitive movements and simple exploratory activity, usually seen during a child's first two years.

constructive play
A form of play that involves the creation of new objects, often by combining already existing objects.

symbolic play
A form of play that begins around 3 years of age in which children use objects as symbols to stand for something else.

rough-and-tumble play A form of physical play, such as wrestling, tumbling, and running.

Parten's social categories of play • Figure 5.16

Ask Yourself

If two girls are sharing the same set of building blocks to build towers but are building separate towers, what type of play are they engaging in?

a. parallel play
b. co-operative play
c. non-social play
d. associative play

Jupiter Images/Getty Images

▲ **a.** Between the ages of 1 and 2 years, play seems to be **non-social**. This can take two forms: **solitary play**, in which the child plays without interacting with others, or **onlooker play**, in which the child watches and comments on others' play but does not join in.

Ekaterina Monakhova/iStockphoto

▲ **b.** As they grow older, children start looking at other children and appear to be comfortable sitting next to them. Parten called this **parallel play**.

Raymond Gehman/NG Image Collection

▲ **c.** Between the ages of 4 and 5, increased interaction occurs between children, although they are not performing a joint activity. Parten called their play **associative**.

Bob Thomas/iStockphoto

▲ **d.** Finally, from age 5 on, we often observe **co-operative play**, in which children work together toward a common goal.

non-violent. However, for children exposed to violence on TV and in books, in their families, or in war-torn nations, undirected play may involve violent themes (**Figure 5.19**).

Regardless of play's specific content, the evidence in support of its importance is overwhelming. Nevertheless, thanks to our high-tech commercialized world and increasingly competitive global economy (Elkind, 2007), time for play, especially undirected play, has been significantly reduced, particularly among school-age children (Barros, Silver, & Stein, 2009). Add to this a practice of discipline by removing recess privileges and

some children even get less time (Ginsburg, 2007). One study found that 96 percent of schools had at least one recess time period in 1989, but just 10 years later, only 70 percent of schools still did (Pellegrini, 2005). The trend away from recess has continued (McMurrer, 2007). This is unfortunate, as a good deal of research links physical activity, such as children playing during recess, to higher academic performance (see Jensen, 2000, for a review; see also Caterino & Polak, 1999; Dwyer et al., 2001; Etnier, 1997). In addition, as we will learn later in this chapter, exercise is a key means of preventing childhood obesity.

Cognitive categories of play • Figure 5.17

Ask Yourself

A child who sings into a hairbrush is demonstrating what cognitive category of play?
a. functional play   **c.** symbolic play
b. constructive play   **d.** games with rules

a. Functional play correlates with Piaget's sensorimotor period, which is why it is often called **practice play** or **sensorimotor play**. In this type of play, infants engage in repetitive actions such as shaking a rattle or clapping hands. The two children in this photo delight in hearing their feet bang against the metal slide, over and over again.

> **practice play** or **sensorimotor play** A type of play with repetitive actions, such as shaking a rattle or clapping hands.

David Alan Harvey/Magnum Photos,Inc.

Ebby May/Getty Images

Image Source/Getty Images

Tomasz Tomaszewski/NG Image Collection

b. Preschoolers often create things through their play, such as forts made out of bedsheets. This is called constructive play, and creative imagination emerges from this kind of play. Constructive play often co-occurs with more structured activities, such as games with rules.

c. Symbolic play, also known as pretend play, emerges as children enter the preoperational stage of cognitive development. In this type of play, objects stand for something else. A tennis racket might become a guitar, as in this photo. More advanced types of symbolic play, with storylines such as playing "house," soon follow (Kavanaugh, 2006).

d. Piaget believed that games with rules appear during the concrete operational stage of development. These games take various forms, from little plastic pieces on a board to several human bodies running around. For example, these South African children have rules for who can and cannot go underneath their "bridge." Rule-based games help children learn co-operation and competition.

Early-Childhood Education

Prior to 1960, the education of young children was seen as the responsibility of parents. Today, the majority of children in Canada between the ages of 3 and 4 attend a centre-based program before entering kindergarten. Centre-based programs, also known as preschools or nursery schools, operate within a variety of contexts—churches, public schools, independent non-profit organizations, for-profits, and **Head Start**. Children may attend these programs for only a couple of hours once or twice per week, or for as many as 10 hours per day seven days a week

(**Figure 5.20**). Aboriginal Head Start programs demonstrate how local projects controlled by First Nations provide preschool children with a positive sense of themselves, a desire for learning, and opportunities to thrive. Aboriginal Head Start projects typically provide structured half-day preschool experiences for First Nations children

> **Head Start** A program that seeks to promote school-readiness among disadvantaged children through the provision of educational, nutritional, and social services. Aboriginal Head Start programs include local control by First Nations and teaching in Aboriginal culture and language.

Rough-and-tumble play • Figure 5.18

Their faces show that these children are not angry when they play at fighting. Rough-and-tumble play may help children develop physical and socio-emotional skills (Pellegrini & Smith, 1998).

Think Critically Why might rough-and-tumble play benefit children's socio-emotional development?

Photo and Co/Photodisc/Getty Images

Gun play • Figure 5.19

Children's play often deals with big and serious issues, such as death, power, and destruction. Gun play and other make-believe violence, a cross-cultural phenomenon, may provide important opportunities to explore these themes (Jones, 2002).

Think Critically What are your personal opinions on gun play?

Ingram Publishing/ Age Fotostock

in six program component areas: Aboriginal culture and language, education, health promotion, nutrition, social support, and parental involvement (Greenwood, 2006).

Effectiveness of early-childhood education As non-parental early-childhood education becomes more commonplace, developmentalists and families alike wonder how these programs affect children's learning and development. Of the many types of early-childhood education, one that has received a great deal of research attention is Head Start (Zigler & Styfco, 2004). Many developmental scholars have found that Head Start enhances children's cognitive ability and social competence (e.g., Zhai, Brooks-Gunn, & Waldfogel, 2011). However, it is unclear how long these benefits last. Some studies have shown that increases in IQ fade out over time, but other studies have demonstrated long-term decreases in special education placements and grade retention, or in being "held back" to repeat a grade in school (see Barnett & Hustedt, 2005, for a review).

A variety of factors affect the success of children enrolled in Head Start programs. One factor is duration

of enrolment, which has been linked to academic outcomes. In a recent study, the majority of children (approximately 80 percent) showed no significant changes in their school-readiness skills over the first year of attendance (McWayne, Hahs-Vaughn, Cheung, & Wright, 2011). The approximately 20 percent of children who did experience a significant change experienced *either* improvements *or* declines in their functioning. But children who entered Head Start at age 3 and stayed for two years showed better academic outcomes than those enrolled later or for less time (Lee, 2011). Benefits were also greatest among children with more family risk factors and when Head Start programs involved parents in the intervention (Starkey & Klein, 2000).

Even those in favour of Head Start agree that there is room for improvement (Mervis, 2011). Research on the effectiveness of Head Start and of other pre-kindergarten centre-based programs has helped scholars to identify a number of best practices in early-childhood education that may help improve children's outcomes.

Inclusive early-childhood education Best practices in early-childhood education (ECE) support learning and development in *all* children, including those with widely varying developmental needs. In Canada, early-childhood education services are provincially and territorially fragmented (Underwood, Valeo, & Wood,

Best practices in early-childhood education • Figure 5.20

A review of research on early-childhood education recommends taking the following steps for program success (Barnett, 2002).

a. Keep class sizes small and child–teacher ratios low.

c. Make parents active partners in their children's education.

Think Critically Are there other "best practices" that you would add to this list?

b. Develop comprehensive curricula that address children's interrelated developmental needs—emotional, social, cognitive, and physical.

2012). Generally, the commitment among governments has been to deinstitutionalize children with various developmental needs and to integrate them into community settings. In 2000, the Agreement on Early Childhood Development Initiatives was signed by the federal government and provincial/territorial governments, except Quebec. The agreement acknowledged the need for all levels of government to work together to support Canadian families (Uppal, Khan, & Visentin, 2010). Across the provinces and territories, publicly funded ECE programs generally incorporate a commitment to

> **inclusion** An approach to educating students with special educational needs based on the idea that all individuals have a right to be educated in regular classroom settings.

inclusion; children with special needs involved in mainstream programs are to be integrated to the fullest extent possible (Human Resources and Skills Development Canada, 2010).

In recent years, support for the inclusion of children with **autism spectrum disorder (ASD)**, as well as other special needs, in regular educational settings has become widespread. Children with ASD experience impaired social communication and interaction, such as responding inappropriately in conversations and misreading non-verbal cues (American Psychiatric Association, 2013).

> **autism spectrum disorder (ASD)** A neurodevelopmental disorder characterized by impaired social communication and interaction, and repetitive behaviours.

These children also have restricted and repetitive behaviour, interests, and activities. The prevalence of ASD has increased over the past two to three decades; approximately 1 in 94 Canadian children are diagnosed with ASD (Ghali et al., 2014). Each person with an ASD is unique and will have different abilities (Autism Society Canada, 2014) so that the symptoms may be quite mild in one person and severe in another. Early detection and intervention can improve the cognitive outcomes and adaptive behaviour of children diagnosed with ASD (Dawson et al., 2010). Early diagnosis also helps educators develop **individualized education programs** based on each child's specific needs and strengths.

individualized education program
A written statement that defines the individualized educational goals of a child with a disability.

As these disorders are demystified, more and more families are advocating for the right of their children with ASD to be educated in regular classroom settings (Bauer & Shea, 2003). Philosophical and political support for the inclusion of children with ASD is strong (Ferraioli & Harris, 2011), but only a modest body of research about the effective inclusion of children with ASD currently exists.

Nevertheless, it points to some potential benefits of inclusion. Children with ASD in inclusive preschool programs make significant gains in language skills, social interaction skills, play skills, and IQ (Harris et al., 1991; Stahmer & Ingersoll, 2004; Whitaker, 2004).

Many of the best practices listed in Figure 5.20 are applicable to children with ASD. In addition, teachers can help these children by creating predictable routines and structured learning environments, and by teaching peers how to effectively interact with children with ASD (Wetherby & Prizant, 1999). Some parents worry that including children with special needs will make early-childhood education less effective for everyone. Research suggests, however, that inclusion does not harm the social and academic outcomes of typically developing peers and may actually promote them (**Figure 5.21**). As inclusive classrooms become the norm, early-childhood educators will need to expand their skill sets in order to ensure that all children receive the effective support and education they deserve.

In addition to effective early-childhood education, scientific findings indicate that children thrive when they have access to healthy foods and exercise and when they have the opportunity to learn and grow in safe contexts that are free of harmful toxins and the risk of

Inclusive classrooms • Figure 5.21

In one study of 19 inclusive education programs, typically developing children demonstrated positive social-emotional growth and made the same academic gains as students in non-inclusive classrooms (Hunt & Goetz, 1997).

Robin Nelson/PhotoEdit

Put It Together *Review the figure on best practices in early-childhood education and answer the following question:* What best practices do you think are important in inclusive classrooms?

unintentional injury. We now turn to some common health risks of early childhood. Families, policy-makers, and educators alike play a key role in addressing these common health and safety concerns.

Common Health and Safety Concerns of Early Childhood

Obesity, unintentional injury, and lead poisoning undermine health at all stages of the lifespan. However, the prevalence of these health concerns during early childhood is of note. We turn first to the issue of obesity.

Obesity

Obesity in childhood has become a global epidemic (Wang & Lobstein, 2006), as well as a major concern in Canada (**Table 5.3**). About 22 percent of Canadian children aged 2 to 5 years are considered **overweight** or **obese** (Booth et al., 2000) according to their **body mass index (BMI)**. For the most recent Canadian Community Health Survey, BMI was derived using the formula BMI = (weight in kg)/(height in m). Calculating overweight and obesity in children and adolescents is different from establishing adult cut-offs because it is not clear which BMI levels are associated with health risks at younger ages. The most recent Canadian statistics have attempted to correct for this challenge by using the International Obesity Task Force's new approach to measuring overweight and obesity among children and adolescents (Cole, Bellizzi, Flegal, & Dietz, 2000). Overweight cut-offs for children ages 2 to 6 vary by sex. For males, BMI cut-off starts at a high of 18.41 at age 2, systematically decreases to 17.42 at age 5, then incrementally goes up to 17.55 at age 6. For females, BMI cut-off starts at 18.02 at age 2 to a low of 17.15 at age 5, to 17.34 at age 6. The obese cut-off for BMI also varies according to sex and age: males are classified as obese if at age 2 the BMI is equal to or greater than 20.09, and this systematically decreases to 19.26 at age 4.5 and rises to 19.78 at age 6; the female BMI obese cut-off ranges from 19.81 at age 2 to a low of 19.12 to

> **overweight** or **obesity** A classification based on the association of various BMI cut-offs with health risks; varies in children by age and sex.
>
> **body mass index (BMI)** A measure used to determine healthy body weight that is calculated by dividing a person's weight (in kilograms) by the square of their height (in metres) BMI = weight(kg)/height²(m)²

19.65 at age 6. Why do you think the cut-offs for children vary by age and sex?

Many factors contribute to childhood obesity, and factors vary from one child to the next. Genetic predisposition and a sedentary lifestyle contribute to childhood obesity. Recent studies have looked at the association between exposure to unhealthy foods, such as sugary breakfast cereals, that are developed and marketed directly to children, and rates of childhood obesity. Researchers have found that the average preschooler today sees 642 ads for such foods each year, with the most heavily marketed cereals being the least healthy ones (Harris, Thompson, Schwartz, & Brownell, 2011). In addition, advertising influences how much children eat. In one study, children who watched a show that contained food commercials ate 45 percent more snacks than did those who watched an ad-free show (Harris, Bargh, & Brownell, 2009).

Overweight children are at higher risk than normal-weight children for psychological problems, including depression, low self-esteem, being bullied, and dysfunctional social skills (Daniels, 2006). Further, poor nutrition and being overweight in early childhood are health risk factors known to be associated with the chronic diseases of adulthood, including heart disease, osteoporosis, diabetes, impaired liver function, and asthma (Burrowes, 2007). Before 1990, diet-related type 2 diabetes was rarely seen in children. But with obesity rates on the rise, we have seen an increase in the number of children diagnosed with this disease (Centers for Disease Control and Prevention, 2013). The Canadian Diabetes Association (CDA, 2015) provides recommendations for healthy living intended to help Canadians reduce the risk of developing type 2 diabetes. The CDA states that moderate weight loss and regular physical activity can reduce the risk of type 2 diabetes by more than 50 percent. It recommends simple lifestyle changes that can make a big difference in health:

- Switch from regular pop to sugar-free pop or water.
- Switch to lower-fat dairy products, such as 1 percent or skim milk.
- Offer children healthy snack choices, such as fresh fruits and cut-up veggies.
- Model healthy eating and activity habits for your children.
- Leave the car at home; walk or bike whenever possible.
- Gradually reduce screen time (such as watching television and using computers) and replace it with active play time. Try a family walk after dinner.

Childhood obesity rates over time   Table 5.3

The percentage of children in Canada classified as overweight or obese has been increasing in recent decades. Although young children are not experiencing as sharp an increase as older children and adolescents, the early-childhood years set the stage for later eating and exercise habits.

Ask Yourself

1. BMI is calculated using weight and _____.
2. Girls under age 6 with a BMI of 18.05 would be classified as _____.
3. Boys under age 6 with a BMI of 20.1 would be classified as _____.
4. What are some ways to encourage children to develop appropriate eating and exercise habits?

		Overweight		Obese		Overweight/Obese	
	Estimated population '000	%	95% confidence interval[d]	%	95% confidence interval	%	95% confidence interval
Total	6,184	18.1	16.8, 19.3	8.2	7.3, 9.1	26.2	24.8, 27.7
Sex							
Boys[a]	3,178	17.9	16.0, 19.8	9.1	7.7, 10.5	27.0	24.6, 29.3
Girls	3,007	18.3	16.4, 20.1	7.2	6.1, 8.4	25.5	23.4, 27.6
Age group							
Total 2–5	1,348	15.2	12.3, 18.0	6.3	4.6, 8.0	21.5	18.3, 24.6
Boys[a]	684	13.1	9.4, 16.9	6.3[b]	3.9, 8.6	19.4	15.0, 23.7
Girls	664	17.3	12.9, 21.6	6.4[b]	4.0, 8.8	23.6	19.1, 28.2
Total 6–11	2,321	17.9	15.8, 19.9	8.0	6.4, 9.6	25.8[c]	23.4, 28.3
Boys[a]	1,173	17.0	13.9, 20.0	8.5	6.0, 11.0	25.4	21.6, 29.2
Girls	1,148	18.8	15.9, 21.6	7.5	5.2, 9.8	26.3	22.8, 29.8
Total 12–17	2,515	19.8	17.8, 21.8	9.4	7.9, 10.9	29.2	26.9, 31.5
Boys[a]	1,320	21.1	18.3, 24.0	11.1	8.8, 13.4	32.3	28.9, 35.6
Girls	1,195	18.3	15.6, 21.0	7.4[c]	5.6, 9.3	25.8[c]	22.6, 28.9

[a] Reference group

[b] Coefficient of variation between 16.6% and 33.3% (interpret with caution)

[c] Significantly different from estimate for reference group (p < 0.05)

[d] Confidence Interval is the range of values within which a particular measure for the group is likely to fall. For example, in this table the total percentage of overweight-classed people is 18.1% but this measurement can vary reliably between 16.8 % and 19.3%. Thus confidence intervals give you a clearer sense of how much a group varies on particular measures.

Source: Margot Shields, *Measured Obesity: Overweight Canadian Children and Adolescents* (Table 1, page 33, Statistics Canada, 2004), retrieved from www.statcan.gc.ca/pub/82-620-m/2005001/pdf/4193660-eng.pdf.

- Follow Health Canada's *Eating Well with Canada's Food Guide* as explored in this chapter's *Where Developmentalists Click* and the *Canadian Physical Activity and Sedentary Behaviour Guidelines* from the Canadian Society for Exercise Physiology.

Clearly a first step in prevention is *diet*. Researchers from areas as diverse as public health, neurobiology, and psychology have begun to reach a consensus that food choices are more important than exercise in losing weight (Cloud, 2009). Why? One answer comes from a study of Boston-area adolescents: The more the students exercised, the more they ate. In fact, they ate about 100 calories more than they burned (Sonneville & Gortmaker, 2008). Unfortunately, the eating habits of children in Canada are often well outside the parameters of what could

Factors affecting the physical activity of children and youth • Figure 5.22

Patrick Foto/Shutterstock

Monkey Business Images/Shutterstock

Realistic Reflections/Getty Images

▲ **Physical Activity Levels**
- Active transportation
- Organized sport and physical activity participation
- Active play and leisure

▲ **Influences**
- School
- Family and peers
- Community and built environment policy

▲ **Individual Characteristics**
- Disability
- Ethnicity
- Race
- Urban/rural living
- Socio-economic status
- Gender
- Age

Kyle Lee/Shutterstock

◀ **Outcomes**
- Mental health
- Body weight
- Physical health
- Academic performance
- Skill development
- Physical literacy
- Fun

Corepics VOF/Shutterstock

Ask Yourself

What do you notice about the role of the environment in prevention?

◀ **Sedentary Behaviour**
- Screen-based sedentary behaviours
- Non-screen-based sedentary behaviours

Source: 2012 Active Healthy Kids Canada Report Card on Physical Activity for Children and Youth.

---

be considered a healthy diet (Taylor, Evers, & McKenna, 2005).

Another key method of prevention is *activity*. Along with emerging evidence about the importance of healthy eating habits in the struggle against being overweight or obese, exercise certainly has its place. A combination of healthy eating and physical activity seems to be the most powerful approach. **Figure 5.22** illustrates the many factors that affect the physical activity of children and youth.

A valuable preventive element is the *family*. Through observational learning, children come to value certain foods and decide about the importance (or lack of importance) of physical activity. Thus, parents and other family members should educate themselves about proper nutrition, learn about healthy food preparation, and model healthy exercise habits (Klesges, 1984).

Obesity across cultures Socio-economic status is also related to children's risk of being

socio-economic status The combination of a person's income, education, and occupation relative to others.

unintentional injury Any type of physical trauma that is determined to have been caused by circumstances other than abuse or maltreatment.

overweight or obese. Canadian researchers have found that children in low-income families may be at higher risk for experiencing childhood obesity (Dutton & McLaren, 2011), and have observed that the socio-economic conditions under which a family lives can constrain the availability of healthy food choices (Willows, Hanley, & Delormier, 2012). This relationship was also found among Russian children. In China, however, high-income children were at the greatest risk of becoming obese (Wang, 2001). Such variation within and across cultures underscores the powerful influence of social and environmental factors on childhood obesity.

Unintentional injury Just as children's families can play a key role in preventing childhood obesity, they are also vital in preventing and treating injury and illness. **Unintentional injuries** are the leading cause of death in children and adolescents in Canada and a major cause of morbidity (Yanchar, Warda, & Fuselli, 2012). It is the fourth leading cause of hospitalization of children between the ages of 1 and 4

Health Canada

Health Canada has created an extensive nutrition resource for citizens and educators alike on its website. The site has a section for First Nations Inuit, and Métis that includes traditional foods as well as store-bought foods found in rural or remote locations in Canada. The website's interactive environment includes a mobile app section and provides healthy eating and activity guidelines. To create a personalized food guide, select an age and sex category, and then select the various foods you eat in each of the four food groups. Next, select the kinds of activities you enjoy. What results is an individualized set of recommendations.

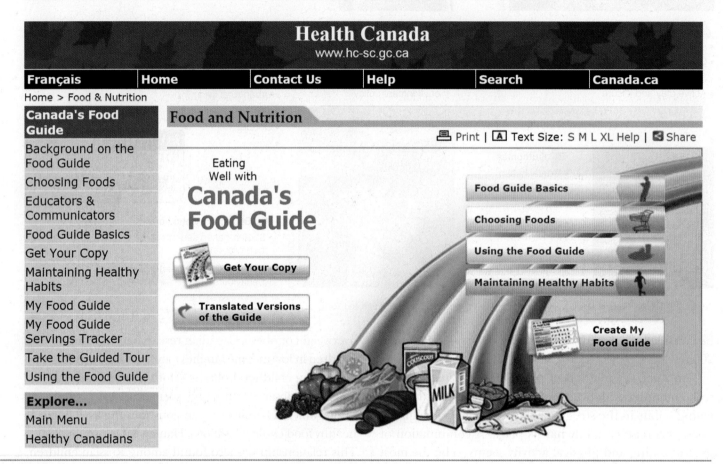

(360 per 100,000), and almost 25 percent of all deaths of children in this age range are due to injury (Public Health Agency of Canada, 2008b). Evidence has shown that these injuries are not the "accidents" we tend to dismiss as unlucky or unfortunate, but predictable events that are frequently preventable (Rivara & Grossman, 1996). Assessing the most effective injury prevention strategies requires an understanding of the factors that contribute to both injury occurrence and compliance with injury prevention measures (e.g., use of seat belts, booster car-seats, and bicycle helmets). The significance of the evidence regarding these factors and any resulting policy decisions is becoming more apparent as injury control practitioners debate whether injury prevention programming should target a whole population or be adapted for a specific population of interest, such as "high-risk" groups. As this debate heats up, the need for a clearer understanding increases. The link between economic prosperity and child health is very well established (Reading, 1997). In 1991, 18 percent of Canadian children under the age of 18 were living in poverty, and those living in the poorest income areas were at the greatest risk of dying from injuries (Canadian Institute of Child Health, 1994). This link remains apparent in Canada; low-income children continue to be more likely to die as a result of unintentional injuries (Canadian Paediatric Society, 2009).

CHALLENGES IN DEVELOPMENT
Unintentional Injury

Three-year-old Marcus plays quietly by himself while his Aunt Loretta makes dinner. Suddenly she hears a loud bang. She rushes into the living room and finds Marcus sprawled on the floor with one arm askew. He appears to have been playing on the staircase and fallen. Like many children his age, Marcus will be rushed to the hospital with an unintentional injury. Although Marcus may emerge with little more than a cast, many of his peers are not so fortunate.

The single best way to reduce the rate of unintentional injuries is through prevention. The Public Health Agency of Canada is working to decrease the incidence of death and hospitalizations among children through the development of resources for parents, teachers, and care workers. Its website addresses a number of factors in accident prevention. It provides resources for assessing safety in the home, in play spaces, and while transporting children, and addressing farm safety and environmental health issues. It has a special section on emergency preparedness, and provides specific fire and water safety tips. The agency's work also includes creating safe and healthy media images, conducting research on making communities safer, and finding better ways to prevent injuries.

The health and well-being of children depends on the safety and quality of their homes, schools, and communities. Research by King and colleagues (2001) has shown that home visits by injury prevention experts, such as trained nurses, can reduce injury rates. During a home visit, the expert focuses on five key issues: (1) parental knowledge of what causes injury; (2) potential hazards in the home; (3) the presence or absence of safety items, such as smoke detectors, in the home; (4) the number of injuries that have occurred in the home to date; and (5) the cost effectiveness of instituting prevention (King et al., 2001).

Of course, no amount of precaution can prevent all injuries. With supervision, however, children can be given vital opportunities to explore while being kept as safe as possible.

Think Critically This child is about to suffer an unintentional injury. How could this accident be prevented? During an injury prevention home visit, one issue focused on is the cost of instituting prevention. What would you see as key challenges in conducting this assessment?

Lead poisoning Another health concern of early childhood is exposure to toxins, such as lead, that damage brain neurons. Often called the silent epidemic, lead poisoning among children has been a major public health concern for almost half a century. Although health officials linked lead-based paint to lead poisoning around the beginning of the twentieth century, the use of lead-based household paint was not regulated in Canada until 1976, and many homes built prior to that time still harbour old, lead-based paint. In October 2010, the federal government amended the Surface Coating Materials Regulations to significantly lower the level of total lead allowed in paints and other surface coating materials to a concentration of 0.009

percent. This Canadian lead limit is among the strictest in the world (O'Grady & Perron, 2011).

Although severe poisonings leading to seizures, coma, mental retardation, and death are rare these days, many young children today are exposed to lead levels that result in cognitive damage, learning disabilities, and attention-deficit hyperactivity disorder (Bellinger, Stiles, & Needleman, 1992; Braun et al., 2006; Lanphear et al., 2005). In addition to affecting the cognitive system, lead exposure can lead to physical deficits, such as poor gross- and fine-motor coordination (Dietrich, Succop, & Berger, 1993), as well as social and emotional problems (Burns et al., 1999).

WHAT A DEVELOPMENTALIST SEES
Preventing Injuries at Home

Bed railings can prevent active sleepers from falling out of tall beds.

Young children become interested in constructive play. Their paints, crayons, markers, and other art supplies should be nontoxic, in case a curious child wonders how they taste. Adults should help children cut things, such as the cardboard to make this spaceship.

Symbolic or pretend play is important in early childhood. Dress-up clothing should not present choking hazards or obstruct vision the way these clothes do.

As children's language skills grow, they love to look at books. Bookshelves and dressers should be attached to walls so that

they will not topple if a child tries to climb or play on them.

Electrical sockets should have safety plugs. A child at play could stick items into the socket and be electrocuted or cause a fire.

Second-floor and higher windows should have locks that prevent children from opening them wide enough to fall through.

Cords for blinds and hanging draperies should be secured out of reach of small children, who can get tangled in them and choke.

Tall lamps can fall and injure children. Also, lamp cords should be in good condition (not frayed or torn) in order to avoid fire or electrocution.

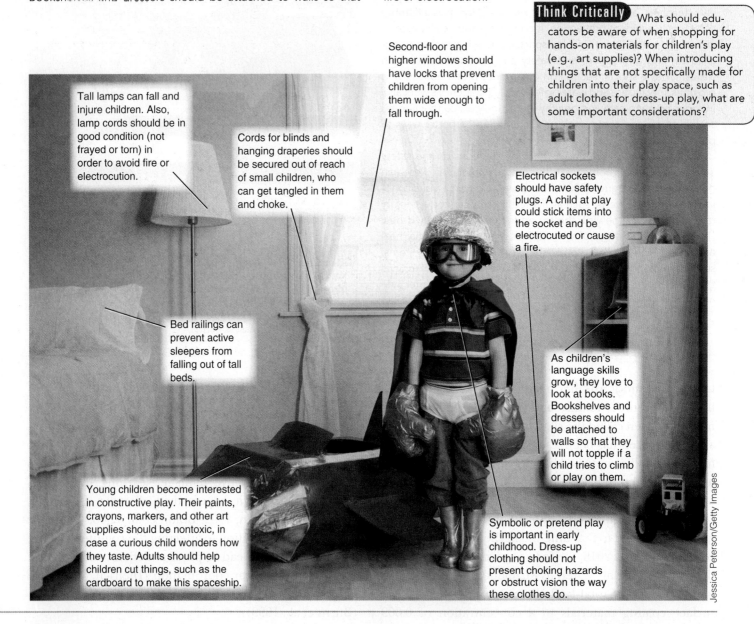

Think Critically What should educators be aware of when shopping for hands-on materials for children's play (e.g., art supplies)? When introducing things that are not specifically made for children into their play space, such as adult clothes for dress-up play, what are some important considerations?

Tall lamps can fall and injure children. Also, lamp cords should be in good condition (not frayed or torn) in order to avoid fire or electrocution.

Cords for blinds and hanging draperies should be secured out of reach of small children, who can get tangled in them and choke.

Second-floor and higher windows should have locks that prevent children from opening them wide enough to fall through.

Electrical sockets should have safety plugs. A child at play could stick items into the socket and be electrocuted or cause a fire.

Bed railings can prevent active sleepers from falling out of tall beds.

As children's language skills grow, they love to look at books. Bookshelves and dressers should be attached to walls so that they will not topple if a child tries to climb or play on them.

Young children become interested in constructive play. Their paints, crayons, markers, and other art supplies should be nontoxic, in case a curious child wonders how they taste. Adults should help children cut things, such as the cardboard to make this spaceship.

Symbolic or pretend play is important in early childhood. Dress-up clothing should not present choking hazards or obstruct vision the way these clothes do.

Jessica Peterson/Getty Images

What makes child lead poisoning especially frightening is that the effects appear to be irreversible. Researchers have found a treatment that successfully lowered children's blood lead levels, but they have been unable to reduce the cognitive, behavioural, and neuropsychological damage caused by lead exposure (Rogan et al., 2001).

Unless work is carried out with caution, renovating older homes containing lead-based paint can produce fine dusts, fumes, and paint chips that children—and adults—can ingest or inhale (Marino et al., 1990). Unfortunately, many families are unaware of the dangers of lead poisoning. It is vital, then, that practitioners educate families about the dangers of lead, its sources and means of absorption, and precautions necessary to prevent exposure.

CONCEPT CHECK

1. **What** are the two major categorization schemes for play, and **how** do they group the various types of play?

2. **What** are the benefits of inclusive early-childhood education?

3. **How** might being overweight or obese affect a child?

4. **Why** is injury prevention particularly important during early childhood compared with other segments of the lifespan?

5. **What** is the main source of lead poisoning today?

Summary

1 Physical Development 152

- **Synaptic pruning** continues throughout life but slows after infancy, beginning in the preschool years. Young children's brains grow as a result of increases in dendrites and continuing **myelination**. These processes enable young children to perform more complex and faster thinking and actions than they could as infants.

Myelination of the cerebellum • Figure 5.2

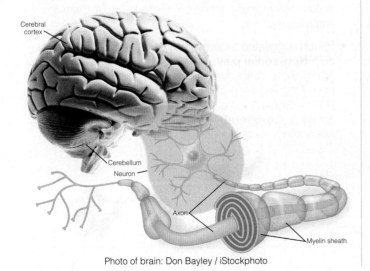

Photo of brain: Don Bayley / iStockphoto

- The brain hemispheres continue **lateralization**, which leads to hand preference, or **handedness**.

- All children's bones grow longer, wider, and thicker during childhood, although individual children's bone growth may vary greatly due to both genes and environmental influences, such as nutrition. Physicians can use measures of **ossification** to determine bone maturation and predict a child's adult height.

- Slow and steady growth of muscles leads to increasingly coordinated gross- and fine-motor skills.

2 Cognitive Development 157

- Piaget suggested that the second stage of cognitive development, the **preoperational stage**, is divided into two substages. In the first substage, **symbolic function**, children use symbols in play and thought, as shown here. **Intuitive thought** follows as the child begins to think about how the world works.

An example of symbolic thinking • Figure 5.4

Dan Bellack

- Piaget identified several cognitive qualities of preoperational thinking, including **centration** and **irreversibility**, which he demonstrated through tests of children's **conservation** abilities.

- Other cognitive qualities identified by Piaget included **egocentrism**, **animism**, and **artificialism**. More recent researchers have suggested that Piaget underestimated young children's thinking abilities and that the processes of cognitive development he described may not be demonstrated universally across cultures.

- In contrast to Piaget, Vygotsky emphasized the importance of a child's social environment. Vygotsky suggested that **guided participation** and **scaffolding** by more experienced thinkers can help children accomplish tasks in their **zone of proximal development**.

- Vygotsky also emphasized the importance of language, including **private speech**, in cognitive development. Although Piaget, who described a **collective monologue**,

and some subsequent researchers, disagreed, suggesting that private talk is egocentric, research results tend to support Vygotsky's view.

- Young children's developing **theory of mind** also suggests that their thinking is less egocentric than Piaget believed. Researchers who take an information-processing approach have also noted gradual improvements in young children's memory abilities and their ability to pay attention to less salient features of problems.

- Children's vocabularies increase dramatically during early childhood. **Categorization** abilities and **fast mapping** may contribute to the **vocabulary spurt**, also known as a **naming explosion**. At the same time, children are learning language rules, and they may **overgeneralize** them at first. Some researchers report a **noun bias** in early childhood. Children also come to understand the social functions, or **pragmatics**, of language as they age. Learning two or more languages can give children cognitive advantages, but it is best if the languages are learned simultaneously rather than one at a time.

- Fast mapping offers a biological explanation of language development based on the work of the famous linguist Noam Chomsky, who believed that humans have an innate mechanism for processing words, which he called a language acquisition device (LAD). Critics supporting a functional language approach argue that children learn language because they live in a social world that requires it.

3 All the Systems Working Together 169

- Play is an essential part of the preschool years and has many physical, cognitive, and socio-emotional benefits for children, particularly when they are allowed to direct their own play. Unfortunately, many schools in Canada are decreasing unstructured time.

- Parten suggested a developmental sequence of types of play. **Non-social play**, in which a child is absorbed in play with objects, precedes **parallel play**, in which two children play alongside each other. **Associative play** develops as children interact more, though still engaging in their own activities. **Co-operative play** follows, in which children interact in pursuit of a common goal.

Parten's social categories of play • Figure 5.16

Raymond Gehman/NG Image Collection

- Other researchers point out that older children engage in all of Parten's types of play, and suggest, instead, a cognitive classification of types of play, ranging from the least cognitively complex, **functional play**, through **symbolic play** and **constructive play**. Another form of identified play is rough-and-tumble-play—a form of physical play, such as wrestling, tumbling, and running.

- Today, many Canadian children between the ages of 3 and 4 attend centre-based programs, also known as preschools or nursery schools. One such program, **Head Start**, seeks to promote school-readiness among disadvantaged children through the provision of educational, nutritional, and social services.

- **Autism spectrum disorder (ASD)** is characterized by impaired social communication and interaction, and restricted and repetitive behaviour, interests, and activities. Support for the **inclusion** of children with ASD in regular educational settings has recently become widespread. Early diagnosis also helps educators develop **individualized education programs** based on each child's specific needs and strengths. A small body of research suggests that inclusion appears to benefit both children with ASD and their typically developing peers.

- Childhood body weight issues, such as being **overweight** or struggling with **obesity** as defined by the **body mass index**, represent a major health concern in Canada.

- Several health risks, including type 2 diabetes, are associated with being overweight. Overweight children are also at risk of depression, low self-esteem, and poor social skills. Medical professionals recommend preventing obesity through a healthy diet and physical exercise.

- **Unintentional injury** is the leading cause of death among preschool children, and is associated with the **socio-economic status** of a child's family. Eliminating common hazards in children's home environments can help prevent some injuries.

- Exposure to **toxins** or poisonous substances during early childhood illustrates the complex interaction between genetic and environmental factors. For example, **lead poisoning** is an environmental factor that interacts with genes to produce cognitive deficits in children.

Key Terms

- animism 158
- artificialism 161
- associative play 171
- autism spectrum disorder (ASD) 175
- body mass index (BMI) 177
- categorization 167
- centration 158
- collective monologue 162
- conservation 158
- constructive play 171
- co-operative play 171
- egocentrism 158
- fast mapping 168
- functional language 169
- functional play 171
- guided participation 161
- handedness 154
- Head Start 173

- inclusion 175
- individualized education program 176
- intuitive thought 157
- irreversibility 160
- language acquisition device (LAD) 168
- lateralization 154
- lead poisoning 154
- myelination 153
- naming explosion 165
- non-social play 171
- noun bias 167
- obesity 177
- object permanence 157
- ossification 155
- overgeneralization 167
- overweight 177
- parallel play 171
- practice play 173

- pragmatics 167
- preoperational stage 157
- private speech 161
- rough-and-tumble play 171
- scaffolding 161
- sensorimotor play 173
- socio-economic status 179
- symbolic function 157
- symbolic play 171
- synapses 153
- synaptic pruning 153
- theory of mind 163
- toxin 154
- unintentional injury 179
- vocabulary spurt 165
- zone of proximal development (ZPD) 161

Critical and Creative Thinking Questions

1. What are the various factors involved in the development of handedness?

2. Have you noticed any of the cognitive qualities of preoperational thinking, such as animism or centration, among your peers? How, if at all, do they differ from those displayed by young children?

3. How have you used your theory of mind today?

4. What advice would you give to parents who want to improve their young child's language skills? What would you tell them if they were interested in teaching the child two languages?

5. How much has play changed since you were a child? What types of play activities that were prevalent in your youth do you no longer see?

6. Look around the room you are in now. What hazards might it present for a curious, active preschooler? How could those hazards be reduced?

What is happening in this picture?

This child may be having more fun than Santa is during this visit. According to Piaget, what does this child probably believe about Santa Claus?

Joel Sartore/National Geographic Creative

Think Critically

1. Pulling off Santa's hat seems to be fun for this boy. Which of Parten's categories of play might this represent? Which cognitive category of play might it represent?

2. Does this boy seem to be left-handed or right-handed? What brain developments are related to his hand preference?

3. Does this child realize that Santa cannot see when his hat is pulled over his eyes?

4. What are some new words that a child might learn through fast mapping during a trip to visit Santa?

REAL  Development

Physical Development and Health in Early Childhood

In these video activities, you will observe preschoolers' physical and cognitive development.

In the first activity, you are the new director of a preschool. One of your first initiatives concerns nutrition. Using the charts provided, you will compare the body mass index of children in your school with a nationally representative sample.

In the second and third activities, you are an assistant teacher at a preschool. One of your responsibilities is to evaluate your students' readiness to enter kindergarten. As you know, children undergo a number of changes during the preschool years related to motor and cognitive development. Your task is to determine whether your students are developing at normal rates. In the second activity, you have designed a series of activities to identify students' fine and gross motor skills, and you will assess their development based on these activities. In the third activity, you will help the teacher evaluate students' thinking and reasoning skills.

WileyPLUS Go to WileyPLUS to complete the REAL Development activity.

03.01

Self-Test

(Check your answers in Appendix A.)

1. Myelination of the _____, shown here, helps the two halves of the brain work together, improving young children's coordination and speed.

   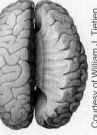

   Courtesy of William J. Tietjen, Ph.D., Bellarmine University

   a. anterior cerebellum

   b. bilateral bifurcatum

   c. corpus callosum

   d. diencephalon divider

2. A preference for the left or right hand occurs as a result of brain hemisphere _____.

   a. fibre complexity

   b. lateralization

   c. diffusion

   d. compartmentalization

3. Doctors can use X-rays of areas of cartilage that will turn into bone to determine a child's _____.

   a. skeletal age

   b. gross-motor stability

   c. bone myelination rate

   d. dominant gross-motor hemisphere

4. A child who believes that everyone feels the same way he or she does is exhibiting _____.

   a. animism

   b. centration

   c. egocentrism

   d. overregularization

5. Inability to understand that even after a balloon is blown up it can still return to its original shape when the air is let out is an example of which of the following?

   a. irreversibility

   b. decentration

   c. operationality

   d. overcompensation

6. Vygotsky referred to the range of tasks shown on this graph, which a child cannot perform alone but can accomplish with help, as the _____.

a. zone of private talk

b. guided participatory zone

c. zone of proximal development

d. scaffolding assistance zone

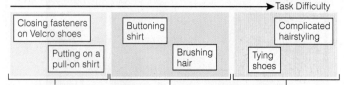

7. As shown here, Anne moves the ball her friend Sally put into the basket. A child who believes that Sally will come back and look for the ball in the box has not yet developed _____.

a. false beliefs

b. a theory of mind

c. information processing

d. a collective monologue

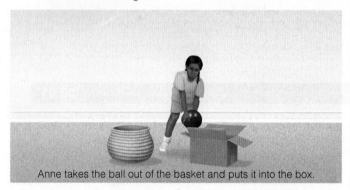

Anne takes the ball out of the basket and puts it into the box.

8. When 6-year-old Mei wants to make sure her 3-year-old brother, Jian, understands something, she speaks more slowly, in a higher-pitched voice than usual, and repeats herself more often than she would with her friends. Mei's use of child-directed speech with Jian shows her growing grasp of _____.

a. pragmatics

b. egocentrism

c. monolingualism

d. syntactic bootstrapping

9. The child shown above right learns the word "dragonfly" through the process of _____.

a. regularizing

b. fast mapping

c. conditioning

d. telegraphing

Richard Drury/Getty Images

10. According to Parten's development categories, the type of play that occurs when two children work together to build a sand castle is _____.

a. non-social play

b. parallel play

c. associative play

d. co-operative play

11. Which type of cognitive play is this?

a. functional play

b. symbolic play

c. constructive play

d. games with rules

Dan Bellack

12. Rough-and-tumble play includes _____.

    a. running

    b. wrestling

    c. tumbling

    d. all of these

13. The measure used to determine whether a child is obese or overweight is his or her _____.

    a. weight

    b. body mass index

    c. coronary functioning

    d. daily calorie consumption

14. Which of the following is most important in preventing obesity?

    a. activity

    b. family

    c. genes

    d. diet

15. The leading cause of death of preschool children in Canada is _____.

    a. cancer

    b. suicide

    c. SIDS

    d. unintentional injury

16. What systems of development can be damaged through lead exposure?

    a. physical

    b. cognitive

    c. social/emotional

    d. all of these

THE PLANNER ✓

Review your Chapter Planner in the chapter opener and check off your completed work.

Socio-emotional Development in Early Childhood: Two to Six Years

People often comment on all the ways in which twins Hayley and Harper Cash differ. Hayley is outgoing and personable, ready to strike up a conversation with just about anyone. Harper, on the other hand, is quiet and shy. During a preschool parent showcase, Hayley is eager and ready to perform in full view of everyone while Harper hangs back and hesitates to take the stage. Why are Hayley and Harper—two children born at the same time, from the same womb, and raised in the same household—so different?

For one thing, there are major genetic differences between them: The girls are fraternal twins. Yet even if Hayley and Harper were identical twins, we should not be surprised to see substantial differences in their personalities. Nature and nurture interact to produce unique individual personalities, differing even between twins.

In this chapter we will explore the aspects that developmental theorists believe form the core of our personalities. We will also consider the roles that parenting styles, non-parental child care, media, gender, culture, and other environmental factors play in shaping who we are. Finally, we will take a look at how we each develop our own "emotion vocabulary" and learn ways of keeping our emotions in check.

Dan Bellack

CHAPTER PLANNER ✓

- ❑ Study the picture and read the opening story.
- ❑ Scan the Learning Objectives in each section:
  p. 192 ❑   p. 199 ❑   p. 213 ❑
- ❑ Read the text and study all visuals. Answer any questions.

Analyze key features

- ❑ Where Developmentalists CLICK, p. 194
- ❑ Development InSight, p. 201
- ❑ Challenges in Development, p. 204
- ❑ What a Developmentalist Sees, p. 208
- ❑ Process Diagram, p. 215
- ❑ Stop: Answer the Concept Checks before you go on:
  p. 199 ❑   p. 213 ❑   p. 220 ❑

End of chapter

- ❑ Review the Summary and Key Terms.
- ❑ Answer the Critical and Creative Thinking Questions.
- ❑ Answer *What's happening in this picture?*
- ❑ Complete the Self-Test and check your answers.

Personality Development

LEARNING OBJECTIVES

1. **Describe** how behaviour geneticists study the contributions of heredity to personality.

2. **Explain** the underlying assumptions of behaviourism and social-cognitive theories as they relate to personality.

3. **Describe** what changes occur in Erikson's third stage of psychosocial development.

4. **Characterize** young children's self-concepts and self-esteem.

During the early-childhood years, the differences in children's personalities become increasingly apparent, thanks to their growing cognitive sophistication and mastery of language. Like Hayley and Harper, young children differ in how outgoing they are, how comfortable they are in new situations, and in several other ways. **Figure 6.1** describes some of the factors that make up our personalities. Children's sense of self and evaluations of themselves also become more complex during this period. Seeing all of this budding personality in action, we find it difficult to keep from wondering what, exactly, shapes children's personalities. We will begin by exploring this question through three different lenses: biological, behavioural and social-cognitive, and psychodynamic.

A Biological Perspective

As we discussed in Chapter 2, the science of genetics has been instrumental in understanding deviations from normal development. For example, scientists know that certain chromosomal and genetic abnormalities, such as Down's syndrome, are associated with a variety of behavioural, as well as physical, outcomes (Malouff, Rooke, & Schutte, 2008; Nussbaum, McInnes, & Willard, 2007). Such findings have led some scholars to believe that genes might also play a role in the expression of personality. In fact, many researchers in the field of **behaviour genetics** suggest that genes and biology are the *predominant* influences on a good deal of our behaviour, including personality. Behaviour geneticists have studied the role of genetics in producing a range of complex behavioural traits in young children, including intelligence, morality, temperament, and even television watching (Buss & Plomin, 1984; Jensen, 1998a & b; Plomin, Corley, DeFries, & Fulker, 1990; Wilson, 1975).

> **behaviour genetics** An area of science that studies the nature of the relationship between genes and behaviour.

Behaviour geneticists are concerned with the genetic causes of individuality, or the differences among individuals, as depicted in **Figure 6.2** (Plomin, 1986). Although they admit that genes and environments may interact, the aim of most behaviour genetics research is to determine the proportion of the differences among people that is due to our genes and how much is due to our environments.

Personality differences • Figure 6.1

Important factors of our personalities are already noticeable in early childhood, including our levels of openness to new experiences, extraversion or introversion, and agreeableness (Costa & McCrae, 2011).

Think Critically Can you think of examples of such personality differences among young children you know, or from your own past?

Blend Images - Ariel Skelley/GettyImages

"Sorting" the independent effects of genes and environments • Figure 6.2

Benjamin **(a)** has a sunny disposition, while Fred **(b)** tends to be somber. Behaviour geneticists want to know what proportion of these differences is due to genes and what proportion is due to the environment.

a.

b.

Ask Yourself

1. Behaviour geneticists look at differences _____ people in a specific trait.
   a. within
   b. between

2. According to behaviour geneticists, the effects of genes and environments are _____.
   a. multiplicative
   b. independent
   c. equal

heritability estimate A calculation used by behaviour geneticists to denote the independent contribution of genes to differences seen among people in a given trait.

Behaviour geneticists use a statistic called a **heritability estimate** to represent the independent contribution of genes to differences seen *between* people in a given characteristic. Heritability estimates say nothing about the extent to which genes determine a personality trait *within* an individual. **Figure 6.3** shows the heritability estimates calculated by one team of behaviour geneticists who studied **prosocial behaviour**, or the helping of others, in early childhood and beyond (Knafo & Plomin, 2006). The heritability estimates in Figure 6.3 suggest what percentage of the difference in prosocial behaviour among all the boys studied was due to genetic

prosocial behaviour Voluntary behaviour that is intended to benefit another person.

The heritability of prosocial behaviour in early childhood • Figure 6.3

Researchers who studied prosocial, or helping, behaviour among young boys reported that genetics explain 37 percent of the differences they saw among 2-year-old boys (Knafo & Plomin, 2006). Among the 7-year-old boys, genes explained 72 percent of the differences seen.

Ask Yourself

According to this chart, what proportion of the differences in prosocial behaviour among 4-year-old boys is explained by factors *other* than genetics?

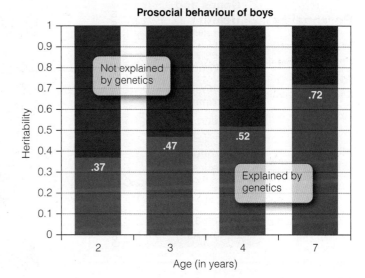

Prosocial behaviour of boys

Not explained by genetics

Explained by genetics

.37 .47 .52 .72

Heritability

Age (in years)

Where Developmentalists CLICK

GeneWatch UK

Genetic science and technologies are regarded by some as the solution to a wide range of problems—from hunger and crime to cancer. GeneWatch UK, a not-for-profit policy research and public interest group, is concerned with the effects of these technologies on individual health and society. GeneWatch believes that overemphasizing genetic explanations of complex behavioural traits can mean that underlying social, economic, and environmental influences are ignored. Through a variety of resources, including regular reports and news releases, GeneWatch keeps developmentalists and others abreast of the issues. Access the site by going to the homepage of GeneWatch UK. Click on "Human Genetics," then "Genes and Health," and peruse the recent articles and resources.

GeneWatch UK

UK

Home

About GeneWatch

GM Crops and Food

GM animals

Human Genetics

Genes and Health
  Twin studies

Genes and Marketing

Privacy and Discrimination

Genetic Research

Reproductive Genetics

Genes and the NHS

Genes and behaviour

differences among them. The heritability estimate cannot be used to find out the genetic contribution to the prosocial behaviour of any one particular boy in the study.

Twin studies are the most common method used by behaviour genetics researchers to obtain heritability estimates. Fraternal or **dizygotic (DZ)** twins share up to 50 percent of their genes. Hayley and Harper Cash, described at the beginning of this chapter, are DZ twins. Identical or **monozygotic (MZ)** twins have identical DNA; they share all of the same genes. If MZ twins are more likely than DZ twins to share a particular behavioural characteristic, behavioural geneticists conclude that genetic heritability affects the likelihood that a young child will exhibit that characteristic (DiLalla, 2004; Malouff, Rooke, & Schutte, 2008; Pedersen, Plomin, McClearn, & Friberg, 1988).

> **dizygotic (DZ)** Twin siblings who share up to 50 percent of their genes.
>
> **monozygotic (MZ)** Twin siblings who share identical DNA.

Heritability estimates are controversial, and the research methods of behaviour genetics studies are strongly criticized (Lerner, 2012 a & b; Malouff, Rooke, & Schutte, 2008). Twin studies, for example, fail to account for the effects of shared family environments (Collins, Maccoby, Steinberg, Hetherington, & Bornstein, 2000)—an especially strong influence on early childhood socio-emotional development, as we learn later in this chapter. Most young pairs of twins are raised in the same home, by the same parents, providing both children with very similar environments.

Most importantly, genes do not work in a way that supports the assumptions made by behaviour geneticists (Lerner & Warren, in press). Genes do not translate—through cells, tissues, organs, the individual, and his or her actual context—into real-time behaviours. Rather, behaviour and personality in early childhood (and throughout the lifespan) are the result of a dynamic interaction—or fusion—between genes and the environment (Lerner & Warren, in press). For these reasons, behaviour genetics has fallen out of favour among many lifespan developmentalists (Greenberg, 2011; Lerner, 2006, 2012a; Lerner & Warren, in press; Overton, 2011).

Nevertheless, many scientists continue to conduct behaviour genetics research (e.g., Plomin, 2000; Plomin, Defries, McClearn, & McGuffin, 2008; Rowe, 1994). In *Where Developmentalists Click*, we highlight one website that monitors new developments in genetics research and analyzes its effects from a public interest and human rights perspective.

Behaviour genetics assumes that genes play the main role in young children's personality development. At the

Behaviourism in action • Figure 6.4

Some siblings share while others quarrel. Behaviourists point to the role of the environment in explaining these differences.

Ask Yourself

According to behaviourists, is early personality development the result of nature or nurture?

▼ **a.** Perhaps the children in this set of photos were praised by their parents every time they shared.

Rich Reid/NG Image Collection

Rich Reid/NG Image Collection

▼ **b.** These children may not have faced consistent punishment for their fighting behaviour and may have received attention—a form of reinforcement—when they fought.

Nick Nichols/NG Image Collection

Nick Nichols/NG Image Collection

opposite end of the nature–nurture continuum lies the assumption that a child's environment is the major shaper of his or her personality. Let us take a look now at some perspectives that emphasize environmental influences on young children's personality.

Behavioural and Social-Cognitive Perspectives

Behaviourist John Watson is often quoted as saying, "Give me a dozen healthy infants, well-formed, and my own specified world to bring them up in and I'll guarantee to take any one at random and train him to become any type of specialist I might select—doctor, lawyer, artist—regardless of his talents, penchants, tendencies, abilities, vocations and race of his ancestors" (Watson, 1930, p. 104). His statement could well be the tagline for the behaviourist movement.

According to behaviourists, including Watson's famous successor B. F. Skinner, we are shaped purely by environmental forces such as reinforcement and punishment, which we discussed in Chapter 1. Our personality does not result from what is inside us, they claim, but rather from what happens to us. A child who is rewarded for helpful behaviour is more likely to perform prosocial acts in the future, for example. This is the reason that Watson claimed he could raise any baby to become any type of person by carefully controlling his or her environment. Parents have a great deal of direct influence over their children's environment during the early-childhood years, so it is particularly interesting to view young children's personality traits through a behavioural lens, as shown in **Figure 6.4** (Skinner, 1938; Watson, 1930).

Following the behaviourist tradition, scholars have conducted research on behaviour modification through

Bandura's classic research on modelling in early childhood • Figure 6.5

Children who are exposed to aggressive adult models may tend toward aggressive behaviour.

Think Critically How might Bandura's research inform parents' selection of media for their children?

Courtesy Albert Bandura

rewards and punishment. These studies have examined a range of behaviours, including eating habits, impulse control, and aggression (Bandura, 1973; Kendall & Braswell, 1993; Lindsay, Sussner, Kim, & Gortmaker, 2006). The results of these studies suggest that learning principles do contribute to young children's personality development.

Unlike strict behaviourists, who assume that environment is the only force that shapes personality, social-cognitive theorists, such as Canadian-born Albert Bandura, focus on the role of socialization forces that mediate the influence of the environment on the developing child. According to social-cognitive theorists, the environment influences the individual through others who model and teach young children the rules and expectations of society. **Figure 6.5** illustrates Bandura's classic study demonstrating the importance of modelling (Bandura, Ross, & Ross, 1961).

Bandura and his colleagues asked 3- to 6-year-old children to watch adults play with a variety of toys and then to play with the same toys themselves. Some of the adults displayed aggression, repeatedly hitting an inflatable clown, called a Bobo doll, with a mallet. Other adults played non-aggressively. The researchers found that children who had been exposed to aggressive adult models were much more likely to behave aggressively

than children who had witnessed no aggression. This tendency was more evident among the boys who participated in the study than in the girls (Bandura, Ross, & Ross, 1961). We'll see later in this chapter that modelling is important in helping children understand the gender roles and emotional rules of their cultures. Some observers are also concerned about the power of media models to influence young children.

Bandura's research has led some scholars to wonder if young children simply copy what they see, or whether their own thinking influences how much they adopt as their own of the behaviour that they observe (Bandura, 1973; Bandura, Ross, & Ross, 1961; Barr & Hayne, 2003; Meltzoff, 2007). For example, one research team had 24-month-olds watch live and televised models as they performed a task (Nielsen, Simcock, & Jenkins, 2008). In one of the televised conditions, the models behaved as if they were interacting with the children through the screen. Another set of televised models were aloof. The researchers found that children were more likely to imitate the live models and the interactive televised models than they were to copy the aloof televised models. This finding is consistent with other research, suggesting that children may evaluate the sources of behaviour, rather than simply copy whatever they witness (Nielsen, 2006; Slaughter & Corbett, 2007).

A Psychodynamic Perspective

Like behaviourists, psychodynamic theorists consider the role of the environment in shaping personality, especially the early environment. However, these theorists emphasize the expectation that societies have for individuals to gain greater and greater control over themselves as their biological maturation allows. Erik Erikson's psychosocial theory, an example of psychodynamic theory, proposes that young children face the developmental task of resolving the **initiative versus guilt stage**. During this stage of development, children may begin to take more *initiative*, or show more responsibility for their behaviour (Erikson, 1950).

> **initiative versus guilt stage** Erikson's third stage of psychosocial development, in which the 3- to 6-year-old child must learn to take responsibility for his or her own behaviour without feeling guilty for the outcomes of that behaviour.

Young children's assertive actions, however, can cause difficulties and create conflict between themselves and their caregivers. One example of this conflict is depicted in **Figure 6.6**. Through these conflicts, young children begin to develop initiative and to understand and adopt for themselves key rules of conduct. If they are punished for their well-meaning actions, young children may instead develop a sense of guilt. We will discuss guilt more fully later in this chapter.

Our personalities are observable features of ourselves that can be noticed by others. As young children, we also began to develop our own internal, subjective perceptions of ourselves.

Erikson's stage of initiative versus guilt • Figure 6.6

Erikson believed that the best outcomes of the initiative versus guilt stage happen when parents respond positively to young children's initiatives, regardless of their success or failure.

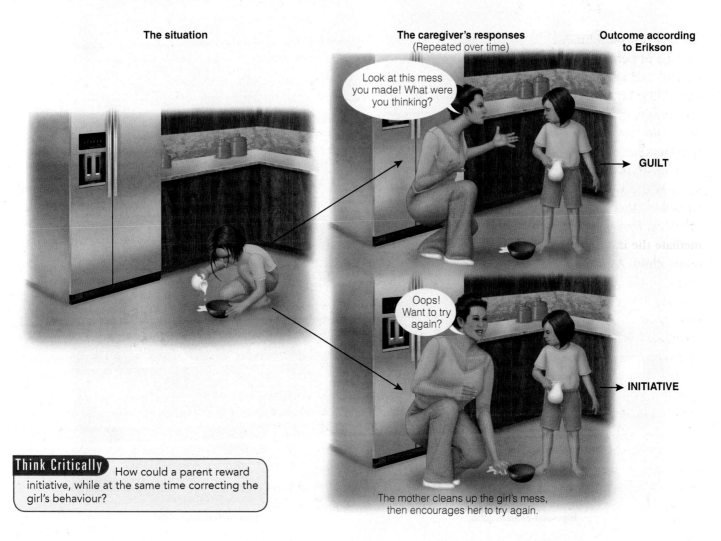

The situation

The caregiver's responses (Repeated over time)

Outcome according to Erikson

Look at this mess you made! What were you thinking?

→ GUILT

Oops! Want to try again?

→ INITIATIVE

The mother cleans up the girl's mess, then encourages her to try again.

Think Critically How could a parent reward initiative, while at the same time correcting the girl's behaviour?

Development of Self-Understanding

Young children understand the self as a collection of separate attributes (Harter, 2006). This impression of their own personalities is called **self-concept**. The emergence of a positive self-concept is fundamental to socio-emotional development (Harter, 2006; Kagen, Moore, & Bredekamp, 1995). Children who

> **self-concept** One's multidimensional impression of one's own personality, of the attributes, abilities, and attitudes that define one's self.

have a sense of themselves are better able to use that awareness as a behavioural and relational guide (Eder & Mangelsdorf, 1997).

Across development, self-concept becomes increasingly complex (Harter, 2006). During early childhood, children construct self-definitions that include only observable features of the self. A child might say, for example, "I have hazel eyes, and I live in a white

Self-esteem behaviours in young children • Figure 6.7

Children with high self-esteem are typically eager to try new things. When frustrations or disagreements arise, these children tend to handle them well. In contrast, children with low self-esteem often hang back, as they lack the confidence to initiate activities. These children can become easily frustrated and react to stressful situations with immature behaviour.

> **Think Critically** Considering the discussion of personality, is it possible for a child to have high self-esteem and still prefer familiar situations to new ones?

Active displays of confidence, curiosity, initiative, and independence...

Adaptive reaction to change or stress...

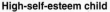

High-self-esteem child

Failure to display confidence, curiosity, initiative, and independence...

Difficulty in reacting to change or stress...

Low-self-esteem child

house with a red door." These definitions of self that refer to concrete external attributes are known as the **categorical self**. As we will see in Chapter 8, it is not until middle childhood that children can integrate separate attributes into an abstract representation of the self (Harter, 2006). An older child, for example, might say something such as, "I'm really shy except around my friends."

> **categorical self**
> Self-definitions based on concrete external attributes.
>
> **self-esteem**
> Judgements of worth that children make about themselves and the feelings that those judgements elicit.

As soon as children possess a categorical self, they begin to evaluate it. This evaluative component of the self-concept is called **self-esteem**. Young children's self-esteem is most easily seen in their behaviour (Harter, 2006). Behaviours that are common among children with high self-esteem and behaviours typical of children with low self-esteem are summarized in **Figure 6.7** (Harter, 1999).

Theory and research point to a number of personal and social influences on the development of early self-concept (Harter, 2006; Thompson & Goodvin, 2005; Verschueren, Doumen, & Buyse, 2012). However, the role of the family has received the most attention. Recall from Chapter 4 our discussion of babies' attachment to their caregivers. One of the first attachment theorists, John Bowlby (1969/1982), believed that children's emerging representations of self are directly tied to their early interactions with primary caregivers. According to Bowlby, children who experience responsive and emotionally supportive caregiving are more likely to view themselves as lovable and worthy of such support. Later research has shown that secure attachment to one's caregiver is associated with positive self-perceptions and self-esteem (e.g., Goodvin, Meyer, Thompson, & Hayes, 2008; Verschueren et al., 2012; Verschueren, Marcoen, & Schoefs, 1996; Clark & Symons, 2000).

In addition to the family context, children's school or preschool context is linked to their early self-concepts. The quality of teacher–child relationships is related to children's academic self-concept, and acceptance by peers is related to their social self-concept (Verschueren et al., 2012). In a small-scale observation study of 5-year-olds, developmentalists found that children who displayed more positive emotions during teacher–child interactions held more positive perceptions of themselves (Colwell & Lindsey, 2003).

These studies about context and early self-concept begin to reveal the various social influences affecting young children's social and emotional development. In the next section, we take a closer look at some of these key influences.

CONCEPT CHECK STOP

1. **Why** are the research methods of behaviour genetics criticized?

2. **What** do behaviourists and social-cognitive theorists agree and disagree about with regard to personality development?

3. **How** do children develop initiative according to Erikson?

4. **How** does the family influence positive self-concept?

Social Influences

LEARNING OBJECTIVES

1. **Discuss** Baumrind's parenting styles and their effects on children.

2. **Explain** what developmental scientists have found about the effects of non-parental child care on children.

3. **Describe** how media exposure may affect young children.

4. **Describe** gender differences in early childhood.

P arents, non-parental child care, media, and gender all play key roles in young children's social and emotional development. In this section we discuss these major forces, as well as other contributors to socio-emotional development in early childhood.

Parenting

Who has the biggest influence on socio-emotional development? Of all the social influences in our lives, developmentalists and intuition alike suggest that parenting is the most significant (Belsky, 1998; Brazelton & Cramer, 1990). Caregivers' sensitivity to the full range of children's behaviours shapes the development of social competence and positive adjustment (Belsky, 1998).

However, it is not news that parent–child relationships can be complicated. When delving into such complexity, developmentalists often begin by describing what they see. Researcher Diana Baumrind did just this, observing hundreds of interactions between parents and their children and categorizing the patterns of these interactions (Baumrind, 1966, 1967, 1985, 1991).

Parenting styles In her series of studies on parenting, Baumrind (1966, 1967, 1985, 1991) found that parents differ in two key areas: **demandingness**, the level and consistency of demands they place on children; and **responsiveness**, how quickly and sensitively parents address their children's needs (Baumrind, 1991). Based on these two dimensions, Baumrind initially identified three different parenting styles, which she named **authoritarian**, **authoritative**, and permissive. Later researchers have suggested that the permissive style actually includes two different types of parents: **permissive-indulgent** and **permissive-neglectful** (Maccoby & Martin, 1983). The characteristics of the four resulting parenting styles are depicted in **Figure 6.8**.

Moving beyond description, developmental scientists have also examined the consequences of the various parenting styles. Studies have found that responsive parenting correlates with social competence and positive adjustment. Demanding parenting is also correlated with positive outcomes, such as high levels of school achievement and behavioural control (Darling, 1999). Children of parents who are highly responsive but make no demands, however, show reduced social competence. In addition, high-demand, low-responsive parenting has been correlated with negative outcomes, including low self-esteem and depression (Darling, Cumsille, & Martinez, 2008).

Among middle-class majority families in Western nations, the high-demand, high-responsiveness of authoritative parenting is associated with significantly more positive outcomes than the other parenting styles (Darling et al., 2008; Weiss & Schwarz, 1996). These positive outcomes appear to persist throughout childhood and well into adolescence (Darling et al., 2008). Authoritarian and permissive styles may lead to better outcomes in non-Western cultures than in Western cultures. For example, Asian parenting has been labelled using terms that match Baumrind's (1971) authoritarian parenting style. Yet, unlike Western children raised by authoritarian parents, Asian students tend to do quite well in school (Chao, 1994). Similarly, in a study conducted in rural Nepal, developmental scientists noticed that many children had tantrums and "out-of-control" behaviour in front of their passive, unconcerned parents (Cole & Tamang, 1998). Although this behaviour matches a Western definition of permissive parenting, the Nepali community studied is known to raise positive, compassionate, and egalitarian individuals. Cross-cultural studies of parenting styles are a reminder that children's development is complex and affected by multiple layers of their environments. Broad cultural influences affect the outcomes of parents' social influence on the personality development of their children. In the next section we turn to another complex issue, that of discipline.

demandingness The level of demands parents make on their children. The number, intensity, and consistency of demands can all vary along a continuum, from very low to very high.

responsiveness The speed, sensitivity, and quality with which parents attend to the needs of their children. Like demandingness, responsiveness ranges along a continuum, from very low to very high.

authoritarian parenting A style of parenting that is characterized by high demands but low responsiveness. Authoritarian parents demand obedience from their children and are consequence-oriented, quick to punish disobedience.

authoritative parenting A style of parenting that is characterized by high demand and high responsiveness. Authoritative parents create rules and expectations while explaining reasons for their rules.

permissive-indulgent parenting A style of parenting that is characterized by high responsiveness and very low demand. Indulgent parents are involved, caring, and loving but provide few rules and little guidance.

permissive-neglectful parenting A style of parenting that is low in both demand and responsiveness. Neglectful parents are uninvolved and distant, often unaware of their child's activities.

Development InSight   Baumrind's parenting styles • Figure 6.8

When we look at the two dimensions of demandingness and responsiveness, four types of parenting styles emerge, as depicted here.

a. Authoritarian parents have strict rules for their children's behaviour and sometimes use corporal punishment when rules are broken. Some experts refer to them as "because-I-said-so" parents, since many of their rules are made and punishments delivered without explanation. These parents also use **psychological control**—behaviours that violate and manipulate children's feelings, thoughts, and attachments to parents (Barber & Harmon, 2002).

psychological control
Associated with authoritarian parenting, behaviours that violate and manipulate a child's feelings, thoughts, and attachments to parents.

b. Authoritative parents make reasonable deman(that are appropriate to their children's developmen stage and the context in which behaviour occurs. They explain rules, expectations, and consequence and the reasons for them. They involve children in decision-making and are responsive to children's changing needs, adapting rules as children grow older and begin to understand personal responsibilities.

b. Authoritative parents

a. Authoritarian parents

High

Demandingness

Responsiveness

High

c. Permissive-indulgent parents

Parenting styles

Low

Low

d. Permissive-neglectful parents

d. Permissive-neglectful parents tend to disavow parental responsibility for their children and neither impose nor enforce rules or standards of behaviour. Children of these parents are most likely to be unsupervised, leading to long-term behavioural problems (Barber, 1996).

c. Permissive-indulgent parents appear to be loving, involved, and caring, but they do not apply any boundaries to their children's behaviour. Children of these parents are typically immature, self-centred, and demanding.

Photo credits: a. U.Baumgarten/Getty Images; b. Jose Luis Pelaez Inc./Getty Images; c. LifesizeImages/iStockphoto; d. Lihee Avidan/Getty images.

Put It Together   *Looking at this figure and at the margin definitions of the four parenting styles, answer the following questions:*
1. The two parenting styles high in responsiveness are _____ and _____.
2. What is the primary difference between the authoritarian parenting style and the permissive-neglectful parenting style?

induction A rational form of discipline in which adults use reasoning and explanations to help children understand the effects of their misbehaviour on others.

Discipline Before we delve into how parents deal with unwanted behaviour, we must first distinguish between discipline and punishment. Discipline refers to teaching children to control their behaviour and follow rules. Punishment refers only to the unpleasant consequences of failing to follow the rules. Thus, although the two concepts are related, there can be discipline without punishment.

Discipline takes many forms, from **induction** to behaviourist practices, such as consistently rewarding positive behaviour, to requiring **time outs**, during which the child is removed from reinforcing stimuli, events, or conditions for a short period of time (Horton, Ray, & Cohen, 2001; Warzak, Floress, Kellen, Kazmerski, & Chopko, 2012). Whatever its form, we have seen that having clearly communicated boundaries and rules, especially in conjunction with parental warmth and sensitivity, yields positive outcomes.

The age-old question among parenting experts and parents, however, is what role punishment should play,

time outs A disciplinary measure in which the child is removed from reinforcing stimuli, events, or conditions for a short period of time.

Prohibition of corporal punishment across the globe • Figure 6.9

An increasing number of countries around the world have implemented policies or laws that protect children from all forms of corporal punishment. As of January 2014, 35 countries around the world have made such legal reforms (Global Initiative to End All Corporal Punishment of Children, 2014).

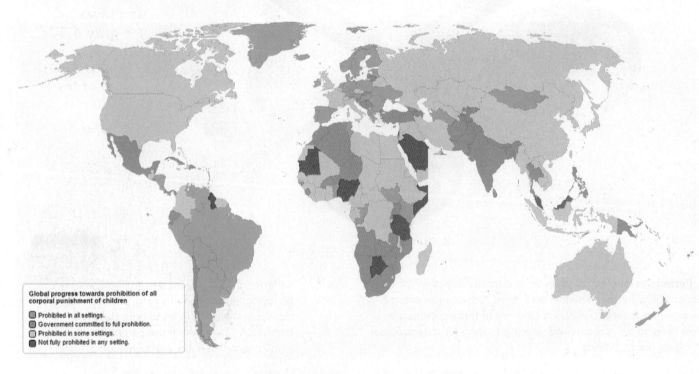

Global progress towards prohibition of all corporal punishment of children

- Prohibited in all settings.
- Government committed to full prohibition.
- Prohibited in some settings.
- Not fully prohibited in any setting.

Global Initiative to End All Corporal Punishment of Children (2016). Accessed 10/13/16 at http://www.endcorporalpunishment.org/interactive-map. Reproduced by permission of Global Initiative to End All Corporal Punishment of Children, http://www.endcorporalpunishment.org/

Think Critically What might be some roadblocks to prohibiting corporal punishment in all settings?

corporal punishment The use of physical force to cause pain or discomfort in order to punish unwanted behaviour.

physical abuse Non-accidental physical injury as a result of caretaker acts such as shaking, slapping, punching, beating, kicking, biting, or burning.

sexual abuse The involvement of children and adolescents in sexual activities that they do not understand and for which they cannot give informed consent.

neglect Failure of caretakers to provide for a child's fundamental needs, such as adequate food, housing, clothing, medical care, emotional well-being, or education.

emotional/ psychological abuse Continual verbal harassment and intimidation of a child by means of disparagement, criticism, threat, or ridicule.

if any, in this discipline (Greven, 1991). Historically, the authoritarian parenting style assumed that strict punishment led to well-behaved children. "Spare the rod, spoil the child" was the motto, and punishments were applied regularly. **Corporal punishment**, or the infliction of physical damage as a means of punishment, was even allowed in schools. Support for the use of corporal punishment is still found in Canada, while, as **Figure 6.9** shows, countries worldwide have begun to ban the practice.

While some scholars and practitioners believe corporal punishment is effective and desirable (e.g., Baumrind, 1997; for a review, see Larzelere, 2000), others have concluded that corporal punishment is ineffective and, indeed, harmful (e.g., American Academy of Pediatrics, 1998; Straus, 2000). For example, studies have suggested that the use of corporal punishment increases children's risk of internalized aggression, anger, withdrawal, and criminal behaviour (Agnew, 1983; Donaldson, 1997; American Academy of Pediatrics, 1998). Corporal punishment also models physical aggression for children, potentially teaching them that it is acceptable to hit others.

Finally, corporal punishment has been shown to be a major risk factor for **physical abuse** (Straus, 2000). Along with **sexual abuse**, **neglect**, and **emotional/psychological abuse**, physical abuse is a form of child maltreatment and the topic of this chapter's *Challenges in Development* (Litrownik et al., 2005).

Teachers and child care providers are among the mandated reporters of child maltreatment in Canada. They are also, as we'll see next, a major influence on the socio-emotional development of young children in their care.

Non-parental Child Care

In Chapter 5, we considered the role of early-childhood education in young children's learning and development. We turn now to the broader category of early **non-parental child care**.

non-parental child care Any type of child care that is carried out by someone other than the primary child care provider.

Dramatic changes in child-rearing have taken place in Canada and in other industrialized nations over the past several decades. Perhaps the most dramatic change is the rise of dual-income families. With few fathers taking parental leave and more mothers returning to work, the result is an increase in the use of non-parental child care (Laughlin, 2011; Leibowitz & Klerman, 1995). There is much variation in the cost, quality, and general environment of non-parental child care. As shown in **Figure 6.10**, the most common type of non-parental child care performed by non-relatives is

Child care arrangements for Canadian children of working parents • Figure 6.10

Children experience a variety of nonparental childcare arrangements (U.S. Department of Education, National Center for Education Statistics, 2012). As shown here, centre-based care is most common.

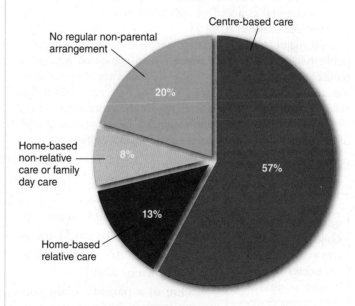

Think Critically What are your opinions of the most common challenges faced by parents seeking child care arrangements and centre-based care?

CHALLENGES IN DEVELOPMENT
Child Maltreatment

We all share in the duty of protecting children from harm; everyone has a responsibility to report child abuse and neglect (Canadian Child Welfare Research Portal, 2011). All Canadian provinces and territories have enacted mandatory reporting laws that require professionals working with children, such as teachers and health care providers, to report suspected cases of child abuse to authorities (Sinha, 2012). Unfortunately, there can be significant variations in levels of reporting due to both subjective and legal differences in what constitutes suspected maltreatment (Levi & Portwood, 2011).

An in-depth United Nations study confirms that violence against children—including physical violence, psychological violence such as insults and humiliation, discrimination, neglect, and maltreatment—exists in every country and cuts across culture, class, education, income, and ethnic origin (Pinheiro, 2006). The majority of violent acts against children are perpetrated by people they know: parents, schoolmates, teachers, employers, boyfriends or girlfriends, as well as parents' spouses and partners. One study conducted in the Republic of Korea found that 90 percent of parents thought corporal punishment was necessary (Kim, 2000). In another report from Yemen, nearly 90 percent of children said that physical punishment was the main form of discipline used by their families, with beating as the most common method (Habasch, 2005). When surveyed, Canadians generally report negative attitudes toward the physical disciplining of children (Bell & Romano, 2012; Durrant, Rose-Krasnor, & Broberg, 2003). However, approximately 25 percent of parents still use corporal punishment with children ages 2 to 11 years (Fréchette & Romano, 2015).

Child maltreatment has been identified as an understudied public health problem in Canada. When compared with other parts of the world, a limited number of studies are conducted and the data are less diverse (Afifi, 2011). The most recent Canadian child maltreatment data are from the Canadian Incidence Study of Reported Child Abuse and Neglect (CIS), a national sample of child maltreatment investigations by child welfare collected in 2008 (Trocmé et al., 2008). According to this study, most maltreated children in Canada suffer from neglect (34 percent; **Figure a**) or witnessing violence in their home (34 percent). Although many cases of abuse are still not reported to either police or child welfare authorities, data from police reports and child welfare authorities is still the most important source of information about child abuse. The CIS uses data from child welfare authorities to estimate the extent of child abuse in Canada. In its third iteration, the CIS is an important resource in providing a

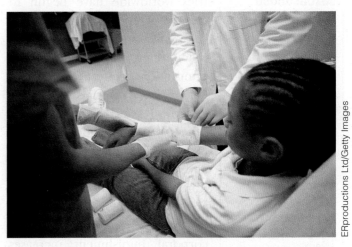

a. A next-door neighbour brings 7-year-old Thomas to the emergency room. Like the estimated 235,000 other children every year, Thomas is suffering from child maltreatment (Trocmé et al., 2008). For some children, child maltreatment is fatal. Thankfully, this number has been on the decline in recent years.

---

centre-based child care Child care that is provided at a location away from home, generally including four or more children and a qualified child care provider.

centre-based child care, in which children are cared for at a child care centre (Clarke-Stewart & Allhusen, 2002).

One of a parent's main concerns after deciding to have a child is how to provide non-parental care. One of the most significant social changes in Canadian history has been the rise of women entering the paid workforce. In 2014, women represented 47.3 percent of the labour force, which is up from 45.7 percent in 1999 and 37.1 percent in 1976. Consequently, there has been steady growth in labour force participation among women with young children. In 2009, 64.4 percent of Canadian women with children under the age of 3 were employed, more than double the proportion of 27.6 percent reported in 1976 (Status of Women Canada, 2015). Public policy has been slowly catching up to these social changes. In 2000, changes to the federal Employment Insurance Act extended the duration of benefits for parents to be able to care for their infant. If each parent of a newborn took the maximum national picture of child abuse. In 2008, an estimated 235,842 maltreatment-related investigations were conducted across Canada, representing a rate of 39.16 investigations per 1,000 children. Not all investigations were substantiated. In 2008, approximately 85,440 cases were substantiated. **Figure b** shows that the two most common forms of abuse were witnessing intimate partner violence (34 percent) and neglect (34 percent) followed by physical abuse (20 percent), emotional maltreatment (9 percent), and sexual abuse (3 percent). Aboriginal heritage was documented by the CIS-2008 in an effort to better understand some of the factors that bring Aboriginal children into contact with the child welfare system. Aboriginal children were identified as a key group to examine because of concerns about their over-representation in the foster care system. Twenty-two percent of substantiated cases (an estimated 18,510 investigations) involved children of Aboriginal heritage.

Girls and boys seem to be affected differently by abuse. Girls are more likely to internalize their response to violence, and experience, for example, suicidal ideation, eating disorders, low self-esteem, and psychological disorders. Boys are more likely to externalize their response to violence, displaying, for example, increased aggression, delinquency, and spousal abuse. Boys who have been exposed to violence in their homes are more likely to be violent in their adolescent and adult relationships than boys not exposed to violence (Status of Women Canada, 1999; Dauvergne & Johnson, 2001).

Children and youth in Canada are most likely to be killed by members of their own family. Between 2000 and 2010, the rate of family homicide was highest among infants under one. Over this same 10-year period, the vast majority of homicides of infants (98 percent) and toddlers aged 1 to 3 (90 percent) were committed by parents (Sinha, 2012). Maltreated children are also at increased risk for later developing alcoholism, drug abuse, eating disorders, obesity, depression, suicide, sexual promiscuity, and other chronic disorders (Finkelhor, 1990; Kydd, 2003). The effects of abuse may appear right away, or surface only in adolescence or adulthood. Further, the effects may differ according to the nature of the response to the abuse, and whether the abuse was disclosed or reported (Latimer, 1998). In addition, adults who were maltreated as children are more likely to abuse their own children (Dubowitz, Feigelman, Lane, & Kim, 2009).

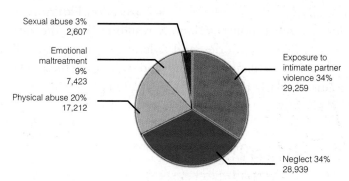

Child Maltreatment in Canada in 2008

Sexual abuse 3%
2,607

Emotional maltreatment
9%
7,423

Physical abuse 20%
17,212

Exposure to intimate partner violence 34%
29,259

Neglect 34%
28,939

b. The CIS-2008 found that witnessing intimate partner violence and being neglected were the two more common forms of child maltreatment in Canada. Source: *Canadian Incidence Study of Reported Child Abuse and Neglect 2008* (Trocmé et al., 2008). Accessed at http://www.phac-aspc.gc.ca/cm-vee/csca-ecve/2008/index-eng.php

Think Critically If you were in charge of a government agency that targets child maltreatment, what three initial steps would you take to begin to address the problem?

leave allowed at separate times, the baby would have a parent at home for 89 consecutive weeks (17 weeks of pregnancy leave for the birth mother, plus 35 weeks of parental leave for the birth mother, plus 37 weeks of parental leave for the other parent). Still, Canada lacks a national early childhood education program and parents struggle to find quality child care spaces, which are particularly sparse for infant care. About 54 percent of children under age 5 have regular non-parental care (Bushnik, 2006). When parents have higher incomes, they tend to pay for daycare outside of their family, whereas lower income Canadians tend to rely on care by a relative (Canadian Council on Learning, 2009).

In 2011, almost half (46 percent) of Canadian parents reported using some type of non-parental child care arrangement for children under the age of 14. The majority (86 percent) of parents using child care relied on the service on a regular basis, which translated into approximately 30 hours of non-parental care per week (Sinha, 2014). The average number of hours Canadian children spend in non-parental care arrangements has remained relatively stable, with 31 hours reported for 1994–1995, and 29 hours reported for 2002–2003 (Bushnik, 2006). The median cost of full-time child care varies greatly by geographic location, ranging from a low of $152 per month in Quebec to a high of $677 in Ontario. The majority (98 percent) of Canadian parents report satisfaction with the overall quality of their child care arrangement (Sinha, 2014).

Since so many children spend time away from their parents in child care, it is important to determine what constitutes a high-quality daycare centre. Developmentalists have identified a number of characteristics, including qualified daycare workers, licensing, a low child-to-caregiver ratio, an educational mission, and, of course, safety. This chapter's *What a Developmentalist Sees* highlights how to evaluate these aspects during a visit to a daycare centre.

The child care choices that parents make are influenced by the social policies of the countries in which they live. In turn, national child care and family policies reflect the prevailing norms and practices of societies (Himmelweit, 2007). For example, in order to boost maternal employment numbers and in response to increasing pressure from parents and advocacy groups, France has been steadily increasing its public support to working mothers since the 1990s (Fagnani, 2012). Currently, the French government subsidizes both individual child care arrangements, such as nannies, and centre-based care. With the growth of state-supported child care, maternal employment has been increasing in France: 47 percent of mothers living in France who have at least one child less than 3 years of age work at paying jobs (OECD, 2010). Germany, on the other hand, lags far behind France in child care provision and benefits, and only 15 percent of German parents of children under 6 years of age support the idea of full-time employment for mothers (Institut für Demoskopie Allensbach, 2007). Fewer German mothers (32 percent) are in paid work and the majority of these mothers are employed on a part-time basis, while more than 73 percent of their counterparts in France work full-time (Fagnani, 2012; OECD, 2010).

As noted above, Canada has no national program or overall approach to early childhood education. **Figure 6.11** outlines the funding variations resulting from the fact the provinces, territories, and federal government are all involved in regulating, funding, and structuring these programs. Similarly, the number of regulated family child care

Allocation to regulated child care per child 0–12 years, 2011–2012, by province/territory • Figure 6.11

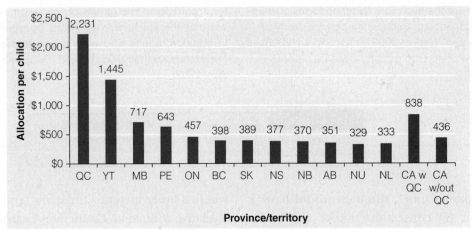

Source: Ferns & Friendly (2014). Figure 7: Allocation to regulated child care per child 0–12 years, in *The State of Early Childhood Education and Care in Canada 2012: Moving Childcare Forward Project* (A joint initiative of the Childcare Resource and Research Unit, Centre for Work, Families and Well-Being at the University of Guelph, and the Department of Sociology at the University of Manitoba), p. 12. Retrieved from http://childcarecanada.org/sites/default/files/StateofECEC2012.pdf.

Think Critically How might national disparity in funding for regulated child care spaces impact children and their families?

spaces varies dramatically between jurisdictions. The province of Quebec uniquely and consistently offers residents a universal low-fee child care program (**Figure 6.12**). This province's spending on child care has accounted for more than 50 percent of the total provincial/territorial spending on child care for more than a decade. Comparatively, public spending for early childhood education across the rest of country remains low. However, responsibility for child care has continued to shift away from the community service sector to the education ministries of Canada; six provinces have now integrated full-day kindergarten into primary education (Ferns & Friendly, 2014).

Research on the effects of non-parental child care has been controversial, to say the least (Vandell, 2004). Some studies report that early child care, especially high-quality care and care for economically disadvantaged children (e.g., Campbell, Pungello, Miller-Johnson, Burchinal, & Ramey, 2001), is a source of both intellectual and social enrichment (e.g., Burchinal, Roberts, Riggins, Zeisel, Neebe, & Bryant, 2000; Peisner-Feinberg et al., 2001). However, developmental researchers have long pointed to a number of developmental risks associated with non-parental care in early childhood, especially when such care is extensive and begins early in life (Bates, Marvinney, Kelly, Dodge, Bennett, & Pettit, 1994; Belsky et al., 2007; Haskins, 1985; Vandell & Corasaniti, 1990). For example, children who experienced early, extensive, and continuous non-maternal care had less harmonious parent–child relations and higher levels of aggression and non-compliance during the toddler, preschool, and early primary school years, compared with children who attended less child care (Belsky, 2001).

Studies have often focused on two aspects of non-parental care: quantity and quality. Studies that focused solely on quantity of care—that is, how many hours a week a child spends in such care—found that more non-parental care was related to poorer parent–child relationships, more behavioural problems, and problematic peer relationships (Belsky et al., 2007; Bradley & Corwyn, 2005; Lucas-Thompson & Clarke-Stewart, 2007). However, the National Institute of Child Health and Human Development (NICHD) has noted that just examining the effects of quantity in isolation makes it "impossible to determine if the seemingly adverse effects of substantial hours in child care

Number of regulated family child care spaces in Quebec and Canada • Figure 6.12

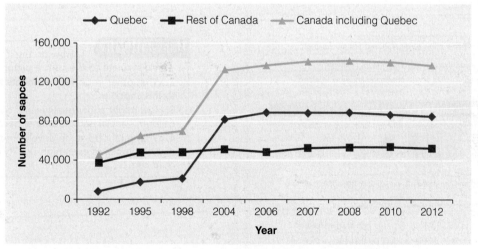

Source: Ferns & Friendly (2014). Figure 5: Number of regulated family child care spaces in Canada and Quebec: Allocation to regulated child care per child 0–12 years, in *The State of Early Childhood Education and Care in Canada 2012: Moving Childcare Forward Project* (A joint initiative of the Childcare Resource and Research Unit, Centre for Work, Families and Well-Being at the University of Guelph, and the Department of Sociology at the University of Manitoba), p. 9. Retrieved from http://childcarecanada.org/sites/default/files/StateofECEC2012.pdf.

Think Critically Are there research questions which would be ideal to study based on the knowledge of disparity between provincial jurisdictions?

WHAT A DEVELOPMENTALIST SEES
Evaluating the Quality of Centre-Based Care

Developmental researchers and practitioners have identified a number of specific elements of high-quality centre-based child care. Checklists of these indicators, such as this one from the National Association of Child Care Resource and Referral Agencies, are designed to help parents evaluate the centres they are considering for their children's care.

Is This The Right Place For My Child?

(Make a copy of this checklist to use with each program you visit.)

Place a check in the box if the program meets your expectations.

Will my child be supervised?

Are children watched at all times, including when they are sleeping?[15]

Are adults warm and welcoming? Do they pay individual attention to each child?[40]

Are positive guidance techniques used?
Do adults avoid yelling, spanking, and other negative punishments?[16]

Are the caregiver/teacher-to-child ratios appropriate and do they follow the recommended guidelines:

➤ One caregiver per 3 or 4 infants
➤ One caregiver per 3 or 4 young toddlers
➤ One caregiver per 4 to 6 older toddlers
➤ One caregiver per 6 to 9 preschoolers[19]

Have the adults been trained to care for children?

If a center,

➤ Does the director have a degree and some experience in caring or children? [27/28/29]
➤ Do the teachers have a credential*** or Associate's degree and experience in caring for children?[27/28/29]

If a family child care home:

➤ Has the provider had specific training on children's development and experience caring for children?[30]

Is there always someone present who has current CPR and first aid training?[32]

Are the adults continuing to receive training on caring for children?[33]

Have the adults been trained on child abuse prevention and how to report suspected cases?[12/13]

Will my child be able to grow and learn?

For older children, are there specific areas for different kinds of play (books, blocks, puzzles, art, etc.)?[21]

For infants and toddlers, are there toys that "do something" when the child plays with them?[41]

Is the play space organized and are materials easy-to-use? Are some materials available at all times?[21]

Are there daily or weekly activity plans available? Have the adults planned experiences for the children to enjoy? Will the activities help children learn?[22]

Do the adults talk with the children during the day? Do they engage them in conversations? Ask questions, when appropriate?[43]

Do the adults read to children at least twice a day or encourage them to read, if they can read?[43]

Is this a safe and healthy place for my child?

Do adults and children wash their hands (before eating or handing food, or after using the bathroom, changing diapers, touching body fluids, eating, etc.)?[4]

Are diaper changing surfaces cleaned and disinfected after each use?[5]

Do all of the children enrolled have the required immunizations?[6]

Are medicines labeled and out of children's reach?[7]

Are adults trained to give medicines and keep records of medications?[7]

Chris Cheadle/Getty Images

"Is this the Right Place for My Child?: 38 Research-Based Indicators of Quality Child Care" has been provided by Child Care Aware, a program of the Child Care Aware of America.

Think Critically
1. How do the items on this checklist relate to the centre pictured here?
2. What other important elements would you add to this checklist?
3. How might a low-quality child care centre affect children's social and emotional development?
4. What might be some developmental disadvantages of even high-quality centre-based child care?

are a function of poor quality care or particular types of care" (NICHD, 2002, p. 134).

To explore questions about the importance of both quality and quantity of early child care, the NICHD conducted one of the most comprehensive longitudinal studies of child care settings to date. The NICHD study of more than 1,000 children examined the relationships between quality and quantity of child care and outcomes that included pre-academic skills (such as identifying letters and words) and problem behaviours (such as being too fearful and anxious) (NICHD, 2002). As shown in **Figure 6.13**, the NICHD study found that high-quality early child care was associated with stronger pre-academic skills, regardless of children's gender, ethnicity, socio-economic status, and the quality of parenting they received. The study also found, consistent with previous research, that children who spent a large quantity of time in non-parental child care were more likely to show problem behaviours (NICHD, 2002).

On the whole, caregivers—parents and child care workers alike—typically have the best interests of the child in mind. But what can be said of media programs? Preschoolers today have more access to media than ever in human history. In the next section, we will consider how this media access may be affecting them (Van den Bulck & Van den Bergh, 2000).

Media Exposure

Children these days are exposed to a variety of media options, including TVs, computers, DVD players, and handheld devices such as tablets and video games. On a typical day, 27 percent of 5- to 6-year-olds use a computer (for an average of 50 minutes), 32 percent watch videos/DVDs (for 1 hour and 20 minutes, on average), and 75 percent of children watch television (Vandewater, Rideout, Wartella, Huang, Lee, & Shim, 2007). Television watching continues to be the most

Quality and quantity of early child care: Developmental benefits and risks • Figure 6.13

When we examine both the quality and the quantity of early child care, a more nuanced picture emerges.

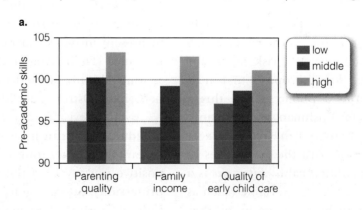

a. High-quality child care is associated with better pre-academic skills than low-quality child care.

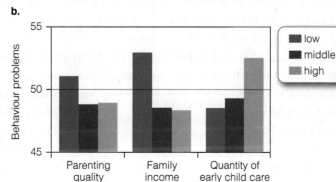

b. However, high quantity of child care is associated with more behaviour problems than low quantity of chilld care.

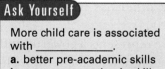

Ask Yourself

More child care is associated with _____.
a. better pre-academic skills
b. worse pre-academic skills
c. more behaviour problems
d. fewer behaviour problems

popular option and has received the most research attention. Developmentalists have studied the effects of television media on aggressive behaviour, cognition, and prosocial behaviour (Eisenberg, Fabes, & Spinrad, 2006; Lemish, 2006).

Television media and aggression Violence abounds in children's movies, videos, and television shows, which average 14 violent acts per hour (Wilson et al., 2002). By the time they are 18 years old, regular viewers will have witnessed an average of 200,000 acts of televised violence, including 40,000 murders (Huston et al., 1992). Developmental researchers, in one of the most significant longitudinal studies of the associations between violent television and aggressive behaviour, recruited a group of 8-year-olds who watched at least four hours or more of violent television each day and studied the same participants for the next 40 years (Huesmann, Moise, Podolski, & Eron, 2003). Amazingly, over 60 percent of the original sample remained involved in the study during the entire period. Based on interviews with friends, teachers, parents, and relatives of the participants, the researchers concluded that there was a clear correlation between watching violent television and aggressive behaviour (Huesmann et al., 2003).

Although correlation does not mean TV watching *causes* aggression, a number of developmentalists believe that media violence is a risk factor for aggressive behaviour, and some propose that it is worthy of being considered a public health threat (e.g., Anderson et al., 2003; Bushman & Huesmann, 2001). Researchers have compared the effect size of media violence on aggression with the effect sizes of some common threats to public health. *Effect size* is a measure of how much change in one variable (such as aggression) is brought about by a change in another variable (such as media violence). The effect size of media violence on aggression was second only to the effect size of cigarette smoking on lung cancer. Media violence also appears to be associated with other negative behaviours, such as desensitization to real violence, aggressive thoughts, and conflict with parents, siblings, and peers (for a complete review see Gentile, 2003).

Aggressive behaviour may involve physical contact, as we discuss in greater detail later in this chapter, but it may also take the form of verbal affronts, called **relational aggression**

> **relational aggression** Subtle harmful acts, such as manipulating, gossiping about, or creating public humiliation for another individual.

(Galen & Underwood, 1997; Ostrov, Gentile, & Crick, 2006). Relational aggression is most common among older age groups, but it does occur in early childhood. Using parental reports, teacher ratings, and observation, one research team found that preschoolers' violent media exposure was related to both physical and relational aggressive behaviour (Ostrov et al., 2006).

Television media and cognition Developmental scientists have also examined the link between watching television and how children think. Studies show that television is associated with gender identity, gender roles, worldviews, creativity, imagination, ability to take the perspective of others, and perceptual skills, among other aspects of thought (Lemish, 2006). Television also appears to be associated with children's attention, memory, and perception (Anderson & Lorch, 1983).

Television media and prosocial behaviour Developmentalists have often focused on problems associated with children's television, but studies have also shown that certain types of television shows may have some interpersonal benefits. Many researchers have studied the effects of the long-running public television show *Sesame Street*, as well as other educational television shows. Producers of these shows often work with psychologists to present images of prosocial behaviour, diversity, and tolerance (Fisch, Truglio, & Cole, 1999). High levels of viewing educational media have been linked to prosocial behaviour (Ostrov et al., 2006).

Even television shows that are not intended to be educational can have some benefits. For example, researchers have found that television can create positive portrayals of the medical and mental health professions, often engendering a more accepting attitude of those workers among viewers (Vogel, Gentile, & Kaplan, 2008). In addition, children from low–socio-economic-status families who watch television improve their vocabularies and gain information about geographical areas that are otherwise unavailable to them (Van Evra, 2004).

Media exposure represents a powerful and pervasive influence on development throughout the lifespan, so we will return to a discussion of media influences in later chapters. In the next section, we examine another powerful influence on socio-emotional development during the early childhood years, gender.

Gender

Young children tend to develop both a **gender identity**, a perception of themselves as male or female (Zucker & Bradley, 2005), and a sense of their **gender role**, the specific behaviours a culture expects from genders (Ghosh, 2012). However, as noted in Chapter 4, the relationship between sex and gender—indeed the conception of sex and gender as categories—is not uncomplicated.

Gender identity Shortly after their second birthday, most children can communicate their assigned sex, or identify themselves as a boy or girl, but the beginnings of gender identity are evident even earlier for many children (Campbell, Shirley, & Caygill, 2002). By the time a child has reached the age of 3, gender identity may be fairly well established (Zucker & Bradley, 2005). At this age, children also understand the idea of **gender constancy**, meaning that gender does not change over time (Kohlberg, 1966). A 2-year-old boy might think that he could decide to become a girl, for example, but an older boy who understands gender constancy knows that his gender will most likely stay the same. Children's perception of gender constancy has been observed as being related to their awareness of the role genitalia plays in constituting one as a boy or girl (Bem, 1989). Research suggests that the more significance and positivity children associate with their assigned gender, the more they understand gender as a stable construct (Halim, Ruble, Tamis-LeMonda, Zosuls, Lurye, Greulich, 2014).

Of course for some children, gender identity is not a straightforward process, but is met with ambivalence and questioning. At the most basic level, gender identity is constructed from one's anatomy, but for children born with ambiguous genitalia (intersex conditions) or for boys who lack a penis because of a surgical accident or genetic condition, gender identity may not follow a usual course (Ruble, Martin, & Berenbaum, 2006). These children were often raised as females because it is easier to construct female genitalia from ambiguous genitalia than male genitalia. This approach has been questioned in recent years. While it was long assumed that children's gender identity was based on rearing, more recent research shows that gender identity is not directly determined by either

gender identity A perception of one's gender category.

gender role Specific behaviours or appearances that are expected of children, based on their culture's beliefs about gender.

gender constancy The belief that one's gender is permanent and unchanging.

gender schema theory A cognitive approach to understanding gender development that centres on children's own constructions of gender.

gender schemas Children's mental representation of gender categories.

biology or rearing and may change even later in the lifespan (Reiner & Gearhart, 2004).

There are also children whose biological sex is not in question, but whose understanding of self is incongruent with their biological sex (Ruble et al., 2006). Transgender children begin showing gender-atypical behaviour during the preschool years, such as wearing opposite-sex clothes and being preoccupied with opposite-sex toys. Boys are referred for treatment more often than girls, possibly because there is less tolerance for gender-atypical behaviour among boys than among girls.

Despite these variations, most children develop and reflect a perception of self as male or female, and tend to follow the gender roles associated with their assigned sex. However, cross-cultural research suggests that in play contexts, most children bend and play with gender (Eunsook & Dong Haw, 2004). Unfortunately, girls continue to display more confidence in playing outside of gender lines than boys because of the widespread value placed on masculinity and the corresponding intolerance for feminine masculinities (Eunsook & Dong Haw, 2004; Kane, 2006).

Gender role development One influential viewpoint, **gender schema theory**, focuses on the combined role of environmental influences and children's own cognitions about gender development (Martin, Ruble, & Szkrybalo, 2002). Recall from Chapter 1 that Piaget used the term "schemas" to describe mental structures, such as categories or thoughts. According to gender schema theory, young children observe the gender-related preferences and behaviours of parents, teachers, and others around them, but they do not passively adopt these behaviours. Instead, children organize their observations and experiences into **gender schemas**, their own mental representations of masculine and feminine categories. Five-year-old Kimberly thinks of males as forceful and dominant and females as gentle and warm. She uses these gender schemas or sex-linked associations to understand the world around her. Young children's growing understanding of gender roles can be seen in their play.

Gender roles and play Children begin making gender-typed toy selections as early as 18–20 months of age

(Cherney, Kelly-Vance, Gill, Ruane, & Ryalls, 2003). By 3 years of age, children have begun to form stereotypes about gender-appropriate play and gender stereotypes for toys (Fagot, 1974; Cherney, Harper, & Winter, 2006). Toy trucks, for example, are "boy toys." By the time they are 4 or 5 years old, children display what one research team called the "hot potato effect": Children will avoid playing with toys they like if the toys are deemed appropriate for the opposite sex (Blakemore & Centers, 2005). Recall our earlier discussion of the categorical self. The self-concepts of young children tend to be based on their concrete external attributes. So, for example, when a boy plays with a feminine-stereotyped toy, he may think that the external attribute—"I play with dolls"—could define his sex.

Given the central role of toy play in young children's lives, developmental researchers have begun to examine how gendered toys affect children's socio-emotional and cognitive skills. Feminine-stereotyped toys, such as stuffed toys and domestically oriented toys, allow for more communicative play and collaborative role playing (Caldera, Huston, & O'Brien, 1989; Leaper, 2000). Masculine-stereotyped toys, such as vehicles, balls, guns, and construction toys, are thought to inspire competition, aggression, and movement in space (Miller, 1987). One team of researchers evaluated the behavioural complexity of children's play with masculine, feminine, and gender-neutral toys (Cherney et al., 2003). They found that, for both girls and boys, feminine toys, such as a doll, generated the greatest number of different behaviours (child dresses doll, makes doll sit at the table, pours tea for the doll, and then puts the doll to bed). Given that boys typically display stronger same-sex toy preferences than girls, the researchers caution us that boys may have fewer opportunities for complex play (Carter & Levy, 1988; Green, Bigler, & Catherwood, 2004).

Influences on gender roles Parents influence young children's gender roles more than any other factor (Hines, Golombok, Johnston, Golding, & the Avon Longitudinal Study of Parents and Child Study Team, 2002). For example, parents reinforce children's gender-typed toy selections and play behaviours. They may ignore or even dissuade doll play by their sons, while encouraging nurturing and submissive play behaviours in their daughters. They also model "gender-appropriate" play by more readily demonstrating or inviting children to play with parent-same-sex toys (Caldera et al., 1989).

In most areas of Canada, boys are rewarded when they engage in rough-and-tumble play, a form of physical play, such as wrestling, tumbling, and running (Pellegrini & Smith, 1998). Girls are rewarded for quieter activities (Ghosh, 2012). Research suggests that fathers play a significant role in this socialization process, as depicted in **Figure 6.14**.

Fathers and gender role socialization • Figure 6.14

Fathers can have a significant influence on the development of gender roles.

Think Critically Why do you think fathers play such a powerful role in gender socialization?

a. Fathers are more likely than mothers to reinforce behaviour that is consistent with a culture's gender roles, and even to discourage behaviour that does not match gender roles (Ruble et al., 2006).

b. Fathers influence their sons' gender role development in a similar way.

Some research is showing how a machismo and stereotypical pattern of interacting with our children may be contributing to dire social problems. For example, in a meta-analytic study of adherence to the masculine gender role and its connection to sexual assault against women, robust effects were found for two measures of masculine ideology: acceptance of aggression against women and negative, hostile beliefs about women, including agreement that men are dominant over women. Thus the greater extent to which these beliefs were part of a masculine gender identity, the greater the likelihood the man would also commit abuse against women (Murnen, Wright, & Kaluzny, 2002). Research continues to demonstrate a relationship between hegemonic masculinity and violence against women (Murnen et al., 2002; Reidy, Berke, Gentile, & Zeichner, 2014; Reidy, Shirk, Sloan, & Zeichner, 2009). How can we raise our children to think about gender roles in ways that do not promote sexual aggression and hostility?

Parents continue to reinforce gender roles throughout childhood. Parents and other social entities also influence emotional expression and regulation (Holodynski, 2004), the topics we turn to next.

CONCEPT CHECK

1. **What** parenting styles are associated with the best and worst child outcomes in Western nations?

2. **What** factors influence the relationship between non-parental child care and development in early childhood?

3. **How** is media exposure related to aggression, cognition, and prosocial behaviour?

4. **How** do gender roles develop?

Emotional Development

LEARNING OBJECTIVES

1. **Describe** the emotion vocabularies of young children.

2. **Explain** how emotional regulation develops during early childhood.

3. **Explain** the role of moral emotions in early moral development.

As children move through early childhood, they tend to develop increasingly sophisticated emotion vocabularies and greater ability to regulate their emotions and the behaviours associated with them. As we'll see, this leads to the beginnings of moral development.

> **emotion vocabulary** The number of words a person can use to name his or her emotional states and explain the emotional behaviour of self and others.

Developing a Vocabulary to Describe Emotions

Babies smile, frown, grimace, and express their emotions in various ways from an early age, as we discovered in Chapter 4. During early childhood, emotional expression becomes deeper and more varied. Using their burgeoning vocabulary skills and improving cognitive abilities, children begin to describe how they feel about events. That is, children begin to build an **emotion vocabulary** of words that they will use to label their own emotions. Young children also become better at recognizing and labelling the emotions of others (Bretherton, Fritz, Zahn-Waxler, & Ridgeway, 1986).

Research has shown that a high percentage of 28-month-old toddlers are able to use words like "sad," "scared," "happy," and "funny" with regard to themselves, as well as to describe the emotions of others. Children appear to use emotion words as reasons for emotion ("It's dark, I scared"), interventions ("No cry, Mama, it will be all right"), and explanations ("I laugh, Daddy funny") (Bretherton & Beeghly, 1982). These toddlers are describing internal states ("I scared") as well as behavioural expressions of emotion ("I laugh").

Emotion vocabulary: Describing the emotions of self and others • Figure 6.15

This little boy is using his emotion vocabulary to make an emotional attribution about his stuffed animal.

He's sad because he has a boo-boo.

Think Critically How might the development of an emotion vocabulary aid young children's social development?

Sajoiner/iStockphoto

Eventually children begin to use emotion words in play and to make emotional attributions about dolls and other inanimate objects, as we see in **Figure 6.15**. They also learn to use emotion words to deceive, as they come to understand that emotion words can describe the causes and consequences of emotion without a person actually experiencing the emotion (Lemerise & Arsenio, 2000; Stein & Trabasso, 1989). For example, a child who simply doesn't want to go grocery shopping might claim to be afraid of the store.

Some children, however, struggle with expressing and identifying their full range of emotions using words, an occurrence called **alexithymia**. These children typically know the words related to emotions but cannot apply those words to the emotions they are feeling or that they see others expressing.

alexithymia Difficulty understanding, identifying, and describing emotions with words.

somatic complaints Physical problems without physiological cause.

emotion regulation The ability to control the behaviour one displays in response to an emotional state.

In particular, they often have problems distinguishing between positive and negative emotions that tend to feel similar physiologically, such as fear and excitement (Lundh & Simonsson-Sarnecki, 2001). Alexithymia has been found to be related to a number of disorders, including depression and **somatic complaints**, physical problems such as headaches or stomach aches without any physiological cause. The causes of alexithymia are still being studied, but it is currently believed that the problem can result from genetic factors, traumatic experiences in childhood, and early parent–child relationships that negatively affect the development of neural and cognitive systems involved in the processing of emotional information (Taylor & Bagby, 2000; Way, Yelsma, Van Meter, & Black-Pond, 2007; Zlotnick, Mattia, & Zimmerman, 2001). Alexithymia persists into adulthood in about 10–15 percent of people, but most children manage to develop an emotion vocabulary that they can apply to their own and others' emotions (Way et al., 2007).

By the end of early childhood, children typically understand that some people may have different emotions for the same event: "Billy likes it when it rains, so he's happy. But Manuel gets sad when it rains." They also come to notice that emotions have indirect effects on things: "We didn't get to go outside because the teacher was mad at Rasheed." In addition, children become able to make predictions about future emotions: "I'll be very happy when my friend comes over to play."

The development of emotion vocabulary is an indication that children are becoming more astute at understanding the varying uses and contexts of emotion (Bretherton et al., 1986). One of the earliest uses of this developing vocabulary is the regulation of emotions.

Regulating Emotions

Adults, or even school-age children, do not typically throw tantrums when they are frustrated. At some point, most of us have developed the skills of **emotion regulation**, the ability to modify or modulate either the way our behaviour expresses our emotion or our perceptions of the situation that elicit the emotion (Diamond & Aspinwall, 2003; Eisenberg, Fabes, Guthrie, & Reiser, 2000; Gross, 1999a & b). The process of emotion regulation is shown in **Figure 6.16**.

Emotion regulation • Figure 6.16

How will a child react to a potentially aversive situation such as taking a bath? If he or she is poor at emotion regulation, a tantrum might ensue. But if the child has emotion regulation skills, as shown in this diagram, the negative emotions may be dampened.

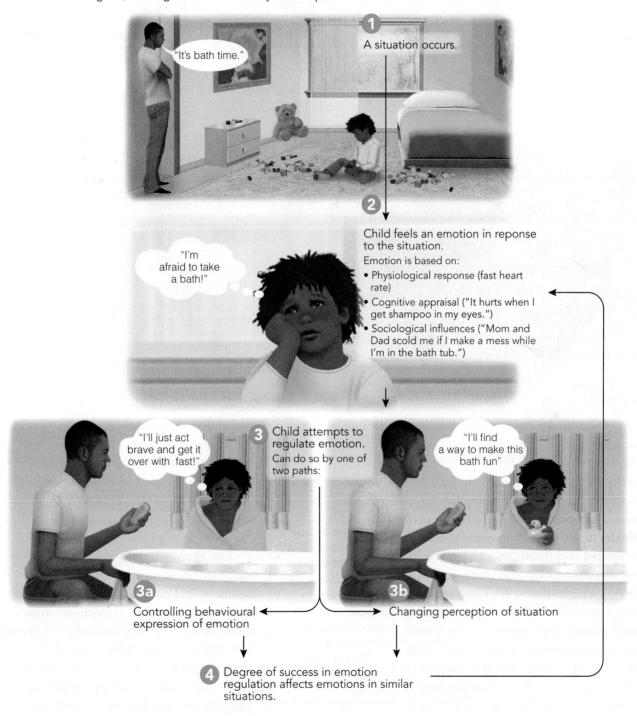

Think Critically In what ways can parents help children develop emotion regulation skills?

Affective social competence is the ability to effectively send and receive emotional cues and manage one's own emotional experience. These abilities play an important role in peer relations.

Experiencing

Neave is excited to join her classmates' play, but is also anxious that her bid for entry will be denied. She manages to keep her anxiety in check, while continuing to smile as she approaches the sand table because that is what people do when they greet each other.

Henry Zoe Neave Angus

Receiving

As Neave approaches her classmates at the sand table, she must be able to distinguish between smiles of welcome and body language signalling potential rejection. Neave knows from past experience that when Henry does not answer a bid for entry into the play scenario, that means "yes," but when Angus does not answer, that means "no".

Sending

Neave realizes that she must send an emotional cue to the other children. She is eager to join them at the sand table and knows that Zoe responds well to her exuberance, while Angus needs to be approached more gently.

Adapted from Halberstadt, A. G., Denham, S. A., & Dunsmore, J. C. *Social Development* 10 (1), 79–119. Copyright © 2002 by John Wiley & Sons, Inc.

Emotion regulation and peer relations Emotion regulation has implications for peer relations (Dunsmore, Noguchi, Garner, Casey, & Bhullar, 2008). The emotions that children communicate verbally, facially, or through other modes provide information during interactions with peers. Emotions are an important source of information for both the person who is communicating and the recipient of that communication (Halberstadt, Denham, & Dunsmore, 2001). Children who are more accurate at sending emotional communications tend to have more friends and better peer relations (Boyatzis & Satyaprasad, 1994). These children may be better able to give their playmates important information about how the play is progressing (Lemerise & Arsenio, 2000). In turn, the ability to receive emotional communications is also linked to positive peer relations (Fabes, Eisenberg, Hanish, & Spinrad, 2001). Receiving others' emotional communications requires knowledge about emotions and

affective social competence The ability to effectively communicate one's own emotions, interpret and respond to others' emotions, and successfully manage the experience of emotions.

the ability to apply that knowledge within a dynamic social context. The ability to effectively send and receive emotional cues and manage one's own emotional experience is called **affective social competence** (Halberstadt et al., 2001). **Figure 6.17** shows the importance of affective social competence in young children's social lives.

The three components of affective social competence—sending emotional cues, receiving emotional cues, and managing emotional experience—may be performed consciously, unconsciously, or automatically (Halberstadt et al., 2001). Young children are likely to enact certain aspects of this process quite deliberately, while adolescents and adults may find that this process becomes rapid and seemingly effortless. Developmental scientists suggest that the same components and processes contribute to affective social competence throughout our lifespans and across cultures. However, the appearance of affective social competence may vary across the lifespan, across cultures and subcultures, and across contexts and specific goals (Halberstadt et al., 2001).

For example, cultures differ in their **display rules** for emotional expression (Ekman & Friesen, 1969; Matsumoto, Yoo, & Fontaine, 2008). One team of researchers found that individualistic cultures, such as those in the United States and Australia, that foster independence, favour personal goals over group goals, and that value personal attitudes as determinants of behaviour were likely to endorse emotional expressiveness (see **Figure 6.18**). Collectivistic cultures, such as those in Indonesia and Hong Kong, that encourage interdependence, emphasize group goals, and that value cultural norms as determinants of behaviour were more likely to favour reserved expression of emotion (Matsumoto et al., 2008).

> **display rules**
> Cultural norms that dictate socially appropriate emotional displays.

At the same time children are sending and receiving emotional communications, they are also experiencing emotions. Children who understand their own emotions and are better able to regulate them have greater peer-related social competence (Smith, 2001). In contrast, children who have trouble regulating their emotions tend to have issues with social functioning, such as aggression

Display rules for emotional expression • Figure 6.18

Exuberant, joyful New Orleans "jazz funerals" call for grand displays of emotional expression.

Ask Yourself

How might a culture support emotional expressiveness?

Andrew Stanfill/Demotix/Corbis

(Bowie, 2010; Eisenberg, Carlo, Murphy, & Van Court, 1995).

Problems with emotion regulation

Children who are either very high or very low in the ability to control the expression of emotion are at risk of developing **internalizing** or **externalizing problems**. These problems form the basis of a number of psychological disorders. For example, externalizing behaviours are a feature of oppositional defiant disorder, and internalizing problems are part of depressive disorders (American Psychiatric Association, 2013).

A more common problem is aggression. Children can be aggressive when they have difficulty controlling their expressions of emotion. Studies reveal that physical aggression is most common among children 24 to 42 months old, ages when many children are still developing their emotional regulation abilities (for a review, see Tremblay, 2004). Most early aggressive behaviour falls into two categories: **instrumental (or proactive) aggression** and **hostile (or reactive) aggression**. Instrumental aggression occurs when a child is actively attempting to achieve a goal or obtain something. For example, a child who wants a toy that another child is holding might quickly and forcibly grab the toy and express frustration if the one holding it refuses to let go.

Hostile aggression is a purposeful action intended to cause harm to another. Hostile aggression can include **overt aggression**, harmful physical acts or threats, such as hitting, and relational aggression, which we discussed earlier (Crick, 1996; Galen & Underwood, 1997). Girls tend to be more involved in relational aggression, whereas boys tend to be more overtly aggressive (Crick, Bigbee, & Howes, 1996).

> **internalizing problems** Problems that result when children overcontrol the expression of emotions, including depression, social withdrawal, anxiety, and somatoform disorders.
>
> **externalizing problems** Problems that result when children undercontrol the expression of emotions, including aggression and delinquency.
>
> **instrumental (or proactive) aggression** A goal-oriented act through which a person or object is harmed.
>
> **hostile (or reactive) aggression** An intentional act that harms a person or object.
>
> **overt aggression** A direct and obvious harmful act, such as hitting, kicking, biting, or verbally threatening.

Factors influencing emotion regulation A number of developmentalists have studied the factors that influence the development of emotion regulation (Aspinwall & Taylor, 1997; Cumberland-Li, Eisenberg, Champion, Gershoff, & Fabes, 2003; Eisenberg, Fabes, Guthrie, & Reiser, 2000; Spinrad, Eisenberg, & Gaertner, 2007). Parental socialization of emotion has been found to be the most important influence (Campos, Frankel, & Camras, 2004). Parents' beliefs about emotion intimately affect their children's emotional tendencies. Some parents believe that emotions should be controlled, while others welcome their expression. This dimension of suppression versus expression can vary from one emotion to another. For example, some families allow the expression of sadness but not the expression of anger (Eisenberg, Cumberland, & Spinrad, 1998). Given these data, it is not surprising to learn that emotional relationships with family members lie at the heart of early moral development.

Emotions and Early Moral Development

While moral development researchers used to focus on children's cognitive processes (Kohlberg, 1984), many scholars today have turned their attention to the role of emotions, especially as they occur within the context of early family life (Eisenberg, Fabes, & Spinrad, 2006; Laible & Thompson, 2002; Lane, Wellman, Olson, LaBounty, & Kerr, 2010; Nussbaum, 2005). By the time they are 2 to 3 years of age, children have internalized moral rules about what to do and what not to do in various situations (Emde, Biringen, Clyman, & Oppenheim, 1991). Three-year-old Finn knows that at Grandma's house he can have as many cookies as he desires, but at home he is only allowed to take one from the cookie jar after dinner. His actions are guided by his feelings of right and wrong, which are based on his understanding of the rules. Emotions are at the core of young children's morality.

By the age of 4 to 5 years, Finn will likely experience the **moral emotions** of guilt and shame when acting against his internalized moral rules (Eisenberg, 2000). Moral emotions, such as guilt, shame, and empathy, are believed to play a fundamental role in

morality (Eisenberg, Spinrad, & Sadovsky, 2006; Tangney, Stuewig, & Mashek, 2007). Guilt and shame belong to a family of moral emotions called **self-conscious emotions**. Self-conscious emotions arise when we scrutinize and evaluate ourselves with respect to moral standards. When we break a rule or act badly somehow, the self-conscious emotions of guilt and shame provide us with immediate feedback about our moral acceptability.

Guilt and shame An important self-conscious emotion that develops during early childhood is **guilt**, the emotional response to one's own wrongdoing. Guilt is a feeling of regret that arises when one causes, anticipates causing, or is associated with a negative act that is inconsistent with one's moral standards (Ferguson & Stegge, 1998). For example, 5-year-old Jehan, a true animal lover, felt terribly guilty after stepping on his cat's tail. Research has demonstrated that the development of guilt is an essential factor in children's adjustment (Eisenberg, Fabes, & Spinrad, 2006; Kochanska, Forman, Aksan, & Dunbar, 2005). Both young children's personalities and their parents' behaviour affect the internalization of guilt (Kochanska & Aksan, 2006). When parents are warm toward their children and the children have fearful temperaments, guilt is enhanced. Parents who are authoritarian and exert power over a child's behaviour, however, appear to undermine the internalization of guilt.

Developmental researchers often compare guilt and **shame**. For example, guilt is more task-related and internal, whereas shame is related to some self-other relationship (Tangney & Dearing, 2002). We can feel guilty about something we have done while alone, but generally feel ashamed only in the presence of another person. Shame focuses more on others' negative perceptions of the self than on the harm that one has caused to others. Six-year-old Rebecca felt shame when she dropped her sister's birthday cake at the party in front of everyone. Later that day, she snuck off with one of her sister's gifts, but then returned it with an apology because she felt guilty. Guilt and shame also differ in terms of how "moral" they are as emotions (Tangney et al., 2007). Guilt appears to be the more adaptive emotion. While guilt can benefit the individual and his or her relationships by prompting constructive actions such as confessions and apologies, as

moral emotions Emotions believed to play a fundamental role in morality.

self-conscious emotions Moral emotions that are evoked by self-reflection and self-evaluation.

guilt A feeling of regret or remorse arising from perceptions of having done something wrong.

shame A feeling that the whole self is a failure or bad, which can lead to defensiveness and social withdrawal.

in the case of Rebecca, shame has a number of hidden costs (Baumeister, Stillwell, & Heatherton, 1995). For example, shame promotes defensiveness and interpersonal separation (Tangney, Wagner, Hill-Barlow, Marschall, & Gramzow, 1996). After Rebecca dropped the cake, she claimed that someone had tripped her and then she stomped off. Shame is also correlated with anger, aggression, and the tendency to blame one's troubles on factors beyond the self (Bennett, Sullivan, & Lewis, 2005; Furukawa, Tangney, & Higashibara, 2012; Tangney & Dearing, 2002).

There is some disagreement among scholars about the age at which guilt and shame emerge. One theorist proposes that both moral emotions emerge around 3 years of age, at the point when children (1) understand that the self is different from other people, (2) possess some moral standards of behaviour, and (3) have the cognitive abilities to evaluate their own behaviour against these standards (Lewis, 1998). Others argue that the precursors of guilt and shame may be seen even in the second year of life (Barrett, 1998; Hoffman, 1998). The moral emotion of empathy has also been observed among children in the second year of life (Zahn-Waxler, Radke-Yarrow, Wagner, & Chapman, 1992).

> **empathy** The capacity to understand or feel what another person is feeling from their perspective.
>
> **sympathy** Feelings of pity for another person's misfortune.

Empathy The emotional response of **empathy** is based on one's comprehension of another's emotional state and is similar to what the other person is feeling, or might be expected to feel (Eisenberg et al., 1994). A child experiences empathy, for example, when she or he feels sad in response to a peer's sadness. In contrast, **sympathy** is a feeling of sorrow or concern for another, as opposed to feeling the same emotion as the other person (Eisenberg, Fabes, et al., 2006). Some developmental scientists have made a distinction between two types of empathic reactions: other-oriented empathy and self-oriented personal distress (Batson & Coke, 1981; Eisenberg et al., 1989). Other-oriented empathy, which involves perspective-taking and the vicarious experience of another's emotions, typically leads to helping behaviours. Self-oriented personal distress, where the empathizer is preoccupied with his or her own empathic response and not the experiences and needs of the other person, does not lead to such helping behaviours and may even interfere with their occurrence (Eisenberg et al., 1990, Eisenberg, Spinrad, & Sadovsky, 2006). Studies, including the one summarized in **Figure 6.19**, suggest this is true for preschoolers in both Western and non-Western cultures.

Empathy, distress, and prosocial behaviour across cultures • Figure 6.19

One research team looked at the relationship among empathy, distress, and prosocial behaviour among 5-year-olds in two Western cultures (Germany and Israel) and two Southeast Asian cultures (Indonesia and Malaysia) (Trommsdorff, Friedlmeier, & Mayer, 2007).

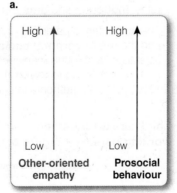

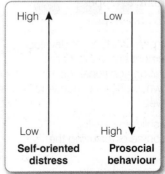

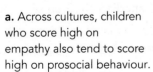

a. Across cultures, children who score high on empathy also tend to score high on prosocial behaviour.

b. However, in most of the cultures studied, children who show high levels of distress in response to another's misfortune are less likely to engage in prosocial behaviour.

Think Critically Why might distress prevent prosocial behaviour?

Research on the socialization of empathy has focused on the role of various parenting practices. Investigators have found that a secure attachment relationship between mother and child is positively associated with children's empathy and guilt (Eisenberg Fabes, & Spinrad, 2006; Kochanska & Aksan, 2006). In addition, the development of empathy in children has been linked to (1) parenting that encourages children to understand others' emotions, (2) low levels of angry emotions in the home, and (3) parental practices that help children manage their negative emotions (for a review of findings, see Eisenberg Fabes, & Spinrad, 2006).

In this chapter we have seen that social and emotional development are inextricably linked during early childhood. As we will see in upcoming chapters, they are inextricably linked throughout the lifespan.

CONCEPT CHECK

1. **What** does the emotion vocabulary of a 3-year-old most likely contain?
2. **What** are the steps in emotion regulation?
3. **How** does guilt compare to shame?

THE PLANNER

Summary

1 Personality Development 192

- **Behaviour genetics** researchers use family, adoption, and twin studies involving **monozygotic (MZ)** and **dizygotic (DZ) twins** to calculate **heritability estimates** of various personality and other traits. Heritability estimates refer to differences seen between people in a specific trait, such as **prosocial behaviour** shown in the figure (Knafo & Plomin, 2006).

The heritability of prosocial behaviour in early childhood • Figure 6.3

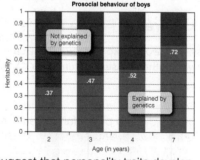

- Behaviourist theories suggest that personality traits develop through the processes of reinforcement and punishment, while social-cognitive theorists posit an additional role for cognition, such as that displayed when children choose to imitate behaviour they have observed.

- Erik Erikson proposed that young children develop personality characteristics in the course of resolving the **initiative versus guilt stage**.

- **Self-concept** becomes increasingly abstract with age. Young children construct concrete self-representations that include only observable features of the self. These definitions of self are known as the **categorical self**, and the evaluations that children make about themselves is called **self-esteem**.

- Children's emerging representations of self are directly tied to their early interactions with primary caregivers.

2 Social Influences 199

- Diana Baumrind's research identified three categories of parenting—**authoritarian, authoritative**, and permissive—based on parents' **demandingness** and **responsiveness**. More recently, developmental scientists have distinguished between two permissive parenting styles: **permissive-indulgent** and **permissive-neglectful**. In Canada, the authoritative style is generally associated with positive outcomes for children. In other cultures and subcultures, however, other styles are linked with positive outcomes.

- Discipline and punishment are related concepts, but not the same thing. Discipline refers to teaching children to control their behaviour and follow rules, whereas punishment refers only to the unpleasant consequences of failing to follow the rules. **Induction** and **time outs** are two forms of discipline.

- The authoritarian parenting style emphasizes strict discipline and the use of **corporal punishment**. Developmental scientists have found many negative effects of corporal punishment, and the **psychological control** also associated with authoritarian parenting.

Child care arrangements for Canadian children of working parents • Figure 6.10

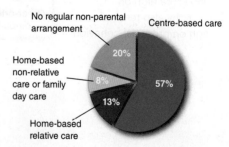

- Young children are vulnerable to many types of maltreatment, including **physical abuse**, **sexual abuse**, **neglect**, and **emotional/psychological abuse**. Parents, family friends, and relatives most often commit such abuse.

- Approximately half of preschool-age Canadians spend time in a variety of **non-parental child care** arrangements, as shown in the figure.

- Developmental scientists have identified a number of elements that indicate high-quality **centre-based child care**. Studies show that both the quality of care and the amount of time spent in non-parental child care affect children's outcomes.

- Watching violent television has been linked to physical and **relational aggression** among young children, but watching educational programming is linked to prosocial behaviour. Television also has a variety of influences on children's thinking and other cognitive abilities.

- Sex characteristics are those related to biological factors, while **gender** is a socio-cultural way of categorizing people. **Gender identity** is a person's perceptions or understanding of their own gender, and **gender constancy** is the belief that one's gender is a relatively permanent characteristic. **Gender roles** are the specific behaviours expected of children by a particular culture based on gender. One influential approach to understanding gender role development is **gender schema theory**, where the focus is on the combined role of environmental influences and children's own cognitions, or gender schemas, about gender categories.

- Feminine-stereotyped toys and play allow for more communicative play and collaborative role playing, while masculine-stereotyped toys and play, such as **rough-and-tumble play**, is thought to inspire competition, aggression, and movement in space.

3 Emotional Development 213

- Young children begin to develop an **emotion vocabulary** that they use to label their own and others' emotions. A small percentage of children and adults fail to develop adequate emotion vocabularies. This condition is known as **alexithymia**, which may be related to the development of psychological problems, including depression and **somatic complaints**.

Emotion regulation • Figure 6.16

Controlling behavioural expression of emotion

Changing perception of situation

- Throughout early childhood, children develop **emotion regulation** skills. There are two general ways that children regulate emotions, as shown in the figure.

- **Affective social competence**, the ability to effectively send and receive emotional cues and manage one's own emotional experience, is important for young children's positive peer relations. The appearance of affective social competence may vary across cultures, which have different **display rules** for emotional expression.

- Children who overcontrol their emotions may be at risk for **internalizing problems**, and those who undercontrol their emotions may be at risk for **externalizing problems**.

- Emotions play an important role in young children's peer relationships. Children who understand their own emotions and are better able to regulate them have greater peer-related social competence. In contrast, children who have trouble regulating their emotions tend to have issues with social functioning, such as aggression.

- Aggression peaks between 24 and 42 months and typically falls into two categories: **instrumental** (or **proactive**) **aggression** and **hostile** (or **reactive**) **aggression**. Hostile aggression can be further categorized as **overt** or **relational**.

- Scholars have identified a number of **moral emotions** that are believed to play a fundamental role in morality, such as **guilt**, **shame**, and **empathy**. These emotions belong to a family of moral emotions called **self-conscious emotions**. Empathy is distinguished from **sympathy**, and can be subdivided into two types of empathic reactions: other-oriented empathy and self-oriented personal distress.

Key Terms

Critical and Creative Thinking Questions

1. If genes determine social class, as some behaviour geneticists believe (e.g., Rowe, 1994), what early childhood social and educational policies might result? Why might genetic technologies be a human rights issue?

2. What style(s) of parenting did you experience as a child? How did you feel about the parenting style(s) you experienced? What style do you, or would you, use as a parent?

3. What are your opinions about using corporal punishment to discipline young children?

4. Based on what you have read in this chapter, what would you say to a parent of a young child who asked your advice about non-parental child care?

5. What recommendations would you give to a parent of a young child regarding television and media use?

6. Can you think of any popular parenting practices that might inhibit the development of empathy in young children? What are some practices that are likely to foster empathy?

What is happening in this picture?

Think Critically

1. What factors may have influenced this child to choose this costume?

2. What, if anything, might this costume say about this boy's emerging personality?

3. What kind of TV show is most likely to be this boy's favourite?

4. What gender role is this boy portraying? What factors likely influenced how he learned that gender role?

5. What emotions does this child seem to be experiencing? Based on what you've learned in this chapter, is it likely that he could describe these emotions in words?

Photodisc/Getty Images

REAL  Development

Socio-emotional Development in Early Childhood

In this video activity, you are interested in learning more about peer interactions and how they develop. A developmental psychologist at your school, Dr. Jones, has done a great deal of research on different types of play. You will read about different types of play and then use these descriptions to help Dr. Jones identify the forms of play that take place in Adeline's preschool classroom.

John Wiley & Sons, Inc.

WileyPLUS Go to WileyPLUS to complete the REAL Development activity.

03.01

Self-Test

(Check your answers in Appendix A.)

1. What information is provided by heritability estimates?
   a. the personality traits two parents should expect their child to have
   b. how much of any individual person's behaviour is due to their genetics
   c. the likelihood of two parents having monozygotic or dizygotic twins
   d. how much of the differences among people in a given trait are due to genetics

2. What is the most common method used by behaviour genetics researchers?
   a. family studies
   b. twin studies
   c. adoption studies
   d. all of these

3. Bandura's classic research shown here demonstrated that
   _____.
   a. rewards are more influential than punishment in determining what behaviour children will learn
   b. the threat of punishment is the most effective way to teach children new behaviours
   c. children can learn new behaviours by observing the behaviour of others
   d. models need to be extremely similar to children in order to teach new behaviours

Courtesy Albert Bandura

4. According to Erikson, what will be the outcome if this girl's caregiver responds negatively to her efforts to do things for herself?

a. initiative

b. a superego

c. fixation

d. guilt

5. Children who fail to display confidence, curiosity, initiative, and independence are said to have _____.

a. relational aggression

b. internalizing problems

c. externalizing problems

d. low self-esteem

6. Fill in the blanks with the names of parenting styles described by Baumrind and other researchers.

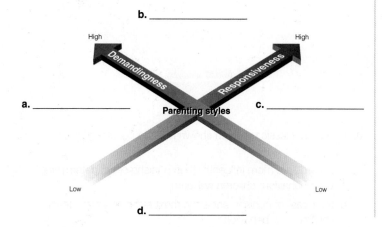

7. Research on the effects of non-parental child care suggests that

a. high-quality non-parental child care is essential for the development of children's future academic and social skills.

b. non-parental child care is a positive social influence on children, regardless of quantity or quality.

c. quantity of time spent in non-parental child care is linked to higher levels of problem behaviours.

d. spending more than four hours a day in non-parental child care has positive effects on children's social behaviour.

8. What have studies shown about young children's viewing of violent television programming?

a. Violent television clearly causes aggressive behaviour in children.

b. Aggressive children choose to watch violent television.

c. Watching violent television and aggressive behaviour by children are positively correlated.

d. Authoritarian parenting styles cause children to watch violent TV and behave aggressively.

9. Watching educational television is positively correlated with young children's _____.

a. aggressive behaviour

b. prosocial behaviour

c. decision-making skills

d. attention span

10. Who is most influential in socializing young children into traditional gender roles?

a. child care providers

b. mothers

c. fathers

d. peers

11. Declan is gradually learning a variety of words to express his feelings and identify the feelings of others. He is in the process of building his _____.

a. initiative

b. alexithymia

c. authoritative style

d. emotion vocabulary

12. Modulation of the behaviour we show in response to an emotional state is called _____.

a. emotion control

b. emotion regulation

c. emotion awareness

d. emotion cognition

13. Children who overcontrol their emotions are at risk for developing _____.

a. alexithymia

b. the emotion of guilt

c. internalizing problems

d. externalizing problems

14. In order to join a group of classmates playing at the sand table, Neave will need to send emotional cues, receive emotional cues, and manage her emotional experience. These are the three components of _____.

a. self-conscious emotions

b. affective social competence

c. moral emotions

d. display rules

Experiencing
Neave is excited to join her classmates' play, but is also anxious that her bid for entry will be denied. She manages to keep her anxiety in check, while continuing to smile as she approaches the sand table because that is what people do when they greet each other.

Henry   **Zoe**   **Neave**

Sending
Neave realizes that she must send an emotional cue to the other children. She is eager to join them at the sand table and knows that Zoe responds well to her exuberance, while Angus needs to be approached more gently.

Angus

Receiving
As Neave approaches her classmates at the sand table, she must be able to distinguish between smiles of welcome and body language signalling potential rejection. Neave knows from past experience that when Henry does not answer a bid for entry into the play scenario, that means "yes," but when Angus does not answer, that means "no".

Adapted from Halberstadt, A. G., Denham, S. A., & Dunsmore, J. C. *Social Development* 10 (1), 79–119. Copyright © 2002 by John Wiley & Sons, Inc.

15. A goal-oriented act through which a person or object is harmed is called _____ aggression.

a. overt

b. relational

c. hostile

d. instrumental

THE PLANNER ✓

Review your Chapter Planner in the chapter opener and check off your completed work.

Physical and Cognitive Development in Middle and Late Childhood: Six to Eleven Years

The melodic sounds of Miles Davis's *Kind of Blue* ooze from the speakers on a Friday afternoon in Room 107. Students gather their art supplies and find a comfortable spot around the classroom. It is "classic album Friday," and Mr. Warren has given his Grade 5 students the assignment to use the music as inspiration for their drawing and painting. Marisol chooses to paint blueberries, blue birds, and a blue sky. Victor draws trumpets and other instruments with musical notes coming out of them.

Clearly, Victor and Marisol are a great deal more advanced than they were during early childhood. In this chapter, we will explore the developmental processes that make "classic album Friday" possible. We will consider the brain changes that lead the children to make complex connections, the increased fine motor

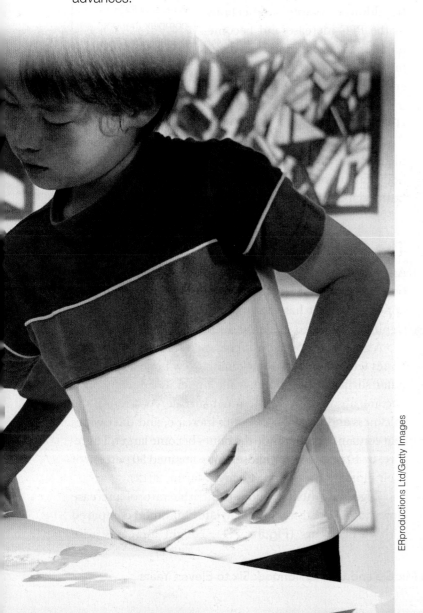

skills that allow them to paint and draw, and the enhanced representational skills that enable them to visualize and create visuals of the music they hear. We will also reflect on how reading skills, memory abilities, and intelligence permit them to learn about the musical genre of jazz. Finally, we will explore the ways that health and well-being play a vital role in supporting all of these advances.

ERproductions Ltd/Getty Images

CHAPTER PLANNER ✔

- ❏ Study the picture and read the opening story.
- ❏ Scan the Learning Objectives in each section:
  p. 228 ❏   p. 231 ❏   p. 243 ❏
- ❏ Read the text and study all visuals. Answer any questions.

Analyze key features

- ❏ Process Diagram, p. 236
- ❏ What a Developmentalist Sees, p. 248
- ❏ Challenges in Development, p. 249
- ❏ Stop: Answer the Concept Checks before you go on:
  p. 231 ❏   p. 243 ❏   p. 254 ❏

End of chapter

- ❏ Review the Summary and Key Terms.
- ❏ Answer the Critical and Creative Thinking Questions.
- ❏ Answer *What's happening in this picture?*
- ❏ Complete the Self-Test and check your answers.

Physical Development

LEARNING OBJECTIVES

1. **Explain** how the brain changes during middle and late childhood.

2. **Describe** height and weight changes during this period of the lifespan.

3. **Describe** the development of the muscular system during middle and late childhood.

During middle to late childhood, curiosity and intelligence find new outlets just as more intense responsibilities, such as schoolwork, appear. Simultaneously, the physical self changes as chubby bodies lengthen and physical abilities become more complex. Not visible, but just as notable, are the changes occurring within the brain.

The Nervous System

Compared with young children, school-aged children are better at waiting in line and listening to the instructions of a teacher. This increase in self-control is perhaps the most dramatic outcome of the developing nervous system. Although the high level of brain plasticity that we saw in early childhood begins to slow between 5 and 7 years of age, it remains present throughout this developmental period (and throughout the lifespan). This brain plasticity allows children and adults to adapt to varied environments. In fact, during childhood, neuron density first increases and then decreases as synapses are pruned to accommodate environmental demands (Johnson, 2008). An increase in myelin, the fatty coating on axons, contributes to the efficiency of this adaptation (Chevalier et al., 2015). As we previously discussed in Chapters 3 and 5, although myelin increases most significantly during the first two years of life, there is evidence that myelin growth continues through childhood and adolescence (Johnson, 2005, 2008).

Myelination occurs in two parts of the brain, colourfully referred to as **grey matter** and **white matter**. Myelination in grey matter allows for the faster action of neurons, resulting in a more complex and efficient pathway for neural connections. Efficient pathways allow children to learn to carry out a variety of complex activities. Myelination of white matter results in faster communication between the left and right hemispheres of the brain via the corpus callosum. White matter pathways that connect the brain and spinal cord also become more myelinated, improving coordination.

Behavioural changes also result from developments in the **prefrontal cortex (PFC)** of the brain. This area of the brain is responsible for planning, thinking, and a variety of specific cognitive functions. During middle and late childhood, the neurons of the PFC become increasingly myelinated. In addition, synaptic connections in the PFC increase and become more specialized. These changes may be responsible for the increased self-knowledge, enhanced social awareness, and more efficient cognitive processing seen in older children (Pfeifer, Lieberman, & Dapretto, 2007; Tsujimoto, 2008).

Many changes take place in the brain during middle and late childhood. Meanwhile, other systems in the body, including the skeletal system, are also undergoing both quantitative and qualitative changes.

> **grey matter** The parts of the brain that contain neuron cell bodies and some of their connections.
>
> **white matter** The spongy tissue that connects various areas of the brain to one another as well as to parts of the spinal cord.

> **prefrontal cortex (PFC)** The frontmost part of the frontal lobe that is responsible for complex thought, planning, and problem solving.

The Skeletal System

As children approach puberty, their skeletons expand both in width and in length. The result is a physical appearance that has more adult-like proportions and a significantly improved sense of coordination.

A great many of these appearance changes result from bones lengthening and thickening. New bone adds to the outer surface of the bone, while minerals simultaneously become absorbed from the inner surface. As a result, the thickness and diameter of bones increase, and the cavities that contain marrow inside the bones become larger. Therefore, by 10 years of age children have attained 50 percent of their ultimate bone mass (Cech & Martin, 2012).

Regarding height and weight, the rate of increase slows down slightly in middle to late childhood compared with earlier years (**Figure 7.1**). Height increases arise

Height and weight changes during middle and late childhood • Figure 7.1

From 6 to 12 years of age, there is a steady increase of about 8 lbs and 2 to 3 in (3.5 kg and 5 to 8 cm) per year. As you can see, males and females do not differ significantly until age 10, when female bodies begin to prepare for puberty. Around this age, girls' pelvises and hips also begin to widen to accommodate the expanding reproductive system.

Think Critically What are some potential psychosocial consequences of sex differences in rate of change in height?

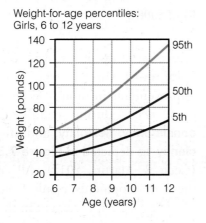

Weight-for-age percentiles: Girls, 6 to 12 years

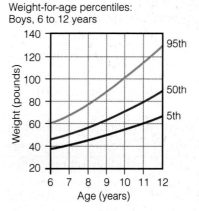

Weight-for-age percentiles: Boys, 6 to 12 years

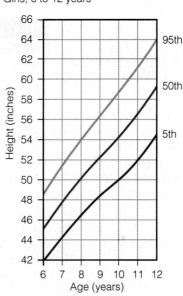

Height-for-age percentiles: Girls, 6 to 12 years

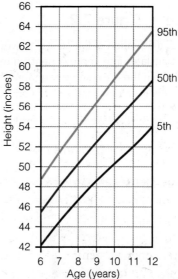

Height-for-age percentiles: Boys, 6 to 12 years

Source: Developed by the National Center for Health Statistics in collaboration with the National Center for Chronic Disease Prevention and Health Promotion (2000).

mainly from a lengthening in the lower part of the skeleton, particularly the pelvis and long bones of the legs. Variations in height can be influenced by race and ethnicity (Shih et al., 2005).

Several interrelated factors contribute to the development of the skeletal system during childhood, including genetics, nutrition, and hormone levels. The hypothalamus and pituitary gland stimulate the production of several types of hormones, including human growth hormone. This hormone stimulates organs to increase cell production in the bones, causing lengthening and enhanced mass. In addition, studies have shown that physical activity contributes to an increase in the mineral content and density of bones in childhood (Bouxsein & Marcus, 1994). Physical activity plays a similarly important role in the development of muscles.

The Muscular System

The muscular and skeletal systems follow similar developmental paths during middle and late childhood. Bone growth precedes muscle growth (Cech & Martin, 2012) and causes muscles to stretch. Muscle fibres lengthen and become more differentiated, resulting in improved motor skills. Although there are individual differences in the timing of particular motor milestones, motor development is a sequential process that follows universal patterns, including the cephalocaudal and proximodistal patterns discussed throughout this book (Cech & Martin, 2012).

Motor development Motor development unfolds as children face environments that require new physical adjustment and adaptation, including school. They are now expected to use pencils, type on computer keyboards, and play sports that require flexible and complex actions. During these middle- and late-childhood years, fine motor and gross motor skills (introduced in Chapter 3) significantly improve (**Figure 7.2**) (Piek, Baynam, & Barrett, 2006; Kim, 2008).

Improvements in motor development Three types of improvements in motor development occur during childhood: **consistency**, **flexibility**, and **efficiency**, as depicted in **Figure 7.3** (Cech & Martin, 2012). All of these developments result from a continuing improvement in the

consistency The ability to physically repeat an action in the same way with the same level of function.

flexibility The ability to perform a physical act in a variety of contexts with similar outcome.

efficiency The muscular and cardiovascular system energy expended to perform a physical action.

Hand–eye coordination • Figure 7.2

Ask Yourself

The differences in these two writing samples reflect improvements in _____ motor skills.

From early to middle childhood, maturation of the central nervous system supports improved hand–eye coordination, which translates into improvements in the writing abilities of children. Maturation of the connections within the brain and throughout the central nervous system can be observed in differences in the way children are able to communicate their thoughts.

a. At 5 years and 4 months, Maria's ability to write a story about four girls having a play-date is dictated both by her ability to spell words she wants to use and her ability to write those words.

b. By the time Maria turned 9, her writing demonstrates significant brain maturation. Her brain has access to the words she needs to communicate her thoughts and improvement in her fine motor skills allows her to write significantly more clearly.

Courtesy Jennifer Tanner

Courtesy Jennifer Tanner

Improvements in motor development during middle to late childhood • Figure 7.3

Three types of motor development improvements occur in childhood (Cech & Martin, 2012):

a. Consistency
This girl must learn to use fine motor skills involving discrete muscles over repeated intervals. Early muscle development mirrors the plasticity of the brain, which is why children can learn to play the piano more quickly than adults.

b. Flexibility
This boy is drawing with a magic marker. Paint brushes, pencils, and charcoal require similar motor movements but slightly different hand positions.

c. Efficiency
Swimming requires a coordination of fine and gross motor skills that, at first, is inefficient. As this child becomes more efficient at swimming, she will increase speed and endurance and displace less water.

Kali Nine LLC/iStockphoto

Marjorie Kamys Cotera/PhotoEdit

Fine art/Alamy

Ask Yourself
1. A child who can catch a soccer ball, a tennis ball, and a large bouncy ball is exhibiting _____.
2. Increases in speed and endurance reflect improvements in _____.

coordination and interaction of the nervous and skeletal systems, as well as from genetic and environmental influences. Myelination is also a contributing factor in these changes. Once again, the predispositions set forth by nature are inseparable from the outcomes of the tasks presented by nurture. Similarly, as we will see in the next section, a child's cognitive development relies on a combination of both innate and external factors.

CONCEPT CHECK STOP

1. **What** is the role of myelination in brain development during middle and late childhood?
2. **What** types of skeletal changes affect height?
3. **What** muscular changes are responsible for the improvement in handwriting as children get older?

Cognitive Development

LEARNING OBJECTIVES

1. **Review** the major hallmarks of concrete operational thought.
2. **Identify** the major forms of social support for cognitive development.
3. **Describe** the changes that occur in information processing during middle and late childhood.
4. **Explain** how intelligence is conceptualized and tested.
5. **Report** the primary approaches to teaching reading.

For developmental psychologist Jean Piaget, thinking *operationally* means thinking logically. Logical thought involves the ability to group objects by their properties, to create categories to organize them, and to be able to reverse thinking about objects. As we will see, children in the concrete operational stage are able to understand these logical processes in relation to tangible, physical objects, but not yet in relation to abstractions (Inhelder & Piaget, 1958; Gruber & Vonèche, 1977).

A classification scheme • Figure 7.4

Classification is a hallmark of concrete operational thought and is the ability to group objects according to their shared properties.

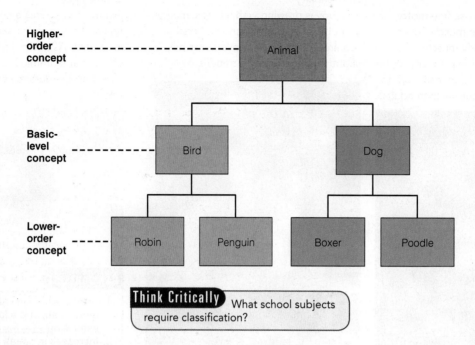

Higher-order concept — — — — — — — — — Animal

Basic-level concept — — — — — — — Bird | Dog

Lower-order concept — — — — Robin | Penguin | Boxer | Poodle

Think Critically What school subjects require classification?

Piaget's Concrete Operational Stage

As in earlier stages in Piaget's theory, children progress from the preoperational stage to the **concrete operational stage** via their interactions with the world. For example, they may start to see similarities and differences in objects around them. They may come to recognize that one person can be happy at the same time as another person is sad. They may realize that, when their brother Tommy is wearing a Halloween mask, he is still Tommy. That is, with experience in the world, children construct a new theory about the way objects work (Piaget, 1926a & b).

> **concrete operational stage** Piaget's third stage of cognitive development, in which school-age children begin to think logically about concrete events.

Evidence of concrete operational thought is found in children's ability to understand conservation, which is the awareness that objects, places, and things remain constant even though their physical properties change (discussed in Chapter 5). According to Piaget, children in the concrete operational stage not only recognize the conservation of objects but also have the ability to defend it (Piaget, 1954). For example, children at this stage are able to explain how a ball of clay can be flattened into a pancake and remain the same amount of clay.

Along with this understanding of conservation, concrete operational thinkers comprehend that tangible objects have the property of **reversibility**, meaning that they can return to original shapes. For example, a child in the concrete operational stage knows that the pancake-shaped piece of clay can be made back into a ball (Piaget, 1928; Gruber & Vonèche, 1977).

Another hallmark of concrete operational thought is the ability to group objects based on similar properties, a process called **classification** (**Figure 7.4**). Classification involves two key abilities. The first is the ability to identify the particular property that defines the class. The second is the ability to identify specific members of the class. Understanding how the world is classified is necessary for survival. We must know the difference, for example, between hot and cold, good and bad, dangerous and safe.

Another key quality of concrete operational thought is **seriation**, a type of logic that requires the arrangement of items by using a system of quantitative relationships,

> **reversibility** The ability to understand that tangible objects can return to their original form.
>
> **classification** The ability to create groups or classes of objects and sort them by similar properties.
>
> **seriation** The ability to sort objects using a rule that determines an increasing magnitude of one or more dimensions.

such as size or amount. The logic required to understand seriation also underlies key principles in arithmetic; among these is the idea of **transitivity**. Both seriation and transitivity are depicted in **Figure 7.5** (Williams, Morgan, & Kalthoff, 1992).

> **transitivity** The logical rule that says, if A is greater than B and B is greater than C, then A is greater than C.

Concrete operational thinking is qualitatively different from preoperational thinking. With this qualitative shift, children's worlds expand and their knowledge base becomes more complex. There remain, however, some limitations. Concrete operational thinkers base their decisions about the world on their own reality or experiences. For example, try asking an 8-year-old child to describe what someone from another planet might look like. Her description will likely involve known but exaggerated qualities, like a gigantic head with 40 eyes. There is little that is truly creative about such a response (Piaget, 1954).

As we discussed in Chapter 5, Vygotsky offers an important contrast to Piaget's focus on qualitative shifts happening within the individual child. Vygotsky (1987) looked beyond the child to consider the role of social and cultural experiences in children's thinking.

Seriation and transitivity • Figure 7.5

Seriation and transitivity are two hallmarks of Piaget's concrete operational stage.

a. If asked to place sticks in order by size, preoperational children do not focus on both the top and bottom of the sticks, ending up with the sticks aligned in a chaotic order. Concrete operational children, on the other hand, are able to demonstrate seriation by ordering the sticks according to size.

b. Transitivity is assessed, for example, by showing a child Card 1 and then Card 2, and then asking a child if A is bigger than C. A concrete operational child will say "yes," whereas a preoperational child will likely say "I don't know" or give the wrong answer.

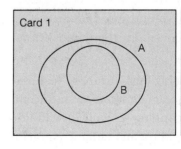
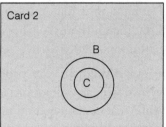

Lisa Passmore

Ask Yourself

When Ms. Khan asks her Grade 5 class to line themselves up according to height, she assumes her students have what concrete operational ability?

The Social Basis of Cognitive Development: From Vygotsky to Now

Vygotsky's (1978) socio-cultural theory, and the research it inspired, has led to a growing appreciation of cognitive development as a social process (Gauvain, Perez, & Beebe, 2013). That is, children develop their thinking in the context of other people. For school-age children, these social influences become increasingly diverse, from parents to teachers and peers to members of the larger community. Social support for cognitive development during these years takes many forms, from modelling, demonstration, and formal instruction, to less formal approaches, such as scaffolding, casual conversations, and participation in cultural institutions (Gauvain et al., 2013; see also Rogoff, 1998).

Researchers have identified five key features of scaffolding students' learning environments:

1. sharing a common goal,
2. conducting ongoing diagnosis of students' progress,
3. offering dynamic and adaptive support,
4. maintaining dialogues and interaction, and
5. fading and transfer of responsibility (Puntambekar & Kolodner, 2005).

Like Vygotsky, you probably envision these features as involving a student and a teacher. However, in recent years, teachers have used technology-enhanced scaffolding in their classrooms to build on and enhance human scaffolding.

One team of researchers studied how Grade 6 students use different types of scaffolds to solve scientific problems in everyday classroom settings (Kim & Hannafin, 2011). The students in this study participated in a science project in which they had to solve the problem of a local community's growing wolf population. Students used teacher and peer scaffolds, as well as technology-enhanced scaffolds designed to help students reflect on and assess their own thinking process, as described in *Where Developmentalists Click.*

In general, the combination of teacher-, peer-, and technology-supported scaffolds helped Grade 6 students investigate problems and find solutions (Kim & Hannafin, 2011). Each type of scaffold served different, but complementary, purposes. Teacher scaffolds helped students monitor their progress, remain on task, and refine strategies, whereas peer scaffolds inspired and challenged students' thinking. Technology-based scaffolds helped students to visualize their understandings, identify resources,

and manage the number of items that require their attention at a given moment in time, also known as **cognitive load**.

> **cognitive load**
> The total number of items that must be attended to by one's working memory, where information is temporarily stored and manipulated.

Whether scaffolds come in the form of other people or technologies designed by other people, Vygotsky's contributions have led researchers to appreciate that problem solving, and learning in general, are social processes. We turn now to the information-processing perspective, which offers another way of thinking about problem-solving and other cognitive abilities during middle and late childhood.

Information-Processing Perspective

As we have discussed in earlier chapters, the information-processing perspective examines increases in cognitive abilities such as attention, reasoning, problem solving, memory, and metacognition. For children in this age group, the school environment requires use of all of these cognitive abilities. Information-processing approaches focus on describing the changes necessary for success in school, as well as for other aspects of a child's life, such as games and sports (Borkowski & Burke, 1996).

Problem solving According to information-processing theorists, problem-solving abilities improve in four key areas across childhood: selective attention, automatization, strategy construction, and strategy selection. We will consider each in turn.

Selective attention is a child's ability to make a decision about what is relevant and what is irrelevant among a series of competing stimuli. As we discussed earlier, changes in brain structure result in increasing control over cognitive processes, aiding in selective attention. In addition, direct instruction in attention can help children improve their selective attention abilities (Huang-Pollock, Nigg, & Carr, 2005).

> **selective attention** The ability to attend to a particular item in the environment while inhibiting other distracting stimuli.
>
> **automatization**
> The allocation of fewer attentional resources to perform simple, repetitive behaviours.
>
> **reaction time**
> The time involved in responding to a stimulus.

Automatization is the ability to allocate less attentional capacity to tasks. With practice and repetition, tasks become routine, **reaction time** decreases, and automatization

Technology-Enhanced Scaffolding in a Classroom Setting

The Web-based Inquiry Science Environment (WISE) is an Internet-based platform that helps students solve problems through guided inquiry activities, visualization tools, embedded communication features like hints, and other technology-enhanced scaffolding (Kim & Hannafin, 2011). Since 1997, WISE has served a growing community of science teachers, researchers, and curriculum designers, as well as 100,000+ K–12 students around the world. Access the site by going to the WISE homepage (https://wise.berkeley.edu/). Click on one of the WISE Features and learn more about this virtual learning environment.

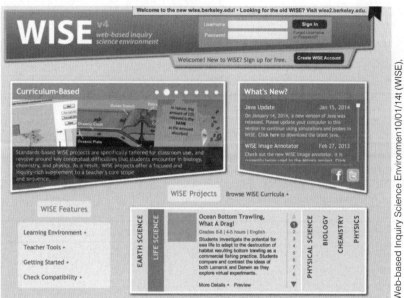

Web-based Inquiry Science Environmen10/01/14t (WISE), http://wise.berkeley.edu

improves. For example, once a child has mastered pedalling and steering a bicycle, he can then turn attention to other bicycling skills like using hand signals or manoeuvring around objects (Moores, Nicolson, & Fawcett, 2003).

In addition to improvements in selective attention and automatization, use of strategies advances during childhood. A **strategy** is a consciously available, effortful plan deliberately used to solve a specific problem (Bjorklund, 1990). Strategy construction in childhood is fairly basic, such as **maintenance rehearsal**, in which a child repeats words (or images, behaviours, and so on) over and over in order to remember them. That is not to say that children do not use more complex strategies. Bjorklund (1990) and his colleagues (Bjorklund, Muir-Broaddus, & Schneider, 1990) suggest that there is a continuum of strategies, from simple ones to those requiring more effort and resulting in more effective outcomes.

strategy An effortful plan deliberately used to solve a specific problem.

maintenance rehearsal A retention strategy in which a child repeats the thing to be remembered (words, images, actions) in order to remember them.

metamemory One's understanding of one's own memory process.

But even if a strategy has been constructed, it does not mean it will be effectively employed. Selecting the correct strategy to solve a problem requires a level of cognitive awareness unavailable earlier in development. Children must not only have the ability to store strategies, but they must also be able to access and choose the best one for the problem at hand. However, because strategy selection is difficult to observe objectively, information-processing theorists do not yet agree on what differentiates use of a planned strategy from the non-strategic completion of a task (Bjorklund et al., 1990). An area in which there is greater consensus is memory development.

Memory The most dramatic change in memory ability between the ages of 3 and 10 years is the emergence of **metamemory** (Flavell, 1971; Dixon, 2000; Metcalfe, 2000).

Three categories of memory • Figure 7.6

Information from the outside world flows from the sensory memory to the working memory to the long-term memory. The executive function, which plays a supervisory role, regulates the flow of information.

Executive function

Information enters from the environment

1 Sensory memory
Holds sensory data for a very short time (visual information for less than a second, and auditory information for 2–3 seconds)

Some data move into working memory. Attention helps to determine which data enter working memory and which are lost

2 Working (short-term) memory
Temporary storage and manipulation of information

Encoded information moves into long-term memory for storage and is retrieved from long-term memory for use in working memory

3 Long-term memory
Provides storage of large amounts of information over a long time

Put It Together *Review the section* The Social Basis of Cognitive Development: From Vygotsky to Now *and answer the following question:*
Cognitive load involves what category of memory?
a. sensory memory
b. working (short-term) memory
c. long-term memory
d. all of the above

For example, what do you do when you want to remember something for a long time? How do you help yourself remember the names of people you have just met? You probably have effective strategies for these and many other memory scenarios. Creating these strategies requires metamemory. Metamemory appears in early childhood and gradually increases from elementary school through high school.

Metamemory involves four key functions. They are:

1. knowledge regarding the function of memory and strategies based on that knowledge,

2. awareness of ongoing memory processes,

3. awareness of one's ability to remember things, and

4. knowledge of the relationship between emotion and memory (Hertzog, 1992).

As each of these factors improves, cognitive efficiency also increases.

Although young children have difficulty knowing how much they can remember and developing strategies to improve their memory, with age they come to recognize the importance of strategies and to understand the causes of their errors (Schneider, 1999; Dixon, 2000). In turn, metamemory improvements underlie improvements in all three categories of memory: **sensory memory, working (short-term) memory**, and **long-term memory** (Cowan, 2008) (**Figure 7.6**).

As you saw in Figure 7.6, the **executive function** supervises the memory process, regulating and controlling key processes, including working memory, attention, planning, and problem solving, among others. Within the information-processing perspective, the executive function actually supervises all of the processes that are fundamental to cognitive development, such as attention, planning, problem solving, and metacognition.

sensory memory The ability to briefly store sensory information so that it may be processed.

working (short-term) memory The ability to keep a small amount of information (7 ± 2 items) in an active, ready-to-use state for a short time.

long-term memory The vast and virtually limitless store of knowledge and prior events.

executive function The aspect of the brain that supervises the memory process by regulating the flow of information and controlling key processes.

Metacognition Any discussion of cognitive processes in childhood would be incomplete without a consideration of the overriding process of **metacognition**, or knowing about knowing. Bjorklund (1990) points out that there are very few cognitive processes without a *meta* attached to them. Among the meta processes are communication, imitation, and self-knowledge. He therefore concludes that "metacognition is seen as a cause and consequence of other aspects of cognition" (p. 10). Metacognition leads us naturally to one of the most controversial issues in childhood: the definition and assessment of intelligence.

> **metacognition**
> The process of knowing about knowing.
>
> **general intelligence (g)**
> A construct thought to underlie one's ability to adapt and determine one's competence level.

Intelligence

What is intelligence? How does one define it? Can we measure it? Despite the ubiquity of the concept of *intelligence* in popular society, different definitions abound (see Sternberg & Detterman, 1986). Conventional notions of intelligence define it as a generalized adaptation to the environment (Birney & Sternberg, 2011). Building on this idea, psychometric theories of intelligence (Spearman's, in particular) posit the existence of a **general intelligence** construct (**g**) that underlies one's ability to adapt (**Figure 7.7**; e.g., Jensen, 1998; see also Sternberg & Grigorenko, 2002).

General intelligence or g • Figure 7.7

According to Spearman's model, an individual's general intelligence determines his or her specific ability level.

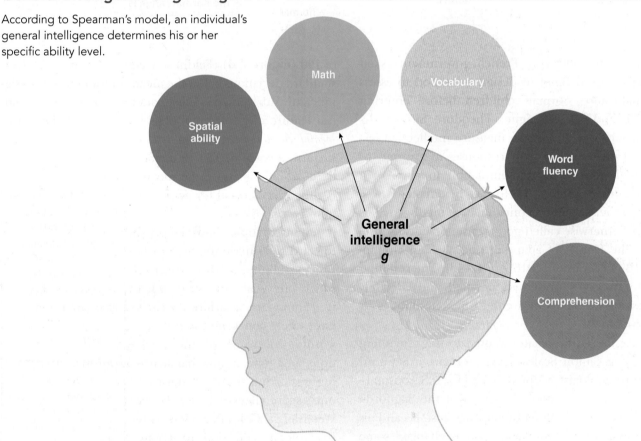

Ask Yourself

According to the general intelligence perspective, if Sébastien's math ability exceeds Yulan's, then we can assume that his general intelligence _____.
a. is lower than Yulan's
b. is equal to Yulan's
c. exceeds Yulan's
d. We cannot assume anything about the difference between Sébastien and Yulan's general intelligence.

The Stanford–Binet Intelligence Test • Figure 7.8

The national average on the Stanford–Binet Intelligence Test is 100, which means that a child is performing at the level expected for his age. Most children score within one standard deviation (15 points) above or below the national average. Few children score lower than 70 or higher than 130, which is why these are the common cut-off points for intellectual disability and genius or gifted categorizations, respectively.

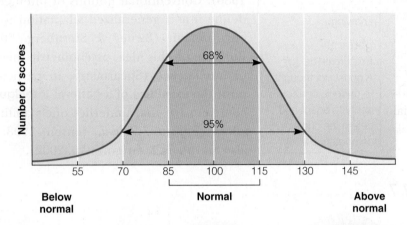

Ask Yourself

The percentage of children scoring within the normal range is _____.

In the early 1900s, the French government asked psychologist Alfred Binet to design a method to assess "subnormal" and "normal" children before entering school. He and his colleague, Theodore Simon, developed a series of 30 tests to measure intellectual levels of children based on their responses to a variety of things ranging from tactile stimulation to parts of a picture (Binet & Simon, 1916). As he created these measures, Binet began to conceptualize intelligence as "judgment, otherwise called good sense, practical sense, initiative, the faculty of adapting one's self to circumstances" (Binet & Simon, 1916, pp. 42–43). The resulting Binet–Simon Scales presented detailed and precisely constructed assessments of a child's mental abilities or levels of judgment.

Because the United States wanted to use something like the Binet–Simon Scales, Lewis Terman, a Stanford University psychologist, adapted the test for U.S. consumption and named it the Stanford–Binet Intelligence Test. He and his graduate students changed some questions and used the term "mental age" rather than level to assess the outcomes. His work led to the concept of **intelligence quotient**, or **IQ**, which is a child's mental age (MA) divided by his or her chronological age (CA) multiplied by 100, resulting in an average score

intelligence quotient (IQ) A score calculated from results on an intelligence test originally derived from the formula of (mental age/chronological age) × 100, resulting in an average score of 100.

of 100 (**Figure 7.8**) (Feldhusen, 2003). A score of 70 (two standard deviations below the mean) or lower indicates significantly subaverage intellectual functioning and is a central feature of **intellectual disability** (formerly known as *mental retardation*; American Psychiatric Association, 2013). In turn, a score of 130 (two standard deviations above the mean) is a theorized cut-off for genius or **gifted** categorization.

Many people have stepped forward to criticize the Stanford–Binet's validity, or the extent to which the scale measures what it claims to measure. Critics have been concerned about the wording of some of the questions and have noted that learning test-taking skills can improve one's score (Becker, 2003). David Wechsler, a Columbia University psychologist, decided to create alternate measures, called the **Wechsler Intelligence Scales**. These scales are now widely used, and there are different versions for various age groups. In Wechsler's view, intelligence involves a "global capacity to think rationally" (Wechsler, 1944, p. 3).

intellectual disability A disorder characterized by significantly below-average intellectual functioning (an IQ of 70 or lower) and impaired adaptive functioning, with onset prior to 18 years of age.

gifted Significantly above-average intellectual functioning as indicated by an IQ of 130 or higher.

Wechsler Intelligence Scales Popular psychometric test purporting to measure the global capacity to think rationally.

Sternberg's triarchic theory of successful intelligence • Figure 7.9

Intelligence has three components according to Sternberg's theory: Analytical (strength in problem solving and analysis); practical (having street smarts, or the ability to fit in well with one's environment); and creative (the ability to come up with novel solutions and to be inventive).

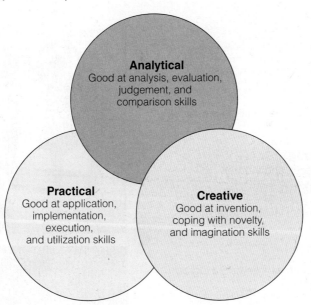

Analytical
Good at analysis, evaluation, judgement, and comparison skills

Practical
Good at application, implementation, execution, and utilization skills

Creative
Good at invention, coping with novelty, and imagination skills

Ask Yourself

Children with vibrant imaginations are demonstrating _____.

---

triarchic theory of successful intelligence A theory of intelligence advanced by Robert Sternberg emphasizing three key components: analytical, practical, and creative.

analytical intelligence Abstract, verbal, mathematical, and logical types of thinking.

practical intelligence Common sense needed for real-world situations that require adaptation and basic knowledge.

creative intelligence Divergent, novel, and problem-solving–oriented thinking.

Concerned with the narrowness of the general intelligence construct, a growing number of scholars have sought to expand the theoretical foundations of intelligence (e.g., Gardner, 1993a & b; Sternberg, 2003). In his **triarchic theory of successful intelligence**, depicted in **Figure 7.9**, Stanford University psychologist Robert Sternberg proposed that intelligence is the ability to have a successful life by balancing **analytical**, **practical**, and **creative intelligence** (Birney & Sternberg, 2011).

Harvard psychologist Howard Gardner also questioned and rejected the conventional notion of intelligence as a single, global capacity. He posited eight different intelligences in his **theory of multiple intelligences**, described in **Figure 7.10**: linguistic, spatial, bodily/kinesthetic, intrapersonal, logical/mathematical, musical, interpersonal, and naturalistic (Gardner, 1993a & b, 1999). Later, he reflected on the possibility of a ninth intelligence: spiritual/existential (Gardner, 1999, 2011).

Despite excitement regarding the newer perspectives on intelligence, criticisms continue regarding defining and testing intelligence. One of the most pointed criticisms concerns research on intelligence that ignores the cultural context and draws false and hasty generalizations (Sternberg, 2004). These critics warn that intelligence research conducted within a single culture may fail to recognize the full range of skills and knowledge that constitute intelligence in other cultures. Accordingly, intelligence must be understood within its cultural context. We will explore more deeply the question of bias in intelligence testing in future chapters. For now, we return to a topic we last examined during early childhood: language development.

theory of multiple intelligences A theory of intelligence advanced by Howard Gardner suggesting the existence of at least eight distinct intelligences.

Language Development

Unlike earlier periods of the lifespan, middle and later childhood is a time for the broadening and expansion

Gardner's theory of multiple intelligences • Figure 7.10

Gardner's multiple intelligences are conceptualized as somewhat independent, though their interaction may lead to intelligent behaviour.

TYPE OF INTELLIGENCE

Linguistic
Language, such as speaking, reading a book, writing a story

Spatial
Mental maps, such as figuring out how to pack multiple presents in a box or how to draw a floor plan

Bodily/kinesthetic
Body movement, such as dancing, soccer, and football

Intrapersonal
Understanding oneself, such as setting achievable goals or recognizing self-defeating emotions

Logical/mathematical
Problem solving or scientific analysis, such as following a logical proof or solving a mathematical problem

Musical
Musical skills, such as singing or playing a musical instrument

Interpersonal
Social skills, such as managing diverse groups of people

Naturalistic
Being attuned to nature, such as noticing seasonal patterns or using environmentally safe products

Spiritual/existential
Attunement to meaning of life and death and other conditions of life

Source: Gardner 1993, 1999, 2011.

Courtesy Jennifer Tanner

Michael Freeman/Corbis

Horizon Images/Motion/Alamy

Put It Together *Review Figure 7.9 and answer the following question:*
Sternberg's analytical intelligence is most similar to Gardner's _____ intelligence.

of already existing language skills. Whether these skills are related to speech comprehension, language production, or the understanding of words on a page, the changes may be more subtle than those observed during infancy and early childhood. They are, however, just as important.

Improvements in speech and linguistic understanding
The most obvious change in the development of language during childhood is vocabulary size. Children continue to build upon the techniques of early word learning that rely on comparison of categories of objects (Hall & Rhemtulla, 2014) and their word learning is facilitated by their

expanding working memory and attentional control (Rabi & Minda, 2014) as they enter school. When children start Grade 1, their vocabulary is approximately 14,000 words on average. By the time they reach Grade 4, it has grown to 40,000 words (Pianta, Belsky, Vandergrift, Houts, & Morrison, 2008). The role that vocabulary plays in both thinking and understanding has been a recurring debate within developmental scholarship. From questions surrounding the accuracy of measuring a child's vocabulary (Bornstein & Haynes, 1998) to research into the relationship between vocabulary and academic competency (Beitchman et al., 2008), attempts to infer meaning from this increase in vocabulary has led to many competing viewpoints.

Another language event for children is a change in their ability to understand the context of words, or to understand the pragmatics of language, a concept we introduced in Chapter 5. Understanding of pragmatics becomes increasingly evident as a child enters school and begins to learn more about the nature of language (Levinson, 2011). For example, a young child may ask her uncle, "Why is your nose so big?" or say, "You smell funny." With age, however, the child realizes that these statements may be inappropriate. That is, children come to realize that certain situations require a different tone of speech and that certain questions should be withheld to protect a person's feelings.

Children also experience a greater understanding of how language works, called metalinguistic awareness (Zipke, 2007). This knowledge about language improves largely because of direct instruction in school. In addition, around 6 years of age children begin to realize that there is more to the meaning of what someone says than just the literal definition; they learn that tone, context, and word choice are important components of communication (Cain, Oakhill, & Elbro, 2003).

metalinguistic awareness Understanding the complexity of language and the fact that language relies on context as well as individual word meaning.

bilingual Able to speak two languages.

multilingual Able to speak more than two languages.

Additional-language learning

For children growing up **bilingual**, metalinguistic awareness increases with regard to two languages. Children are bilingual either because they have learned two languages at the same time from an early age or because they learned a second language after acquiring the first. The same holds for **multilingual**

development. The percentage of multilingual homes is growing in Canada. According to census documents, in 2006 approximately 4.5 million people spoke at least two languages at home. This percentage rose in 2011 to 17.5 percent (approximately 5.8 million people, Statistics Canada, 2011).

Research examining the case of later **second-language learning** has documented a suppression of the native language, called *first-language attrition* (Levy, McVeigh, Marful, & Anderson, 2007). Pallier et al. (2003) reported that children adopted in middle childhood who learn the language of their parents often have no memory of their native language when they are adults.

In the public school system, Canadian children have opportunities for French and English language instruction. All provinces, for example, offer minority-language education programs, a form of **bilingual education**, aimed at students whose native language is French in provinces other than Quebec and whose native language is English in Quebec. During the 2008/2009 school year, approximately 244,000 students were enrolled in minority-language education programs wherein the language spoken at home was their classroom instruction language and it was a minority language in their community (McMullen & Brockington, 2011). These programs may also provide helpful education options for new Canadians who will not only be faced with the daunting challenge of learning a new culture, but may also be learning an additional language. Many Canadian elementary schools offer **English as a second language (ESL)** programs specifically targeting students who have immigrated from non–English-speaking locations; the structure of such programs varies considerably by location, reflecting the diverse rates of immigration found across the country (Burnaby, 2008). **Figure 7.11** shows the most common non-official language in each region of the country. In addition to the original Aboriginal languages, Canada has a rich language diversity. Understanding the language of their adopted country creates issues at home as well as at school. When children learn the new language more

second-language learning The process of learning another, non-native language.

bilingual education Academic instruction in two languages: a native language and a secondary language.

English as a second language (ESL) Language education programs, in which non–English-speaking students are taught English.

A look at Canada without English and French • Figure 7.11

From Tagalog in the Yukon to Spanish in Quebec, there is a rich language diversity throughout Canada (Kuzmin, Motskin, & Gallinger, 2015).

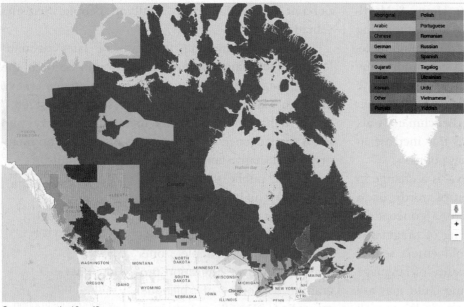

Source: www.the10and3.com

Think Critically How might second-language learning affect children's acclimation to a new culture?

proficiently than their parents, issues of pride and loss of face for the parent can become an added problem for the family (Pedersen, Draguns, Lonner, & Trimble, 2008). The effects of additional-language learning are still being examined. Given that Canada continues to be a land of increasing diversity, multi-language learning will remain a significant topic of research in coming decades.

Language immersion programs are also popular in Canada. The majority of second-language immersion

language immersion
Language education programs in which students are taught academic content exclusively in a non-native language (a language not spoken at home).

programs are aimed at anglophone students in provinces other than Quebec (McMullen & Brockington, 2011). Since the early 1990s, public school enrolment in Canada has been decreasing in line with decreasing population numbers (McMullen & Brockington, 2011); however, French immersion enrolment has

risen by 28 percent (Lepage & Corbeil, 2013). Research points to the educational benefits of second-language instruction (Menken & Solorza, 2014). However, many English-speaking Canadians outside of Quebec do not retain their learned bilingualism as they grow older (Lepage & Corbeil, 2013).

Regardless of the language being learned, middle and late childhood is a time for the deepening and broadening of language skills that were established during early childhood. Burgeoning linguistic abilities are also called upon as a child learns to read (Snowling, 2005).

Reading instruction Learning to read may be one of the most difficult school tasks a child must master. For example, English is a non-intuitive language because words are spelled with silent letters, all rules have exceptions, and sounds produced by certain letter combinations vary, with no particular consistency. Encountering a new problem on each page can lead to frustration and decreased motivation, calling upon a child's temperament, effortful control, and emotion regulation skills. Even when taught by skilled teachers, learning to read requires an academic resilience unlike any other topic in school (McTigue, Washburn, & Liew, 2009).

McTigue, Washburn, and Liew (2009) have identified six classroom characteristics that foster academic resilience and reinforce mastery of reading:

Principle 1: Create a warm, accepting environment. A safe environment encourages new readers to take reading risks.

Principle 2: Assess academic resilience. Measuring behaviours such as engagement, inquiry, and self-monitoring are useful indicators of academic resilience.

Principle 3: Model literacy and self-efficacy. Teachers should demonstrate academic resilience in themselves, as well as helping students overcome roadblocks.

Principle 4: Use effective feedback. Effective feedback is specific and accurate, and emphasizes effort.

Principle 5: Set goals. Target specific and realistic goals and outcomes for student achievement.

phonics approach A form of reading instruction that emphasizes the segments of sounds in words in the learning of reading skills.

whole-language approach A form of reading instruction that emphasizes communication over particular elements of reading and writing, such as spelling or sounds.

Principle 6: Promote self-evaluation. Students should be able to improve reading skills by evaluating what they are doing and how well they do it (McTigue et al., 2009).

You might notice that something is conspicuously absent from these principles: how precisely to teach the reading process. In fact, this question has been a matter of great debate among educators and psychologists. Two key methods of reading instruction have emerged: the **phonics approach** and the **whole-language approach**. The phonics approach teaches reading by breaking down words into their constituent sounds, such as "lie" and "on" for "lion." The whole-language approach, on the other hand, focuses on the meaning and relationships between and among words (Stahl, McKenna, & Pagnucco, 1994; Gray et al., 2007).

Regardless of the approach, improving one's reading skills is a lifelong process. Early positive experience with reading is associated with later academic achievement as well as enhanced vocational success (Zins, Bloodworth, Weissberg, & Walberg, 2004). In the next section, we take a closer look at academic achievement and the developmental context of school.

CONCEPT CHECK 🛑 STOP

1. **What** is the significance of a child understanding conservation, according to Piaget?
2. **What** is a contemporary example of Vygotsky's concept of scaffolding?
3. **What** are the key differences between information-processing theory and Piaget's theory?
4. **Why** is intelligence difficult to define?
5. **How** is reading related to language development?

All the Systems Working Together

LEARNING OBJECTIVES

1. **Review** the major goals of learning in school.
2. **Identify** disorders that make learning in school difficult.
3. **Describe** the factors that promote and threaten children's physical health and well-being.

As we have discussed, there tends to be a slow-down of physical changes in middle to late childhood, allowing for time to improve coordination, to better react to a changing world, and to face new challenges away from the comfort of home. Vitally important to all of these developments is a child's overall health.

In this section, we examine some of the common health issues of childhood. But first we focus on the developmental context of school, examining the issues surrounding this influential institution and its role in the development of children.

The Developmental Context of School

Since 1979, when Bronfenbrenner wrote the first of his landmark papers on the physical and socio-cultural contexts of human development, researchers have become increasingly interested in the developmental context of school (Eccles & Roeser, 2011). And rightly so, when, by middle childhood, the majority of the world's children are spending more time in school than any other setting outside the home.

Schools are complex, multi-level institutions that affect the development of the whole child, including his or her cognitive-intellectual, social-emotional, physical, and behavioural development (**Figure 7.12**; Eccles & Roeser, 2011). We can think of these multiple levels as forming causal chains of influence, where one level affects another, which affects another, and so on (Eccles & Roeser, 2011).

Given the central role of schools in children's lives, it is not surprising that today the goals of learning in school extend beyond the three Rs of reading, writing, and arithmetic. Additional goals of learning in school include moral and character development, the cultivation of certain mental habits like persistence and concentration, and the promotion of social-emotional skills (Blumenfeld, Marx, & Harris, 2006; Eccles & Roeser, 2011).

The goals of learning in school The goals of learning in school, as well as in other learning environments, can be academic, social-emotional, metacognitive, and developmental (Blumenfeld et al., 2006). Academic goals focus on learning particular subject matter and are typically based on standards set forth by professional organizations. For instance, the National Council of Teachers of Mathematics (2000) has outlined standards for teaching mathematics.

Social-emotional goals of learning in school are at the heart of an emerging curriculum movement known as **social and emotional learning (SEL)**

> **social and emotional learning (SEL)** Educational programs seeking to foster the development of five non–subject-matter competencies: self-awareness, self-management, social awareness, relationship skills, and responsible decision-making.

The multiple levels of the school context • Figure 7.12

Eccles and Roeser (2011) identified seven nested levels of the school context that span everything from the student's academic work to the educational policies of his or her nation, state, and local school district.

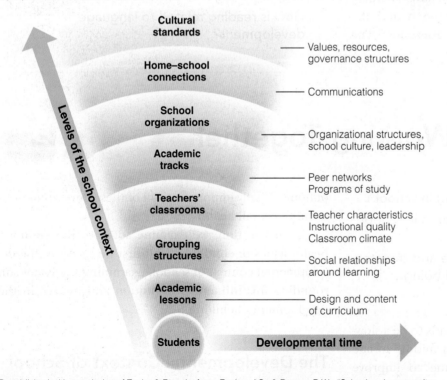

Levels of the school context

- Cultural standards — Values, resources, governance structures
- Home–school connections — Communications
- School organizations — Organizational structures, school culture, leadership
- Academic tracks — Peer networks / Programs of study
- Teachers' classrooms — Teacher characteristics / Instructional quality / Classroom climate
- Grouping structures — Social relationships around learning
- Academic lessons — Design and content of curriculum
- Students — Developmental time

Think Critically At which of the seven levels would you see the greatest parent participation?

Republished with permission of Taylor & Francis, from Eccles, J.S., & Roeser, R.W., "School and community influences on human development." In M.E. Lamb & M.H. Bornstein (Eds.), *Social and personality development: An advanced textbook.* Copyright © 2011. Permission conveyed through Copyright Clearance Center, Inc.

(Durlak, Weissberg, Dymnicki, Taylor, & Schellinger, 2011). SEL programs seek to foster the development of five non–subject-matter competencies: self-awareness, self-management, social awareness, relationship skills, and responsible decision-making (Collaborative for Academic, Social, and Emotional Learning, 2005). Canadian schools are responding to the opportunity to enrich the core competencies of social and emotional learning, and SEL-based programs are currently being delivered in selected schools across Nova Scotia, Alberta, and Manitoba (Canadian Mental Health Association Nova Scotia,

2015). South of the border, Illinois recently became the first state to require SEL programs in every school district. **Table 7.1** summarizes the social and emotional development standards that were added to the Illinois learning standards (Illinois State Board of Education, n.d.). SEL standards are being instituted in other states (such as New York) as well and in other countries (such as Singapore).

In a recent meta-analysis of 213 SEL programs (Durlak et al., 2011) involving more than a quarter million students spanning the middle to late childhood years

Illinois social/emotional learning goals and standards	**Table 7.1**	
SEL goals	**Learning Standards**	
Goal 1: Develop self-awareness and self-management skills to achieve school and life success.	A. Identify and manage one's emotions and behaviour. B. Recognize personal qualities and external supports. C. Demonstrate skills related to achieving personal and academic goals.	
Goal 2: Use social-awareness and interpersonal skills to establish and maintain positive relationships.	A: Recognize the feelings and perspectives of others. B: Recognize individual and group similarities and differences. C: Use communication and social skills to interact effectively with others. D. Demonstrate an ability to prevent, manage, and resolve interpersonal conflicts in constructive ways.	
Goal 3: Demonstrate decision-making skills and responsible behaviours in personal, school, and community contexts.	A: Consider ethical, safety, and societal factors in making decisions. B: Apply decision-making skills to deal responsibly with daily academic and social situations. C: Contribute to the well-being of one's school and community.	

BSIP/UIG/Getty Images

Heidi Velten/Age Fotostock

Sasse/laif/Redux

and beyond, SEL participants had significantly improved socio-emotional skills, attitudes, behaviour, and academic performance. Consistent with previous research (Eisenberg, 2006; Guerra & Bradshaw, 2008), these findings suggest that meeting socio-emotional goals of learning in school also helps students meet intellectual and behavioural goals.

Metacognitive goals have to do with promoting certain habits of mind, ways of thinking, and reasoning that support learning (Blumenfeld et al., 2006). Examples of these mental habits include maintaining concentration and using strategies to monitor progress and revise one's approach when needed. Finally, developmental goals focus on students' progression in terms of their levels of knowledge and the sophistication of their thinking (Blumenfeld et al., 2006).

Teachers' beliefs about the goals of learning in school have important implications for their instructional behaviour and interpersonal style in the classroom (Eccles & Roeser, 2011). As we will see, there are grade-related differences in these beliefs.

The elementary school years (ages 5 to 10) As children transition into elementary school, they encounter a number of important changes (Eccles & Roeser, 2011). Classes are age stratified, making social comparison among age-mates easier to do. Elementary school children are also grouped for the first time based on their abilities (for example, reading group assignment) and begin receiving formal evaluations of their performance. Studies have shown that ability grouping is based not only on ability, but also on other personal characteristics, such as temperament, ethnicity, gender, and social class (e.g., Alexander, Entwisle, & Dauber, 1994; Rist, 1970). And one's particular group placement, after controlling for differences in beginning competence, significantly affects academic achievement, motivation, and behaviour even years later (Alexander et al., 1994).

Teachers' perceptions about the goals of learning in school influence their classroom behaviour (Eccles & Roeser, 2011). Two contrasting achievement goals espoused by teachers have received the most scientific attention: **mastery goals** and **performance goals** (**Figure 7.13**). Mastery goals centre on self-improvement and skill development, and

mastery goal An achievement goal that focuses on self-improvement and skill development, while downplaying ability level and peer comparison.

performance goal An achievement goal that emphasizes ability level and competition among peers.

racialized People or communities that are treated poorly or experience violence because of racism or a belief that they are inferior.

de-emphasize current ability level and social comparison (Ames, 1992). Elementary teachers of mastery-oriented classrooms are more likely to stress the intrinsic value of learning, promote peer collaboration, and tailor instruction to their students' developmental levels and interests (Meece, 1991). Not surprisingly, these practices are associated with intrinsic motivation—motivation that comes from within the self rather than from an external source—and persistence in the face of difficulty (Elliott & Dweck, 1988; Murayama & Elliot, 2009).

In performance-oriented classrooms, on the other hand, the goal is to demonstrate one's abilities and to outperform peers (Covington, 1984). Teachers who hold performance goals for their students are more likely to group their students by ability level, publicly assess performance, and use academic competitions and rewards for top performers (Ames, 1992). In turn, their students are more likely to be anxious and to use self-handicapping strategies, such as intentionally withdrawing effort (Urdan, Midgley, & Anderman, 1998). Taken together, these findings suggest that long-term and high-quality learning is promoted by a mastery goal orientation. And, yet, as children move through elementary school and eventually into middle school (ages 10 to 14 years), there appears to be a shift away from mastery goals to performance goals, competition, and social comparison (e.g., Midgley, 2002).

Another shift we see during these years concerns teachers' beliefs about their professional role. Elementary school teachers tend to see themselves as socializers, whereas teachers of older grades identify most often with the role of academic instructor (McPartland, 1990). At the same time, students' sense of belonging and perceptions of emotional support from their teachers are on the decline (Burchinal, Roberts, Zeisel, & Rowley, 2008). Sense of belonging, which is tied to motivation to learn (Osterman, 2000), may be particularly important for students of minority groups.

Poverty, ethnicity, culture, and achievement gaps Poverty and its correlates may help to explain the ongoing achievement gaps that we see between students from different racial, ethnic, and linguistic backgrounds (Eccles & Roeser, 2011). **Racialized** Canadians continue to face disproportionate representation within national poverty ratings (Employment

Mastery versus performance goals • Figure 7.13

Mastery and performance goals represent two contrasting ways of thinking about and engaging in learning activities (Ames, 1992).

a. Children with mastery goals tend to think that effort leads to success (Ames & Archer, 1988). They are more likely to prefer challenging tasks and to view learning in a positive light.

Eduardo Verdugo/AP Photos

b. On the other hand, children with performance goals tend to think that superior performance leads to success (Dweck, 1986). These children are more likely to avoid challenging tasks and to tie their self-worth to their ability to perform.

Andersen Ross/Blend Images/Getty Images

Ask Yourself

1. Peer collaboration is more likely to occur when teachers hold _____ goals for their students.
2. When children define success as doing better than everyone else, they most likely hold _____ goals.

and Social Development Canada, 2013), and Canadian researchers continue to report a persistent and positive relationship between socio-economic status and academic achievement (Caro, McDonald, & Willms, 2009; Edgerton, Peter, & Roberts, 2008).

Achievement gaps are also apparent among different cultural groups worldwide (Provasnik et al., 2012). Students from Asian countries, for example, tend to outperform Canadian students in science on standardized **achievement tests** (Canadian Council on

> **achievement test** A measure of children's knowledge about particular academic subjects, such as reading, writing, or mathematics.

Learning, 2005; Frase, 1997). Why does such a discrepancy exist? Chao (2000) suggests that Asian children simply spend more time in school. However, time in school does not seem an adequate explanation; if we look within systems that have the same amount of time in school, we will still see achievement discrepancies. For example, regional achievement gaps also exist in Canada; the Atlantic provinces have been observed as performing below the Canadian average in most domains (Canadian Council on Learning, 2005;

WHAT A DEVELOPMENTALIST SEES
Specific Learning Disorders

Specific learning disorder in children who are otherwise developing typically is the most frequently occurring developmental disorder of childhood (Berninger, 2006). Some learning disorders are specific to one academic domain, whereas others involve more than one domain.

a. The specific learning disorder dyscalculia is difficulty in learning or understanding how we use numbers to represent, communicate, and manipulate quantitative information. Approximately 3 to 6 percent of the population meets criteria for dyscalculia, although not every child with the disorder is diagnosed. One symptom of dyscalculia in school-aged children is a deficiency in understanding quantity. This may be observed as a slow ability to compare the quantity of two numbers. For example, an 8-year-old student with dyscalculia would take longer to answer this question correctly than a student who does not have dyscalculia.

Which number is larger?

3   8

b. Brain research provides insight into cognitive processes and learning disorders. These two fMRI scans show the activity of two brains during intelligence testing. The higher-IQ brain on the right (the high-IQ brain) shows less activity than the lower-IQ brain on the left, illustrating that lower-IQ brains work harder, but not as efficiently. Although we cannot yet cure learning disorders, uncovering such brain differences may help us to understand the difficulties that plague thousands of schoolchildren.

Courtesy Richard J. Haier, University of California-Irvine

Think Critically What types of cognitive and social developmental impairments are likely to occur if, for example, a reading disorder is left untreated?

Edgerton et al., 2008). International and domestic comparisons are valuable in highlighting areas for improvement, but it is essential to place them in context. Different locations can have different priorities, education systems, educational values, and strategies for achieving success (Canadian Council on Learning, 2005).

Clearly, there seems to be more to achievement than just hours of work. Parental expectations, cultural beliefs, and level of involvement also play a role in supporting or undermining student success (Sy & Schulenberg, 2005). The powerful role parents play in shaping children's in-school learning is also illustrated by the special education movement in Canada, the topic to which we turn next.

autism spectrum disorder (ASD) A neurodevelopmental disorder characterized by impaired social communication and interaction, and repetitive behaviours.

Children with Special Learning Needs

Throughout this book, we have discussed the various domains of development: cognitive, physical, emotional, and social. Examining these domains helps us to understand whether children are developing and learning in a typical way or whether they are facing some developmental challenges. In this section of the chapter, we will discuss some of the most common learning and developmental challenges faced by school-aged children.

Autism spectrum disorder (ASD) As discussed in Chapter 5, children with **autism spectrum disorder (ASD)** experience impaired

CHALLENGES IN DEVELOPMENT
Attention-Deficit/Hyperactivity Disorder (ADHD)

Cindy is an 8-year-old girl who is having trouble in school (**Figure a**). She fidgets, is distracted, and often talks excessively or blurts out answers before the teacher has finished asking the question. At home things are no better: she is forgetful and has great difficulty concentrating on household tasks or even play activities, moving from one thing to the next without completion of the activity. Cindy has attention-deficit/hyperactivity disorder (ADHD), a persistent pattern of inattention and/or hyperactivity and impulsivity that emerges prior to 12 years of age and causes impairment in multiple contexts (American Psychiatric Association, 2013).

According to the American Psychiatric Association (2013), ADHD occurs in approximately 5 percent of the childhood population. However, recent studies in the United States report a rate that is more than double that—approximately 11 percent of (6.4 million) children between the ages of 4 and 17 years have been diagnosed with ADHD (Centers for Disease Control and Prevention [CDC], 2013). The rate is slightly lower during middle and late childhood (**Figure b**). The upward trend in ADHD diagnosis and pharmaceutical intervention is also occurring in Canada. Recent research reports that the prevalence of prescribed ADHD medications for Canadian children aged 3 to 9 significantly increased between 1994 and 2007 (from 1.3 to 2.1 percent). Rates of ADHD diagnoses for that age group also jumped between 2000 and 2007 from 1.7 to 2.6 percent (Brault & Lacourse, 2012).

Some health care professionals interpret the rising rate as evidence that we are seeing improvements in accurate diagnosis of this neurodevelopmental disorder. But there is some concern that current diagnostic practices may lead to overdiagnosis. A leading concern is that misdiagnosis will result in medication treatment when it is not medically necessary (Schwarz, 2013).

Ariel Skelley/Blend Images/Getty Images

a. Cindy shows signs of inattentiveness in the classroom, a characteristic of ADHD.

b. In 2010, approximately 8 percent of 5- to 11-year-olds were diagnosed with ADHD.

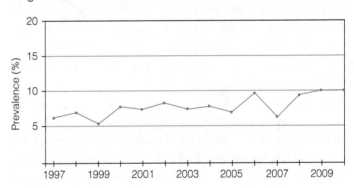

Think Critically What are your opinions about the rising rates of ADHD diagnosis and prescriptions?

---

social communication and interaction, such as responding inappropriately in conversations and misreading non-verbal cues (American Psychiatric Association, 2013). These children also have restricted and repetitive behaviour, interests, and activities. For example, they may be overly dependent on routines and extremely sensitive to changes in their context. To receive a diagnosis of ASD, symptoms must be present early on in development, even if symptoms are not recognized until later in the lifespan.

Frequencies of ASD reported around the world have approached 1 percent in recent years (American Psychiatric Association, 2013). That is a substantial portion of the population when you consider that the symptoms of ASD can make participation in school more difficult, especially when learning takes place in the context of social interactions. Many children with ASD need one-on-one assistance throughout the day and often require specialized therapies, such as occupational and speech therapy.

Specific learning disorders There is another special population of children who face difficulties learning in school, but who fall *within* the expected range for each domain of development (Berninger, 2006). These children have a **specific learning disorder**, the topic of this chapter's *What a Developmentalist Sees*. Disorders of reading and writing are the specific learning disorders most common in middle childhood (Berninger, 2006).

Attention-deficit/hyperactivity disorder (ADHD) Another disorder that affects learning in school is **attention-deficit/hyperactivity disorder (ADHD)**, which we discuss in *Challenges in Development*. The symptoms of ADHD are usually most salient during the elementary school years, though this disorder can continue throughout adulthood (American Psychiatric Association, 2013). Barkley (2015) notes that 84 percent of children with ADHD that persists to adulthood have at least one other disorder, with 61 percent having two disorders, and 45 percent having three co-occurring diagnoses. By adolescence and adulthood, symptoms tend to be less obvious. For example, hyperactivity symptoms may morph into inner feelings of restlessness rather than excessive gross motor activity.

Children with ADHD typically achieve lower test scores than their intellectual ability would predict because ADHD interferes with ability to optimally perform, and, eventually, they obtain less schooling (American Psychiatric Association, 2013). When symptoms centre on inattention, children suffer most from academic problems. On the other hand, hyperactivity and impulsivity are most closely associated with peer rejection, and sometimes with accidental injury.

The birth of inclusive education Changes to the educational opportunities available for students with unique needs can be traced to the 1960s normalization movement in Canada. This movement, in which parents of children with diverse leaning needs played a key advocacy role, espoused the philosophical belief that all individuals should be provided with a typical learning environment (Winzer, 2008). However, official Canadian policy was slow to catch up. The Canadian Charter of Rights

> **specific learning disorder** A specific difficulty with reading, writing, or math that is indicated when academic functioning is substantially below what is expected for age, IQ, and schooling.
>
> **attention-deficit/ hyperactivity disorder (ADHD)** A neurobehavioural disorder characterized by inattention and/ or hyperactivity-impulsivity that emerges prior to 12 years of age and causes impairment in multiple contexts.

and Freedoms requires that all Canadian provinces and territories have education laws to ensure that *all* students receive free and appropriate education, but interpretations of what that means has historically varied by location. In 1999, the Social Union Framework Agreement developed an agenda for how the federal and provincial/territorial governments would work to establish a social policy framework targeting, among other social issues, both children and disability. Across the country, the public school system operates with a commitment to inclusion. However, there continues to be much variability between the provinces and territories in terms of the funds and services available to children with special needs (Uppal, Khan, & Visentin, 2010).

Unfortunately, a number of challenges exist regarding the identification of students with special learning needs and their education (Berninger, 2006). Many schools hire paraprofessionals (persons trained in a professional task but not qualified members of a given profession) to teach students with learning disorders (Berninger, 2006). Paraprofessionals' limited training in child development and as general educators may make them less effective in addressing the changing developmental needs of these diverse students.

In addition to quality staff, the effectiveness of a school depends on the health and well-being of its students. Common ailments of childhood, such as asthma, are responsible for school absenteeism (CDC, 2011).

Physical Health and Well-Being

Canadian children can expect to live longer from the time of their birth than any other generation; however, increasing health risks for chronic disease are raising concerns about their quality of life (Decady & Greenberg, 2014). One such health risk is related to weight. As illustrated in **Figure 7.14**, Statistics Canada reports that in 2004 the overweight rate for the 2 to 17 age group was 18 percent (an estimated 1.1 million), with 8 percent being obese (about half a million)—a combined rate of 26 percent (Shields, 2008). This represents a stark increase from 1979, when 12 percent of 2- to 17-year-olds were overweight, and 3 percent were obese—a combined

Overweight and obesity rates, by population aged 2 to 17, Canada excluding territories, 1978/79 and 2004 • Figure 7.14

Canada's overweight and obesity rates for 2- to 17-year-olds showed a stark increase from 1979 to 2004.

Think Critically What factors might explain this increase in obesity rates?

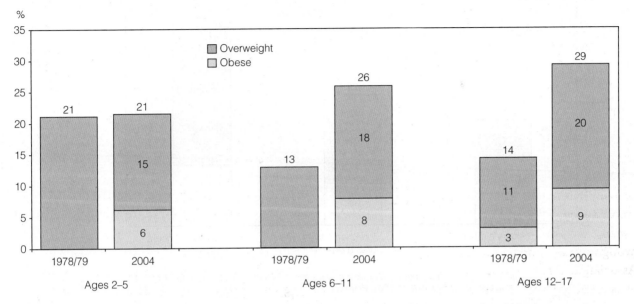

Source: Shields, M. (2008). *Measured obesity: Overweight Canadian children and adolescents*, Chart 2. Statistics Canada Catalogue no. 82-620-MWE2005001. Retrieved from www.statcan.gc.ca/pub/82-620-m/2005001/pdf/4193660-eng.pdf.

overweight/obesity rate of 15 percent. In 2013, the combined overweight/obesity rate was 31 percent for Canadians aged 5 to 17. Based on the body mass index (BMI), measured as part of the Canadian Health Measures Survey, 26 percent of children ages 5 to 11 were overweight (Statistics Canada, 2014). How do you create interventions to reverse such trends? An examination of the figure shows that the rates differ at various ages. What are the implications of this knowledge?

Ethnic minority and low-income communities experience the highest rates of childhood obesity. Researchers point to various environmental factors that disproportionately affect disadvantaged and minority children, and thus help explain disparities in obesity rates. For example, neighbourhoods where low-income and minority children live often have more fast-food vendors and fewer healthy food options than more affluent or predominantly Caucasian neighbourhoods (for a review, see Kumanyika & Grier, 2006). Although eating habits certainly contribute to overweight and obesity, choices about physical activity also play an important role. Unsafe streets, few recreational facilities, and the absence of

green spaces represent obstacles to physical activity for children living in disadvantaged neighbourhoods (Lovasi et al., 2013).

Leisure time Before there were computers, the Internet, social media networks, and televisions in every room, children spent the majority of their free time out on the playground. When children are outside they play longer, move more, and sit less (Smith, Nichols, Biggerstaff, & DiMarco, 2009). Since the 1980s, the time a 10-year-old child spends outdoors has decreased by 70 percent and there has been a decline in local neighbourhood games in which adults are not present (Strong et al., 2005; Castelli, Hillman, Buck, & Erwin, 2007). **Figure 7.15** illustrates the relationship between screen time and weight concerns. Canadian children ages 6 to 11 spend approximately 7.6 hours a day being sedentary, and only 24 percent of those children are meeting the guideline of two hours of screen time or less per day (ParticipACTION, 2015).

According to the most comprehensive assessment of child and youth physical activity in Canada, the ParticipACTION Report Card on Physical Activity for

Overweight and obesity rates, by daily hours of screen time, household population aged 6 to 11, Canada excluding territories, 2004 • Figure 7.15

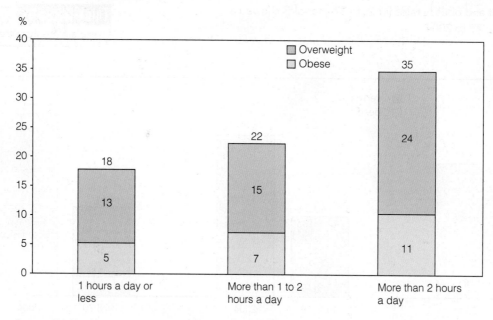

Source: Shields, M. (2008). *Measured obesity: Overweight Canadian Children and Adolescents*, Chart 12. Statistics Canada Catalogue no. 82-620-MWE2005001. Retrieved from www.statcan.gc.ca/pub/82-620-m/2005001/pdf/4193660-eng.pdf.

Children and Youth, 70 percent of children ages 3 to 4 get the recommended 180 minutes of daily activity at any intensity level. However, as the guidelines change to 60 minutes of moderate to vigorous activity per day for children ages 5 and up, rates plummet: only 14 percent of children ages 5 to 11 are meeting these activity guidelines. Overall, only 9 percent of 5- to17-year-olds get the 60 minutes of heart-pumping activity they need each day to stay healthy. Why might this trend of decreasing activity with increasing age occur? Canada's grade for overall physical activity remained at a D– for three recent years in a row because the majority of children and youth were not meeting the Canadian Physical Activity Guidelines (ParticipACTION, 2015).

Physical activity aids in a variety of types of physical development, including developing the cardiovascular system, improving muscle strength, and allowing for healthy tissue growth. Exercise also initiates the most important process in the body: oxygenation. Because children have less hemoglobin—the oxygen-carrying molecules in blood—than adults, children's bodies are less efficient than adults' at extracting oxygen, making exercise especially important (Cech & Martin, 2012).

The cardiovascular system also increases significantly during childhood (Cunningham, Paterson, & Blimke, 1984), and exercise can play a role in this expansion.

Most contemporary after-school activity is time-limited and follows proscribed rules under adult supervision. However, participation in organized activity is not equal across income levels. What do you notice in **Figure 7.16** illustrating income and participation in organized sports? Sports participation is highest among children from high-income households, at 68 percent, and lowest among children from lower income households, at 44 percent. Family income and also gender interact as the participation gap between boys and girls narrows with household income. This suggests that girls from lower-income families are particularly disadvantaged when it comes to sports participation (Clark, 2008).

Participation in sports has benefits far beyond the physical domain. Sports help a child improve cognitive skills by teaching strategies, planning, and goal formation. Team sports such as baseball, soccer, and hockey also help children understand the fundamental ideas of competition and teamwork. Finally, an emphasis on the importance of an active lifestyle early in a child's life can

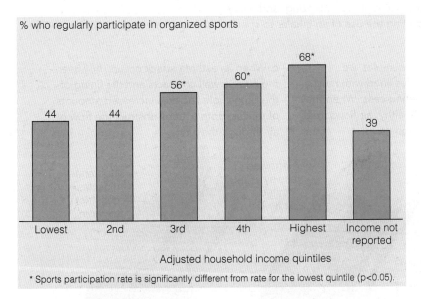

% who regularly participate in organized sports

Adjusted household income quintiles

* Sports participation rate is significantly different from rate for the lowest quintile (p<0.05).

Ask Yourself

What might account for the disparities in organized sports participation?

Source: Clark, W. (2008). Chart 2. Statistics Canada Catalogue no. 11-008-X. Retrieved from www.statcan.gc.ca/pub/11-008-x/2008001/article/10573-eng.pdf.

promote a habit of healthy behaviour that may continue into adulthood (Bell & Suggs, 1998; Wold & Anderson, 1992). The benefits of sports cut across all domains of development: physical, cognitive, and socio-emotional. Unfortunately, physical activity decreases across childhood, especially on weekends (Nader, Bradley, Houts, McRitchie, & O'Brien, 2008). In addition, physical activity can at times be impeded by physical ailments, such as asthma, the topic to which we now turn.

Asthma The most recent global estimate of **asthma** indicates that as many as 334 million people have asthma.

> **asthma** A chronic illness in which the airways of the lung constrict, resulting in decreased airflow.

The historical view of asthma as a disease of high-income countries no longer holds: most people affected are in low- and middle-income countries and rates seem to be increasing rapidly as the world becomes more Westernized (Global Asthma Network, 2014). The prevalence of diagnoses in Canada has increased to over 2.4 million (Statistics Canada, 2015). Asthma is most common during childhood; slightly less than 12 percent of Canadians aged 12 to 19 were diagnosed with asthma in 2010 (Statistics Canada, 2013). Asthma continues to be a major cause of hospitalization for children in Canada, responsible for 18 percent of all admissions for children ages 0 to 14. However, children younger than 5 years of age have the highest hospitalization rates for asthma. In Canada, death resulting from asthma is uncommon for children and youth but it does present a greater risk for older adults managing the disease (Public Health Agency of Canada, 2007).

There are socio-economic status (SES) differences in cases of asthma, with children from lower-SES households experiencing significantly higher incidence than children living in middle- and upper-SES families (Bloom, Cohen, & Freeman, 2011). These differences can be partially understood in terms of disadvantageous conditions. Maternal smoking and exposure to cockroach and mouse antigens, for example, are associated with both lower SES and the prevalence of asthma (Lin et al., 2004). Other researchers have suggested that the relationships among poverty, psychological stress, and immune pathways creates asthmatic vulnerability in lower-SES families (Chen, Hanson, Paterson, Griffin, Walker, & Miller, 2006).

Figure 7.17 explains what happens in the lungs during an asthma attack. The most common causes of these attacks are infection, allergies, exercise, weather conditions, and second-hand smoke. Peterson-Sweeney (2009) suggests that family intervention and education can reduce and prevent future episodes. Through this process, families work (1) to reduce exposure to trigger

What happens during an asthma attack • Figure 7.17

During an asthma attack, a child experiences chest tightness, coughing, wheezing, and the feeling of being unable to take in a breath, often necessitating the use of an inhaler to speed the delivery of medication directly to the lungs.

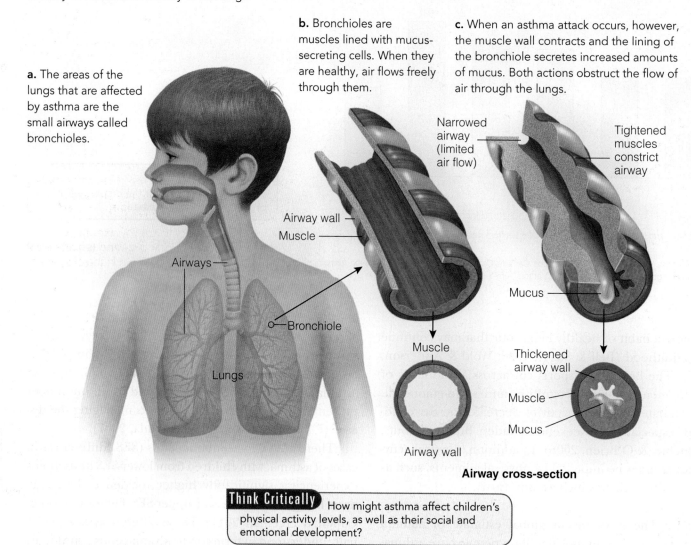

a. The areas of the lungs that are affected by asthma are the small airways called bronchioles.

b. Bronchioles are muscles lined with mucus-secreting cells. When they are healthy, air flows freely through them.

c. When an asthma attack occurs, however, the muscle wall contracts and the lining of the bronchiole secretes increased amounts of mucus. Both actions obstruct the flow of air through the lungs.

Airways

Bronchiole

Lungs

Airway wall

Muscle

Narrowed airway (limited air flow)

Tightened muscles constrict airway

Muscle

Airway wall

Mucus

Thickened airway wall

Muscle

Mucus

Airway cross-section

Think Critically How might asthma affect children's physical activity levels, as well as their social and emotional development?

elementsin the environment, such as dirty carpets, insect infestations, cigarette smoke, and pets; and (2) to strengthen medication maintenance schedules by improving family organization and routines. Given the prevalence and high instances of hospitalization in Canada, it is not hard to imagine asthma's pervasive influence on all the systems, affecting not only children's physical development, but also their socio-emotional development, the focus of our next chapter.

CONCEPT CHECK STOP

1. **How** do mastery goals of learning in school differ from performance goals?

2. **What** are the key issues surrounding autism spectrum disorder?

3. **What** factors contribute to increased obesity in children?

Summary

1 Physical Development 228

- The plasticity of the brain begins to diminish compared with early childhood, but the brain is still changing. The number of synapses rises and falls as connections are added and pruned. Myelination continues in both **grey matter** and **white matter**. The **prefrontal cortex (PFC)** develops, which may be linked to increased self-knowledge and more efficient cognitive processing.

- Children's bones grow longer and thicker, resulting in more adult-like body proportions, even though height and weight gains do not take place as quickly as they did in early childhood. It is not until around age 10 that males and females begin to differ markedly in terms of height and weight.

- Muscle growth follows bone growth in childhood. Muscle fibres lengthen and differentiate from one another, aiding both fine motor skills, such as writing, and gross motor skills.

- Increasing coordination and interaction of the nervous, muscular, and skeletal systems improve the **consistency** (demonstrated in the photo in the figure), **flexibility**, and **efficiency** of children's motor skills.

Improvements in motor development during middle to late childhood • Figure 7.3

Marjorie Kamys Cotera/PhotoEdit

2 Cognitive Development 231

- The ability to understand and explain conservation—that objects can stay the same even if their physical appearance changes—is the hallmark of Piaget's third stage of cognitive development: the **concrete operational stage**. Children in this stage not only understand the ideas of conservation and **reversibility**, but have also mastered **classification** and **seriation**, which requires an understanding of **transitivity**.

- Contrasting with Piaget's focus on the inner workings of the child, Vygotsky focused on the role of social and cultural experiences in children's thinking. Social support to help

children manage their **cognitive load** during middle–late childhood comes in many forms, including modelling, formal instruction, and scaffolding, both human and technology-enhanced.

- Children make gains in a number of information-processing skills. Improvements in **selective attention**, **automatization**, **reaction time**, **strategy** construction, and strategy selection all help children become better problem solvers. **Maintenance rehearsal** is an example of basic strategy construction. Children also develop key meta-skills, or abilities to think about their own cognitive processes, including **metamemory** and **metacognition**.

- This is the age when young children deploy **executive function** to utilize **sensory memory**, **working (short-term) memory**, and **long-term memory** (shown in the diagram in the figure) with greater mastery.

Three categories of memory • Figure 7.6

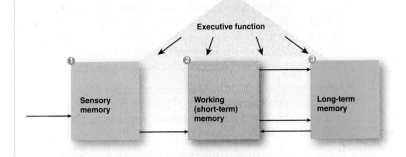

- Intelligence is hard to define. Psychometric theories of intelligence, such as Spearman's, suggest the existence of a **general intelligence (g)**. Intelligence tests, like the **Wechsler intelligence scales**, which yield **intelligence quotient (IQ)** scores, assume that intelligence is a single, unified characteristic. These tests define average intelligence, as well as thresholds for **intellectual disability** and **giftedness**. Such tests have elicited a variety of criticisms. Robert Sternberg's **triarchic theory of successful intelligence** suggests that there are three kinds of intelligence: **analytical**, **practical**, and **creative**. Howard Gardner's **theory of multiple intelligences** suggests that there are eight.

- With regard to language development, children develop knowledge about language, called **metalinguistic awareness**, and an increased understanding of pragmatics.

- Learning to read is one of the most difficult tasks children face in school. Researchers have identified six key elements of teachers and classrooms that effectively support beginning readers. Two key approaches to reading instruction are the **whole-language approach** and the **phonics approach**.

- Canada is a **bilingual** nation and many Canadian children grow up in multilingual homes. Programs in **English as a second language (ESL)**, **language immersion**, and **bilingual education** highlight the cultural, racial, and ethnic diversity in Canadian schools and the complex issues that arise from **second (additional) language learning**.

3 All the Systems Working Together 243

- Schools are complex multi-level institutions that affect the development of the whole child. The goals of learning in school can be academic, social-emotional, metacognitive, and developmental. **Mastery goals** and **performance goals** are two contrasting ways of thinking about and engaging in learning activities.

- Interest in international and domestic academic comparison has led to the inclusion of **achievement tests** in primary education. These tests reveal gaps in the performance of students from different regions in Canada. Poverty and its correlates may help to explain the ongoing achievement gaps between children of different socio-economic backgrounds. Canadian schools also focus on **social and emotional learning (SEL)**. These educational programs seek to foster the development of five non–subject-matter competencies: self-awareness, self-management, social awareness, relationship skills, and responsible decision-making.

- Autism spectrum disorder (ASD) is a neurodevelopmental disorder characterized by impaired social communication and interaction, and repetitive behaviours. The symptoms of ASD can make participation in school more difficult.

- **Specific learning disorders** in children who are otherwise typically developing are the most frequently occurring developmental disorder of childhood. Another disorder that affects learning in school is **attention-deficit/hyperactivity disorder (ADHD)**, a disorder characterized by inattention and/or hyperactivity-impulsivity.

- Federal legislation guarantees access to free and appropriate schooling for all students, including those with special learning needs. Unfortunately, a number of challenges exist regarding the identification of students with special learning needs and their education.

- Children's unsupervised outdoor play has decreased substantially in recent decades and changes with age.

- Only 14 percent of Canadian children ages 5 to 11 are meeting physical activity guidelines. Children's participation in athletics or high-intensity play offers many physical benefits, including oxygenation, which is especially important because children's bodies are less efficient than adults' at carrying and extracting oxygen. Sports also offer cognitive and social benefits and can lay a foundation for lasting healthy habits.

Income and participation in organized sports • Figure 7.16

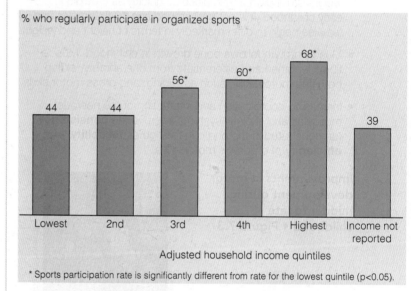

% who regularly participate in organized sports

* Sports participation rate is significantly different from rate for the lowest quintile (p<0.05).

- **Asthma** is most common during childhood. Research has suggested a relationship among poverty, psychological stress, and immune pathways creates asthmatic vulnerability in lower-SES families.

Key Terms

- achievement test 247
- analytical intelligence 239
- asthma 253
- attention-deficit/hyperactivity disorder (ADHD) 250
- autism spectrum disorder (ASD) 248
- automatization 234
- bilingual 241
- bilingual education 241

- classification 232
- cognitive load 234
- concrete operational stage 232
- consistency 230
- creative intelligence 239
- efficiency 230
- English as a second language (ESL) 241
- executive function 236

- flexibility 230
- general intelligence (*g*) 237
- gifted 238
- grey matter 228
- intellectual disability 238
- intelligence quotient (IQ) 238
- language immersion 242
- long-term memory 236
- maintenance rehearsal 235

Critical and Creative Thinking Questions

1. What recommendations would you give to parents or caregivers about how best to support their children's skeletal and muscular development?

2. Describe your own intelligence: Name your primary triarchic intelligence and your strongest of Gardner's multiple intelligences.

3. List potential advantages and disadvantages for children who participate in team sports during the elementary-school years. How might the disadvantages be overcome?

4. What do you think should be the most important goal of schools? Which, if any, of the goals listed in this chapter do you believe schools should *not* accept?

What is happening in this picture?

Children are more likely today than in the past to participate in supervised, organized sports like soccer than to play unsupervised pick-up games.

Christopher Futcher/iStockphoto

Think Critically 1. What physical and cognitive developments contribute to children's improving soccer skills during middle to late childhood?
2. How are these children benefiting, physically and in other ways, from playing soccer?
3. Do you think the trend toward more supervised activities in recent decades is a positive one? Why or why not?

REAL  Development

Physical and Cognitive Development in Middle and Late Childhood: Six to Eleven Years

In these video activities, you learn more about physical and cognitive development in middle to late childhood.

In the first activity, you are a nutritional consultant for Eagle Glen Elementary School. The school is required to adopt new nutritional standards released by Health Canada. Acting as a liaison for the department, you will evaluate the school's current lunch offerings and provide guidance on how the school can meet the new federal guidelines.

In the second activity, you are a student intern in the school district. One of your assignments is to visit classrooms and observe the teaching–learning process. In this activity, you will visit Mr. Timberlake's Grade 3 science classroom, where his students will be studying fish behaviours. Your task is to observe Mr. Timberlake interacting with students, keeping in mind what you have learned in this chapter about cognitive development during middle childhood.

John Wiley & Sons, Inc.

WileyPLUS Go to WileyPLUS to complete the REAL Development activity.

03.01

Self-Test

(Check your answers in Appendix A.)

1. Which component of the brain is made up of neurons and their connections?

    a. myelin

    b. white matter

    c. grey matter

    d. synapses

2. During childhood, children's bones _____.

    a. grow longer

    b. grow thicker

    c. add and absorb minerals

    d. do all of these

3. As shown in this graph, compared with earlier in development, weight gains during childhood tend to _____.

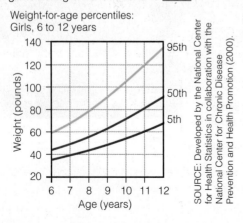

Weight-for-age percentiles: Girls, 6 to 12 years

SOURCE: Developed by the National Center for Health Statistics in collaboration with the National Center for Chronic Disease Prevention and Health Promotion (2000).

    a. stop entirely

    b. spurt upward rapidly

    c. speed up slightly

    d. slow down slightly

4. This child's smoother and less splashy swimming stroke is a result of improvements in the _____ of her motor skills.

    a. efficiency

    b. consistency

    c. flexibility

    d. plasticity

Kali Nine LLC/iStockphoto

5. For which concrete-operational thinking ability is this child being tested?

Lisa Passmore

a. conservation

c. seriation

b. classification

d. reversibility

6. A child's ability to focus on just one thing, in spite of all the surrounding distractions, is called _____.

a. selective attention

c. transitivity

b. automaticity

d. metacognition

7. Understanding how one's own thoughts work, or knowing about knowing, is called _____.

a. metamemory

c. metacognition

b. metalinguistics

d. awareness

8. This graph of intelligence scores indicates that the mean score is _____.

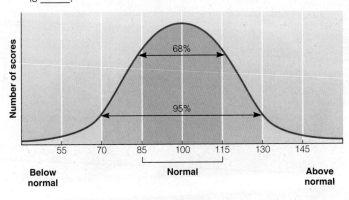

a. 70

c. 130

b. 100

d. 15

9. Howard Gardner believes that all of the following are intelligences except _____.

a. linguistic

c. intrapersonal

b. cultural

d. naturalistic

10. A teacher who breaks down words into their constituent sounds is using the _____ approach for teaching students to read.

a. phonics

c. whole-language

b. triarchic

d. metalinguistic

11. This figure depicts the multiple levels of the school context. Fill in the blanks where they appear:

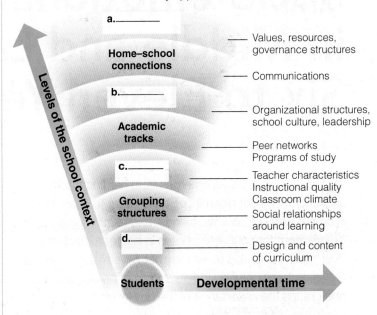

Republished with permission of Taylor & Francis, from Eccles, J.S., & Roeser, R.W., "School and community influences on human development." In M.E. Lamb & M.H. Bornstein (Eds.), Social and personality development: An advanced textbook. Copyright © 2011. Permission conveyed through Copyright Clearance Center, Inc.

12. The goals of learning in school can be _____.

a. academic

c. metacognitive

b. social-emotional

d. all of these

13. Physical activity _____.

a. aids in developing the cardiovascular system

c. initiates oxygenation

d. all of the above

b. improves muscle strength

14. Compared with their parents, today's children show increases in all of these except _____.

a. life expectancy

c. obesity

b. asthma

d. chronic stress

15. Health promoters are concerned about the activity levels of youth because _____.

a. the average 10-year-old now spends more time outdoors than in 1980

b. almost no children between ages 9 and 11 get the recommended amounts of moderate to vigorous physical activity every day

c. schools have increased their requirements for physical education to ensure that children meet recommendations for daily amounts of activity

d. every year after age 11, children reduce the time spent in daily moderate to vigorous physical activity by about 40 minutes

THE PLANNER

Review your Chapter Planner in the chapter opener and check off your completed work.

Socio-emotional Development in Middle and Late Childhood: Six to Eleven Years

Eight-year-old Sylvia emerges from her first track and field meet gleaming. She is eager to share the moment with her parents, friends, and relatives, posing before them for countless photos in her team track suit. Just years earlier this event may not have meant much to Sylvia, but now, as her understanding of herself deepens, she grasps the importance of the day in the context of her athletic lifestyle. Sylvia is beginning to develop and understand her abilities, including both her strengths and her weaknesses. She now has a clear and identifiable personality, and will not hesitate to tell you what she does—and does not!—like. When she gets her report card from school, she knows she worked hard for her grades and is pleased to show off the fruits of her labour to others.

As we will see in this chapter, school-age children like Sylvia have progressed considerably from the early-childhood years. They can describe their personality, they have *best* friends, and they have a complex vocabulary to tell you how they feel. Our first stop in examining this new level of awareness is a consideration of personality and the self.

Image Source Salsa/Alamy Stock Photo

CHAPTER PLANNER ✓

- ❑ Study the picture and read the opening story.
- ❑ Scan the Learning Objectives in each section:
  p. 262 ❑   p. 268 ❑   p. 277 ❑
- ❑ Read the text and study all visuals.
- ❑ Answer any questions.

Analyze key features

- ❑ Process Diagram, p. 266
- ❑ Challenges in Development, p. 270
- ❑ Development InSight, p. 280
- ❑ Stop: Answer the Concept Checks before you go on:
  p. 268 ❑   p. 277 ❑   p. 281 ❑

End of chapter

- ❑ Review the Summary and Key Terms.
- ❑ Answer *What is happening in this picture?*
- ❑ Answer the Critical and Creative Thinking Questions.
- ❑ Complete the Self-Test and check your answers.

Personality Development

LEARNING OBJECTIVES

1. **Describe** the key developments related to the self that occur during middle and late childhood.

2. **Explain** Piaget's and Kohlberg's theories of moral development, discussing as well Gilligan's critique of Kohlberg's theory.

3. **Discuss** Erikson's stage of industry versus inferiority.

We begin this chapter with a focus on how school-age children think about and define their own personalities. As these children move out into the world and engage classmates and teachers, issues of morality play an increasing role in their personality development. From a psychodynamic perspective, these social experiences affect the quality of one's personality.

Development of the Self

Early in development, self-analysis is virtually absent. With age, however, a complex understanding of self emerges (Harter & Bukowski, 2012). Preschoolers in Piaget's preoperational stage have an egocentric sense of the self that focuses on physical qualities, such as "I have black hair," or on possessions, such as "I have a dog named Rufus." Preoperational self-awareness is immediate and in the moment (Pomerantz, Ruble, Frey, & Greulich, 1995).

As a child begins to think more operationally in middle to later childhood, self-descriptions also change. Behaviours and abilities become the focus. Now we hear children say things like "I am a fast runner," or "I like chocolate better than vanilla." Self-knowledge includes more general categories, such as "I'm smart," as well as more connections between categories, such as "I get good grades because I'm smart" (Pomerantz et al., 1995).

Preschoolers tend to focus on positive self-descriptions rather than the negative ones, whereas older children have a more realistic self-knowledge (Butler & Gasson, 2005). For example, a preschooler might say "I'm the fastest runner in the school," or "I'm the strongest!" without any evidence to back him up. By the time they move into the later grades of elementary school, however, children are quite aware of their strengths and weaknesses (Harter & Bukowski, 2012).

One reason children shift toward a less positive, more realistic sense of self is due to **social comparison** (Pomerantz et al., 1995). For example, when a group of schoolchildren gets math tests back from their teacher, they come to realize that some scored well whereas others did not. A child with a low score might begin to say things like "I'm good at writing but not good at math."

As we first discussed in Chapter 6, **self-concept** is a set of descriptive beliefs about one's own personality and abilities that have evolved through social interactions and personal perceptions. Parental influences (Siegel, 1999), peer feedback (Berndt & Perry, 1990), culture (Kenny & McEachern, 2009), and selective memories (Klein & Loftus, 1988) all provide information that children use to create a self-concept. When the child starts evaluating the self-concept, self-esteem becomes involved (Damon & Hart, 1982; Trautwein, Lüdtke, Köller, & Baumert, 2006).

You will also recall from Chapter 6 that **self-esteem** is the value children place on the self and the emotional responses they have to these values. Self-esteem underlies factors that contribute to a child's sense of self-worth, capabilities, success, and personal significance (Coopersmith, 1967; Park & Maner, 2009). Just like self-concept, a child's self-esteem has varying sources of influence. Among these influences are parental interactions (Grusec, 2002) and social comparisons (Pomerantz et al., 1995), which appear to have the most significant impact. There are several outcomes related to high and low self-esteem, shown in **Figure 8.1**.

One specific self-evaluation, **self-efficacy**, reflects the child's sense of agency, the belief that the child can actively accomplish goals and competently complete tasks.

> **social comparison** The process of learning about one's abilities and characteristics by observing how they compare with others'.
>
> **self-concept** One's multidimensional impression of one's own personality, of the attributes, abilities, and attitudes that define one's self.

> **self-esteem** Judgements of worth that children make about themselves and the feelings that those judgements elicit.
>
> **self-efficacy** One's perceived ability to be successful in accomplishing specific goals.

Correlates of self-esteem during middle and late childhood • Figure 8.1

Think Critically What other variables are likely to correlate with self-esteem during middle and late childhood?

Self-esteem is correlated with a number of important variables, as we see here. Given that much of the research about self-esteem is correlational, we cannot determine the direction of cause. For example, does high self-esteem cause a child to have more friends, or does having more friends cause a child to have high self-esteem?

Correlates of high self-esteem

- Feeling happier (DeNeve & Cooper, 1998)
- Doing better in school (Baumeister, Campbell, Krueger, & Vohs, 2003)
- Demonstrating lower anxiety (Greenberg et al., 1992)
- Performing better in sports (Cassidy & Conroy, 2006)
- Having more friends (Hubbard & Coie, 1994)

Steve Debenport/iStockphoto

Correlates of low self-esteem

- More likely to engage in delinquent behaviour (Baumeister et al., 2003)
- Feeling depressed more often (Whisman & Kwon, 1993)
- Higher incidence of eating disorders (Wade, Bulik, Prescott, & Kendler, 2004)

PhotoAlto/Thierry Foulon/Getty Images

Self-efficacy develops during middle to late childhood but, from a developmental systems perspective, has its roots in toddlerhood and even earlier in the lifespan. One's particular belief of self-efficacy often continues into adolescence and is tied to a sense of agency in adulthood (Bandura, 1997).

As children move into adolescence, beliefs about the self undergo significant transformations, as we will see in subsequent chapters. Another transformation occurs in children's understanding of right and wrong.

Moral Development

How did you learn the difference between right and wrong? In childhood, most of us relied on our parents to make this determination. As we got older, we internalized ideas about behaviours that are acceptable and behaviours that are not. What influences inform a child's concept of morality? In this section, we examine three prominent theories that seek to answer this question.

Piaget's theory of moral development Piaget believed that moral development mirrors a child's cognitive abilities. He identified two overlapping stages of morality, preceded by a pre-moral period. During this pre-moral period, which occurs prior to about 4 years of age, children do not have any concept of what is right or wrong and are relatively devoid of any moral sensibility. Decisions about right and wrong come from an authority figure who directly attaches meaning to an event or behaviour. For example, a parent might say, "Taking candy from your sister's bag is wrong!" This specific, immediate information from a respected individual enables a young child to begin to understand what rules are and how they work (Piaget, 1997).

The first moral stage, which Piaget called the stage of **moral realism**, is characterized by **heteronomous morality**. A child with heteronomous morality believes that rules are absolute and unchangeable. The child also focuses on the consequences of actions rather than intentions. For example, if Erin's brother Jamal steps on her hand, no explanation by Jamal will prevent Erin from being upset. "I didn't do it on purpose!" Jamal says, but these words do not ease Erin's anger (Piaget, 1997). Children in this stage are moral non-relativists; that is, the specifics of the situation at hand have no bearing on what is right and wrong.

moral realism The idea that there are moral facts that refer to objective, rather than subjective, features of the world.

heteronomous morality Piaget's description of a child's first idea of what is right and wrong and the sense that morality is an external, unchangeable set of rules with a focus on consequences of behaviour.

moral relativism
The idea that morality is subjectively grounded and contextually dependent.

autonomous morality Piaget's observation that as children get older they begin to see morality as more flexible and consider the intentions of other people's behaviour.

However, children develop in the direction of **moral relativism**, Piaget's next stage of moral reasoning, during which right and wrong depend very much on the situation at hand. Children now consider intentions when assigning the labels of right and wrong (Piaget, 1997). Returning to our earlier example, if Erin was in the stage of moral relativism she would be comforted to know that Jamal did not mean to step on her hand. Moral relativism is characterized by **autonomous morality**. Autonomous morality emphasizes a democratic approach in which rules are human-made and can change if everyone agrees. Games can now be made up: "That tree is first base, the rock is second."

To determine a child's stage of morality, Piaget presented children with a dilemma, similar to the one we see in **Figure 8.2**. The dilemma asked children to focus on either the consequences of actions or the intentions of actions.

Piaget's work on moral development led to another cognitive theory about moral development. This theory also has levels and uses dilemmas to understand moral reasoning, but it conceptualizes the reasoning process rather differently (Piaget, 1997).

Kohlberg's theory of moral development Harvard psychologist Lawrence Kohlberg brought moral development into the consciousness of the academic world and expanded on the work of Piaget. Kohlberg believed that cognitive development and moral development follow similar patterns. Like Piaget, Kohlberg divided the development of moral reasoning into separate levels, each with a specific underlying set of beliefs.

An example of Piaget's study of moral development • Figure 8.2

Is it worse to break more dishes accidentally, as Laurent does, or to break fewer dishes while doing something that is "naughty," as Celine does? Children with heteronomous morality (ages 4–10 years) would generally say Laurent is naughtier, because they would focus on the outcome and that he broke more dishes; whereas children with autonomous morality (more than 7 years) would generally say Celine is naughtier because intention matters more than outcome. Note that the stages overlap between 7 and 10 years of age, when children may show elements of each type of thinking (Piaget, 1997).

Think Critically How would we expect Laurent's mother to react to the broken dishes?

Laurent was helping his mother clean dishes when he accidentally bumped a stack of *15 dishes* and broke all of them.

Celine snuck into the kitchen to steal a cookie from the cookie jar. As she leaned across the counter, she knocked *one dish* on the floor and broke it.

The levels build upon each other and do not vary, also like Piagetian structure.

Kohlberg even used Piaget's idea of studying morality through the use of a dilemma. He typically used one called the Heinz dilemma (Kohlberg, 1963). Kohlberg told participants that Heinz's wife was dying of a rare kind of cancer and would be dead by morning unless he got her a specific drug that was recently discovered by a local druggist. Heinz went to the druggist and told him the situation. The druggist had the drug but inflated the price to $2,000, 10 times what the drug cost him to make. Heinz could not afford the drug and was unable to borrow enough to buy it, so he tried to reason with the druggist. But the druggist would not give in. Finally, out of desperation, Heinz broke into the store and stole the drug to save his wife. Kohlberg then asked participants whether Heinz was right or wrong to steal the drug and requested an explanation of their answer. Kohlberg was less concerned about whether participants thought Heinz was right or wrong than he was about the reasoning they gave for their decisions.

After listening to the various reasons participants gave for their answer to the Heinz dilemma, Kohlberg developed his now famous theory of moral development. The theory includes three levels—**preconventional morality**, **conventional morality**, and **postconventional morality**— each of which has two stages, as shown in **Figure 8.3** (Kohlberg, 1981). In stages 1 and 2, moral judgement is self-centred. For example, young Emilio believes it is wrong to torment the family cat because he is punished for it. In stages 3 and 4, moral judgement becomes other-centred. For instance, Armada believes that behaving well gains people's approval and respect, so she "does the right thing" in order to ensure the social order. Finally, in stages 5 and 6, moral judgement is based on personal standards for right and wrong. Ari, for example, believes that a person can justifiably break laws that deny certain people dignity and freedom.

How would you answer the Heinz dilemma? Do you think your gender affected your answer? As we will see, psychologist Carol Gilligan believes it probably did (Gilligan, 1982).

preconventional morality Level 1 of Kohlberg's theory of moral development, in which moral reasoning is guided by personal rewards and punishments.

conventional morality Level 2 of Kohlberg's theory of moral development, in which moral reasoning is guided by laws and social norms.

postconventional morality Level 3 of Kohlberg's theory of moral development, in which moral reasoning is guided by universal ethical principles.

Gilligan's different voice In her 1982 book *In a Different Voice*, psychologist Carol Gilligan criticized Kohlberg's theory of moral development for gender bias, arguing that Kohlberg underestimated the level of maturity of a woman's response to the Heinz dilemma (Gilligan, 1982). She believed that whereas the male view of morality focuses solely on justice, the female view of morality is based on care and relationships (Gilligan, 1982). For example, according to Gilligan, when presented with the Heinz dilemma, men might be more likely to say, "Heinz was wrong because stealing is against the law." Gilligan argued that women, on the other hand, tend to see morality as complex and situational and include human factors when making moral decisions. A woman might be more likely to say, "It depends," or "I need more information. The druggist may have reasons we don't know about."

Gilligan is thought of as a pioneer of gender studies. Many feminists fear that focusing on the differences between males and females will justify existing inequities. Gilligan's perspective, now known as *difference feminism*, highlights gender differences but calls for an equal valuing of them. Gilligan's critique has come under scrutiny in recent years, given the lack of empirical evidence supporting a gender difference in moral reasoning (Colby & Damon, 1994; Walker, 2006). Nevertheless, Gilligan's work launched a conversation among scholars that is ongoing about the multiple, interacting influences on moral development (Jorgensen, 2006). A series of studies has shown that care-oriented morality is valuable for human growth and a balanced consideration of the needs of self as well as others appears to develop gradually across childhood into young adulthood (Skoe, 2014). People have both justice and care orientations available and use them differentially depending on various background and contextual factors (Jaffe & Hyde, 2000). Culture is another such influence.

Morality and culture How do you think your culture might have affected your answer to the Heinz dilemma? Culture appears to play a significant role in moral reasoning (Dong, Anderson, Kim, & Li, 2008). For example, in a collectivist society, Heinz's decision would not be just about Heinz and his wife, but about the entire community and the shame he would bring to his family by stealing the drug (Ames & Rosemont, 1999). Cross-cultural investigations suggest that moral decision-making is influenced by a convergence of cultural forces (Gross, 1996).

Kohlberg's stages of moral reasoning • Figure 8.3  THE PLANNER

Kohlberg theorized that moral reasoning evolves from reliance on external, immediate sources of moral information to a more internalized understanding of what is right and wrong. Everyone has Level 1 reasoning at some point in their lives, but only some people progress to Level 2, and even fewer make it to Level 3.

PRECONVENTIONAL LEVEL

(Stages 1 and 2—birth to adolescence) Moral judgement is *self-centred*. What is right is what one can get away with, or what is personally satisfying. Moral understanding is based on rewards, punishments, and the exchange of favours.

1 Punishment-obedience orientation

Focus is on self-interest—obedience to authority and avoidance of punishment. Because children at this stage have difficulty considering another's point of view, they also ignore people's intentions.

2 Instrumental-exchange orientation

Children become aware of others' perspectives, but their morality is based on reciprocity—an equal exchange of favours.

CONVENTIONAL LEVEL

(Stages 3 and 4—adolescence and young adulthood) Moral reasoning is *other-centred*. Conventional societal rules are accepted because they help ensure the social order.

3 Good-child orientation

Primary moral concern is being nice and gaining approval, and judges others by their intentions—"His heart was in the right place."

4 Law-and-order orientation

Morality based on a larger perspective—societal laws. Understanding that if everyone violated laws, even with good intentions, there would be chaos.

POSTCONVENTIONAL LEVEL

(Stages 5 and 6—adulthood) Moral judgements are based on *personal standards for right and wrong*. Morality is also defined in terms of abstract principles and values that apply to all situations and societies.

5 Social contract orientation

Appreciation for the underlying purposes served by laws. Societal laws are obeyed because of the "social contract," but they can be morally disobeyed if they fail to express the will of the majority or fail to maximize social welfare.

6 Universal-ethics orientation

"Right" is determined by universal ethical principles (e.g., non-violence, human dignity, freedom) that *all* religions or moral authorities might view as compelling or fair. These principles apply whether or not they conform to existing laws.

Sources: Adapted from Kohlberg, L. "Stage and Sequence: The Cognitive Developmental Approach to Socialization," in D. A. Goslin, *The Handbook of Socialization Theory and Research.* Chicago: Rand McNally, 1969, p. 376 (Table 6.2).

Think Critically Based on your response to the Heinz dilemma, which level and which stage do you best fit into?

Obviously there is more to personality than just morality. With that in mind, we return to one of the key originators of personality theories: Erikson (Erikson, 1950).

A Psychodynamic Perspective

You will recall from previous chapters that psychodynamic theorists consider the role of the environment in shaping personality. Specifically, they emphasize the expectation that societies have for individuals to gain greater and greater control over themselves as their biological maturation allows. We've been discussing Erik Erikson's psychosocial theory as an example of this perspective, in which each period of the lifespan is characterized by a crisis. In middle to late childhood, children face the developmental task of resolving the **industry versus inferiority stage** (**Figure 8.4**) (Erikson, 1950).

On the industry side of the crisis, a child experiences a growing sense of skill, self-knowledge, and desire to be an industrious member of a class. When Yasmin started Grade 1, she loved it. She easily learned spelling, was in the best reading group, and enjoyed going to school each day. According to Erikson, Yasmin's industry will lead to the emergence of competence and well-being (Erikson, 1950).

Inferiority, on the other side, breeds low self-esteem and less enthusiasm about the school process and any

> **industry versus inferiority stage** Erikson's fourth stage of psychosocial development, leading to a sense of competence or a move away from social interactions.

Industry versus inferiority • Figure 8.4

According to Erikson, social experiences affect personality development.

a. Alex, recognized for his accomplishments in the National Geographic Bee, has the appearance of confidence and success. His sense of industry will greatly impact his ability to internalize competence and social achievement (Erikson, 1950).

b. Roger, however, appears despondent and distant because he was not chosen to play during a hockey game. He is struggling with feelings of inferiority.

Tom Horan/AP Photo

Thomas Barwick/Ionica/Getty Images

Think Critically What do you think is the relationship between Erikson's industry versus inferiority stage and self-esteem?

other social interactions. Abdul hated going to school. His teachers always picked on him, he could not read well, and he did not even like recess. Inferior-feeling children like Abdul may think of themselves as less competent. These children tend to feel fear and anxiety around their teachers and to have few friends (Erikson, 1950).

As in all of Erikson's stages, there is still hope for a child like Abdul. As we see next, a variety of social influences are interacting to mould his life and personality.

CONCEPT CHECK ⬛STOP

1. **What** influences self-concept during middle and late childhood?
2. **What** is one criticism of Kohlberg's stages of moral development?
3. **Where** do children sort out the crisis of industry versus inferiority according to Erikson?

Social Influences

LEARNING OBJECTIVES

1. **Describe** the changes in parenting that occur during middle and late childhood.
2. **Examine** the effects of divorce on the parent–child relationship.
3. **Discuss** the role of siblings during middle and late childhood.
4. **Outline** the peer statuses identified by researchers.

Social influences on development become increasingly dynamic and multi-faceted during the middle and late childhood years, expanding to include influences beyond those that have been around since birth. Teachers and peers become increasingly important in late childhood, when children spend longer periods of time away from home and family. During these years and into adolescence, parents remain a central influence on development. Their role changes but is not replaced by new social relationships (Lamb & Lewis, 2011). Recent developmental science offers exciting insights into the role that families, siblings, and peers (discussed later in this section) play in the social lives of tweens.

tween A term used in the popular media to describe a preadolescent, or a young person who shares characteristics of both children and teenagers.

In Chapter 5, we learned about the rising prevalence of autism spectrum disorder (ASD) in Canada, the value of inclusion in regular educational settings for all children, especially for their social development, and how the school transition for children with ASD places demands on children, parents, and school settings. Extending our understanding of the diversity of Canadian culture, we must also find valuable ways to support children with ASD from culturally diverse backgrounds who require support systems and interventions to better facilitate their school entry and resulting social development (Fontil & Petrakos, 2015). With a growing culturally diverse demographic in Canada, children with disabilities often come from diverse backgrounds and have to cope with challenges above and beyond those related to their disability, including language and communication issues and disparities between teacher and parent values (Dyches, Wilder, Sudweeks, Obiakor, & Algozzine, 2004).

Fontil and Petrakos (2015) explored the experiences of Canadian and immigrant families of children with ASD, during their school transition. Their research illustrated the value and the complexity of establishing empathetic and caring home–school relationships wherein parents felt they were working with educators who genuinely cared for and supported the needs of their children. Importantly, language was a concern for both Canadian and immigrant families, although in differing ways; the prospect of learning a new language was incredibly daunting. Immigrant families were also concerned with their own communication and language skills and its impact on home–school collaboration. Immigrant families also seemed less clear about the path of communication between different community resources and the school. Support and intervention research is a growing topic of concern as children's spheres of influence shift into a wider social environment, a topic to which we now turn.

The Changing Role of Parents During Middle and Late Childhood

Compared with parents of younger children, parents of school-age children are less likely to use physical coercion with their children and are more likely to appeal to their self-esteem or try to arouse guilty feelings (Maccoby, 1992). During these years, parents are more effective when they monitor their children as opposed to directing them (Baumrind, 1991; Hetherington & Clingempeel, 1992). Children tend to be defiant in response to directive maternal strategies, whereas the children of mothers who rely on reasoning and suggestions are more likely to use negotiation (Kuczynski, Kochanska, Radke-Yarrow, & Girnius-Brown, 1987). These middle and late childhood years also mark a gradual increase in children's responsibilities and decision-making power within the family (Goodnow, 1996).

The ways in which children interact with their parents also change during this period of development. Compared with younger children, school-age children are less likely to express their frustrations toward their parents (Lamb & Lewis, 2011). Yet parental involvement continues to play an important role in development. There is accumulating evidence that caring, supportive parent–child relationships protect against poor mental health and strained intimate relationships later in life (Elgar, Craig, & Trites, 2013; Johnson & Galambos, 2014; Raudino, Fergusson, & Horwood, 2013). Children with disengaged parents are more immature, irresponsible, and socially incompetent. And these effects extend beyond the family—these children also do worse in school and have poorer peer relationships (Baumrind, 1991; Rubin, Coplan, Chen, Bowker, & McDonald, 2011).

Interventions aimed at improving parent–child communication and quality relationships are also showing promising results in the promotion of mental health and the prevention of behavioural issues in children and adolescents (Morgan, Brugha, Fryers, & Stewart-Brown, 2012). Despite the critical role of strong parent–adolescent relationships in mental health promotion during adolescence, there are significant gaps between Canadian provinces in terms of the availability of supports and funding, which may be particularly challenging for newcomers to Canada (Ruiz-Casares, Kolyn, Sullivan, & Rousseau, 2015). Existing mental health organizations may have difficulty in reaching ethnocultural communities because of language (Avila & Bramlett, 2012), cultural mistrust (Murry, Heflinger, Suiter, & Brody, 2011; Soorkia, Snelgar, & Swami, 2011), and the stigma (Sandhu et al., 2013), including among refugee families (Ellis et al., 2011), that is associated with mental health and parenting programs.

Parenting style and the education and income of parents are only a few factors that contribute to the diversity of twenty-first-century families. In recent decades, developmental science has been called upon to help us identify family factors that contribute to the health and well-being of children. Over the past few decades, more children are being raised in families with gay and lesbian parents (Gates, 2013). Research indicates that children nurtured in homes where both parents are the same sex have similar childhood experiences and outcomes compared with peers raised in families with parents of the opposite sex (Patterson, 2006). The most important factors contributing to child well-being and life satisfaction are higher levels of parental involvement and quality of parental contact (Goldberg, 2009; Patterson, 2006). In middle and late childhood, healthy parent–child relationships facilitate child happiness and reduce negative outcomes. In particular, communication, expressions of affection, monitoring of activities, a sense of safety, and consistency of parenting are of utmost importance (Holden & Miller, 1999; Murrin, 2007). Understanding the importance of parent involvement and parent–child relationship quality in middle and late childhood helps us see why children have more difficulties during these years when they lack parent support. Another pervasive influence on development is poverty, the topic of this chapter's *Challenges in Development*.

Effects of Divorce

Divorce, or the end of parental cohabitation, has the potential to temporarily interrupt supportive parenting, but divorce does not negate the possibility of co-operative co-parenting and supportive parenting during and after parental separation. In Canada, there has been an overall increase in the divorce rate in any given year, with 5 percent of the adult population experiencing divorce in 1981, and 11.5 percent experiencing divorce in 2011 (Milan, 2013). However, the structure of the Canadian family has also continued to evolve. Cohabitation, or common-law partnerships, with and without children also gained in popularity across the country during this time. In 2011, common-law couples accounted for 16.7 percent

CHALLENGES IN DEVELOPMENT
Growing Up in Poverty

What does it mean to live in poverty? Canada does not have an official "poverty line," but Statistics Canada produces several measures of low income. There are two sets of low-income cut-offs (LICO). The first is based on before-tax income including government transfers, such as tax credits. The second is based on after-tax income, which defines the income level at which a family may be considered in distressed circumstances because it has to spend a greater proportion of its income on necessities (food, clothing, shelter) than the average family does. There is about a 5-percentage-point difference in child poverty rates between these two measures. The 2013 LICO after tax for one parent with one child in a large urban centre was $24,066. It is important to note that the LICO is currently based on 1992 spending patterns and has not been adjusted since then (Statistics Canada, 2014). How might poverty rates change under a rebased LICO that reflected current conditions?

In 2011, the most recent Statistics Canada data available at the time of writing, nearly 3 million Canadians, or 8.8 percent of the population, have low income (Statistics Canada, 2013a). Internationally, Canada ranks in the bottom third of industrialized nations on measures of child poverty. With an estimated 14 percent of children living in poverty, Canada ranked 24th out of the 35 countries evaluated by UNICEF in 2012 (UNICEF Innocenti Research Centre, 2012). Child poverty rates have continued to climb in Canada, with numbers reported in 2014 approaching 19 percent, or more than 1.3 million children (Campaign 2000, 2014). For Indigenous children, poverty rates are even higher, with 40 percent of, or 171,000, First Nations children living in poverty. For First Nations children living on reserve, in communities where the federal government plays a major role in funding income support and community services, 50 percent are living in poverty (Macdonald & Wilson, 2013).

In Canada's labour market, full-time jobs with benefits that prevent poverty and enable parents to lift themselves out of low-income situations are being replaced by low-waged jobs, precarious work, and part-time employment (Campaign 2000, 2014). Therefore, work is not an assured route out of poverty; a low-income worker is a person whose work effort is high throughout the year, but whose family income is below the LICO. Lone parents and workers whose spouses do not work are most likely to be low-income workers. Additionally, the more dependent children there are in a home, the greater the probability it is a low-income family, whether there are two income earners or not (Fleury & Fortin, 2013). In 2004, more than 40 percent of children living in low-income families had at least one parent who worked a minimum 910 paid hours during the year, and more than 20 percent lived in families with at least two earners (Fleury, 2008). The majority of low- and modest-income families do not have access to affordable, secure housing or high-quality early childhood education services. Children of recent immigrants, from racialized families, in female lone-parent families, and with a disability are at a higher risk of living in poverty. Low- and modest-income students face steep barriers as the costs of post-secondary education rise (Campaign 2000, 2014).

---

of census families, and for the first time the number of common-law families (1,567,910) exceeded the number of lone-parent families (1,527,840) living in Canada (Statistics Canada, 2012). As such, the dissolution of a family unit may be more meaningful to Canadian families than the legal process of divorce, which is often not the component of a parental separation to cause difficulties for children.

Observing interparental conflict causes great stress for children (**Figure 8.5**) (Amato & Booth, 2001; Amato & Cheadle, 2008; Hetherington & Kelly, 2002). Children have been found to react to parental fighting with fear, anger, and an inhibition of normal emotional expression (Cummings, 1987). Younger, more egocentric children tend to blame themselves for the conflict (Grych & Fincham, 1990), and older children tend to show aggressive behaviour with peers and in other social situations (Amato & Cheadle, 2008).

In addition, divorce or leaving a partnership is not a single event. The time leading up to, during, and after a split relationship is marked by a clear decline in effective parenting (Grych, 2005). Parents in conflict are more likely to use harsh and inconsistent punishment for a child's behaviour. In some cases, parents will use children to deliver negative messages to the other parent, putting the child in an awkward and stressful position. As a result, children are often confused about how to engage parents to discuss personal problems, peer relationships, and school issues (Amato & Booth, 2001).

One overriding factor in reducing the negative effects of parental split on children is the availability of the non-custodial parent. In cases that do not involve abuse or neglect, seeing the non-custodial parent on a regular basis can facilitate some continuity while mediating some of the stress for the child (Amato & Booth, 2001; Deutsch, 2008). Parent education programs are now available in

Think Critically What social and economic circumstances in Canada might have accounted for the peak rate of 22 percent of children being in low-income families in 2004?

Defining poverty in these purely economic terms is controversial, however. Many developmentalists use a more encompassing definition that takes into account not only material assets, but also one's capacity for cultural identity, social belonging, dignity, and education (Engle & Black, 2008). Another controversy surrounds whether poverty should be considered an individual condition, or whether it is more productive to take a developmental systems theoretical approach to studying poverty and consider the contextual factors that prevent certain groups of people from escaping poverty.

However one defines it, poverty is a persistent problem in Canada and worldwide, negatively affecting family life and children's developmental outcomes (Engle & Black, 2008). Children raised in conditions of poverty are more likely to be abused, to drop out of school, and to turn to crime than those from higher financial statuses (Fass, 2009). Children in poverty are also less connected to their communities due to recurrent homelessness, evictions, or foreclosures.

Despite the overwhelming evidence that poverty represents a major challenge to children's positive development, there are many examples of children living below the poverty line who managed to overcome these challenges (Luthar, Cicchetti, & Becker, 2000). How families cope with poverty and the individual characteristics of the children themselves help to explain these differences.

Children in low-income families in Canada, 2000–2012

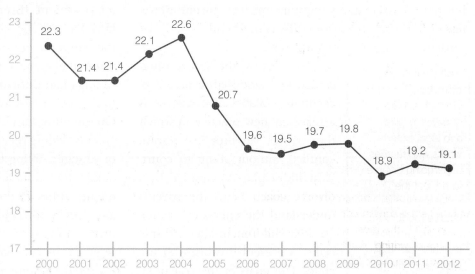

Source: Campaign 2000, *2014 Report Card on Child and Family Poverty in Canada*, p. 3, Chart 3. Data from Statistics Canada, CANSIM Table 111-0015, using Low Income Measure A-T, T1FF data. Accessed at http://campaign2000.ca/report-cards/national.

Conflict versus divorce • Figure 8.5

It seems obvious that this child is probably experiencing stress from watching parents argue. But we might think, "At least the parents are still together." Is the child indeed better off than a child of divorced parents? Actually, some research suggests that the level of interparental conflict may be more important than family composition in determining child outcomes (Phares, 2007).

Joel Sartore/National Geographic Creative

Think Critically What other factors are likely to determine child outcomes in the case of divorce?

every province and territory to help parents understand the importance of parental continuity in spite of long-lasting interparental conflict. These education programs also help parents become aware of the effects of conflict on their children, better understand co-parenting, and solve legal issues (Deutsch, 2008). Early indications are that parent education programs improve parent awareness of how their behaviour affects their children, which translates to less conflict and stress.

collaborative divorce A process in which a team of psychological and legal experts works with families undergoing divorce to protect the child(ren) and resolve roadblocks, facilitating an amicable divorce with minimal legal entanglements.

To address the stress often caused by traditional divorce proceedings, **collaborative divorce** is a relatively new practice in which the parties attempt to resolve conflicts without going to court. A multidisciplinary team led by a divorce coach helps the parents understand the effects of divorce on their children, and a child specialist is present to work with the child. The goals of the collaboration are to reduce conflict and to improve parenting through stress management and open communication. One key rule is that the collaboration ends if traditional divorce litigation occurs (Deutsch, 2008).

Unfortunately, there is no guaranteed solution for reducing the negative effects of divorce and interparental conflict on children. Developmental scientists are continuing to investigate possible strategies to effectively reduce the long-term effects. In the meantime, one coping mechanism children use is support from siblings, the topic we now consider (Jacobs & Sillars, 2012).

Sibling Relationships

In most cases, children's relationships with siblings are the longest-lasting relationships of their lives (Dunn, 2002) and children spend more time with their siblings than anyone else, including parents (Buist, Deković, & Prinzie, 2013). How many Canadian children have siblings? According to the 2011 census, 27 percent of families had two children and 9 percent had three or more children (Statistics Canada, 2013b). Most of these siblings are biological, but many children also have step-, adopted, or foster siblings. Approximately 86 percent of Canadian children have at least one sibling, whether they are biological, step, adopted, or foster (Statistics Canada, 2013b).

How well do you get along with your sibling(s)? Developmental researchers take a strong interest in this question, aiming to discover why some sibling relationships are positive whereas others are not. They have found that two key factors in determining the quality of sibling relationships are parent–child interaction and sibling temperament (Brody, Stoneman, & Gauger, 1996; Jenkins, Rasbash, Leckie, Gass, & Dunn, 2012). In particular, the temperament of the older sibling seems to be highly influential. One research team found that when older siblings had difficult temperaments, sibling relationship quality was rated as more negative (Brody et al., 1996). On the other hand, when older siblings had easy temperaments, sibling relationship quality was positive regardless of younger sibling temperament. The quality of parent–child interactions also correlated with sibling relationship quality, although difficult temperaments continued to be a challenge for family harmony regardless of the quality of those interactions (Brody et al., 1996). Since sibling interactions can be both a risk and a protective factor for the development and maintenance of emotional and behavioural problems, it is important to identify potential areas for intervention (Feinberg, Solmeyer, & McHale, 2012). Promising research shows how interventions can improve sibling relationships and that doing so can be beneficial for a range of social and emotional outcomes (Dirks, Persram, Recchia, & Howe, 2015).

Sibling rivalry can add tension to a sibling relationship, especially early in life. With age, however, sibling rivalry tends to dissipate as older siblings become teachers and mentors to younger siblings. Siblings have a shared, intimate history that they carry with them into adulthood.

sibling rivalry The competitive quality found in some sibling relationships.

Moving beyond the family context, we now consider the role of peers. Experiences with peers influence cognitive, physical, and socio-emotional development in distinct ways in middle childhood. The peer context also affects adjustment, not only during the middle- and late-childhood years, but later in the lifespan as well (Rubin, Bukowski, & Parker, 2006).

Peers

Peers are an important context of childhood development (Rubin et al., 2006). For the majority of children in Western cultures, peer interactions dramatically increase during the school years (Rubin et al., 2011). Peer groups

Peer statuses in childhood   Table 8.1

Status and outcomes	Rated as "liked"		Rated as "disliked"	

Popular children
• Remain popular over time
• Have fewer problems
• Do well in school
• Exhibit continued social competence
• Assertive
• Adept at mediating social conflict
  (Newcomb, Bukowski, & Pattee, 1993; see Rubin et al., 2006,
  for a review).
	Many nominations		Few nominations	

Rejected children • Poor students • Get into trouble • Have a high risk of juvenile delinquency (Kupersmidt & DeRosier, 2004).	Few nominations		Many nominations	

Neglected children
• May be socially unskilled
• May be introverts who don't often choose to
  socialize but when they do, they are able to do so
• Can gain social skills with healthy peers
  (Sandstrom & Zakriski, 2004)
	Few nominations		Few nominations	

Controversial children • Unclear	Many nominations		Many nominations	
Average children • Average outcomes	Medium number of nominations		Medium number of nominations	

---

sociometric measurement
A type of measurement of interpersonal relationships through social group survey.

popular children
Children with high numbers of positive nominations and low negative nominations in a sociometric analysis.

rejected children
Children with high numbers of negative nominations and low positive nominations in a sociometric analysis.

become considerably larger, more diverse, and less closely supervised by adults (Bergin & Bergin, 2009; Grossmann & Grossmann, 2000). We also see a shift in the range of settings. Whereas preschool children interact with peers primarily in the home setting and, for some, in daycare centres, school-age children interact with peers across a variety of settings—at school, travelling to and from school, talking on the telephone, playing sports, attending parties, and just hanging out (Zarbatany, Hartmann, & Rankin, 1990).

Research interest in how children relate to their peers has existed since at least the 1930s (Moreno, 1933). A primary

method of assessing the nature of peer relations is **sociometric measurement**, a type of survey in which children are asked to rank other members of their class in terms of whom they like most or least (Cillessen & Bukowski, 2000; see also Rubin et al., 2006). A set of five peer statuses has emerged from these rankings: **popular**, **rejected**, **neglected**, **controversial**, and **average**. **Table 8.1** shows the five types of peer statuses based on the number of children who rate a particular peer as "liked" or "disliked." As shown in the table, peer statuses have predictive significance for future social relations and other outcomes (Coie,

neglected children Children with few negative or positive nominations in a sociometric analysis.

controversial children Children with high numbers of positive nominations and high negative nominations in a sociometric analysis.

average children Children who get slightly more nominations in a sociometric analysis than neglected children but not enough to rank in one of the categories.

rejected-aggressive
Children who are rejected by peers for their aggressive behaviour.

rejected-withdrawn
Children who are rejected by peers for their withdrawn behaviour.

Dodge, & Coppotelli, 1982; De-Rosier & Thomas, 2003). Rejected children can be further categorized as **rejected-aggressive** (children who are rejected by peers for their aggressive behaviour) and **rejected-withdrawn** (children who are rejected by peers for their withdrawn behaviour; Dodge et al., 2003).

Children's peer status is linked to a variety of important characteristics and behaviours. For example, sociometrically popular children are more likely to be seen as friendly, co-operative, sociable, and sensitive by their teachers and peers (see Rubin et al., 2006, for a review). When conflicts do arise, these children tend toward negotiation and compromise. Many of these positive qualities also describe controversial children. Yet controversial children are, at the same time, reported to show more aggression, propensity to anger, and social withdrawal (Coie & Dodge, 1988).

Although few specific behaviours are consistently linked to neglected status, we find a strong association between aggression and rejection (e.g., Newcomb, Bukowski, & Pattee, 1993). In fact, aggression is one of the strongest predictors of peer rejection (e.g., Dodge, 1983; Coie & Kupersmidt, 1983). But that's not the whole story. Children who show some aggression, but balance that with positive qualities that facilitate peer connection, may not end up rejected by their peers (Farmer, Estell, Bishop, O'Neal, & Cairns, 2003). And, as children approach the adolescent years, aggression is decreasingly associated with rejection, particularly among boys (e.g., Sandstrom & Coie, 1999). Another behaviour linked to peer rejection is victimization (Kochenderfer-Ladd, 2003).

Bullying and victimization Were you bullied in school? Perhaps you were instead on the other side, acting as a bully during your school years? Or maybe you were a *bully/victim*, both a perpetrator and a victim. Bullying is widespread in Canada. In the 1990s, Canadian researchers determined that the bullying rates and frequencies suffered by students merited interventions (Craig, Peters, & Konarski, 1998; Sudermann, Jaffe, & Schieck, 1996). Canadian data suggest that the prevalence of bullying

behaviour, outside of cyberbullying, in terms of reported victimization declines from grades 6 to 10 (Craig & Mc-Cuaig, 2012). Data reported by the World Health Organization show that 17 percent of 11-year-olds report being bullied in Canadian schools. This level of bullying resulted in Canada's international ranking of 29th out of the 39 countries evaluated (Currie, Zanotti, Morgan, Currie, Looze, & Roberts, 2012) when it comes to a lack of bullying, which means we are near the bottom of the pack and have a long way to go to improve students' experiences. Current definitions of **bullying** vary considerably, which makes it hard for developmental researchers to document the prevalence and impact of bullying and to track trends over time (Law, Shapka, Domene, & Gagne, 2012). The World Health Organization has defined bullying as the assertion of interpersonal power through aggression. Aggression involves negative physical or verbal actions that have hostile intent and cause distress to victims. The World Health Organization additionally suggests that power relationships become consolidated with repeated bullying (Currie et al., 2012). Bullying inflicts physical, psychological, social, or educational harm and can take place in person or through technology, as **cyberbullying**. Although face-to-face aggression is still more common than electronic aggression, studies suggest that cyberbullying is an emerging public health concern (David-Ferdon & Hertz, 2009; Kulp, 2014). Further, researchers have cautioned that more research is required to understand the similarities and the differences between the two so that better interventions can be created (Law, Shapka, Hymel, Olson, & Waterhouse, 2012).

bullying Unwanted aggressive behaviour by another youth or group of youths that involves a power imbalance and is repeated multiple times.

cyberbullying
Bullying that takes place through technology, such as email, chat rooms, text message, or social media.

Bullying is a serious problem in Canada. The Canadian Institutes of Health Research reports that at least one in three adolescent students report recent experiences of bullying victimization; that the bullying experienced by youth who identify as lesbian, gay, bisexual, trans-identified, two-spirited, queer, or questioning (LGBTQ) is three times higher than heterosexual youth; and that any participation in bullying can increase rates of suicidal ideas in youth (Canadian Institutes of Health

Children's drawings of friendship • Figure 8.6

Across cultures, children's drawings of themselves with a friend show that similarity is an important feature of friendship (Pinto, Bombi, & Cordioli, 1997). As one team of researchers puts it, "No evidence exists to suggest that opposites attract" (Hartup & Abecassis, 2002, p. 291).

Think Critically Why might similarity be an important feature of friendship?

a. The artist who made this drawing is a 7-year-old boy from Bolivia. Note the figures' similar clothing.

b. A 10-year-old girl from Lebanon drew this picture of herself and a friend. Despite cultural, gender, and age differences between artists, similarity appears to be a universal feature of friendship.

Pinto, G., Bombi, A. S., & Cordioli, A. (1997). Similarity of Friends in Three Countries: A Study of Children's Drawings, *International Journal of Behavioral Development*, 20(3), 453–469.

Research, 2012). The problem does not have geographic boundaries. Researchers have observed bullying in most cultures (see also Rubin et al., 2006). Given the severity and spread of bullying, an increasing amount of research has been devoted to understanding this form of peer interaction.

Bullying and victimization are in full bloom by middle childhood (Espelage, Bosworth, & Simon, 2000). Children who engage in bullying behaviour have themselves typically experienced harsh parenting by caregivers (CDC, 2014). These children may be more accepting of violence and exhibit defiant and disruptive behaviour. Bullying behaviour centres around the quest for dominance, in which the bully aims to be at the top of a social hierarchy (Pellegrini & Bartini, 2000). Indeed, bullies typically like the fact that they are bullies (Veenstra, Lindenberg, Munniksma, & Dijkstra, 2010).

The majority of victims are males, though females are victims as well (Veenstra et al., 2010). Victimization is most common among children who are viewed by their peers as different or quiet (CDC, 2014). They typically have low self-esteem and poor peer relationships. Interestingly, victimization is also common among aggressive children, and this finding appears to be universal across cultures (e.g., Hanish & Guerra, 2004; Khatri & Kupersmidt, 2003). One explanation for this association is that children are victimized when their behaviour does not promote the basic functioning of the group. Aggressive children are seen as an obstacle to the group's coherence, harmony, and evolution, and so they are victimized (see Rubin et al., 2006).

Peer group norms are powerful tools shaping aggressive and non-aggressive anti-social behaviour and have important implications for prevention purposes (Vitaro, Brendgen, Girard, Boivin, Dionne, & Tremblay, 2015). Many schools have implemented prevention programs to reduce the incidence of bullying. Research points to four promising program elements (Farrington & Ttofi, 2010).

1. Improve supervision of students.

2. Use school rules and behaviour management techniques to identify and address bullying.

3. Have a whole-school anti-bullying policy and consistently enforce the policy.

4. Promote co-operation between school staff and parents.

Swedish psychologist Dan Olweus created one such bullying-prevention program (Olweus, 2005). Assessments of the Olweus Bullying Prevention Program report moderate success, as discussed in *Where Developmentalists Click* (Olweus, 2005).

Victimization is more common among friendless children (Boulton, Trueman, Chau, Whitehand, & Amatya, 1999). In turn, friendship serves many protective functions (Rubin et al., 2011). Middle and late childhood marks a dramatic shift in children's understanding of friendship. We turn now to this important form of peer relationships.

Friendship Friendship involves a voluntary, close, and mutual relationship (Rubin et al., 2011). A defining feature of friendship is reciprocity—an equal giving-and-taking between partners (Hartup & Stevens, 1997). When asked, "What is a best friend?" (Bigelow, 1977), children of all ages include the idea of reciprocity in their definitions. Similarity of friends is another consistently strong feature of friendship, which seems to foster both friendship formation and longevity (Kupersmidt, DeRosier, & Patterson, 1995; **Figure 8.6**). The big change we see across childhood is that young children's friendships are based in the here and now, tied to particular social activities, whereas school-age children's friendships transcend specific activities (Rubin et al., 2011).

At the beginning of middle childhood, children focus on the rewards and costs of friendship (Bigelow, 1977). Friends are rewarding to be with—they live nearby, have interesting toys, and like to engage in the same types of play. Non-friends, on the other hand, are

Where Developmentalists CLICK

Olweus Bullying Prevention Program

Although the best source for strong research is peer-reviewed journals, the lag time between data collection and publication in a journal can be years. Therefore, developmentalists often watch for updated research reports online, especially on topics with heightened policy implications like bullying. The website for the Olweus Bullying Prevention Program both summarizes current findings and provides citations for peer-reviewed journal articles, which you then can look up. Access the site by going to the homepage of the Olweus Bullying Prevention Program (www.violencepreventionworks.org). Click on "Key Resources," "Olweus," and then "Latest Research" and peruse the research summaries. Visiting the site also offers a good opportunity to use your critical thinking skills. For example, what are the potential conflicts of interest when a scientist provides a fee-for-service such as this bullying program? How might these inevitable conflicts best be managed, both by the researchers and by the field of lifespan development as a whole?

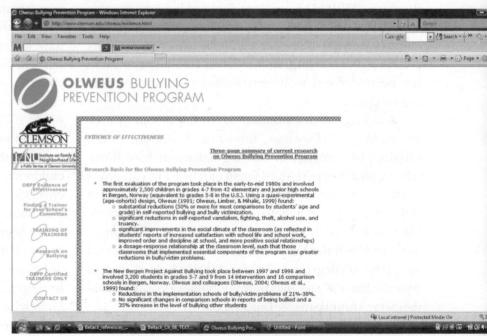

perspective taking The increasing ability to take on other people's viewpoints.

hard or boring to be with. During middle childhood and into early adolescence, children begin to appreciate the importance of loyalty and shared values (Rubin et al., 2011). What explains this developmental shift in children's ideas about friendship? Some developmental scientists argue that it has to do with the development of **perspective taking**, the ability to take on other people's viewpoints (Selman & Schultz, 1990). Other researchers have argued that children's understanding of friendship develops in conjunction with their understanding of reciprocity (e.g., Youniss, 1980). At the most basic level, this shift seems to reflect Piaget's ideas about children's movement from a concrete understanding of the world to a more abstract one (Rubin et al., 2011).

There are some interesting gender differences in the quality of boys' and girls' friendships. Girls report more caring, intimacy, and conflict resolution compared with boys (Parker & Asher, 1993; Rubin, Dwyer, Booth, Kim, Burgess,

& Rose-Krasnor, 2004). Girls also report more **co-rumination** than boys (Rose, 2002). Even so, boys and girls do not significantly differ in their satisfaction with these relationships (Parker & Asher, 1993; Rose & Rudolph, 2006). Gender differences are also evident in school-age children's emotional development.

co-rumination The act of dwelling on negative occurrences and feelings.

CONCEPT CHECK 🛑 STOP

1. **What** qualities of parent–child relationships facilitate child happiness and reduce negative outcomes?
2. **How** can parents mitigate the negative effects of splitting up?
3. **What** determines the quality of sibling relationships?
4. **What** is the relationship between peer rejection and aggression?

Emotional Development

LEARNING OBJECTIVES

1. **Explain** how a child's emotional vocabulary affects developmental outcomes.
2. **Define** resilience in childhood, discussing factors related to its development.

Although the lives of young children are emotionally rich, school-age children have an even better understanding of their own and others' emotions. As we will see, this emotional understanding has implications for children's coping and resilience.

Emotional Understanding

Improved cognitive abilities, including verbal skills, enable many emotional gains during middle and late childhood (Izard, 2001). Most school-age children have a basic **emotional vocabulary**. They can also correctly identify emotional situations, facial expressions, and behaviours (Fabes, Eisenberg, Nyman, & Michealieu, 1991).

Verbal ability in particular may be associated with greater emotional knowledge, **emotional regulation**, and emotional coping (Mostow, Izard, Fine, & Trentacosta, 2002). For example, in order to comfort an unhappy friend, a child must first recognize the unhappiness, know the appropriate words to say, and have the skill to moderate her own emotions. Children with strong vocabularies appear to be better at this task than those who have weak vocabularies (Schultz, Izard, & Ackerman, 2000). Children with strong verbal skills report happy and adaptive social interactions, good coping skills, and healthy friendships. On the other

emotional vocabulary The increasing ability to identify and label complex emotions.

emotional regulation The ability to adapt to changing situations with a range of constructive emotional responses.

Self-conscious emotions • Figure 8.7

Self-conscious emotions require a deeper understanding of the world than do primary emotions (Davidson, 2006). They also require some external social filter, through which an individual considers another's perspective in relation to his or her behaviour.

	Envy	Embarrassment	Pride	Guilt
Vibe Images/Alamy	Philip felt envious when he saw how much Simone was enjoying her ice cream cone.	Violet felt embarrassed when she accidentally dropped her sister's birthday cake in front of a crowd of singing friends and family.	Adeline felt proud when her teacher complimented her short story in front of her classmates.	Sajid felt guilty when the family cat escaped from the house because he forgot to latch the door as he was supposed to do.

Put It Together *Review the section on Piaget's theory of moral development and answer the following question:*
Violet's sister, the birthday girl, is in the stage of moral realism. In response to the dropped birthday cake, we would expect her to be _____.
a. understanding   **c.** focused on the intentions behind the action
b. upset   **d.** comforted to know that Violet did not mean to drop the cake

---

hand, children with poor verbal abilities falter when it comes to emotional knowledge. They have a hard time coping with stress and experience less satisfying social interactions (Izard, Fine, Schultz, Mostow, Ackerman, & Youngstrom, 2001).

As we discussed in Chapter 4, primary emotions emerge early in the lifespan. As children get older, they begin to observe subtle changes in emotional expression and start to recognize feelings like embarrassment and envy, known as **self-conscious emotions** (**Figure 8.7**). Self-conscious emotions increase with age. One researcher asked 4-, 6-, and 8-year-old children to give an example of an embarrassing situation (Griffin, 1995). Only the 8-year-olds made reference to an audience—a person or group of people who had witnessed the embarrassing situation. Thus, as children get older they begin to realize the context of emotional displays and the subtle differences in situations that result in varied emotional expressions (Griffin, 1995).

self-conscious emotions Emotions that involve internal and external evaluations of the self.

Emotion continues to evolve and become more complex throughout childhood. Children come to recognize situations that may elicit emotional outbursts and to develop strategies to mediate these events. Emotional regulation is closely tied to coping and resilience.

Risk, Resilience, and Coping

Imagine a child growing up in a context of significant disadvantage: violence in his neighbourhood, a lack of social support, physical and verbal abuse from a parent—all identified risk factors. Now we visit him 40 years later. How is he doing? Perhaps he is battling alcoholism and trying to shake a criminal record. Or maybe instead he is thriving, with a strong career, a healthy and loving family, and an enviable financial situation. What causes a child to go down one of these paths or the other? That is the question that many developmentalists are now asking as they look for ways to promote **resilience**.

resilience Positive adjustment in the face of significant risk.

Before we continue, let's get a couple things straight. Children are *not* resilient. You read that right. And resilience is also *not* a feature of the context. Rather, resilience refers to the *relationship* between a child and his or her context. When the characteristics of the child fit with the features of the context in such a way as to bring about positive adjustment in the face of significant risk (**Figure 8.8**), then we're talking about the phenomenon of resilience (Lerner et al., 2013; Luthar et al., 2000).

Using Statistics Canada's National Longitudinal Survey of Children and Youth, Bellamy and Hardy

The relationship between risk and resilience • Figure 8.8

When children face high levels of adversity, those who have extraordinary coping skills will demonstrate high levels of achievement despite significant risk exposure.

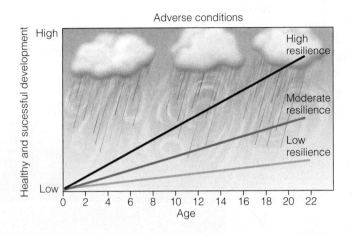

Ask Yourself

1. According to this figure, children who are extremely healthy and successful despite adversity can be described as _____.
2. True or false? Resilience is a phenomenon applicable to most children.

(2015) identified several factors that increase risk of the development of depression symptoms in both boys and girls. They found, however, that girls showed a greater risk of developing depression. Negative parental experiences, such as maternal depression or loss of a parent, as well as conduct disorder and aggression, place girls at higher risk of developing depression than girls who do not experience these stressors. Childhood symptoms of anxiety and depression place children at risk for depression in late adolescence, boys especially so; boys with lower levels of self-esteem and perceptions of parental rejection are at increased risk for depression. The study showed evidence for continuity of depressive symptoms over time, with early symptoms in childhood continuing into adolescence and adulthood (Bellamy & Hardy, 2015).

Some of the most comprehensive studies of risk and resilience were undertaken by Emmy Werner and colleagues (e.g., Werner & Smith, 2001). In 1955, they began collecting data on every single child born that year on the island of Kauai in Hawaii. Werner et al. found that the early-childhood years lay the foundation for resilience. They noted, however, that there were possibilities for recovery later in life, especially in the context of effective support systems. They also found that boys tended to fare worse than girls. In particular, males were more likely to have behavioural problems in adolescence and less likely to experience resilience as adults compared with females (Werner & Smith, 2001).

Building on these findings, developmental scientists have identified a number of specific **risk factors** and **protective factors** that contribute to the process of resilience. **Figure 8.9** covers the major risk and protective factors. These factors combine to affect the development of resilience (Hansson et al., 2008).

As noted in Figure 8.9, one way that individuals contribute to the process of resilience is by adopting positive coping strategies (Rutter, 2007). Coping and emotional regulation are closely related, if not interchangeable, concepts (e.g., Brenner & Salovey, 1997)—both are involved when children use strategies to manage stressful experiences or negative emotions. Coping researchers have come up with different categories of coping strategies (e.g., Lazarus, 1999; Marriage & Cummins, 2004). For example, **Table 8.2** presents the four categories of coping strategies that children use to deal with peer rejection (Sandstrom, 2004).

With age, children get better at coping (see Saarni, Campos, Camras, & Witherington, 2006, for

risk factor A negative factor in a child's life that endangers his or her well-being and likelihood for resilience, such as insecure attachment to a primary caregiver, parental death, and neighbourhood violence.

protective factor A positive factor in a child's life that bolsters his or her well-being and likelihood for resilience, such as high self-efficacy, authoritative parenting, and competent and caring friends.

Risk factors and protective factors interact to increase or decrease the likelihood of resilience. For example, Jorge lives in a neighbourhood where there is frequent violence, and his father struggles with mental illness, which makes their relationship difficult. All of these pose risk factors for Jorge. At the same time, he is intelligent, with a loving extended family and a supportive group of friends, all of which serve as protective factors. The risk and protective factors for Jorge in particular are indicated by arrows pointing to items on the generic lists.

Risk factors

Individual characteristics
- Having a difficult temperament
- Having an insecure attachment with primary caregiver
- Having genetic predispositions to a psychopathology

Family characteristics
- Being exposed to parental psychopathology
- Experiencing parental death
- Being exposed to family dysfunction
- Being a victim of abuse or neglect
- Being exposed to interparental conflict

Community characteristics
- Having inadequate educational resources
- Being exposed to neighbourhood violence
- Living in poverty/Low SES

Protective factors

Individual characteristics
- Being of average or above-average intellectual functioning
- Being sociable and easygoing
- Having faith
- Having high self-efficacy
- Having a positive coping style (seeking help from others when necessary)
- Possessing talent(s)
- Having the ability and willingness to problem solve

Family characteristics
- Having socio-economic advantages
- Having connections to the extended family
- Having a close relationship with a parental figure
- Having a parent who uses authoritative parenting style

Community characteristics
- Attending effective schools
- Having connections to prosocial organizations
- Having bonds to prosocial adults
- Having competent, caring friends

Denis Jr. Tangney/Getty Images

Tim Kitchen/Getty Images

Think Critically Do you think it is a better use of public resources to create programs that enhance protective factors or to create programs that decrease risk factors? Why?

Coping with peer rejection	Table 8.2
Active coping	• Problem solving • Seeking help/support
Aggressive coping	• Teasing • Retaliation
Denial coping	• Pretending not to care • Ignoring the issue
Ruminative coping	• Worrying • Withdrawal

a review). They become more effective at eliciting social support and managing negative emotions. They also get better at distinguishing between and dealing with controllable and uncontrollable stressors (Aldwin, 1994). Younger children deal with uncontrollable stressors by trying to escape them, such as hiding under the bed to avoid a negative event. Older children, on the other hand, are more likely to use active coping strategies like reframing—adopting a new, more positive point of view (Marriage & Cummins, 2004).

Many interrelated factors converge to determine whether or not an individual will thrive after childhood. A child's sense of self, experiences in school, and family life interact to foster or impede healthy development. As we will see, these influences continue into the adolescent period.

CONCEPT CHECK

1. **What** is the connection between emotion and cognition?

2. **How** do risk factors and protective factors affect the development of resilience?

 THE PLANNER

Summary

1 Personality Development 262

- Self-understanding grows more complex with age. **Social comparison** leads to more realistic self-knowledge, and contributes to self-esteem. Children base their self-esteem and self-concepts on information from parents, peers, and other interactions. **Self-efficacy** reflects the child's sense of agency, the belief that the child can actively accomplish goals and competently complete tasks.

- Piaget suggested that children move from a **moral realism** marked by **heteronomous morality** to a **moral relativism** marked by **autonomous morality**. Kohlberg used moral dilemmas to identify three levels of moral development, each of which has two stages: **preconventional morality**, **conventional morality**, and **postconventional morality**.

- Critics of Kohlberg's theory include Carol Gilligan, who suggested that males focus on a morality of justice, whereas females use a care-based moral framework. Other critics have called attention to the influence of cultural factors on moral decision-making.

- In the **industry stage versus inferiority**, Erikson believed that children must avoid a sense of inferiority and work toward industry, as this boy in the figure has done.

Industry versus inferiority • Figure 8.4

Tom Horan/AP Photo

2 Social Influences 268

- Although parenting changes in a number of ways during the **tween** years, parental involvement is still very important.

Children living in poverty and children with disengaged parents suffer a variety of negative developmental outcomes. Research reveals no differences between the children of heterosexual parents and the children of homosexual parents.

- The parental conflict leading up to a divorce can lead to poor parenting behaviours and cause great stress for children. **Collaborative divorce**, parent education programs, and other steps to promote effective co-parenting can reduce the negative effects of divorce on children.

- Approximately 86 percent of Canadian children have at least one sibling, whether they are biological, step, adopted, or foster. Parent–child interactions and older-sibling temperaments affect how well siblings get along. **Sibling rivalry** also tends to be related to age.

- Researchers conduct **sociometric measurement** to analyze children's status among their peers. **Popular**, **neglected**, **controversial**, **average children**, and **rejected children**—subdivided into **rejected-aggressive** and **rejected-withdrawn children**—all tend to have different characteristics and outcomes.

- Many students are involved in **bullying**, whether as victims, bullies, or bully/victims. Electronic aggression, or **cyberbullying**, appears to be an emerging public health concern.

- Friendship involves a voluntary, close, and mutual relationship. Similarity of friends is a defining feature of friendship, as illustrated by children's drawings across cultures, such as those in the figure.

Children's drawings of friendship • Figure 8.6

Pinto, G., Bombi, A. S., & Cordioli, A. (1997). Similarity of Friends in Three Countries: A Study of Children's Drawings. *International Journal of Behavioral Development*, 20(3), 453–469.

- Young children's friendships are based in the here and now, whereas school-age children's friendships transcend specific activities. As children move from a concrete understanding of the world to a more abstract one, they better understand **perspective taking** and begin to appreciate the importance of loyalty and shared values. One notable gender difference in children's friendships is that girls report more **co-rumination** than boys.

3 Emotional Development 277

- Improvements in verbal skills are linked to increases in **emotional vocabulary** and development during childhood. **Self-conscious emotions** like embarrassment also arise during childhood. Emotions become more complex and children become more aware of **emotional regulation**.

- Developmentalists have identified a number of specific **risk factors** and **protective factors** that contribute to **resilience**, or positive adjustment in the face of significant risk, as shown in the diagram in the figure.

The relationship between risk and resilience • Figure 8.8

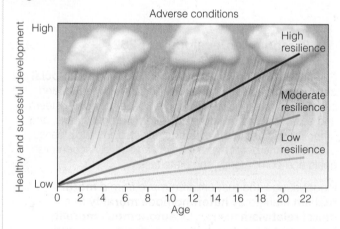

- Coping is one way that children contribute to their own resilience.

Key Terms

- autonomous morality 264
- average children 273
- bullying 274
- collaborative divorce 272
- controversial children 273
- conventional morality 265
- co-rumination 277
- cyberbullying 274
- emotional regulation 277
- emotional vocabulary 277
- heteronomous morality 263
- industry versus inferiority stage 267
- moral realism 263
- moral relativism 264
- neglected children 273
- perspective taking 277
- popular children 273
- postconventional morality 265
- preconventional morality 265
- protective factor 279
- rejected children 273
- rejected-aggressive children 274
- rejected-withdrawn children 274
- resilience 278
- risk factor 279
- self-concept 262
- self-conscious emotions 278
- self-efficacy 262
- self-esteem 262
- sibling rivalry 272
- social comparison 262
- sociometric measurement 273
- tween 268

Critical and Creative Thinking Questions

1. What can parents and teachers do to enhance children's self-esteem?

2. Which theory of moral development holds the most appeal to you and why?

3. If you knew someone who was married and considering divorce, what advice would you give them about helping their children best cope with the issue?

4. If you have a sibling, how would you describe your relationship? How did the relationship change as you grew older? If you do not have siblings, what have you noticed about the relationships between siblings you know?

5. What risk factors and protective factors characterized your own childhood and those of people you know?

What is happening in this picture?

These children are riding in a parade in their community.

Think Critically **1.** What emotions do they appear to be feeling? How might their emotions differ from those of younger children in this situation?
2. How might this activity contribute to their self-esteem and self-concepts? How might Erik Erikson view this activity in relation to the main challenge faced by children?
3. This community seems to offer protective factors. What other protective factors might these children benefit from?

XPACIFICA/National GeographicCreative

REAL  Development

Socio-emotional Development in Middle and Late Childhood: Six to Eleven Years

In this video activity, you are a student intern at Abegweit Middle School interested in learning more about socio-emotional development in middle to late childhood. You will help the school counsellor select an appropriate brochure on bullying. The brochure will be distributed to students and their parents. As part of your research on students' existing perceptions, knowledge, and experiences of popularity and bullying, you gather a group of students to serve as a focus group. Your task is to select which brochure you will recommend to the school counsellor, taking the students' input into account.

John Wiley & Sons, Inc.

WileyPLUS Go to WileyPLUS to complete the REAL Development activity.

03.01

Self-Test

(Check your answers in Appendix A.)

1. Which self-description is LEAST likely to come from an elementary-school-aged child?

a. I like to play drums and sing.

b. I'm better at math than some of the other kids in my class.

c. I'm getting really good at bike jumps because I practise a lot.

d. I'm the strongest boy in the world.

2. Which of the following is correlated with high self-esteem in children?

a. feeling happier

b. doing well in school

c. having more friends

d. All of these are correlated with high self-esteem.

3. Erikson believed that children who experience growing self-esteem and a sense of their own skill are developing _____.

a. industry   c. inferiority

b. latency   d. morality

4. During Piaget's stage of moral relativism, children are able to consider intentions when judging actions and can make up their own rules for games. These are characteristics of _____.

a. autonomous morality

b. heteronomous morality

c. absolutist morality

d. hegemonious morality

5. Aiden does a favour for his friend only when his friend does a favour for him. Aiden is reasoning using which of Kohlberg's orientations?

a. universal ethics   c. social contract

b. instrumental-exchange   d. good-child

6. In Carol Gilligan's critique of Kohlberg's theory, she suggested that female moral reasoning is based on _____.

a. rules made by external authorities

b. concepts of justice

c. care and relationships

d. collectivist input from community

7. Which of the following is a typical change in the parent–child relationship during middle and late childhood?

a. Children's responsibilities and decision-making power increase within the family.

b. Parents are less likely to use physical coercion.

c. Children are less likely to express their frustrations toward their parents.

d. All of these are typical.

8. Which of the following causes stress for children whose parents divorce?

a. the parents' conflict before the divorce

b. lack of access to one parent after the divorce

c. confusion and poor parenting practices during the divorce

d. All of these cause stress.

9. Research shows that when _____ siblings have _____ temperaments, sibling relationship quality is _____.

a. older; easy; positive

b. younger; difficult; positive

c. younger; easy; negative

d. older; easy; negative

10. Fill in each peer status in the table.

	Liked	**Disliked**
a. _____	Many nominations	Few nominations
b. _____	Many nominations	Many nominations
c. _____	Few nominations	Many nominations
d. _____	Few nominations	Few nominations
e. _____	Medium amount of nominations	Medium amount of nominations

11. Ennis is a student in Grade 6 who shows defiant and disruptive behaviour. His dad tends to push him around at home, which makes Ennis feel a strong need to dominate somebody else. Ennis is most likely to be _____.

a. a bully

b. a victim of a bully

c. a witness to bullying

d. completely uninvolved in bullying

12. _____ is an equal giving and taking between partners and a defining feature of friendship.

a. Co-rumination

b. Reciprocity

c. Similarity

d. Perspective taking

13. This child is displaying an emotion that requires an understanding of an audience, known as a _____ emotion.

Vibe Images/Alamy

a. self-esteem

b. self-concept

c. self-conscious

d. self-deprecating

14. Resilience is a feature of the _____.

a. child

b. context

c. parent

d. child–context relationship

15. Fill in the blanks in the table.

a. _____	• Problem solving • Seeking help/support
Aggressive coping	• Teasing • Retaliation
Denial coping	• Pretending not to care • Ignoring the issue
b. _____	• Worrying • Withdrawal

THE PLANNER

Review your Chapter Planner in the chapter opener and check off your completed work.

Physical and Cognitive Development in Adolescence

After weeks of shopping, a day of primping, and an afternoon posing for photos, the teens shown here are finally ready to embark on the Canadian adolescent ritual of senior prom. These adolescents have already faced many challenges before getting to this day.

As we will see in this chapter, they have experienced changing brain landscapes, growth spurts, pubertal transformations, and completely new ways of thinking that cast everything they knew into a new light. And now here they are, ready to celebrate the end of their

high school careers and their teen years by dressing in their finest. Regardless of whether an adolescent excitedly prepares for the prom or unconditionally rejects the tradition, this rite of passage marks the end of high school and foreshadows the transition to adulthood.

Bikeriderlondon/Shutterstock

CHAPTER OUTLINE

CHAPTER PLANNER ✓

- ❏ Study the picture and read the opening story.
- ❏ Scan the Learning Objectives in each section:
  p. 288 ❏   p. 298 ❏   p. 303 ❏
- ❏ Read the text and study all visuals. Answer any questions.

Analyze key features

- ❏ Development InSight, p. 290
- ❏ Process Diagram, p. 301
- ❏ What a Developmentalist Sees, p. 309
- ❏ Challenges in Development, p. 312
- ❏ Stop: Answer the Concept Checks before you go on:
  p. 298 ❏   p. 302 ❏   p. 314 ❏

End of chapter

- ❏ Review the Summary and Key Terms.
- ❏ Answer *What is happening in this picture?*
- ❏ Answer the Critical and Creative Thinking Questions.
- ❏ Complete the Self-Test and check your answers.

Physical Development

LEARNING OBJECTIVES

1. **Describe** the physical and hormonal events of puberty, including the significance of timing.
2. **Describe** changes in the nervous system during adolescence.
3. **Explain** changes in the skeletal system during adolescence.
4. **Outline** muscle development during adolescence, including differences between the sexes.

Of the many rapid physical and physiological changes occurring in adolescence, puberty is perhaps the most profound. Pubertal maturation transforms the young person from looking like a child to appearing and, in some ways, feeling and acting like an adult. It is this striking transformation that has captured the attention of scholars, artists, the media, and parents alike, and inspired an array of cultural rites of passage. The biologically based process of puberty affects all—physical, cognitive, and socio-emotional—domains of development (Susman & Dorn, 2009). The general sequence of pubertal changes is the same for most people, but, as we will learn, there is great variation in their timing and impact (Katchadourian, 1977; Tanner, 1991).

Puberty

The word **puberty** comes from the Latin word "pubertas," meaning adult. Although adolescents are not yet adults,

> **puberty** A hormonal process resulting in reproductive competence and related physical development.
>
> **adolescence** The transitional period in which young people move into adult cognitions, emotions, and social roles.

puberty endows adolescents with reproductive competence and, therefore, marks the potential for significant adult responsibilities associated with sexuality. Adolescence and puberty are not interchangeable terms. Puberty, at a basic level, is a brain–neuroendocrine (hormonal) process resulting in sexual maturation and related physical development (Susman & Dorn, 2009). **Adolescence**—a broader concept that encompasses puberty—is a transition into adult cognition, emotions, and social roles.

The timing of pubertal changes varies among individuals. Within Canada, some adolescents go through puberty during elementary school, whereas others are just beginning the transition during their senior year in high school (Ellis & Essex, 2007). Before we look more deeply at these individual differences, let's first examine the universal physical changes of puberty.

The physical changes of puberty The five key changes that occur during puberty are (Marshall, 1978):

1. The development of specific organs in the body responsible for reproduction (male and female reproductive systems), which are called **primary sex characteristics**. For males, these changes are in the penis and testes and, for females, these changes occur in the ovaries, fallopian tubes, vagina, and cervix.

2. The development of **secondary sex characteristics**, which are associated with sex hormones but not reproduction. These changes appear in skin, vocal cords, body hair, and breasts.

3. Growth spurts in both height and weight.

4. Changes in the distribution of fat and muscle.

5. Changes in circulation and respiration.

When some of the changes are underway, but most have yet to occur, the young person is in the **prepubescent phase** of puberty (Schonfeld, 1969). The **pubescent phase** is marked by the initiation of most of these bodily changes and, when most of these changes are complete, the young person is said to be in the **postpubescent phase**. This final phase ends when all the bodily changes of puberty are complete (Schonfeld, 1969).

> **primary sex characteristic** A physical characteristic, such as the internal and external genitalia, directly associated with reproduction.
>
> **secondary sex characteristic** A physical characteristic associated with sex hormones but not directly associated with reproduction.
>
> **prepubescent phase** When some of the changes associated with puberty are underway, but most have yet to occur.
>
> **pubescent phase** When the majority of the changes associated with puberty are occurring.
>
> **postpubescent phase** When the majority of the changes associated with puberty have been experienced and are complete.

Hormones A number of significant **hormones** increase during puberty as the endocrine reproductive system becomes more active. Endocrine glands begin to release hormones along a pathway established before birth called the **hypothalamus-pituitary-adrenal (HPA) axis**, which is named for the major glands that are involved: the hypothalamus, pituitary, and adrenal glands (HPA) (**Figure 9.1**). These hormones are like time-release capsules that have waited for the appropriate moment to activate various structures of the body, including the **gonads** or sex glands (testicles in males and ovaries in females). The organizational influence of hormones, however, begins much earlier than adolescence (Cesario & Hughes, 2007).

During the embryonic stage of prenatal development, the brain produces steroid hormones that create neural circuits in the brain (Sisk, 2006). These circuits tend to develop along gender-specific parameters. During puberty, the rise in hormones finishes these circuits, allowing for reproductive capacity and influencing adolescent behaviour (Day, Chiu, & Hendren, 2006; Sisk, 2006).

Of the many hormones that are active during puberty, GnRH (gonadotropin-releasing hormone) is a particularly important one (Sisk, 2006). GnRH directs the release and synthesis of the two key hormones— LH (luteinizing hormone) and FSH (follicle-stimulating hormone)—that together stimulate the gonads to increase production of androgens and estrogens (male and female sex hormones) and complete the development of sperm and eggs. We typically associate androgens, such as **testosterone**, with males and estrogens, such as **estradiol**, with females. However, both types of sex hormones are present in both males and females, though to varying degrees.

> **hormone** A chemical that travels in the bloodstream to target organs, helping them regulate a variety of bodily functions such as reproduction, sleep, hunger, and stress.
>
> **hypothalamus-pituitary-adrenal (HPA) axis** A communicative pathway between three endocrine glands: the hypothalamus, the pituitary gland, and the adrenal glands.
>
> **gonads** Testicles in males and ovaries in females, also known as the sex glands.

> **testosterone** An androgenic sex hormone produced by the gonads (but in much lower levels in females) that is responsible for primary and secondary sex characteristics.
>
> **estradiol** A potent form of estrogen produced by the gonads (but in much lower levels in males) that is responsible for primary and secondary sex characteristics.

The HPA axis in puberty • Figure 9.1

The release of hormones along the HPA axis triggers the noticeable maturation of male and female sex characteristics.

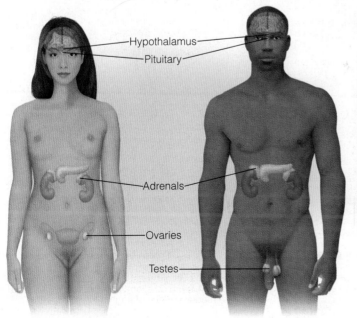

Ask Yourself

1. Which part of the body releases androgens?
   a. pituitary **b.** adrenals **c.** hypothalamus
2. What part of the brain stimulates the pituitary gland?
   a. ovaries **b.** adrenals **c.** hypothalamus

Hypothalamus	Produces LHRH (luteinizing hormone releasing hormone), a chemical that stimulates the secretion of hormones from the pituitary.
Pituitary	Releases LH (luteinizing hormone) and FSH (follicle-stimulating hormone) into the bloodstream, which stimulate the gonads to secrete sex hormones.
Adrenals	Release androgens, which trigger maturation of primary and secondary male and female sex characteristics.
Ovaries	Release estrogens, which trigger maturation of primary and secondary female sex characteristics.
Testes	Release testosterone, which triggers maturation of primary and secondary male sex characteristics.

All of this hormonal activity is associated with dramatic physical changes, as well as social and emotional ones. Parent–child conflict, sensation-seeking, and the development of romantic interests have been shown to coincide with pubertal maturation more than with age, leading some developmental scientists to consider the role of hormones in behavioural patterns characteristic of adolescence (Dahl & Spear, 2004; Goddings, Heyes, Bird, Viner, & Blakemore, 2012; Steinberg, 1988). However, we know that hormones do not exert their influence in a vacuum, but rather interact with the context to produce the patterns we see (Forbes & Dahl, 2010). Hormones also interact with the context to produce the physical changes of puberty, primary and secondary sex characteristics, as depicted in **Figure 9.2** (Kramer, Perry, Golbin, & Cushing, 2009).

Primary sex characteristics As noted previously, primary sex characteristics are directly related to reproduction. For girls, these characteristics involve the maturation of the eggs in their ovaries, and an increase in volume and maturity of the fallopian tubes, lining of the uterus, and cervix. The external female sex organs exhibit significant growth as well (Roney, 2005).

Menarche is the first menstrual period in females, but it

> **menarche**
> (pronounced *me-när-kē*) The first menstrual period of human females, signalling the beginning of fertility.

Development InSight

The development of primary and secondary sex characteristics • Figure 9.2

Normal pubertal development proceeds in terms of sequence, timing, and tempo through a sequence of five stages referred to as the Tanner stages (Tanner, 1973). Stage 1, for both males and females, is a point when no signs of puberty are present. Stage 5 is full maturity of adult genitalia and the presence of pubic hair, adult in type, quantity, and spread.

a. Female pubescence

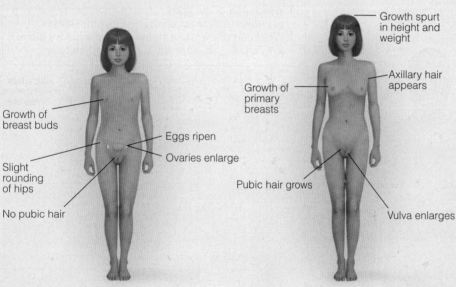

Prepubescent phase
Stage 2: Breast buds appear, with elevation of breast and enlargement of areola; sparse growth of long, slightly pigmented pubic hair along labia

Growth of breast buds
Eggs ripen
Ovaries enlarge
Slight rounding of hips
No pubic hair

Pubescent phase
Stage 3: Further enlargement of, but no separation in contour between, breast and areola; darker, coarser, more curled hair over pubic area

Growth spurt in height and weight
Axillary hair appears
Growth of primary breasts
Pubic hair grows
Vulva enlarges

Postpubescent phase
Stage 4: Areola forms a secondary mound above level of breast; pubic hair, adult in type, but covering smaller area than adult (no spread to medial surface of thighs)

Most changes in primary and secondary sexual characteristics are complete
Decrease in the rate of growth in height
Axillary hair development is complete
Fertile
Pubic hair development is complete

ovum A mature female reproductive cell, also known as an egg, released from the ovary during ovulation.

does not necessarily indicate the release of the first mature **ovum** (egg) and, thus, the ability to reproduce. Ovulation does not typically accompany the first menstrual cycle, nor does it occur regularly at first. Once ovulation does occur regularly as a part of the menstrual cycle, the release of eggs then proceeds from alternating ovaries on approximately a 28- to 32-day menstrual cycle. Research has shown a slight difference in timing of menarche among Caucasian, African American, and Hispanic girls, with the latter two groups experiencing menarche somewhat earlier (Chandra, Martinez, Mosher, Abma, & Jones, 2005).

The timing of menarche is also linked to body fat. Girls with more body fat are more likely to have earlier menses (Leitão, Rodrigues, Neves, & Carvalho, 2013). In Canada, the first national study of menarche was conducted in 2000–2001 and we do not have trend data to compare any shifts in the onset of menarche (Al-Sahab, Ardern, Hamadeh, & Tamim, 2010). However, recent research indicates that girls may currently be experiencing menarche and other signs of puberty—such as breast development—earlier than girls born in the previous three decades (Biro et al., 2010; Sex Information and Education Council of Canada, 2015).

In Canada, the mean age at menarche is approximately 12.72 years, with significant inter-provincial differences in

THE PLANNER

Put It Together *Review Figure 9.1 and answer the following questions:*

1. In males, maturation of primary and secondary sex characteristics is triggered by _____ released by the testes.

2. In females, the _____ release estrogen, which trigger the primary and secondary sex characteristics we see here.

b. Male pubescence

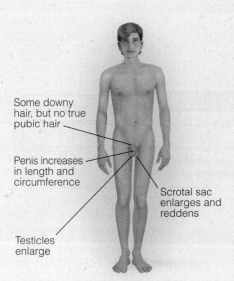

Some downy hair, but no true pubic hair

Penis increases in length and circumference

Scrotal sac enlarges and reddens

Testicles enlarge

Prepubescent phase

Stage 2: Enlargement of scrotum and testes; scrotum skin reddens and changes in texture; darker, coarser, more curled hair over pubic area

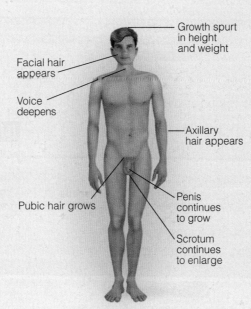

Growth spurt in height and weight

Facial hair appears

Voice deepens

Axillary hair appears

Pubic hair grows

Penis continues to grow

Scrotum continues to enlarge

Pubescent phase

Stage 3: Lengthening of penis; further growth of testes; darker, coarser, more curled hair over pubic area

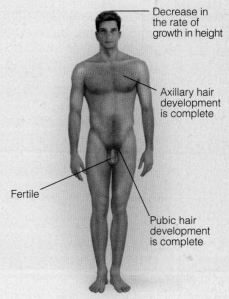

Decrease in the rate of growth in height

Axillary hair development is complete

Fertile

Pubic hair development is complete

Postpubescent phase

Stage 4: Increased size of penis (breadth); development of glans; testes and scrotum larger; scrotum skin darker; pubic hair, adult in type, but covering smaller area than adult (no spread to medial surface of thighs)

the onset, as shown in **Figure 9.3**. Researchers are trying to understand what may be underlying these substantial differences among the provinces. Out of all the socio-economic indicators, only income was found to have a significant association with age at menarche. High income was associated with lower early menarche rates but higher rates for late menarche. Almost 14.6 percent of Canadian girls were classified as early menarche (< 11.53 years), while 17.4 percent were late maturers (> 13.91 years) (Al-Sahab et al., 2010). At a population health level, this

is significant information to track because menarche serves as an intermediate health outcome that affects well-being in later stages of life (Adair, 2001; Senie, 2014). Early menarche is among the few established risk factors for breast cancer (Magnusson et al., 1999; Rockhill, Moorman, & Newman, 1998; Santen, Yue, & Wang, 2015), has been associated with risk variables for metabolic syndrome (Frontini, Srinivasan, & Berenson, 2003; Senie, 2014), and is linked with weight-related issues and obesity (Bralić et al., 2012; Mueller et al., 2015). In

Menarche rates across Canadian provinces, 2000/2001 • Figure 9.3

a. Percentage of girls undergoing early menarche (at 11.53 years old or younger)

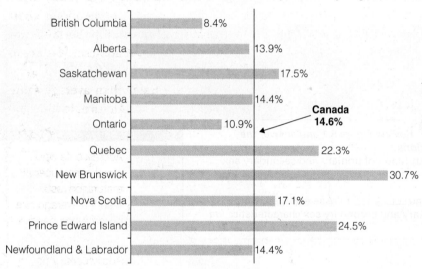

b. Percentage of girls undergoing late menarche (at 13.91 years or older)

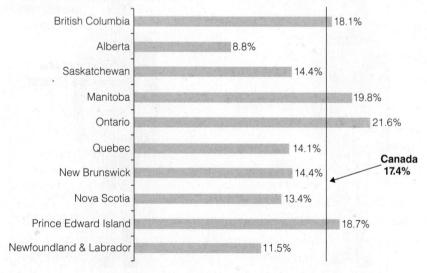

Think Critically What aspects of income might be contributing to the different rates of menarche among the provinces? What are other environmental factors that could be associated with income to influence maturation rates?

Source: Al-Sahab, B., Ardern, C. I., Hamadeh, M. J., & Tamim, H. (2010). Age at menarche in Canada: Results from the National Longitudinal Survey of Children and Youth. *BMC Public Health, 10*(1), 736, p. 4, Figures 2 and 3. Retrieved from www.biomedcentral.com/content/pdf/1471-2458-10-736.pdf.

the next section we will examine social impacts as well.

For males, the first indication of a change in primary sex characteristics is a lengthening of the penis and internal growth of the testes. Males have no sperm in the testes at birth and begin to produce mature sperm during puberty, a process called **spermatogenesis**. The first ejaculation of sperm (usually between 11 and 16 years of age; Kinsey, Pomeroy, & Martin, 1948), called **spermarche**, occurs at the onset of puberty. The production of sperm gradually increases to approximately 350 million per day. The prostate gland also grows and the muscles around it get stronger (Carreau et al., 2007).

Secondary sex characteristics The secondary sex characteristics are the parts of the body influenced by sex hormones but not directly involved in reproduction. In females, the breasts, areoles, and nipples enlarge. There are some breast changes in males as well. Both males and females also show changes in hair growth, especially in the pubic area and underarms (called *axillary hair*), and while males grow more hair on their chests, females do have some chest hair, around the nipples in particular (Gordon & Laufer, 2005). Some females have some hair on other areas as well: abdomen, lower back, neck, and cheeks. Hirsutism is a medical term for excessive hair growth in women and it is usually a sign of other underlying issues that might be accompanied by irregular menstruation or weight gain (Rosenfield, 2005).

All experience a change in muscle-to-fat ratio. Males experience an increase in muscle because androgens are anabolic and create tissue growth. Females, meanwhile, develop more fat and less muscle because estrogens are catabolic and break down tissue while increasing fat (Epel, Burke, & Wolkowitz, 2007). In fact, by the time she reaches her twenties, 20–25 percent of an average, healthy female's body mass is made up of fat tissue. In contrast, only about 15–18 percent of an average male's body is composed of fat (Koeslag, 2007).

Skin changes occur, with an increase in sebaceous gland production causing skin to be more oily and rougher than in prepubescence and sometimes leading to skin diseases such as acne (Cameron, 1990). In addition, the voice deepens because of a larger larynx, especially in males.

Now that we have an understanding of the general sequence of pubertal changes, let's look at individual differences in the timing of these changes.

Individual differences in pubertal timing What does a 12-year-old look like? As we see in **Figure 9.4**, this question can be difficult to answer because, although the sequence of physical changes during puberty is fairly predictable, the timing of that sequence is not (Ellis, 2004; Jones, 1957; Steinberg, 2007a). It is obvious to teens, and everyone else, who has matured early and who has matured late. This knowledge may affect teens' self-perceptions, as well as others' perceptions about them. The psychological significance of pubertal timing is a favourite topic among scholars of adolescent development (Susman & Dorn, 2009).

Adolescents who develop faster than average same-age peers are called **early maturers**. In turn, **late maturers** develop more slowly than average, whereas **on-time maturers** experience pubertal maturation at an average rate. These differences are due to genetic differences, as well as social and cultural differences (Comite et al., 1987).

Developmental researchers have investigated the effects of pubertal timing on psychosocial functioning (e.g., Brooks-Gunn, Petersen, & Eichorn, 1985; Ge, Brody, Conger, Simmons, & Murry, 2002). In general, early-maturing girls are at greater risk for psychosocial challenges than late or on-time maturing girls (see Susman & Dorn, 2009, for a review). Studies report lower self-esteem, poorer **body image**, and higher rates of sexual promiscuity, depression, smoking, and drinking among girls who mature early compared with their on-time peers (Collins & Steinberg, 2006; Tither & Ellis, 2008). Substance use is more prevalent among early-maturing girls and boys, and this pattern is seen across cultures (van Jaarsveld, Fidler, Simon, & Wardle, 2007; Wiesner & Ittel, 2002). Why might early

Differing rates of pubertal development • Figure 9.4

Different rates of pubertal maturation lead to dramatic differences in bodily appearance.

a. At age 12, some females have matured less than average, some may be on time or average with respect to their peers, whereas others will have matured more than average.

b. Although on average males go through puberty later than girls, boys may also vary at age 14 with respect to their pubertal maturation.

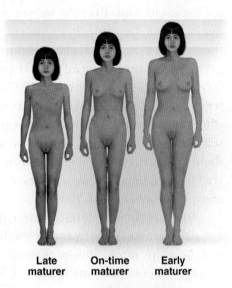

| Late maturer | On-time maturer | Early maturer |

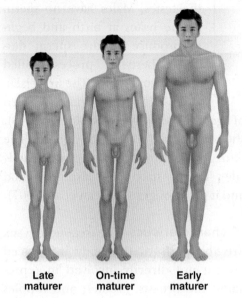

| Late maturer | On-time maturer | Early maturer |

Think Critically How might these differences in bodily appearance affect teens' perceptions of self?

menarche be associated with these kinds of health and social concerns?

The findings for boys, however, are inconsistent. Compared with on-time and later-maturing boys, early-maturing boys reported more internalized distress and hostile feelings (Ge, Conger, & Elder, 2001). This finding is inconsistent with earlier research showing that boys seem to benefit from early pubertal maturation.

The early-timing hypothesis was proposed to try to explain the disadvantages, particularly among girls, of early pubertal maturation (Brooks-Gunn et al., 1985; Petersen & Taylor, 1980). This hypothesis points to the mismatch between the physical development of early maturers and their cognitive and emotional development. Speeding through the stages of pubertal development, early maturers may find themselves cognitively and emotionally unprepared to deal with the complex pressures associated with looking more mature.

rite of passage A ritual that symbolizes the transition from one period of the lifespan to another.

separation The first stage marking the transition to adulthood involving the distancing of an adolescent from the earlier social context physically and/or psychologically.

It is important to keep in mind, however, that pubertal maturation does not necessarily lead to certain cognitive, emotional, and behavioural changes. This relationship is not direct and inevitable (e.g., Crockett & Petersen, 1987; Petersen, 1985, 1987). Individual differences in the effects of puberty on behaviour are dependent on familial, socio-economic, historical, and cultural contexts of the developing adolescent. We turn next to the cultural contexts surrounding pubertal maturation.

Cultural rites surrounding puberty Regardless of specific timing, most cultures mark the process of becoming an adult using **rites of passage** (Weisfeld, 1999; Susman & Rogol, 2004). Although the substance of these rites differs by culture, most rites can be separated into three stages: separation, transition, and incorporation (van Gennep, 1909/1960; Weisfeld, 1999).

Separation is the distancing of the adolescent from his or her earlier social context

transition The second stage marking the transition to adulthood, where the adolescent learns about how to be an adult.

physically and/or psychologically, as discussed in **Figure 9.5** (Weisfeld, 1999). During the next stage, **transition**, the adolescent learns about how to be an adult. The time it takes for this stage varies by culture. In Western culture, the time of transition has become quite variable. Increasingly, a "gap year" (Jones, 2004; King, 2011) is used as a transitional time when school leavers take time out from study or formal work after completing high school. This gap year often involves structured activities such as "volunteer tourism" and unstructured activities such as leisure. The gap year is a fairly privileged transition that is not common among working-class and poorer students (Heath, 2007; Reay, David, & Ball, 2005), but it appears to serve as an effective transition facilitating focus and motivation for students who continue their education (King, 2011). Some adolescents graduate high school and leave their childhood community to go on in school, to work, or to travel but later

incorporation The final stage marking the completed transition into adulthood, where new or more permanent responsibilities that signify adulthood are taken up.

return to live at home again for another period, sometimes staying there until well into their 20s.

The final stage is **incorporation**, in which the transitioned adult takes up either new or more permanent responsibilities that signify adulthood in his or her culture. For some, this may

include a return to the home community or country. Incorporation is the entry process into more enduring community connections, such as setting up a home with a partner, birthing and raising children, and contributing to community organizations and structures in meaningful ways. Notably, industrialized nations offer blurry boundaries between adolescence and adulthood. The agency and personal independence that come with traditional rites of passage appear to be absent because of many historical and sociological events over the last 100 years (Kagitçibasi, 2002). Even coming-of-age Western religious ceremonies, such as confirmation and bar/bat mitzvah, lack the requirements of separation, transition, and incorporation. One thing that is inescapable, however, is what happens to our nervous, skeletal, and muscular systems over the course of adolescence.

The Nervous System

Until relatively recently, the only way that scientists could visualize the human brain was through autopsy. Although autopsies provided insight into adult brains, research on post-mortem adolescent brains was fairly scarce (Sowell et al., 1996). With the invention of functional magnetic resonance imaging (fMRI), researchers now have a way of recording images of the brain while it is functioning, such as performing a cognitive task (Kalbfleisch & Iguchi, 2008; Malhi et al., 2008). These techniques have provided clear pictures of activity and growth in the brains of living children and adolescents.

The first step in becoming an adult • Figure 9.5

Separation is the beginning of becoming an adult in many cultures. In industrialized nations, separation typically takes the form of (a) university or college attendance, (b) leaving home for a job, or (c) taking a "gap year" between high school and further education.

Think Critically How might separation help an individual transition from one developmental period to the next?

a.	b.	c.

XiXinXing/iStockphoto	Wavebreakmedia/Shutterstock	Sturti/iStockphoto

During adolescence, **grey matter** gradually decreases because of synaptic pruning (**Figure 9.6**) (Paus, 2009). This decrease happens in specific areas of the cortex, most notably the prefrontal cortex, which is responsible for complex cognitive processes (Zecevic & Rakic, 2001). Meanwhile, the same areas show a continuous increase in **white matter**, largely due to increased amounts of myelin, the substance that speeds neural connections (Blakemore & Choudhury, 2006).

Researchers have found a number of links between brain changes (as seen in fMRIs) and behaviour during adolescence. For example, changes in white matter are linked to language development, whereas the growth of grey matter in the prefrontal cortex is linked to increases in executive functioning (Paus, 2009). Developmentalists who study the links during adolescence between brain and behaviour caution us not to assume that one is necessarily the cause of the other (Paus, 2009; Paus, Gachter, Starmer, & Wilkinson, 2008). Even if there is a causal relationship, we do not know whether brain changes cause behavioural changes or whether behavioural changes cause brain changes. From a developmental systems perspective, both directions of influence are plausible.

As the brain develops in complexity, other systems are also changing to make way for new challenges and adventures of adolescence. One such system is the skeletal system.

The Skeletal System

Although the physical activity of adolescents varies widely from individual to individual, adolescents' behaviours tend to result in increased bone density. Their active lifestyle also leads to increased risks to skeletal integrity. In other words, adolescents' bones are getting denser, but they are also more likely to get broken.

Adolescents also experience a **growth spurt**, during which height and weight suddenly increase (**Figure 9.7**). At the peak of the growth spurt, an adolescent is growing at about the

> **growth spurt** A sudden and intense increase in the rate of growth in weight and height.

same rate as a toddler. For boys the rate averages 10.4 cm a year, and for girls about 8.9 cm (Steinberg, 2007a). The closing of the ends of the long bones signals the conclusion of the growth spurt (Shih et al., 2005).

fMRI imaging of developmental brain changes • Figure 9.6

Grey matter decreases as the brain matures. Note the timing of these changes in the prefrontal cortex, an area responsible for thinking, planning, and reasoning.

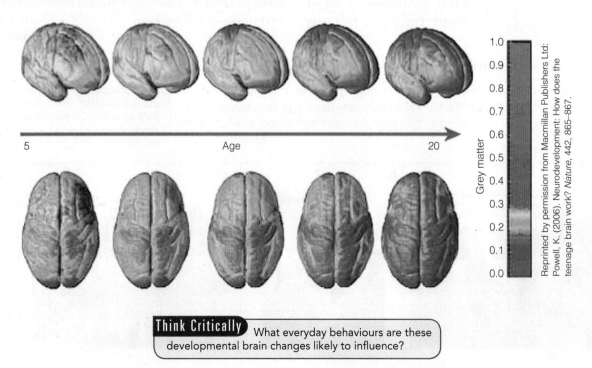

Think Critically What everyday behaviours are these developmental brain changes likely to influence?

Adolescent growth spurt • Figure 9.7

As shown in this chart, the rate of girls' height changes peaks at approximately age 12, whereas boys continue their spurt until about age 18. The reasons for these sex differences are contextual as well as evolutionary (Weisfeld, 1999). For example, females' bodies grow earlier in order to prepare for reproduction, making space for the expansion of the fallopian tubes, ovaries, and uterus.

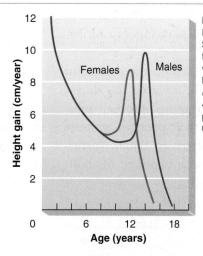

From Tanner, J. N., Whitehouse R. N., and Takaishi, M. Standards from birth to maturity for height, weight, height velocity, and weight velocity: British children, 1965. I. *Archives of Diseases in Childhood, 41,* 454–471, 1966. Reproduced with permission from BMJ Publishing Group Ltd.

Think Critically What might be some contextual reasons for the sex differences we see here?

---

asynchronicity
With reference to physical development during adolescence, the process of uneven growth of physical systems. The term can also describe asymmetrical changes among physical, socio-emotional, and cognitive systems.

Another interesting aspect of bone growth during adolescence is **asynchronicity**, in which some parts of the body do not grow at the same rate as other parts. The combination of rapid growth and asymmetrical changes frequently creates a series of odd movements, resulting in the awkwardness sometimes seen in teens. Eventually, these changes reach an equilibrium, bringing the adolescent to a more normal state of balance (Steinberg, 2007a). As we will see, great changes are also occurring in the muscular system of the body.

The Muscular System

As the skeletal system expands, the muscles must do what they can to keep the tension on those spurting bones. As a result, between the ages of 6 and 18, muscles become stronger, longer, and more flexible. To accomplish these changes, muscles add new fibre or sarcomeres, which are the basic units of protein, and other key chemicals that give muscles flexibility and strength (Harris et al., 2005).

There are clear sex differences in muscle development (**Figure 9.8**), and there are many reasons for these differences. Hormones such as androgens, produced in higher amounts in males, build muscle, whereas hormones such as estrogens, produced in higher amounts in females, increase fat tissue. Other hormones, such as

---

Sex differences in muscles • Figure 9.8

Forearm muscle growth takes a gender-specific course during puberty, indicating that it is influenced by hormonal changes. Muscle mass accelerates with puberty in both males and females, with more pronounced acceleration noted in males (Neu, Rauch, Rittweger, Manz, & Schoenau, 2002).

Put It Together *Review the section* The physical changes of puberty *and answer this question:* Are male and female muscle changes during puberty considered a primary sex characteristic or a secondary sex characteristic?

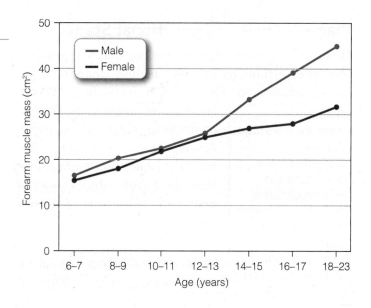

HGH, insulin, and thyroid hormones, also influence male muscle development. In addition, ethnic background and activity level contribute to muscle changes in adolescence (Thigpen, 2009).

Although the media have focused on the decline in physical fitness of Canadian youth, research has shown that many teens are motivated to strengthen their muscles in order to compete against their peers in athletics (Ricciardelli, McCabe, Holt, & Finemore, 2003). Participating in team sports is an important context for both physical and cognitive development.

1. **How** does pubertal timing affect psychosocial functioning?
2. **What** adolescent behaviours are linked to changes in grey and white matter?
3. **What** are some potential consequences of asynchronous physical development?
4. **Why** are there sex differences in muscle and fat tissue development?

Cognitive Development

LEARNING OBJECTIVES

1. **Describe** Piaget's stage of formal operations.
2. **Compare** Elkind's view of adolescent egocentrism with Piaget's preoperational egocentrism.
3. **Explain** how adolescents make decisions, especially about risky situations.

As we are learning, adolescents face dramatic changes to their bodies that affect every facet of their lives. They must try to make sense of these changes, and of the choices, challenges, and risks that characterize this period of the lifespan (Kuhn, 2009). What cognitive processes help teens cope with their new bodies and new sense of autonomy?

Piaget's Formal Operational Stage

How do you explain a type of thinking that requires that very type of thinking in order to fully understand it? Sound complicated? That is exactly the challenge Piaget faced while creating his **formal operational stage** of cognitive development. As they enter adolescence, some children begin to think in a more abstract way, a defining characteristic of formal operational thought.

> **formal operational stage**
> Piaget's fourth stage of cognitive development, in which adolescents and near-adolescents begin to think abstractly and to use hypothetical-deductive reasoning.

Abstract reasoning Central to understanding Piaget's stage of formal operations is the concept of **abstract thinking**, or the ability to think about possible situations, ideas, and objects that are not immediately present or obvious. Piaget extends conservation of objects to a conservation of reasoning and logic. For example, concrete thinkers base their definitions on prior experiences and specific information based on those experiences, such as "A horse is a horse" (of course). However, abstract thinkers can apply prior experience to new possibilities. For example, "John is a horse when he comes to work." In the second situation, the word "horse" takes on a different logical definition. Understanding this metaphor is an example of the emergence of abstract reasoning and formal operational thought (Piaget, 1972).

> **abstract thinking**
> The ability to think about possible situations, ideas, and objects that are not immediately present or obvious.

Many school subjects rely on abstract thinking, including advanced mathematics. Concrete operational thinkers understand numbers and their use in addition, subtraction, multiplication, and division. They see 2 + 2 = 4 and easily recognize the meaning and logic. When individuals move to algebra and beyond, formal operational thought is required. Now there's a variable *x* that can have various meanings. The equation $2 + x = y$ is abstract because of the variability of *x* and *y*. Can you think of other academic subjects that require formal operational thought?

In some cases, however, young adolescents lack the formal operational thought necessary for success in these endeavours (Piaget, 1972; Keating, 2004; Kuhn & Franklin, 2006). What other concepts are central to formal thinking?

Hypothetical-deductive reasoning Hypothetical thinking is at the core of formal thought because it requires the ability to think about things that are not immediately observable. This is a key difference between concrete and formal thinkers. Piaget noted that young children tend to solve problems using a rudimentary **trial-and-error**

> **trial and error** A type of elementary problem solving in which the solver attempts different immediate solutions with no systematic plan.
>
> **hypothetical-deductive reasoning** The ability to formulate varying solutions in one's mind and to think through the effectiveness of each possible solution.

method. For example, if asked to balance a T-scale, they would place and remove weights until they balanced the scale. **Hypothetical-deductive reasoning** instead involves the ability to create a variety of possibilities in one's own mind and evaluate all the dimensions of a problem, such as the mass of the weights and how far the weights are placed from the centre of the scale. Understanding all of the possible combinations in a problem requires the ability to hypothesize events, such as in the example shown in **Figure 9.9**.

Hypothetical-deductive reasoning is an extension of the metacognition we discussed in Chapter 7. The formal operational thinker evaluates his or her thinking and begins to improve thought strategies and reasoning ability. Thus, the adolescent is not just thinking about thinking as much as understanding the basic process of thinking, controlling thoughts, and refining thinking. Now this individual can create categories and create categories for categories. Formal thinking has no limits or boundaries, making it invaluable for imagination, creativity, and problem solving (Dimaggio et al., 2009; Nixon et al., 2008).

Obviously, space prohibits us from delving too deeply into the complex world of formal operations. We conclude this section with one of the key issues raised by critics of Piaget: who can think formally and who cannot?

Using the mind to hypothesize • Figure 9.9

How many possible colour combinations can you make using red, yellow, and blue paint? Formal operational thinkers do not have to physically blend the colours to answer this question. They can do it in their heads. Can you?

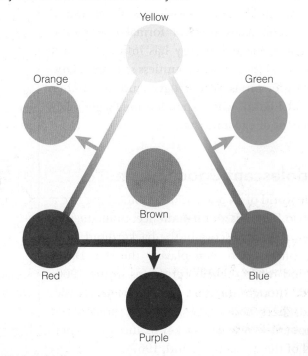

Ask Yourself

1. In order to answer the question using only your thoughts (without physically touching the paints), you must use _____ reasoning.

2. Young children would most likely use _____ to answer the question posed in this figure.

Who can think formally? Although Piaget asserted that adolescence is the time during which formal operations emerge, he did note, as have others, that not everyone achieves this level (Keating, 2004; Kuhn & Franklin, 2006; Martorano, 1977; Overton & Newman, 1982). For example, cross-cultural studies in the 1960s and 1970s revealed that some cultures do not reach formal operations without schooling and, specifically, without exposure to the type of scientific thinking found in science classes (e.g., Laurendeau-Bendavid, 1977). Piaget (1972) responded to these studies by retracting his claim that his stages of cognitive development are universal among humans.

Piaget (1972) also concluded that formal operations might be present in some situations but absent in others. Critics have questioned, however, whether his formal operational tasks were of sufficient relevance to the test-taker (Kuhn, 2008). When tasks are personally relevant, younger adolescents have shown moderate formal operational ability (Overton, 1990). Having such capability, however, does not necessarily imply use of it (Keating, 2004; Kuhn & Franklin, 2006).

Although debate continues about attainment and assessment of formal operational thought, Piaget's theory has influenced and informed the work of countless scientists. One such person is psychologist and researcher David Elkind, who expanded on Piaget's key concept of egocentrism.

Adolescent Egocentrism

The world of an adolescent is something like a movie. There is a rapt audience, dramatic tension, a musical score in the background, and, of course, each teen playing the star. David Elkind made these observations in the 1960s and, though the cast of characters, music, and dress code have changed, **adolescent egocentrism** remains a key feature of this period of the lifespan (Elkind, 1967).

Although the origins of adolescent egocentrism are arguably cognitive, this construct has affective

adolescent egocentrism Elkind's term to describe the adolescent perception that one is at the centre of the social world.

imaginary audience Elkind's term to describe the adolescent's assumption that his or her preoccupation with personal appearance and behaviour is shared by everyone else.

personal fable Elkind's term to describe the adolescent belief that one is special and unique and, thus, invulnerable.

(emotional), noncognitive characteristics, including self-consciousness, invulnerability, and speciality (Elkind, 1967, 1978). The concept of adolescent egocentrism was introduced, in part at least, in an attempt to tie cognitive development to emotional aspects of adolescent personality.

Within the Piagetian theory of cognitive development, egocentrism is broadly defined as a lack of differentiation in self–other relations that takes a unique form and is reflected in a unique set of thoughts and actions at each stage of mental development (Piaget, 1962a, 1962b). In Chapter 5 we discussed the egocentrism of the young child. With the emergence of formal operations during adolescence, we see a new type of failure of differentiation.

Elkind (1967) proposed a theory of adolescent egocentrism with two distinct, but related, constructs—the **imaginary audience** and the **personal fable**, as shown in **Figure 9.10**. He and his colleagues constructed an Imaginary Audience Scale and administered it to subjects in Grades 4, 6, 8, and 12 (Elkind & Bowen, 1979). As expected, eighth-grade participants scored significantly higher than did the other age groups. These results were

Imaginary audience and personal fable • Figure 9.10

Elkind's theory of adolescent egocentrism involves two ideas—imaginary audience and personal fable.

a. The presence of an admiring or fault-finding (imaginary) audience helps to account for the heightened self-consciousness characteristic of early adolescence.

b. The personal fable gives rise to a sense of invulnerability and specialness, which is associated with behavioural risk-taking (Alberts, Elkind, & Ginsberg, 2007).

Yellow Dog Productions/GettyImages

Jay P. Morgan/Getty Images

Think Critically Based on Elkind's ideas about the distinct features of adolescent thinking, what might the teen in part a. be thinking about herself while waiting her turn in the spelling bee?

The stages of substance use • Figure 9.11

The stages of substance use are differentiated by the primary motivation for use. The stages typically occur in order; it is highly unlikely that a person will jump into the compulsive stage without first going through earlier stages. Certainly, however, not everyone who uses a substance proceeds to the later stages. A person might be in different stages for different substances.

Think Critically Should substance abuse recovery programs aim to help people return to earlier stages of use or to stop using altogether?

Lyndsay Russell/Alamy

❶ Experimental stage

- Use is due to curiosity, peer pressure, or risk-taking.
- In this stage the use is infrequent.
- This stage marks a point in development when an adolescent discovers substances and learns that alcohol or drugs can produce a pleasant mood swing.
- Substances are sought because the adolescent is curious and because there is excitement associated with using a substance that is off-limits.

❷ Social stage

- Use is with friends or in social situations.
- At this stage, use is situational.
- Motivation to use substances is the desire for social acceptance. Use of substances may be what bonds adolescents together, serving as a reason to share time and space with others.

Jimmy Anderson/iStockphoto

❸ Instrumental stage

- Substance is used in order to alter feelings or behaviour.
- Use at this stage becomes regular.
- At this stage, the user is seeking a mood swing. Hedonistic use occurs when an adolescent seeks out and uses a substance because it produces a pleasurable or euphoric state.
- Compensatory use occurs when an adolescent uses a substance to reduce or numb unwanted emotions. There are few, if any, indicators that substance use is associated with serious problems in the adolescent's life.

❹ Habitual stage

- A habit has developed, and other facets of life begin to be neglected. Brain changes have typically occurred to make the user crave the substance.
- This stage is characterized by habitual use.
- The adolescent's peer group changes from non-users to users.
- At this stage, substance use has crossed the line between use and misuse. Adolescents at this stage habitually seek the mood swing associated with the substance. Behaviour and lifestyle changes are made to accommodate use.
- Tolerance has developed; the adolescent needs increasing amounts of the substance to achieve the same effect.
- Dysfunction in one or more domains of life is apparent (for example, problems in school, with family, with the law).

Janine Wiedel Photolibrary/Alamy

❺ Compulsive stage

- The individual becomes focused on gaining access and ignores nearly all other aspects of life.
- This stage is marked by loss of control. The adolescent is unable to abstain from regulate, or reduce the substance use.
- Loss of control results in addiction. The adolescent engages in extreme behaviour to get the substance, including breaking the law, selling drugs, or prostitution. He or she may experience withdrawal.
- The interpersonal life of the adolescent is chaotic at this stage of substance use. As a result of substance use, the adolescent may experience a loss of social support and suffer from low self-esteem.

PROCESS DIAGRAM

replicated by other studies (Enright, Shukla, & Lapsley, 1980; Gray & Hudson, 1984; Ryan & Kuczkowksi, 1994).

The personal fable is a natural consequence of the imaginary audience. Thinking of himself or herself as the centre of attention, the adolescent comes to believe that it is because he or she is special and unique. "Other people will not realize their ambitions, but I will; other people will grow old and die but not me; other people will get hooked on drugs but not me." Thanks to this personal fable, the young adolescent believes that his or her feelings and emotions are different, more intense and excruciating, than those of others. Elkind's theory of adolescent egocentrism predicts a curvilinear pattern between childhood and middle-to-late adolescence. That is to say, preadolescents and late adolescents are expected to score significantly lower on the dimensions of adolescent egocentrism than those early teenagers just acquiring formal operations. Subsequent research has provided support for this predicted developmental pattern (Elkind & Bowen, 1979; Enright et al., 1980; Green, Morton, Cornell, & Jones, 1986).

Some psychologists maintain that the behaviours described by Elkind, rather than being the result of a form of cognitive egocentrism, are actually an adaptive social-cognitive strategy for coping and developing self-worth (Aalsma, Lapsley, & Flannery, 2006). From this perspective, the qualities associated with the personal fable (uniqueness, omnipotence, and narcissism) are an attempt by adolescents to maintain boundaries, integrity, and cohesiveness of the self as they facilitate the process of separation from family/parental control (Aalsma et al., 2006; Lapsley, 1993; Lapsley & Rice, 1988). Despite these potential benefits, personal fables may also be related to internalizing problems such as depression, especially for girls. In addition, perceptions of invulnerability may lead to risk-taking behaviour, the topic to which we turn next (Aalsma et al., 2006; Alberts et al., 2007).

Decisions and Risks

During the earlier years, others make decisions for children. Parents typically make decisions for children about what to eat, when to play, and even whom to have as friends. This process changes dramatically during adolescence, when teens are away from home more frequently and are confronted with riskier situations (Eaton et al., 2008). Therefore, the ability to assess risk becomes a key aspect of adolescent decision-making. Unfortunately, research on why adolescents take risks and make questionable decisions has been less than comprehensive, although some key findings can be extracted (Reyna & Farley, 2006).

First, how well do teens estimate risk of activities like smoking or substance use, as discussed in **Figure 9.11**? The research here is mixed. Some studies suggest that adolescents tend to underestimate risks, whereas others find that adolescents overestimate risks (Steinberg, 2007b). Generally speaking, however, adolescents are not very good at assessing actual risk in relation to long-term consequences. For example, they may know that driving drunk is a risk, but the likelihood that negative consequences will occur tends not to be part of their decision-making (Reyna & Farley, 2006).

Researchers wonder why adolescents might be more prone to risk-taking. Some suggest that the immature adolescent brain may be responsible for teens' tendency toward risk (National Research Council, 2006; Steinberg, 2008). But others argue that no evidence can validate such a brain–behaviour relationship and instead look toward the social context and parenting as key reasons for adolescent risk-taking (Males, 2009).

Despite all the controversy, one fairly consistent finding from adolescent risk research is the **optimistic bias**. When compared with others who engaged in the same risky behaviour, adolescents tend to believe that they are less likely to suffer negative consequences. In fact, this same finding occurs among adults, especially if the immediate benefits are high (Crisp & Barber, 1995; Rothman, Klein, & Weinstein, 1996).

> **optimistic bias** A tendency for people to underestimate their own risk and overestimate the risk to someone else engaged in the same type of behaviour.

Although risk-taking behaviours are a feature of adolescence, it is important not to lose sight of the many strengths that adolescents possess. These strengths are the focus of cutting-edge developmental science about positive youth development, which we turn to next.

CONCEPT CHECK

1. **How** does abstract reasoning differ from concrete operations?

2. **Why** is adolescent egocentrism associated with risk-taking behaviours?

3. **How** does the optimistic bias explain adolescent risk-taking?

All the Systems Working Together

LEARNING OBJECTIVES

1. **Differentiate** between the early storm-and-stress view of adolescence and the current positive youth development perspective.

2. **Explain** the considerations and risks involved in adolescent sexuality, including methods of sex education.

3. **Identify** key health issues in adolescence, discussing both challenges and prevention.

A dolescence is a period of multiple transitions, a time when the majority of one's biological, cognitive, psychological, and social characteristics are in flux. All of these simultaneous changes make adolescence a prime period of the lifespan to study the interconnectedness of physical, cognitive, and socio-emotional systems. This interconnectedness is a central feature of the positive youth development perspective, the first topic we discuss. Adolescent sexuality, including the challenges associated with teen pregnancy, will serve as another illustration of the interactions among developmental systems during adolescence. We end this chapter with a discussion of three common health concerns of adolescence—drug use, disordered eating, and sleep—and their pervasive implications for the developing adolescent.

Positive Youth Development

Historically, adolescence was characterized as a universal period of "storm and stress" (Hall, 1904). From this point of view, adolescents were seen as antagonistic, emotionally unstable, and in need of continuous monitoring and moulding to avoid adult psychopathology (Susman & Dorn, 2009). Framed by developmental systems theories of human development (discussed in Chapter 1), a new perspective on the study of adolescence emerged in the early 1990s and has led to a significant reconceptualization of this period of the lifespan (e.g., Lerner, 2009; Lerner, von Eye, Lerner, Lewin-Bizan, & Bowers, 2010; Phelps et al., 2009). The **positive youth development (PYD)** perspective views young people "as resources to be developed . . . not as problems to be managed" (Lerner, Phelps, Forman, & Bowers, 2009, p. 542; see also Roth & Brooks-Gunn, 2003a, 2003b). This perspective stands in sharp contrast to the early storm-and-stress view of adolescence espoused by G. Stanley Hall (1904), the founder of the scientific study of adolescent development (Lerner & Ohannessian, 1999). The PYD perspective involves two overarching hypotheses.

> **positive youth development (PYD)** A positive strengths-based perspective view of adolescence as a life stage involving two overarching hypotheses: the Five Cs and youth–context alignment.

The Five Cs The first hypothesis associated with the PYD perspective is that of the Five Cs—competence, confidence, connection, character, and caring (**Table 9.1**). Together they indicate the presence of PYD (Lerner et al., 2005). These Cs are consistent with reviews of

The Five Cs of positive youth development	Table 9.1
Competence	A positive view of one's actions in specific areas, including social, academic, cognitive, health, and vocational. Social competence involves interpersonal skills (e.g., conflict resolution). Academic competence involves school performance as shown, in part, by school grades, attendance, and test scores. Cognitive competence involves cognitive abilities (e.g., decision-making). Health competence involves using nutrition, exercise, and rest to keep oneself fit. Vocational competence involves work habits and exploration of career choices.
Confidence	An internal sense of overall positive self-worth and self-efficacy.
Connection	Positive bonds with people and institutions that are reflected in exchanges between the individual and his or her peers, family, school, and community in which both parties contribute to the relationship.
Character	Respect for societal and cultural norms, possession of standards for correct behaviours, a sense of right and wrong (morality), and integrity.
Caring/compassion	A sense of sympathy and empathy for others.

Lerner, J. V., Phelps, E., Forman, Y., & Bowers, E. (2009). Positive youth development. In R. M. Lerner & L. Steinberg (Eds.), *Handbook of adolescent psychology: Vol. 1: Individual basis of adolescent development* (3rd ed., pp. 524–558). Hoboken, NJ: Wiley.

the adolescent development literature (Eccles & Goot-man, 2002; Lerner, 2004a, 2004b; Roth & Brooks-Gunn, 2003b). They are also salient terms used by practitioners, parents of adolescents, and adolescents themselves when asked to define "thriving" among youth (Alberts et al., 2006; King et al., 2005).

Richard M. Lerner and colleagues at the Institute for Applied Research in Youth Development at Tufts University conducted a longitudinal investigation of the PYD perspective, called the 4-H Study of PYD. They provided empirical evidence of the Five Cs of PYD and of their relationship to a sixth C, contribution (Jelicic, Bobek, Phelps, Lerner, & Lerner, 2007; Lerner et al., 2005). That is, youth who are developing positively—who exhibit the Five Cs over time—will also make contributions to themselves, their families, their immediate communities, and the larger society (Lerner, 2004a, 2004b).

Youth–context alignment The second hypothesis asserts that, when the strengths of youth are aligned with resources for healthy development within their context (their home, school, and community), PYD may be enhanced (e.g., Lerner et al., 2005). These resources, known as **developmental assets**, provide the necessary nutrients for the positive development of youth (Benson, 2003; Benson, Scales, Hamilton, & Semsa, 2006). There is some debate about the number of developmental assets that may exist and about whether certain assets may be more important than others in certain settings (Benson, Leffert, Scales, & Blyth, 1998; Theokas et al., 2005). Despite this controversy, there is agreement among scholars and practitioners that community-based programs (e.g., 4-H, Boys and Girls Clubs, and Scouting) represent an important source of developmental assets (Lerner et al., 2009). Unfortunately, such a positive perspective is still underrepresented in the literature on adolescent sexuality (but see Meier, 2007; Smiler, Ward, Caruthers, & Merriwether, 2005).

> **developmental assets** Resources that encourage and enhance positive youth development.

Adolescent Sexuality

Within contemporary Western culture, adolescent sexuality is often portrayed as a dangerous activity leading to a host of negative outcomes, such as sexually transmitted infections and teen pregnancy (Diamond & Savin-Williams, 2011). Educational campaigns have sought to discourage sex among adolescents and have shied away from open discussions about early sexual desire and experiences. Similarly, conventional research on adolescent sex has avoided a non-judgmental analysis of normative sexual development and sexual health promotion. The focus, instead, has been on amassing data about the state of adolescent sex (the who, what, when, and where of adolescent sexual activity) and its negative consequences.

The state of sex among adolescents The majority of Canadians have their first heterosexual intercourse during their teen years (Maticka-Tyndale, 2008, Rotermann, 2008), although the trend is declining: the rate was 70 percent in 1996/1997 versus 68 percent in 2010 (Rotermann, 2012). Oral sex tends to happen at about the same time as intercourse, but up to a quarter of teens begin their sexual explorations with oral sex (Maticka-Tyndale, 2008). While sexual activity is a normalized activity across adolescence, unfortunately many adolescents still engage in risky sexual behaviours that can lead to negative health outcomes. The data in **Figure 9.12** are taken from the 2009/2010 Canadian Community Health Survey; 32 percent of youth age 15 to 24 did not use a condom during their last experience of intercourse (although condom use had improved from 2003; see **Figure 9.13**). Additionally, approximately one-third of those surveyed reported having more than one sexual partner over the previous 12 months (Rotermann, 2012).

Among Canadian youth aged 15 to 24 who have had intercourse, the average age for first heterosexual intercourse for both males and females is 16.5 years (Rotermann, 2005). In developing countries, however, we see girls are more likely than boys to have had sex at an early age (**Figure 9.14**). Early sex increases the risk of HIV infection and unintended pregnancy (United Nations Children's Fund, 2012).

Sexually transmitted infections Sexually transmitted infections (STIs) continue to be a significant public health concern in Canada. Reported cases of chlamydia, gonorrhea, and infectious syphilis have all been increasing since the late 1990s (Public Health Agency of Canada, 2014). STIs impact Canadians of all genders, backgrounds, and socio-economic categories

Sex/Age group/ Province/Territory	Multiple partners in past year								Condom used at last sexual intercourse							
	2003				2009/2010				2003				2009/2010			
	Number		95% confidence interval		Number		95% confidence interval		Number		95% confidence interval		Number		95% confidence interval	
	'000	%	from	to	'000	%	from	to	'000	%	from	to	'000	%	from	to
Total	739.6	30.9	29.5	32.4	818.4	32.5	30.8	34.1	1,268.2	62.2	60.4	63.9	1,416.3	67.9‡	66.2	69.6
Sex																
Males†	436.0	36.7	34.4	38.9	508.6	39.0	36.7	41.3	720.0	67.3	64.8	69.8	817.4	72.5‡	70.2	74.7
Females	303.6	25.3*	23.5	27.0	309.8	25.4*	23.4	27.4	548.2	56.5*	54.1	58.9	598.9	62.5*‡	60.1	65.0
Age group																
15 to 17†	108.0	35.1	31.8	38.3	110.6	34.7	31.2	38.2	239.0	78.5	75.7	81.3	252.6	79.9	76.9	82.9
18 to 19	164.7	34.9	31.9	37.9	194.1	39.4	36.0	42.8	304.3	67.6*	64.7	70.4	349.3	73.7*‡	70.8	76.7
20 to 24	466.9	29.0*	27.1	30.9	513.8	30.0*	28.0	32.1	725.0	56.4*	54.0	58.8	814.3	62.8*‡	60.4	65.3
Province/Territory																
Newfoundland and Labrador	11.7	26.8	19.2	34.4	13.5	31.1	24.9	37.2	27.9	70.4*	63.0	77.8	25.9	70.0	62.4	77.7
Prince Edward Island	3.9	36.6	26.9	46.4	3.3	36.1	24.4	47.8	6.7	72.5	61.8	83.3	5.7	68.3	57.6	78.9
Nova Scotia	22.7	31.3	24.4	38.2	19.8	28.7	21.5	35.9	45.5	71.4	63.8	79.1	37.7	66.8	59.0	74.7
New Brunswick	19.0	31.5	24.8	38.3	17.5	33.2	27.1	39.3	31.6	61.1	53.7	68.6	30.1	73.1‡	66.2	80.0
Quebec	207.4	31.8	28.6	34.9	224.4	34.3	31.1	37.5	304.0	55.7*	51.9	59.6	326.0	59.9*	56.2	63.6
Ontario	273.7	31.0	28.5	33.5	275.3	30.4	27.6	33.2	504.9	65.1*	62.0	68.3	551.2	72.6*‡	70.0	75.2
Manitoba	22.7	27.0	20.3	33.8	24.9	32.6	25.1	40.2	46.3	63.6	55.6	71.5	43.3	64.9*	57.8	72.1
Saskatchewan	20.4	28.7	23.5	33.9	25.7	32.3	26.7	37.9	37.9	66.1	59.3	72.9	42.3	68.9	62.0	75.8
Alberta	63.4	26.9*	23.3	30.5	113.3	34.8‡	29.9	39.6	112.1	59.6*	54.1	65.1	190.2	72.5*‡	68.2	76.7
British Columbia	91.0	34.2	29.5	38.9	96.8	32.6	28.0	37.2	146.5	63.7	59.3	68.1	158.4	65.5	60.2	70.9
Yukon	1.0	39.0	25.4	52.5	1.5	54.0*	42.7	65.2	1.5	73.4	58.4	88.3	1.7	71.2	60.1	82.3
Northwest Territories	1.6	38.2ᵉ	26.6	49.7	1.5	38.6	27.6	49.5	2.1	66.8	53.5	80.2	2.5	78.4*	69.2	87.7
Nunavut (10 largest communities§)	0.9	36.4	26.8	46.0	0.9	36.6	26.5	46.8	1.2	72.7	54.9	90.6	1.4	79.1*	63.2	95.1

† reference category
* significantly different from reference category or from rest of Canada in same year (p<0.05)
‡ significantly different from 2003 (p<0.05)
§ Iqaluit, Cambridge Bay, Baker Lake, Arviat, Rankin Inlet, Kugluktuk, Pond Inlet, Cape Dorset, Pangnirtung, Igloolik
ᵉ use with caution
Sources: 2003 and 2009/2010 Canadian Community Health Survey.

Source: Rotermann, M. (2012). Sexual behaviour and condom use of 15- to 24-year-olds in 2003 and 2009/2010. Statistics Canada Catalogue no. 82-003-X. Health Report, Vol.23, no. 1, March 2012. Retrieved from www.statcan.gc.ca/pub/82-003-x/2012001/article/11632-eng.pdf.

Think Critically What do you notice about similarities and differences among the provinces and territories? What might account for some of these differences?

(**Table 9.2**) (National Institute of Allergy and Infectious Diseases, 2012). Young Canadians have the highest reported rates of STIs, although impacted age groups and common infection types vary among the Canadian provinces and territories (Public Health Agency of Canada, 2013). Between 2002 and 2011, for example, the overall rate of reported cases of gonorrhea increased by 40.8 percent. Females between the ages of 15 and 24 (and males between the ages of 20 and 24) accounted for the highest proportion of diagnoses, and the highest rate was observed in the Northwest Territories (Public Health Agency of Canada, 2014). STIs result primarily from penetrative intercourse, but can also be transmitted during other types of sexual activity, such as oral sex. When compared with the general population, STI prevalence is higher within Aboriginal communities. Particularly concerning is the overrepresentation of Aboriginal persons with new HIV diagnoses, the rate of which is estimated to be 3.5 times higher than for the non-Aboriginal population (Public Health Agency of Canada, 2013).

Condom use at last sexual intercourse • Figure 9.13

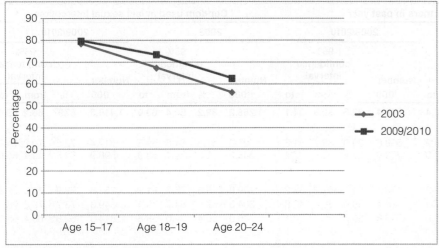

Source: Rotermann, M. (2012). Sexual behaviour and condom use of 15- to 24-year-olds in 2003 and 2009/2010. Statistics Canada Catalogue no. 82-003-X. Retrieved from www.statcan.gc.ca/pub/82-003-x/2012001/article/11632-eng.pdf.

Think Critically What developments across the teen and emerging adulthood years might explain the decrease in condom use as youth get older?

There is no one-size-fits-all prevention method for STIs. For some of the STIs that are viral, vaccines are being developed to prevent outbreak. The most effective method, of course, is changing behaviour. The debate over how best to educate teens about sex is heated, but research indicates that **comprehensive sexuality education**—those programs that go beyond an abstinence-only message to teach safe sex techniques—is much more effective at promoting

comprehensive sexuality education Sex education programs that present information about both abstinence and safe-sex practices.

healthy sexual behaviours and reducing risky sexual behaviours when compared with **abstinence-only sex education** (Carter, 2012). Comprehensive sexuality education can result in a delayed start to sexual activity, a reduced number of partners (Alford, 2008; Kirby, 2001), and increased condom and

abstinence-only sex education Sex education programs that promote only abstinence and that do not teach safe-sex techniques.

Sex in adolescence in the developing world • Figure 9.14

There are 1.2 billion adolescents worldwide. Nearly 90 percent live in developing countries. In the least developed countries, the illiteracy rate is around 30 percent and unemployment is high. These factors significantly influence the sexual experiences of young people in these countries. Here we see that before age 15, female adolescents are more likely than male adolescents to have had sex.

Think Critically How might adolescents' opportunities for education and employment influence sexual behaviour during the teen years?

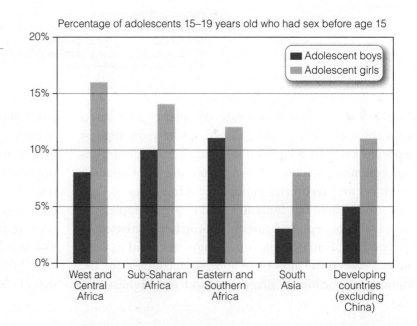

Percentage of adolescents 15–19 years old who had sex before age 15

The most prevalent STIs	Table 9.2
Chlamydia	• Most frequently reported bacterial infection in Canada • Curable if treated early • Affects both males (causes penile discharge) and females (causes infertility)
Gonorrhea	• After 20 years of decline, the rates of reported cases of gonorrhea have risen more than 53 percent between 2006 and 2016. This increase can be partly attributed to improved lab tests and screening methods. • Results from bacterial infection. • Early treatment results in a complete cure. • Disproportionately affects sexually active youth and young adults under 24. • Females experience slightly milder symptoms than males.
Genital herpes	• Results from a virus. • Transmitted through intercourse, as well as other types of contact. • Transmission is more likely during active episodes. • Incurable at this time.
Human papilloma virus (HPV) and genital warts	• One of the most common sexually transmitted infections in Canada and worldwide. • Many types of HPV have been identified, with some leading to cancer and others to skin lesions such as genital warts. • Two vaccines are available in Canada to help prevent some types of HPV, including those that cause 70 percent of cervical cancers and 70 to 90 percent of anogenital warts. • There is no cure for HPV infections.
Syphilis	• Rates have been on the rise in Canada since 2001 when outbreaks began occurring in urban centres across the country. • Disproportionately affects men in Canada, particularly those over 30. • A treatable bacterial infection and the oldest known STI. • Symptoms include sore throat, tiredness, swollen glands, and ulcerated "shanker" sores on penis or vagina. • Antibiotics such as penicillin are the best and most effective treatment.
Human immunodeficiency virus/acquired immunodeficiency syndrome (HIV/AIDS)	• The syndrome results from a virus that attacks the immune system. • The size of this virus and its ability to adapt to antiviral vaccines have made cures elusive. • In 2011, the estimated number of new HIV infections in Canada was 3,175, which is the lowest number of annual HIV cases since reporting began in 1985. The median time from infection to AIDS diagnosis now exceeds 10 years (Public Health Agency of Canada, 2012). • The disease is far more widespread in parts of Africa and Asia.

contraceptive use (Kirby, Lads, & Rolleri, 2007). Abstinence-only sex education, on the other hand, lacks empirical evidence of effectiveness (Collins, Alagiri, Summers, & Morin, 2002; Klein & American Academy of Pediatrics Committee on Adolescence, 2005), and has been associated with higher rates of youth pregnancy and STI transmission (Carter, 2012). The overwhelming evidence from a meta-analysis of 174 studies examining the impact of different types of sexual health promotion interventions found that comprehensive programs do not inadvertently increase the frequency of sexual behaviour (Kohler, Manhart, & Lafferty, 2008) or number of sexual partners (Smoak, Scott-Sheldon, Johnson, & Carey, 2006).

The Public Health Agency of Canada states that our sexual health is vital to our overall health and well-being:

"Sexual health is a key aspect of personal health and social welfare that influences individuals across their lifespan. It is thus important that health promotion programs focusing on enhancing positive sexual health outcomes and reducing negative sexual health outcomes are available to all Canadians regardless of their age, race, ethnicity, gender identity, sexual orientation, socioeconomic background, physical/cognitive abilities, religious background or other such characteristics" (Public Health Agency of Canada, 2008a, p. 2). The agency developed the Canadian Guidelines for Sexual Health Education, which are intended to inform sexual health programming. It encourages education that focuses on the self-worth, respect, and dignity of the individual; is provided in an age-appropriate, culturally sensitive manner that is respectful of individual sexual diversity, abilities, and choices; helps individuals to become more sensitive and aware of the impact their behaviours and actions may have on others and society; and does not discriminate on the basis of age, race, ethnicity, gender identity, sexual orientation, socio-economic background, physical/cognitive abilities, and religious background in terms of access to relevant, appropriate, accurate, and comprehensive information (Public Health Agency of Canada, 2008a).

In principle, all Canadians, including youth, have a right to the information, motivation/personal insight, and skills necessary to prevent negative sexual health outcomes (e.g., sexually transmitted infections including HIV, unplanned pregnancy) and to enhance sexual health (e.g., positive self-image and self-worth, integration of sexuality into mutually satisfying relationships). The Society of Obstetricians and Gynaecologists of Canada hosts a sexual health website (SexualityandU. ca) with a number of interactive educational tools and resources (see *Where Developmentalists Click*).

Teen pregnancy Teen pregnancy rates are used as a direct indicator of young women's opportunities and capacity to control this aspect of their sexual and reproductive health. In Canada, the pregnancy rate (the number of live births, induced abortions, and fetal loss) for both younger (age 15–17) and older (age 18–19) teenage women has fallen significantly over the last several decades (McKay, 2012). More recently, the pregnancy rate among 15- to 19-year-old females declined from 47.6 per 1,000 in 1995 to 14.2 per 1,000 in 2009 (Statistics Canada, 2012; Sex Information and Education Council of Canada, 2010). The highest rates of teen pregnancy in North America tend to occur in places that have high rates of poverty and

Where Developmentalists CLICK

SexualityandU.ca

The Society of Obstetricians and Gynaecologists of Canada hosts an interactive educational website with a variety of tools that focuses on positive sexuality (www.sexualityandu.ca/). Developmentalists can use this in their teaching or their practice working with people and their contraceptive needs. One tool in particular, Choosing Wisely, creates a personal profile that helps you to select from 20 birth control methods. The website gives details on each birth control method and helps you compare various options. A survey asks questions about your medical history as well as your ability to manage birth control and the implications for you personally should you have an unintended pregnancy. The printout at the end of the survey can be used to have a discussion with your health care provider. You find out the pros and the cons of various recommendations as well as the list of options that are likely not suitable for you.

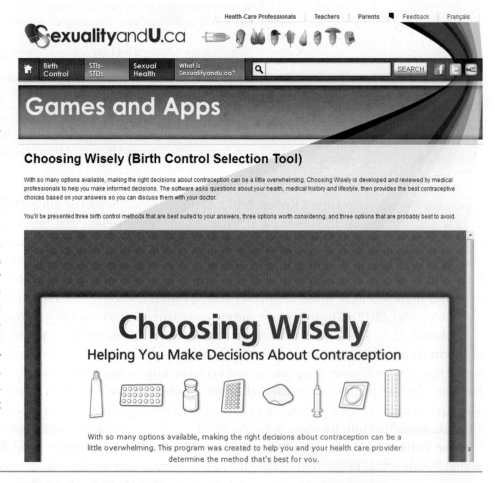

that typically de-emphasize comprehensive sex education programs in favour of abstinence-only sex education programs (United Nations Statistics Division, 2011).

Childbearing teens and their children face a number of health, economic, and social challenges (Hoffman, 2008; Martin et al., 2012). Compared with her peers, a teenage mother has a higher likelihood of dropping out of school, having a lower lifetime income, and having another baby while a teenager. Nearly one in five teen births are repeat births, which poses even greater challenges to both mother and child (Centers for Disease Control and Prevention, 2013). Whether the first teen birth or a repeat birth, risks to the fetus or infant include perinatal death, brain damage, and low birth weight (discussed in Chapter 2). In addition, individuals who were born to teen mothers have a higher likelihood of becoming a teen parent themselves, of becoming a high school dropout, and of abusing drugs (Santelli, Orr, Lindberg, & Diaz, 2009).

Most research on teen pregnancy has focused on teenage mothers and their children. When teen fathers are the focus, studies show that they face similar risk factors as teen mothers. For example, they have reduced income potential, poorer academic performance, and higher school dropout rates (Castiglia, 1990; Fagot, Pears, Capaldi, Crosby, & Leve, 1998; Xie, Cairns, & Cairns, 2001). Given these significant risks to teen parents and their children, a number of programs have been enacted to help prevent teen pregnancy (see *What a Developmentalist Sees*).

WHAT A DEVELOPMENTALIST SEES
Preventing Teen Pregnancy

When developmentalists look at teenage pregnancy rates, they see the opportunity to step in and make changes. Some pregnancy prevention programs focus only on girls, whereas others include both boys and girls in the classroom.

a. Abstinence-only sex education

One major type of program is known as *abstinence-only sex education*, which stresses the message that the only way to prevent STIs and pregnancy is to abstain from sex until marriage. Some programs urge students to sign so-called virginity pledges. These programs do not provide information about contraception or disease prevention. Based on research findings, many developmental researchers believe this approach is unrealistic in the lives of today's adolescents. What do you notice about the images used in such campaigns and who the target audience might be as shown below?

Andreas Keuchel/Alamy

Peter Dazeley/Getty Images

b. Comprehensive sexuality education

Other programs, commonly called *skills-based comprehensive sexuality education*, focus on providing students with information and skills. The condom demonstration shown here is commonly used to teach students proper condom use.

Research suggests that programs effective in preventing unwanted youth pregnancy address risk factors, and seek to prevent risky behaviour, while simultaneously promoting the development of individual skills and competencies (Catalano et al., 2012). They are multi-faceted, educationally based, and comprehensive; such programs may include communication skill building, strategies for effective decision-making, and information on effective contraception use, and encourage delaying the start of sexual activity (Lavin & Cox, 2012). Ethical cautions have been voiced by researchers interested in the impacts of prevention programs that they do not inadvertently create greater stigma and social burdens on adolescent parents (Chabot, Shoveller, Johnson, & Prkachin, 2010).

Ask Yourself

1. Programs that focus primarily on providing students with information and skills are called _____.
2. Virginity pledges are most often associated with _____.

Trends in binge drinking and illicit drug use among Canadian youth • Figure 9.15

The use of alcohol and drugs is common among youth in Canada. Alcohol is the most prevalent substance used, but experimentation with multiple substances is widespread among contemporary youth (Leatherdale & Burkhalter, 2012).

> **Think Critically** Based on the above data, what can be said about the current substance use trends of young Canadians? What do you notice about the definition for binge drinking used in the table and how might this impact the results?
>
> Based on the above data, how would you design a substance use prevention program targeting Canadian youth? When would you introduce your program and what would you focus on?

Common Health Concerns of Adolescence

When it comes to lifestyle decisions, adolescents have much more freedom than they had earlier in their lives. From what to eat to what to drink to when and how to sleep, teens make myriad choices that affect the quality and safety of their day-to-day lives. We begin our discussion by considering a class of temptations to which most individuals are first seriously exposed during adolescence: alcohol and illicit drugs (Nasrallah, Yang, & Bernstein, 2009) (**Figure 9.15**).

Alcohol and illicit drug use Adolescent illicit drug use remains a prominent concern, with 60 percent of illicit drug users in Canada being between the ages of 15 and 24 (Tjepkema, 2004). Underage alcohol use is also a concern. For example, in the 2012–2013 Youth Smoking Survey (which also asks about alcohol and drug use), an alarming 46.2 percent of high school students reported alcohol use categorized as binge drinking (Health Canada, 2014), although that rate was down from the 69.8 percent reported in 2006–2007 (Health Canada, 2008). Binge drinking is defined as consuming five alcoholic drinks per sitting for men and four drinks per sitting for women, and is associated with

a. Binge drinking trends over a recent period (in this chart, binge drinking is defined as consuming five or more drinks on one occasion)

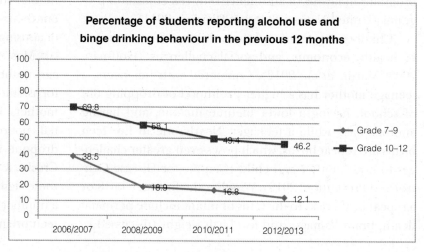

b. Trends for marijuana use

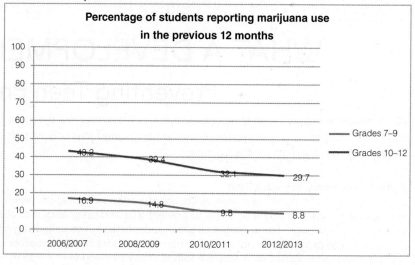

c. Trends for use of illicit substances excluding marijuana

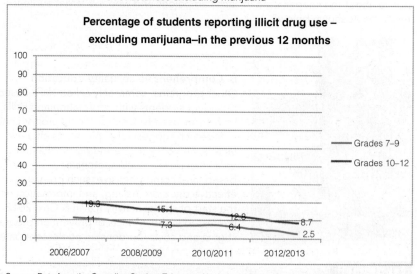

Source: Data from the Canadian Student Tobacco, Alcohol and Drugs Survey (conducted by a consortium of researchers across Canada and coordinated centrally by the Propel Centre for Population Health Impact at the University of Waterloo). Retrieved from https://uwaterloo.ca/canadian-student-tobacco-alcohol-drugs-survey/information-researchers/results.

cardiovascular problems, memory loss, loss of concentration, depression, unintentional injury, and death. Excessive alcohol consumption is particularly dangerous for youth, accounting for 69 percent of drug-related hospital stays among 10- to 19-year-olds in 2004 (Hunter & Francescutti, 2013).

Adolescents who are engaged in school, have friends, and have good communication with parents are less likely to use drugs (Bond & Sheridan, 2007; Ennett et al., 2006). The question that remains is how best to promote these characteristics among teens. Responses to youth drug use in Canada can be broadly categorized into four key groups: prevention, treatment, enforcement, and harm reduction. Intervention services, other than those involving the justice system, fall under provincial and territorial jurisdiction. Although this allows for localized responses to youth substance use, it also translates into significant differences in approach and funding allocation. Consequently, substance interventions specifically targeting youth continue to be underfunded, fragmented, and often based on adult treatment models that may not work for youth (Canadian Centre on Substance Abuse, 2007). Religious involvement has also been shown to moderate the use of drugs, although the relationship is only correlational (Merrill, Folsom, & Christopherson, 2005).

Ultimately, the choice to use substances is a personal one. Family background and parent practices are a part of the equation, but the nature of adolescence creates a context of curiosity and risk-taking (Al-Halabi Diaz et al., 2006). Unfortunately, this context also sets the stage for the emergence of eating disorders.

Disordered eating behaviours It is often during adolescence that eating disorders emerge. According to a 2002 survey, 1.5 percent of Canadian women aged 15 to 24 had an eating disorder (Government of Canada, 2006). The most common forms of these disorders are **anorexia nervosa** and **bulimia nervosa** (Bryant-Waugh, 2000), which we discuss in *Challenges in Development*. Anorexia nervosa has the highest mortality rate of any psychiatric illness. It is estimated that 10 percent of individuals with anorexia nervosa will die within 10 years of the onset of the disorder

anorexia nervosa
An eating disorder defined by excessive concern about gaining weight and restriction of food intake leading to extremely low body weight.

bulimia nervosa
An eating disorder that involves repeated episodes of binge eating followed by self-induced vomiting or another compensatory behaviour to prevent weight gain.

(Sullivan, 2002). Girls are at higher risk for developing an eating disorder and adopting disordered eating patterns. When asked about body image, for example, 34 percent of adolescent girls (Grades 6 to 10) described themselves as "too fat." This perception increased with age; 25 percent of Grade 6 girls described themselves in this way compared with 40 percent of Grade 10 girls (Public Health Agency of Canada, 2008b). Additionally, adolescent girls are hospitalized for eating disorders more than six times the rate of any other population category (Butler-Jones, 2011). However, body preoccupation and a desire to alter one's body affect both genders. In a 2002 study, 4 percent of boys in Grades 9 and 10 reported anabolic steroid use (Boyce, 2004), and it is estimated that 5 to 15 percent of eating disorder patients are male (Butler-Jones, 2011).

Weight-related teasing is unfortunately a common experience for young people. Both overweight and underweight youth reported higher levels of teasing than those of average weight (Neumark-Sztainer et al., 2002). In a survey of adolescents in Grades 7 to 12, 30 percent of girls and 25 percent of boys reported being teased by peers about their weight. Such teasing has been found to persist at home as well: 29 percent of girls and 16 percent of boys reported having been teased by a family member about their weight (Eisenberg & Neumark-Sztainer, 2003). Meta-analysis research has highlighted a positive association between teasing and body dissatisfaction and between teasing and disordered eating (Menzel et al., 2010). Excessive eating, overeating, and binge eating are also examples of disordered eating behaviours. Studies point to both short- and long-term health consequences of poor diet and inactivity among adolescents, including type 2 diabetes, high cholesterol, and hypertension (high blood pressure) (see Ozer & Irwin, 2009, for a review). Of course, not all teens struggle with substance use problems or disordered eating. However, there is one topic to which most adolescents in Canada can relate: lack of sleep.

Sleep How did you feel each day when the alarm rang for your day at high school? If you were like most teens, you desperately wanted another hour or two of sleep. In fact, if adolescents are allowed to fall asleep when it feels

CHALLENGES IN DEVELOPMENT
Bulimia Nervosa and Anorexia Nervosa

Eating disorders typically emerge during adolescence or early adulthood (National Institute of Mental Health, 2011). Bulimia nervosa is diagnosed when an individual repeatedly takes in large amounts of food and then compensates through vomiting, laxative use, excessive physical exercise, or other means (American Psychiatric Association, 2013). The anorexia nervosa diagnosis includes a failure to maintain normal body weight for one's age, sex, developmental trajectory, and physical health; a distorted body image (see the photo); an intense fear of gaining weight; and irregular menstruation among females (American Psychiatric Association, 2013). Individuals with anorexia tend to be young, high-achieving females, but about one in four anorexia nervosa sufferers are male (Raevuori et al., 2008; National Institute of Mental Health, 2011). Unfortunately, males tend to wait until their symptoms are much more severe than females before seeking help (Raevuori et al., 2008). The physical consequences of eating disorders are substantial. Anorexia nervosa can lead to problems with bone thinning and loss, anemia, and damage to the cardiovascular system. The most common cause of death among anorexia nervosa patients is cardiac arrest (Birmingham, Su, Hlynsky, Goldner, & Gao, 2005). Bulimia nervosa can lead to gastrointestinal problems and tooth decay (Leon, 1991).

Despite the seriousness of these disorders, health professionals remain uncertain about the causes (National Institute of Mental Health, 2011). Finding effective treatment methods has proven equally elusive. Researchers report that anorexia nervosa patients admitted to hospitals are often unmotivated to undergo treatment and that treatment yields poor results unless patient motivation is high (Rieger & Touyz, 2006).

Clearly, this feature reflects just the tip of the iceberg concerning the challenges faced by individuals with these life-threatening disorders. If you have questions or concerns about eating disorders in your own life, you can visit the website of the National Eating Disorder Information Centre at www.nedic.ca or call its toll-free helpline at 1-866-633-4240.

Abnormal self-perception in anorexia nervosa

Adolescents with anorexia nervosa often have distorted body images, believing themselves to be heavier than they actually are.

BSIP/Science Source

Think Critically How might Elkind's concepts of imaginary audience and personal fable help explain eating disorders such as anorexia nervosa?

---

phase delay
The shift to later natural sleeping and waking times that is typically seen among adolescents.

natural to them, they tend to delay both bedtime and risetime (as we see in **Figure 9.16**), a shift researchers call a **phase delay**. When you couple a later bedtime with an estimated need of 9 hours and 15 minutes of sleep a night and earlier school start times, you end up with a very tired group of high schoolers. From a developmental systems perspective, this is a great example of how human development is shaped by, and at the same time, shapes interactions between people and their contexts (as discussed in Chapter 1). Adolescents' need for more sleep and schools' earlier start times create a developmental mismatch that leads to daytime sleepiness and undermines adolescents' readiness to learn (Eccles & Roeser, 2011).

The sleep pattern of adolescents varies notably from that of prepubescent children. Adolescents tend to be more tired than prepubescent children, as indicated by the smaller number of minutes it takes them to fall asleep (National Sleep Foundation, 2000). They also tend to have greater irregularities in their sleep patterns across the course of the week than children. For example, 18-year-olds sleep about two hours longer on the weekends than on the weekdays. This large discrepancy can cause difficulties falling asleep or staying asleep, and it can disrupt sleep quality (Crowley, Acebo, & Carskadon, 2007; National Sleep Foundation, 2000). While a national study by Williams (2001) found that Canadian youth age 15 to 24 averaged 8.5 hours of sleep, Gibson and colleagues (2006) found that 70 percent of high school students in their Ontario study had less than 8.5 hours sleep.

Developmental changes in sleep/wake patterns • Figure 9.16

Across adolescence we see a phase delay in natural sleeping and waking times (National Sleep Foundation, 2000). This shift has been documented in other countries around the world (Andrade, Benedito-Silva, Domenice, Arnhold, & Menna-Barreto, 1993; Laberge, Petit, Simard, Vitaro, & Tremblay, 2001; Van den Bulck, 2004).

> **Think Critically** If you were in charge of making educational policies, what changes would you propose to accommodate adolescent phase delay?

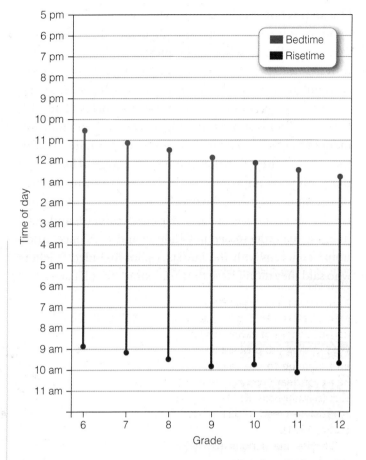

Fatigue can have many detrimental effects. For example, lack of sleep is linked to car accidents (National Sleep Foundation, 2000). Approximately 20 percent of fatal collisions in Canada involve driver fatigue (CCMTA, 2010), and in the United States at least 100,000 motor vehicle accidents each year are principally attributed to fatigue, with younger drivers causing about half of those sleep-related accidents. In addition, teens who do not get enough sleep have a higher tendency toward irritability and depression, and are more likely to turn to stimulants and alcohol. Insufficient sleep has also been associated with being overweight (Chen, Beydoun, & Wang, 2008).

How can we help teens cope with their unique sleep needs? Some schools have set back their start times in order to better match teens' natural circadian rhythms. In 2009, Toronto's Eastern Commerce Collegiate Institute ran a pilot project starting classes an hour later (10 a.m.) than other high schools in the city to determine if getting extra sleep actually improves not just student attendance, but their grades as well. Eastern has one of the latest start times of any North American school, and classes end most days at 4:15 p.m. Preliminary results show teens at Eastern get half an hour more sleep each night—for an average total of seven hours and 50 minutes—and almost one quarter of Eastern students sleep nine hours a night, 2.5 times more than teens in the control group (ABC school) (**Figure 9.17**). The principal has reported that "the most important thing is that the kids are in a better place, and

Differences in start times and student sleep patterns • Figure 9.17

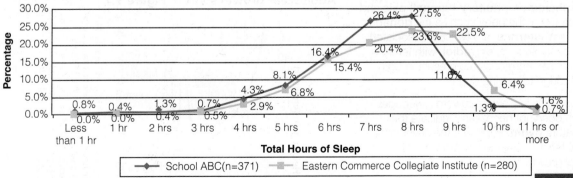

> **Ask Yourself** What other factors might be contributing to the grade improvements?

I mean psychologically, emotionally and physically, and for optimizing learning—that's number one." In comparison with other district schools, the increased sleep is credited with a 4- to 9-percent increase in passing a course/credit accumulation for Grade 9 and 10 students, higher than the Toronto District School Board overall. In Grades 11 and 12, Eastern students showed the highest percentage improvement in English and math compared with the entire board, though they are still below the board average. This means these students improved markedly compared to the rest of the students in the board. However, standardized test results remained the same in Grades 9 and 10, and class marks actually decreased in Grade 11 and 12 science. Additional concerns with the late-start pilot included teachers who said they didn't have time for extracurricular activities, and teachers who ended up staying at school until 7 p.m. (Brown et al., 2011). Other jurisdictions across Canada have examined the evidence and have opted to adopt the later start times for high school students (CBC, 2012).

Getting enough rest will benefit adolescents' social and emotional lives, the topic to which we turn in Chapter 10.

CONCEPT CHECK STOP

1. **What** are the two overarching hypotheses of the positive youth development perspective?

2. **How** do STIs differ from one another?

3. **Why** might campaigns that encourage students simply to say no to drugs fail in their mission?

Summary

1 Physical Development 288

- **Puberty** is a hormonal process resulting in reproductive competence. It differs from the broader concept of **adolescence**, which is a transition into adult cognition, emotions, and social roles. The experience of puberty can be subdivided into three phases: **prepubescent**, **pubescent**, and **postpubescent**.

- Puberty involves the development of **primary sex characteristics** and **secondary sex characteristics**, as well as growth spurts in height and weight, changes in the distribution of fat and muscle, and changes in circulation and respiration. The activity of several **hormones** increases during puberty. Endocrine glands begin to release hormones along the **HPA (hypothalamus-pituitary-adrenal) axis** and activate various structures of the body such as the **gonads**. Androgens, such as **testosterone**, are typically associated with males and estrogens, such as **estradiol**, with females. However, both types of sex hormones are present in both males and females, though to varying degrees.

- There is a trend among girls in Canada toward lower ages for **menarche**, which does not necessarily indicate the release of the first mature **ovum**. For boys, the development of primary sex characteristics includes lengthening of the penis and internal growth of the testes, leading to **spermatogenesis** and **spermarche**. Secondary sex characteristics include changes in breasts, particularly for females, and lowering of voice, particularly for males.

- The timing and experience of puberty vary widely among individuals, but are often described in three broad groups: **early maturers**, **late maturers**, and **on-time maturers**. Cultural **rites of passage** also tend to have three universal stages: **separation**, **transition**, and **incorporation**.

- Grey matter increases until middle adolescence, then levels off, due to synaptic pruning, particularly in the frontal cortex. White matter continues to increase throughout adolescence. Myelination and pruning in the prefrontal cortex affect emotional understanding, behavioural control, and executive control of working memory.

- All adolescents experience **growth spurts**, as shown in the figure. These growth spurts can include **asynchronicity** among body parts, leading to physical awkwardness.

Adolescent growth spurt • Figure 9.7

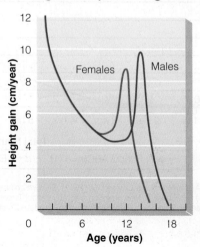

From Tanner, J. N., Whitehouse R. N., and Takaishi, M. Standards from birth to maturity for height, weight, height velocity, and weight velocity: British children, 1965. I. *Archives of Diseases in Childhood*, 41, 454-471, 1966. Reproduced with permission from BMJ Publishing Group Ltd.

2 Cognitive Development 298

- **Abstract thinking** is the hallmark of Piaget's **formal operational stage** of cognitive development, allowing for advanced studies like mathematics.

- Many school subjects require students to use abstract thinking skills, such as **hypothetical-deductive reasoning**, rather than relying on **trial and error**.

- **Adolescent egocentrism** makes teens feel as though they are the stars of their own movies. Adolescents often feel as though they are observed by an **imaginary audience** and are the centre of their own **personal fable**. Such thinking may allow teens to engage in risky behaviours, as we see in the photo in the figure.

- As parents and teachers make fewer choices for them, adolescents need to learn to assess risks and make decisions. Like many adults, most adolescents have difficulty assessing risks accurately, often displaying an **optimistic bias**. Education, formal thinking, and age may contribute to less risk-taking among older adolescents.

Imaginary audience and personal fable • Figure 9.10

Jay P. Morgan/Getty Images

3 All the Systems Working Together 303

- The **positive youth development (PYD)** perspective challenges and seeks to replace the early storm-and-stress view of adolescence. The PYD perspective involves two overarching hypotheses: (1) PYD is made up of the Five Cs of competence, confidence, connection, character, and caring; and (2) youth–context alignment enhances PYD through the provision of **developmental assets**.

- Nearly half of all sexually transmitted infections (STIs) occur among people ages 15 to 24. **Comprehensive sexuality education** and **abstinence-only sex education programs** aim to prevent the spread of STIs, as well as teen pregnancy. Teen pregnancy and parenthood pose physical and other risks to both teens and their babies. For this reason, there are many programs designed to help prevent teen pregnancy.

- Binge drinking and marijuana and illicit drug use among youth remain a concern in Canada. Alcohol and marijuana are among the most popular substances used by Canadian youth.

- Drug use can progress in stages, from experimental to compulsive. Being involved in school, having friends, having good communication with parents, and having religious involvement are related to less drug use.

- Eating disorders, such as **bulimia nervosa** and **anorexia nervosa**, are another risk for adolescents, especially females. A distorted **body image** often accompanies anorexia nervosa.

- Teens may struggle to get enough sleep. As shown in the figure, a **phase delay** makes it difficult for them to fall asleep early enough to get the nine or more hours of sleep they need before they must wake for school. Even with optimal sleep, adolescents experience greater daytime sleepiness than earlier in life.

Developmental changes in sleep/wake patterns • Figure 9.16

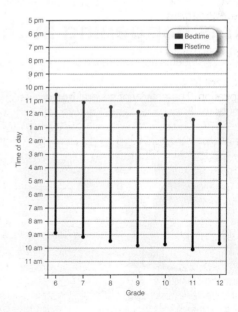

- Sleep deprivation and irregular sleep patterns can put teens at risk for car accidents, depression, substance abuse, and becoming overweight.

Key Terms

- abstinence-only sex education 306
- abstract thinking 298
- adolescence 288
- adolescent egocentrism 300
- anorexia nervosa 311
- asynchronicity 297
- body image 293
- bulimia nervosa 311
- comprehensive sexuality education 306
- developmental assets 304
- early maturers 293
- estradiol 289
- formal operational stage 298
- gonads 289

- grey matter 296
- growth spurt 296
- hormone 289
- hypothalamus-pituitary-adrenal (HPA) axis 289
- hypothetical-deductive reasoning 299
- imaginary audience 300
- incorporation 295
- late maturers 293
- menarche 290
- on-time maturers 293
- optimistic bias 302
- ovum 291
- personal fable 300
- phase delay 312

- positive youth development (PYD) 303
- postpubescent phase 288
- prepubescent phase 288
- primary sex characteristic 288
- puberty 288
- pubescent phase 288
- rite of passage 294
- secondary sex characteristic 288
- separation 294
- spermarche 293
- spermatogenesis 293
- testosterone 289
- transition 295
- trial and error 299
- white matter 296

Critical and Creative Thinking Questions

1. What do you remember as the most awkward moments of puberty for you or your friends? What were the best parts?

2. How would an effective substance-use prevention program take into consideration adolescents' emerging abstract thinking abilities as well as their egocentrism and optimistic biases?

3. What are the social and political implications of the positive youth development perspective? How do they differ from the major implications of the storm-and-stress view of adolescence?

4. Describe what you believe would be the ideal sexuality education program for young adolescents between the ages of 11 and 14 years. In what setting would this program be presented? Who would lead it? What information would be included, and how would it be taught?

5. Why do you think eating disorders such as anorexia nervosa are so much more prevalent among females than males?

What is happening in this picture?

These Grade 12 students are celebrating their prom and shopping for their big night.

Fstop123/Getty Images

Think Critically

1. Based on what you can see in the picture, would research suggest that the timing of these young people's puberty was most likely late, early, or on time?

2. How does the prom show these students' formal operational thinking abilities?

3. How do you think the presence of a large, real audience at prom might affect the students' thoughts about their personal fables and conviction of an imaginary audience?

REAL  Development

Physical and Cognitive Development in Adolescence

In these video activities, you want to contribute to the research on physical and cognitive development in adolescence.

In the first activity, you have been asked to interview professionals who can provide insight into aspects of adolescent sexuality so that you can start to develop a sex education awareness initiative. The nurse and counsellor at Jenna's school have agreed to answer your questions on sex education.

In the second activity, you are studying to be a child psychologist. You have been asked to observe a history lesson. As you complete the activity, consider what you have learned about students' cognitive development during adolescence based on the Piagetian, Vygotskian, and information processing models of cognitive development.

John Wiley & Sons, Inc.

WileyPLUS Go to WileyPLUS to complete the REAL Development activity.

03.01

Self-Test

(Check your answers in Appendix A.)

1. Label the three parts of the HPA hormonal axis.

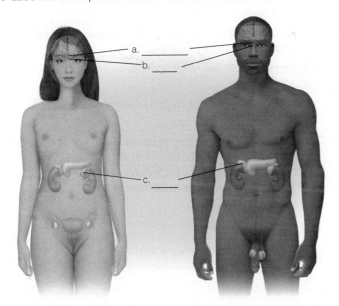

2. Which hormone directs the release and synthesis of other key puberty hormones, leading to an increase in androgens and estrogens?

a. follicle-stimulating hormone (FSH)

b. luteinizing hormone (LH)

c. gonadotropin-releasing hormone (GnRH)

d. androgen hormone (AH)

3. Which of the following is NOT a key change associated with puberty?

a. growth spurts in height and weight

b. changes in the distribution of fat and muscle

c. changes in circulation and respiration

d. increases in emotional instability

4. Pubertal changes in a girl's _____ are an example of secondary sex characteristic development.

a. ovaries

b. breasts

c. vulva

d. fertility

5. The diagrams show young people in the _____ phase of puberty.

a. spermatogenesis

b. pubescent

c. postpubescent

d. prepubescent

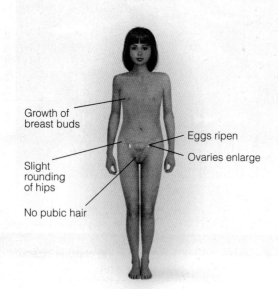

Growth of breast buds

Eggs ripen

Ovaries enlarge

Slight rounding of hips

No pubic hair

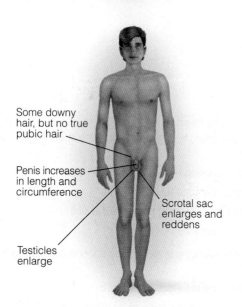

Some downy hair, but no true pubic hair

Penis increases in length and circumference

Scrotal sac enlarges and reddens

Testicles enlarge

6. Changes in the _____, depicted here, are associated with increased skills in thinking, planning, and reasoning.

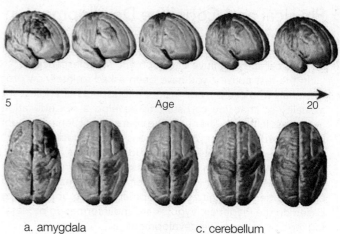

Reprinted by permission from Macmillan Publishers Ltd: Powell, K. (2006). Neurodevelopment: How does the teenage brain work? *Nature, 442,* 865–867.

a. amygdala

b. hypothalamus

c. cerebellum

d. prefrontal cortex

7. Asynchronicity is the process of uneven growth of _____ systems during adolescence.

a. physical

b. socio-emotional

c. cognitive

d. all of the above

8. Understanding the metaphor in the statement, "I wish I could be a fly on the wall in the teachers' lounge," requires _____.

a. abstract thinking abilities

b. hypothetical-deductive reasoning

c. trial-and-error problem solving

d. an understanding of conservation and reversibility

9. Elkind's theory predicts that adolescent egocentrism will _____.

a. increase between childhood and middle-to-late adolescence

b. be significantly lower among preadolescents and late adolescents

c. decrease between childhood and middle-to-late adolescence

d. be significantly higher among preadolescents and late adolescents

10. Oulette knows that her friends drive really badly after they've been drinking, but she believes that she is unlike them, because a few beers at a party don't affect her driving ability at all. Oulette's thinking is a demonstration of _____.

a. adolescent impulsivity

b. a personal fairy tale

c. an imaginary audience

d. an optimistic bias

11. An internal sense of overall positive self-worth and self-efficacy is which of the Five Cs of PYD?

   a. competence

   b. confidence

   c. connection

   d. character

12. Which of the following sexually transmitted infections is caused by a virus?

   a. chlamydia

   b. gonorrhea

   c. herpes

   d. all of these

13. What type of pregnancy prevention program is shown by research to be most effective?

   a. abstinence-plus programs

   b. abstinence-only sex education programs

   c. comprehensive sexuality education programs

   d. No pregnancy prevention program has been shown to be more effective than another.

14. Binge drinking among high school students has been on a decline. Illicit drug use _____.

   a. is unrelated to the trend we see in alcohol use

   b. has been increasing since the early 1980s

   c. generally mirrors the trend we see in alcohol use

   d. has reached historic proportions in recent years

15. Label the stages of substance use.

1. _____ Use is due to curiosity, peer pressure, or risk taking.

2. _____ Use is with friends or in social situations.

3. _____ Substance is used in order to alter feelings or behaviour.

4. _____ A habit has developed, and other facets of life begin to be neglected. Brain changes have typically occurred to make the user crave the substance.

5. _____ The individual becomes focused on gaining access and ignores nearly all other aspects of life.

THE PLANNER ✓

Review your Chapter Planner in the chapter opener and check off your completed work.

Socio-emotional Development in Adolescence

Everything about being an adolescent—well, almost everything about it anyway—is the interesting thing about being a person. You feel you're on a process of discovery towards something, and you have things that you really love and you organize your life around things you really love.

—Ira Glass (Conversations, 2009)

A key word in Ira Glass's quotation and the key experience in most adolescents' lives is *discovery*. Some of this discovery is literal, as is reflected in the girls in this photo learning archery skills

at summer camp, just as they learn math, science, and arts skills each day in high school. These girls are also experiencing more abstract discoveries, including a burgeoning sense of self and a new-found understanding of relationships. Who adolescents become depends on the myriad discoveries they make during the dynamic teenage years.

Despite the popular belief that adolescence is a stage of turmoil and conflict, these years are about responding to one of the most significant, critical challenges of

lifespan human development—answering the question, "Who am I?" As cognitive and physical changes exert their influence, adolescents are challenged to evaluate their understanding of themselves. In response to all the changes happening in their bodies and their minds and their social worlds, adolescents must work hard to learn to control their emotions and their behaviours. It's no small task to discover "who I am." But at the end of it all, adolescents have the sense of self they will need to navigate the transition to adulthood.

CHAPTER PLANNER ✔

- ❏ Study the picture and read the opening story.
- ❏ Scan the Learning Objectives in each section:
  p. 322 ❏   p. 330 ❏   p. 340 ❏
- ❏ Read the text and study all visuals. Answer any questions.

Analyze key features

- ❏ Development InSight, p. 325
- ❏ Challenges in Development, p. 337
- ❏ Process Diagram, p. 338
- ❏ What a Developmentalist Sees, p. 344
- ❏ Stop: Answer the Concept Checks before you go on:
  p. 330 ❏   p. 340 ❏   p. 346 ❏

End of chapter

- ❏ Review the Summary and Key Terms.
- ❏ Answer the Critical and Creative Thinking Questions.
- ❏ Answer *What is happening in this picture?*
- ❏ Complete the Self-Test and check your answers.

Bob Daemmrich/PhotoEdit

Personality Development

LEARNING OBJECTIVES

1. **Evaluate** early thinking about the period of adolescence.

2. **Compare** classic theories of how identity develops during adolescence.

3. **Explain** the influences on adolescent identity development.

dolescence, from the Latin verb meaning *to grow up*, is a life stage defined by both physical and psychological change. The natural state of the adolescent is flux rather than stasis.

Adolescence

Adolescence has been recognized as a distinct stage of the lifespan for just over a century. G. Stanley Hall, a psychologist and university president, originated and described this life stage in over 1,300 pages of his text, *Adolescence: Its Psychology and Its Relations to Physiology, Anthropology, Sociology, Sex, Crime, Religion and Education* (1904). This work revolutionized scientific understanding of the teen years by detailing biological and social changes that occur from the early teens through adulthood.

Despite Hall's elaborate and intricate study of adolescence, it would not be accurate to say that he was a fan of the adolescent. As we first mentioned in Chapter 9, Hall borrowed the phrase "storm and stress"—or *Sturm und Drang* in the original German—to emphasize the volatility of this stage, which, from his perspective, manifests in parent–adolescent conflict, moodiness, and risky behaviour. Hall's view of adolescence as an inherently tumultuous stage of development has more recently been challenged (**Figure 10.1**). Despite contemporary arguments in favour of a more moderate view of adolescence as a stage that is neither more nor less chaotic than other stages, Hall's original emphasis on the instability of adolescent emotions and behaviours influenced a century of research on adolescent development and adjustment, perpetuating the idea of adolescents as troublemakers.

Adolescence was a different experience in the early 1900s, when Hall introduced the concept. Life expectancy was 47 (U.S. Bureau of the Census, 1975; see also Rosenfeld, 2006), and the age of legal adulthood was 16. The majority of adolescents lived in a state of semi-dependence on their parents, during which time they contributed to the economic activities of their families, or they lived and worked under another family's authority (Rosenfeld, 2006). In 1900, a sizeable minority of adolescents ages 10 to 15 were employed: 26 percent of boys and 10 percent of girls. The increase in employment among adolescents reflected the impact of the Industrial Revolution and the growing labour market needs in cities. These jobs attracted young people old enough to live independently, but young enough not to have families of their own. As work life shifted from agriculture to manufacturing, the government took a more active role in determining the activities of children and adolescents. By 1900, all U.S. states had adopted compulsory education laws, with exemptions available for youth who remained involved in agrarian family life and work. Child labour laws were also passed, restricting the employment activities of adolescents. Hall's work responded to the role of mandating education and restricting employment of adolescents. He recognized that these social changes affected the length of time adolescents spent in a state of semi-dependence on parents.

Hall's work set the stage for other psychologists to accumulate rich data about adolescents. From this research we know that adolescent personality begins with a key question: Who am I?

Identity in Adolescence

Ask an adolescent who she is and you might get a response similar to this one from a 13-year-old girl who sees herself in many roles and identities:

Savannah Cash is me; daughter, student, sister and friend. A Jew for life and a passionate religious person (Kosher, too). A student of everything and anything. A sister to her siblings, a daughter to her parents, and a friend to many more. Unique, in more ways than one, with many talents which are; music, language arts, and mathematics (Yes, a girl who loves math!). Never perfect, but good enough for her friends and family. [Savannah Cash, age 13]

"Storm and stress" or "healthy and normal"? • Figure 10.1

Many researchers since G. Stanley Hall have viewed adolescence as a time of storm and stress characterized by three key issues: parental conflict, moodiness, and risk-taking. According to Hines and Paulson (2006), however, these may actually be normative responses to adolescence (Arnett, 1999; Steinberg, 2007).

Spencer Grant/Getty Images

a. Parental conflict

Steinberg (1990) suggests that conflict does not dominate parent–adolescent relationships. Instead, parents and teens tend to have insignificant disagreements over superficial issues such as curfews, clothes, and music. Basic values are not affected by this bickering, and the majority of these adolescents report positive feelings toward parents.

Catchlight Visual Services/Alamy

b. Moodiness

The moodiness often associated with adolescence actually results largely from emerging autonomy that meets resistance from parents (Hines & Paulson, 2006). In addition, researchers find that how parents cope with their child's developing independence has a significant impact on the perceived moodiness of the adolescent.

Verge Images/Alamy

c. Risk-taking

There appears to be an exaggeration of adolescent involvement in high-risk behaviour and other dangerous activities. As Hines and Paulson (2006) neatly sum up, "A majority of adolescents may admit to breaking a rule or committing a deviant act; however, for most these are not frequent occurrences and the majority does not participate in seriously delinquent behaviour" (p. 599).

Ask Yourself

Which of the following is *not* a part of the storm-and-stress view of adolescence?
a. conflict with parents
b. moodiness
c. risky behaviour
d. rational thought

Savannah seems to have an understanding of who she is becoming. Defining **identity** is a challenging task, whether you're an adolescent or a developmental scientist. Researchers have struggled to identify a single definition because identity is an abstract concept composed of numerous social and psychological processes (Côté, 2009). In addition, researchers have approached the study of identity from a variety of perspectives. As a result, a number of theoretical approaches have been proposed to examine the development of identity. We first turn to Erik Erikson's theory that identity, like other elements of personality, results from the decision to move toward or away from others (Erikson, 1963).

identity An individual's understanding of self in relation to his or her social context.

Erik Erikson's stage of identity versus role confusion

As we have discussed in previous chapters, Erikson suggests that individuals face specific crises at different junctures in their lives. These crises centre on social issues related to lifespan-specific events, played out against the cultural context of the current time period. By the time adolescence begins, a pattern of social crisis resolution has already developed, providing the underlying structure for future crisis resolution (Erikson, 1963).

identity versus role confusion Erikson's fifth stage of psychosocial development, during which the adolescent must adopt a coherent and integrated sense of self.

The crisis of adolescence, according to Erikson, is **identity versus role confusion**. The challenge for the adolescent is to function with a coherent and integrated sense of self and purpose. Thus, key questions of adolescence include: Who am I? What do I want to be? How do I let others know my identity?

The trusting adolescent, already versed in choosing social interaction over withdrawal, must answer these questions by weighing incoming information from parents, other family members, friends, teachers, media, and self-observation. An active search to find oneself ensues, called an **identity crisis**. The adolescent identity crisis demonstrates itself in many ways, including frequent changes in preferences for music, clothing, friends, and hairstyles. With age, identity explorations typically move away from superficial choices and begin to centre on decisions about vocation and post–high school life. Erikson believed the adolescent identity crisis can be seen as a good crisis and is a requirement of adolescence (Erikson, 1970/1975). In fact, many psychologists believe that if one does not have an identity crisis during adolescence, it will appear later in the form of a mid-life crisis (Steinberg, 2007). However, recent research suggests that this is unlikely; identity development is an ongoing process and a level of continuing questioning and uncertainty exists well beyond high school graduation (Louden, 2005). Contextual factors can both open and close opportunities for identity exploration. As mentioned in Chapter 1, economic changes have altered the social expectations around work and education for young Canadians, resulting in a trend of prolonged transitions into adulthood. This kind of emerging adulthood can lengthen identity exploration and delay identity formation (Côté & Bynner, 2008).

identity crisis A crisis that entails an evaluation of possible choices concerning vocation, relationships, and self-understanding.

Although many teenagers eventually forge a sense of identity, some teenagers instead experience **role confusion**. "The danger of this stage is role confusion," Erikson (1970/1975, p. 253) stated. "To keep themselves together they temporarily over-identify, to the point of apparent complete loss of identity, with the heroes of cliques and crowds." Identity-confused adolescents are uncertain about who they are, what they want, and where they are going. They appear lost in their social world.

role confusion An adolescent's inability to define an identity, resulting in a lack of direction and focus.

James Marcia's identity statuses Although Erikson's theory of identity development has had great influence, one frequent criticism is that his concept of identity is too narrow and needs more substance to be relevant (Hoover, 2004). That criticism led theorist and researcher James Marcia (1966, 1976, 1980) to extend the concept of identity in adolescence. Marcia suggests that four distinct identity statuses emerge while searching for answers to the question, "Who am I?"

According to Marcia, two dimensions determine a person's particular identity status at any given time. **Exploration** involves a positive search for options, whereas **commitment** is an individual's conscious choice about a particular aspect of identity. One must go through a process of exploration before making a true commitment. The four identity statuses and their relation to exploration and commitment are explained in **Figure 10.2**. At any one time, the teenager is likely to have different statuses for different domains. For example, he might be in **identity moratorium** about religion (for example, he has begun to explore his religious identity but has yet to make a commitment), in **identity diffusion** about politics (for example, he has not yet thought about his political orientation), and in **identity foreclosure** regarding vocation (for example, he has committed to becoming a doctor like his father without exploring other options).

exploration One of the two dimensions suggested by Marcia as determining a person's identity status at a particular time; it is a positive search for identity options.

commitment One of the two dimensions suggested by Marcia as determining a person's identity status at a particular time; it is a conscious choice made about a particular aspect of identity.

identity moratorium As described by Marcia, an individual who has begun to explore his or her identity but has yet to make a commitment.

identity diffusion As described by Marcia, an individual who has neither made a commitment about nor begun to explore his or her identity.

identity foreclosure As described by Marcia, an individual who has made a commitment about his or her identity without even exploring options.

Development InSight

Marcia's identity statuses • Figure 10.2

This figure shows identity development as described by Marcia related to the domain of vocation. Other domains of identity also go through these statuses, including religion, political views, and musical preferences.

a. Exploration versus commitment

Marcia's four identity statuses are determined by the presence or absence of exploration and commitment.

EXPLORATION

	NO	YES
NO	IDENTITY DIFFUSION	IDENTITY MORATORIUM
YES	IDENTITY FORECLOSURE	IDENTITY ACHIEVEMENT

COMMITMENT

b. Identify diffusion

Identity diffusion is a state of static non-growth. The individual has not yet made a commitment about or begun to explore his or her identity. For example, we might infer that this young man is avoiding identity work. He's sitting still, in a room that lacks organization, disconnected from others and his social world.

Image Source/Getty Images

c. Identity moratorium

In this status, a person actively searches out options for his or her identity, but has yet to make a commitment. In relation to career, this may take the form of intense thought, university internships, military service, or taking a number of part-time jobs to see which one fits. The process can be painful, but it is healthy and is necessary to achieve identity.

d. Identity foreclosure

There is no exploration in this status because parents, teachers, or the like make a commitment to a particular direction for the individual. For example, this woman has chosen the same career as her father. That was the easy choice for her, one she made without considering alternatives.

Jodi Cobb/National GeographicCreative

e. Identity achievement

Marcia considered this status to be the ultimate goal, characterized by having an identity gained through exploration. Identity achievement results after challenging struggles with long-term choices and an eventual understanding of who you are and what you want.

David J. Green/Alamy

Juice Images/Alamy

Think Critically Can you think of examples from your own life of people whose identities match the four different statuses?

identity achievement
As described by Marcia, an individual who has made a commitment about his or her identity following a process of exploration.

Once **identity achievement** occurs, Marcia suggests that we are still not done with identity development. As we go through life, new crises arise and we begin to question our identity all over again. In some cases, we quit our jobs and go back to school. Marcia calls these events the *MAMA cycle* because they entail a new moratorium followed by achievement. The take-home message? Identity development may be most notable during adolescence, but it never ends.

Influences on Identity Development

Thus far, we have discussed approaches to identity development that were designed to capture what is believed to be universal about identity formation. The limitations of these approaches are brought to light when we consider that the content of identity formation can differ substantially among various subpopulations (Côté, 2009).

Ethnic identity Every adolescent has an ethnicity, but its meaning in the lives of adolescents is largely dependent on society and, thus, varies considerably (Côté, 2009). Is an adolescent's ethnicity related to minority or majority status? Is the minority status belittled or held in high esteem? And what are the adolescent's perceptions of his or her ethnic group? These questions reveal **ethnic identity** as a dynamic construct, involving "complex and subtle interactions between different elements of ethnic identity and external forces" (Phinney & Rosenthal, 1992, p. 148).

ethnic identity A component of identity and self-concept that acknowledges a unique connection to a specific ethnic group and the values and beliefs associated with that group.

Based on Marcia's identity statuses, noted researcher Jean Phinney developed a three-stage model of ethnic minority identity formation (**Table 10.1**; Phinney, 1993, 2006). According to her model, ethnic identity develops through the processes of exploration and commitment. The adolescent is faced with the developmental task of resolving positive and negative views about ethnic group membership. Phinney (1993) notes that the best outcome is reached when the adolescent has both an achieved ethnic identity and a positive view of the majority culture.

Ethnic identity is a central thread in Canada's social fabric. Our long history of intercultural contact, stretching from the diverse Aboriginal cultures through generations of immigration, is reflected in our official policy of multiculturalism (*Canadian Multiculturalism Act*, 1985). This policy aims to give diverse peoples a framework in which to celebrate both their unique cultural heritages and their sense of shared identity as Canadians. Multiculturalism suggests that a strong and positive heritage identity should be no barrier to an equally strong and positive Canadian identity. In this way, this policy sets identification with two cultures—known as biculturalism—as a reachable goal for Canadians. This formal policy does not necessarily show itself in the interactions that immigrants have in Canadian society, however, because immigrants continue to encounter discrimination in Canada (e.g., Nangia, 2013; Oxman-Martinez et al., 2012). Research (Stroink & Lalonde, 2009) indicates that bicultural identity or simultaneous identification is associated with well-being but that this is a challenging process. What might facilitate or undermine simultaneous identification or the development of a bicultural identity?

A good deal of research on ethnic identity focuses on **acculturation**, or the process of a minority culture adopting the values of the majority culture (García-Vásquez, 1995). One of the prime areas of acculturation research investigates how ethnicity affects self-concept and self-esteem (Cavazos-Rehg & DeLucia-Waack, 2009; Cheryan & Tsai, 2007; Phinney, 1990, 1995, 1998).

acculturation A process for people within a minority culture wherein they adopt values from a majority culture.

Ethnic minority identity formation	Table 10.1
Stage 1: Unexamined ethnic identity	Ethnicity remains unexamined by the adolescent, who may accept without question the values and opinions of the majority culture. Such unquestioned acceptance is similar to Marcia's identity foreclosure. Identity diffusion may also characterize this stage, if the adolescent shows a lack of interest in exploring his or her ethnic identity.
Stage 2: Ethnic identity search/moratorium	Ethnic identity exploration is typically triggered by an experience of prejudice or discrimination. This stage is consistent with Erikson's identity crisis and Marcia's moratorium status.
Stage 3: Ethnic identity achievement	Ethnic identity achievement is obtained after the adolescent resolves uncertainties and develops a secure sense of his or her ethnic background.

For example, American Latino adolescents enrolled in bilingual education programs were found to have enhanced self-esteem (Cavazos-Rehg & DeLucia-Waack, 2009). This finding matches research indicating that having a bicultural identity is healthier than disowning either culture. Another factor that affects our sense of identity is our gender.

Gender identity In earlier chapters we discussed how young people begin to take on behaviours often associated with their assigned gender, including gender-related activity preferences, personality traits, and attitudes (Signorella & Frieze, 2008). As they move toward and through adolescence, gender identity, defined and discussed in Chapter 6, can further intensify, becoming increasingly rigid (Martin, Ruble, & Szkrybalo, 2002). Or, in other cases, influences such as media, peer relations, and parental role models can create a more flexible attitude toward gender identity.

Researchers call the shift toward stereotypical, gender-specific behaviours **gender intensification** (**Figure 10.3**; Galambos, Almeida, & Petersen, 1990). This movement toward

> **gender intensification**
> A process wherein a person becomes more rigid in their gender performance, behaving in stereotypical ways for their identified gender.

increasing rigidity in gender may arise partly from peer and parental pressure. For example, one research team found differential treatment, with males being encouraged to be independent and females being encouraged to be compliant (Crouter, Manke, & McHale, 1995). This research supports the social learning and contextual models of gender identity, which suggest that gender identity results from a number of social and environmental factors, such as parental modelling, socio-economic status, and family composition (Signorella & Frieze, 2008).

As we first discussed in Chapter 6, gender schema theories present a cognitive approach to gender development that centres on the individual's own constructions of gender. These theories emphasize the role of self-understanding and gender-related ideology of masculinity and femininity (Signorella & Frieze, 2008). Individuals become more or less rigid about their gender identity based on their particular gender schema, or "stored framework or body of knowledge" about gender (Ashcraft, 1989, p. 309).

Gender identity during adolescence • Figure 10.3

Some adolescents experience gender intensification, in which their behaviours fall more in line with gender stereotypes.

a. Female adolescents may do this by learning homemaking skills traditionally practised by women.

b. Male adolescents may do this by engaging in leisure activities that typically bring men together.

> **Ask Yourself**
>
> Which of the following factors is *not* a likely factor that influences the flexibility of one's gender identity?
> a. peer relations
> b. parental role models
> c. functioning of the prefrontal cortex
> d. media

Where Developmentalists CLICK

The Kinsey Institute

Developmentalists visit the Kinsey Institute website to download the institute's latest research findings in areas including sexual arousal, contraception use, and sexual disorders, and also to gain access to Dr. Kinsey's original pioneering research. Access the site by going to the homepage of the Kinsey Institute (www. kinseyinstitute.org). Click on the Research tab and read about the Institute's research on various topics, such as sexual decision-making, definitions of sex, and condom use errors and problems.

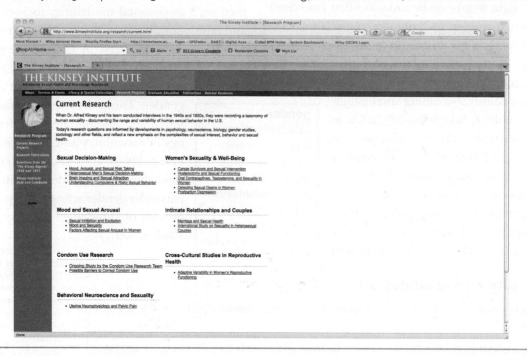

A large body of clinical evidence indicates that many people experience uncertainty around their gender identities. Individuals may waver back and forth between a desired and assigned gender identity, seek sexual reassignment in order to adopt an alternative gender identity, embrace a gender identity inconsistent with their assigned sex (Meyer-Bahlburg, 2010), or adopt a fluid gender identity (Eliason & Schope, 2007). Transgender, transsexual, and gender queer identities challenge the stability of sex as the underpinning of gender identity and disrupt the male-female gender binary (Diamond & Butterworth, 2008). Many researchers agree that trans identity development begins with an awareness of the self as different. However, stage-based models of divergent gender identity development, which often end with the integration of a stable gender identity, have been criticized for assuming an innate gender ordination, positioning masculinity and femininity as irreconcilable, and being too rigid to fit gender queer identities (Diamond & Butterworth, 2008; Eliason & Schope, 2007).

Which model is right? It's hard to say. The incredible variation in gender identity among adolescents has yielded inconclusive research results. At this point, more research examining gender identity is underway, helping add some clarification to this elusive area (Signorella & Frieze, 2008). One area that has inspired much research is sexual orientation and its intersection with gender identity.

Sexual orientation One of the first people to conduct research on sexual orientation and sexual behaviour was Dr. Alfred Kinsey, who published his original research in 1948 and 1953, and founded the still-cutting-edge research foundation, the Kinsey Institute, in 1947. This institute was the first to perform in-depth research on human sexual behaviour. Today the Kinsey Institute has an active program of research that spans various topics, including sexual arousal, contraception use, and sexual disorders (see *Where Developmentalists Click*).

Current research on sexual orientation tends to be divided into several categories. Major areas of research include genetic and environmental influences on sexual orientation, the impact of sexual orientation on attachment and relationship satisfaction, psychological issues related to sexual orientation and homosexual identity, and changing public opinion about gay and lesbian culture (Boegart, 2006; Francis, 2008; Garnets, 2002; Gonsiorek, 1991; Matte, Lemieux, & Lafontaine, 2009; Pillard & Bailey, 1995; Shackelford & Besser, 2007).

A growing area of research aims to clarify the definition of sexual orientation (Heath & Euvard, 2008). This research is key to determining how many people fall into the category of *homosexual*. Is someone homosexual if he has ever engaged in a homosexual act, or only if he self-identifies as homosexual? The definition of homosexuality falls into what Heath and Euvard (2008) call the "inadequate trichotomy of homosexual, bisexual, and heterosexual" (p. 633). This inadequacy results from the assumption that sexual identity is a static component of a person's overall identity. In fact, research suggests that sexual orientation is a fluid and changing form of identity rather than an enduring, predisposed trait (Garnets, 2002). Alfred Kinsey's pioneering work on sexuality found that 28 percent of males and 17 percent of females reported at least one homosexual experience between puberty and 20 years of age, which is consistent with the view that sexual orientation is fluid (Garnets, 2002; Kinsey, Pomeroy, & Martin, 1948).

Although Canadian researchers have contributed much to the body of scholarship focused on sexual orientation, to date there have been no large-scale studies of lesbian sexual behaviour in Canada, and data concerning men's sexual behaviour is dated. Myers and colleagues, for example, undertook "Men's Survey '90" to study gay and bisexual Canadian men (Myers, Lucker, Orr, & Jackson, 1991). They surveyed the sexual practices of approximately 1,300 men recruited from 12 bars and three bathhouses in Toronto. About 48 percent reported sex only with

men in their lifetime, another 35 percent had previously had sex with women but had only had sex with men in the past year, and 13 percent were bisexual.

If researchers struggle so much with the definition of homosexuality, it is no wonder that many individuals struggle with their self-definition. Approximately 11 percent of high school students between the ages of 12 and 18 report uncertainty about their sexual orientation (Remafedi, Resnick, Blum, & Harris, 1992). In order to define one's own sexual orientation, the individual must be able to differentiate behaviour from thoughts or fantasies and realize that sexual orientation may not be a dichotomous dimension (Heath & Euvard, 2008).

Researchers interviewed 60 gay and lesbian Toronto-area youth age 15 to 22 about their self-identification process. Multiple factors were named as contributing to their labelling themselves as gay or lesbian (Schneider, 1991) (**Figure 10.4**).

Factors Contributing to Self- Identification of Gay and Lesbian Youth • Figure 10.4

- Emergence of same-sex attraction and feelings was mentioned most often by both sexes, but males were more likely to identify this as "general same-sex attraction" (7 percent of females versus 73 percent of males), whereas females associated their sexual feeling with falling in love with someone of the same sex (83 percent of females versus 10 percent of males).

Lise Gagne/Getty Images

- Lack of interest in a different-sex partner (10 percent of females versus 33 percent of males) was a relevant factor in that most had dated heterosexually and were aware of their disinterest, but it was less influential as a salient clue in self-identification because many assumed early on that they would eventually be attracted to hetero-sex partners.

- Same-sex sexual experience was identified by 33 percent of females and 37 percent of males as a validation of their ability to experience pleasure with the same sex and of the sense that "it seemed right for them." Males were more likely than females to identify "casual and anonymous sex over an extended period of time" as a factor in their self-identification as gay (0 percent of females versus 40 percent of males).

BraunS/Getty Images

- More than half identified "contact with lesbians/gays" (67 percent of females versus 50 percent of males) as an important influence, suggesting that positive role models reinforce self-acceptance. This seems likely since such contact was also the most common contributor to their feeling positive about their lesbian/gay identity (93 percent of females versus 80 percent of males).

- First long-term relationships contributed to self-identification for 73 percent of females and 37 percent of males (Schneider, 1991).

> **coming out** The process by which a homosexual person makes his or her orientation known to self, friends, and family.

Once a self-definition has been reached, the process of **coming out** can pose a dilemma. The coming-out process entails a series of personal and social steps that often have a major impact on one's relationships and self-concept. Despite the visible presence and growth of gay and lesbian communities and greater awareness of sexuality, Canadian youth are still at tremendous peril for bullying and gay bashing (Abramovich, 2012; Taylor et al., 2008) regardless of whether they identify as gay, lesbian, queer, or questioning.

Hate crime in Canada continues to be very much a youth phenomenon, as both victims and those accused are concentrated between the ages of 12 and 24. This has led organizations such as Egale to bolster efforts across Canada to educate youth and foster inclusivity within schools (Egale, 2010). According to the Canadian Centre for Justice Statistics report *Hate Crime in Canada, 2013*:

- Sexual orientation was one of the top three motivations for hate crimes, accounting for 16 percent of the hate crimes reported to police in 2013.
- Incidents motivated by hatred of a sexual orientation were more likely to be violent (66 percent) than those motivated by hatred of a race/ethnicity (44 percent) or religion (18 percent).

Between 2010 and 2013:

- 83 percent of victims of a violent hate crime motivated by sexual orientation were male, and 48 percent were under the age of 25
- 61 percent of victims of a violent hate crime motivated by sexual orientation identified the accused as a stranger, and nearly half (46 percent) sustained injuries
- 91 percent of those accused of hate crimes motivated by sexual orientation were male, and 64 percent were under the age of 25 (Allen, 2015).

Clearly, the process of determining one's own sexual orientation can be complex and difficult. We will discuss both heterosexual and homosexual romantic relationships later in this chapter, but first we turn to the role of social influences on adolescent development.

CONCEPT CHECK STOP

1. **How** did G. Stanley Hall characterize the adolescent period?
2. **What** factors contribute to an adolescent's identity according to Erikson?
3. **What** definitional challenges do researchers face when studying sexual identity development?

Social Influences

LEARNING OBJECTIVES

1. **Describe** how traditional high schools shape adolescent motivation and learning.
2. **Explain** how parent–child relationships change during adolescence.
3. **Outline** key topics of peer interactions during adolescence, including group dynamics and technology use.
4. **Describe** the development of romantic relationships in adolescence.

The social influences in adolescence take a unique turn when compared with earlier development. The most important difference has to do with freedom. The independence of adolescence comes with a new context of influence. For the first time in life, peers know things about adolescents that even their parents don't know. Friends, cliques, and sexual interests create a social milieu that adolescents take with them for the rest of their lives. The place it all starts is in high school.

that typically de-emphasize comprehensive sex education programs in favour of abstinence-only sex education programs (United Nations Statistics Division, 2011).

Childbearing teens and their children face a number of health, economic, and social challenges (Hoffman, 2008; Martin et al., 2012). Compared with her peers, a teenage mother has a higher likelihood of dropping out of school, having a lower lifetime income, and having another baby while a teenager. Nearly one in five teen births are repeat births, which poses even greater challenges to both mother and child (Centers for Disease Control and Prevention, 2013). Whether the first teen birth or a repeat birth, risks to the fetus or infant include perinatal death, brain damage, and low birth weight (discussed in Chapter 2). In addition, individuals who were born to teen mothers have a higher likelihood of becoming a teen parent themselves, of becoming a high school dropout, and of abusing drugs (Santelli, Orr, Lindberg, & Diaz, 2009).

Most research on teen pregnancy has focused on teenage mothers and their children. When teen fathers are the focus, studies show that they face similar risk factors as teen mothers. For example, they have reduced income potential, poorer academic performance, and higher school dropout rates (Castiglia, 1990; Fagot, Pears, Capaldi, Crosby, & Leve, 1998; Xie, Cairns, & Cairns, 2001). Given these significant risks to teen parents and their children, a number of programs have been enacted to help prevent teen pregnancy (see *What a Developmentalist Sees*).

WHAT A DEVELOPMENTALIST SEES
Preventing Teen Pregnancy

When developmentalists look at teenage pregnancy rates, they see the opportunity to step in and make changes. Some pregnancy prevention programs focus only on girls, whereas others include both boys and girls in the classroom.

a. Abstinence-only sex education

One major type of program is known as *abstinence-only sex education*, which stresses the message that the only way to prevent STIs and pregnancy is to abstain from sex until marriage. Some programs urge students to sign so-called virginity pledges. These programs do not provide information about contraception or disease prevention. Based on research findings, many developmental researchers believe this approach is unrealistic in the lives of today's adolescents. What do you notice about the images used in such campaigns and who the target audience might be as shown below?

Andreas Keuchel/Alamy

Peter Dazeley/Getty Images

b. Comprehensive sexuality education

Other programs, commonly called *skills-based comprehensive sexuality education*, focus on providing students with information and skills. The condom demonstration shown here is commonly used to teach students proper condom use.

Research suggests that programs effective in preventing unwanted youth pregnancy address risk factors, and seek to prevent risky behaviour, while simultaneously promoting the development of individual skills and competencies (Catalano et al., 2012). They are multi-faceted, educationally based, and comprehensive; such programs may include communication skill building, strategies for effective decision-making, and information on effective contraception use, and encourage delaying the start of sexual activity (Lavin & Cox, 2012). Ethical cautions have been voiced by researchers interested in the impacts of prevention programs that they do not inadvertently create greater stigma and social burdens on adolescent parents (Chabot, Shoveller, Johnson, & Prkachin, 2010).

Ask Yourself

1. Programs that focus primarily on providing students with information and skills are called _____.
2. Virginity pledges are most often associated with _____.

Trends in binge drinking and illicit drug use among Canadian youth • Figure 9.15

The use of alcohol and drugs is common among youth in Canada. Alcohol is the most prevalent substance used, but experimentation with multiple substances is widespread among contemporary youth (Leatherdale & Burkhalter, 2012).

> **Think Critically** Based on the above data, what can be said about the current substance use trends of young Canadians? What do you notice about the definition for binge drinking used in the table and how might this impact the results?
>
> Based on the above data, how would you design a substance use prevention program targeting Canadian youth? When would you introduce your program and what would you focus on?

Common Health Concerns of Adolescence

When it comes to lifestyle decisions, adolescents have much more freedom than they had earlier in their lives. From what to eat to what to drink to when and how to sleep, teens make myriad choices that affect the quality and safety of their day-to-day lives. We begin our discussion by considering a class of temptations to which most individuals are first seriously exposed during adolescence: alcohol and illicit drugs (Nasrallah, Yang, & Bernstein, 2009) (**Figure 9.15**).

Alcohol and illicit drug use Adolescent illicit drug use remains a prominent concern, with 60 percent of illicit drug users in Canada being between the ages of 15 and 24 (Tjepkema, 2004). Underage alcohol use is also a concern. For example, in the 2012–2013 Youth Smoking Survey (which also asks about alcohol and drug use), an alarming 46.2 percent of high school students reported alcohol use categorized as binge drinking (Health Canada, 2014), although that rate was down from the 69.8 percent reported in 2006–2007 (Health Canada, 2008). Binge drinking is defined as consuming five alcoholic drinks per sitting for men and four drinks per sitting for women, and is associated with

a. Binge drinking trends over a recent period (in this chart, binge drinking is defined as consuming five or more drinks on one occasion)

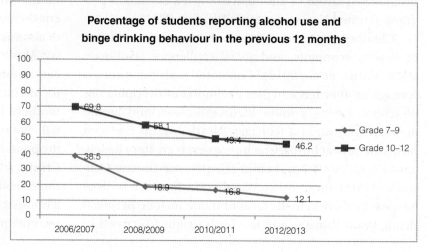

b. Trends for marijuana use

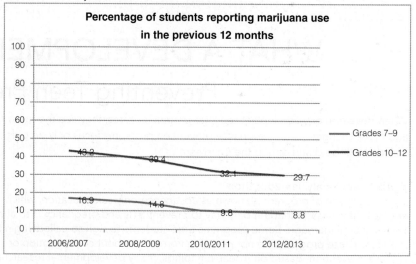

c. Trends for use of illicit substances excluding marijuana

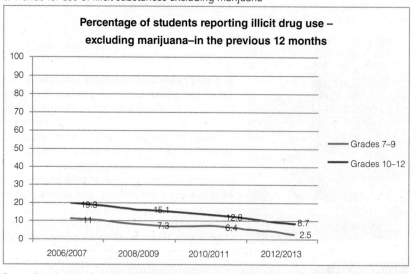

Source: Data from the Canadian Student Tobacco, Alcohol and Drugs Survey (conducted by a consortium of researchers across Canada and coordinated centrally by the Propel Centre for Population Health Impact at the University of Waterloo). Retrieved from https://uwaterloo.ca/canadian-student-tobacco-alcohol-drugs-survey/information-researchers/results.

High School

Educators have long considered how best to educate adolescents. As one noted researcher wrote, "Not only are schools the chief educational arena for adolescents in America, but they also play an extremely important role in defining the young person's social world and in shaping the adolescent's developing sense of identity and autonomy" (Steinberg, 2007, p. 216). Clearly, what goes on in school will have long-lasting effects on the developing adolescent. And yet studies point to declines in early adolescents' academic motivation and achievement as they transition to junior high or middle school (see Eccles & Roeser, 2011). Academic failure and dropout are particularly salient problems among some racial/ethnic groups.

Canada's high school dropout rate has been falling over the last few decades, but it is still a problem among Aboriginal youth. Statistics Canada began collecting data in 1990 that allow for the calculation of high school dropout rates (**Figure 10.5**). At that time, nearly 340,000 young people aged 20 to 24 (16.6 percent), or one out of every six young adults, had not obtained a high school diploma. Since that time, dropout rates have been falling.

Data collected in 2009/2010 showed that dropout rates had been cut in half; one in 12 (8.5 percent) Canadians aged 20 to 24 had not obtained their high school diploma. New Canadians are less likely to drop out of high school than Canadian-born students (6.2 percent and 9.1 percent, respectively, in 2009/2010). However, Aboriginal students have a much higher dropout rate compared with non-Aboriginal youth. From 2007 to 2010, the dropout rate among First Nations people living off-reserve aged 20 to 24 was 22.6 percent, compared with 8.5 percent for non-Aboriginal youth (Gilmore, 2010).

Scholars have offered various explanations for these changes in academic achievement and motivation across adolescence. Some blame the seemingly unavoidable storm and stress of adolescence (e.g., Blos, 1965), whereas others suggest that these declines result from multiple simultaneous changes, such as when adolescents experience dramatic changes in pubertal development right when they transition to junior high school (Simmons & Blyth, 1987). More recently, scholars have pointed to certain features of traditional high schools that may create a poor fit between adolescents and their classroom environments, thus leading to declines in academic

High school dropout rates, provinces and territories • Figure 10.5

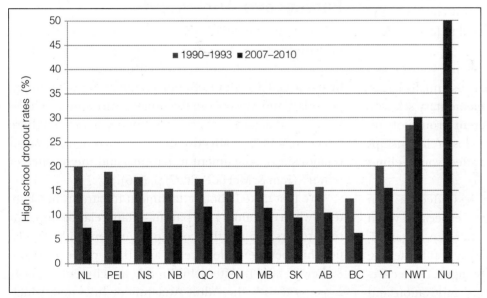

A dropout is defined as a 20- to 24-year-old without a high school diploma and not in school.

Data for 1990–1993 for Yukon are not available; data used are for the years 1992–1995.

Data for 1990–1993 for Northwest Territories are not available; data used are for the years 2001–2004.

Source: Statistics Canada, Labour Force Survey. Data retrieved from www.statcan.gc.ca/pub/81-004-x/2010004/article/11339-eng.htm.

Think Critically Considering various levels of an adolescent's social world, can you think of microsystem and exosystem factors that might explain changes in high school drop out rates? What do you notice about locations with predominantly Indigenous youth? Can you think of systemic issues impacting Indigenous youth differently than non-Indigenous youth?

motivation and achievement (Eccles & Midgley, 1989; Eccles & Roeser, 2011). These features range from grading practices and the structure of classroom activities, to the goals of learning in school (see Eccles & Roeser, 2011, for a review). In Chapter 7 we introduced mastery goals (which emphasize self-improvement and skill development) and performance goals (which emphasize ability level and competition). High schools are more likely to promote performance goals than elementary schools (Midgley, 2002). Yet students and teachers alike feel more effective when mastery is the goal of classroom learning. The one central person who ties all of these features together is the teacher.

Increasing teacher control Imagine you are a junior high or middle school student. You are more mature than you were as an elementary school student, and you certainly desire more autonomy and control, but your teachers actually give you *fewer* opportunities for decision-making and self-management. How might this mismatch affect your motivation to learn?

One team of researchers sought to answer this question by looking at how students' interest in mathematics changed across the junior high school transition (MacIver & Reuman, 1988). Students who reported a decrease in decision-making opportunities during this transition also reported the largest decreases in interest in mathematics. The takeaway: increasing teacher control can leave the control-seeking adolescent less motivated to learn.

Decreasing teacher efficacy Now picture yourself as a junior high school teacher. You have substantially larger classes than your colleagues in the elementary schools, and each day you teach several different groups of students, making it doubly hard to form close relationships with any one of them. How might this affect your feelings of effectiveness as a teacher?

Junior high school teachers feel less effective than their elementary school counterparts, especially when they have low-achieving students (Juvonen, Le, Kaganoff, Augustine, & Constant, 2004; Midgley, Feldlaufer, & Eccles, 1988). Because teachers' feelings of effectiveness are associated with their students' motivation and achievement (Ashton & Webb, 1986), we should not be surprised to see declines in students' academic motivation and achievement as they transition into high school. What about the transition to high school?

The high school transition Many of the same issues appear to continue across the transition to high school (see Eccles & Roeser, 2011, for a review). High schools are usually larger than junior high and elementary schools, so it becomes even harder for students to receive the guidance and support they need from non-familial adults. High schools also often sort students into different curricular tracks. Because track assignments can have more to do with students' ethnic group and socio-economic status than their abilities and interests (Lee & Smith, 2001), curricular tracking may actually reinforce ethnic and socio-economic status differences in academic achievement.

One equalizer of school success among adolescents occurs at home (Leung & Leung, 1992). Although exactly how much impact parents have on academic success remains uncertain, it appears that adolescents in intact families (where the original parents are raising their children) experience higher academic achievement and subjective well-being (Suldo et al., 2009). Attitudes about academic achievement held by parents appear to have significant impact on school success, particularly in minority families (Strom, Strom, & Beckert, 2008). Clearly, parents play an important and continuous role in adolescents' lives.

Parents and Adolescents

Throughout the childhood years, parents had the final say with their children on who to have as friends, where to go, what to eat, and even what to wear. Adolescence brings a new freedom of choice coinciding with longer periods of time away from the home environment. That is not to say that parents have no influence. However, there is a change in "the affective quality of parent–adolescent relationships, attachment to parents, and the balance of power" (Kan & McHale, 2007, p. 566).

We first talked about attachment to parents in Chapter 4, when examining the parent–infant relationship. But researchers also use this concept to understand the relationship between adolescents and their parents (Lamb & Lewis, 2011). After childhood, attachment security is assessed with the Adult Attachment Interview, which determines adolescents' ability to integrate their early memories of parental attachment into a realistic, positive working model of relationships (George, Kaplan, & Main, 1985; Main & Goldwyn, 1994). Adolescents are classified

**secure/
autonomous** An
attachment category
in which adolescents
display the ability to
recognize both the
positive and negative
aspects of childhood
attachment figures.

**insecure/
dismissive**
An attachment
category in which
adolescents minimize
considerations of
early experiences
and relationships,
or downplay the
importance of
early attachment
experiences.

**insecure/
preoccupied**
An attachment
category in which
adolescents display
preoccupation with
early experiences and
attachment figures,
but experience
difficulty evaluating
those relationships.

as **secure/autonomous** (able to freely evaluate their early attachments), **insecure/dismissive** of their attachment relationships, or **insecure/preoccupied** with these relationships. Autonomous or securely attached adolescents are rated by their peers as less anxious, hostile, and aggressive, and more prosocial and resilient (Dykas, Ziv, & Cassidy, 2008; Kobak & Sceery, 1988). These adolescents report higher levels of social support and lower levels of distress. On the other hand, adolescents in the dismissive group are rated by their peers as high on hostility and low on resilience. Preoccupied adolescents are also rated by peers as low on resilience, but they report higher levels of distress than the dismissive group. These categories seem to be passed down through the generations, in that autonomous adults tend to respond more sensitively to their infants, who in turn are more likely to be securely attached (see van IJzendoorn, 1995).

One key research question in the literature on parent–adolescent relationships is how parental gender affects communication and development (Sim, 2003). As in childhood, mothers tend to spend more time with their adolescent children than do fathers, although this may be changing in some families (Lewis, 2009; Parke, 2004). In an investigation of how parental gender and child gender interact, one research team found that daughters tended to experience more pressure from fathers and more emotional support from mothers. Sons experienced more conflict with fathers than did daughters and felt more support from mothers (McKinney & Renk, 2008).

In general, however, although mother–daughter and father–son differences may exist, style of parenting appears to be a more powerful predictor of adjustment in adolescence (McKinney & Renk, 2008). Indeed, the way parents communicate with their adolescent child seems to follow a developmental pattern that began in early childhood, a pattern that is coloured by parental style (Baumrind, 1993).

Recall our discussion of Baumrind's parenting styles in Chapter 6 and think about what these styles might look like in adolescence. Baumrind (1993) suggests that the consistency and clarity on limit setting of authoritative parenting provide a stable context for the adolescent. Authoritarian parenting, on the other hand, is characteristically punitive and inconsistent, and associated with internalizing problem behaviours. In short, if trust, honesty, and openness were present earlier in life, they tend to continue into adolescence (Parke, 2004).

Scholars used to think that peer influence gradually replaced parental influence during adolescence (Coleman, 1961; Freud, 1958). The biological changes associated with puberty, together with intergenerational conflict over values and behaviour, theoretically led to parental detachment and conflict. This emotional upheaval between adolescents and their parents was even seen as a necessary part of the transition from childhood to adulthood. Here, again, we see the powerful influence of G. Stanley Hall's storm-and-stress view of adolescence as an inherently tumultuous stage of development. These ideas have not been supported by research, however. Most adolescents continue to look to their parents for support, advice, and emotional intimacy, even as peer culture plays an increasingly important role (Maccoby & Martin, 1983; McGrellis, Henderson, Holland, Sharpe, & Thomson, 2000).

Peer Culture

What group of peers did you hang out with in high school? What groups of peers did you not like? These questions get at a well-researched and pervasive element of adolescent peer culture: the **crowd**. A crowd shares certain qualities such as athletic skill (jocks), popularity (populars), or drug use (druggies) (**Figure 10.6**). Crowds

crowd A group of
people who may or
may not be friends
but who share similar
attributes to one
another.

have a hierarchical structure and individuals often receive status based on identification with particular levels. The benefits of being in a high-status crowd are many. Generally, the jocks, the highest-status crowd, set the norms for

High school crowds • Figure 10.6

Classic research on peer culture identified these five common crowds, listed from highest to lowest in peer status (Brown & Lohr, 1987). Crowds have powerful implications for the lives of adolescents. For example, the self-esteem of crowd members is directly related to the status of their crowd.

a. Jocks, members of the highest-status crowd, are athletically oriented students and may be a part of a sports team.

b. Populars tend to be well-known students who organize and play a leading role in social activities.

Maggie Steber/National Geographic Creative

ZUMA Press, Inc./Alamy

the entire peer culture, decide what is or is not cool, and are in the enviable position to dictate who gets in and who does not. Members of a crowd may or may not actually be friends with one another.

Another feature of adolescent peer culture is the **clique**. In some cases, cliques have been together for years, may live close to one another, and belong to the same church. Members of cliques typically identify strongly with fellow members (Bishop et al., 2004).

clique A tight-knit group of friends who share similar values and behaviours.

There are two major differences between peer groups in childhood and peer groups in adolescence (Eccles & Roeser, 2011). First, adolescents spend substantially more time in peer groups than do children. Second, adolescents are much more preoccupied with being accepted by their peer groups. In fact, social acceptance is one of the biggest predictors of self-esteem during adolescence,

even more so than perceiving oneself as cognitively competent (Harter, 1990).

Adolescents tend to form peer groups with those who share similar activity preferences and motivations. And then these peer groups reinforce members' preferences and motivational values (Berndt & Keefe, 1995). As we see in **Figure 10.7**, this reinforcement can be positive if the peer group is characterized by positive values and behaviours (Eccles, Barber, Stone, & Hunt, 2003). But what would we expect in the case of an anti-social peer group?

Peer group influences may help to explain certain ethnic differences during adolescence (Steinberg, Dornbusch, & Brown, 1992). For example, European-American youths' higher academic performance may be better explained by ethnic differences in peer support than ethnic differences in parental support. Adolescents across ethnic groups report strong parental support for academics,

c. Normals are average students who make up the majority.

Pablo Corral Vega/National Geographic

Brooke Auchincloss/Onoky/Getty Images

d. Druggies/toughs are known among their peers for illicit drug use and/or delinquent behaviour.

Steve Stanford/Alamy

e. Nobodies, belonging to the lowest status crowd, tend to have poorer social skills and academic performance.

Think Critically Now that it's been over 20 years since this classic research was conducted, would you add or remove any crowds? Would you reorder the peer status of these crowds? How relevant was this to your experiences?

but Hispanic-American and African-American students report less support from peers than European-American and Asian-American students (Steinberg et al., 1992).

What rules govern crowds and cliques? To explore this question, one research team interviewed over 100,000 middle and high school students and found the following (Bishop et al., 2004):

1. *Boundaries* Crowds have clear boundaries that are defined by key members of the crowd. The boundaries are most fluid during the transition from middle school to high school. Often new members of upper-status crowds have to abandon former friends and behave in a new way to please fellow members. Lower-status crowds are more fluid and easier to enter.

2. *Crowd membership* The factors that determine crowd membership generally focus on specific characteristics. For example, qualities that often enable a person to

become a member of a high-status crowd include having higher socio-economic status, having athletic ability, being attractive, and having high academic performance. Individuals who possess none of the required qualities to be in high-status crowds often are labelled *losers, geeks,* or *freaks,* and are viewed as outcasts by the popular crowds. There are other subgroups called *posers* who dress, act, and behave like popular crowds but do not have membership.

3. *Peer pressure* Crowd membership can result in peer pressure to behave in negative ways (Bishop et al., 2004). For example, there may be pressure to de-emphasize academics or to harass members of lower-status crowds. Peer pressure during adolescence appears to be strongest in the context of peer groups. Adolescents are more likely to take risks when they are in groups (Gardner & Steinberg, 2005).

Positive and negative peer group influences • Figure 10.7

Whether or not peer group reinforcement is positive depends on the type of behaviours and values that characterize the group (Eccles et al., 2003).

a. High-achieving Marcus is part of a clique made up of other high achievers. His academic accomplishments motivate his friends to try even harder, and their hard work inspires Marcus.

b. Rebecca has very little motivation to do her schoolwork, which is also true for the members of her clique. Since they began hanging out freshman year, Rebecca and her friends have started skipping school and getting into trouble.

DAVID PULLIAM/KRT/Newscom

Tom Carter/Alamy

Think Critically What types of behaviours and values characterized your high school peer groups?

---

problematic Internet use
An excessive preoccupation with Internet use that leads to socio-emotional maladjustment, academic difficulties, and physical health problems.

Technology has revolutionized adolescent peer culture, opening up a whole new virtual stage on which peer group dynamics play out. Instant messaging and chatting have become the new norm for socializing among teens (Thomas, 2013). And, now, as shown in *Challenges in Development*, with the increasing popularity of social media like Snapchat, Vine, and Instagram, researchers have revealed a new phenomenon among adolescents who cannot seem to unplug—**problematic Internet use** (Hsu & Shi, 2013; Widyanto & Griffiths, 2006; Young, 1998).

We turn now to another social influence in the lives of adolescents. Romantic relationships are at the forefront of most adolescents' minds.

Romantic Relationships

Only about a third of 15- and 16-year-olds report currently having a boyfriend or girlfriend (Feiring, 1996). But even if they are not in a dyadic relationship with a significant

other, adolescents are often already on the road toward such relationships, as we explore in **Figure 10.8**.

A four-phase model was advanced to describe the stages of building a romantic relationship (Brown, 1999). In the first, **initiation phase**, early adolescents begin to notice and become comfortable with sexually attractive others. The focus during the initiation phase is more on the self than on the relationship. Young teens explore whether they have the confidence and self-esteem to be friends with someone they are attracted to and whether a relationship beyond friendship is possible (Seiffge-Krenke, 2003).

As adolescents get older and move into dyadic relationships, they enter the **status phase**. This phase follows Elkind's (1967) idea of the imaginary audience, discussed in Chapter 9. Here the concern is about dating the right people. One must not be

initiation phase
The first phase in a four-phase model of early romantic relationships in which adolescents begin to notice and become comfortable with others perceived as sexually attractive.

status phase The second phase in a four-phase model of early romantic relationships in which crowd and status influence how an adolescent couple develops.

CHALLENGES IN DEVELOPMENT
Problematic Internet Use

Ninety-three percent of youth between the ages of 12 and 17 years are online, spending an average of 14 hours per week on the Internet (Milani, Osualdella, & Di Blasio, 2009; Strasburger, Jordan, & Donnerstein, 2010). Researchers have wondered if the attractiveness of the Internet, especially highly interactive applications like online chatting, could be addictive for some young people (for a review, see Thomas, 2013). Four components of problematic Internet use have been identified (see the photo; Block, 2008; Yu, Kim, & Hay, 2013).

Problematic Internet use can interfere with adolescents' academic performance and sleep, and can increase the likelihood of depressive symptoms (Cheung & Wong, 2011; Huang & Leung, 2009; Park, 2009). Adolescents addicted to the Internet are lonelier and have lower self-esteem and poorer social skills than adolescents who are moderate users (Ghassemzadeh, Shahraray, & Moradi, 2008). Another concern is that problematic Internet use puts adolescents at risk for sexual solicitation and cyberbullying (Leander, Christianson, & Granhag, 2008; Mesch, 2009).

Parental relationships and gender may also be tied to problematic Internet use. Adolescents who perceive their parents as intrusive, punitive, and lacking warmth were more likely to exhibit problematic Internet use (Huang, Zhang, Li, Wang, Zhang, & Tao, 2010). Similarly, adolescents addicted to Internet games were more likely to perceive their parents as hostile and were less likely to perceive them as affectionate (Kwon, Chung, & Lee, 2011). The findings regarding gender differences in problematic Internet use are less consistent. However, a majority of studies show that male adolescents tend to be more addicted to the Internet than female adolescents (Chou, Condron, & Belland, 2005; Hawi, 2012; Li, Zhang, Li, Zhen, & Wang, 2010).

Four components of problematic Internet use

Whether the focus is excessive gaming or email and text messaging, problematic Internet use involves four components (Block, 2008; Yu et al., 2013).

| **1. Excessive use** |
| Losing sense of time and neglecting basic needs |
| **2. Withdrawal** |
| Feeling angry, tense, and/or depressed when the computer is unavailable |
| **3. Obsession** |
| Needing better equipment, more computer software, or more hours on the Internet |
| **4. Negative consequences** |
| Lying, social isolation, fatigue, and poor achievement, among others |

Alen Ajan/Getty Images

Think Critically Problematic Internet use can be hard to treat and is associated with high relapse rates. Why do you think this is the case?

---

affection phase
The third phase in a four-phase model of early romantic relationships in which the emphasis shifts away from the influence of peers to the development of a meaningful connection between two individuals.

seen with someone in a different crowd. During this phase, the couple gets to know one another and either moves closer or terminates their relationship. Values, behaviours, and similarity are explored during this phase.

If they make it through the status phase, the couple enters the **affection phase**. Here a shift in emphasis occurs from the

contextual influence of the crowd to a meaningful connection between two individuals. There is a higher likelihood of sexual activity in this phase as the couple begins to communicate and express mutual romantic feelings.

If they are still together through the affection phase, they may make it to the final phase: bonding. The **bonding phase**

bonding phase
The fourth phase in a four-phase model of early romantic relationships in which relationship becomes characterized by a high level of commitment and a future orientation.

Shifts in social relationships through adolescence • Figure 10.8

The developmental progression toward dyadic romantic relationships tends to occur in a series of overlapping stages (Feinstein & Ardon, 1973; McCabe, 1984).

Cultura/Benedicte Vanderreydt/Getty Images

1 Same-gender friends: Younger adolescents tend to spend time with people most like them.

Jeff Greenberg/Photo Edit

2 Mixed-gender friends: Spending time with a range of friends regardless of gender then becomes more commonplace.

PYMCA/Alamy

3 Dating: Eventually, couples pair off and begin dating, which may occur in groups.

Tassii/iStockphoto

4 Exclusive attachment: Finally, an exclusive romantic attachment develops between just two people (called a *dyad*).

Think Critically How might an adolescent's working model of relationships affect his or her progression through these stages?

entails a commitment not seen in earlier phases. This phase contains "the possibilities of remaining together with a romantic partner for a lifetime" (Seiffge-Krenke, 2003, p. 520). Obviously, the bonding phase will only occur after a couple has been together for a reasonable amount of time and is of an age when considerations of commitment are meaningful.

Although this model provides insights into the development of adolescent romances, it does have limitations. First, the model does not specify actual ages associated with these phases. Second, it is unclear what variables influence

dissolution or resolution in the event of dissatisfaction. Finally, we must be mindful that emerging homosexual attraction typically follows a different trajectory due to the general lack of social acceptance of such relationships.

Emerging homosexual attraction Emerging homosexual attraction follows a different course than that of heterosexual attraction. We depict the typical stages of homosexual attraction in **Figure 10.9**. Despite follow-up research to further understand these steps (e.g., Rosario, Schrimshaw, Hunter, & Braun, 2006), homosexual

Emerging homosexual attraction • Figure 10.9

✓ THE PLANNER

The steps here were proposed by Cass (1984) to describe the course of homosexual attraction. Although a person may progress linearly through the steps, he or she may also skip steps or cycle back through steps over and over.

ColorBlind Images/The Image Bank/Getty Images

Image Source/Alamy

Epa european pressphoto agency b.v./Alamy

1 Identity confusion

In this stage, adolescents experience confusion, as previously held identities regarding sexual orientation are questioned. The adolescent will either entertain the possibility of a homosexual identity or reject this possibility and foreclose further development of a homosexual identity. (Foreclosure is possible in each stage of development.)

2 Identity comparison

Having accepted the possibility of a homosexual identity, adolescents may then face feelings of isolation as they compare themselves with non-homosexual adolescents.

3 Identity tolerance

This stage is characterized by tolerance of a homosexual self-image, but not yet acceptance of it. Increasing tolerance leads adolescents to begin to make contact with other homosexuals to fulfill socio-emotional and sexual needs. But often two separate images are maintained: a public heterosexual image and a private homosexual one.

4 Identity acceptance

Increased contact with the gay subculture leads to a more positive view of homosexual identity. Adolescents begin to selectively disclose their sexual orientation to significant others.

5 Identity pride

In this stage, adolescents feel pride for their homosexual identity and hold homosexuals as a group in high regard. The stigma around homosexuality generates feelings of anger and may lead to confrontation with non-homosexuals.

6 Identity synthesis

Homosexual identity is no longer seen as the overarching identity. Adolescents see themselves as multi-dimensional people, only one dimension of which involves homosexuality. Public and private self-images are synthesized into one cohesive identity, leading to a sense of peace and stability.

Think Critically Do you think heterosexual development, like homosexual development, is non-linear? Why do you think this may or may not be the case?

development remains less researched and understood than heterosexual development.

It is evident in Figure 10.9 that sexual orientation minority groups such as lesbian, gay, bisexual, transgender, queer, and questioning (LGBTQ) adolescents face certain challenging life conditions that influence their sexual identity (Shenkman & Shmotkin, 2013).

Stigma, prejudice, and discrimination create a stressful context for these minority groups and can lead to mental health problems (Meyer, 2003). Compared with their heterosexual counterparts, homosexual adolescents are more concerned about being victimized, lacking social and family support, failing to find love, and having poor health (Shenkman & Shmotkin, 2013). Internal stressors, such as the failure to accept one's sexual orientation, can also affect LGBTQ adolescents' well-being. We turn now to teen dating violence, a phenomenon that affects both homosexual and heterosexual adolescents.

Teen dating violence Despite efforts to address it, **teen dating violence** remains a significant public health concern that causes both immediate harm to youth and puts them at risk for negative developmental outcomes, such as educational difficulties (Banyard & Cross, 2008; Centers for Disease Control and Prevention, 2012). Although estimates vary, most studies reveal that teen dating violence affects both males and females. In Canada, there has been a rise in reported incidences of dating violence. Between 2004 and 2008, for example, police-reported dating violence against female persons increased by 40 percent (Mahony, 2010). In 2013, dating violence accounted for 53 percent of police-reported incidents of intimate partner violence, surpassing reports of spousal violence (47 percent). Approximately four in 10 female victims (41 percent) of violent crimes were victimized by an intimate partner, a proportion that was 3.5 times higher than for men (12 percent), who are more frequently victimized by a friend or acquaintance (40 percent), or a stranger (36 percent). Young adults have the highest rate of dating violence, with the risk of intimate partner victimization decreasing with age. In 2013, the highest rate of police-reported dating violence involved victims aged 20 to 24 years (653.7 per 100,000 population). Those aged 15 to 19 reported dating violence at a rate of 398.7 per 100,000 (Canadian Centre for Justice Statistics, 2015). This is down from 2010, when this age group reported the highest rates of dating violence of any age category at 948 per 100,000 (Sinha, 2012). The drop may be due in part to the different databases used to report on the issue, with the Sinha paper including both police databases and a general survey of the population.

These data make it clear that romantic relationships during adolescence can involve some serious challenges. But even when they appear rosy, adolescents' romantic relationships are marked by intense and shifting emotions, the topic we explore next.

> **teen dating violence** Physical assault by a boyfriend or girlfriend against his or her romantic partner that may include psychological and sexual violence.

CONCEPT CHECK 🛑 STOP

1. **How** does increasing teacher control influence adolescents' academic motivation and achievement?
2. **What** are some correlates of Baumrind's parenting styles during adolescence?
3. **What** is the difference between a crowd and a clique?
4. **How** are the developmental patterns of homosexual and heterosexual attraction similar and different?

Emotional Development

LEARNING OBJECTIVES

1. **Differentiate** emotion from emotion regulation in adolescence.
2. **Discuss** the appearance of depression during adolescence.
3. **Discuss** adolescent suicide, including differences between males and females.

There is no doubt that adolescence is a period of transformation and change. As we have discussed, puberty, social interactions, and a continuing struggle for identity can be heavy burdens for a developing teen. How do these challenges relate to an adolescent's emotional development? As we will discuss in a moment, most teens successfully regulate their emotions and consequently control their behaviours well. In some situations, this is harder than others; a **young offender** would likely be an adolescent who struggled with emotional or behavioural control for various complex reasons.

Youth who have been charged with criminal behaviour and who are under the age of 18 used to be categorized as young offenders. Canadians have historically struggled with our priorities about how the system should respond to young offenders—rehabilitation or repression, treatment or punishment (Bala, 1997). From 1984 to 2003, youth under the age of 18 were governed by the Young Offenders Act (YOA). But in 2003, the YOA was replaced by the Youth Criminal Justice Act (YCJA), which did away with the term "young offenders." The YCJA differs from the YOA on three key points. First, it focuses on diverting youth away from the court system through community-based responses to non-violent offences and crime prevention programs. Second, it aims to improve decision-making at all levels of the justice system to ensure meaningful consequences that reinforce accountability and reduce the use of custody. Third, it introduces a simplified process for applying adult sentences to extremely violent offenders.

Has the YCJA accomplished its goals? In terms of reducing the number of youth who are accused of crimes from actually being charged, it seems to have succeeded. **Figure 10.10** shows the trends hovering at or above 60 percent for the majority of years leading up to the implementation of the YCJA, after which it fell to below 50 percent and remained stable. Under the YOA, the use of courts and custody had risen, and in the early years of the millennium, Canada had one of the highest rates of youth in custody in the world. Under the YCJA, the rate of youth in custody has decreased without an increase in reported youth crime (Bala, Carrington, & Roberts, 2009). In 2010/2011, there were approximately 14,800 youth (aged 12 to 17 at the time of the offence) in Canada's correctional system, a rate of approximately 79 youth per 10,000. This rate was 6 percent lower than the rate reported in 2009/2010, and 12 percent lower than in 2005/2006 (Munch, 2012). The discussion continues about how to handle youth who have committed crimes. Some advocate for an abolition approach where alternatives outside of the justice system are the default, whereas others continue to focus on how the existing approach can be modified.

Parenting behaviours are strongly correlated with youth crime (Hoeve, Dubas, Eichelsheim, van der Laan, Smeenk, & Gerris, 2009). From a meta-analysis of 161 studies, researchers concluded that parents who reject their children and/or who do not supervise their children are particularly likely to raise children who commit

Proportion of Canadian chargeable youth who were charged (1986–2007) • Figure 10.10

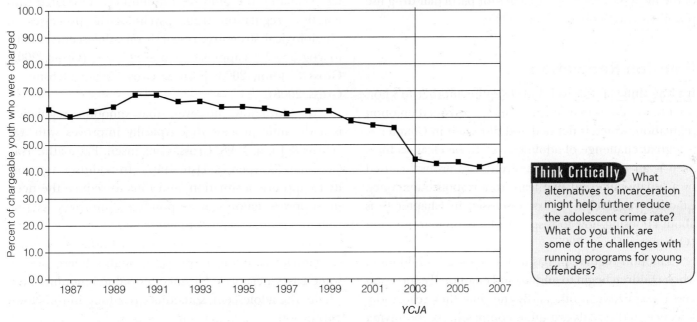

Think Critically What alternatives to incarceration might help further reduce the adolescent crime rate? What do you think are some of the challenges with running programs for young offenders?

Source: Statistics Canada, Canadian Centre for Justice Statistics, Uniform Crime Reporting Survey.

crimes. This link was strongest in the earlier years of life, with parents seeming to have less influence during later adolescence (Hoeve et al., 2009).

Individuals who have been abused or neglected are at particular risk of engaging in criminal behaviour. In fact, they are 38 percent more likely to commit violent crimes if no intervention occurs (Widom, 1992). The more forms of abuse a particular child has experienced, the more likely he or she is to become delinquent. Maltreated individuals who have experienced academic problems, substance abuse issues, or mental health problems; who have run away from home; and/or who have associated with deviant peers seem to be most likely to become involved in delinquent acts (Bender, 2010).

Treating young offenders can be difficult, but it is necessary because without intervention, 60 to 80 percent will reoffend (Jenson & Howard, 1998). Unfortunately, current treatment techniques that typically make use of group therapy may lead to increased criminal activities. In a process called *deviancy training*, young offenders often teach each other how to be even more deviant. Research continues in order to determine how best to improve treatment outcomes. It seems that having an adult present during all group sessions and having well-structured sessions may help to reduce some negative effects of group treatment (Cécile & Born, 2009). Given that illicit drug use is implicated in recidivism, it is unfortunate that only some programs have a substance use component; programs for Aboriginal youth that offer multisystemic approaches, where many societal issues are considered, create some of the most innovative approaches for particular drug use problems (Erickson & Butters, 2005).

Emotion Regulation

It's one thing to feel sad, but it's quite another to know what to do about that feeling. The latter, called emotion regulation, which is defined and discussed in Chapter 8, is a great challenge of adolescence. To be clear, sadness itself is an emotion, or an awareness of arousal caused by a situational event that leads to a response tendency. Emotion regulation, as first discussed in Chapter 6, is about choosing how to respond to a particular emotion (Ochsner & Gross, 2008).

Emotion regulation has its roots in early childhood, when children begin to understand emotional expression and recognize it in others. By the time they reach adolescence, individuals are quite competent at identifying emotions in themselves and others. In addition, the cognitive developments of adolescence enable the young adolescent to attach a number of possible meanings to each emotion. This ability can be both a curse and a blessing. Is a friend angry because a boy didn't ask her out, or because of something you did (or didn't do!)? Decisions about how to act toward this friend are likely to ride largely on interpretation. Thus, without a stable and reliable peer group with whom to talk these issues out, emotion regulation can be particularly difficult (Yap, Allen, & Sheeber, 2007).

Researchers have identified two key strategies in the process of emotion regulation (Gross & John, 2004). The first is **cognitive reappraisal**, in which one reassesses the emotion-causing situation. The second, **expressive suppression**, focuses on suppressing the emotional response tendency. Both are challenges for adolescents (**Figure 10.11**).

Young adults who choose appraisal over suppression appear to be psychologically healthier than those who choose suppression. One's tendency toward appraisal or suppression is related to factors such as temperament, family communication patterns, and intelligence (John & Gross, 2004). Although there are many research studies evaluating the individual differences associated with emotion regulation from psychological processes to physiological structure, research on adolescents' ability to cognitively reappraise remains scarce (Gross, 2002; Gross & John, 2003; John & Gross, 2004; Ochsner & Gross, 2008).

We do know, however, that emotion regulation is a dynamic process that typically improves with age (Gross & John, 1998; Gross, Carstensen, Pasupathi, Tsai, Götestam Skorpen, & Hsu, 1997). In addition, the ability to appraise a situation, and thus to reduce the need to suppress emotional responding, improves as one becomes more socially competent and less prone to emotionality (Gross, 2002; Saarni, 1993). Although the ability to regulate emotion improves through adolescence, in some cases negative and uncomfortable emotions overwhelm the adolescent, sometimes resulting in full-blown depression.

cognitive reappraisal The ability to re-evaluate the cause of an emotional state and mediate the response.

expressive suppression An emotion regulation strategy that inhibits one's emotional response without reducing the level of emotion.

Emotion regulation strategies • Figure 10.11

These illustrations show how the two key emotion regulation strategies—cognitive reappraisal and expressive suppression—play out in the real world. As shown, both strategies successfully regulate emotions but lead to very different behavioural outcomes.

a. When Jennifer does not return Samuel's wave, he evaluates the situation from a different, more positive perspective and thereby reduces any negative emotions.

b. Dante, on the other hand, negatively interprets Yibing's lack of response and then suppresses his negative emotional response.

Think Critically In what types of situations might cognitive reappraisal be a less healthy strategy?

a.

b.

Depression

Given all of the issues adolescents must cope with on a daily basis, the risk of depression is high (Horowitz & Garber, 2006; Yap et al., 2007). In fact, one out of four adolescents reports a depressive disorder (Van Voorhees, Smith, & Hickner, 2008). Females are more likely to experience depression, though males certainly become depressed as well (Angold & Costello, 2001).

As shown in *What a Developmentalist Sees*, depression causes a number of symptoms. The causes of depression in adolescence vary greatly and can include genetic vulnerability, family dysfunction, and cognitive attribution style, or the adolescent's explanation of the causes of behaviour and events (Phares, 2002). The physiological changes of adolescence may also be responsible for depressive symptoms in some adolescents (Compton, March, Brent, Albano, Weersing, & Curry, 2004).

Treatment for depression among adolescents also has its complexities. This age group has been found to be particularly sensitive about the stigma associated with seeing a therapist—they don't want their friends to know—but they are less concerned than people in other age groups about using antidepressant medications (Van Voorhees et al., 2008). This can be problematic because short-term relief may be attainable through medication, but the best long-term prognosis arises from a combination of medication and therapy (Phares, 2002). Indeed, even after treatment with antidepressants, depression often continues to be a source of family conflict, impaired functioning in relationships and school, and increased risk of drug use (Van Voorhees et al., 2008).

WHAT A DEVELOPMENTALIST SEES

Signs of Depression

You might think this teenager is just a typically sleepy adolescent (see the photo). But if this fatigue continued over time in combination with other symptoms (see the table), a clinical psychologist might consider a diagnosis of depression.

Although most people experience some signs of depression at some point in their lives, full-blown major depressive disorder is only diagnosed when a person experiences five or more symptoms every day for at least two weeks (American Psychiatric Association, 2013). Teenagers may be diagnosed with a number of other mood disorders, including a less intense but longer-lasting depressive disorder called *dysthymia*.

Joel Sartore/NG Image Collection

Think Critically What behaviours indicative of depression might a clinical psychologist look for in a teenager to ensure the validity of the diagnosis?

Nine symptoms of depression
(American Psychiatric Association, 2013)

1. Depressed mood, such as feelings of sadness, emptiness, and hopelessness.

2. Decreased interest in most activities.

3. Significant weight loss without dieting or significant weight gain.

4. Insomnia or excessive tiredness.

5. Observable restlessness or psychomotor retardation (appearing slowed down).

6. Loss of energy or fatigue.

7. Feeling worthless or excessive guilt.

8. Diminished concentration or persistent indecisiveness.

9. Recurrent thoughts of death, suicidal thoughts, or a suicide attempt.

In addition, there is concern that use of antidepressants in adolescents may increase the risk of suicide (Healy, 2009). Several research studies suggest that psychotherapies are a safer and more effective way of combating depression and suicidal thoughts that can stem from a depressed mood (Fergusson et al., 2005; Healy, 2009; Van Voorhees et al., 2008). In fact, Health Canada (2004) has ordered that warnings now be included on all antidepressants in order to alert physicians and patients to the suicide risk and to highlight the fact that Health Canada does not approve of the use of antidepressants for patients under 18 years of age. The use of antidepressants with people under age 18 is called off-label use and is recognized as a tool that doctors may use with caution. But untreated depression may be even riskier. In acknowledgement of this reality, the Canadian Paediatric Society has released a position paper focused on selective serotonin reuptake inhibitor use, which advises the use of balanced decision-making, the careful documentation of baseline symptomology before starting pharmacotherapy, and ongoing detailed monitoring following the start of pharmacotherapy (Korczak, 2013).

Adolescent Suicide

One tragic, though rare, response to the helplessness that some adolescents feel during these years is suicide. For young Canadians, suicide is one of the leading causes of death. In 2009, among those aged 15 to 34, suicide was the second leading cause of death, preceded only by accidental death. Suicide among those aged 15 to 19 represented almost a quarter (23 percent) of all deaths for this age group in 2009, up from 9 percent in 1974 (Navaneelan, 2012). Teen suicide rates remained stable between 2009 and 2011 (Statistics Canada, 2014). Males continue to outnumber females in completed suicides, although females attempt suicide more frequently. The methods range from firearms, which are used more by males, to hanging and overdosing, which are used more by females.

Health agencies continue efforts to educate parents, schools, and health professionals about the precursors to teen suicide and the complicated set of variables involved. Some warning signs of suicide include statements that life no longer has meaning, sudden efforts to give away possessions, saying goodbye to friends, and/or talking about death (Haugaard, 2000). Many suicides, however, occur with no obvious warning signs.

Suicide statistics also suggest that youth who are marginalized are at particular risk. For example, **Figure 10.12** shows the increased risk for suicidality among lesbian, gay, bisexual, transgender, two-spirited, or queer youth. Also, members of racial minorities tend to be more likely to attempt suicide than Caucasians (Garcia, Skay, Sieving, Naughton, & Bearinger, 2008). In Canada, First Nations youth are five to six times more likely to commit suicide than non-Aboriginal youth. Suicide rates for Canada's Inuit youth are among the highest in the world, and are 11 times the national average (Health Canada, 2015). Researchers report high rates of **suicidal ideation**, attempts, and emotional distress in minorities, particularly among individuals who describe themselves as mixed race (Garcia

> **suicidal ideation** A continued obsession with thoughts of suicide, including the methods, time, and place of the suicide.

et al., 2008). Of these individuals, ninth-grade females appear especially prone to suicidal ideation.

Along with untreated psychological illness, the thought processes associated with adolescent egocentrism (see Chapter 9) are sometimes partly responsible for this desperate act. An adolescent's life can be filled with drama, and the imaginary audience is there to see all the failures and rejections. Research focused on prevention and awareness can be critical in determining the futures of so many bright young lives.

The devastation left behind when an adolescent commits suicide is immeasurable. Thankfully, adolescent suicide is actually very rare (Males, 2009). Much more common among adolescents is **non-suicidal self-injury** (Wilkinson & Goodyer, 2011). The onset of non-suicidal self-injury typically occurs between the ages of 12 and 16 years, though it can begin in early to middle childhood (Barrocas, Hankin, Young, & Abela, 2012; Giannetta et al., 2012; Klonsky, Muehlenkamp, Lewis, & Walsh, 2011). Self-cutting is one of the most common forms of non-suicidal self-injury. Although sharp physical

> **non-suicidal self-injury** Deliberate self-injury with no suicidal intent for the purpose of self-punishment, managing negative emotions, or communicating personal distress.

LGBTQ youth and suicide • Figure 10.12

Darrin Henfry/iSockphoto

Source: Centre for Suicide Prevention, www.suicideinfo.ca

Lesbian, gay, bisexual, transgender, two-spirited, or queer youth are at increased risk for suicide. D'Augelli and colleagues (2001) found that:

- 42 percent of LGBTQ youth studied had thoughts of suicide at some time
- 25 percent had thoughts of suicide in 2000
- 48 percent said thoughts of suicide were clearly or to some degree related to their sexual orientation
- 54 percent of suicide attempts occurred before parents knew of the youth's sexual orientation.

Youth who are lesbian, gay, bisexual, transgender, two-spirited, queer, or unsure of their sexual orientation were 3.4 times more likely to report a suicide attempt in the previous 12-month period.

Think Critically How is sexual orientation discussed in your circles? How might communities, families, and friends create conversations about sexual orientation that are supportive of youth?

pain can temporarily distract adolescents from difficult feelings, non-suicidal self-injury can have long-term emotional consequences, such as leading to feelings of guilt and shame toward the self. Depressive symptoms are consistently associated with non-suicidal self-injury during adolescence and into adulthood, the next period of the lifespan we examine (Klonsky, Oltmanns, & Turkheimer, 2003; Marshall, Tilton-Weaver, & Stattin, 2013).

1. **How** do adolescents attempt to regulate emotions?

2. **What** are the nine symptoms of depression?

3. **What** are some warning signs of adolescent suicide?

Summary

1 Personality Development 322

- Adolescence, a life stage defined by both physical and psychological change, was only relatively recently recognized as a distinct stage of the lifespan. G. Stanley Hall, who first identified this stage, used the phrase "storm and stress" to describe adolescence as an inherently tumultuous period of development. Hall's more negative view of adolescence is not supported by contemporary research.

- Defining one's **identity** is an important task during adolescence. Erik Erikson believed that adolescents must resolve an **identity crisis** through which they either forge a sense of identity or risk **role confusion**. Amid critiques that Erikson's **identity versus role confusion** was too narrow a concept, James Marcia instead posited four distinct identity stages: **identity diffusion**, **identity foreclosure**, **identity moratorium**, and **identity achievement**. A teen's status is based on whether the teen has undertaken an **exploration** of his or her identity, and the degree to which he or she has made a **commitment** to an aspect of identity. Marcia suggested that we can repeat tasks in the identity development process, leading to what he called the MAMA cycle.

- A person's **ethnic identity** is related to his or her level of **acculturation** to a mainstream or dominant culture.

- Across adolescence, gender identity can further intensify, becoming increasingly rigid, or be explored, becoming increasing fluid. However, many teens show **gender intensification** in their behaviour, as shown in the photo in the figure. Social learning theories suggest that gender intensification results from conditioning and modelling, whereas gender schema theories suggest that self-understanding can lead to either increases or decreases in gender rigidity.

- Many adolescents report uncertainty about their sexual orientation, and some researchers suggest that sexual identity can evolve and change, much as our self-concepts do. Teens who adopt a non-heterosexual self-definition may begin the process of **coming out** to their families and friends.

Gender identity during adolescence • Figure 10.3

David Grossman/Alamy

2 Social Influences 330

- High schools and teachers have long-lasting effects on adolescents. Adolescents' academic motivation and achievement decline across the High school transition. Scholars have pinpointed certain features of traditional High schools that may affect students' academic motivation and achievement, including increasing teacher control and decreasing teacher efficacy. The figure shows the student drop out rates and trends across the nation.

High school dropout rates, provinces and territories •
Figure 10.5

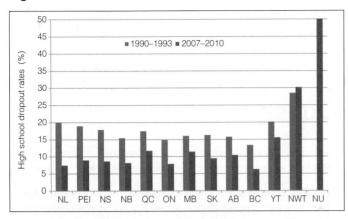

- Researchers use the concept of attachment to understand the adolescent–parent relationship and determine whether an individual is **secure/autonomous**, **insecure/dismissive**, or **insecure/preoccupied** with these relationships. Researchers also apply Baumrind's parenting styles to the adolescent period. Authoritative parenting provides a stable context for the adolescent, whereas authoritarian parenting is associated with internalizing problem behaviours.

- Teens identify with large **crowds** that tend to influence and define status. They spend time with smaller **cliques** of peers who share similar values and behaviours. Both cliques and crowds are characterized by boundaries, membership characteristics, and peer pressure.

- Instant messaging, chatting, and social media have revolutionized adolescent group dynamics, but **problematic Internet use** poses academic, socio-emotional, and physical health risks as adolescents become increasingly preoccupied with technology.

- Many teens follow a set of steps from spending most of their time with same-sex friends toward romantic attachment, usually involving sexual attraction. One four-phase model proposes that teens move through an **initiation phase**, **status phase**, and **affection phase** before moving into a **bonding phase** with a romantic partner. Homosexual attraction may follow a different trajectory.

- **Teen dating violence** is a major public health concern that affects both heterosexual and homosexual adolescents. Females experience higher rates of victimization, which can include psychological as well as sexual violence. However, males also report dating violence victimization.

3 Emotional Development 340

- Cognitive developments in adolescence can make it difficult to decide how to interpret and respond to emotions. A peer group can help adolescents interpret events and emotions. **Cognitive reappraisal** and **expressive suppression** are two possible strategies for emotional regulation. Cognitive reappraisal is usually a healthier response, and emotional regulation abilities improve with age.

- Adolescents, especially females, can become depressed. Symptoms of major depressive disorder include depressed mood, significant weight loss, and excessive tiredness, as shown in the photo. Many adolescents feel less stigma about taking antidepressant medications than about seeing therapists, but drugs can increase suicide risk, and are not as helpful alone as they are when combined with therapy.

What a Developmentalist Sees: Signs of Depression

Joel Sartore/NG Image Collection

- Teens may give warning signs before attempting or committing suicide. Suicide attempts and **suicidal ideation** are more common among minority and female adolescents. Adolescent thought processes may contribute to suicidal thoughts and actions. Much more common than adolescent suicide is **non-suicidal self-injury**, such as self-cutting.

Key Terms

Critical and Creative Thinking Questions

1. Which of Marcia's identity statuses best describes you? Why?

2. How do you feel that your ethnic identity affects or affected your own dating patterns? Did your own or your friends' dating histories seem to follow any of the models described in this chapter? How closely?

3. How would you define the term "homosexual" and why?

4. Based on your own experience or knowledge, what are some of the best ways for teachers to show support to their students?

5. Do your experiences and the experiences of people you know tend to support adolescence as healthy and normal or a time of storm and stress? How much and what kinds of conflicts with parents, moodiness, and risky behaviour do you recall, for example?

What is happening in this picture?

These girls are celebrating Christmas by going swimming in ice-cold water.

KeenPress/NG Images Collection

Think Critically

1. Would Erikson likely conclude that these girls have found their identity, are in identity crisis, or have identity confusion? Why do you think so?

2. What evidence for or against gender intensification is found in this picture?

3. Do you think these girls are part of a clique? Why or why not? What crowd would you guess they are in?

4. Do these girls seem to be experiencing storm and stress in their adolescence? Do they show any evidence of depression?

REAL  Development

Socio-emotional Development in Adolescence

In this activity, you will be learning about the socio-emotional development of adolescents.

In the first activity, you are a guidance counsellor in training. The sex education awareness initiative you developed was so successful that the school district has decided to institute a new program to address other issues important to teens. The nurse and guidance counsellor have asked you to observe interview sessions with Jenna and Michaela and analyze them to discover important issues.

In the second activity, you would like to offer parenting classes in the Eagle Glen school district. To begin the process, you will review parenting research and then analyze your findings. You are interested in the qualities, techniques, and outcomes related to different parenting styles.

John Wiley & Sons, Inc.

WileyPLUS Go to WileyPLUS to complete the REAL Development activity.

03.01

Self-Test

(Check your answers in Appendix A.)

1. Who famously said that adolescence is a period of storm and stress?

a. Erik Erikson

b. Sigmund Freud

c. G. Stanley Hall

d. James Marcia

2. Erikson believed that adolescents need to evaluate and choose among possible vocations, relationships, and other ways of understanding themselves. Erikson called this _____.

a. an identity crisis

b. identity confusion

c. a MAMA cycle

d. a moratorium

3. Fill in the four possible identity statuses defined by James Marcia.

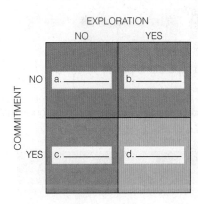

EXPLORATION

4. One factor that affects adolescents' ethnic identity is their level of _____.

a. acculturation

b. foreclosure

c. crisis

d. dating

5. Teens who shift toward more gender-stereotyped behaviour are exhibiting _____.

a. waning rigidity

b. compliance reinforcement

c. sexual orientation

d. gender intensification

6. Quentin has come to define himself as gay, and now he is beginning to inform his friends and relatives about his sexual orientation. Quentin is in the process called _____.

a. sexual identity commitment

b. libido orientation

c. gender outing

d. coming out

7. Academic failure and dropout are particularly salient problems among _____.

a. jocks

b. Aboriginal youth

c. populars

d. secure/autonomous adolescents

8. Name one key feature of traditional high schools that distinguishes them from elementary schools.

a. small classroom sizes

b. increasing teacher efficacy

c. increasing teacher control

d. mastery goals

9. Which of the following affects how well teens get along with their parents?

a. age of the teen

b. gender of the teen and the parent

c. parenting style of the parent

d. all of these

10. These students' shared participation in sports makes them part of a _____.

Maggie Steber/National Geographic Creative

a. clique

b. crowd

c. crisis

d. all of these

11. What stage of emerging social relationship is shown in this photo?

Tassii/iStockphoto

a. exclusive attachment

b. dating

c. mixed-sex friends

d. same-sex friends

12. The adolescents pictured here have begun to make contact with other homosexuals to fulfill socio-emotional and sexual needs. But they still maintain two separate self-images: a public heterosexual image and a private homosexual one. They are in the _____ stage of emerging homosexual attraction.

Image Source/Alamy

a. identity synthesis

b. identity pride

c. identity tolerance

d. identity confusion

13. Beryl just heard from Ruby that Khaled said something mean about her. Instead of acting strained around Khaled, Beryl pauses to wonder if Ruby might have misunderstood what Khaled said. Beryl is regulating her emotions with a strategy called _____.

    a. co-regulation

    b. clique reorientation

    c. cognitive reappraisal

    d. expressive suppression

14. Which of the following parent behaviours in a child's earlier years are more likely to produce delinquency in adolescence?

    a. rejection

    b. abuse or neglect

    c. lack of supervision

    d. all of the above

15. Tanara is pondering whether death would come faster if she took an overdose of pills or hanged herself. Tanara's thoughts show evidence of _____.

    a. the imaginary audience

    b. cognitive restructuring

    c. identity foreclosure

    d. suicidal ideation

THE PLANNER ✓

Review your Chapter Planner in the chapter opener and check off your completed work.

11
Physical and Cognitive Development in Emerging and Young Adulthood

These two young men are graduating from high school tonight. Around the globe, young people go through a variety of transitions as they leave adolescence and make their way into adulthood.

The first steps into adulthood take each young person in a different direction, although they are all travelling to the same place. No longer is adulthood far off in the future.

The late teens and 20s are years filled with transitions. Good health and increasing well-being help young people manage all of the changes—the graduations, the setbacks, the breakups, and the commitments. Strength of both the body and the mind are on the side of young people. Yet some will face more challenges than others, and many will experience hardships as they struggle to become an adult.

In this chapter we will explore what it means to become an adult in different cultures. We will consider the transition between adolescence and adulthood. We will see the brain continue to grow, the body peak in physical strength, and the mind find ways to make sense of the adult world. We will also take a look at stresses and outlets that young adults share.

Jeff Gritchen/Long Beach Press-Telegram

CHAPTER OUTLINE

CHAPTER PLANNER ✔

- ❑ Study the picture and read the opening story.
- ❑ Scan the Learning Objectives in each section:
  p. 354 ❑   p. 360 ❑   p. 368 ❑   p. 371 ❑
- ❑ Read the text and study all figures and visuals. Answer any questions.

Analyze key features

- ❑ Challenges in Development, p. 365
- ❑ Process Diagram, p. 369
- ❑ What a Developmentalist Sees, p. 370
- ❑ Development InSight, p. 376
- ❑ Stop: Answer the Concept Checks before you go on:
  p. 360 ❑   p. 367 ❑   p. 371 ❑   p. 377 ❑

End of chapter

- ❑ Review the Summary and Key Terms.
- ❑ Answer the Critical and Creative Thinking Questions.
- ❑ Answer *What is happening in this picture?*
- ❑ Complete the Self-Test and check your answers.

Theory: The Transition to Adulthood

LEARNING OBJECTIVES

1. **Describe** the role culture plays in defining the transition to adulthood.

2. **Debate** Arnett's theory of emerging adulthood.

3. **Discuss** markers of young adulthood.

The question of when adulthood begins is not easy to answer. Adulthood begins at different times for young people, depending on the social world in which they live.

Cultural Context of Adulthood

Culture plays a key role in determining the line between adolescence and adulthood. Cultures prepare young people for adulthood through **socialization**. Socialization is the

> **socialization** The process of acquiring the skills needed to adapt behaviours and expectations to fit the norms of a given culture.

process by which parents, teachers, and community members encourage young people to control their behaviours, develop healthy habits, and contribute to their families, schools, and communities. These messages implicitly promote taking responsibility, a key marker of adult status (Arnett, 2007).

The way each culture prepares young people for the transition to adulthood depends on that culture's needs and values. In some cultures, crossing the border into adulthood is marked with a cultural ceremony. Such cultures define the rite of passage into adulthood in various ways. Some cultures test the strength and stamina of young people, looking for evidence that the young person is prepared for the physical strain of adulthood. Other cultures come together for ceremonies and celebrations when a young person reaches a specific age of maturity, usually between 16 and 21 (**Figure 11.1**). In these cultures, the line between youth and adult is clearly demarcated. This results in a shared, cultural understanding of who is an adult and who is not.

Not all cultures have social ceremonies to mark the transition from youth to adult. In some cultures, there is no shared rite of passage that marks the transition to adulthood, and there is no clear line between adolescence and adulthood. In such cultures, becoming an adult is a personal, individualized experience, not easily observable by others. Broadly speaking, the process involves establishing oneself in the adult social world by committing to adult social roles such as employee, spouse, parent, and community member.

A rite of passage • Figure 11.1

In Japan, young people become adults in a coming-of-age ceremony known as *seijen shiki*. Coming-of-age day is celebrated on the second Monday of January. Young people transition to adulthood at age 20 when they gain the legal rights to smoke, drink, and vote.

Wdeon/Shutterstock

Think Critically 1. In Canada, what rights are granted at various ages during the transition to adulthood?
2. What messages do these rights convey about what is acceptable adult behaviour versus youth behaviour?

Mother's age at birth of first child • Figure 11.2

In 2011, the average age of mothers at the birth of their first child was 28.5 years—5 years greater than the average in 1965 (Milan, 2013).

a. This young woman, pregnant in 1965, would have approximately 4 years out of high school when she conceived her first child.

Armstrong Roberts/ClassicStock/The Image Works

b. This young woman, pregnant for the first time in 2009, had been out of university for a few years before giving birth to her first child.

Kenhurst/iStockphoto

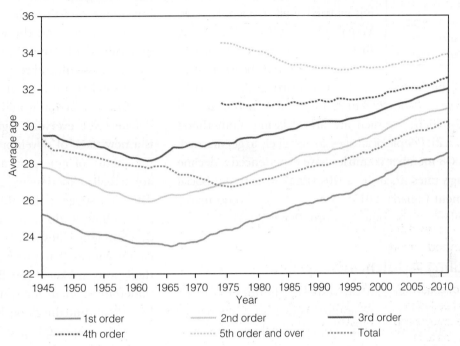

Average age of mother by birth order, Canada, 1945 to 2011

——— 1st order   ——— 2nd order   ——— 3rd order
········· 4th order   ········· 5th order and over   ········· Total

Note: Births to mothers for whom the age is unknown were prorated.
Source: Milan, A. (2013). Fertility: Overview, 2009 to 2011. Statistics Canada Catalogue no. 91-209-X. Retrieved from www.statcan.gc.ca/pub/91-209-x/2013001/article/11784-eng.pdf.

Think Critically   **1.** How are the lives of 23-year-old and 28-year-old mothers different?
2. How might greater age at first birth change the experiences young people have during the transition to adulthood?

Cultures have always varied in the extent to which becoming adult is viewed as a social, shared event or as a personal, individually determined passage. Even so, the transition to adulthood has significantly changed in the past 50 years. Global social and economic forces have altered the pathways to adulthood in Canada and beyond.

In North America, through the 1960s, young people entered careers, got married, and had children in their early to mid-20s in a relatively predictable set of transitions into adult roles. Times have changed. Today young people more often delay their entry into careers. According to Statistics Canada (2005), the restructuring of the Canadian economy over the past quarter century has had an impact on the demand for a university education. Many more entry-level jobs in today's economy require post-secondary qualifications than in the past. This means that enrolment in post-secondary education continues to climb (Statistics Canada, 2005), and it also means that youth need a way to finance this additional education.

New social norms have emerged. Now young people are much more likely to **cohabit** before marriage, and more

cohabit To live together and have a sexual relationship without being married.

young people leave their 20s not having married at all (Copen, Daniels, Vespa, & Mosher, 2012). Examining first-time marriages for Canadian couples, we see that between 1972 and 2008 the average age for first marriage increased by roughly 6 years (from 22.5 to 29.1 for women and from 24.9 to 31.1 for men). Women are also delaying motherhood (**Figure 11.2**). People of all ages are less likely to get married; all of the G8 member countries have experienced a decline in marriage rates since the 1970s (Employment and Social Development Canada, 2015). Among those who do marry, premarital sex has become the norm (Finer, 2007).

Emerging Adulthood

So what does all this mean with respect to the question, when do young people become adults? As discussed in Chapter 1, changes in the way young people are making transitions to adulthood led a developmental psychologist to argue that young people in industrialized countries in their late teens and 20s experience a stage of development between adolescence and adulthood—emerging adulthood. Based on findings from surveys (Arnett, 1997, 1998, 2000) and

qualitative interview A research method used to gain an understanding of the way others think about a topic.

qualitative interviews with over 300 young people ages 20 to 29 (Arnett, 2004), Jeffrey Arnett concluded that emerging adulthood is a new, twenty-first-century stage of life in between adolescence and young adulthood. His findings and observations led him to describe emerging adulthood as a time in life when young people explore possibilities in love

and work, and they delay committing to relationships and careers. Arnett (2004) identified five key characteristics of emerging adulthood, described in **Table 11.1**.

In the span of a decade, a new research field exploring emerging adulthood has been launched. One important question that was raised and examined by researchers around the world is, how widespread is the experience of emerging adulthood? As **Figure 11.3** shows, cross-cultural research finds evidence of emerging adulthood around the globe.

But scholarship wouldn't be complete without a good debate. Not everyone agrees that emerging adulthood is a new stage of development. One counter-argument to the theory of emerging adulthood is that young people are actually experiencing arrested, or delayed, adulthood. This view suggests that the delay in taking on adult roles has nothing to do with a new stage of exploration in the developmental lifespan, but rather is the result of economic circumstances that prevent young people from entering the labour market (Côté, 2000). High unemployment and underemployment for young people have fuelled massive protests around the globe. For example, a movement known as the Arab Spring began in 2011 and led to the overhaul of many Middle Eastern and North African governments. The Arab Spring was fuelled by massive demonstrations led primarily by people in their 20s. These emerging adults were protesting what **Figure 11.4** shows is a worldwide problem: high rates of joblessness that disproportionately affect young people between the ages of 15 and 24. Protesters argued that governments encourage youth to invest in attaining twenty-first-century education and training, but fail to provide twenty-first-century job opportunities. In countries such as Morocco, the more education a young person attains, the less likely he or she is to be employed (Dhillon & Yousef, 2009). These world developments have led many observers to conclude that emerging adulthood is not a result of young people actively selecting to delay their

The characteristics of emerging adulthood Table 11.1	
Characteristic	**Explanation**
Identity exploration	An exploration of "who am I?" especially with regard to love and work.
Instability	Work, education, and love tend to be in flux.
Self-focused	Few responsibilities and great autonomy translate into much time to attend to the self.
Feeling in-between	Emerging adults typically do not feel like adolescents, but they do not fully feel like adults either.
A time of possibilities	As emerging adults begin to create their own lives, they tend to feel great optimism about their futures.

Emerging adulthood across the globe • Figure 11.3

There is evidence of emerging adulthood from across the globe. Research findings identify variations in what young people in different countries view as markers of "being an adult."

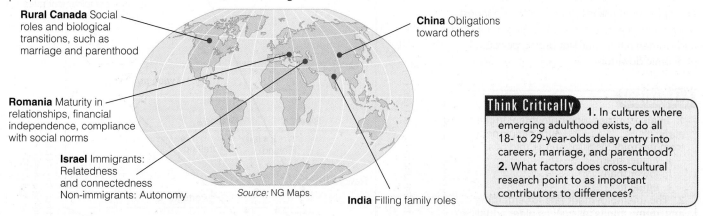

Rural Canada Social roles and biological transitions, such as marriage and parenthood

Romania Maturity in relationships, financial independence, compliance with social norms

Israel Immigrants: Relatedness and connectedness Non-immigrants: Autonomy

Source: NG Maps.

China Obligations toward others

India Filling family roles

Think Critically 1. In cultures where emerging adulthood exists, do all 18- to 29-year-olds delay entry into careers, marriage, and parenthood? 2. What factors does cross-cultural research point to as important contributors to differences?

entry into adulthood. Instead, their development is stalled due to lack of available job opportunities.

So the debate continues. Do the years between adolescence and young adulthood represent a stage of development or a delay in development? Future research on transitions to adulthood around the world will refine

our understanding and help us answer that question. New organizations, such as the Society for the Study of Emerging Adulthood featured in *Where Developmentalists Click,* support investigations of the ways young people become adult in all parts of the world. These organizations also train new researchers who want to optimize development

Where Developmentalists CLICK

The Society for the Study of Emerging Adulthood

Members of the Society for the Study of Emerging Adulthood (SSEA) study the development of people between the ages of 18 and 29. Developmentalists seek out the society's website (www.ssea.org) for the latest research, publications, and announ-cements about emerging adulthood around the globe. You can better understand emerging adulthood through cross-cultural comparisons using this website.

SSea Society for the Study of Emerging Adulthood

| HOME | ABOUT SSEA | RESOURCES | MEMBERSHIP | CONFERENCE | CONTACT US |

ABOUT SSEA

The Society for the Study of Emerging Adulthood (SSEA) is a multidisciplinary, international organization with a focus on theory and research related to emerging adulthood, which includes the age range of approximately 18 through 29 years. The primary goal of the Society is to advance the understanding of development in emerging adulthood through scholarship, education, training, policy and practice. This goal is promoted through Biennial Meetings, the flagship journal Emerging Adulthood, and a website that includes information on topics, events, and publications pertaining to emerging adults from diverse backgrounds, cultures, and countries. Membership is open to researchers, policy makers, educators and practitioners with special interests in development during this period of life.

Become a Founding Member

As a member, you will contribute to building a non-profit organization dedicated to advancing the understanding of development in emerging adulthood through scholarship, education, training, policy, and practice.

JOIN THE SSEA

Global unemployment •
Figure 11.4 _____

In countries with globalized economies, unemployment risk is highest for the youngest people in the labour force. Emerging adult men and women are hit hardest during periods of economic downturn.

Ask Yourself

1. In all countries, unemployment in the early 20s is _____ unemployment from the mid-20s through the mid-50s.
   a. higher than
   b. lower than
   c. equal to
2. The unemployment rate for emerging and young adults, as well as older adults, is highest in _____.
   a. Israel
   b. Sweden
   c. Spain
3. Identify the three countries where youth unemployment decreased between 2008 and 2012.
4. What country experienced the largest change in youth unemployment between 2008 and 2012?

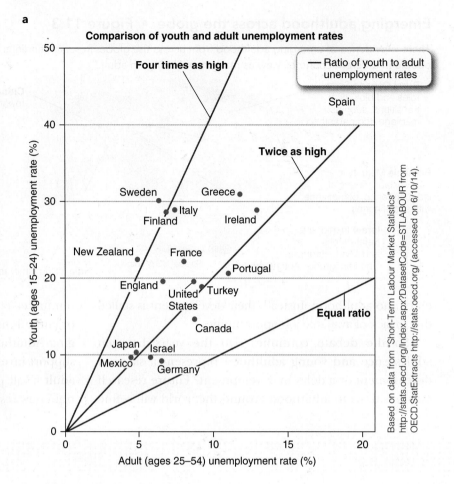

a

Comparison of youth and adult unemployment rates

Based on data from "Short-Term Labour Market Statistics" http://stats.oecd.org/Index.aspx?DatasetCode=STLABOUR from OECD.StatExtracts http://stats.oecd.org/ (accessed on 6/10/14).

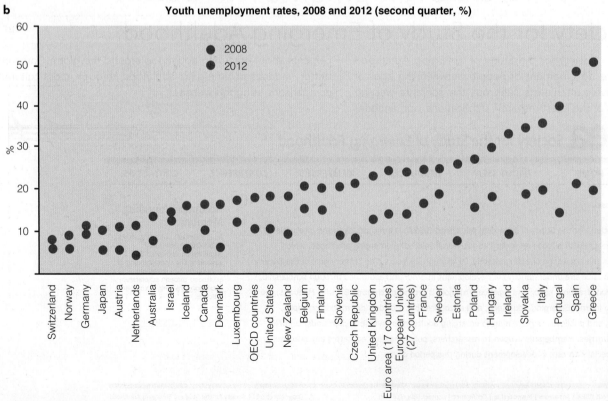

b

Youth unemployment rates, 2008 and 2012 (second quarter, %)

Source: Adapted from International Labour Organization, *Global Employment Trends for Youth 2013: A generation at risk*, Figure 5, p. 11. Retrieved from www.ilo.org/ wcmsp5/groups/ public/---dgreports/ ---dcomm/ documents/ publication/ wcms_212423.pdf.

in emerging adulthood as a way to make adult lives better—because, in the end, the vast majority of young people find their way into young adulthood.

Young Adulthood

In contrast to adolescence or emerging adulthood, **young adulthood** is a stage of

> **young adulthood**
> A stage of the lifespan when the adult is committed to one or more adult social roles, including employee, homeowner, committed partner, and parent.

the lifespan characterized by commitment to adult roles and responsibilities. Commitments to careers, marriages, and parenting are considered key markers of entry into young adulthood. The vast majority of individuals have entered into young adulthood by age 30. **Figure 11.5** shows the results of one community study that followed participants

Pathways to adulthood • Figure 11.5

When we graph emerging adults' transitions to residential and financial independence, committed relationships, and parenthood, it's easy to see how many different pathways (grey lines) there are to young adulthood. But if we think about a single person (red lines), we are reminded that the transition to adulthood involves making progress in multiple domains. And when we think about emerging adults as a group, we see that, on average (blue line), people become more independent and committed to adult roles from the late teens through the 20s.

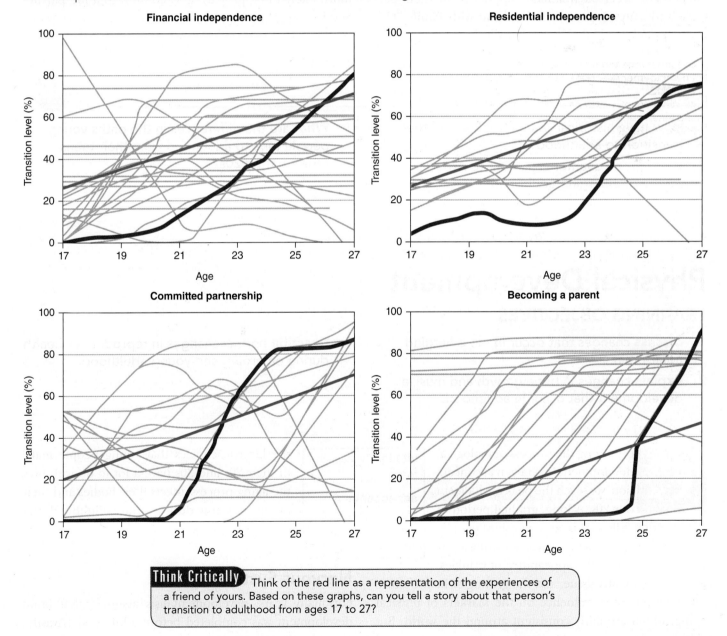

Think Critically Think of the red line as a representation of the experiences of a friend of yours. Based on these graphs, can you tell a story about that person's transition to adulthood from ages 17 to 27?

from age 17 to age 27 (Cohen, Kasen, Chen, Hartmark, & Gordon, 2003). In this study, young people completed a life chart, providing information about the events and experiences that describe how their lives changed. These narratives were coded by researchers to generate information about the level of independence and responsibility each emerging adult demonstrated across those 10 years.

The vast majority of emerging adults made progress toward independence and greater responsibility from ages 17 to 27. By the time the people in the study were 27, only 16 percent identified themselves as students. Eighty percent were employed (mostly full time). Nearly all participants were financially independent; fewer than 10 percent received financial support from their parents, and only 15 percent were living with family. The participants had also made personal commitments. Half were or had been married, and 40 percent had at least one child.

As Figure 11.5 shows, however, this study also found a great deal of variation in the paths that individual participants followed from adolescence into adulthood. Family background, including socio-economic status, gender, and race, can affect when people take on roles associated with adulthood. In general, researchers found that gains in one domain are related to gains in others (Sneed, Hamagami, McArdle, Cohen, & Chen, 2007). For example, young people who achieve greater financial independence from their parents through their 20s are also likely to have moved out of their parents' home and more likely to be preparing to commit to a life partner and to parenthood.

CONCEPT CHECK STOP

1. **How** have historical changes influenced the transition to adulthood?

2. **What** is one counter-argument to Arnett's theory of emerging adulthood?

3. **What** are the differences in the paths young people take to adulthood from their teens through their 20s?

Physical Development

LEARNING OBJECTIVES

1. **Discuss** changes that occur in the emerging adult brain.

2. **Explain** changes in bone growth and muscle development that occur in adulthood.

3. **Describe** normal changes in reproductive health during emerging and young adulthood.

Continuing the process of biological development that began at conception, we reach the peak of **vitality** in our 20s. A long, gradual period of **senescence** follows this peak. For most people, noticeable signs of aging surface during their 30s. These include the appearance of wrinkles, an increase in fatty tissue, and the greying of hair. Culture has relatively little influence on the markers of physical aging, which are fairly consistent around the world. But

vitality The capacity to live.

senescence A gradual age-related decline in physical systems.

the lifestyle choices that young people make in their 20s and 30s have a lot to do with how the aging process affects their bodies and their brains, not only during young adulthood, but also in later years.

Nervous System

For many years, developmentalists assumed that brain development was completed before adulthood (Avasthi,

Srivastava, Singh, & Srivastava, 2008). We now understand that our brains show potential for continued growth and maturation well into our 20s, and even beyond. Recently, brain researchers have paid increasing attention to the **plasticity** of our brains during our 20s and 30s. **Figure 11.6** shows that the brain sculpting begun in early childhood continues into adulthood. Brain changes through the 20s and beyond occur primarily in the prefrontal cortex as a result of ongoing pruning (Petanjek et al., 2011) and increasing white matter volume (Lebel & Beaulieu, 2011).

As the prefrontal cortex develops, the **executive system** evolves. Maturation of the executive system involves increasingly complex coordination of two or more areas of the brain. The executive system matures as a result of the types of experiences young people have during the transition to adulthood. Emerging adulthood puts demands on executive functioning abilities: emotional control, organization, planning and prioritizing, goal-directed persistence, and time management (Hedden & Gabrieli, 2004). Some emerging adults have more sophisticated executive systems than others. Underdeveloped or poor executive functioning skills can impede progress toward becoming more responsible during the transition to adulthood. Problems with executive functioning are most often associated with attention-deficit/hyperactivity disorder (ADHD), but are also seen in others who do not meet the criteria for ADHD (**Figure 11.7**). Executive functioning abilities play a role in predicting educational and occupational attainment in the 20s, 30s, and mid-life (Andersson & Bergman, 2011).

Brain development influences and is influenced by the development and aging of other biological systems. As you learn more about changes in muscles, bones, and the reproductive system across the 20s and 30s next, keep in mind the fact that the workings of all biological systems are interrelated.

plasticity A process whereby the brain continues to change.

executive system A set of complex and sophisticated cognitive control and management abilities that require coordination of more than one region of the brain to perform.

Brain development into the 20s • Figure 11.6

a. The blue areas of these brain scans represent loss in grey matter volume. Losing grey matter in specific brain areas indicates that those areas of the brain are maturing. **b.** In emerging adulthood, maturation is primarily located in the prefrontal cortex, the region responsible for coordinating communications between different areas of the brain.

a.

5 yrs

AGE

20 yrs

>0.5
0.4
0.3
0.2
0.1
0.0

Grey Matter Volume

Courtesy Paul Thompson (USC) and Judith Rapoport (NIMH)

b. **Parietal lobe**
Touch, taste, pain, pressure, hot and cold

Frontal lobe
Speech, thought, short-term memory

Prefrontal lobe
Planning, prioritizing, complex decision-making

Temporal lobe
Sound and language coordination

Occipital lobe
Vision

Think Critically What are the implications of these findings for policies that set age minimums for certain activities, such as the minimum age of 16 for adult sexual consent, 17 to apply for Canadian military service, 18 to vote in provincial and federal elections, and 19 to purchase and drink alcohol in most provinces?

Problems with executive functioning • Figure 11.7

Impairments in executive functioning make it more difficult for university or college students to organize their responsibilities and manage their time. Some young adults with impaired executive functioning don't feel overwhelmed until they have the stress of managing a family and a career at the same time.

Activation
Organizing, prioritizing, and initiating work or projects
Focus
Sustaining and shifting attention
Effort
Regulating alertness, sustaining effort, and processing information
Emotion
Managing frustration and modulating emotions
Memory
Utilizing and accessing short-term memory
Action
Monitoring and self-regulating action

Think Critically How might emerging adults in university with very good versus very poor executive functioning skills differ when faced with final exams? How does executive function help this student to parent and study?

Jim Craigmyle/Corbis

Skeletal System

Throughout childhood and adolescence, our bones grow longer and gain mass. Bone lengthening slows tremendously after adolescence, and it is complete around 25 years of age. As shown in **Figure 11.8**, the enlarged ends of the long bones, called **epiphyses**, fuse and stop producing new growth (Cech & Martin, 2002).

Our adult height is determined primarily by bone length, so by emerging adulthood, we are as tall as we are going to get. Females tend to reach their maximum heights slightly earlier than males because bone growth is closely related to hormones, particularly estrogen, found in higher quantities in females (Cutler, 1997).

Bone mass also peaks in early adulthood. The timing of skeletal maturity can vary greatly, but approximately 80 percent of bone mass is achieved by age 20. Bone mass reaches its peak around age 30, for both men and women. At this point, the rate at which we lose bone tissue and the speed with which we

epiphyses The enlarged ends of a long bone, initially growing separately from the shaft.

bone mineral density The amount of minerals, such as calcium, in an individual's bones as he or she ages.

produce new bone are about equal, unlike earlier stages during which creation of bone tissue outpaced loss. After this peak, we begin to lose bone mass. For the majority of young adults, bone mass deterioration has begun by the mid-30s.

The structure of our bones, as well as their stiffness and strength, helps our skeletons to meet the functional demands of movement. Maintaining the bone mass you accumulate before deterioration begins is one way to slow the effects of aging on the skeletal system. Loss of bone mass occurs naturally, due to body chemistry and environmental factors such as physical stress, diet, and activity. The good news is that health behaviours in the 20s and 30s can stave off bone loss. Young adults can protect their bones by maintaining hormonal balance and emotional health. Medical practitioners also recommend eating a healthy diet rich in alkaline-forming foods, tapering off the intake of sugar and alcohol, consuming adequate calcium, and maintaining regular exercise to maintain **bone mineral density**.

Bone growth in emerging adulthood • Figure 11.8

Epiphyseal plates made of cartilage rest on the ends of the epiphyses. Our bones stop lengthening when the cartilage in the epiphyseal plates hardens and stops producing new bone.

Epiphyseal plate

Think Critically What advice would you give a 25-year-old emerging adult male who is hoping to grow a few more centimetres so that he will be taller than his older brother?

Not surprisingly, many of the same health behaviours that help maintain skeletal health also help maintain the muscular system through the earliest stages of adulthood.

Muscular System

Just as in the skeletal system, muscle mass and strength peak in the 20s. It is no wonder that professional athletes typically deliver their most efficient performances during this period of life. As **Figure 11.9** shows, the vast majority of Olympic medals are won by emerging and young adults (Miller, 2008). By emerging adulthood, muscles make up a significant component of our overall body mass, approximately 34 percent for females and 42 percent for males 18 to 29 years old (Janssen, Heymsfield, Wang, & Ross, 2000). Variation in muscle mass among people in their 20s results from differences in genetic and environmental contributions to growth during their earliest years of development and from the influence of hormones on development during adolescence (for example, estrogen).

After peak muscle mass is achieved in our 20s, muscle becomes subject to the effects of aging. Atrophy, or decrease, of muscle begins at age 25, when muscle fibres begin to shrink and we lose muscle tissue altogether (Lexell,

Taylor, & Sjostrom, 1988). Although we lose between 0.5 and 1 percent of our muscle per year, the loss starts slowly during the 20s and 30s, and it is relatively

Olympic success by age • Figure 11.9

During emerging adulthood, high levels of physical fitness can be harnessed to achieve world records in a wide variety of athletics. At the London 2012 Olympics, the average athlete was 26 years old. Fewer than 2 percent of the Olympians (187 of the 10,383 who competed) were over the age of 40.

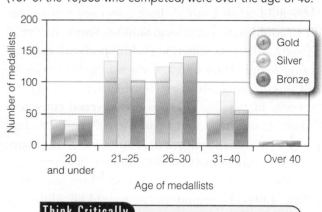

Think Critically In what ways do peak physical fitness levels in emerging adulthood benefit the average non-Olympian?

unnoticeable until the mid-40s (Janssen et al., 2000). The smaller muscles, such as those in the arms, lose tissue more slowly than the larger muscles found in the legs (Lynch et al., 1998).

As we have noted, some of the same strategies for maintaining bones help us hang on to muscles, too. Maintaining musculoskeletal health is key for preventing injuries in the later years of adulthood. Healthy bones and muscles also provide strength to help those in their 20s and 30s meet the demands of giving birth to and raising children.

Reproductive System

Like other biological systems, the reproductive system begins to mature at conception, fully matures in adolescence, and starts to age during the mid-20s. Unlike other body systems, men and women have different reproductive systems. Also unlike other biological systems, the potential of the reproductive system can be controlled to a great extent through human behaviour. Even within a single country, different cultures influence norms for sexual behaviour and access to education and contraception. Norms, education, and contraception play significant roles in the different **reproductive health** challenges that emerging and young adults face.

reproductive health A responsible, satisfying, and safe sex life, including the capability to reproduce, and the freedom to decide if, when, and how often to do so.

Reproductive health Between the ages of 18 and 30, humans are at the height of active sexuality, including reproductive abilities (Tortora, 2008). Sexual activity and fulfillment of family goals are both associated with quality of life in adulthood (Eisenberg, Shindel, Smith, Breyer, & Lipschultz, 2010). By emerging adulthood, the majority of young people report an active sex life. Approximately half of emerging adults are sexually active by age 18, 90 percent by age 25. There is no universal consensus on what sexual behaviours constitute "sex," although age, gender, and sexual orientation seem to influence how "sex" is conceptualized and defined (Sanders, Hill, Yarber, Graham, Crosby, & Milhausen, 2010; Sanders & Reinisch, 1999). Emerging adults, indeed all adults, engage in a range of sexual activities. The combination of being single and having autonomy often results in sexual experimentation during emerging adulthood (Lefkowitz & Gillen, 2006).

For many young adults, an active sex life includes heterosexual intercourse (Center for Sexual Health Promotion, 2010). Young adult men and women between the ages of 25 and 45 have **coital sex**, on average, six times per month. At this time of life sexual intercourse and orgasm are at their most frequent for males; females continue to experience an increase in orgasmic abilities into their later adulthood (Herbenick, Reece, Schick, Sanders, Dodge, & Fortenberry, 2010). However, young adults rarely engage in only one sex act per sexual event. In 2010, the National Survey of Sexual Health and Behavior reported more than 40 combinations of sexual activity that respondents described as their most recent sexual experience. Additionally, while approximately 7 percent of female respondents and 8 percent of male respondents identified as bisexual, lesbian, or gay, the proportion of individuals who reported sexual interactions with someone of the same sex was higher (Herbenick et al., 2010).

coital sex The sexual union between a male and a female involving insertion of the penis into the vagina.

Sexual activity is more frequent for men and women in marriages and committed partnerships than among single adults (Eisenberg et al., 2010). Healthy sexuality and reproductive justice includes opportunities for protected sex, often with a condom or **dental dam** to guard against sexually transmitted infections (STIs). STIs have serious health consequences, such as impaired fertility and adverse pregnancy outcomes, including low birth weight and prematurity and transmission of disease to children (Goldenberg, Andrews, Yuan, MacKay, & St. Louis, 1997). For heterosexual vaginally penetrative interactions, contraception is another pressing issue in order to avoid an unintended pregnancy. For women wishing to conceive, emerging adulthood is a very fertile period and many women become mothers during this period of development.

dental dam Originally manufactured for use in dentist offices, a small, thin, square-shaped latex barrier that allows sensation without skin-to-skin contact; it is effective for oral-vaginal or oral-anal-contact to protect from sexually transmitted infections.

For those not wishing to become pregnant, there is a wide array of methods of contraception, with differing degrees of efficacy (Society of Obstetricians and Gynaecologists of Canada, 2012). Ready access to contraception

CHALLENGES IN DEVELOPMENT
The Most Common Causes of Infertility

Infertility problems are often complex, due to more than one factor. And well over 10 percent of infertility cases have no known cause (Centers for Disease Control [CDC], 2012a). The chart shows diagnosed causes of infertility in those who were using fertility treatment with assisted reproductive technology.

Think Critically With respect to the relationship between age and infertility, are men or women more likely to be aware of their body's potential fertility?

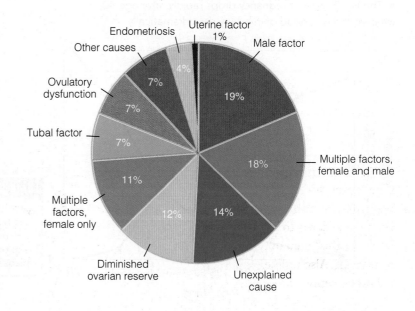

Endometriosis
Uterine factor 1%
Other causes
Male factor 19%
Ovulatory dysfunction
7%
4%
7%
Tubal factor
7%
Multiple factors, female and male 18%
11%
Multiple factors, female only
12%
14%
Diminished ovarian reserve
Unexplained cause

---

is an important part of women's health (United Nations General Assembly, 2011). Unfortunately, contraception can fail, or circumstances can be such that a woman conceives an unplanned pregnancy. Women must then decide within the complexity of their lives what this means. For some, it may be possible to rearrange their lives, have the necessary supports, and be healthy enough to continue the pregnancy to term. For others, the pregnancy is unwanted and they must make arrangements to terminate as quickly as possible. Despite the fact that abortion is legal in Canada, access to the procedure varies markedly among the provinces and in rural and remote regions (Kaposy, 2010). The best evidence indicates that abortion does not increase a woman's mental health problems but unwanted pregnancy does (Academy of Medical Royal Colleges, 2011). The United Nations General Assembly (2011) cites barriers to abortion access as a pressing health concern for women. Unintended pregnancies put young people and their babies at risk for delayed prenatal care, premature birth, and negative physical and mental health effects (Ventura, Curtin, Abma, & Henshaw, 2012).

Often by the mid-20s, many people's reproductive health goals focus less on preventing unwanted outcomes and more on planning and spacing pregnancies. By the mid-20s, sexual activity takes on new meaning as many young people begin to prepare for childbearing. The other end of the spectrum of reproductive justice is infertility, the subject of this chapter's *Challenges in Development*, which explores the inability to conceive or to take a pregnancy to term.

Fertility and the ability to form a family play an important role in reproductive health. Approximately 12 percent of women ages 15 to 44 are faced with **infertility** (Chandra, Martinez, Mosher, Abma, & Jones, 2005). Doctors can identify a single reason or multiple factors to explain about 80 percent of infertility cases. Infertility is often associated with age. As the graph in **Figure 11.10** shows, a woman's likelihood of getting pregnant decreases significantly after her 30s. However, genes and disease can also increase the risk for infertility.

fertility The natural capability to produce offspring.

infertility Medically defined as not conceiving a pregnancy after one year of unprotected sexual intercourse.

Pregnancy, infertility, and age • Figure 11.10

Through the 30s, women's fertility significantly influences the specific choices partners make with respect to family planning. With age, infertility plays an increasingly consequential role in shaping options for childbearing.

a. The likelihood of pregnancy drops rapidly after age 40, whereas the likelihood of infertility rises dramatically.

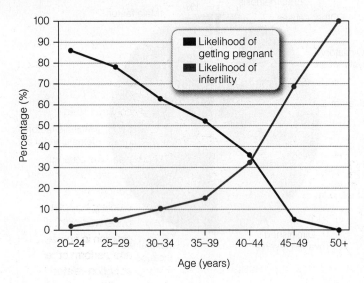

Think Critically 1. What implications does emerging adulthood have with respect to the biological window of fertility?
2. How might spending more years exploring her choices affect a woman's plans for having children?

b. Fertility rates have varied over time when we compare emerging adult years and later years.

Age-specific fertility rates, Canada, 1989 to 2009

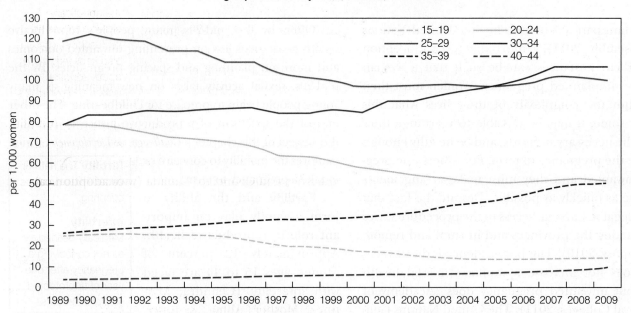

Source: Age-specific fertility rates, Canada, 1989 to 2009. Statistics Canada, CANSIM table 102-4505 and Births, Catalogue no. 84-210-X. Retrieved from http://www.statcan.gc.ca/pub/84f0210x/2009000/ct002-eng.htm.

Experiencing infertility is stressful (Kraaij, Garnefski, & Vlietstra, 2008) and is often associated with a decrease in marital and sexual satisfaction (Holditch-Davis, Sandelowski, & Glenn-Harris, 1999). When faced with infertility, many couples turn to alternative pathways to becoming parents: infertility treatment and adoption. In the pursuit of parenthood, same-sex couples confront unique considerations involving fertility and reproductive technologies (Gates, 2012).

Infertility treatments Approximately 90 percent of cases of infertility can be treated (Gordon et al., 2008). Depending on the underlying cause, treatment options

> **assisted reproductive technology (ART)** A method of infertility treatment in which eggs are removed from the woman's body, are combined with sperm, and are reintroduced into the body.
>
> **in vitro fertilization (IVF)** The manual combination of an egg and sperm in a laboratory dish.

include surgery, ovulation induction, intrauterine insemination, and **assisted reproductive technology (ART)** (CDC, 2010; Gordon et al., 2008). ART involves fertility procedures in which both sperm and eggs are handled by medical staff. The most frequent form of ART, used in 99 percent of cases (CDC, 2010), is **in vitro fertilization (IVF)**.

Women in their 30s are much more likely to seek infertility treatments than are those in their 20s. A variety of factors affect the likelihood that couples will pursue infertility treatments and which treatments they choose, including economic status, religious beliefs, ethical considerations, and the individual needs of the couple.

Child-rearing options for same-sex couples In Canada, approximately 9.4 percent of same-sex couples are engaged in child-rearing. Female same-sex couples are nearly five times more likely to have a child at home (16.5 percent) than males (3.4 percent) (Statistics Canada, 2011). Today, gay men often achieve fatherhood through foster care placements, adoption, and surrogacy (Patterson & Tornello, 2010). Although many lesbian couples pursue motherhood through adoption (Jennings, Mellish, Tasker, Lamb, & Golombok, 2014), they are more likely to use intrauterine insemination with a sperm donor, or ART such as IVF (Tarín, García-Pérez, &

Cano, 2015; Touroni & Coyle, 2002). Evidence suggests that both lesbian and gay couples have higher success with ART than heterosexual couples because such methods are often used without the presence of fertility issues (Tarín et al., 2015).

Adoption Adoption is another pathway to becoming parents. Although approximately one-third of all women of childbearing age (18–44) have considered adoption, only 2 percent of all women have adopted a child. Women who actually seek to adopt children are more likely than those who do not begin the adoption process to be infertile and to have previously used infertility services (Jones, 2008). Adoption also offers a pathway to parenthood for singles and, as previously mentioned, many gay and lesbian couples.

> **adoption agency** An organization licensed by a province to prepare adoptive parents, counsel birth parents, perform home studies, complete paperwork, place children in homes, and perform other adoption-related functions.
>
> **adoption counsellor** A therapeutically skilled and trained professional who is also knowledgeable about adoption issues and dynamics.

Adoption requires that parents be physically, mentally, and legally fit. Many potential parents seek children through an **adoption agency**. Potential adoptive parents are also advised to work with experienced **adoption counsellors** who are trained to help parents navigate and manage the adoption process. Adoption and child welfare come under provincial jurisdiction, so each province has its own laws and regulations. An excellent resource for would-be adoptive parents is the Adoption Council of Canada (www.adoption.ca).

CONCEPT CHECK

1. **What** role does the executive system play in the developing emerging adult brain?
2. **How** does bone growth during the 20s and 30s affect height and aging?
3. **What** options for starting a family are available to couples who experience infertility?

Cognitive Development

LEARNING OBJECTIVES

1. **Differentiate** postformal thinking from Piaget's formal operational thinking.

2. **Discuss** Perry's theory of adult intellectual development.

3. **Describe** creativity during emerging adulthood.

R ecall that we covered the final stage of Piaget's theory, formal operational thought, in Chapter 9. Piaget believed that this highest level of cognitive functioning was attained during adolescence. From its development and through the 1950s, Piaget's model of cognitive development was consistent with prevailing beliefs about aging. At this time, **gerontologists** operated under the assumption that intellectual development peaked in the late teens and early 20s, after which people underwent a noticeable decline in intellectual functioning.

Cognitive Development in Adulthood

During the second half of the twentieth century, research began to challenge the assumption that we experience only cognitive decline after our 20s. In 1956, K. Warner Schaie gave tests of mental abilities to 500 adults ages 22 to 70 in the Seattle area to collect information he needed to finish his doctoral study at the University of Washington. At the time, he didn't know that he would study this same group of adults for more than 50 years in the Seattle Longitudinal Study of Adult Intelligence. Over the past half-century, Schaie and colleagues have published hundreds of studies showing that cognitive decline is not a given (see Schaie & Willis, 2011). In fact, some cognitive abilities increase through our 20s and 30s, and most cognitive decline does not occur until after the 60s.

Postformal Thought: Beyond Piaget

From the 1960s through the 1970s and 1980s, a number of developmental scientists studied the thinking of American college students in an effort to better understand how adult cognition might change as a function of learning after age 18. Laurence Kohlberg and his colleagues

> **gerontologist** A professional who studies the social, psychological, and biological aspects of aging.
>
> **world view** The lens or overall perspective an individual uses to see and interpret the world; a personal philosophy of life.

found changes in students' thinking over the course of the college years. Interestingly, college students' thinking seemed to regress after their entry to college. Their once clear and certain ways of knowing and understanding the world became less organized (Kohlberg & Kramer, 1969). Later studies led the researchers to revise their conclusion that these changes represented a regression.

William Perry (1970), in his studies of Harvard University students, recognized a similar shift in the way students changed their thinking. As shown in **Figure 11.11**, upon entry into university, students were assured of their **world view**; they entered with firm, black-and-white views about moral issues. People could act and believe in ways that were either right or wrong, true or false. As they progressed through university, students' dualistic thinking was challenged. They began to feel destabilized and less sure of their ways of seeing things. And, as their dualistic thinking became less and less useful, students adopted a more subjective world view that required them to understand the context and multi-dimensionality of an issue.

In sum, studies of college students through the end of the twentieth century showed that age and education are both associated with increased moral development and cognitive complexity (Dawson, 2002).

At the same time, other developmental scientists continued to use Piaget's framework to study cognitive maturation. Gisela Labouvie-Vief examined adults' performance on Piagetian tasks. When presented with the conservation of liquid volume task (see Chapter 5), a task that Piaget believed children mastered around 7 years of age, adult subjects would sometimes make mistakes. The adults' explanations for their errors intrigued Labouvie-Vief (Sinnott, 1984), who began to study why formal operations, as defined by Piaget, did not account for adults making errors on predicting the amount of water in a wide beaker. When asked why

University student thinking • Figure 11.11

Perry (1970) concluded that there are three main positions of adult intellectual growth. As university students progressed, Perry observed that they shifted their views about knowledge. That is, university students' thinking develops through three predictable stages.

David Butow/Corbis

1 Dualism

Core feature: Either/or thinking

Students believe there is a single right answer to any question. Students receive knowledge when professors teach it to them. At this stage, students believe that learning involves taking notes, memorizing facts, and demonstrating knowledge of facts on their exams.

Corey Rich/Aurora/Getty Images

2 Multiplicity

Core feature: Knowledge is subjective

Students believe that knowledge is an opinion. Students and professors are equally entitled to their own opinions. Students at this stage rebel against critique of their work, believing that such feedback is opinion.

Huntstock/Getty Images

3 Relativism

Core feature: Knowledge is constructed

Students believe that opinions are based on values, experiences, and knowledge. Students can argue their perspective and can consider the relative merit of opinions by evaluating evidence. These students view faculty as having better-informed opinions in their area of expertise and believe that professors are valuable in their ability to teach students how to evaluate knowledge.

Ask Yourself

Match each student with a type of thinking according to Perry's model.
1. Samira looks forward to discussing points of disagreement with her professors.
2. Santiago expects his professor to tell him exactly what he needs to know.
3. Benoît is frustrated when his professors don't respect his opinion.

a. dualism
b. multiplicity
c. relativism

---

they gave their incorrect answer, some adults took into account factors other than the water and the beaker. They mentioned potential evaporation, the temperature of the beakers, and other issues. In essence, adults were relying on life experiences, as well as on physical features of the objects.

These findings led Labouvie-Vief and others (Labouvie-Vief, 2003; Wu & Chiou, 2008) to wonder whether they might observe changes in the way young people experienced and understood themselves after adolescence, during the transition to adulthood and beyond. Labouvie-Vief (2006) has since concluded that the emerging adult years in particular present the opportunity for **postformal thought** to manifest and mature, under conditions of opportunity. As a result of this

postformal thought A quality of thinking beyond Piaget's formal operational stage that includes cognitive flexibility, practicality, and relativism.

WHAT A DEVELOPMENTALIST SEES
Creative Productivity

There is much emphasis on becoming an adult by acting like an adult. Training for a career is considered a marker of success (**Figure a**). Pursuing a creative interest or talent may be viewed as chasing a dream rather than focusing on reality (**Figure b**). A developmentalist sees emerging adulthood as a stage of the lifespan during which creativity has its place (**Figure c**).

Stuart Pearce/Age FotostockAmeric, Inc.

a.

DragonImages/iStockphoto

b.

c.

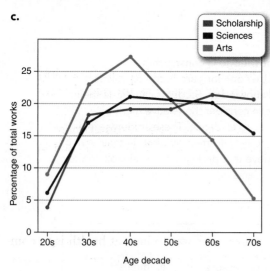

Put It Together *Review the section on the nervous system and executive functions and answer these questions:*
1. What advice would you give to parents concerned that their emerging adult wants to be a professional musician?
2. How would your advice differ if you learned the emerging adult had never taken a music lesson?

---

cognitive flexibility An executive function that allows an individual to piece together elements of knowledge to fit the demands of a given situation.

new way of seeing, young people become less rigid in their world views and they gain **cognitive flexibility** (Spiro, Feltovich, Jacobson, & Coulson, 1995).

Creativity

Creativity results when there is a specific combination of genetic predispositions, environmental factors, and

opportunity (Amabile, 1996). With the ability for relativistic and flexible thinking peaking, it's not surprising that, as discussed in *What a Developmentalist Sees*, creativity begins to rise during emerging and young adulthood (Csikszentmihalyi, 2002; Kurtzberg & Amabile, 2001). What is creativity? The definition varies depending on who is providing it (Amabile, 1996; Csikszentmihalyi, 1988; Kurtzberg &

creativity The state or quality of being able to generate new and valuable ideas or things.

Amabile, 2001; Sternberg & Lubart, 1995; Torrance, 1979). A classic definition of creativity (Torrance, 1979) identifies a combination of fluency, flexibility, elaboration, and novelty. Another definition suggests that creativity is a novel response that is appropriate to the situation (Sternberg & Lubart, 1995); in other words, creative people can think outside of the box.

Despite differences in the way creativity is defined, researchers agree that there are developmental patterns in the evolution of creativity and that the emerging and young adult years are a critical period for producing highly creative work. Examples of highly creative acts by emerging adults abound. Bill Gates and Paul Allen were 20 when they completed the BASIC computer language program, enabling them to start Microsoft. During Mozart's 19th year, he wrote four violin concertos, a mass, and an opera. Before he reached the age of 30, former Beatle Paul McCartney had written and performed 29 number-one songs in the United States and the United Kingdom.

CONCEPT CHECK

1. **How** do our cognitive abilities change during emerging and young adulthood, according to Schaie?

2. **What** are the key characteristics of postformal thought?

3. **When** does creativity peak?

All the Systems Working Together

LEARNING OBJECTIVES

1. **Describe** how differences in emerging adult health and well-being are shaped by earlier life experiences.

2. **Name** the leading causes of death in emerging adulthood.

3. **Discuss** the relationship between physical health and psychiatric disorder in emerging adulthood.

4. **List** four health risk behaviours in emerging adulthood that increase risk for poor health later in life.

5. **Compare** and **contrast** health outcomes associated with fitness and lack of fitness in emerging adulthood.

At the transition to adulthood, for the first time, young people become responsible for regulating their own lives and lifestyle patterns. The ability to self-regulate one's sleep, weight, and food intake can affect health and well-being in a number of ways. As we've seen, physical development peaks in many ways during the 20s and 30s, but good health during these years is not assured.

> **morbidity** The rate of disease in a population.
>
> **life course health approach** A model that uses people's trajectories of health from conception through death to study and understand the development of disease and promotion of health.

Health and Well-Being

Our view of the role of health in the lives of emerging and young adults very much depends on the lens we use. One way to look at health is to compare levels of **morbidity** among different age groups. When viewed this way, the years between 18 and 30 look good. Most North Americans are relatively disease-free during this time of life (Tejada-Vera & Sutton, 2010) compared with later stages of adult development.

Another way to look at health is more longitudinal. A **life course health approach** considers each person's individual health history, or trajectory, beginning in the years before transition to adulthood and stretching through periods after early adulthood, as shown in **Figure 11.12**. From this view, you can see that risk and protective factors from people's

Health across the lifespan • Figure 11.12

The life course health approach encourages us to view emerging adult health in relation to earlier and later stages of development. In emerging adulthood, health differences among young people can be predicted by individuals' exposure to risk factors or protective factors. The exposed trajectory describes the health pathway of someone who was exposed to more risk factors than protective factors. In contrast, the protected trajectory describes someone exposed to more protective than risk factors.

Think Critically Write descriptions of two emerging adults, one who is characterized by an exposed health trajectory and one who is characterized by a protected health trajectory. You might consider some common diseases, such as cancer, diabetes, or heart disease, in your descriptions.

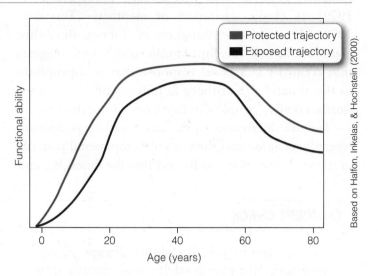

Based on Halfon, Inkelas, & Hochstein (2000).

earliest years make important contributions to their health during their 20s and 30s. Moreover, you can see how one's health trajectory in emerging adulthood establishes a health pathway that continues well into adulthood.

Mortality

Along with low morbidity, **mortality** is relatively low in the 20s and 30s compared with older adults, as shown in **Figure 11.13**. In emerging adulthood, the leading causes of death for ages 19–29 are consequences of high-risk behaviours. The top three causes of death are (1) unintentional injury, (2) homicide, and (3) suicide. Unintentional injuries account for over 80 percent of deaths, and include motor vehicle accidents and drug and alcohol poisoning (CDC, 2009). Likewise, the majority of nonfatal injuries to those ages 19–29 occur as a result of unintentional behaviours, including falls, being struck (hit by any human or object), being in a motor vehicle accident, and overexertion (CDC, 2012b). The consequences of deaths and injuries of people in their 20s and 30s are especially tragic and disproportionate because of the many **potential years of life lost** to premature mortality.

Particularly disturbing is the sex difference in mortality rates. About 75 percent of the people who die during their emerging and early adult years are male (Tejada-Vera & Sutton, 2010). The gender difference is

mortality The rate of death in a population.

potential years of life lost An estimate of the average years a person would have lived if he or she had not died.

psychiatric disorder A mental disorder or mental illness that is a pattern of feelings, thoughts, or behaviours that cause distress or disability.

particularly pronounced for homicide; males are over six times more likely than females to die this way (Tejada-Vera & Sutton, 2010). Given this trend, and considering what the leading causes of death in this age range are, Heuveline (2002) concludes that "individuals' risk behavior is most gendered during their twenties" (p. 180).

Sex differences account for some risk for risky behaviours and mortality in emerging adulthood; mental health problems also play a significant role.

Psychiatric Disorders

Whereas physical disorders are rare, **psychiatric disorders** are common during emerging adulthood. During an average 12-month period, 44 percent of 18- to 29-year-olds will meet the criteria for a psychiatric disorder. The rate is higher than in any other adult age group.

Clinicians use the *Diagnostic and Statistical Manual* (*DSM*), published by the American Psychiatric Association ([APA], 2013), to determine whether a set of symptoms or behaviours meet the criteria for a psychiatric diagnosis. The most common psychiatric disorders diagnosed among 18- to 29-year-olds are anxiety disorders (22 percent), characterized by abnormal, pathological worry and fear; substance use disorders (22 percent), which involve the overuse and in some cases physiological dependence on nicotine, alcohol, and/or drugs; mood disorders (13 percent), in

Mortality across the lifespan • Figure 11.13

Mortality rates provide us with information about the likelihood of death given a person's age. Mortality rates are low in emerging adulthood and increase linearly across adulthood.

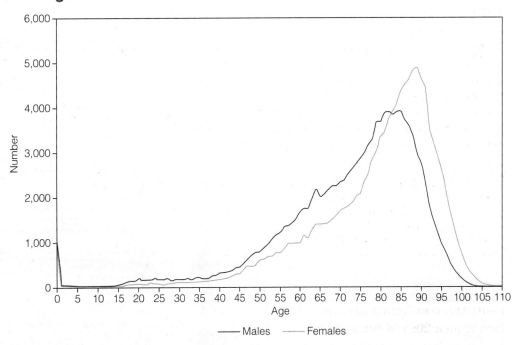

Notes: Deaths for which the province or age of death was unknown were prorated using the observed distribution.

Source: Number of deaths by age and sex, Canada, 2011. Statistics Canada, Canadian Vital Statistics, Deaths Database, 2011, Survey 3233. Retrieved from www.statcan.gc.ca/pub/91-209-x/2013001/article/11867/fig/fig3-eng.htm.

Think Critically **1.** If you changed the graph to include a second set of lines showing the association between potential years of life lost and age, what would the new line look like compared with the existing line? **2.** What would these two sets of lines together tell us about the likelihood and the impact of a death in emerging adulthood?

which the primary symptom is a disturbance in mood, such as major depressive episode or bipolar disorder; and impulse control disorders (12 percent), characterized by losing control and failing to resist an impulse that may be harmful to self or others (Kessler, Chiu, Demler, Merikangas, & Walters, 2005).

Psychiatric disorder is a key concern for those interested in understanding how we can promote health and development during the transition to adulthood. Psychiatric disorders impede emerging and young adults' overall well-being, as well as their performance in specific domains, such as school or relationships (Tanner, Reinherz, Beardslee, Fitzmaurice, Leis, & Berger, 2007; Vander Stoep, Beresford, Weiss, McKnight, Cauce, & Cohen, 2000). In addition, psychiatric disorders often co-occur with physical illnesses, including pain, gastrointestinal issues, and respiratory disorders (McCloughen, Foster, Huws-Thomas, & Delgado, 2012).

The life course approach to health can help us understand psychiatric, as well as physical, disorders. As

Figure 11.14 shows, early experiences increase risk for psychiatric disorder; likewise, protective factors decrease risk. Approximately 75 percent of those who experience a psychiatric disorder in emerging adulthood already have a developmental history of psychiatric problems (Kessler, Berglund, Demler, Jin, Merikangas, & Walters, 2005). In this respect, a significant proportion of emerging-adult psychiatric disease is due to spillover from the first two decades. In fact, psychiatric disorders have been called "the chronic diseases of youth" (Insel & Fenton, 2005). The other 25 percent of psychiatric disorders appear for the first time during the person's 20s. Disorders in which first episodes are likely to occur during the 20s, such as schizophrenia and bipolar disorder, are often severe and debilitating (APA, 2013).

Health Behaviours

In general, as people move from adolescence into emerging adulthood, they engage in fewer behaviours to

Protective and risk factors for psychiatric disorder during the transition to adulthood • Figure 11.14

Mental health problems seen during the transition to adulthood often have a developmental history that can be traced back to childhood or adolescence. Experiences during the transition to adulthood also increase risk for psychiatric disorder during these critical years. Biological and psychological risks exert influence from within the developing person in interaction with external influences, including family, school, and community.

Think Critically How might emerging adulthood—a stage of exploration before commitment—promote or undermine mental health?

	Protective factors	Risk factors
Societal		
Community	Connectedness to community, opportunities for leisure, positive cultural experiences, positive role models, rewards for community involvement, connection with community organizations	Urbanization, community disorganization, discrimination and marginalization, exposure to violence
School	Opportunities for involvement in school life, positive reinforcement for academic achievement, identification with school or need for educational attainment	Academic failure, failure of schools to provide appropriate environment to support attendance and learning, inadequate or inappropriate provision of education, bullying
Family	Family attachment, opportunities for positive involvement in family, rewards for involvement in family	Inconsistent caregiving, family conflict, poor family discipline, poor family management, death of a family member
Psychological	Ability to learn from experience, good self-esteem, high level of problem-solving ability, social skills	Learning disorders, maladaptive personality traits, abuse and neglect, difficult temperament
Biological	Age-appropriate physical development, good physical health, good intellectual functioning	Exposure to toxins during pregnancy, genetic risk for psychiatric disorder, head trauma, birth complications, illnesses and diseases, malnutrition, substance use
Individual		

Data from Patel, Flisher, Hetrick, & McGorry (2007).

improve their health and more behaviours that can harm their health. As the life course approach suggests, poor health habits during a person's 20s affect their health not only during emerging adult years, but also in their later adult years. Four modifiable health risk behaviours of many emerging adults—lack of physical activity, poor nutrition, tobacco use, and excessive alcohol consumption—are particularly likely to increase the risk for illness, suffering, and early death in the adult years.

Fitness

Many people understand and accept the benefits of physical activity (Sloan et al., 2009), yet emerging adults particularly struggle with fitness once they leave high school. The World Health Organization and Canadian guidelines recommend that to achieve health benefits, adults aged 18 and older should accumulate at least 150 minutes of moderate- to vigorous-intensity aerobic physical activity per week, in bouts of 10 minutes or more (Statistics Canada, 2011). Only 15 percent of Canadian adults meet the recommended guidelines, and the amount of physical activity declines with age (and is markedly lower among women) (**Figure 11.15**). What are some of the factors you think might account for the decrease in activity levels among young adults? As young people age through their 20s, staying fit often becomes even more difficult. Suddenly days are filled with work duties, a free gym is not located just a quad away, and the scheduled routine of team sports involvement has typically ended. Transitions to adult roles take their toll on fitness, too (**Figure 11.16**).

Levels of physical activity across age groups • Figure 11.15

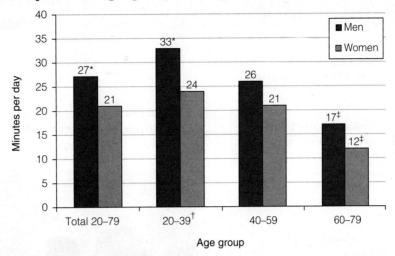

Source: Health fact sheets: Physical activity levels of Canadian adults 2007–2009, 2011. Statistics Canada Catalogue no. 82-625. Retrieved from www.statcan.gc.ca/pub/82-625-x/2011001/article/11552-eng.pdf.

† Reference category
* Significantly different from estimate for women (p<0.05)
‡ Significantly different from estimate for reference category (p<0.05)

For some people, the search for identity in emerging adulthood extends into the arena of drug use. Substance use is a problem behaviour that begins in adolescence. Many emerging adults see drug experimentation as the last chance for free expression and sensation-seeking before they become settled into long-term romantic partnerships and careers. Most people who use substances do not go on to have recurring problems, but some young adults do (Simpson, 2004). When substance use interferes with a young person's functioning, he or she has developed a **substance use disorder** (**Figure 11.17**; APA, 2013).

The difficulties caused by lack of exercise are hard to underestimate. Exercise helps control weight, a growing problem for emerging and young adults (CDC, 2011). Since 1971, obesity rates in emerging adults have tripled. Currently, about 17 percent of emerging adults in America are obese, and an even larger percentage are overweight (Navaneelan & Janz, 2014; Flegal, Carroll, Ogden, & Curtin, 2010). Clearly, exercise has a number of physical benefits, including

substance use disorder A mental disorder that occurs when substance use interferes with a person's daily life or functioning.

improvement of cardiopulmonary function (Mandic et al., 2009; Rees, Taylor, Singh, Coats, & Ebrahim, 2004), central nervous system function, and as we saw earlier in this chapter, skeletal and muscle function (Cech & Martin, 2002). In addition, although emerging adults tend to be quite healthy, poor fitness habits set up during these years can have serious negative health consequences in future years. With decreased physical activity comes increased risk of heart disease, high blood pressure, type II diabetes, and some types of cancer, to name just a few.

Staying fit can also positively affect mental health. Exercise has been shown to be related to lower rates of depression (Craft & Landers, 1998) and anxiety (Calfas & Taylor, 1994). People who engage in regular physical activity also tend have higher self-esteem than those who do not (Spence, Poon, & Dyck, 1997). It remains unclear whether the relationship between mental health and exercise is causal or merely correlational, but exercise certainly does not hurt. Regular exercise also stands out as one of the most common suggestions for reducing stress. Perhaps most important, fitness plays a significant role in maintaining health, delaying aging, and preventing disease.

Emerging adulthood is an in-between stage with respect to physical activity and fitness. Physical activity decreases from adolescence to emerging adulthood.

a. Sports

From a list of over 30 sports, participation in only three did not decrease from age 15 to age 23: walking, weight training, and working hard (such as gardening).

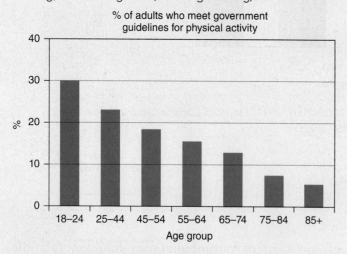

% of adults who meet government guidelines for physical activity

Age group: 18–24, 25–44, 45–54, 55–64, 65–74, 75–84, 85+

b. Employment

When emerging adults start work, they are more sedentary and have fewer hours to exercise.

Caro/Photoshot

c. Romantic relationships

The transition to couplehood is associated with a reduction in exercise because couples begin organizing their lives around each another.

2/Tim Klein/Ocean/Corbis

d. Having a baby

Parenthood is associated with significant decreases in leisure time, especially time for active exercise.

SHARON WASHINGTON/GettyImages

Think Critically Based on the graph in figure a., what type of hypothesis can you make about the association between age, taking on adult roles, and change in physical activity?

When substance use is substance abuse • Figure 11.17

Emerging adults use drugs more frequently than teens. Despite small variations in rates of drug use over the past decade, rates have remained relatively stable among emerging adults. The *DSM-5* lists a set of criteria for a diagnosis of a substance disorder. At a minimum, meeting two or more of the following criteria may indicate a substance disorder.

Criteria for a substance disorder

- Taking the substance in increasing amounts
- Wanting but not managing to cut down
- Spending a lot of time getting, using, or recovering
- Experiencing cravings and urges to use the substance
- Not meeting your responsibilities at home or work
- Using despite it causing problems in your relationships
- Giving up important activities because of substance use
- Using substances even when it puts you in danger
- Continuing to use, even when you know you have a physical or psychological problem
- Needing more of the substance to get the effect you want (tolerance)
- Developing withdrawl symptoms that can be relieved by taking more of the substance

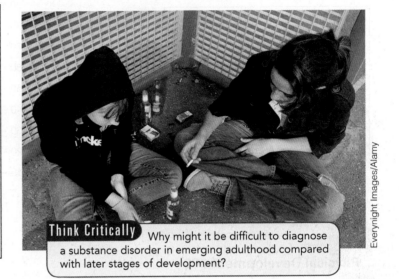

Everynight Images/Alamy

Think Critically Why might it be difficult to diagnose a substance disorder in emerging adulthood compared with later stages of development?

CONCEPT CHECK STOP

1. **How** does the life course approach view health during emerging and young adulthood?

2. **What** is the relationship between behaviour and the leading causes of death in emerging adulthood?

3. **What** influence do psychiatric disorders have on the lives of emerging adults?

4. **How** do emerging adults' health risk behaviours predict health outcomes in later adulthood?

5. **How** can emerging adults protect themselves against aging?

 **THE PLANNER**

Summary

1 Theory: The Transition to Adulthood 354

- Culture and **socialization** processes play a significant role in shaping the transition to adulthood. In some cultures, young people go through a rite of passage after which they are recognized as full adults. In other cultures, there is no line between adolescence and adulthood. Around the world, the transition to adulthood is an individual process that is marked in different ways.

- The theory of emerging adulthood proposes that, in some cultures, young people experience a new stage of life in between adolescence and adulthood, during which they explore possibilities in love and work before settling into adult roles and commitments. Based on surveys and **qualitative interviews** with young people, researchers have found that emerging adulthood is characterized by identity exploration, instability, self-focus, instability, and possibilities.

- **Young adulthood** marks the end of the transition to adulthood. Young adulthood is marked by progress toward financial independence, residing outside of the parental home, making commitments to careers and romantic relationships, and entering parenthood. Cultural shifts in the past 50 years are apparent in the rising numbers of young people **cohabiting** before marriage and an increased proportion of young women delaying motherhood. As shown in the figure, individuals take widely varying paths toward these goals of independence.

Pathways to adulthood • Figure 11.5

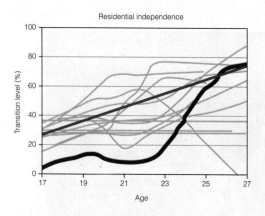

licensed **adoption agencies** and professional **adoption counsellors** can help parents navigate this process.

Pregnancy, infertility, and age • Figure 11.10

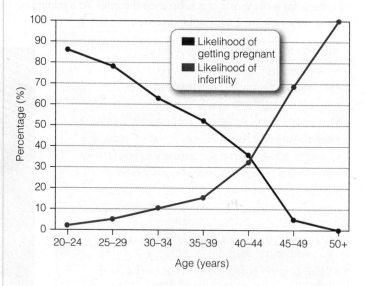

2 Physical Development 360

- The adult brain continues to grow through the 20s and even the 30s. The most significant growth occurs in the prefrontal cortex, which demonstrates continued plasticity. As a result of brain changes, the **executive system** ramps up its abilities to combine functions from two different regions of the brain in order to carry out more complex tasks, such as prioritizing.

- During emerging and early adulthood, our major physical systems peak in **vitality** and then begin to show the first signs of **senescence**.

- Bone lengthening slows after adolescence, and it is complete around 25 years of age when the enlarged ends of the long bones, called **epiphyses**, fuse and stop producing new growth. Most people's muscle mass and strength also peak during their 20s and decline beginning in their 30s. Diet and other lifestyle factors can affect the likelihood of developing low **bone mineral density**, especially for women, who are at much higher risk than men. Activity and weight control may also slow muscle loss and lessen risks of injuries.

- By age 25, 90 percent of young adults are actively engaging in a range of sexual activities, which may include **coital sex**. Emerging adult **reproductive health** is primarily focused on preventing unwanted pregnancy and sexually transmitted infections. By the mid-20s, the goals of sexual behaviour may shift toward reproduction. The vast majority of all reproduction occurs in emerging and young adulthood. **Fertility** is a critical component of reproductive health. About 10 percent of couples face **infertility**, and as the graph in the figure shows, risk increases with age. Most cases of infertility can be treated using **assisted reproductive technology (ART)** such as **in vitro fertilization (IVF)**, which is also used by some same-sex couples trying to begin a family. Infertile couples, same-sex couples, and singles can also become parents via adoption. Provincially

3 Cognitive Development 368

- Some **gerontologists** have suggested that **postformal thought** goes beyond Piaget's formal operations stage and that it happens when adults rely on experience and flexibility, as well as logic, to help them think about issues.

- Life experiences help emerging and young adults to develop **world views**, or unique systems of values and beliefs. Life experiences can also contribute to **cognitive flexibility**, constructing knowledge to meet changing demands in our environments.

- William Perry suggested that thinking develops through three main positions of adult intellectual growth: dualism, multiplicity, and relativism.

- **Creativity** often begins to rise during emerging and early adulthood, as demonstrated by the young artist in the photo.

What a Developmentalist Sees: Creative Productivity

DragonImages/iStockphoto

4 All the Systems Working Together 371

- When we examine **morbidity** rates between younger and older adults, young adults are shown to be relatively disease-free compared with older adults. A **life course health approach** considers a person's health from birth to death and reveals how risk and protective factors from an individual's earliest years affects his or her health in young adulthood.

- Although the **mortality** rate is relatively low, as shown in the figure, compared with that of older adults, young adults' death rates are twice those of adolescents, and some researchers suggest that risky behaviour is to blame. The top causes of young adult death are accidents, especially motor vehicle accidents, as well as homicide and suicide. Males' death rates are far greater than those of females, although increasing numbers of females are dying in motor vehicle accidents. Like childhood deaths, young adult deaths are particularly tragic because of the **potential years of life lost**.

- **Psychiatric disorders**, including mood, anxiety, and impulse control disorders, are common in emerging adulthood. Risk and protective factors accumulate from childhood and adolescence to increase risk for mental health problems in emerging adulthood. Emerging adulthood carries distinct risks associated with the stressors of becoming adult. Psychiatric disorders present an immediate threat to well-being in emerging adulthood and predict a cascade of risk across the adult lifespan.

- Young adults tend to engage in fewer behaviours to improve their health and more behaviours that can harm their health. Many young people experiment with drugs as part of their identity exploration, and some develop **substance use disorders**.

- Exercise and fitness offer clear physical and mental health benefits, but only 15 percent of adult Canadians get the recommended amount of exercise. Emerging and young adults face many new stressors, including starting post-secondary education, jobs and careers, and relationships or marriages, that can make healthy living more challenging.

Mortality across the lifespan • Figure 11.13

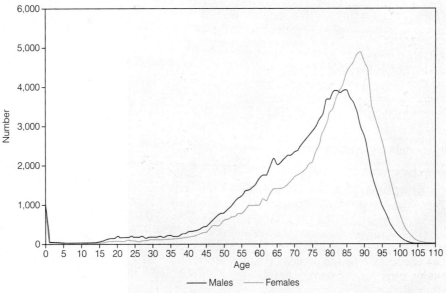

Key Terms

Critical and Creative Thinking Questions

1. What personal or other milestones do you believe define adulthood? Why?

2. Based on what you have read in this chapter, what diet and lifestyle recommendations would you make to a friend who wanted to maintain his or her peak of physical fitness and to cope well with stress during young adulthood?

3. What methods, if any, do you believe would be effective in getting emerging and young adults to reduce their risky behaviours, such as substance use, poor fitness habits, or reckless driving?

4. What examples of postformal thought, cognitive flexibility, or Perry's stages or positions of intellectual growth have you noticed among emerging and young adults you know?

What is happening in this picture?

This person is a Peace Corps volunteer, working with local people in Burkina Faso.

Peace Corps

Think Critically

1. Is emerging adulthood a more likely time for people to join an organization such as the Peace Corps, a two-year volunteer program?

2. How might the transition to adulthood in this village, where young people complete their formal education at a significantly younger age, be different from the transition to adulthood in North America?

3. What type of cognitive abilities might this young person develop as a result of her experience as a Peace Corps volunteer?

REAL  Development

Physical and Cognitive Development in Emerging and Young Adulthood

In this video activity, you are an intern for Dr. Chris Willard, a clinical psychologist from Tufts University who specializes in stress and anxiety in students. You are visiting a university to conduct research into how stress affects physical and cognitive development in young adults. You will shadow Dr. Willard at work as he helps university students assess their stress levels. You are asked to draw conclusions about the level of stress experienced by university students.

You will also watch Dr. Willard define and explain stress. At the end of the lecture, the students share a list of coping mechanisms that they use to deal with their stress. You will analyze the benefits of various coping mechanisms, including physical activity.

Finally, you follow up with Eliza about her experiences with stress in university. As a counselling intern, you are asked to provide Eliza with feedback and cognitive strategies for coping with stress.

WileyPLUS Go to WileyPLUS to complete the REAL Development activity.

03.01

Self-Test

(Check your answers in Appendix A.)

1. Which of the following characterizes emerging adulthood?
   a. a search for identity
   b. a focus on one's self
   c. an optimistic feeling of possibilities
   d. all of these

2. Based on information from this chapter, which is the most correct advice for parents of graduating university students?
   a. "It's quite likely that your adult child will never become an adult."
   b. "Almost all young people become 'adult,' but the road to adulthood is now longer and less predictable."
   c. "As long as your adult child has the same values and beliefs as you, he or she will become an adult very quickly."
   d. "Your university graduate is very likely to become an adult very quickly because education is the primary criterion for becoming 'adult.'"

3. Regular physical activity during young adulthood can help people slow down losses of _____.
   a. bone mineral density
   b. muscle mass
   c. muscle strength
   d. all of these

4. Fill in the blanks on the accompanying figure with the five leading causes of infertility.

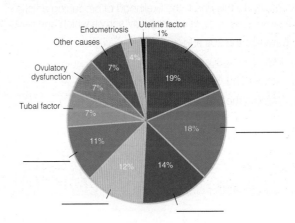

5. The most commonly used assisted reproductive technology, in which eggs and sperm are mixed together in a laboratory dish, is called _____.

    a. ovulation induction

    b. in vitro fertilization

    c. ex-corporis adoption

    d. intrauterine insemination

6. According to this graph, which best describes the physical activity of a typical man in his late 30s?

    a. He was more active in emerging adulthood than he is now.

    b. He was more active in his early 30s than during emerging adulthood.

    c. He is more active now than he was during his 20s.

    d. He is less active now than he will be during his 40s.

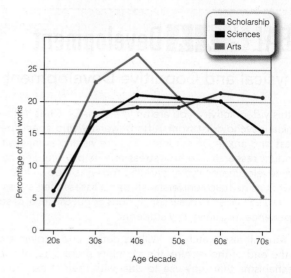

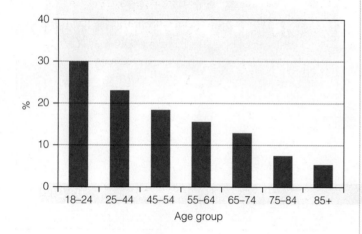

7. University students who experience challenges to their black-and-white thinking are likely to experience cognitive maturation via gains in their _____.

    a. cognitive flexibility

    b. dualistic thinking

    c. postformalism

    d. world views

8. According to this chart, the likelihood of producing artistic output increases most dramatically across which age period?

    a. between the 20s and 30s

    b. between the 30s and 40s

    c. between the 40s and 50s

    d. between the 50s and 60s

9. Emerging adult health is _____.

    a. unpredictable because there is no relationship between childhood health and emerging adult health

    b. equivalent for all young people because childhood risks don't affect adult health

    c. influenced by early health trajectories

    d. influenced by emerging adult health risk behaviours, exclusively

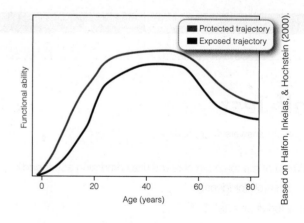

10. Which physical activity is not practised at the same rate through emerging adulthood?

    a. running

    b. walking

    c. yard work

    d. weight training

11. Fill in the blanks with the one-word names for categories of risk factors that contribute to the likelihood that a psychiatric disorder will emerge before adulthood.

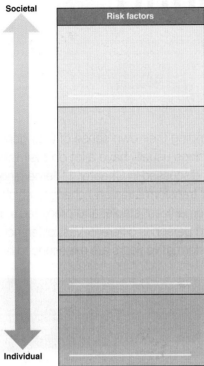

Data from Patel, Flisher, Hetrick, & McGorry (2007).

12. Substance use disorders undermine healthy functioning in emerging adulthood. All of the following are criteria for substance use disorder *except*:

a. taking the substance in increasing amounts

b. not meeting responsibilities at home or at work

c. wanting but not managing to cut down

d. spending more money on the substances than on education

13. The leading causes of death during emerging and young adulthood include all of these *except* _____.

a. cancer

b. accidents

c. suicide

d. homicide

14. The most common psychiatric disorders in emerging adulthood include all of the following *except* _____.

a. anxiety disorders

b. substance use disorders

c. mood disorders

d. ADHD

15. Mental health problems during the transition to adulthood are _____.

a. not likely to first appear until after age 28

b. most often triggered by post-secondary education stress

c. often related to a history of risk exposure

d. quite rare, compared with physical problems

THE PLANNER

Review your Chapter Planner in the chapter opener and check off your completed work.

Socio-emotional Development in Emerging and Young Adulthood

What are these young women talking about? If research into emerging and young adulthood can give us any clues, they are most likely discussing their social lives and plans for their futures. These topics serve as the focal points of emerging and young adults' lives. Whether negotiating the challenges of love and living arrangements, working through a potential quarter-life crisis, or finding their own sense of their gender roles, 20-somethings usually have a lot on their minds.

As we discussed in Chapter 11, emerging adulthood is a time of transformation and change, which gives way to a more organized, stable, and predictable adult life. Yet each young person is different. Vast differences in the way these transformative years are experienced have a great

deal to do with personality and the preparedness of young people to establish a sense of "Who am I?" and "Who do I love?" For some, these years are overwhelming; for others, they represent an opportunity to begin the life they have planned. For the vast majority, in a short time, life will calm down. At that time, they will drop anchor and remain in adulthood for the rest of their lives.

John Powell/Topfoto/The Image Works

CHAPTER PLANNER ✓

- ❑ Study the picture and read the opening story.
- ❑ Scan the Learning Objectives in each section:
  p. 386 ❑   p. 389 ❑   p. 408 ❑
- ❑ Read the text and study all visuals. Answer any questions.

Analyze key features

- ❑ Process Diagram, p. 390
- ❑ Development InSight, p. 396
- ❑ What a Developmentalist Sees, p. 408
- ❑ Challenges in Development, p. 412
- ❑ Stop: Answer the Concept Checks before you go on:
  p. 388 ❑   p. 407 ❑   p. 414 ❑

End of chapter

- ❑ Review the Summary and Key Terms.
- ❑ Answer the Critical and Creative Thinking Questions.
- ❑ Answer *What is happening in this picture?*
- ❑ Complete the Self-Test and check your answers.

Personality Development

LEARNING OBJECTIVES

1. **Identify** the Big Five personality traits.
2. **Compare** and **contrast** intimacy vs. isolation.
3. **Describe** change in personality from adolescence into adulthood.

A s we learned in Chapter 11, the transition to adulthood takes many different shapes across many different cultures. But transitions to adulthood also vary to a great extent within cultures. After all, becoming an adult is an individual journey. For some, becoming adult will seem exciting, and for others the challenge will seem overwhelming. **Personality** plays a role in determining how a young person will experience this critical life stage.

> **personality** A combination of emotional, attitudinal, and behavioural response patterns of an individual.

unlike me." A personality inventory yields a **personality profile**, an overall portrait of a person that describes and predicts the way that person is likely to think, act, or feel across a variety of situations. Emerging and young adults might complete personality inventories to help them determine which careers best match their personality. As **Figure 12.2**

> **personality profile** The unique combination of personality traits that describes the more and less dominant features of an individual's personality and dominance of the Big Five traits relative to one another.

Personality Traits

One way of understanding what personality is and how it influences our daily lives is to think about the characteristics that most and least describe us. This is how personality psychologists, particularly those who use trait theory to explain personality, understand what makes each of us unique. Trait theorists operate from the assumption that a very small number of traits, or characteristics, combine in an endless number of ways to distinguish one person from another. The most well-known personality trait theory is the **Big Five** or **five-factor model of personality**, shown in **Figure 12.1** (Costa & McCrae, 1997; McCrae & Costa, 1990).

To assess emerging and young adults' personalities, researchers ask people to complete **personality inventories** in which they rate descriptions of feelings, thoughts, and behaviours on a scale from "very like me" to "very

> **Big Five** or **five-factor model of personality** A theory that there are five personality traits that combine to express personality: openness to experience, conscientiousness, extraversion, agreeableness, and neuroticism.

> **personality inventory** A questionnaire used to rate a person on a set of characteristics that make up a respondent's personality.

The Big Five personality traits • Figure 12.1

Big Five traits are often remembered using the acronym OCEAN: openness to experience, conscientiousness, extraversion, agreeableness, and neuroticism.

Big Five traits	Low scorers	High scorers
1 **O**penness	Down-to-earth Uncreative Conventional Uncurious	Imaginative Creative Original Curious
2 **C**onscientiousness	Negligent Lazy Disorganized Late	Conscientious Hard-working Well-organized Punctual
3 **E**xtraversion	Loner Quiet Passive Reserved	Joiner Talkative Active Affectionate
4 **A**greeableness	Suspicious Critical Ruthless Irritable	Trusting Lenient Soft-hearted Good-natured
5 **N**euroticism	Calm Even-tempered Comfortable Unemotional	Worried Temperamental Self-conscious Emotional

> **Think Critically** Using the Big Five, how would a character in a book behave, think, and feel if that character had the personality opposite yours on the Big Five?

Personality inventories • Figure 12.2

Trait theory has informed the development of many personality tests other than those assessing the Big Five personality traits. Tests that deliver personality profiles can provide important, even essential, information useful in a variety of settings.

a. The **Myers-Briggs Type Indicator (MBTI)** is a well-known personality test that types individuals according to responses on four dimensions: (1) introversion vs. extraversion, (2) sensing vs. intuiting, (3) thinking vs. feeling, and (4) judging vs. perceiving. The Myers-Briggs is commonly used to assess career interests and match people with careers that are most likely to fit them.

> **Myers-Briggs Type Indicator** A personality test that maps people along four dimensions and is commonly used in career counseling.

b. The **Minnesota Multiphasic Personality Inventory—Second Edition (MMPI-2)** is used in clinical settings to assess personality traits known to be associated with mental illnesses. The MMPI-2 is also used to select candidates for positions that require top security clearance for organizations such as the U.S. Central Intelligence Agency.

> **Minnesota Multiphasic Personality Inventory** A personality test used by clinicians for the purpose of assessing traits associated with mental illness.

> **Think Critically** How might a personality inventory help you at this stage of your life?

ISTJ	**ISFJ**	**INFJ**	**INTJ**
Responsible, sincere, analytical, reserved, realistic, systematic. Hardworking and trustworthy with sound practical judgement.	Warm, considerate, gentle, responsible, pragmatic, thorough. Devoted caretakers who enjoy being helpful to others.	Idealistic, organized, insightful, dependable, compassionate, gentle. Seek harmony and co-operation, enjoy intellectual stimulation.	Innovative, independent, strategic, logical, reserved, insightful. Driven by their own original ideas to achieve improvements.
ISTP	**ISFP**	**INFP**	**INTP**
Action-oriented, logical, analytical, spontaneous, reserved, independent. Enjoy adventure, skilled at understanding how mechanical things work.	Gentle, sensitive, nurturing, helpful, flexible, realistic. Seek to create a personal environment that is both beautiful and practical.	Sensitive, creative, idealistic, perceptive, caring, loyal. Value inner harmony and personal growth, focus on dreams and possibilities.	Intellectual, logical, precise, reserved, flexible, imaginative. Original thinkers who enjoy speculation and creative problem solving.
ESTP	**ESFP**	**ENFP**	**ENTP**
Outgoing, realistic, action-oriented, curious, versatile, spontaneous. Pragmatic problem solvers and skilful negotiators.	Playful, enthusiastic, friendly, spontaneous, tactful, flexible. Have strong common sense, enjoy helping people in tangible ways.	Enthusiastic, creative, spontaneous, optimistic, supportive, playful. Value inspiration, enjoy starting new projects, see potential in others.	Inventive, enthusiastic, strategic, enterprising, inquisitive, versatile. Enjoy new ideas and challenges, value inspiration.
ESTJ	**ESFJ**	**ENFJ**	**ENTJ**
Efficient, outgoing, analytical, systematic, dependable, realistic. Like to run the show and get things done in an orderly fashion.	Friendly, outgoing, reliable, conscientious, organized, practical. Seek to be helpful and please others, enjoy being active and productive.	Caring, enthusiastic, idealistic, organized, diplomatic, reponsible. Skilled communicators who value connection with people.	Strategic, logical, efficient, outgoing, ambitious, independent. Effective organizers of people and long-range planners.

Subscales of the MMPI-2

Clinical scales	Typical interpretations of high scores
1. Hypochondriasis	Numerous physical complaints
2. Depression	Seriously depressed and pessimistic
3. Hysteria	Suggestible, immature, self-centred, demanding
4. Psychopathic deviate	Rebellious, nonconformist
5. Masculinity-femininity	Interests like those of other sex
6. Paranoia	Suspicious and resentful of others
7. Psychasthenia	Fearful, agitated, brooding
8. Schizophrenia	Withdrawn, reclusive, bizarre thinking
9. Hypomania	Distractible, impulsive, dramatic
10. Social introversion	Shy, introverted, self-effacing

shows, personality inventories also help clinicians assess whether the way a person's personality is organized warrants the attention of a mental health professional.

Trait theories and the Big Five model of personality dominate personality research. However, there is an alternative way of thinking about personality. Rather than consider a set of traits, developmentalists often view personality as a set of strengths that can be acquired as we progress through the different stages of the lifespan.

Psychosocial Development

Theories of **psychosocial development** assume that personality is shaped throughout the lifespan. Through specific challenges we face at each life stage, our personalities can become more adaptive and more sophisticated, improving our ability to control impulses and respond to the demands of our social worlds. A number of psychosocial stage theories have outlined the different tasks people encounter at different life stages. Erik Erikson's (1950) model of psychosocial development is the best known. As you have learned, Erikson divided the lifespan into eight stages, with each stage defined by one central task.

The central task of adolescence, according to Erikson, is establishing a personal identity. The critical questions a young person is trying to answer at this life stage are "Who am I?" and "What can I become?" According to Erikson, the identity crisis begins in the teen years but is often not resolved until the 20s. Identity achievement contributes to healthy personality development. Erikson believed those who fail to resolve questions about their identity experience a sense of **role confusion**, appearing adrift, aimless, and without direction.

psychosocial development A set of theories that assume personality is shaped through experience and interactions with the environment throughout the lifespan.

role confusion The lack of a secure sense of self and identity, according to Erikson.

intimacy vs. isolation stage Erikson's sixth stage of psychosocial development, leading to the capacity to share oneself with another or not.

In young adulthood, as we try to find our place in the world through both love and work, we also face the **intimacy vs. isolation stage**. The young adult grapples with the question, "Can I love?" In Erikson's view, achieving intimacy has little to do with marriage or taking a romantic partner, but rather is an outcome of knowing oneself and having the ability to share oneself with another. In this way, it is clear how achieving a solid sense of self, an identity, is an essential step in achieving true intimacy with another.

Young people strive for intimacy in different ways, as you can see in **Figure 12.3**. Resolving both identity and intimacy in emerging and young adulthood predicts healthy adjustment not only in the 20s and 30s, but later into adulthood as well. Findings from the Rochester Adult Longitudinal Study revealed that identity and intimacy in the early 20s were associated with well-being and relationship satisfaction in the 50s (Sneed, Whitbourne, Schwartz, & Huang, 2012).

Personality Change

One of the major questions of personality psychology is "Does personality change?" (Mayer, 2007) Knowing whether or not personality changes, particularly during emerging and young adulthood, is useful information because it helps us understand what normal development looks like during these years. Findings from numerous studies tell us that personality continues to change through the transition to adulthood and that it changes more through the 20s than it does in later stages of adulthood. Researchers find this same pattern across cultures. With respect to the Big Five traits, conscientiousness and agreeableness tend to increase during these years (Srivastava, John, Gosling, & Potter, 2003), perhaps because young people are trying hard to establish their careers and build relationships with others. Extraversion and openness to experience decrease as we move through the transition to adulthood, which may reflect progress in selecting pathways, settling down, and exploring less (Donnellan & Lucas, 2008). Neuroticism decreases after adolescence and throughout adulthood (Soto, John, Gosling, & Potter, 2011).

Knowing these general trends, however, does not make it easy to predict which of your friends is going to change the most, how each will change, or in what direction. People change over time in many different ways. For example, one friend may make huge gains in conscientiousness, whereas another friend may become less conscientious during the same years (Roberts & DelVecchio, 2000). Think of all the things that happen to us during our 20s. There are a great number of influences that shape our personalities. It makes sense that personality remains open and flexible through our 20s and less so after young people make commitments to the adult roles that organize and stabilize their lives. After age 30, people change much less relative to one another. The way friends behave, think, and feel about life becomes more and more predictable with age.

CONCEPT CHECK

1. **Which** five personality traits are referenced by the mnemonic OCEAN?

2. **What** are the three forms of intimacy identified by Erikson?

3. **How** does personality change during emerging and young adulthood?

Erikson's three forms of intimacy • Figure 12.3

Erikson believed intimacy to be critical for the young adult's healthy personality development. Intimacy can take many forms, including the three shown here.

a. Physical intimacy is most notable during the early stages of a relationship. Erikson suggested that young adults achieve intimacy mainly through physical acts, including sex, and that true intimacy does not appear until later (Capps, 2004; Sneed, Whitbourne, & Culang, 2006).

DonyKuo/iStockphoto

Warren Goldswain/Shutterstock

b. As a relationship grows stronger, **intellectual intimacy** may emerge. This form of intimacy is based on having shared attitudes, opinions, and preferences, such as this couple's love for outdoor adventures. Intellectual intimacy forms the basis of social relationships and is driven by a need for humans to connect with others (Hawkley, Browne, & Cacioppo, 2005).

Think Critically To be able to have true emotional intimacy, which of Erikson's earlier stages of psychosocial development need to be resolved successfully? Why?

PeopleImages/iStockphoto

c. The final and most substantive type of intimacy is **emotional intimacy**. This type of intimacy forms as people share information about themselves, like these university students discussing their goals and dreams with one another. Erikson believed that emotional intimacy rarely appears during the emerging adult years.

Social Influences

LEARNING OBJECTIVES

1. **Describe** the role of family in emerging and young adulthood.
2. **Understand** the factors that determine the selection of adult friendships.
3. **Define** the components of love proposed by Sternberg's triangular theory of love.
4. **Explain** different pathways to marriage.
5. **Identify** the challenges young people face when they become parents.

Relationships matter. At the transition from adolescence into emerging adulthood, relationships take on new meanings as young people are challenged to develop self-sufficiency and responsibility for themselves.

Relationship experiences and quality of relationships influence a person's developing sense of self in relation to others; reciprocally, a person's sense of self in relation to others influences the quality of relationships a person has with friends, families, partners, and co-workers.

Family

Family relationships change significantly as teens approach adulthood. The **family life-cycle** model shown in **Figure 12.4** is useful in understanding how **first-order change**—development of the individual—is related to **second-order change**—changes in the family. **Differentiation** takes centre stage in families as adult children face the transition to adulthood. Healthy differentiation is more likely to occur in families with histories of high cohesion and low conflict (Aquilino & Supple, 2001; Fosco, Caruthers, & Dishion, 2012). In families characterized by high warmth, respect for personal boundaries, and low conflict,

First order change The development of the individual in a family life-cycle.

Second order change In the family life-cycle, these are changes in the family.

family life cycle The stages of development a family goes through as a function of the aging and maturation of individual family members.

differentiation The ability to maintain a sense of self while in a relationship with others.

PROCESS DIAGRAM

The family life cycle • Figure 12.4

✓ THE PLANNER

Similar to Erikson's proposition that the individual lifespan is divided into tasks that are common at different life stages, the family life cycle describes the predictable stages of a family through a generation.

Think Critically **1.** Which of these eight family life-cycle stages correspond to emerging adulthood?
2. Which correspond to young adulthood?

1 **Family-of-origin experiences**
- Maintain relationships with parents, siblings, and peers
- Determine education and training goals
- Develop the foundations of model family life

2 **Leaving home**
- Differentiate self from family of origin
- Develop adult-to-adult relationships with parents
- Develop intimate peer relationships
- Begin work, developing work identity and financial independence

3 **Premarriage**
- Select a partner or decide to remain single
- Establish relationship intimacy
- Make a plan for establishing a family home

4 **Childless couplehood**
- Develop a way to live together practically and emotionally
- Adjust family of origin and peer relationships to include partner
- Make decisions about adding a child to the partnership

5 **Family with young children**
- Realign family system to make space for children
- Adopt and develop parenting roles
- Realign family relationships with families of origin to include parenting and grandparenting roles

6 **Family with adolescents**
- Adjust parent–child relationships to allow adolescents more autonomy
- Adjust family relationships to focus on mid-life relationship and career issues
- Take on responsibility for caring for families of origin

7 **Launching adult children**
- Negotiate adult-to-adult relationships with children
- Adjust to living as a couple again
- Adjust to include in-laws and grandchildren
- Deal with disabilities and death in the family of origin

8 **Later family life**
- Adjust to children taking a more central role in family maintenance
- Value wisdom and experiences of older adults
- Deal with loss of spouse and peers
- Prepare for death

Support from parents • Figure 12.5

Parents provide support in different ways in emerging and young adulthood.

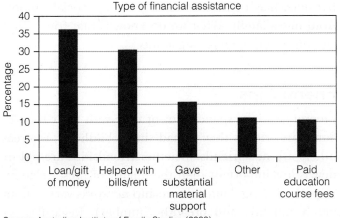

Type of financial assistance

Source: Australian Institute of Family Studies (2009).

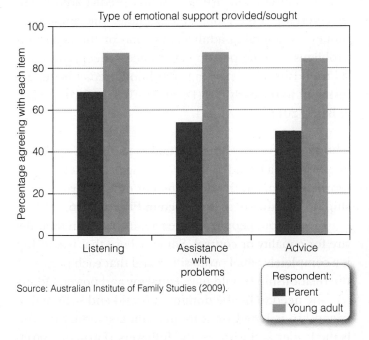

Type of emotional support provided/sought

Source: Australian Institute of Family Studies (2009).

Respondent:
■ Parent
■ Young adult

a. Parents provide financial support to their adult children. Over one-third of parents report giving their adult child a loan or gift of money in the past year.

b. Parents also provide their adult children with emotional support. In fact, adult children report receiving higher levels of emotional support from their parents than parents report.

Think Critically What are the pros and cons of parents extending support into their children's 20s? Think about costs and benefits to adult children and to their parents.

children are encouraged and expected to become responsible for themselves in emerging adulthood and to develop a set of beliefs and values all their own.

On average, emerging adults' relationships with their parents get better after adolescence, as conflict decreases (Whiteman, McHale, & Crouter, 2011). Emerging adults' relationships with parents are most positive after they have made significant gains in establishing themselves as adults—they have moved away from home, are employed, have partnered—and before there are any children in the picture.

During the transition to adulthood, parents may be important sources of **affective**

affective support
Emotionally based expressions of interest, care, and concern.

instrumental support The provision of tangible assistance.

support, providing comfort and concern, as well as **instrumental support**, including money and goods—or both (Sage & Johnson, 2012)—as shown in **Figure 12.5**. The type of support emerging and young adult children receive changes across the transition to adulthood. Parents provide scaffolding and safety nets as their adult children make progress toward taking responsibility for themselves. Parents give less support to young people who make greater gains in becoming financially independent and romantically independent—that is, those who make progress setting up households of their own (Swartz, Kim, Uno, Mortimer, & O'Brien, 2011).

The amount of support an emerging adult will receive from parents varies from family to family. Emerging adults from two-parent households receive more support because those families are likely to have greater financial resources available (Johnson & Benson, 2012). The amount of financial support young people get from their parents does not appear to differ for young men and women or for emerging adults from different races and ethnic backgrounds. What does make a difference is parents' education. Emerging adults whose parents have higher levels of education receive significantly more financial support than emerging adults whose parents have less education. This pattern has not changed significantly over the past 30 years (Wightman, Patrick, Schoeni, & Schulenberg, 2013).

At the same time, parent–child relationship quality and the emerging adult's ability to achieve responsibility also play a role in determining the amount of support that is provided, and in a very interesting way. Within families, it appears that the squeaky wheel gets the grease—parents provide more financial assistance to adult children who need more support (Fingerman, Miller, Birditt, & Zarit, 2009). Emerging adults who experience more employment problems and more negative life events get more support from parents than those who have fewer problems (Swartz et al., 2011).

For young adults, the transition to parenthood is unique in its effect on the parent–adult child relationship, and specifically with respect to support. When emerging adults have a child, the decrease in parent financial support is less significant than the reduction we see when adult children make other transitions, such as career and relationship transitions (Hartnett, Furstenberg, Fingerman, & Birditt, 2010). The transition to parenthood is associated with an increase in practical support; for example, in the form of help with housework and child care (Bucx, van Wel, & Knijn, 2012). This type of intergenerational support and care requires adult children and their parents to renegotiate boundaries to accommodate the parent and grandparent roles and exchange of new types of need and support (Breheny, Stephens, & Spilsbury, 2013).

Perhaps not surprisingly, however, young people whose earlier relationships with their parents were problematic (higher in negative emotions and lower in positive emotions) continue to have less positive relationships (Belsky, Jaffee, Caspi, Moffit, & Silva, 2003).

Changes in support from parents occur in the context of broader changes in the emerging adults' network of close social relationships. Despite the significant changes in social relationships that are common in emerging adulthood, we know very little about the way relationships with others, including friends and intimate partners, may contribute to low or high social support from one's family. What we do know is that friendships are important to emerging adults.

Friendships

Emerging adults spend a lot of time with their friends. Some are friends they've had since childhood, whereas others are new friends. Whether friendships are old or new is less important than the quality of these relationships. Emerging adults' friendship networks vary in both depth (quality) and breadth (number). Regardless of other resources and risk factors that predict adjustment in emerging adulthood—for example, the amount of money an emerging adult's family has or the behaviour problems a young person experiences—deep, meaningful friendships in emerging adulthood predict better adjustment in the early 20s (Pettit, Erath, Lansford, Dodge, & Bates, 2011).

Choosing friends But what makes us choose a particular person as a friend? Fehr (1996) suggests that there are four key factors in the development of long-term friendships in adulthood, as described in **Figure 12.6**.

In addition, people choose friends based on their desire for equality or control. Some believe that friendship is a completely equal proposition and that each person in the relationship should have equal say and power. Others feel the need to be the dominant friend and believe that friendship is based on a mutual understanding of who is the leader and who are the followers (Furman, 2001). Friendships also vary based on the individual's desire for communion, agency, and individuation. **Communion** is the levels of closeness and equality people want in their friendships. **Agency** is the amount of control a person asserts over his life. **Individuation** is the extent to which individuals actualize their true selves (Adams & Blieszner, 1994; Zarbatany, Conley, & Pepper, 2004). When two people fit together on these factors, they are more likely to become friends.

> **communion** The levels of closeness and equality people want in their friendships.
>
> **agency** The amount of control individuals perceive and assert over their life.
>
> **individuation** The extent to which individuals actualize their true selves.

Who do we pick as friends? • Figure 12.6

Researcher Beverly Fehr (1996) identified four key factors in the formation of adult friendships.

a. Physical attractiveness
People tend to select friends with similar levels of attractiveness.

b. Proximity
People choose friends who are geographically near.

Tom Carter/Photo Edit

Peathegee Inc/Blend Images/Corbis

c. Frequent exposure
People are more likely to be friends when they spend time together.

d. Exclusionary criteria
People who do not share values are unlikely to become friends. Exclusionary criteria often include religious, racial, political, and/or lifestyle factors, such as smoking.

Fotoluminate LLC/Shutterstock

Martinan /iStockphoto

Think Critically Given these factors underlying friendship, imagine a specific emerging adult and describe the friends your imaginary person is most likely to have.

Another key issue related to friendships is gender. In general, women are likely to have more friends than men. They are also more likely than men are to see friendship as a process of support and emotional connection (Cramer & Donachie, 1999; King & Terrance, 2008). Compared with women, men are more likely to engage in active gatherings with their friends, such as sports, and are more likely to keep both physical and emotional distance.

But what happens when men and women are friends? Through much of North American history, most adult friendships were same sex (Wright, 1982), continuing the patterns typically set in childhood and adolescence (Bukowski, Newcomb, & Hartup, 1996). However, in modern times, more diverse-sex friendships are likely to occur. Some men report that having female friends helps them develop romantic relationships with other women. Meanwhile, women report that male friends require less maintenance than their romantic relationships. All in all, both sexes report fulfilling and educational benefits in cross-gender friendships, though potential conflicts with romantic heterosexual partners remain a concern (Samter & Cupach, 1998).

Social networks Regardless of sex, one contemporary development that appears to be affecting how friends of every type interact is social networking. Although online

> **social network** A group of people who identify themselves as connected because of some similar demographic, such as religion, age, ethnicity, or common interest, and who interact regularly.
>
> **social networking site (SNS)** An Internet-based community in which people can join and connect with others, share information, and interact socially online.

social networking is relatively recent, the idea of social networks is not new. A person's **social network** was originally viewed by social scientists as a social structure composed of individuals who share some type of demographic connection (Wellman & Berkowitz, 1988). In the 1960s and 1970s, individuals in the same social group, high school organization, chamber of commerce, student union, or book club would have been referred to as a *social network*. At that time, the primary connection between members of social networks was physical geography. Clearly, the Internet has changed all of that.

As you're most likely aware, the twenty-first century has brought an explosion of **social networking sites (SNSs)**, Internet-based interactive venues for people to connect with others of similar ethnicity, age, sexual orientation, or any number of demographic, social, and/or business-related variables (**Figure 12.7**; Barker, 2009). The most popular of these venues is Facebook, with over 1.3 billion monthly active users (Statistic Brain, 2014). Other popular SNSs include Twitter and Instagram, with new sites frequently gaining and losing popularity.

Given the cost of travelling great distances, or even across town, SNSs can provide us with opportunities to strengthen our social ties, become aware of social issues, and, in some cases, even improve physical and mental health (Ellison, Steinfield, & Lampe, 2007). Researchers have found that people use SNSs to create new relationships, often forming offline friendships from online

Social networking • Figure 12.7

Social networking is now a common means of connecting with others for the vast majority of emerging and young adults. The use of social networking sites has increased significantly in recent years. Emerging adults make up the largest proportion of users of all the social networking sites. Over 90 percent of emerging adults use at least one social networking site. Which sites do you and your friends prefer?

Think Critically Reflecting on Fehr's model of long-term friendship, what role can social networking sites play in providing a context for such relationships?

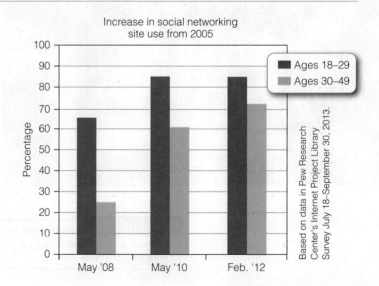

meetings, as well as to maintain old relationships that were initially formed offline (Ellison et al., 2007; Parks & Floyd, 1996). Not all results of using SNSs are positive, however. Some observers have worried that SNSs detract from users' face-to-face relationships (Nie, 2001) and increase their risks of becoming victims of identity theft or Internet stalking. All in all, though, current research seems to support SNSs as a forum for adding to our social support systems and self-esteem (Barker, 2009).

In addition to the rise of SNSs, instant message-exchange systems have become increasingly popular. Text messaging, instant messaging, and Twitter are all social options in which individuals share bits of information about themselves electronically. Emerging adults report that the most positive aspect of this type of communication is that it affords control over social relationships (Madell & Muncer, 2007). That is, the asynchronous nature of electronic communication allows more freedom than face-to-face interaction. You don't necessarily have to answer a text immediately, for example, but your in-person conversation partner would likely be disturbed if you took several minutes or even hours to respond. Regardless of how they choose to connect with others, having a rich social life is important for the health and life satisfaction of emerging and young adults (Hawthorne, 2008; Helson & Kwan, 2000).

Romantic Relationships

By the time we reach emerging adulthood, we are familiar with the role love plays in relationships. However, adult love is multi-faceted. *Love* doesn't mean the same thing to all emerging and young adults. And young people may be looking for different types of love as they explore the way they relate intimately to others.

Consummate love is romantic love, or love that involves sexual relations with a partner—a different type of love than the love people feel for friends or their children. One of the most well-known theories of consummate, or romantic, love was developed by psychologist Robert Sternberg. As shown in **Figure 12.8**, Sternberg's **triangular theory of love**

> **consummate love** A relationship involving both emotional and physical intimacy.
>
> **triangular theory of love** Sternberg's (1997) theory suggesting that various types of love reflect different combinations of passion, intimacy, and commitment.

(Sternberg, 1997, 2006) consists of three components: passion, intimacy, and commitment.

Dating Who do you ask out on a date? When and why? Historically, in heterosexual dating, men did much of the asking when it came to dating (Miller, 2001). By the 1980s, women were increasingly likely to initiate dates (Buss, 1985; Cram & Jackson, 2003). Today, dating may be less likely to conform to tradition, but the practice of dating remains common—over 70 percent of university and college students report dating (Siebenbruner, 2013).

Regardless of who does the asking, physical attraction tends to be a key factor in a person's desire for a date (Swami & Furnham, 2008; Wilson & Cousins, 2003). People also tend to date and mate with someone similar to themselves, a process called **assortative mating** (Caspi & Herbener, 1990). Indeed, people are more satisfied with others who share similar values, education, personality traits, religion, and ethnicity than with those who differ on such variables (Bleske-Rechek, Remiker, & Baker, 2009).

> **assortative mating** A process throughout the animal kingdom in which species seek out similar partners as mates.

Coupling Making commitments to romantic partners, along with establishing a work identity, is a task that gains significance in emerging adulthood compared with developmental tasks they continue to work on, such as academics, peer relationships, and conduct (Roisman, Masten, Coatsworth, & Tellegen, 2004). Although we might be tempted to assume that emerging adult relationships share the same qualities, they vary with respect to timing, duration, and frequency. Researchers followed a group of children into their 20s. They identified five distinct groups of emerging adults based on the timing, duration, and frequency of their romantic relationships from ages 18 to 25: those who were (1) steadily involved (22 percent), (2) later involved (28 percent), (3) sporadically involved (13 percent), (4) frequently involved (16 percent), and (5) long-term committed (21 percent) (Rauer, Pettit, Lansford, Bate, & Dodge, 2013).

Coupling in emerging adulthood is influenced by developmental histories of relating to close personal others. Over 40 percent of emerging adults were consistently involved with, on average, one or two partners.

Development InSight
Sternberg's triangular
theory of love • **Figure 12.8**

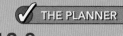 ✓ THE PLANNER

According to Robert Sternberg's triangular theory of love, various types of love can be created by different combinations of passion, intimacy, and commitment.

a. Passion is the physical component of love, characterized by lust, physical attraction, and sexual desire. Passion is accompanied by high heart rates, constant thoughts of the beloved, and the need for proximity to that person.

Passion The physical component of love.

b. Intimacy is characterized by an emotional connection as a result of attachment and bonding. Intimacy is promoted by sharing personal feelings, beliefs, and values.

Intimacy The emotional connection of love.

Liking

INTIMACY

Romantic love

Companionate love

CONSUMMATE LOVE

Intimacy + Passion + Commitment

PASSION

COMMITMENT

Infatuation

Empty love

Fatuous love

Commitment The decision to maintain a connection with another person.

c. Commitment is a conscious decision to maintain a connection with another person. Short-term commitment is characterized by the decision to have a focused and often mutually exclusive relationship with someone. Long-term commitment involves a greater investment and acknowledgement of a shared future.

Ask Yourself

With respect to the triangular theory of love, which type of love is characterized by physical, emotional, and cognitive attachments to another?

During childhood and adolescence, these emerging adults reported positive relationships with their mothers and their peers. In contrast, emerging adults with more partners and intermittent or sporadic romantic relationships reported, in adolescence, that they received support from their peers and reported that their peers engaged in more deviant behaviours. Harsh parenting in childhood and low parental monitoring were also associated with less steady romantic relationships in emerging adulthood (Rauer et al., 2013).

hook-up A sexual encounter that involves mutual consent and mutual agreement that no relationship commitment is expected.

Hooking up Nowadays—in the **hook-up** era (Bogle, 2008)—sexual behaviour without commitment is normative in emerging adulthood. Hooking up is relatively common among university and college students, ranging from 50 percent to 85 percent (Owen, Rhoades, Stanley, & Fincham, 2010). Importantly, the four-year university setting tends to discourage relationships and makes hooking up appealing; likely this is part of the reason it is the site of much research about the phenomenon; however, it also reflects a privileged path to adulthood and may be less common in other contexts (Hamilton & Armstrong, 2009). Hooking up is an ambiguous term used to refer to a wide range of sexual behaviours. In one study of university students, approximately 70 percent of male students reported hooking up during a semester at school and 73 percent of those were penetrative hook-ups involving either oral sex or intercourse (Olmstead, Pasley, & Fincham, 2012).

Male and female university students are equally likely to hook up (Owen et al., 2010). However, women and men who choose to hook up face different social perceptions. As has been historically true, men who have multiple sexual partners are still seen more positively than are women (Epstein, Calzo, Smiler, & Ward, 2009). University women report less positive hooking-up experiences than men (Owen et al., 2010).

Much of the research on hooking up and sexual behaviour of emerging adults, in general, focuses on what we know about heterosexual sexual behaviours. Hooking up might be experienced differently depending on whether an emerging adult is looking for a heterosexual or same-sex hook-up partner. For example, university students looking for hetero-sex partners were more likely to find partners on campus, at parties, or at bars; whereas university students looking for same-sex encounters, men and women, were more likely to find partners online (Kuperberg & Padgett, 2014). This likely indicates that gay, lesbian, transsexual, and transgender emerging adults face different odds in their quest to hook up on or off campus in a sexually **heteronormative** world.

heteronormative Assuming that heterosexual behaviour is the norm and that men and women fall into traditional sex roles in life.

Some university students are more likely than others to hook up. Caucasian emerging adult students are more likely to hook up than students from all other races and ethnicities (Owen et al., 2010). In addition, emerging adult students who come from families that have more money are more likely to hook up than students whose families reported less income. Whether or not parents are divorced isn't a significant factor in predicting who hooks up while attending university; perhaps surprisingly, neither is religious background a material factor. A much less surprising finding is that emerging adults who hold favourable views of hooking up and those who drink more alcohol are more likely to hook up (Owen et al., 2010).

Outcomes of hook-ups vary greatly. By definition, sexual hook-ups have no strings attached. Sexual exploration is normative in emerging adulthood; these are opportunities for learning about oneself as a sexual adult and an opportunity to learn how to relate sexually to another. However, it's not always the case that no strings are attached. For example, sometimes relationships characterized by repeated hooking up—sometimes called *friends with benefits* (FWBs)—really are relationships that one or both partners want to transform into a more exclusive relationship (Epstein et al., 2009; Mongeau, Knight, Williams, Eden, & Shaw, 2011). In other cases, one partner desires an outcome the other partner does not. In most cases, such unwanted affection is merely annoying to the disinterested partner, but dangerous consequences remain a potential concern. When extreme emotions are triggered by a lack of return of the same feelings, other factors may be playing a role in the intensity, such as sex addiction, drugs, and anger (Evans, Grace, Higman, & Evans, 2009).

Canadian cohabitation trends in terms of married and common-law couples, 1981–2011 • Figure 12.9

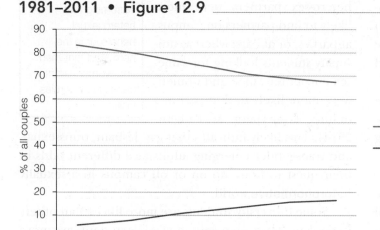

Source: Statistics Canada (2013). Fifty years of families in Canada: 1961 to 2011. Statistics Canada catalogue no. 98-312-X2011003. Retrieved from www12.statcan. gc.ca/census-recensement/2011/as-sa/98-312-x/98-312-x2011003_1-eng.cfm.

Cohabitation Over the last decade, a greater number of emerging adults in North America have lived with an intimate partner, in **cohabitation**, before or as an alternative to marriage (Popenoe, 2009; Williams, Sassler, & Nicholson, 2008). **Figure 12.9** shows the Canadian cohabitation trends in terms of married and common-law couples. Statistics Canada began collecting cohabitation information in 1981.

> **Cohabitation**
> The commitment to live with an intimate partner (without a marriage certificate).

The majority of those who cohabit are young romantic partners (Popenoe, 2009). **Figure 12.10** illustrates changes in the perception of cohabitation over time.

There are few differences in cohabitation patterns between different racial or ethnic groups (Kroeger & Smock, 2014). When socio-economic status is taken into consideration, differences by race and ethnicity in the rate of transitioning from cohabitation to marriage become irrelevant. This is because economic resources do matter. For more socio-economically advantaged adults, cohabitation is more likely to be a step toward marriage. For those less socio-economically advantaged, cohabitation is more likely to be an end (Kroeger & Smock, 2014).

For decades, researchers have reported that heterosexual couples who go on to marry after living together premaritally were more likely to divorce. However, that risk disappears when researchers take age into consideration. The older a person is when making a first commitment, the less likely the person is to divorce (Kuperberg, 2014). That is, the longer a couple waits to make a commitment, the less likely they are to undo it.

Problems in romantic relationships Intimate relationships in the transition to adulthood may be a source of stress, resulting in tension and conflict. One team of researchers who followed a group of young people from the same community over several years found that partner conflict increases between ages 19 and 25 and then decreases through the early 30s. Several background characteristics are associated with relationship conflict in emerging adulthood: having a family history of low socio-economic status, being an only child, and experiencing a parental divorce. In addition, the demands of a relationship contribute to the likelihood of experiencing stress and conflict. Between ages 17 and 27, emerging adults who got married, got divorced, or became parents during this time experience a greater increase in relationship conflict than emerging adults who did not make these transitions (Chen et al., 2006). What this means is that managing life for one is hard, but managing partnerships and parenting is even more challenging.

Some young people will find it easier than others to establish relationships that are healthy and relatively low in stress and conflict. Think back to what you learned in earlier chapters about attachment theory, particularly the expectation that early attachment experiences influence the way we relate to others in later relationships. Adult attachment theory works from the assumption that **interpersonal schemas**

> **interpersonal schema** An expectation about whether intimate relationships satisfy or deny emotional and psychological needs.

Perceptions of cohabitation over time • Figure 12.10

Over the past several decades, it has become increasingly common for romantically involved, non-married couples to live together whether or not they intend to get married.

a. Increasing numbers of young adults are living together without getting married.

Christopher Clem Franken/Visum/The Image Works

b. Part of the increase in cohabitation may be due to more positive perceptions of the practice. For example, in a survey of Grade 12 students taken in 2005, as shown in this chart, more than 60 percent either "agreed" or "mostly agreed" that it was a good idea to live together before getting married (Popenoe & Whitehead, 2007), compared with fewer than 40 percent in the 1970s.

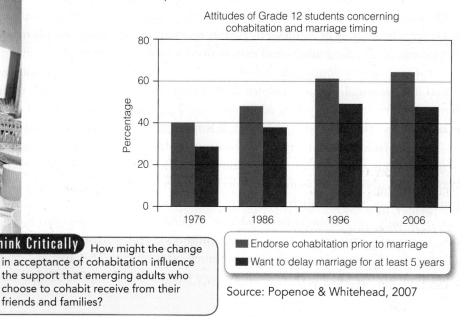

Attitudes of Grade 12 students concerning cohabitation and marriage timing

■ Endorse cohabitation prior to marriage
■ Want to delay marriage for at least 5 years

Source: Popenoe & Whitehead, 2007

Think Critically How might the change in acceptance of cohabitation influence the support that emerging adults who choose to cohabit receive from their friends and families?

---

developed in the first year of life are carried over into adult romantic relationships. These expectations based on past ways of relating—whether healthy or unhealthy—affect the way young adults relate to their intimate partners. Young people with healthy schemas seek relationships that validate those schemas; young people with unhealthy schemas seek to replicate those damaged ideas about how people relate intimately to one another. For example, when young people who experienced abuse in their early years perceive a threat in their current relationships, they are primed to expect rejection (Berenson & Andersen, 2006).

Relationship churning—on-again, off-again relationships in which intimate partners break up and get back together—mimics the approach–avoidance type of relationship found in some types of insecure attachment between infants and caregivers. For almost

relationship churning An on-off pattern found in some intimate relationships where partners frequently break up and reconcile.

personality disorder A long-term pattern of relating that causes problems in relationships and at work.

half of emerging adults, breakups don't necessarily mean the end of the relationship. One study of 17- to 24-year-olds in intimate relationships revealed that 44 percent of emerging adults who had been in a relationship in the past two years experienced at least one reconciliation with their partner (Halpern-Meekin, Manning, Giordano, & Longmore, 2013). Of those who experienced a reconciliation, more than half (53 percent) reported that they had sex with this ex. Relationship churning may also be a signal of conflict that goes beyond normal and healthy arguments between partners.

Psychopathology can also contribute to relationship problems. Approximately one in five (20 percent) 18- to 25-year-olds meet the established criteria for a **personality disorder** (Blanco et al., 2008). Although personality disorders disrupt many domains of a person's life, they are particularly insidious in close interpersonal relationships.

Extreme cases of dysfunctional relating can result in intimate partner violence. Partner violence happens in all types of intimate relationships, at all ages, and to people of all genders. As shown in **Figure 12.11**, it takes many forms. Rates of partner violence are dramatically higher among young adults ages 18 to 24 than in other age groups (Catalano, 2012). Following over 4,000 adolescents into emerging adulthood, the National Longitudinal Study of Adolescent Health revealed that 40 percent of all young adults had experienced sexual or physical violence by young adulthood: 8 percent experienced interpersonal partner violence only during adolescence, 25 percent only in young adulthood, and 7 percent in both stages (Halpern, Spriggs, Martin, & Kupper, 2009).

Partner violence in emerging and young adulthood is not random. The victims are predominantly female. People who grow up in families headed by other than two biological parents, such as a stepfamily or single-parent family, are at increased risk for experiencing interpersonal partner violence by young adulthood. The strongest predictors of interpersonal violence by young adulthood are having a greater than average number of romantic partners and beginning sexual activity before age 16 (Halpern et al., 2009).

Marriage

Romantic relationships that aren't formally affirmed are different from those recognized by marriage. Marriage elicits a social acceptance from many people, who feel it signifies that a young person has joined the ranks of adults who have committed to sharing a life with another. In most cultures, there's a lot of pressure to get married, and marriage affords many social, legal, and financial rewards. For example, convergent sources of information report that married people live longer, are happier, and are better off economically than single people (Amato, 2005; Popenoe, 2008; Williams et al., 2008). However, **Figure 12.12** shows that the number of new marriages has been declining in Canada (Kelly, 2012) and those who do marry are waiting longer than ever to make the commitment to marriage (Employment and Social Development Canada, 2015).

Declining marriage rates may reflect young adults' widespread recognition that marriage can be a source of distress as well as happiness. Many who marry will divorce. The average marriage lasts approximately 8 years, and half of all first marriages among emerging adults end in

---

Intimate partner violence • Figure 12.11

Almost half of emerging adult couples report some type of partner violence in one year.

a. Intimate partner violence is not uncommon in emerging adulthood.

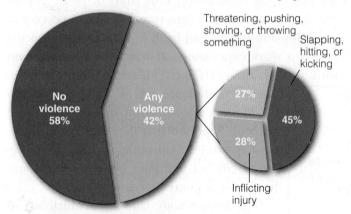

No violence 58%
Any violence 42%

Threatening, pushing, shoving, or throwing something — 27%
Slapping, hitting, or kicking — 45%
Inflicting injury — 28%

Source: Berger, A., Wildsmith, E., Manlove, J. & Steward-Streng, M.A. (June 2012). Relationship Violence Among Young Adult Couples, Child Trends Research Brief.

b. There are a number of types of intimate partner violence.

- **Sexual violence** includes rape, being made to penetrate someone else, sexual coercion, unwanted sexual contact/non-contact, and unwanted sexual experiences.

- **Physical violence** includes behaviours ranging from slapping, pushing, or shoving to severe acts such as being beaten, burned, or choked.

- **Stalking** involves a pattern of harassing or threatening tactics used by a perpetrator that both is unwanted and causes fear and safety concerns for the victim.

- **Psychological aggression** includes expressive aggression (such as name calling, insulting, or humiliating an intimate partner) and coercive control, which includes behaviours that are intended to monitor and control or threaten an intimate partner.

- **Control of reproductive or sexual heath** includes the refusal by an intimate partner to participate in safer sex strategies. In heterosexual relations, it also includes the intentional pursuit of pregnancy without the consent of both partners.

Think Critically Compared with other stages of the lifespan, what characteristics of emerging and young adulthood make these years particularly likely to be a time during which intimate partner violence occurs?

Changes in the Canadian population over time for marriages, divorces, and age of first marriage • Figure 12.12

Almost half of emerging adult couples report some type of partner violence in one year.

a. Number of marriages and divorces, Canada, 1926–2008

Source: Kelly, M. B. (2012). Divorce cases in civil court, 2010/2011. Statistics Canada catalogue no. 85-002-X. Retrieved from www.statcan.gc.ca/pub/85-002-x/2012001/article/11634-eng.htm.

Note: *Since 2003, the definition of marriage has been changed in some provinces and territories, and since 2005 for all of Canada, to include the legal union of two persons of the same sex. Age at first marriage for same-sex couples has been higher than for opposite-sex couples.*

b. Average age of first marriage, by gender, 1921–2008 (years)

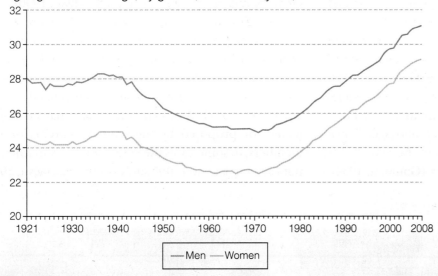

— Men — Women

Sources: Marriage and conjugal life in Canada, Statistics Canada, 1992 (catalogue no. 91-534E) Statistics Canada, Demography Division; Mean age and median age of males and females, by type of marriage and marital status, Canada, provinces and territories, annual (CANSIM Table 101-1002), Statistics Canada, 2008; Canadian Vital Statistics, Marriage Database and Demography Division (population estimates), Statistics Canada, 2011; Indicators of well-being in Canada: Family Life—Marriage, Employment and Social Development Canada, retrieved from http://well-being.esdc.gc.ca/misme-iowb/.3ndic.1t.4r@-eng.jsp?iid=78.

Think Critically

1. How might the developmental challenges of emerging adulthood impact affect on the rates of marriage, divorce, and age of first marriage?

2. What are some questions that may be raised when examining the changes in marriage and divorce rates over time?

3. The average age at first marriage has been steadily climbing. How do you think the average age of first marriage as shown here interacts with rates in the graph in figure b? What kind of research would be needed to understand the impact of age at first marriage on divorce rates if population level data aren't providing a complete picture?

divorce by age 30 for women and 32 for men (Kreider & Ellis, 2009; Stevenson & Wolfers, 2007). Perhaps emerging adults have less mature coping skills, or perhaps their choice of marital partners puts them at greater risk for divorce than those who marry later.

Although being married can be challenging, marriages can be and often are successful. Research has shown that striving for agreed-upon goals and making a mutual commitment to one another typically strengthens a marriage (Gottman, 2006; Heyman, Sayers, & Bellack, 1994). But sometimes partners differ in their ability to handle marital stress, and differences don't necessarily mean that the couple is doomed (Bodenmann, Pihet, & Kayser, 2006). Rather, newlyweds who feel that their partner understands them report high relationship quality regardless of how much their partner actually does know them (Pollmann & Finkenauer, 2009). What this suggests is that after a commitment has been made, a positive bias toward feeling understood is one helpful coping mechanism.

Psychiatrist Roberta Gilbert (1992) suggests that strong relationships contain the qualities of separateness, equality, and openness in order to succeed. **Separateness** is the creation of boundaries such that each person in the relationship has self-direction and self-esteem. **Equality** is the perception that each partner holds equal status regardless of income, age, or traditional gender associations. Finally, relationships must have the quality of **openness**, an interactive sharing of ideas without the fear of emotional consequences. High levels of openness can result only when there is trust and honesty in the relationship.

> **separateness**
> A dimension of self in which individuals in a relationship maintain their boundaries.
>
> **equality**
> A reciprocal acceptance of each person's worth in the relationship.
>
> **openness**
> A clear, honest, and relevant process of communication.

One marriage researcher, John Gottman, has worked with hundreds of newlyweds to understand which marriages last and which ones don't. What's the secret? It's not the absence of anger or conflict. Gottman found that most couples fight; happy couples get angry just as frequently as other couples do. Interestingly, after 10 years of marriage, 69 percent of happy couples say they fight about the same things they've been fighting about for 10 years (Gottman, 1994).

But happy couples, in contrast to those headed for divorce, know how to successfully reconcile after a fight (Gottman, 2007). Specifically, they can return to a neutral state after a fight. Partners don't have to kiss and make up and feel amazing; rather, it's important to get back to normal.

Arranged marriages In some cultures, young people are not exclusively responsible for initiating marriage or deciding on a marital partner. In one of the oldest forms of marriage, **arranged marriage**, family members and religious leaders make decisions regarding the marriages of young people to one another (Batabyal, 2006). For many people in Canada, India is the first place that comes to mind when arranged marriages are mentioned (**Figure 12.13**). In fact, arranged marriages are also found in the Middle East, parts of Africa, and East Asian countries such as Japan, Korea, and China (Xiaohe & Whyte, 1990).

> **arranged marriage** A cultural or religious tradition in which family members and religious leaders, rather than a couple, plan matrimonial arrangements.

Couples in arranged marriages often are not passive participants; instead some have a level of input and decision-making in the process. Some cultures use the terms "family-initiated" and "couple-initiated" marriage to distinguish between arranged and nonarranged marriages (Hortaçsu, 2007). Although a marriage may be family-initiated, or proposed by the couple's parents or family members, in some cases the couple has a say in whether or not the marriage will ultimately occur (Hortaçsu, 2007).

Arranged marriages • Figure 12.13

Arranged marriages are common in several cultures, including much of India, and are anchored within a heteronormative framework. Some families choose mates for their children the day the baby is born, or even before.

Think Critically Describe the differences in taking responsibility for planning one's adult life—in arranged vs. non-arranged marriages. How might partnering traditions support or undermine individual emerging adult development?

Jihan Abdalla/Blend Images/Getty Images

One study of couples in arranged, or family-initiated, marriages found that they believed that love is a process that grows over time, rather than a requirement for beginning a marriage, and that they rate love as less important to marital satisfaction than did couples in choice, couple-initiated marriages (Myers, Madathil, & Tingle, 2005). Thus the emotion of love might be present in some form in all marriages, but the timing of the emotion's appearance may vary greatly.

Research on marital satisfaction in arranged or family-initiated vs. choice or couple-initiated marriages reveals mixed results. One team of researchers compared arranged marriages in India with marriages of choice in the United States and found equal marital satisfaction in the two groups (Myers et al., 2005). In a study of family-initiated vs. couple-initiated marriages in Turkey, however, clear differences in satisfaction were found between the two (Hortaçsu, 2007). In particular, people in couple-initiated marriages reported higher satisfaction and more egalitarian roles over the course of the marriage than did people in family-initiated marriages.

Notably, divorce rates are lower in countries with arranged marriages than in nations where most marriages are couple-initiated (Myers et al., 2005). The lower divorce rates may not, however, be solely related to marital satisfaction.

Factors including familial pressure and lower religious and political tolerance of divorce probably play a role. All in all, though, it seems that couples all over the world are simply looking for dependability, emotional support, kindness, and stability from a spouse, regardless of whether their marriage is arranged or chosen (Buss et al., 1990).

Same-sex marriage Same-sex couples and heterosexual couples have similar desires to find love, friendship, and acceptance in marriage. Gay males and lesbian females report very similar issues to those of heterosexuals with regard to attraction, commitment, and reasons for getting married (Alderson, 2004; Mohr, 2009; Peplau, 1993). And many committed gay couples, like many heterosexual common-law partners, perceive themselves as married even without a marriage certificate.

In 2005, same-sex marriage was legalized across Canada after years of controversy and struggle for equal rights. Much of the opposition appears to have been based on religious and moral grounds as well as certain prejudices, stereotypes, and misunderstandings about homosexual lifestyle (Pope, 2008). **Figure 12.14** shows the pattern of rights for gay and lesbian couples across the country and the year that same-sex marriage was legalized for each province and territory.

Same-sex marriage in Canada • Figure 12.14

a. Marriage equality
The twenty-first century has seen increased marriage inclusion of same-sex couples compared with pre-2000 levels (Alderson, 2004; Green & Mitchell, 2009; Peplau, 1993).

LUKE MACGREGOR/Reuters/Landov

b. Legalization of same-sex marriage
By 2005, same-sex marriage was legalized in each province and territory.

Think Critically Use the image in **figure b** to think about the difference in legalization and inclusion of same-sex marriage in Canada from 2003 to 2005. Now think about a same-sex couple who wants to be married. Can you describe potential differences in what they might encounter today vs. in the 1990s?

Source: Data from CBCNews. Retrieved from www.cbc.ca/news2/interactives/map-samesex-marriage.

Delayed parenting • Figure 12.15

The percentage of adults with children at home has decreased for both women and men.

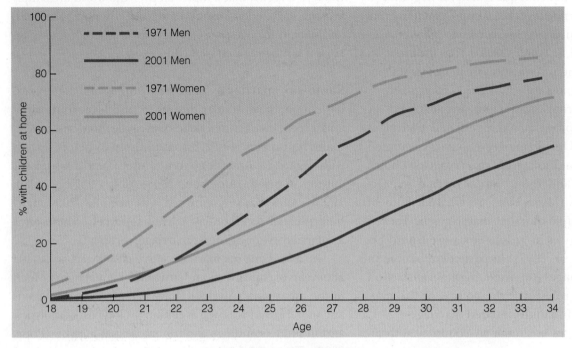

Source: Clark, W. (2007, September). Delayed transitions of young adults. *Canadian Social Trends*, Statistics Canada catalogue no. 11-008. Retrieved from www.statcan.gc.ca/pub/11-008-x/2007004/c-g/10311/4097917-eng.htm.

Think Critically How do the trends for women compare to those for men? What might account for some of the differences across time and between genders?

It is difficult to say much about the experiences of same-sex couples compared with heterosexual couples in emerging and young adulthood because we don't have good information. The limited research findings we do have indicate that same-sex and heterosexual commitments are more similar than different. However, gay and lesbian couples do report greater fidelity and monogamy than straight couples (Alderson, 2004; Peplau, 1993).

More and more same-sex marriages are including children (Pope, 2008). Research on gay and lesbian parenting suggests that children thrive in this situation and that there are few, if any, differences when compared with heterosexual parenting (Barret & Robinson, 2000).

Parenthood

The growing trend in Canada is for young adults to delay having children. As **Figure 12.15** shows, the percentage of adults with children at home has decreased for both women and men. The delay in parenting may be linked to increased education and labour force participation and that elusive work–life balance, particularly for women

(Ravanera, & Rajulton, 2006). Young adults who wait to parent may be able to reach a higher level of maturity that enables them to understand the emotional roller coaster that accompanies parenting. The most dramatic changes in women waiting longer to have their first babies occurred from the 1970s to the 1990s (Mathews & Hamilton, 2009). **Figure 12.16** shows the trends in the average age of mothers. Although fewer than 10 percent of men and women expect to remain child-free, near the end of the fertility window (40–44), 15 percent of women and 24 percent of men have not had a biological child (Martinez, Daniels, & Chandra, 2012).

For new parents of any age, and in all living situations, becoming a parent signals the beginning of a new life stage. Regardless of when parenting begins, the transition to caring for an infant involves significant adjustment. The joy that comes with the arrival of a new infant is accompanied by increased demands on parents' time, finances, and ability to function on less sleep. New parents can feel especially stressed when mothers return to work after taking a parental leave (Claxton &

Trends in the average age of mothers • Figure 12.16

a. Average maternal ages for all births since 1944

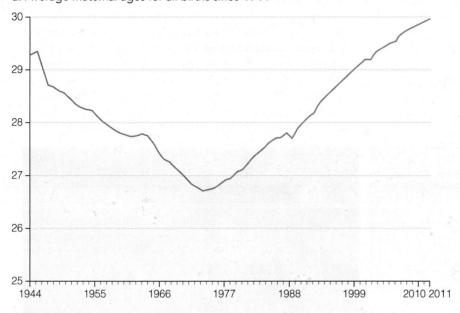

Source: Employment and Social Development Canada (2015). Indicators of well-being in Canada: Family life – Age of mother at childbirth. Retrieved from http://well-being.esdc.gc.ca/misme-iowb/.3ndic.1t.4r@-eng.jsp?iid=78.

b. Percentage of births to mothers over age 30-since 1974

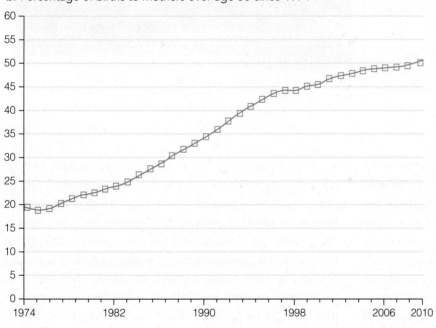

Think Critically How do the challenges of emerging adulthood match the challenges of parenting?

Perry-Jenkins, 2008). These new demands may put a couple's relationship to the test. One of the more well-known myths is that a baby will solve problems between intimate partners (DeGenova & Rice, 2008). But that is myth. Relationship researcher John Gottman (2008) reports that, for couples, the most significant predictor of parenting adjustment is the quality of connection the couple enjoyed before the baby arrived. If the relationship was fragile to begin with, the demands of caring for a newborn add strain to the already stressed relationship (Morse, Buist, & Durkin, 2000).

Having a newborn requires couples to negotiate a new division of household labour (**Figure 12.17**). A new baby also brings increases in familiar household duties, such as laundry, cleaning, and meal preparation. Research has shown that agreement about the division of labour between men and women in heterosexual relationships is associated with better transitioning to parenthood (Gottman & Gottman, 2009). Same-sex couples and heterosexual couples report different division-of-labour formulas but equal levels of satisfaction (Patterson & Farr, 2011).

Division of labour: Separate but equal • Figure 12.17

The division of labour, or the way family responsibilities are divided between partners, has implications for relationship satisfaction.

a. A number of studies have used the *Who Does What?* measure (Cowan & Cowan, 1988) to understand how couples divide household and child care responsibilities as they shift from living together as partners to living together as parents.

Who does what? (Cowan & Cowan, 1988)								
I do it all						My partner does it all		
1	2	3	4	5	6	7	8	9

a Deciding about our child's meals

b Mealtimes with our child

c Changing our child's diapers; dressing our child

d Bath time with our child

e Deciding whether to respond to our child's cries

f Responding to our child's crying in the middle of the night

g Taking our child out: walking, driving, visiting

h Choosing toys for our child

i Playtime with our child

j Doing our child's laundry

k Arranging for babysitters or child care

l Dealing with the doctor regarding our child's health

b. The Atlantic Coast Families Study showed that both heterosexual and lesbian parents were satisfied with the divisions of labour in their parenting partnerships, but that the two types of couples divided labour differently. Heterosexual couples tended to have uneven distributions of child care in the home and work out of the home, with women tending to do more of the child care and men more out-of-home work. Lesbian couples were more likely to have equal labour duties both inside and outside the home (Patterson & Farr, 2011).

Jim Young/Reuters/Corbis

Think Critically How might division of labour in a household shape young adult partners' self-understanding over the course of the marriage?

Becoming a parent for the first time is associated with significant changes in the new parent's social network, as detailed in **Figure 12.18**. Parenthood reduces the amount of time people have to stay involved with activities they enjoy and reduces the amount of time spent with partners (Raymore, Barber, & Eccles, 2001).

Changes in support from social support networks may be especially important for the adjustment of new parents in same-sex relationships. Same-sex couples face the same set of stresses as heterosexual couples in the transition to parenthood, with the very real potential for added stress from social stigma associated with same-sex partnerships. Support from friends is related to lower anxiety among same-sex new parents. Same-sex couples who perceive greater workplace and family support and who enjoy higher relationship quality experience fewer depressive symptoms than those who feel less supported. Lower internalized homophobia and more gay-friendly neighbourhoods also contribute to lower depressive symptoms (Goldberg & Smith, 2011).

Single parenting is becoming more common in Canada, as **Figure 12.19** shows. The vast majority, over 80 percent, of lone-parent families are headed by women. Female-headed single-parent households are among the poorest in Canada and have the most instability in income levels, particularly for women under 40. In fact the younger the single mother, the more likely she is to experience income instability and live below the poverty line (Morissette & Ostrovsky, 2007; Morency et al., 2011). Lone parents may be particularly affected by inflexible work hours, long commutes, and, in some communities, limited access to daycare. All these factors and the general strain of lone parenthood are likely to reduce their employment prospects and make them more vulnerable to earnings instability (Morency, Paez, Roorda, Mercado, & Farber, 2011). The stresses and strains of parenting are even more challenging when you must struggle to pay for the basics.

Shifting contexts of the transition to parenthood • Figure 12.18

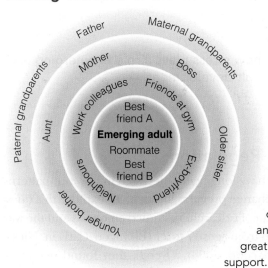

These diagrams show how social networks change in emerging adulthood. Emerging adults get the most support and influence from those closest to them and in the closest contexts.

a. Emerging adulthood is a stage of the lifespan when friends have a great deal of influence and provide a great deal of social support.

b. When emerging adults get involved with a romantic partner, a boundary forms around the couple, requiring even close others to respect the intimacy of the couple.

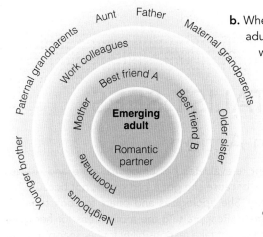

Increasing rates of lone-parent families in Canada • Figure 12.19

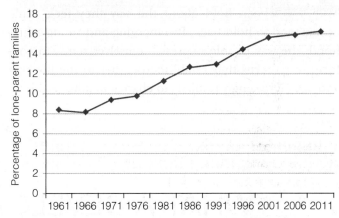

Source: Statistics Canada. (2013). Fifty years of families in Canada: 1961 to 2011. Statistics Canada catalogue no. 98-312-X2011003. Retrieved from https://www12.statcan.gc.ca/census-recensement/2011/as-sa/98-312-x/98-312-x2011003_1-eng.cfm.

Think Critically What are the contexts of becoming a lone parent? How might those contexts change the experiences of parenting?

c. When emerging adults become new parents, they draw closer to relationships that offer the most support.

Think Critically How does this person's social network change as a function of committing to a romantic partner and then becoming a parent?

CONCEPT CHECK STOP

1. **How** do young adults' relationships with their families change during the transition to adulthood?

2. **What** factors predict who will become friends in adulthood?

3. **What** are the components of love in Sternberg's triangular theory of love?

4. **What** traditional and non-traditional intimate partnership arrangements do emerging and young adults participate in?

5. **What** effect does the arrival of a newborn have on the household division of labour?

Emotional Development

LEARNING OBJECTIVES

1. **Describe** the key emotional developments young adults demonstrate.

2. **Distinguish** mental health from psychopathology.

3. **Explain** how stress plays a role in emerging and young adult development.

By the time we reach emerging adulthood, the way we tend to express ourselves is relatively well established. Some people have always been bold about the way they feel, while others tend to hold back. By emerging and young adulthood, the way people express themselves tends to conform to patterns they established earlier in the lifespan and are increasingly unlikely to change in adulthood.

Emotion Regulation

Researchers have long been interested in how our patterns of reacting change over the lifespan. To explore this question, one team of researchers studied emotions and the way they changed from ages 17 to 24 (Blonigen, Carlson, Hicks, Krueger, & Iacono, 2008). Overall, they found decreases in negative emotionality, which measures the person's

WHAT A DEVELOPMENTALIST SEES
Cognitive Reappraisal in Action

Cognitive reappraisal generally matures as we move through emerging adulthood. We come to better understand our typical ways of responding to emotions, and we gain knowledge about other people's motives (John & Gross, 2004). For example, a university student, upset about a bad grade on a test, snaps at the roommate who asked her to make dinner, "I just cooked last night! I am not going to cook again! Stop being so lazy!" (**Figure a**).

The student re-evaluates her emotional state and realizes that she is angry because she got a bad grade, not because her roommate is lazy. She apologizes and offers to cook together with the roommate. Reappraising the motivations for her emotion helped the student take responsibility for her snappish emotional response and seek support from her roommate to bring her out of her bad mood (**Figure b**).

a

Joel Sartore/National Geographic Creative

b

Joel Sartore/National Geographic Creative

Think Critically Can you write a different scenario that illustrates the less-developed cognitive reappraisal that might take place if the roommates were adolescents?

likelihood that he or she will react with anxiety or anger. At the same time, the researchers found increases through the early 20s in constraint, which is the ability to restrain impulsive behaviour and control risk-taking. In other words, young people gain more self-control from the late teens through the 20s.

Emerging adults get better at controlling their emotions because they get a little help from cognitive growth. Specifically, from the late teens through the 20s, we know that emerging adults attain a greater ability to evaluate why they are feeling what they are, a process psychologists call **cognitive reappraisal**. To a great extent, we see very little evidence of cognitive reappraisal in adolescents, but that changes later, as described in *What a Developmentalist Sees*. This increased ability to reflect on one's feelings is particularly important in emerging adulthood because **effortful control**—the ability to regulate our responses to external stimuli—is associated with mental health (Fosco et al., 2012).

cognitive reappraisal The ability to re-evaluate the cause of an emotional state and mediate the response.

effortful control The ability to regulate responses to external stimuli.

Coping with Stress

Emerging adulthood is an exciting time. More than four out of five respondents in a poll of 18- to 29-year-olds in the United States conducted by Clark University agreed that, in their lives, "It all seems as if anything is possible" (Arnett & Schwab, 2012). Along with this wide range of possibilities, however, come challenges. Emerging adulthood can be a stressful period of the lifespan for some. More than half of respondents in the same poll reported that they often feel anxious, and 65 percent said that their lives were full of uncertainty.

The specific goals young people set for themselves are directly associated with the stressors they are each likely to experience. Some young people move straight from high school into lives filled with work and family responsibilities. Others spend some time as either part-time or full-time college or university students.

University and college About half of all emerging adults in North America spend at least the first years of emerging adulthood as students (U.S. Census Bureau, 2010). **Figure 12.20** shows that young people enrolled in post-secondary education at least part-time face a number of stressors in their lives.

Universities and colleges alike provide counselling for their students and have made it a goal for decades to teach their students to use specific skills to cope with the stress of higher education (Miller, Pope, & Steinmann, 2005). Learning to deal with stress can be considered a lifespan skill. Although university and college graduates, on average, report higher job satisfaction, incomes, and life satisfaction than those who did not graduate from higher education (Lounsbury, Fisher, Levy, & Welsh, 2009), graduates eventually face work and relationship stressors. Because staying in school is associated with

Top impediments to academic performance • Figure 12.20

This chart shows that college and university students face a number of difficult issues, as revealed in a study by the American College Health Association (2009). The study also found that most students feel overwhelmed, depressed, lonely, hopeless, or mentally exhausted once or more each month. Many are far from home for the first time in their lives, coping with academic rigours, and dealing with a fast-paced social environment.

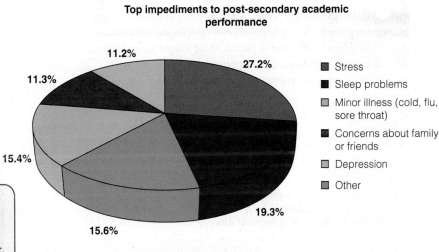

Top impediments to post-secondary academic performance

- 27.2% Stress
- 19.3% Sleep problems
- 15.6% Minor illness (cold, flu, sore throat)
- 15.4% Concerns about family or friends
- 11.3% Depression
- 11.2% Other

Think Critically Make two columns on a piece of paper, labelling the columns "support" and "undermine." Take two minutes to list characteristics of the college or university environment that support or undermine student development and achievement. Which list is longer? What does that mean for post-secondary student mental health?

delays in getting a job and starting a family of one's own, emerging adults who don't take post-secondary education tend to make those transitions earlier (Mills, Rindfuss, McDonald, & te Velde, 2011).

Work What do you want from a job? In one survey, when asking interns what they want to get out of their career preparation experiences, emerging adults reported that, even more than a high income, they wanted interesting work, good benefits, job security, and chances for promotion (Chao & Gardner, 2008). This finding is consistent with results of a study of career expectations in the years following the Great Recession of 2008. Young people were less optimistic about finding work–life balance and an ideal social atmosphere at a job. However, they continued to have high expectations for job content, training, career development, and financial rewards (De Hauw & De Vos, 2010). As shown in **Figure 12.21**, unemployment and underemployment make it less likely they will get what they want.

In addition to the frustration of not reaching their goals, the feeling of economic pressure that many young adults today experience is associated with both anxiety and depressed mood in the transition to adulthood (Stein et al., 2011). Furthermore, decisions young adults make about work in the first years of emerging adulthood

have been found to influence all aspects of their lives for a long time (Niles & Harris-Bowlsbey, 2005). Thus, those whose careers are stalled at the outset by hard times may find it difficult to recover.

We tend to focus on factors that affect the school-to-work transition during emerging adulthood when the transition takes place. However, other factors affect career trajectories in adolescence. One team of researchers has found that early preparation can help young adults reach career goals. They reported that adolescents who already knew what kind of job they eventually wanted were likely to make more money in their 20s than those without a clear career direction (Staff, Harris, Sabates, & Briddell, 2010). Adolescents who were uncertain about their future careers were more likely to be unemployed in their 20s, as well as to have attained lower education and earned lower wages. Perhaps not surprisingly, adolescents with career aspirations that required more years of education were earning more in their 20s than those who aspired to careers that required less education. The researchers also found that students who correctly matched their educational plans to their career goal—for example, understanding whether the career they wanted required a four-year or other degree—were more financially successful in their 20s than those who had under- or overestimated the amount of education needed for a certain career

Unemployment vs. underemployment • Figure 12.21

Unemployment rates get their fair share of media attention, as they should. Today's unemployment rate for emerging and young adults is very high. Less commonly discussed is the rate of underemployment. A person is underemployed when he or she obtains some work and is therefore no longer unemployed, but this work is part-time, doesn't offer benefits, or doesn't utilize the person's education or training.

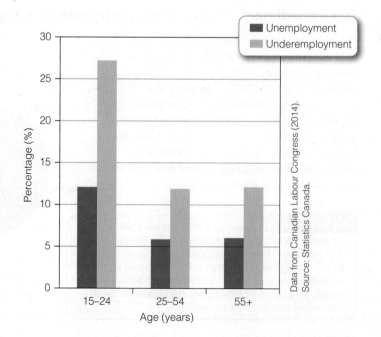

Data from Canadian Labour Congress (2014).
Source: Statistics Canada.

Ask Yourself

1. Unemployment is highest among the _____ to _____ age group.
2. Underemployment is highest among the _____ to _____ age group.
3. The rates of unemployment and underemployment are lower and the same for _____ year-olds and adults older than _____.

(Sabates, Harris, & Staff, 2011). To choose a career goal, adolescents need help. One way that adolescents, young adults, career counsellors, and social scientists research careers in Canada is by using the online Services for Youth, discussed in *Where Developmentalists Click.*

Research on career choice has focused on two key variables that influence decision-making: **career outcome expectations** and **self-efficacy**, or belief in one's ability (Betz, 2001; Feldt & Woelfel, 2009). Career outcome expectations are an individual's realistic beliefs regarding the costs and rewards of a particular occupation (Brooks & Betz, 1990). For example, a person might focus more on the benefits, thinking, "If I choose to go to

career outcome expectations
The process one goes through when deciding about a future career and focusing on costs and rewards involved in career choice.

self-efficacy
Beliefs regarding one's ability to succeed.

law school and become a lawyer, I will be involved in interesting work and make a lot of money." This person would be much more likely to want to be a lawyer than someone who focuses on costs: "As a lawyer I would have to work long hours and sacrifice my personal relationships."

Career outcome expectations are related to self-efficacy. For example, a question related to self-efficacy might be, "Do I have the academic skills to get into law school and pass the classes?" People who answer yes to this question and who think that being a lawyer would be valuable relative to the costs would be highly likely to apply to law school. People choosing a career while in university or college or right out of high school typically

Where Developmentalists CLICK

Services for Youth

The Canadian government provides the Services for Youth (www.youth.gc.ca) website as a portal to information and skills development for a range of life events, including getting an education, finding a job, moving, starting a business, and more. On this website services are also tailored for Aboriginal youth, newcomers, youth with disabilities, and even resources for employers who want to better serve youth. Teachers, guidance and career counsellors, and other developmentalists often help adolescents and emerging adults match their skills and interests with careers that are both personally and financially rewarding. They consult the website to find information about the types of jobs needed in Canada, because encouraging preparation for these specific careers can increase the chances of finding a job once they have completed their education and training.

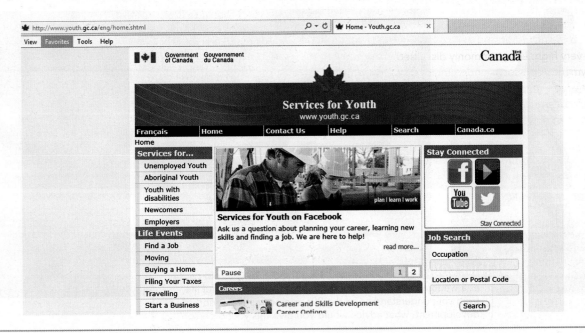

combine career outcome expectations and self-efficacy to evaluate their options.

Post-secondary education and careers can bring emerging adults steps closer to feeling like true adults, but because these new roles and responsibilities also bring challenges and stress, they can create some risks to their mental health.

Mental Health

The term "mental health" describes an overall predominance of positive feelings and positive functioning in life (Keyes, 2002). Mental health is more than the absence of problems—it indicates the presence of positive well-being. For this reason, it is also known as *flourishing*. On average, mental health improves during the transition to adulthood. For example, one study of 18- to 25-year-old Canadians found that their anger and symptoms of depression decreased, and their self-esteem increased, across emerging adulthood (Galambos, Barker, & Krahn, 2006).

As we learned in Chapter 11, however, psychiatric disorder is common during these same years. Because psychiatric disorder interferes with well-being, reducing risks associated with mental health problems is a key ingredient in promoting a healthy emerging adulthood.

CHALLENGES IN DEVELOPMENT
Behind the Quarter-Life Crisis

No empirical evidence supports the idea that there is a universal quarter-life crisis. However, the concept really speaks to 20-somethings who feel pressure to grow up and become adult. What Robbins and Wilner (2001) call the *quarter-life crisis* may very well be pressure to consolidate one's identity.

Emerging adulthood presents a unique challenge to identity. During adolescence, the question "Who am I?" is conceptual. In emerging adulthood, the young person is faced with the task of answering the question, "Who am I in this world?" **Identity consolidation**

> **identity consolidation** The challenge of refining and organizing one's personal identity in response to new adult roles, responsibilities, and contexts.

is the pressure to refine and organize personal identity in response to investing oneself in new adult roles, responsibilities, and contexts.

Identity consolidation is challenging, but it's not a crisis 20-somethings can't handle. Healthy emerging adults might feel as if they are taking one step back every time they take two steps forward, but they are still making progress. Unhealthy identity consolidation feels like being stuck. When identity work is not progressing, seeking support from a professional can help.

Cultura RM/Alamy

Lluckyraccoon/Alamy

Think Critically If you were talking to your 26-year-old cousin at a wedding and he was complaining about his stressful life, from your understanding of the 20s as a normative period of development, what advice would you give this young person?

In order to do so, researchers have considered how stress and decision-making may contribute to psychopathology in emerging and young adults.

Diathesis–stress model Some researchers have suggested that stress plays an instrumental part in the development of psychopathology (Abramson, Metalsky, & Alloy, 1989). As depicted in **Figure 12.22**, the **diathesis–stress**

diathesis–stress model A model suggesting that abnormal behaviour results from a combination of genetic predispositions toward psychopathology and environmental stressors.

model proposes that psychopathology is caused by an interaction among genes, environment, and life experiences. Certainly, the new adult responsibilities and accountability experienced during emerging adulthood can provide plenty of stress.

Quarter-life crisis One reason many people may feel so stressed during emerging and young adulthood is that adulthood is all new, all the

The diathesis–stress model • Figure 12.22

The diathesis–stress model of psychopathologies takes into account genetics, stressors, and coping mechanisms to explain why some individuals develop mental disorders.

Think Critically Use the diathesis–stress model to suggest two hypotheses that might be tested to help explain why rates of psychiatric disorder are higher in emerging adulthood than they are in later stages of adulthood.

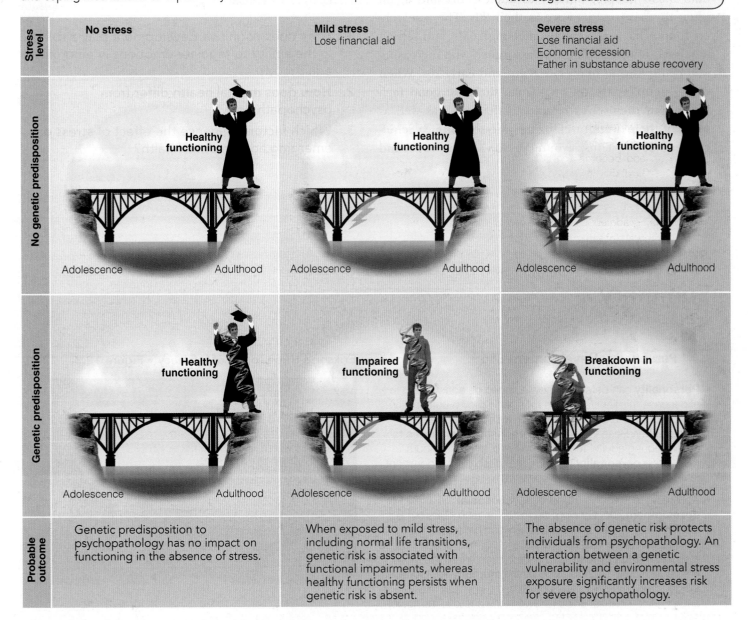

Stress level	**No stress**	**Mild stress** Lose financial aid	**Severe stress** Lose financial aid Economic recession Father in substance abuse recovery
No genetic predisposition	Healthy functioning Adolescence — Adulthood	Healthy functioning Adolescence — Adulthood	Healthy functioning Adolescence — Adulthood
Genetic predisposition	Healthy functioning Adolescence — Adulthood	Impaired functioning Adolescence — Adulthood	Breakdown in functioning Adolescence — Adulthood
Probable outcome	Genetic predisposition to psychopathology has no impact on functioning in the absence of stress.	When exposed to mild stress, including normal life transitions, genetic risk is associated with functional impairments, whereas healthy functioning persists when genetic risk is absent.	The absence of genetic risk protects individuals from psychopathology. An interaction between a genetic vulnerability and environmental stress exposure significantly increases risk for severe psychopathology.

time. In their post-university years, two emerging-adult writers—Alexandra Robbins and Abby Wilner (2001)—

quarter-life crisis The hypothesis proposing that the task of becoming adult is experienced as a personal crisis in the mid-20s.

proposed the popular notion that the very task of becoming adult incites a life crisis. This chapter's *Challenges in Development* takes a closer look at what Robbins and Wilner named the **quarter-life crisis**.

Currently, psychologists have neither validated nor disproven the notion of a quarter-life crisis as a universal, developmental experience. Yet, studies have identified some of the factors that predict increased well-being during this period of life. One team of researchers focused on the importance of goals. They studied more than 5,000 people, initially as adolescents and again when the participants were in their 20s. The researchers found that having goals, meeting goals, and setting new goals for oneself were all associated with increasing well-being during one's late teens and early 20s. When young people gave up on a goal, they lost good feelings about themselves related to that goal, as well as some of their overall well-being (Messersmith & Schulernberg, 2010). Thus, a young person's ability to set and

achieve goals is one factor that contributes to the overall increasing mental health we see during these years (Schulenberg, Sameroff, & Cicchetti, 2004; Skaletz & Seiffge-Krenke, 2010).

Although tackling new roles and responsibilities in emerging and young adulthood can sometimes be overwhelming, each step to adulthood brings with it new and exciting experiences. Mastering these experiences helps to lay a solid foundation for the rest of adulthood, which is important, because well-being during these critical years forecasts what is to come in middle adulthood.

CONCEPT CHECK

1. **How** does cognitive development play a role in the ability to regulate emotions in emerging adulthood?

2. **How** does mental health differ from psychopathology?

3. **Which** factors influence the effect of stress on emerging adult mental health?

✓ THE PLANNER

Summary

1 Personality Development 386

- **Personality** can determine how a young person will experience this life stage. The most well-known personality trait theory is the **Big Five** or the **five-factor model of personality**. Researchers use **personality inventories** to assess young adults' feelings, thoughts, and behaviours, resulting in **personality profiles** that describe the dominant features of an individual's personality.

- According to Erikson's model of **psychosocial development**, identity work begins in the teen years but is often not completed until the 20s. Erikson believed those who fail to resolve questions about their identity experience a sense of **role confusion**. Erikson characterized the move from adolescence to adulthood as the **intimacy vs. isolation stage**. Erikson defined types of intimacy: physical, intellectual, and emotional relationships (shown in the photo in the figure)

Erikson's three forms of intimacy • Figure 12.3

PeopleImages/iStockphoto

with others. Increasing numbers of young people choose to spend more time alone, however, delaying commitment.

- Studies show that personality consistency tends to increase with age and that the **Big Five** personality traits identified in the **five-factor model of personality** tend to remain consistent over the course of the lifespan.

2 Social Influences 389

- Significant changes happen to family relationships as teens approach adulthood. The **family life cycle** goes through changes as teens develop a greater sense of self and **differentiation** from their parents. During the transition to adulthood, parents may be important sources of both **affective support** and **instrumental support**.

- Choosing a friend is based largely on four factors: physical attractiveness, proximity, frequent exposure, and lack of any exclusionary criteria. Friendship is also based on a desire for equality, as well as a person's desire for **communion**, **agency**, and **individuation**.

- **Social networks** are not a new idea, although the modes have undergone a number of changes. **Social network sites (SNSs)** are used to create new relationships and maintain old ones. They can be excellent resources for creating a social support system, but they are not perfect and they carry risks, such as identity theft or online stalking.

- Many people stay single or delay marriage and spend years dating. Dates are primarily chosen based on physical attraction, as well as **assortative mating**—choosing someone similar in values, education, ethnicity, religion, and personality traits. **Hooking up** and having friends-with-benefits relationships have become fairly common and can lead to long-term connections—or, in some extreme cases, dangerous situations. **Relationship churning** can be a sign of an unhealthy relationship or attachment style.

- **Consummate love** is romantic love, or love that involves sexual relations with a partner, and is distinct from the love one has for family and friends. Sternberg's **triangular theory of love** defines three components: passion, the physical aspect of love; intimacy, the emotional connection; and commitment, a conscious decision to stay together in the short term or the long term. As depicted in the diagram, various combinations of these components define different types of love.

- **Arranged marriage** is one of the oldest forms of marriage and continues in some cultural and religious traditions today. In North America, marriage rates are declining, and many emerging adults who marry end up divorcing. Emerging adults may not have the coping skills or maturity to understand that successful marriages require **equality**, **openness**, and **separateness**.

- Marriages can become dysfunctional because of psychopathologies such as **personality disorders** or **interpersonal schemas**—the patterns for relating to other

Sternberg's triangular theory of love • Figure 12.8

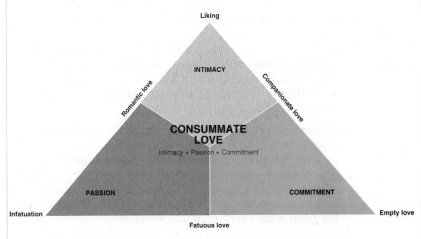

people that we learn from a very young age and carry over into adulthood. The most extreme cases of dysfunctional relating can result in **intimate partner violence**.

- **Cohabitation** has become a viable option for couples in Canada, largely because it has become much more accepted than it used to be. Some couples cohabit to try out the relationship before getting married. For decades, researchers have reported that heterosexual couples who go on to marry after living together prior to marrying were more likely to divorce. However, that risk disappears when researchers take age into consideration.

- In Canada, same-sex marriage was legalized across the country in 2005 and has gained public support and acceptance. However, it is still strongly opposed by many people with religious convictions, or those who cling to traditional **heteronormative** assumptions.

- Young adults are waiting longer than they did in the past to have their first child. If they do have children at an older age, the transition to caring for an infant involves significant adjustment, including changes in the household division of labour and social nesting.

3 Emotional Development 408

- Research has shown that, as a general rule, as people age, their ability to control their emotions increases or strengthens. Our ability to re-evaluate the reasons for our emotions, known as **cognitive reappraisal**, develops, as does our skill in **effortful control** or mediating our responses. This increasing emotional regulation is helpful as we enter into romantic relationships.

- The goals that young people set for themselves can lead to stress. Coping with stress is a lifespan skill. The goal of attaining a degree can lead to stress about delays in getting a job and starting a family of one's own. When young people begin work, they face different stressors.

- Decisions about work and careers increase during this phase of life. Factors in our environment, such as the recent period of economic difficulty in much of the world, can constrain the young adult's career options (as shown in the graph in the figure). Career choice is also influenced by two cognitive variables: **career outcome expectations**—a person's beliefs about the costs and rewards of a specific job—and **self-efficacy**, a person's perception of his or her abilities to achieve and maintain the job.

- Writers have popularized the concept of the **quarter-life crisis**, characterized mainly by a paralysis of thought, as young people struggle with **identity consolidation**. Psychologists continue to study whether the quarter-life crisis exists, but in the meantime have suggested several strategies for coping with this type of life crisis. Goal-setting has been shown to be especially effective.

- Psychopathology is more common during this period of life than during any other. The **diathesis–stress model** suggests that the interaction of genes, environment, and socio-cultural events creates psychopathologies, including anxiety, depression, and substance abuse.

Unemployment vs. underemployment • Figure 12.21

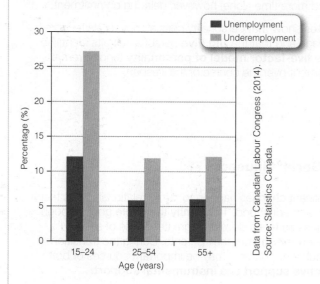

Key Terms

- affective support 391
- agency 392
- arranged marriage 402
- assortative mating 395
- Big Five or five-factor model of personality 386
- career outcome expectations 411
- cognitive reappraisal 409
- cohabitation 398
- commitment 396
- communion 392
- consummate love 395
- diathesis–stress model 413
- differentiation 390
- effortful control 409
- emotional intimacy 389
- equality 402

- family life cycle 390
- first-order change 390
- heteronormative 397
- hook-up 397
- identity consolidation 412
- individuation 392
- instrumental support 391
- intellectual intimacy 389
- interpersonal schemas 398
- intimacy 396
- intimacy vs. isolation stage 388
- intimate partner violence 400
- Minnesota Multiphasic Personality Inventory—Second Edition (MMPI–2) 387
- Myers-Briggs Type Indicator (MBTI) 387

- openness 402
- passion 396
- personality 386
- personality disorder 399
- personality inventory 386
- personality profile 386
- physical intimacy 389
- psychosocial development 388
- quarter-life crisis 388
- relationship churning 399
- role confusion 388
- second-order change 390
- self-efficacy 411
- separateness 402
- social network 394
- social networking site (SNS) 394
- triangular theory of love 395

Critical and Creative Thinking Questions

1. What type of personality changes would indicate that an emerging adult is maturing normally?

2. How do being alone and being isolated differ?

3. What are the characteristics of a healthy romantic relationship?

4. Why are marriage rates declining in Canada, and what might be the results?

5. What are some of the differences between emerging adults who are flourishing and those who are experiencing what feels like a quarter-life crisis?

What is happening in this picture?

Hero Images Inc./Alamy

There is some general concern that emerging adults won't learn to communicate face-to-face because they spend so much time using new technologies; for example, text messaging and social media. However, developmentalists recognize that every generation learns new ways of communicating as new technologies are introduced. Emerging adults are particularly motivated to adopt new ways of relating to one another because keeping up with technological advances helps them prepare for the ever-changing labour market.

Think Critically

1. How might electronic communication methods affect the way we resolve the identity vs. identity confusion stage and the intimacy vs. isolation stage proposed by Erikson?

2. How does in-person communication differ from electronic communication?

3. What advantages and disadvantages are involved in social networking?

4. Why do some people prefer non–face-to-face communication methods (such as the cellphone) to in-person communication methods?

REAL Development

Socio-emotional Development in Emerging and Young Adulthood

In this video activity, you are observing the socio-emotional development of young adults. You are a counsellor in the Counselling and Wellness Centre on campus. The centre is holding a speed-dating event for individuals in their 20s who are current students or graduates of the university, including Eugene Florendo. The director of the Counselling and Wellness Centre has asked you to interview the participants—Eugene, Shahora, and Elena—and report back on what you observe about intimacy, love, and commitment. You will use what you have learned about Erikson's three forms of intimacy and Sternberg's triangular theory of love.

John Wiley & Sons, Inc.

WileyPLUS Go to WileyPLUS to complete the REAL Development activity.

03.01

Self-Test

1. Which Eriksonian stage is depicted in the photo below?

    a. identity vs. identity confusion

    b. industry vs. inferiority

    c. intimacy vs. isolation

    d. trust vs. mistrust

DonyKuo/iStockphoto

2. In which of the family life-cycle stages would a young person develop a work identity and make progress toward financial independence?

    a. family-of-origin experiences

    b. leaving home

    c. premarriage

    d. couplehood

3. Which of the following is not a dimension of the type of intimacy Erikson identified as important in young adulthood?

    a. physical intimacy

    b. geographical intimacy

    c. intellectual intimacy

    d. emotional intimacy

4. How do the Big Five personality traits tend to change after emerging adulthood?

    a. They remain relatively consistent across the lifespan.

    b. They are quite unstable and fluctuate in each stage.

    c. They vary widely from one individual to another.

    d. They lose validity as people merge into full adulthood.

5. When we value personal characteristics of others such as religion or race when choosing friends, we are relying on _____.

    a. physical attractiveness

    b. proximity

    c. frequent exposure

    d. exclusionary criteria

6. According to this graph, what can be concluded about the use of social networking sites during recent years?

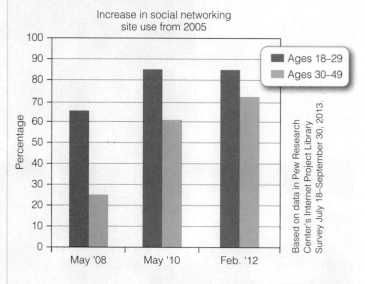

Based on data in Pew Research Center's Internet Project Library Survey July 18–September 30, 2013.

    a. A greater proportion of emerging and young adults are using social networking sites.

    b. A smaller proportion of emerging and young adults are using social networking sites.

    c. Social networking site use has remained stable over the past decade.

    d. Younger people, but not older people, have made greater use of social networking sites.

7. People who use various methods of electronic communication report that their electronic use benefits them most by giving them more _____.

    a. time to pursue other interests

    b. control over social relationships

    c. opportunities to interact with people

    d. practice at fast, high-tech interactions

8. The assortative mating process indicates that people tend to date those who are _____.

    a. extremely attractive

    b. in close proximity

    c. similar to them

    d. unusual and exotic

9. In general, a hook-up involves all of the following *except* _____.

    a. physical intimacy

    b. a lack of commitment

    c. a brief encounter

    d. mutual interests

10. What does the term "self-efficacy" mean in the area of career choice?

    a. perception of one's ability to obtain and maintain a job

    b. beliefs about the costs of a particular occupation

    c. data about the rewards of a chosen career

    d. information about a future profession or field

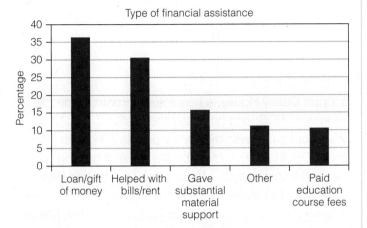

Type of financial assistance

11. Based on the graph, which of these statements about the support parents provide their emerging and young adult children is *false*?

    a. Adult children receive a variety of types of support from their parents.

    b. Almost all young adult children receive loans and gifts of money from their parents.

    c. Less than one-third of parents help their adult children pay bills or rent.

    d. Approximately 10 percent of parents pay tuition for their young adult children.

12. According to Gottman, which is *not* a characteristic of a healthy romantic relationship?

    a. separateness

    b. equality

    c. control

    d. openness

13. What is the key difference between arranged marriages and marriages by choice?

    a. Marriages by choice are done willingly, whereas arranged marriages are forced.

    b. Arranged marriages have a much higher divorce rate than marriages by choice.

    c. Marriages by choice have higher levels of overall marital satisfaction than arranged marriages.

    d. Couples in arranged marriages tend to believe that love is a process rather than a requirement.

14. According to the diathesis–stress model, all of the following factors *except* _____ increase the likelihood of experiencing a psychopathology.

    a. genes

    b. historical period

    c. coping abilities

    d. stressors

15. The quarter-life crisis may be an indicator that emerging adults feel pressure to continue work on which developmental process?

    a. intimacy

    b. identity

    c. industry

    d. autonomy

THE PLANNER

Review your Chapter Planner in the chapter opener and check off your completed work.

13

Physical and Cognitive Development in Middle Adulthood

Well into his 40s, Rick Mercer stands solidly at the height of his career and influence on Canadian society. He has received several prestigious awards and degrees recognizing his influence as a political satirist and comedian through several media, including television and the Internet. His weekly rants on *Rick Mercer Report* inspire many to think critically about contemporary issues and are reposted on many social media profiles. He uses this acclaim to generate change in the world through his many philanthropic works. For example, he assists with bed nets for children in Africa to protect against malaria in the Spread the Net campaign; he helps support Casey House, a hospice in Toronto for people living with AIDS; and he raised the profile of the 2005 Walk For Life to raise money for people living with HIV and AIDS. In 2010, moved by the issue of bullying of gay and lesbian youth, Mercer joined the It Gets Better campaign, to create a series of videos to help overcome bullying (Mcintosh, 2015). Clearly, at mid-life Rick Mercer is doing much to promote health in Canada and around the world. Without a doubt, middle-aged adults have a significant impact on all of our lives.

As we will see in this chapter, the change-filled decades of our 20s and 30s give way to greater stability

in mid-life. In contrast to the earlier years of adulthood, which are spent acquiring information, launching careers, and forming families, mid-life involves applying knowledge and managing one's investments in career and family. Physical systems are beginning to decline, yet health and vivacity typically remain quite strong. Contemporary middle-aged adults often take steps to slow down the aging process through fitness and nutrition regimens. Today's mid-lifers look better, feel better, and see themselves as younger than those in previous generations did. For most, mid-life represents the prime years of adulthood.

Jason Franson/The Canadian Press

CHAPTER PLANNER ✓

- ❏ Study the picture and read the opening story.
- ❏ Scan the Learning Objectives in each section:
  p. 422 ❏   p. 428 ❏   p. 434 ❏
- ❏ Read the text and study all visuals. Answer any questions.

Analyze key features

- ❏ Development InSight, p. 427
- ❏ What a Developmentalist Sees, p. 429
- ❏ Process Diagram, p. 434 ❏   p. 437 ❏
- ❏ Challenges in Development, p. 440
- ❏ Stop: Answer the Concept Checks before you go on:
  p. 428 ❏   p. 433 ❏   p. 443 ❏

End of chapter

- ❏ Review the Summary and Key Terms.
- ❏ Answer the Critical and Creative Thinking Questions.
- ❏ Answer *What is happening in this picture?*
- ❏ Complete the Self-Test and check your answers.

Physical Development

LEARNING OBJECTIVES

1. **Describe** how the nervous system changes as one enters into mid-life.

2. **Explain** key skeletal changes of middle adulthood.

3. **Describe** how the muscular system changes in mid-life.

4. **Distinguish** typical changes in hair and skin related to middle adulthood.

5. **Outline** changes in sensory abilities that occur during mid-life.

The concept of middle age is relative to the average **life expectancy** at birth, which varies between and within countries and across historical periods. Life expectancy is cut short in countries fighting against population health risks, such as poverty, poor nutrition, undeveloped sanitation systems, and communicable disease (for example, HIV/AIDS). In North America, where there are fewer risks, life expectancy pushes 80, and ages from the 40s into the 60s are considered middle age.

In mid-life, people can benefit from good health practices. Exercise and nutrition confer the same benefits

> **life expectancy**
> The average number of years a person can expect to live.

at middle age that they did earlier in life. They can also significantly slow normal biological aging, otherwise known as *senescence*. Despite all population and personal health resources, however, we'll see that by mid-life almost everyone experiences some signs of decline in key physical systems.

The Nervous System

Most people have some signs of physiological decline in the brain during middle adulthood. On average, brain volume decreases (Raz et al., 2005), as **Figure 13.1** shows. However, some people lose more than others. Almost all people in their 20s and 30s have healthy brains. As a result of both genes and exposure to risks, there is more

Brain changes in mid-life • Figure 13.1

Brain volume decreases in mid-life are associated with aging and are accelerated by health risks. The brain shrinks because of atrophy in both grey matter, such as neurons and glial cells, and white matter, the connective tissue of the brain (Kolb & Whishaw, 2011).

Think Critically What are some of the daily tasks adults will find more difficult as they experience decreases in brain volume during middle adulthood?

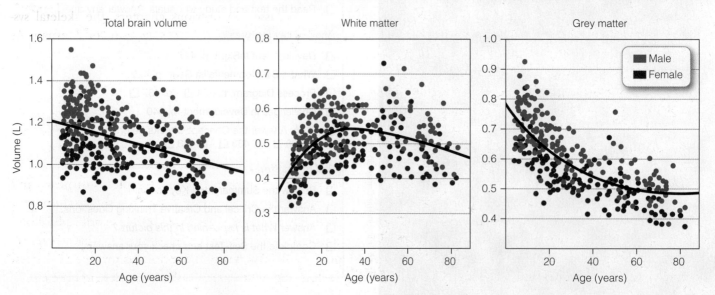

executive functioning Information-processing skills involved in problem solving and strategy design and execution.

variation in the health of mid-life brains. People who lose more brain volume show declines in **executive functioning** skills and ability to make decisions, plan, organize, and focus attention. Through mid-life, smokers show more rapid brain shrinkage than non-smokers. Other health risks are associated with more rapid brain shrinkage as well: depression, stress, high blood pressure, obesity, diabetes, and high cholesterol (Debette et al., 2011).

Some people's brain functioning decreases significantly at mid-life, but in general, the adult brain is capable of learning new things. Adults can certainly perform behaviours that they never before performed. At

neurogenesis The process of generating new neurons from stem cells.

mid-life, our brains demonstrate plasticity, the capacity to rebuild and recover after insult, due in part to our ability to produce new neurons from neural stem cells, a process known as **neurogenesis** (Eriksson et al., 1998; Gould, Reeves, Graziano, & Gross, 1999). Stem cells are undifferentiated cells that can differentiate and specialize, or produce more stem cells.

The discovery that we can grow new neurons is relatively new, and our knowledge of adult brain neurogenesis is still quite limited. Researchers have explored how neurogenesis works only in a limited set of brain regions. Each discovery and each study that provides new insight into the brain's potential to generate new abilities and functions is exciting and promising.

Many people hold hope that new treatments will be discovered to help repair the brains of loved ones who suffer brain damage and dysfunction. For example, strokes become increasingly common after young adulthood and through middle adulthood, although the riskiest years come after age 65. Strokes occur when blood flow to a part of the brain stops. If blood flow stops for longer than a few seconds, the brain stops receiving blood and oxygen. As a result, brain cells begin to die. Historically, the outcome of a stroke has been permanent brain damage.

Strokes can be especially devastating to middle-age adults, who may become disabled in their peak years of work and earning power. Current programs to help people recover often use general techniques such as exercise, which stimulates brain activity (Olson, Eadie,

Ernst, & Christie, 2006). However, these techniques are not specialized enough to target recovery of specific functions. Cutting-edge developmental science is focused on identifying new interventions to stimulate neurogenesis in the specific damaged areas of the brain. For example, some researchers are working to stimulate neurogenesis in ways that reduce cognitive deficits among war veterans who have experienced brain trauma (Sahay et al., 2011).

Research on adult neurogenesis has implications not only for intervention, but also for prevention. For example, it is widely known that obesity is linked to cognitive diseases, such as Parkinson's and Alzheimer's diseases, in later life (Couillard-Despres, Iglseder, & Aigner, 2011). Research suggests that the pathway from obesity to cognitive disease is complex. Obesity increases levels of certain hormones that circulate through the brain. Exposure to these hormones increases risk for dementia by interfering with neurogenesis (Whitmer, Gunderson, Barrett-Connor, Quensberry, & Yaffe, 2005; Whitmer, Gustafson, Barrett-Connor, Haan, Gunderson, & Yaffe, 2008). Now, researchers hope to find ways to disrupt pathways between risks, such as obesity, and unwanted outcomes.

As research on adult neurogenesis matures, we will come to know much more about the dynamic mid-life brain. In the meantime, however, we already know that the best way to prevent cognitive decline and dementia is to reduce poor health habits. Staying active and healthy is good for maintaining not only the mid-life body, but also the mid-life brain.

The Skeletal System

As we discussed in previous chapters, the skeletal system continues to remodel throughout the lifespan. As you may remember, remodelling occurs through the process of **bone resorption** by which bone cells are lost and replaced by new bone cells. As we discussed in Chapter 11, bones reach their maximal length and thickness

bone resorption The process of bone cells breaking down and transforming into a fluid substance that enters the blood.

by young adulthood. In most people, resorption and formation are in a state of balance at the beginning of middle adulthood (Seeman, 2002). As middle adulthood continues, however, bone loss starts to outpace bone replacement. This begins a continuous process of skeletal decline that continues into the later adulthood years.

Bone density as we age • Figure 13.2

This chart shows bone loss in the hip over time. As is shown, women tend to lose more density than men, partly because they have smaller bones on average. Menopause-related decreases in the hormone estrogen also affect women's bone loss, causing many post-menopausal women to develop fragile bones (Seeman, 2002).

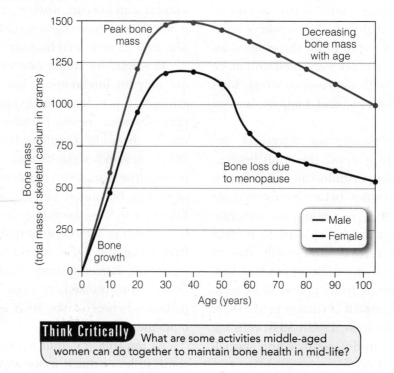

Think Critically What are some activities middle-aged women can do together to maintain bone health in mid-life?

As with other physical systems, our behaviour affects bone health. Bone loss is greater among people who do not engage in weight-bearing activities (Chien, Yang, & Tsauo, 2005). Weight bearing describes any activity you do on your feet that works your bones and muscles against gravity. It may not be as difficult as middle-aged adults think to get in recommended amounts of weight-bearing activity, given that hiking, walking, and yard work are all fine examples of such activities.

Middle-aged adults might benefit from putting weight-bearing activities on their to-do list because they are unlikely to notice changes until later. Although adults lose bone through middle adulthood, the actual size of our bones does not change until later adulthood. Rather than change size, our bones become less dense, as shown in **Figure 13.2**, because the inside of the bone is being lost without replacement (Seeman, 2008).

In addition, both men and women lose height and gain weight during the middle adult years. One way to slow this process is through healthy diet and exercise (Warden & Fuchs, 2009), which we discuss later in the chapter.

As our bones go, so go our muscles. Diminishing bone structure tends to alter the way our muscles stretch, resulting in significant changes in the muscular system at mid-life.

The Muscular System

As we discussed in Chapter 11, muscle strength peaks in the early 30s. Aging brings **sarcopenia**, or age-related muscle loss (Evans, 1995). The rate at which a person experiences sarcopenia varies greatly, depending on the person's gender, the amount of exercise they get, and a host of other variables (Connelly, 2000). As we will see in future chapters, sarcopenia continues into later adulthood, when the percentage of muscle loss increases. Exercise and a healthy diet can help maintain muscle strength, which is important. Muscle strength is an indicator of a person's general health. If you want to assess a person's muscle strength, put out your hand for a handshake. As seen in **Figure 13.3**, hand-grip strength is

> **sarcopenia** The process of skeletal muscle loss due to aging.

Mid-life muscle strength • Figure 13.3

Muscle strength decreases with age. Hand-grip strength is an indicator of general health and a predictor of longevity.

a. Muscle strength is essential for a wide range of personal and work tasks in mid-life. Hand-grip strength is a general indicator of muscle strength throughout the body.

Think Critically As your parents and grandparents age, what information can you learn from holding and shaking their hands when you visit?

Tim Barker/Getty Images

b. A dynamometer is used to test hand-grip strength. Hand-grip strength is a measure of the maximum force a person is able to apply when gripping or pinching an object, such as a coffee cup, a shampoo bottle, or another person's hand during a handshake.

William Mancebo/Cal Sport Media/Newscom

a very good indicator of overall muscle strength and general health, and a good predictor of longevity (Cooper, Strand, Hardy, Patel, & Kuh, 2014; Hairi et al., 2010).

Interestingly, our muscles can get more flexible with age. Over the lifetime, muscles engage in two general types of movement. The first is **concentric muscle movement**, in which muscles contract to lift an object, such as when we lift a suitcase. The second is **eccentric muscle movement**, in which the muscles lengthen or return to their original position, such as when putting a box down. As we get older, we may lose concentric strength, but our eccentric strength, or flexibility of muscles to lengthen, is maintained quite well and may even increase. Of course, there are limits to this lengthening of muscles, and the process slows down as we enter later adulthood.

concentric muscle movement The contraction of muscles during physical activity.

eccentric muscle movement The lengthening of muscles as they return to original position after stretching.

Skin and Hair

Many visible changes occur in our skin as we proceed through mid-life. People in their 40s often notice the appearance of small, often oddly shaped spots on the face, arms, and other exposed areas of skin. These spots are variously called *age spots*, *liver spots*, and *solar lentigines*. They result from years of sun exposure (Farris, 2004). Although such spots are generally not dangerous, any new mole or discoloured area on the skin should be evaluated by a medical professional such as a dermatologist to make sure the change does not signify a more serious condition such as skin cancer.

It's not only the epidermis, the top layer of the skin, that changes due to aging, but also the dermis, right under the top layer of skin. The dermis obtains its elasticity from collagen cells that are scattered throughout skin tissue. With age, the number of collagen cells decreases. In addition, sebaceous glands that produce oil in our skin begin to work less efficiently. Both of these processes cause the skin to lose elasticity and to become dry, leading to cracks and wrinkles, as shown

Signs of aging written all over our faces • Figure 13.4

People who have long careers in the public spotlight provide examples of what happens to all of us with age: our skin changes.

a. Pop culture icon Céline Dion began her singing career in her teens. Her youth is apparent in this photograph of her in her 20s.

b. Seen here in her late 40s, Céline Dion very much remains an icon. Her face has changed. Her cheeks are less full as a result of tissue changes and wrinkles are more evident.

Michel Ponomareff/Ponopresse/Getty Images

Victor Virgile/Getty Images

Think Critically If Céline Dion didn't have access to cosmetics and other interventions that help reduce signs of aging, what other signs of aging might be visible on her face?

in **Figure 13.4**. Once again, the best ways to slow this process are through exercise, because sweating keeps the skin soft and elastic, and through diet.

For many people, their hair, or lack of it, shows the most obvious signs of aging. Each type of hair on our body has an individual growth cycle followed by a resting cycle, during which hair falls out. As a result, we all lose about 100 hairs per day, on average. Usually, new hair replaces the lost hair. For some people, however, hair loss outpaces hair gain, resulting in increasing baldness. In addition, most people's hair tends to change colour with age. The pigment melanin gives hair its colour. As we age, each new replacement hair contains less and less melanin, resulting in hair turning grey. Hair and skin changes are largely cosmetic. Changes to the senses, however, can affect daily functioning.

The Senses

Sight, hearing, smell, and taste all change during midlife, as explored in **Figure 13.5**. In general, the senses become less able to accurately discriminate incoming information. With respect to vision, middle-aged adults often experience three key optical changes:

- **Presbyopia**, the inability to focus on nearby objects, increases (Schachar, 2006). Interestingly, presbyopia is most likely in people who previously had excellent vision.
- **Myopia**, or nearsightedness, may also decrease, allowing some to see objects at a distance better. This change occurs because the eye is gradually getting smaller, changing the focal point on the retina.
- Visual acuity, the ability to discriminate detail, declines continuously as we age (Elliot, Yang, & Whitaker, 1995; Pitts, 1982).

Hearing also declines during middle age, as shown in part b of Figure 13.5. The good news, however, is that the decline is slow.

presbyopia The inability of the eyes to accommodate so that they can focus on objects at a normal reading distance (45–50 cm).

myopia Nearsightedness, or the ability to see close objects clearly but inability to see distant objects clearly.

Our senses become less reactive and process stimuli less accurately as a function of aging in mid-life. Middle age requires adaptations to these changes to maintain prior levels of functioning.

a. Vision

The ability of the eye to accommodate, or to maintain focus on an object, changes dramatically with age. Like many middle-aged adults, the man in this photo holds his reading material at arm's length because he has a hard time focusing on nearby objects. Reading glasses can help solve the problem of presbyopia.

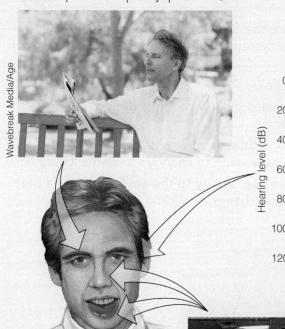

Wavebreak Media/Age

Gordon-Salant, S. (2005) *Journal of Rehabilitation Research & Development*, 42 (4) 9-24. Cruickshanks, KJ, et al, Prevalence of hearing loss in older adults in Beaver Dam, Wisconsin, The Epidemiology of Hearing Loss Study. *Am J. Epidem.* 1998; 148 (9) 879-86, by permission of Oxford University Press.

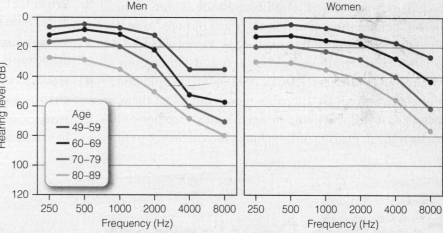

b. Hearing

Age-related hearing loss results in the decreasing ability to hear higher-frequency sounds, such as those that typically accompany speech. The graphs for men and women depict a clear female advantage in retaining hearing sensitivity in mid-life. The graph on the right shows that, although women also experience hearing loss as they age, on average, they have less loss than men.

Dennis McDonald/Photo Edit

c. Smell and taste

As we age, we experience a loss of taste buds and olfactory cells, which are the receptor cells for taste and smell. Because smell and taste combine to create flavour, these receptor changes lead many middle-aged adults to salt and season their food more than they did earlier in life.

Think Critically Picture a middle-aged grandfather interacting with his 6-year-old grandson. Can you describe a few funny moments that happen between the two of them resulting from middle-aged changes in vision, hearing, smell, and taste?

Some people demonstrate excellent hearing into their 70s and 80s (Wingfield, Tun, & McCoy, 2005). Because

<table>
<tr><td>**conductive hearing loss** Hearing loss resulting from conduction impairments in the middle ear.</td></tr>
<tr><td>**sensorineural hearing loss** Hearing loss resulting from loss of hair cells on the basilar membrane of the inner ear.</td></tr>
</table>

declines are slow, middle adults typically do not report perceiving significant hearing loss. When hearing loss does occur, it typically results from impaired conduction in the middle ear, called **conductive hearing loss**, or loss of hair cells along the basilar membrane in the inner ear, called **sensorineural hearing loss**.

Some types of hearing loss can be corrected medically by an otolaryngologist, a specialist in ears and hearing. Current technology has created many other options for middle and older adults with hearing problems. For example, hearing aids are effective for magnifying sound as well as inhibiting noise. There are in the ear, behind the ear, and in the canal options, as well as analogue and digital hearing aids. However, according to the National Institute on Deafness and Other Communication Disorders (NIDCD, 2008), many people who could benefit from hearing aids choose not to get them. Factors that influence middle-aged adults' decisions to use or not use hearing aids include convenience, extent

of hearing disability, expected benefits, and financial costs (Laplante-Lévesque, Hickson, & Worrall, 2010).

Finally, our chemical senses of taste and smell also become less acute, as mentioned in Figure 13.5. Notably, taste and smell sensitivity diminishes for some stimuli but not for all (Mojet, Christ-Hazelhof, & Heidema, 2001). Usually, salty and sweet tastes are lost first, followed by bitter and sour tastes.

In sum, middle adulthood signals the beginning of declines in several areas of physical development. Yet many middle adults refuse to accept these changes sitting down, either literally or figuratively.

CONCEPT CHECK 🛑 STOP

1. **What** are the functional consequences of nervous system changes in middle adulthood?
2. **What** factors affect a person's rate of bone loss at mid-life?
3. **What** causes muscle changes during middle adulthood?
4. **How** do middle-aged adults' appearances change as a result of changes to skin and hair?
5. **How** does sensitivity to the environment via the five senses change in middle adulthood?

Cognitive Development

LEARNING OBJECTIVES

1. **Describe** how our cognitive abilities change during middle adulthood.
2. **Discuss** the processes used to maximize gains and minimize losses associated with aging.
3. **Outline** the attainment of expertise.

J ust as earlier in life, an individual's cognitive ability appears to continue to change as he or she ages. Like most of the dimensions we have studied in this chapter, there is much variability in these changes.

Cognitive Abilities

One of the most difficult processes to define in human development is that of intelligence. As we have seen in

previous chapters, numerous theories of intelligence have been proposed, ranging from Alfred Binet's conceptualization of an intelligence quotient (IQ) to Howard Gardner's theory of multiple intelligences (Gardner, 1993).

Fluid and crystalized intelligence Psychologist Raymond Cattell (1963, 1987) analyzed how individuals reason as they get older. He observed two general dimensions of cognitive abilities that contribute to

WHAT A DEVELOPMENTALIST SEES
Fluid and Crystallized Intelligence

After his plane unexpectedly hit a flock of Canada geese and lost power, 57-year-old Captain Chesley Sullenberger (**Figure a**) successfully piloted it to a safe landing on the Hudson River in New York City in January 2009, saving the lives of all 155 people on board. Sullenberger is a real-life hero. Developmentalists recognize the contribution of crystallized intelligence to Sullenberger's heroic actions. Crystallized intelligence increases with age (**Figure b**). When New York State's deputy secretary for public safety shook Sullenberger's hand and thanked him, Sullenberger replied, "That's what we're trained to do" (Rivera, 2009).

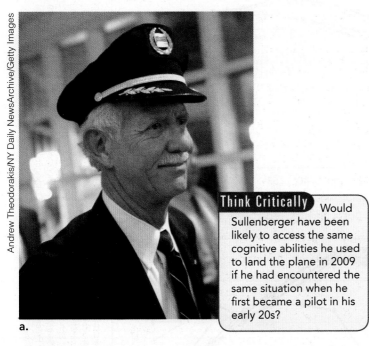

Andrew Theodorakis/NY Daily NewsArchive/Getty Images

Think Critically Would Sullenberger have been likely to access the same cognitive abilities he used to land the plane in 2009 if he had encountered the same situation when he first became a pilot in his early 20s?

a.

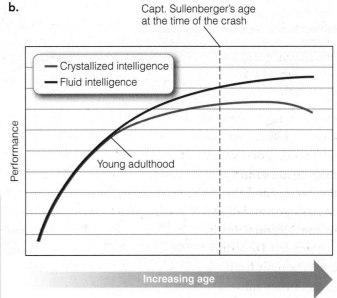

b.

Capt. Sullenberger's age at the time of the crash

— Crystallized intelligence
— Fluid intelligence

Performance

Young adulthood

Increasing age

---

fluid intelligence The category of intelligence that drives reasoning and logic.

crystallized intelligence The category of intelligence that contains basic information that we acquire over time, such as facts and figures.

general intelligence. One dimension—**fluid intelligence**—strongly influences cognitive ability in childhood. Its development looks similar to the development of operative intelligence and learning as described by Piaget. This type of intelligence drives problem solving, pattern recognition, and abstract reasoning. High fluid intelligence is a predictor of the person's likelihood of successfully working through problems of complexity, ambiguity, or uncertainty. Fluid intelligence increases through young adulthood, after which time it steadies and then declines (Baltes, 1993; Schaie, 2005).

Crystallized intelligence, the second dimension of intelligence proposed by Cattell, describes accumulated knowledge—that is, all the skills and knowledge people accumulate through learning and life experience.

Crystallized intelligence increases linearly through middle adulthood (Baltes, 1993; Schaie, 2005). Fluid and crystallized intelligence contribute uniquely to our cognitive abilities. (See *What a Developmentalist Sees.*)

In middle adulthood, we constantly see examples of crystallized intelligence but fewer and fewer instances of fluid intelligence. For example, in the workplace the middle-adult worker is likely to suggest solving a problem by using solutions that have worked in the past. Not surprisingly, younger workers are more likely to approach the problem in novel ways. Of course, younger workers have had fewer problem-solving encounters.

The Seattle Longitudinal Study of Adult Intelligence
Recall from Chapter 11 that the Seattle Longitudinal Study of Adult Intelligence found that some cognitive abilities continue to increase well into adulthood. Data collected during the study suggest that all mental abilities decline over time, but the most significant decline occurs between the ages of 67 and 88. As we move from young adulthood to middle adulthood, only perceptual speed

Changes in intelligence with age • Figure 13.6

The following graphs show average changes in the cognitive abilities of adults from age 25 to 88.

a. Longitudinal data

When the mental abilities of the same individuals were tracked over time, mental abilities remained high until about age 60. They then began a steep decline, with numerical ability declining the most.

b. Cross-sectional data

When people of different ages were studied at one point in time, most abilities began to decline from age 25. As shown in this graph, only numerical and verbal abilities increased until middle age before beginning to decline.

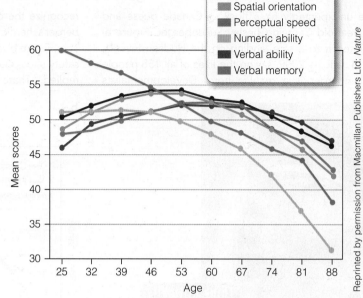

Think Critically 1. If we used only cross-sectional data to understand cognitive abilities in middle adulthood, how would this section of the text be written differently?
2. What might news reporters say about mid-life from the cross-sectional findings?

shows noticeable declines. As **Figure 13.6** shows, another interesting conclusion of the Seattle Longitudinal Study was that longitudinal data indicated a much slower decrease in intellectual abilities than cross-sectional data did (Willis & Schaie, 1999).

Experiences and Goals

Cognitive abilities continue to increase with age in part because new experiences with families, work, health, and friends in middle age continue to encourage cognitive development. A great deal less research has been done on the associations between life experiences and cognitive

changes in middle adulthood than on the associations during later adulthood. We do know, however, that stress (Kremen, Lachman, Pruessner, Sliwinski, & Wilson, 2012) and feeling a lack of control (Windsor & Anstey, 2008) both have negative effects on people's cognitive ability in mid-life, regardless of whether those risks occur at work or, as **Figure 13.7** shows, as part of family life.

Cognitive abilities and experiences are linked in a second interesting way at mid-life. Cognitive abilities are not only shaped by life experiences in mid-life; people also select experiences that maintain and maximize their cognitive abilities during these years. Throughout the lifespan,

selective optimization with compensation (SOC) A theory of successful aging that identifies three processes people use to maximize gains and minimize losses in response to aging.

selection The process of identifying goals that are reasonable and reachable given a person's capabilities.

optimization The process of investing effort and resources in a concentrated attempt to reach a selected goal.

compensation The process of revising a selected goal so that it is better suited to one's ability to reach it.

development involves gains and losses at each life stage. As cognitive abilities begin to decline in middle adulthood, people invoke three processes to help them maximize gains and minimize losses due to aging: selection, optimization, and compensation (Baltes, 1997; Baltes & Baltes, 1990).

Selective optimization with compensation (SOC) is a metatheory, a theory used to organize a number of theories. SOC, proposed by German social scientist Paul Baltes, is a conceptual model particularly useful for describing, explaining, and predicting successful development throughout adulthood (Gestsdóttir, Lewin-Bizan, von Eye, Lerner, & Lerner, 2009). **Selection** is the process of identifying goals that are reasonable and reachable given a person's capabilities. **Optimization** is the process of applying effort and investing personal resources, such as time, in a way that moves the person closer to his or her selected goals. Sometimes, however, we need to adjust our goals. **Compensation** is the process of revising or changing the scope of a

goal so that it is a better match with one's ability to achieve it. Our ability to successfully apply these three SOC processes is a direct determinant of our success and well-being.

The relative emphasis we place on each of these three processes changes as we move through different life stages. Young adults primarily use selection, setting life goals to guide their investments of time and energy. For example, young people set their educational goals before they leave high school. As they reach those goals, they set new goals until they achieve the education for the career they desire. Emerging adults also generally set romantic horizons, such as determining the age by which they expect to commit to a long-term relationship.

Selection strategies can still contribute to success and well-being at mid-life. For example, people who set new goals at work are more likely to advance at their jobs than those who don't. Using selection strategies to advance is especially helpful for people who hold low-complexity jobs that don't have a built-in mechanism to help people move up to new positions (Zacher & Frese, 2011). Gaining experience at higher and higher levels of complexity also helps to keep work interesting and fulfilling. As **Table 13.1** shows, life goals at different stages of the lifespan are different (Staudinger & Fleeson, 1996). Through young adulthood into the mid-50s, family and work are the primary concerns of adults. By the mid-50s, adults shift attention and focus to health concerns.

Although selection remains important, as people age into mid-life, they begin to use optimization and

Sandwiched in middle age • Figure 13.7

During middle adulthood, many people find themselves members of the so-called *sandwich generation*, a name coined to refer to people, usually middle-aged, who are simultaneously caring for their aging parents and their children.

Jae C. Hong/AP Photo

Think Critically How might being a member of the sandwich generation affect the cognitive development of the woman on the left in this photo?

Importance of life domains across the lifespan • Table 13.1					
Priority Rank	Ages 25 to 34	35 to 54	55 to 69	70 to 84	85 to 105
1	Work	Family	Family	Family	Health
2	Friends	Work	Health	Health	Family
3	Family	Friends	Friends	Cognitive fitness	Thinking about life
4	Independence	Cognitive fitness	Cognitive fitness	Friends	Cognitive fitness

Adapted from Staudinger & Fleeson (1996).

compensation processes more often (Ebner, Freund, & Baltes, 2006). Middle-aged adults have to balance competing demands from work and family, which requires them to strategize about the best uses of their time and resources. For example, a middle-aged working parent might have to decide what to do when a child is sick and needs to stay home from school. The parent may use optimization by asking a relative to stay with the child for a few hours while the parent works, and then switch to compensation, leaving work early as soon as an important meeting is over and lowering his or her work goals for the day. Optimization also helps adults to gain expertise.

Expertise

You are lying in a hospital room awaiting the start of a medical procedure. As medical staff enter the room and begin to work on you, you are most likely hoping that every single person providing your medical care is an expert at his or her job. But what exactly defines an *expert*? **Figure 13.8** describes one way in which many

The development of expertise • Figure 13.8

✓ THE PLANNER

Many researchers believe that we develop expertise in a series of steps, as we move from having no knowledge about a particular field to the highest relative level of knowledge (Chi, 2006; Hoffman & Lintern, 2006).

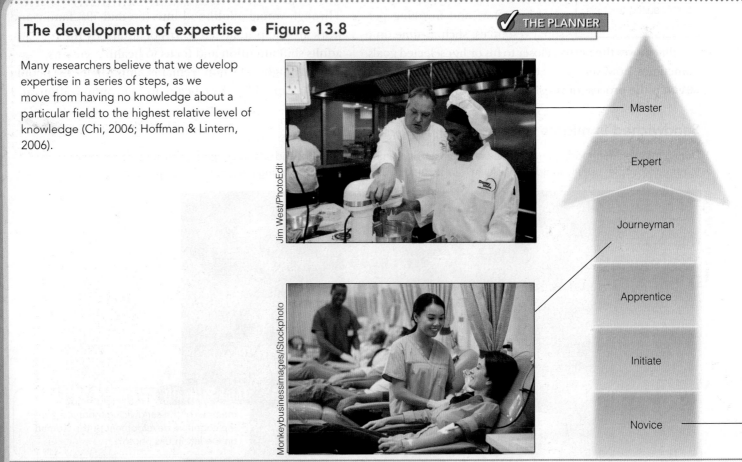

Jim West/PhotoEdit

Monkeybusinessimages/iStockphoto

- Master
- Expert
- Journeyman
- Apprentice
- Initiate
- Novice

psychologists answer this question (Chi, 2006; Hoffman & Lintern, 2006).

According to researcher Peter Fadde (2009), expertise can be found in any area of work. The key ingredient that makes a person an expert is what Fadde calls **recognition-primed decision-making**. In this process, experts are able to make decisions quickly because they are able to recognize the most relevant features of a situation. Fadde (2009) believes that this capability to recognize what is important and then act quickly upon that recognition is what defines expertise.

Another quality of expertise is the ability to do routine actions effortlessly. For example, one study examined expert and novice pilots working on simulators (Endsley, 2006). The researchers found few differences between the groups' actions during emergency-type situations.

recognition-primed decision-making A term used by Peter Fadde to describe a proficiency in decision-making based on the ability to quickly recognize the most relevant features of a situation.

What separated experts from novices, however, was the ease and speed with which experts performed the simple and routine actions required of pilots.

To summarize, expertise appears to be a combination of experience, competence, confidence, and the ability to separate relevant from irrelevant features of a particular situation. And as we will see in Chapter 14, we have the potential not only to become experts at work during middle adulthood, but also to become experts in self-understanding and relationships.

CONCEPT CHECK	STOP

1. **What** key changes in fluid and crystallized intelligence occur from young to middle adulthood?
2. **How** do middle-aged adults use SOC to adapt to physical changes associated with aging?
3. **What** are the characteristics of an expert?

Ask Yourself

1. The _____ is a person who has officially become a student in a set field.
2. By the time a person has reached the level of a(n) _____, he/she can work independently.
3. A(n)_____ is someone whose highly developed knowledge is transferred via teaching others.

6 After reaching expert status, a person may begin to teach others. This teacher is called a **master**.

5 Ultimately, skilled **experts** are admired by peers and are inferior to none (Chi, 2006).

4 A person who can do tasks unsupervised but who remains under others' orders is called a **journeyman**.

3 An **apprentice** works alongside a journeyman and/or expert in order to learn the profession.

2 An **initiates** is an early student in his or her field. Initiates solve problems by referring to rules and facts learned from books or school.

1 A **initiates** knows little about the field. For example, this hospital volunteer has an interest in the medical field but is not yet a medical student.

Monkeybusinessimages/Shutterstock

Cognitive Development **433**

All the Systems Working Together

LEARNING OBJECTIVES

1. **Describe** mid-life health concerns related to weight, exercise, and nutrition.

2. **Outline** typical changes in sexuality and reproductive health for mid-life women and men.

3. **Identify** the leading causes of death in middle adulthood.

4. **Discuss** how health maintenance and stress influence mid-life health and well-being.

P uberty may be the life stage most people associate with hormonal changes, but middle adulthood is also a stage of the lifespan during which changes in hormones and other regulatory systems have a strong influence on life experiences, health, and well-being.

Weight, Exercise, and Nutrition

Unfortunately, too much weight is a major impediment that many Canadians share; based on data collected between 2011 and 2012, one in four adult Canadians, approximately 6.3 million people, were considered obese. This represents an increase of 17.5 percent over data collected in 2003. Between 2003 and 2012, obesity increased more among men than among women

(17.9 percent vs. 16.8 percent, respectively). Canadians ages 35 to 64 are the most likely to be obese (Navaneelan & Janz, 2014). Overweight and obesity can lead to many physical problems and, as we'll see later in this chapter, contribute to the leading cause of death among middle-aged people. The good news is that, at middle age, exercise and good nutrition not only can help control weight, but also, as we saw earlier in the chapter, can slow some of the physical declines of our muscles, bones, and other systems that are associated with aging.

Obesity The World Health Organization (WHO) has been following an epidemic of obesity in both industrial and non-industrial countries, a trend it calls *globesity* (Brownell & Horgen, 2003; WHO, 2009), shown in **Figure 13.9**.

Globesity • Figure 13.9

From 1990 to 2010, obesity rates increased worldwide.

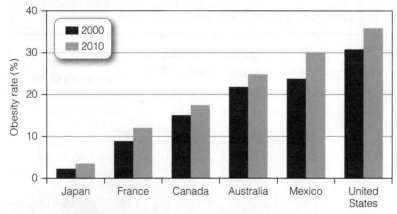

Based on data from OECD (2012), Obesity Update 2012. Retrieved from http://www.oecd.org/health/49716427.pdf.

LUCAS JACKSON/Reuters/Corbis

Ask Yourself

List, in rank order, from highest to lowest, the countries with the highest to lowest increase in obesity rates from 2000 to 2010.

How much should adults exercise? • Figure 13.10

The Canadian Society of Exercise Physiology recommends that adults get at least 150 minutes weekly of physical activity. This also harmonizes with guidelines set by the World Health Organization and other major developed countries like Canada, the United States, Australia, and Britain. There are 24 different diseases, including diabetes, heart ailments, and osteoporosis, that are linked in some way to inertia (Galloway, 2011). Despite recommendations, many adults engage in no physical activity at all, as indicated by this graph, and the percentage of inactive adults increases with age (American College of Sports Medicine, 2011). Inactivity means the person is not engaging in activities beyond daily living and moving about in their environment. Activity means the individual is expending additional energies beyond daily functioning.

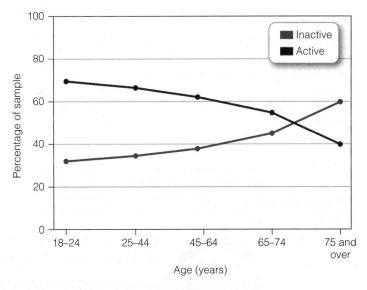

Think Critically What factors make physical activity less likely to occur with increased age?

Exercise in middle adulthood Much research has shown that exercise is correlated with positive health benefits (Pate et al., 1995). This statement is particularly valid for adults entering mid-life (Conn, Valentine, & Cooper, 2002; Dishman & Buckworth, 1996). Unfortunately, as **Figure 13.10** shows, many mid-life adults are missing out on the benefits of exercise.

One key benefit of exercise and physical activity is its role in improving the functioning of the cardiovascular system, which delivers oxygen to muscles. When a person is involved in physical activity or any type of exercise, the muscles in the body require more oxygen and nutrients, strengthening the cardiovascular system.

Given the role of the cardiovascular system in exercise, many organizations suggest that people monitor their heart rates during exercise, aiming to raise the heart rate but not go beyond maximum levels (American College of Sports Medicine, 2011). Most experts suggest that at the beginning of an exercise program, people aim to raise their heart rate during exercise to 70 to 80 percent of maximum (American College of Sports Medicine, 2011). The formula for estimating maximum heart rate is the number 220 minus a person's age. Thus, for a 50-year-old, maximum heart rate should not exceed 170 beats per minute (220 – 50 = 170). Health considerations, such as heart disease or other conditions, should also be taken into account when estimating maximum heart rate.

Exercise and physical activity not only can help lower obesity risk and improve cardiovascular health, but can also improve cognitive functioning, which is, in turn, related

to life expectancy (Singh-Manoux, Hillsdon, Brunner, & Marmot, 2005). Many of the studies in which researchers have observed actual changes in brain structure as a result of exercise have been done with animals (Gil-Mohapel, Simpson, Titterness, & Christie, 2010), but researchers tend to agree that generalizations of this work to humans are valid (Gil-Mohapel et al., 2010). For example, one team of researchers found that exercise actually stimulates prefrontal lobe activity, increasing the speed of processing and the integrity of white matter (Park & Reuter-Lorenz, 2009). Studying humans, another team found a correlation between exercise and cognitive function via scores on intelligence tests (Woo & Sharps, 2003).

Where you live can influence how readily physical activity is part of your daily routine. This is one of the ideas behind defining the factors in an **obesogenic environment** (Powell, Spears, & Rebori, 2010). *Where Developmentalists Click* shows the Canada Mortgage and Housing Corporation interactive website comparing neighbourhoods on their compatibility with active living and for addressing some of the issues creating obesogenic environments. Such information can be help people select better places to live. The environment influences not only how active we can be, but also how readily we can access high-quality nutrition. Exercise must also be accompanied by positive nutrition.

obesogenic environment The aspects of the community that create barriers for physical activity and ready access to highly nutritional food.

Where Developmentalists CLICK

Comparing Neighbourhoods for Active Living

The Canada Mortgage and Housing Corporation (www.cmhc-schl.gc.ca) offers an interactive website where you can compare a range of neighbourhoods on a variety of factors, including how supportive they are for active transportation such as cycling, walking, skateboarding, and non-mechanized wheelchairing, as well as skiing and snowshoeing. Neighbourhoods are ranked based on the proximity of homes to services, recreational opportunities, and workplaces so people can readily make their daily trips without a vehicle. On the website you can find more information about how village environments influence our activities.

Nutrition at mid-life During middle adulthood, nutrition remains just as important as it was during earlier periods of development. The Canadian nutritional guidelines for food intake were discussed in Chapter 5, including an interactive website where people can create personalized age-appropriate suggestions for healthy eating. Although mid-life adults are more likely than younger adults to eat within these guidelines (Ervin, 2011), many people still fall short. Knowing what to eat is not the strongest predictor of nutrition intake. Convenience and enjoyment of eating out apparently outweigh knowledge about healthy food when it comes to choosing to eat fast food (Dunn, Mohr, Wilson, & Wittert, 2008).

According to one study on eating patterns, only about one-quarter of North Americans actually sit down at table to eat meals (Finn, 2000). Instead, most engage in recreational grazing, "snacking on ready-made, hand-held foods" (Finn, 2000, p. 354). Food habits and routines are strong predictors of food choices. Most people have the same food at the same meal for days in a row because meals are embedded in work and family life patterns (Khare & Inman, 2006). As a result, mid-life adults who want to lose weight or maintain weight when physical exercise decreases need to change their habitual eating patterns, as well as follow guidelines for healthy eating.

All in all, a healthy diet and exercise together can translate into better health, positive cognitive function, and higher resistance to disease and the challenges of the aging process.

Reproductive Changes and Sexuality in Middle Adulthood

There are gender differences in reproductive changes during middle adulthood, just as there are during adolescence. For women, reproductive changes are more pronounced and obvious, due to the fact that hormonal changes affect menstruation. For men, changes in hormones and reproductive capabilities take place over a longer period of time—20 to 30 years—compared with women. However, there are fewer external cues in males that these changes are happening inside the body.

In this section we examine normal, expected changes that take place in the reproductive system in middle adulthood. We consider not only the physiological but also the psychological and emotional changes. For example, reproductive changes in mid-life affect sexuality and intimacy. What you learn may surprise you. Many middle-aged adults still report strong sexual interest and desire for intimacy.

Menopause In the same way that menstruation marks the beginning of the reproductive life cycle for adolescent girls, **menopause** signals the end of the reproductive life cycle in middle-aged women. Menopause is not abrupt, but rather takes place over a number of years. Doctors consider a woman to be in menopause after she has had no menstrual period for a year due to changes in her reproductive hormones, and not for any other reason such as breastfeeding or a medical condition. As **Figure 13.11** shows, the two hormones produced in the ovaries, progesterone and estrogen, trigger the onset of menopause. Menopause is a consequence of the reduced production of estrogen and the complete halt of the production of progesterone. Most women begin their

> **menopause** A period of time in which a woman's production of hormones (estrogen and progesterone) begins to decline, causing changes in her reproductive capabilities.

Stages of menopause • Figure 13.11

✓ THE PLANNER

Menopause follows a predictable series of changes in the woman's body that result in the end of menstruation and her childbearing years.

— Estrogen
— Progesterone
● Menstrual period

1 Premenopause
Women are premenopausal during their fertility years until they transition out of this stage in their early to mid-40s. Periods are regular and women are able to bear children. Sex hormones estrogen and progesterone are predictably coordinated. When these ovarian hormones become less cyclically stable, premenopause comes to a close.

2 Perimenopause
Uncoordinated sex hormones associated with irregular periods indicate that a woman has entered perimenopause. The average age of perimenopause is 48, although physical and emotional changes can begin as early as the late 30s. Ovarian hormones become less cyclical and coordinated resulting in irregular periods for all and, for some but not all, dysregulation of mood, sleep, energy, and attention.

3 Post-menopause
In post-menopause, ovarian hormones stabilize. The physiological systems of post-menopausal women no longer cyclically fluctuate throughout the month. After an entire year of not having a period, a woman has reached menopause, the end of menstruation and the childbearing years. Early menopause is defined as having reached this milestone by age 40; late menopause occurs after age 55.

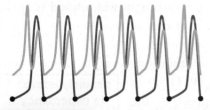

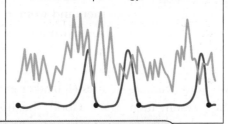

Think Critically If you were a health practitioner explaining the transition through the three stages of menopause to a woman, how would you explain the differences in hormone regulation through the three stages?

PROCESS DIAGRAM

menopausal transition in their late 40s and complete the transition by age 55. For others, the transition through menopause continues into the 60s (Godfrey & Naftolin, 2008).

Approximately two-thirds of women experience some physical symptoms along with the transition to menopause. Some women report weight gain, fluid retention, mood changes, irritability, or hot flashes, but these symptoms do not always rise to the level of life interference. When they do, medical interventions may be prescribed to reduce symptoms. Not too long ago, hormone replacement therapy (HRT), which added estrogen and progesterone into a woman's system by prescription, was a standard treatment. Today, doctors are advised to take into account individual characteristics of each patient to determine when the benefits of HRT will outweigh the costs (Manson et al., 2013). For example, in women going through menopause or those who are in early postmenopause, HRT not only reduces discomfort, but can reduce the risk of heart disease and bone loss, among other medical risks (Boardman, 2014). However, after 60, evidence is mixed as to whether health benefits outweigh potential health risks associated with the intervention (Guallar, Manson, Laine, & Mulrow, 2013).

Menopause is a biological transition that is often experienced as changes not only in one's body, but also in the way one experiences emotions and social life. Some of the earliest research on menopause revealed that many women have negative expectations for this normative biological change (Neugarten, 1996; Neugarten & Datan, 1974; Neugarten & Kraines, 1965). Negative expectations may heighten the risk of experiencing problems at mid-life. Moreover, women having problems for other reasons may attribute these issues to menopause. But not all problems women have at menopause are related to this biological experience, and proper assessment is needed so that women can receive the type of help they actually need rather than the help they are assumed to need (Toffol, Heikinheimo, & Partonen, 2013).

Andropause Men experience a biological transition that is parallel to menopause but not equal to it. Unlike menopause, the andropause transition does not result in the inability to reproduce. Men slowly and gradually lose testosterone through mid-life. As a result, men in their 50s and 60s can still produce enough sperm to impregnate a woman (Sternbach, 1998). The male version of menopause has been given different titles over the last 20 years—most recently, **andropause** (Boul, 2003).

Similar to menopause, symptoms of andropause vary. Men may experience diminished sexual desire, erectile problems, irritability, depression, and anxiety (Boul, 2003). Although many of these symptoms are linked to lower levels of testosterone, some may be due to the aging process more generally.

> **andropause** A decrease in the male hormone testosterone resulting in physiological reproductive changes such as lower sperm count and penile responsiveness.

Sexual relationships in middle adulthood Decreasing hormones at mid-life is associated with a reduction in libido, or desire for sex, in men and women. Pharmaceutical interventions are available for both men and women who want to override this side effect of changing hormones. Most people have heard of Viagra for treating sexual dysfunction in men, and similar prescriptions are available for women (Wincze & Carey, 2012). As with any unwanted consequence of aging-related change, the availability of medication to help reduce the unwanted consequences of hormone changes for sex is likely welcome relief for those seeking help. Sex matters in mid-life because satisfaction with a healthy sex life is associated with good mental health (Thomas, Chang, Dillon, & Hess, 2014).

In mid-life, most adults are still having sex relatively frequently. Men and women report more sex in their 40s and 50s than in later ages. Specifically, men report having sex approximately six times per month in mid-life (44–59) and three times per month in later decades (57–72). Women report having sex approximately five times per month through mid-life (44–59) and less than two times per month at older ages (57–72) (Karraker, DeLamater, & Schwartz, 2011). These figures are lower than those for younger adults in their 20s and 30s. After young adulthood, sexual frequency generally declines. The decrease is due to a number of factors. For both men and women, not surprisingly, widowhood is associated with a decrease in sexual activity. Poor health with age and decreases in happiness are also factors associated with a decrease in the middle-aged adult's sexual activities (Karraker et al., 2011).

Good health predicts the number of years that a person will have a sexually active life. **Sexually active life expectancy** at age 30

> **sexually active life expectancy** The number of years remaining for a person to be sexually active.

is, on average, approximately 34.7 years for women and 30.7 years for men. At age 55, sexually active life expectancy is, on average, approximately 15 for men and 11 for women. The difference between men and women is much smaller for people who remain with a spouse through mid-life. And, again, health matters. Staying physically healthy through mid-life gives men an extra six years and women an extra four years of sexually active life expectancy compared with middle-aged adults in poor or fair health (Lindau & Gavrilova, 2010).

Coming out in mid-life Over the last two decades, same-sex relationships have gained greater acceptance and visibility (Diamond, 2004). Homosexuality, particularly same-sex marriage, has been the focus of legislation, talk radio discussion, books, and films (Diamond & Butterworth, 2008; Tolman & Diamond, 2001). At mid-life, a little over 1 percent of the population, including both men and women, identify themselves as homosexual and a little over 1 percent identifies as bisexual (Mock & Eibach, 2012).

According to University of Utah researcher Lisa Diamond, mid-life is an unusual time to change one's sexual orientation. To better understand changes in sexual identity in adulthood, Marion Armstrong's research at York University in Toronto explored women's mid-life coming-out narratives (2003). In in-depth research conversations, women explored their process of leaving heterosexuality at mid-life and explained how they go through a powerful set of transformations in their self-perceptions and their relationships with others. Women shift their thinking about sexuality and the labels society uses for various forms of sexuality. They also appreciated their mid-life shift to lesbian relationships as rooted in women's greater capacity for intimacy and intimacy needs. They saw their process of coming out as a mature woman as uniquely different from that of younger women. They also acknowledged the impacts of the loss of heterosexual privilege and coming out to family members as well as the significance of redefining what is meant by family (Armstrong, 2003). In recent years, a number of mid-life celebrities have disclosed their gay or lesbian identities. For example, entertainer Ellen Degeneres publicly announced that she was a lesbian in 1997, at age 39. Similarly, television personality Anderson Cooper kept his sexual identity private until 2012 when, at age 45, he publicly announced, "I'm gay, always have been, always will be, and I couldn't be more

happy, comfortable with myself, and proud." Although they only came out publicly in middle age, Ellen Degeneres and Anderson Cooper both emphasized the continuity of their sexual identity from decades prior to mid-life, which reinforces what we have learned from our research: coming out—declaring a sexual identity other than heterosexual—in mid-life is rare. Less than 2 percent of the population reports a different sexual orientation over a 10-year period in mid-life (Mock & Eibach, 2012).

Death and Disease in Middle Adulthood

Director and actor Woody Allen was quoted as saying, "I don't want to achieve immortality through my work... I want to achieve it through not dying." His famous sentiment probably reflects the wishes of many middle adults. For the first time in life, the leading cause of death is not unintentional accidents once we enter middle adulthood. Middle-aged adults are less likely to die from unintentional injuries than are emerging and young adults. As you can see in **Figure 13.12**, by middle adulthood, diseases, particularly cancer and heart disease, have begun to threaten health and well-being.

Heart disease Heart disease (shown in *Challenges in Development*) is a leading cause of death in mid-life (Hall-Baker et al., 2010). Men are more likely to die from heart disease than women. Risk for heart disease is relatively equal for men and women through the early 40s, but then the difference between the sexes widens and men are at higher risk throughout mid-life and later adulthood (National Center for Health Statistics, 2013). However, while most of the risk factors and signs of heart disease are the same for men and women, there are some unique aspects of women's heart health. Estrogen, for example, has a protective effect on women's cardiovascular health. Consequently, women's overall risk of heart disease increases during menopause because of hormonal changes (Heart and Stroke Foundation, 2015). Additionally, women are more likely than men to underestimate their risk for heart disease, misinterpret symptoms, delay seeking medical assistance, and be misdiagnosed by health care providers (Schoenberg, Peters, & Drew, 2003). Understanding the risk factors for heart disease is an important part of preventative care.

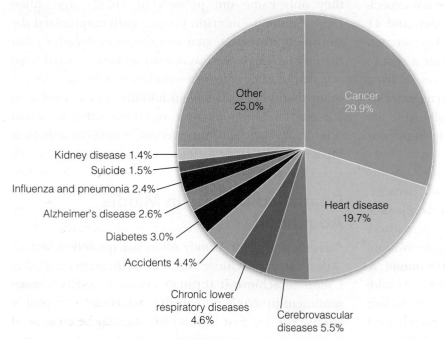

Source: Canadian Cancer Society's Advisory Committee on Cancer Statistics. (2015). Canadian cancer statistics 2015. Retrieved from www.cancer.ca/~/media/cancer.ca/CW/cancer%20information/cancer%20101/Canadian%20cancer%20statistics/Canadian-Cancer-Statistics-2015-EN.pdf.

Think Critically From a prevention perspective, what should be the focus of public health initiatives in young adulthood if our goal is to reduce risk for death in middle adulthood?

CHALLENGES IN DEVELOPMENT
Heart Disease

Heart disease actually begins in the blood vessels (see the figure). As damage progresses, risk for heart attack and stroke increases. Race and ethnicity influence the likelihood of having heart disease and elevated risk for heart attack and stroke. Heart disease, for example, is the leading cause of death for Aboriginal Canadians aged 45 and older (Adelson, 2005; Health Canada, 2011). In a study completed in 2012, the cardiovascular disease mortality rate was 30 percent higher for First Nations men, and 76 percent higher for First Nations women, when compared with non–First Nations Canadians of the same age. Research has also demonstrated a high concentration of risk factors for heart disease, such as diabetes and obesity, within Aboriginal communities. In addition to those well-known risk factors, social influences—such as education, income, and food insecurity—also play a role in the overrepresentation of heart disease among Canada's Aboriginal peoples (Adelson, 2005; Mikkonen & Raphael, 2010; Tjepkema, Wilkins, Goedhuis, & Pennock, 2012).

Health disparities, such as those experienced between Aboriginal and non-Aboriginal Canadians, highlight the underlying causes of such inequalities. The primary factors shaping the health of Canadians are not lifestyle choices, but are more accurately conceptualized as the living conditions experienced by people

and populations. Individuals and populations disproportionally affected by adverse social and material living conditions also experience high levels of physiological and psychological stress, creating illness vulnerability. Heart attacks, for example, are more common among low-income Canadians (Mikkonen & Raphael, 2010). Consequently, risks for developing heart disease at mid-life begin accumulating early in the life course. Some people appear more prone to absorb stress. Adults who reported higher distress tolerance at age 7 were at lower risk for cardiovascular disease in mid-life than those who reported low tolerance (Appleton, Loucks, Buka, Rimm, & Kubzansky, 2013). Healthy lifestyle behaviours through emerging adulthood (from 18 to 30) are protective against cardiovascular disease in mid-life; these behaviours include lower body mass index, no or moderate alcohol intake, higher healthy diet score, higher physical activity score, and no smoking. Those who had one lifestyle risk in emerging adulthood had low risk for cardiovascular disease, at 15 percent. Those who had five lifestyle risks in emerging adulthood had a risk factor of over 60 percent (Liu et al., 2012).

Not all risk for cardiovascular disease is settled prior to middle adulthood. Eating fish twice a week in middle adulthood is protective against cardiovascular disease for women but not for men

Cancers Cancers are the leading cause of death in mid-life. The median age for the diagnosis of most cancers occurs in mid-life. Prognosis and average survival times vary by type of cancer. But a diagnosis of cancer at mid-life is likely to have a very different impact on a person than such a diagnosis at a later age.

Specific strategies for reducing the risk of heart disease and cancer vary depending on a number of factors, including whether or not an individual has a family history of risk for heart disease or a specific type of cancer. There is general agreement, however, that increasing physical activity and avoiding weight gain are general protective strategies for increasing the odds of good health and reducing the risk for cancer (Wei, Wolin, & Colditz, 2010) as well as other chronic diseases. Not surprisingly, fitness at mid-life is associated with a reduced likelihood of developing non-fatal chronic conditions of the heart, kidneys, lungs, and brain (Rantanen, 2013).

Mid-life Health and Well-being

Good health behaviours prior to and during the mid-life years can protect adults against aging processes and disease risk. Being alert to stress exposure and wear and tear on one's body and mind prior to middle age can also be protective.

Maintaining health Traditional health and medicine focuses on the presence of disease and death to the exclusion of health and well-being. The life course health approach (see Chapter 11) is a new, alternative framework for thinking about health and well-being in middle adulthood (Ben-Shlomo & Kuh, 2002). This framework encourages the type of thinking that recognizes mid-life health as a product not only of all the experiences and exposures of mid-life but of all the decades prior to mid-life.

The life course health approach focuses on maintaining health and preventing disease. Health care professionals working from this perspective may be concerned

(Lajous et al., 2013). Coping strategies used in middle adulthood can also be protective or can increase risk in middle adulthood. Use of reappraisal—recognizing and reducing a negative thought about self—is associated with greater health; suppression—holding back negative feelings about self—is associated with increased risk for cardiovascular disease (Appleton, Loucks, Buka, &

Kubzansky, 2014). These findings suggest that it's never too late to shape the trajectories of heart health in a positive direction. However, it is important to be mindful of the fact that opportunities for positive change are not equally distributed; disempowered Canadians will struggle the most in order to change or remove themselves from unhealthy circumstances (Adelson, 2005).

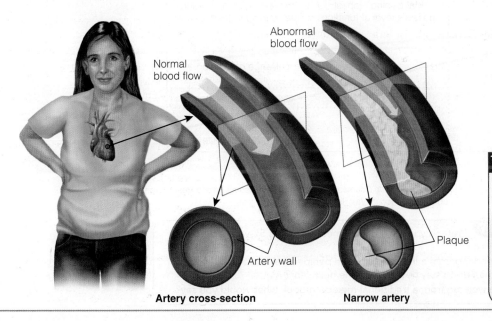

Normal blood flow

Abnormal blood flow

Plaque

Artery wall

Artery cross-section

Narrow artery

> **Think Critically** For an ad campaign designed to increase awareness of risks for heart disease, create two fictional people who portray opposite characters: name and describe the first, "High Risk _____," and the second, "Low Risk _____." Be certain to include all details that distinguish a person who is at high risk for heart disease from one who is at low risk.

with helping their middle-aged patients optimize and maintain **functional capacity**. Functional capacity is an individual's ability to take care of him- or herself. Some specific measures of functional capacity include lung capacity, muscular strength, and cardiovascular output. Functional capacity naturally increases in childhood and peaks in early adulthood. Depending on how well an individual has maintained his or her functional capacity, inevitably, functional capacity will begin to decline (**Figure 13.13**). The rate of decline is largely determined by factors related to adult lifestyle—such as alcohol consumption, smoking, and levels of physical activity and diet.

> **functional capacity** The physiological systems of the body that maintain health and life: digestive system, endocrine system, immune system, lymphatic system, muscular system, nervous system, reproductive system, respiratory system, skeletal system, and urinary system.

Stress Making changes to maintain or improve health is particularly important in mid-life to reduce insults to functional capacity. One specific change mid-life adults can make to reserve functional capacity is to reduce the stress in their lives. Stress increases in adulthood and peaks in mid-life (**Figure 13.14**).

Stress can be a hidden source of risk. It's important to note that high levels of stress do not necessarily mean that a mid-life adult is unhappy. In fact, over 80 percent of adults who feel stressed in their everyday lives are satisfied or even very satisfied with their lives (Statistics Canada, 2001). Moreover, recognizing the burden of stress in mid-life may tell only a partial story of the toll that stress can take on mid-life health. A great deal of research suggests that it is cumulative stress across the lifespan that has the most significant impact on a body's ability to maintain health and well-being.

At all stages of the lifespan, the body's **stress response** protects individuals from the harmful effects of stress. However, the stress response can get overburdened and may even eventually shut down when it is overactivated or activated for inordinately long

> **stress response** A change in the physiological functioning of the body's systems when it perceives an external threat or attack.

Maintaining functional capacity through mid-life • Figure 13.13

With a life course health perspective, individuals are encouraged to maintain and support the health that they have rather than focus on reducing risks for disease. This approach to healthy aging takes the long view and emphasizes how health strategies early in the life course affect mid-life health and how mid-life health affects trajectories of health throughout later adulthood.

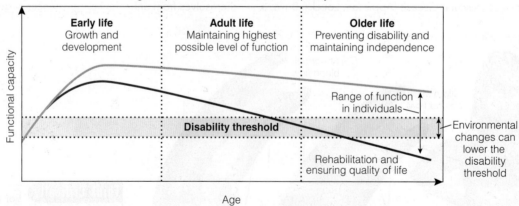

A life course perspective for maintenance of the highest possible level of functional capacity

Reproduced, with permission of the publisher, from *A Life Course Approach to Health*, Geneva, World Health Organization, 2000 (p. 7, http://www.who.int/ageing/publications/lifecourse/alc_lifecourse_training_en.pdf).

Think Critically Pretend you are a doctor meeting with a 55-year-old man for his annual physical.
1. If you are working from a life course health perspective, what would you suggest this man do to stay healthy over the next year?
2. If you were working from a traditional medical model, what would you say?

Stress across the lifespan • Figure 13.14

Middle-aged adults are the most stressed. Over 30 percent of middle-aged adults report feeling that most days are quite or extremely stressful.

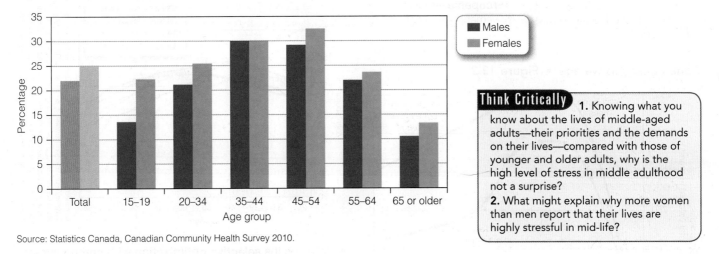

Source: Statistics Canada, Canadian Community Health Survey 2010.

Think Critically 1. Knowing what you know about the lives of middle-aged adults—their priorities and the demands on their lives—compared with those of younger and older adults, why is the high level of stress in middle adulthood not a surprise?
2. What might explain why more women than men report that their lives are highly stressful in mid-life?

periods of time. When activated for an extended period of time, physical wear and tear due to stress exposure takes its toll on the brain and the body. **Allostatic load** is a measure of cumulative stress or physiologic wear and tear on the body over the lifespan. High allostatic load accelerates disease processes and hastens the onset of health problems, whereas low allostatic load across the lifespan is protective of health and well-being in mid-life. Focusing on allostatic load, rather than specific stressors present in mid-life, may help us better respond to the health problems and medical needs of middle-aged adults.

allostatic load
The physiologic wear and tear on the body that is the result of repeated and long-term exposure to stress, the consequence of which is an acceleration of disease processes and health problems.

CONCEPT CHECK

1. **What** health issue has emerged as a global health problem over the past decade?

2. **How** does the reproductive life cycle come to an end for women and men?

3. **How** do the leading causes of death change from young to middle adulthood?

4. **How** does stress contribute to allostatic load by mid-life?

✓ THE PLANNER

Summary

1 Physical Development 422

- **Life expectancy** in North America has pushed up into the 80s, so we consider middle age to be the early to mid-40s through to the mid-60s. During middle age, physical changes occur in all of the body's systems. Physiological decline occurs during this period, including a loss in brain volume and function. People who lose more brain volume show declines in **executive functioning**. However, **neurogenesis** allows the brain to adapt in response to some injuries in mid-life.

- The skeletal and muscular systems also undergo a number of alterations. **Bone resorption** has plateaued by mid-life when bones become less dense, as shown in the figure. Both men and women tend to lose height and gain weight. A number of factors contribute to **sarcopenia**—muscle loss and related reduced muscle movement—in middle adulthood.

Bone density as we age • Figure 13.2

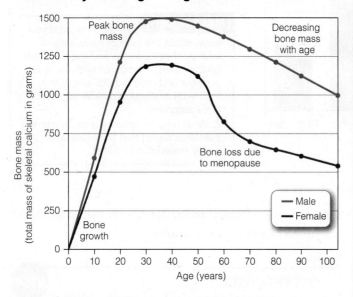

- As we get older, we may lose **concentric muscle** strength, making it more difficult for us to lift objects, but we maintain or increase our **eccentric muscle movement**, or flexibility of muscles to lengthen.

- Skin and hair show changes during mid-life, such as age spots, moles, cracks, and wrinkles. In some people hair loss outpaces hair gain, and, for many, melanin decreases and hair turns grey.

- All of the senses change during this period of life. Vision issues such as **presbyopia** and **myopia** often result in the need for glasses, and visual acuity declines steadily, adversely affecting adults' ability to discern details. **Conductive** and **sensorineural hearing loss** are common, though slow, and hearing aid technology can frequently help with the problem. Finally, both the sense of smell and taste diminish.

2 Cognitive Development 428

- As people age, cognitive ability changes. **Fluid intelligence** decreases with age, whereas **crystallized intelligence** increases. The Seattle Longitudinal Study of Adult Intelligence focused on how mental abilities are affected by age and demonstrated that there is a general decrease in mental acuity with the passing of years, as shown in the figure.

Changes in intelligence with age • Figure 13.6

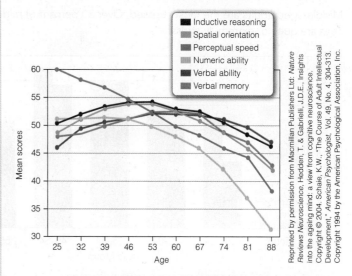

- Based on the **selective optimization with compensation (SOC)** theory, middle-aged adults can use three processes to maximize gains and minimize losses associated with aging. **Selection** is the process people use to set achievable goals, **optimization** is the process they use to allocate resources useful for achieving goals, and **compensation** is the process they use to edit goals in a way that helps them achieve or move on to new goals. Different strategies are used at different ages to increase the likelihood of successful aging.

- Expertise appears to be a combination of experience, competence, confidence, and the ability to recognize relevant and irrelevant actions. According to Peter Fadde, the distinguishing feature of an expert is **recognition-primed decision-making**, the ability to recognize the most relevant features of a situation in order to make decisions quickly.

3 All the Systems Working Together 434

- Although certain physiological changes are inevitable as people age, there are ways to lessen their severity. Obesity can be addressed, for example, through a combination of diet and exercise. Multiple health organizations strongly recommend that all ages include physical exercise in their daily routines in order to lower obesity risk, improve cognitive and cardiovascular functioning, and possibly even increase life expectancy. Nutrition also plays an essential role in weight control and mid-life health. An **obesogenic environment** is not conducive to healthy living.

- Middle age brings reproductive changes, thanks to changes in hormone levels. In women between their late 40s and late 50s, these changes result in **menopause**, preceded by a period known as perimenopause, which can be accompanied by symptoms such as weight gain, fluid retention, mood changes, and hot flashes. The male version of this condition is **andropause**, and it may result in feelings such as depression and anxiety, as well as erectile problems, lowered sexual desire, and other issues.

- Sexual activity decreases from young adulthood across middle adulthood, although the majority of middle-aged adults remain sexually active. Maintaining physical health is key to a longer **sexually active life expectancy**, as is having a partner. It is rare for sexual identity to shift in middle adulthood.

- Mortality is inevitable, of course, and the two leading causes of death during middle adulthood are cancer and heart disease, as shown in the figure.

Causes of Canadian adult deaths, 2011 • Figure 13.12

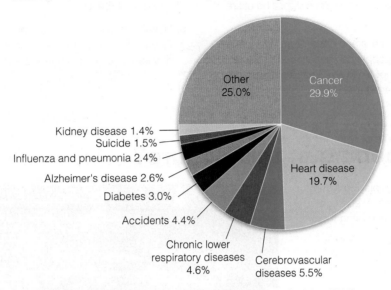

- Other 25.0%
- Cancer 29.9%
- Kidney disease 1.4%
- Suicide 1.5%
- Influenza and pneumonia 2.4%
- Alzheimer's disease 2.6%
- Diabetes 3.0%
- Accidents 4.4%
- Chronic lower respiratory diseases 4.6%
- Cerebrovascular diseases 5.5%
- Heart disease 19.7%

Source: Canadian Cancer Society's Advisory Committee on Cancer Statistics. (2015). Canadian cancer statistics 2015. Retrieved from www.cancer.ca/~/media/cancer.ca/CW/cancer%20information/cancer%20101/Canadian%20cancer%20statistics/Canadian-Cancer-Statistics-2015-EN.pdf.

- The life course health approach looks at mid-life health as a consequence of the experiences and exposures that take place in all the stages preceding mid-life. This model seeks to understand the trajectory of a person's health from birth onward.

- Maintaining **functional capacity** at mid-life is key to good health in middle adulthood and is protective against aging and disease processes across adulthood.

- The body's **stress response**, which protects individuals from the harmful effects of stress by changing the physiological functioning of the body, can shut down if it is activated for too long. Stress is associated with **allostatic load**—pressure on the body's functional systems. High allostatic load increases risk for poor health and accelerated aging; low stress is a protective factor against poor health and accelerated aging.

Key Terms

Critical and Creative Thinking Questions

1. Engaging in regular physical exercise is an important health measure at this time of life. Before engaging in an exercise program, however, what, if any, precautions should be taken, based on what you have learned about skeletal and muscular changes in mid-life?

2. How can cosmetic techniques help a person cope with the typical skin and hair changes of aging? Should they be utilized? Why or why not?

3. The National Institute of Deafness and Other Communication Disorders states that many people can benefit from the use of hearing aids but choose not to do so. What reasons might people have for avoiding hearing aids?

4. How would a decrease in fluid intelligence and increase in crystallized intelligence affect an adult in daily life? What actions and behaviours would be most affected?

5. More North Americans engage in recreational grazing rather than sitting down at a table to eat three meals a day. How does culture support this lifestyle? How might grazing affect the problem of obesity?

6. How could you design a social media campaign—think Facebook and Twitter—to encourage stress reduction and maintenance of functional capacity in middle adulthood?

What is happening in this picture?

These men are concentrating on playing a game of chess. They focus on each move, strategizing which one would be the wisest and bring them closer to victory.

Sonda Dawes/The Image Work

Think Critically

1. What type of intelligence (fluid or crystallized) are they using?
2. How is executive functioning playing a part in this situation?
3. If these men have been playing chess for the last 20 years, how might their play have changed over those decades?
4. How might their skills change in the next 20 years?

REAL 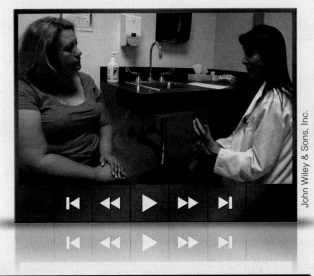 Development

Physical and Cognitive Development in Middle Adulthood

In this video activity, you are interested in looking at physical and cognitive development in middle adulthood. Lyne Borelli has come to the Counselling and Wellness Centre to meet with a physician for an annual checkup. Acting as the physician's assistant, you will help the doctor answer Lyne's questions about development during the middle years. Use your knowledge of physical development during middle adulthood to help answer her questions about menopause, breast cancer, and osteoporosis. You assess the procedures, screenings, tests, and vaccines that the physician is discussing.

WileyPLUS Go to WileyPLUS to complete the REAL Development activity.

John Wiley & Sons, Inc.

03.01

Self-Test

(Check your answers in Appendix A.)

1. Typical brain changes associated with mid-life are accelerated by all of the following *except* _____.
   a. high levels of stress
   b. increased forgetfulness
   c. increased obesity
   d. high cholesterol

2. With respect to neurogenesis, the adult brain _____.
   a. can overcome any trauma
   b. can repair itself only in terms of physical functioning
   c. has some capacity to overcome trauma
   d. can only repair itself in mid-life

3. What process does weight-lifting help to slow down?
   a. sarcopenia
   b. presbyopia
   c. metastasis
   d. perimenopause

4. What causes sensorineural hearing loss?
   a. impaired conduction in the middle ear
   b. chronic exposure to high-intensity volume
   c. loss of hair cells along the basilar membrane
   d. a lack of adequate aural health care in early adulthood

5. According to this chart from the Seattle Longitudinal Study, which age period typically demonstrates the largest decline in mental abilities?

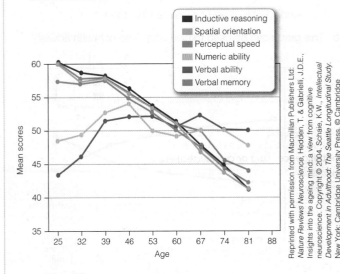

Reprinted with permission from Macmillan Publishers Ltd: *Nature Reviews Neuroscience*, Hedden, T. & Gabrielli, J.D.E., Insights into the ageing mind: a view from cognitive neuroscience. Copyright © 2004. Schaie, K.W., *Intellectual Development in Adulthood: The Seattle Longitudinal Study*. New York: Cambridge University Press. © Cambridge University Press 1996. Reprinted with permission.

   a. 25 to 39
   b. 39 to 53
   c. 53 to 67
   d. 67 to 88

6. With respect to selection, optimization, and compensation, _____.
   a. selection is used predominately in mid-life
   b. optimization and compensation have not yet developed for use in mid-life

c. optimization and compensation are commonly used in mid-life

d. selection and optimization are the only strategies that work in mid-life

7. How do important life domains change in mid-life? Fill in the rankings for ages 55 to 69.

	25 to 34	35 to 54	55 to 65	70 to 84	85 to 105
1	Work	Family	_____	Family	Health
2	Friends	Work	_____	Health	Family
3	Family	Friends	_____	Cognitive fitness	Thinking about life
4	Independence	Cognitive fitness	_____	Friends	Cognitive fitness

8. Expertise is defined by all of the following *except* _____.

a. experience

b. competence

c. confidence

d. deference

9. What is recognition-primed decision-making?

a. spatial orientation, inductive reasoning, and word fluency

b. the ability to quickly know what to do based on relevance

c. a combination of verbal meaning and number skills

d. a blending of fluid and crystallized intelligence

10. This graph can be used to give what type of health advice?

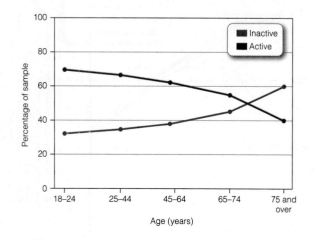

a. Middle-aged adults should prevent a decrease in physical activity.

b. Middle-aged adults should prevent an increase in smoking.

c. Middle-aged adults should prevent an increase in calorie intake.

d. Middle-aged adults should prevent a decrease in muscle strength.

11. All of the following are true about menopause *except* that it _____.

a. can cause psychological symptoms in some women

b. is defined as three months without a menstrual period

c. involves a decrease in production of progesterone

d. causes significant changes to a woman's reproductive capabilities

12. All of the following are true about andropause *except* that it _____.

a. describes the process of losing testosterone

b. often results in lowered sexual desire and depression

c. is the male version of menopause

d. results in the inability to reproduce

13. In the table below, the label for sex has been removed from the legend. For each age group, identify who is most stressed—males or females.

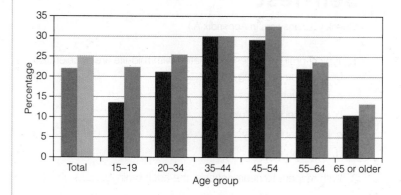

14. Which of the following is *true* about mid-life sexual identity?

a. It is very common to come out as gay at mid-life.

b. It is very uncommon to come out as gay at mid-life.

c. Sexual identity peaks after mid-life.

d. Sexual identity peaks in mid-life.

15. More functional capacity accumulated prior to adulthood predicts that an individual will follow a pathway of _____.

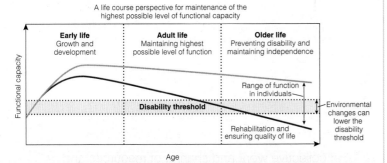

A life course perspective for maintenance of the highest possible level of functional capacity

Reproduced, with permission of the publisher, from *A Life Course Approach to Health*, Geneva, World Health Organization, 2000 (p. 7, http://www.who.int/ageing/publications/lifecourse/alc_lifecourse_training_en.pdf).

a. good health through middle adulthood and late adulthood

b. very poor to very good health

c. very good health that does not decline

d. moderate health that increases through middle adulthood

THE PLANNER ✓

Review your Chapter Planner in the chapter opener and check off your completed work.

Socio-emotional Development in Adulthood

14

Lorraine called the meeting to order and thought with pride how much their social justice group had accomplished in their city and province. Together, they'd organized to lead a project on poverty and poor housing, and now they were organizing for better eye and dental care for people with low income. It had taken a lot of collective work and sharing of resources and skills but together they were making a difference in their community.

In this chapter, we will see how middle adulthood—as Lorraine is experiencing—involves opportunities for growth and adaptation on many

Christopher Futcher/iStockphoto

levels. We will think about how juggling demands of adult children growing up and aging parents needing more help impact the lives of middle-aged adults. Despite these stresses, the middle adult years are often the happiest because they are a time to reflect on all that one has achieved.

CHAPTER PLANNER ✓

❑ Study the picture and read the opening story.

❑ Scan the Learning Objectives in each section:
   p. 452 ❑   p. 456 ❑   p. 468 ❑

❑ Read the text and study all visuals. Answer any questions.

Analyze key features

❑ Development InSight, p. 454

❑ Process Diagram, p. 455

❑ What a Developmentalist Sees, p. 459

❑ Challenges in Development, p. 461

❑ Stop: Answer the Concept Checks before you go on:
   p. 456 ❑   p. 467 ❑   p. 474 ❑

End of chapter

❑ Review the Summary and Key Terms.

❑ Answer the Critical and Creative Thinking Questions.

❑ Answer *What is happening in this picture?*

❑ Complete the Self-Test and check your answers.

Personality Development

LEARNING OBJECTIVES

1. **Discuss** the relationship between personality change, personal development, and well-being in mid-life.

2. **Explain** the crisis of generativity vs. stagnation.

S ince Freud's time, a number of psychologists have come to challenge Freud's belief that development ends after adolescence. Now we know that adults continue to develop well past adolescence. Mid-life is no exception. The change we see in middle adulthood is often in response to significant life events such as divorce and career transitions, whereas change in earlier decades is often in response to physical growth and maturation.

Personality in Mid-life

Until recently, researchers believed that personality traits were fixed by age 30 (Costa & McCrae, 1994). Costa and McCrae (1994) tracked changes in the Big Five personality traits (remembered as OCEAN: openness to experience, conscientiousness, extraversion, agreeableness, and neuroticism) in adults ages 19 to 80 in the Baltimore Study of Aging. They found that among adults followed for more than a decade, the most dramatic changes in personality traits took place in adolescence and early adulthood, followed by less change in the 30s, and then stability from middle through late adulthood (Roberts, Walton, & Viechtbauer, 2006; Specht, Egloff, & Schmukle, 2011).

Although for many years adult personality stability was largely accepted as fact, some researchers were skeptical. They wondered: given all the twists, turns, and transitions that occur in adulthood, could it really be the case that personality doesn't change after age 30? A new set of investigators took a different approach to studying personality trait change in adulthood, and when they did, these different methods confirmed high personality stability between the 40s and 50s. Middle-aged adults tend to stay the same relative to one another, but as a group they continue to become more easy-going—agreeableness and conscientiousness continue to increase (Donnellan & Lucas, 2008; Roberts et al., 2006; Srivastava, John, Gosling, & Potter, 2003).

Different life stages influence personality development in different ways. When you think about how adults change as they take on roles and responsibilities, you might predict that becoming adult encourages people to become more goal-directed, prosocial, and emotionally stable. Indeed, when you tease apart change in the specific traits, researchers find support for this so-called *maturity principle*. In adulthood, conscientiousness and agreeableness increase and neuroticism decreases (Donnellan & Lucas, 2008; Roberts et al., 2006; Srivastava et al., 2003).

Finding that, on average, personality traits increase or decrease through the 30s still doesn't account for a lack of personality change in middle adulthood. We can reasonably argue that there is significant change in the lives of middle-aged adults, so why shouldn't there be change in personality? Another set of researchers hypothesized that we don't see change in personality in mid-life because middle-aged people don't change in the same ways as younger adults. Personality change happens when middle-aged adults **accommodate**—or change their schemas—in response to major life events, such as major illnesses, change in marital status, and major career transitions (Lilgendahl, Helson, & John, 2013). Support for this hypothesis is found when individuals rather than groups are studied (Roberts & Mroczek, 2008; Roberts & Wood, 2006). Studies that estimate intraindividual change, or change within an individual, consistently reveal that some people change a great deal in mid-life, others change less, and some not at all. Why? The Berkeley Longitudinal Study—actually three studies of development following three different groups from preadolescence to mid-life (Eichorn, 1973)—was instrumental in identifying factors that accounted for differences in the way individuals changed through mid-life. These studies asked, what makes middle-aged adults different from one another, and do these differences account for differences in the ways their personalities change through mid-life? They found a number of factors that distinguish those who change a great deal from those who don't, including differences in verbal ability, gender differences, and the timing of life events (for example, completion of education or marriage).

> **accommodate**
> The adjustment of schemas in response to new experiences.

Social context of mid-life personality change • Figure 14.1

The Mills Longitudinal Study found that women's personalities changed significantly during adulthood. Some changes are related to stages of life and individual experiences, but broader social changes also provide an important context for personality change.

a. Personality change

The study showed that between the ages of 21 and 52, women displayed less femininity (interest in and capacity for patience and personal and interpersonal sensitivity) and more dominance (leadership ability, persistence, and social initiative).

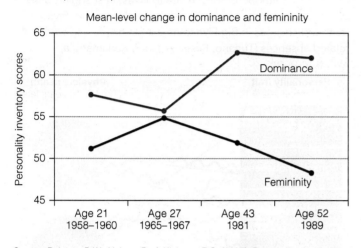

Mean-level change in dominance and femininity

Source: Roberts, B.W., Helson, R., & Klohnen, E.C. (2002). Personality development and growth in women across 30 years: Three perspectives. *Journal of Personality*, 70, 79–102.

b. Societal change

During the period when the study was taking place, the role of women in society was also undergoing a dramatic change, with many more women pursuing post-secondary education.

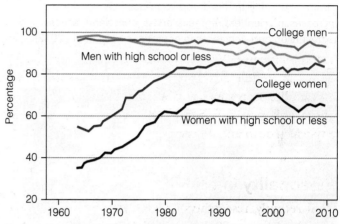

Participation rate in the labour force

Source: Dionissi Aliprantis, Timothy Dunne, and Kyle Fee, The Growing Difference in College Attainment between Women and Men, *Economic Commentary* No. 2011-21 October 18, 2011, http://www.clevelandfed.org/research/Commentary/2011/2011-21.pdf.

Think Critically How might personality change for women in mid-life be different today given that, since the mid-1990s, more women than men earn degrees?

Not surprisingly, the roles that people adopt in adulthood and the historical context in which these roles are adopted also shape adults' lives.

Psychologist Ravenna Helson headed the Mills Longitudinal Study, which followed graduates of an all-women's college in Oakland, California, in order to study changes in women's personalities from the 1960s through the 1990s (Helson, 1999, 2008; Helson & Kwan, 2000). Beginning in 1957, 100 female seniors from Mills College's graduating classes of 1958 and 1960 were interviewed about aspects of their lives, such as creativity, life satisfaction, career development, and family. Over the course of the study, at multiple assessments, the same women completed personality tests and questionnaires (Helson & Cate, 2006). As anticipated, women's personalities changed through their 20s and became more stable in their 30s (Helson, 1993). Changes in personality, however, were not the same across all women. Working in the paid labour force and marital issues (such as marital tension and divorce) predicted differences in personality changes (Roberts, Helson, & Klohnen, 2002). Such changes took place during a historical period when women were making significant gains in accessing higher education and forging new pathways in the work world (**Figure 14.1**).

Mid-life personality traits tell us something about other aspects of an adult's life. Higher levels of extraversion, agreeableness, conscientiousness, emotional stability, and openness are associated with greater self-reported social well-being, or the sense that one has social value (Hill, Turiano, Mroczek, & Roberts, 2012). Very similar relationships are found between life satisfaction and Big Five personality change. Greater life satisfaction is associated with higher levels of traits, as one would predict. In turn, higher levels of these traits—indicators of personality maturity—are associated with greater increases in life satisfaction in adulthood (Specht, Egloff, & Schmukle, 2013). Personality in mid-life is also related to physical health (**Figure 14.2**).

Personality traits influence the way middle-aged men and women experience their lives. Openness to new experiences and extraversion as well as a lack of neuroticism are associated with engagement with work despite approaching retirement age. Personality change during middle adulthood is also associated with life experiences. For example, people who become more conscientious, extraverted, and agreeable report better health.

a. Spending time connecting with others or oneself, as these people are doing in this group yoga class, can facilitate increases in openness, agreeableness, conscientiousness, and Extraversion and decreases in neuroticism (Hill et al., 2012).

b. Middle adulthood is not too late to invest in changing one's personality in positive ways. By varying pathways, Big Five traits and changes in Big Five traits predict health and work-related absences (Turiano, Pitzer, Armour, Karlamangla, Ryff, & Mroczek, 2011).

The Star-Ledger/Aristide Economopoulos/ The Image Works

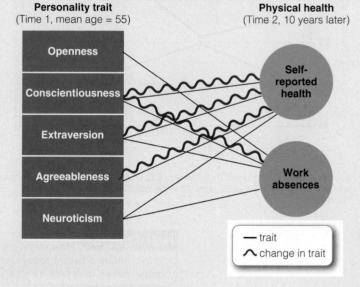

Ask Yourself

1. Which personality traits, with respect to the level of the trait, are associated with work absences?
2. Which personality traits, with respect to change in level, are associated with self-reported health?

Psychosocial Development: Generativity vs. Stagnation

It was Freud's student, Erik Erikson, who first challenged Freud's contention that personality development was fixed at the end of adolescence. Erikson argued that there is indeed opportunity for personal growth at mid-life and that such change depends on how well an individual is able to resolve the seventh of Erikson's eight stages of psychosocial development: generativity vs. stagnation (Erikson, 1963).

Middle-aged adults may experience this psycho-social crisis as an urgency to find something meaning-ful to do with one's talents, abilities, and resources. When people set and strive to meet personal goals that benefit others, society, and future generations, they are demonstrating **generativity**. This is often achieved through investment of self in parenting, careers, or volunteer work, as well as other behaviours, such as donating money.

Stagnation, on the other hand, is characterized by little to no growth, or decline of investment in anything beyond one's own, immediate interests. After having made commitments to career and marriage or other adult roles, the individual who remains focused on self and fulfillment of imme-diate concerns is demonstrating

generativity
The dedication and investment of self and personal resources in the promotion of the health of society and future generations.

stagnation
Remaining focused on day-to-day self-centred activities and interests; a failure to shift one's focus and investment to future- and other-oriented goals.

stagnation. Persons who stagnate are focused on meeting their own needs first and on what they can get from rather than what they can give to others and to the social world.

Summarizing findings from many studies, broadly speaking, we find that generativity increases from the 20s through the 50s, with some evidence suggesting that generativity then decreases in the 60s and 70s. However, there are significant differences in generativity at any age—some people are more generative than others. Within the same person, generativity may be more observable in some areas of life more in others; for example, at home or at work. Life experiences also shape generativity, resulting in differences between people (McAdams, 2006a).

Psychologist Dan McAdams has studied generativity across the lifespan and specifically in mid-life for over two decades. After years of studying generativity, McAdams wanted to know: what pathways lead to generativity at mid-life? To find out, he asked people to tell him the stories of their lives. The developmental stories people told provided him with insight into the characteristics of generative people's lives. One particular pathway is associated with mid-life generativity—the story of what McAdams called the *redemptive self.* Redemption is "the deliverance from suffering to an enhanced sense or state" (McAdams, 2006b, p. 88; **Figure 14.3**).

Empirical studies reveal the important role generativity plays from a lifespan perspective. As Erikson's framework predicts, generativity is associated with general psychosocial maturity and general well-being at mid-life (Dunkel, 2013).

The redemptive self: Pathways to generativity • Figure 14.3   ✓ THE PLANNER

Dan McAdams noted that middle-aged adults who rated higher on generativity, measured on items such as those included here, were significantly different from middle-aged adults who scored lower on generativity on a variety of characteristics related to their relationships and adjustment. Stories of the redemptive self share six specific elements of stories of generative people.

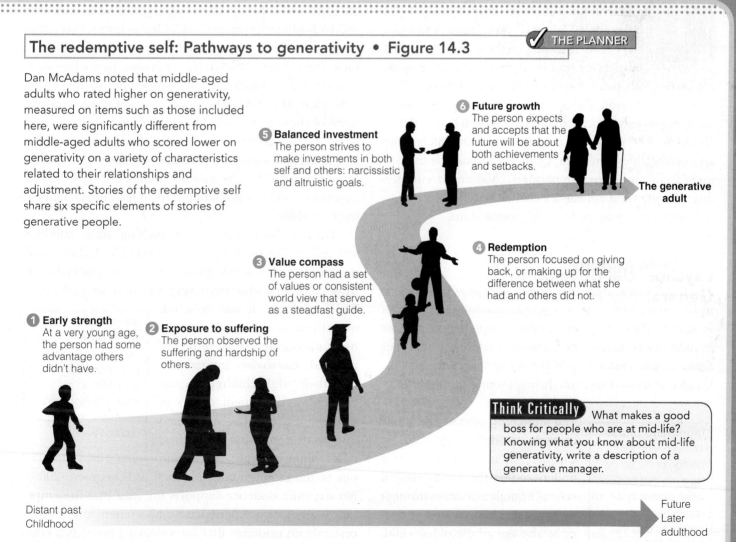

6 Future growth The person expects and accepts that the future will be about both achievements and setbacks.

5 Balanced investment The person strives to make investments in both self and others: narcissistic and altruistic goals.

The generative adult

3 Value compass The person had a set of values or consistent world view that served as a steadfast guide.

4 Redemption The person focused on giving back, or making up for the difference between what she had and others did not.

1 Early strength At a very young age, the person had some advantage others didn't have.

2 Exposure to suffering The person observed the suffering and hardship of others.

Think Critically What makes a good boss for people who are at mid-life? Knowing what you know about mid-life generativity, write a description of a generative manager.

Distant past Childhood

Future Later adulthood

1. **What** mid-life personality changes can be explained by the maturity principle?

2. **How** might generativity appear at home or at work?

Social Influences

LEARNING OBJECTIVES

1. **Characterize** the launching phase of family life, along with the challenges and benefits it brings.

2. **Describe** marital transitions in mid-life, including conflict, divorce, and remarriage.

3. **Describe** the changes that take place in relationships with parents at mid-life.

4. **Outline** the role of adult sibling relationships and friendships at mid-life.

The social lives of middle-aged adults are significantly different from those of younger and older adults. Adults construct most of their social networks during their 20s and 30s, so that by middle age these networks are more stable compared with prior stages of life. In contrast to other stages of adulthood, relationships with family and friends are most strongly associated with mid-life well-being (Ryff & Heidrich, 1997). But this does not mean that all is quiet and predictable in mid-life. Quite the opposite is true. In mid-life, relationships with partners, children, parents, siblings, friends, and colleagues change significantly due to development, aging, and mid-life course shifts.

Family in Mid-life

The families of mid-life men and women show great diversity due to the variety of ways people establish their families in emerging and young adulthood. Young people partner at different ages, have first and last children at different ages, and often make transitions in and out of partnerships, legally recognized and not, through young adulthood.

launching phase
This is a term for a portion of the family life cycle that begins when the first child leaves home and continues until the last child leaves.

The launching phase The family life-cycle model, introduced in Chapter 12, is a useful tool for understanding the developmental tasks of a family as it moves through various stages, determined primarily by the age of the oldest child. For the majority of families, middle adulthood intersects with the **launching phase** of the family life cycle, which begins when the oldest child leaves home and ends when the youngest child leaves home. Given that the age of a first birth in Canada is approximately 28 years for women (Milan, 2013a), half of middle-aged adults have experienced a significant family milestone by their mid-40s—their first child reaching the age of independence, many of them graduating high school, and moving out to begin their adult lives. Also, because the mid-40s mark the end of the transition into parenthood—the majority of all births take place by the mid-40s (Milan, 2013a)—the vast majority of middle-aged adults have at least begun launching by mid-life.

Only a short time ago, launching adult children was believed to be the gateway to mid-life darkness and depression, particularly for mothers and especially for those mothers who were very invested in parenting. These mothers, it was believed, were likely to suffer from **empty nest syndrome** as a result of reduced day-to-day interactions with their adult children. Across cultures, a very small group of women experience emotional distress or depression when their adult children have all moved out of the family home (Mitchell & Lovegreen, 2009). No scientific evidence supports the idea that the empty nest is a negative experience for all women, and there is certainly no evidence that home-leaving predicts a crisis (Mitchell & Lovegreen, 2009). In fact, after children left

empty nest syndrome
Feelings of distress and depression in mid-life as a result of losing the parental role as adult children become independent.

the home, those women who were not worried about children leaving home experienced an increase in positive mood and a reduction in the number of daily hassles (Dennerstein, Dudley, & Guthrie, 2002). This finding may indicate that in some cases the loss of the child from the house is balanced by gains in personal pursuits. For women who are married, the empty nest is associated with increased marital satisfaction due to more time spent with their spouses (Gorchoff, John, & Helson, 2008).

There are a number of additional reasons why the empty nest syndrome is more popular myth than universal truth. Typically, the quality of parent–child relationships improves as children transition into adulthood (Whiteman, McHale, & Crouter, 2010). Most parents continue to be happily invested in their parental roles (Mitchell, 2010). Even when nests are empty, communication is frequent and parents still provide a great deal of support to their adult children (Fingerman, Cheng, Tighe, Birditt, & Zarit, 2012).

Yet another reason the empty nest syndrome is not as prevalent as was once believed may be that fewer nests are empty today than in the past. From 2000 to 2010, the proportion of adult children living with mid-life parents increased by 50 percent percent due to the increasingly common financial dependency of adult children on their parents (Kahn, Goldscheider, & García-Manglano, 2013). The media is full of news stories about these so-called *boomerang kids*, although the phenomenon is not as unprecedented as these stories suggest (**Figure 14.4**). Although the recent rise in adult children living at home happens to correlate with a recession, recessions are not necessarily predictive of young people staying in or returning to the parental home (Payne, 2011). What matters is the economic power of young adults. Unemployment and rates of non-marriage have been associated with adult children remaining at home since the 1940s.

What effect does children's longer co-residence have on parents? Some studies indicate an association between adult children co-residing with their parents and parents reporting lower levels of happiness and self-esteem in mid-life (Nomaguchi, 2011; Pudrovska, 2009). However, what we don't know is whether less happy parents are more likely to have adult children who return home. Future studies will provide us with a better understanding of who returns home and why.

For mid-life parents, the quality of relationships with adult children matters (Koropeckyj-Cox, 2002; Milkie, Bierman, & Schieman, 2008). Positive relationships with adult children at mid-life predicts health and well-being for both mothers and fathers (Bell & Bell, 2012). In mid-life, reciprocity is the rule: adult children's well-being is associated with mid-life parents' well-being, and mid-life parents' well-being is associated with the well-being of their adult children (Knoester, 2003). When adult children are successful in their relationships and their careers, they maintain better relationships with their parents and give them more support as they age (Buhl, 2009; Fingerman, Miller, Birditt, & Zarit, 2009). But when adult children have problems (for example, legal issues or illness) and are less successful at supporting themselves, mid-life parents experience more distress and receive less support (Pillemer & Suitor, 2002).

Adult children's successes and failures impact mid-life parents' well-being cumulatively when parents have more than one child. This supports the adage, "You're only as happy as your least happy child." When mid-life parents have more than one adult child, one successful child does not predict well-being, but the cumulative effects of success

Adult children living at home • Figure 14.4

An increasing number of emerging- and young-adult children are living at home with their parents, but is this new? As you can see from the graph, early ages of home-leaving and a high likelihood of moving out of the parental home in emerging adulthood make the 1960s a unique rather than normal historical period.

Think Critically What social factors and differences in gender roles through different historical periods would account for the greater number of adult men living at home than adult women?

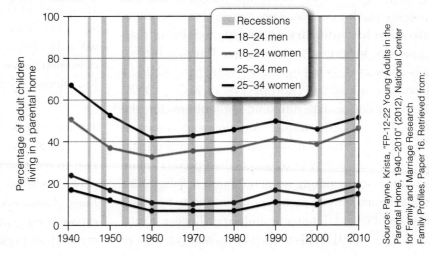

Source: Payne, Krista, "FP-12-22 Young Adults in the Parental Home, 1940–2010" (2012). National Center for Family and Marriage Research Family Profiles. Paper 16. Retrieved from: http://scholarworks.bgsu.edu/cgi/viewcontent.cgi?article=1015&context=ncfmr_family_profiles.

increase parent well-being. In contrast, having one child with problems is associated with lower well-being, and the more adult children who have problems, the lower mid-life parents' well-being (Fingerman et al., 2012).

| relational ambivalence Simultaneous positive and negative feelings about a relationship. |

Approximately half of mid-life parents are extremely happy with being parents. The other half feel relational ambivalence (mixed emotions) (Bengtson, Giarrusso, Mabry, & Silverstein, 2002) toward their adult children (Fingerman, Hay, & Birditt, 2004; Mitchell, 2010). Parents feel more ambivalence about less successful adult children. According to parents, about 20 percent report that at least one of their adult children had a physical or emotional problem (e.g., a serious physical disability or injury or a serious emotional or psychological problem) and approximately 35 percent had one or more lifestyle-behavioural problems (e.g., a drinking or drug problem, financial problems, problems with the police, or divorce or other serious relationship issues) (Birditt, Fingerman, & Zarit, 2010). Parents' ambivalence was elevated when they had higher levels of neuroticism or education, and when they provided more financial support to adult children. Mothers reported greater ambivalence with lifestyle and behavioural problems, whereas fathers reported greater ambivalence related to adult children's physical and emotional problems (Birditt et al., 2010).

Being and remaining childfree in mid-life We have just seen how relationships with adult children affect well-being in many complex ways. Now we examine how being childfree correlates with well-being at mid-life. In general, the well-being of women is similar for those who become mothers and for those who do not. This may be because being childfree has less influence on mid-life well-being than other factors, including possessing good health, feeling socially connected, being financially stable, and having a good partner or husband (Koropeckyj-Cox & Call, 2007).

| childfree Never having birthed or parented a child. |

Being childfree has different implications for the man's well-being. Educational and financial resources don't play a role in predicting why men voluntarily remain childfree, but low access to resources does predict voluntary childfree status among women (Waren & Pals, 2013). Whereas the majority of men report wanting to be a parent, by age 45, 1 in 7 remains childfree (Kessler, Craig, Saigal, & Quinn, 2013). Men's well-being is affected more by partnership than by parenthood status. Being single at mid-life is associated with low well-being above and beyond the influence of childfree status (Dykstra & Keizer, 2009).

When researchers looked more closely at mid-life childfree status, they found that the association was complex. For example, the childfree category is associated with some measures of well-being but not others. In one study of over 5,000 mid-life Norwegian women, neither women with nor women without children reported more negative emotions (depression, loneliness). At the same time, women who remained childfree at mid-life were less satisfied with their lives and reported lower self-esteem than women who had adult children at home or an empty nest (Hansen, Slagsvold, & Moum, 2009).

It appears that some negative impact of childfree status on well-being can be attributed to feelings of control; voluntarily childfree middle-aged adults have higher levels of well-being than those who are involuntarily childless (Jeffries & Konnert, 2002). For men, involuntary childlessness was associated with feelings of loss and a sense of exclusion and isolation (Hadley & Hanley, 2011). Childlessness in men appears to be strongly tied to their relationship status.

The percentage of women and men who wish to remain childfree, roughly 7 percent and 8 percent, respectively, is fairly stable and consistent across the last two decades (Ravanera & Beaujot, 2014; Stobert & Kemeny, 2003). When women remain unmarried and attain high levels of education, being childfree benefits well-being. In these cases, women tend to be very socially connected and highly educated (Koropeckyj-Cox & Call, 2007; Wenger, Dykstra, Melkas, & Knipscheer, 2007). But the protective effects of investments in non-parental domains may be viable in only some contexts. Where negative social attitudes toward a childfree status exist, we are more likely to find poorer well-being among women remaining childfree (Koropeckyj-Cox, 2002). Women retaining a childfree status fare better in terms of their psychological well-being when they live in European countries that are more tolerant of women's choices than when they live in countries that are less tolerant (Huijts, Kraaykamp, & Subramanian, 2013).

Timing of parenthood Looking at mid-life mothers and fathers and adult children, we may pay less attention to early factors that contribute to the influences of parenthood on mid-life adjustment—but we shouldn't. Early transitions to parenthood have an enduring effect on well-being into mid-life. Women who were in their teens (Koropeckyj-Cox, Pienta, & Brown, 2007) or early

20s (Mirowsky & Ross, 2002) when they first gave birth reported lower positive feelings (such as happiness) and more negative feelings (such as loneliness and depression) in mid-life than women who had their first babies later. Numerous studies of teen parenting find short- and long-term implications for early transitions to parenthood.

It's not necessarily young age that introduces risk. Rather, it's the timing of the transition to parenthood, which, when early, coincides with early emerging adulthood, a stage of the lifespan when peers are exploring, preparing, and acquiring resources. Early motherhood is often associated with interruptions in education and career transitions,

which, in turn, undermine women's access to employment and income through mid-life (Koropeckyj-Cox et al., 2007). Early parenthood is also associated with less marital stability. Early mothers not only face poorer economic circumstances, but also are more likely to be unmarried at mid-life and to have experienced marital interruptions while raising their children (Koropeckyj-Cox et al., 2007). A marital interruption could include separations or divorces. But it's also important to remember that not all early marriages end in divorce and not all mid-life marriages remain intact. As with all stages and phases of life, marriage at mid-life is interesting and complex.

WHAT A DEVELOPMENTALIST SEES
Mid-life Marital Biographies

The 40-year high school reunion brings middle-aged adults together to reflect on how much has stayed the same and how much has changed in their lives since they were 18 (**Figure a**). One of the first questions a former classmate might ask is, "Are you married?" Knowing whether or not someone is married at mid-life tells us something about the way he or she lives right now, but developmentalists recognize that people who share the same marital status often have very different stories to tell about their marital histories.

If your classmates are representative of the population, about three in four of them will be married. But you will soon learn that "married at mid-life" doesn't tell the whole story (**Figure b**). In a similar way, those who are not married have a variety of stories to tell about how they came to be single in mid-life (**Figure c**). In other words, the history of entries into and exits out of marriage—a marital biography—tells a lot more about a person than his or her marital status, which is simply a point-in-time snapshot of whether or not someone is legally married.

a. Catching up at a reunion gives a snapshot of classmates' lives but may not tell the whole story.

b. At mid-life, 20 percent of those who are married are in their second marriages: 14 percent following a divorce, 2 percent following the death of their spouse, and another 4 percent having experienced two or more of those events (Hughes & Waite, 2009).

c. At mid-life, of those who report being single, 15 percent have never been married, 39 percent have experienced a divorce, 19 percent are widowed, and 27 percent have experienced two or more of those events (Hughes & Waite, 2009).

Richard J. McCormack/The Jersey Journal/Landov

Think Critically 1. Do your parents share a marital biography?
2. In your own life, would you say that your parents' marital status or marital biographies influenced your own views of marriage? Why or why not?

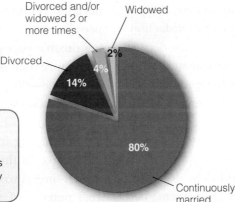

% of those "married" at mid-life

Divorced and/or widowed 2 or more times — 4%
Widowed — 2%
Divorced — 14%
Continuously married — 80%

% of those "single" at mid-life

Never married — 15%
Divorced — 39%
Divorced and/or widowed 2 or more times — 27%
Widowed — 19%

Marriage in Mid-life

The majority of middle-aged adults share a common pursuit—launching their children into adulthood—but fewer share the same marital status. Of middle-aged adults (ages 51 to 61), only 55 percent have been continuously married since their early 20s. Of this 55 percent, many have been married for 30 years or more (Hughes & Waite, 2009). The other 45 percent of 50-somethings vary greatly with respect to their marital statuses and **marital biographies** in mid-life. (See *What a Developmentalist Sees*.)

marital biography
Information about the number, timing, and duration of marriages in a person's life.

In addition to marital status and history, the quality of marriage shapes the lives of those who find themselves married at mid-life. The majority of middle-aged adults celebrating their 30th and then 40th wedding anniversaries have something to celebrate. Two thirds of continuously married mid-lifers report stable and moderate to high levels of satisfaction from the early through the later years of marriage. One-third of mid-life adults who remain in first marriages in mid-life report low satisfaction at some point in their marriages (Anderson, Van Ryzin, & Doherty, 2010); 20 percent report low satisfaction beginning at "I do" (Kamp Dush, Taylor, & Kroeger, 2008). In sum, the majority of marriages that last into mid-life are happy ones, although some go through a rough patch or two, and for others, the rough patch might stretch 30 years or more.

Why would some people stay unhappily married for 30 years? Some research suggests that remaining unhappily married for over a decade is a recipe for personal misery and distress (Hawkins & Booth, 2005). However, happiness with one's marriage is only one determinant of marital continuity. Marital conflict also plays a role in the likelihood of marital dissolution.

In first marriages that stay intact into mid-life, there is more stability in marital conflict than in marital satisfaction. Marital conflict tends to remain stable for the first decade or so and to decrease slightly thereafter. But one study identified three different groups with slightly different patterns of conflict. The majority of marriages (61 percent of the sample) had moderate levels of conflict; these levels were generally stable, with only a slight rise in the later years. By contrast, high-conflict marriages (23 percent) increased in conflict over the first eight years and then decreased over the next 12. Low-conflict marriages (17 percent) had stable, low levels of conflict (Kamp Dush & Taylor, 2012).

The same study showed that the couples' values were correlated with satisfaction and conflict in the marriage. Spouses who believed in lifelong marriage and shared decision-making between partners were more likely to be in the low-conflict group and less likely to be in the high-conflict group. Sharing the same values and husbands sharing in housework predicted that a couple would have a high-satisfaction, low-conflict marriage (Kamp Dush & Taylor, 2012).

John Gottman's marriage research (1994a&b, 2006; Gottman & Gottman, 2009; Gottman, Gottman & DeClaire, 2006) is perhaps best known for stripping away the notion that all marital conflict is bad marital conflict. Rather, Gottman's research taught us that spouses can fight, but that they have to do so constructively or their marriage will suffer. Fighting constructively is not about the intensity of the argument—some couples are indeed very high-conflict but still report high marital satisfaction (Gottman, 1994b). Constructive fighting, in contrast to destructive fighting, involves relationship repair, a coming together after an argument. In the end, those who remain fair are those who know how to make up and stay together even when the going gets rough. More recent research suggests that constructive conflict is only protective against divorce by mid-life if both partners use constructive strategies (Birditt, Brown, Orbuch, & McIlvane, 2010). Eventually, when a spouse feels that the costs of staying in a marriage outweigh the benefits, dissatisfaction triggers divorce. Some couples turn to counselling to resolve conflict and avoid divorce (see *Challenges in Development*).

Divorce By mid-life, approximately 25 percent of the population has been divorced (Hughes & Waite, 2009). However, risk for divorce during mid-life is relatively low compared with risk for divorce in earlier life stages. Mid-life divorce rates have been increasing over the past few decades (**Figure 14.5**). Approximately 12 percent of people between ages 50 and 64 will find themselves signing divorce papers. Some have already divorced once or even more than once. Remarriages are more likely to end in divorce—20 percent, compared with first marriages, 9 percent (Brown & Lin, 2012). Repeat divorces, those involving people who had been divorced at least once before, are accounting for an increasing proportion of divorces in Canada. In the last 30 years, the proportion of repeat to first-time divorces has roughly tripled. Approximately 16.2 percent of men and 15.7 percent of women who divorce do so for a repeat time (Statistics Canada, 2005).

Marital Help-Seeking

Mid-life couples may seek help for different reasons. Some may need help resolving ambivalence, whereas others may seek help to alleviate stress the most common issues for which mid-life couples seek help include issues with communication patterns; complaints of lack of intimacy or emotional distance; challenges that are unique to the couple; and desire for more physical affection and sex (Boisvert, Wright, Tremblay, & McDuff, 2011). Different types of help may be more appropriate depending on a couple's needs (see the **table**). Couples seeking help with relationship problems, including those related to the mental illness of one or both partners, can benefit from therapy. Couples who need information and skills to strengthen their marriage can benefit from family life education. Couples seeking information about family life education can seek information on the website for the National Council on Family Relations.

John shepherd/iStockphoto

	Why? *What's the purpose? What's the goal?*	**What?** *Knowledge base*	**When?** *The timing of work with families*	**For whom?** *Target population for services*	**How?** *Techniques and methods used*
Marriage and family therapy	To reduce relationship problems and/or mental or emotional disorders to achieve stable, long-term, emotionally enriching relationships	Family and relationship theory and research; therapy-focused philosophies and methodologies	Cope with past and current family problems by focusing on past causes and patterns, and improve current and future family functioning	Individuals, couples, and families who have been diagnosed with functional difficulties who are willing to participate in a therapeutic environment	Diagnose family problems; identify a treatment plan
Family life education	To increase knowledge and develop skills so families may build on their strengths to function at optimal levels	Family and lifespan theory and research; teach about knowledge, attitudes, and skills; participants are active in the learning process	Deal with current family needs and challenges to prepare for and improve current and future family functioning	Any individual or family willing and able to function in an educational environment committed to learning	Assess family-related needs; set goals on the basis of family needs and strengths

Source: Myers-Walls, Ballard, Darling, & Myers-Bowman, 2011.

Think Critically Describe one couple that may find the type of help that fits their needs from a marriage and family therapist and one couple that may find a fit between their needs and the type of help a family life educator offers.

Divorce in mid-life •
Figure 14.5 _____

The risk for divorce in younger age groups for both women and men is lower in 2011 than it was in 1981. In contrast, the rates have been increasing especially for individuals aged 50 and over. In other words, divorce rates have decreased for younger people and have increased for older people.

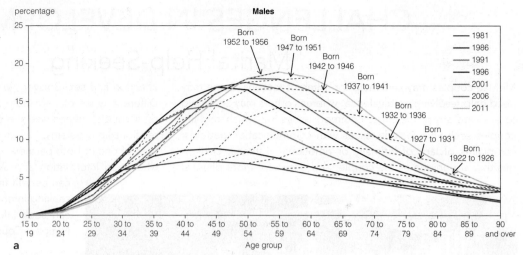

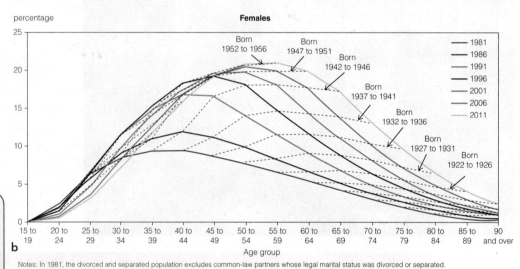

Notes: In 1981, the divorced and separated population excludes common-law partners whose legal marital status was divorced or separated. Less than 4% of the population aged 15 and over lived common-law in 1981. For simplicity, not all birth cohorts are labelled.

Source: Milan, A. (2013b). Marital Status: Overview, 2011. Component of Statistics Canada Catalogue no. 91-209-X. Report on the Demographic Situation in Canada. Statistics Canada, censuses of population, 1981 to 2011. Accessed at www.statcan.gc.ca/pub/91-209-x/2013001/article/11788/fig/fig3-eng.htm.

Think Critically What changes have we seen with respect to transitions to marriage over the past few decades that may be related to differences in the way divorce rates are changing for the baby boomers vs. generations X and Y?

Half of all first marriages that will end in divorce do so within the first eight years (Kreider & Ellis, 2011). Not surprisingly, low-satisfaction marriages, even those that are only moderately unhappy, are more likely to come to an end before couples reach their 20th wedding anniversary (Birditt, Hope, Brown, & Orbuch, 2012), and over 90 percent will be over before the 25th anniversary (Kreider & Ellis, 2011). But it is the state of the marriage in its earliest years that matters most. Even if a marriage makes it to mid-life, couples who were unhappy before the honeymoon was over are more likely than those who were happy in the early years to get divorced in mid-life, regardless of the level of satisfaction they achieve (Hirschberger, Srivastava, Marsh, Cowan, & Cowan, 2009).

Risks for divorce early in a marriage are not the same as risks for later divorce (Gottman & Gottman, 2009). In the early years of marriage, mean fighting is a risk for

divorce. Mean fighting uses contempt and manipulation to control the other person as opposed to fair fighting that is based on solving the problem with respect for the other person's needs. In mid-life, a lack of positive emotion during day-to-day conflict communications predicted divorce (Gottman & Levenson, 2000). Differences in risk factors for divorce between the early and later years of marriage may explain why we see an overall decrease in marital conflict over the course of marriages that remain intact. In the earliest years, big issues get resolved or couples divorce. In the middle years, the big issues have been resolved and couples turn to one another to fulfill the desire and need for warmth and care, and share the work of planning and managing household tasks (Christensen & Miller, 2006; Henry & Miller, 2004).

The three most common reasons for divorce in mid-life are: (1) sexual issues (cheating, sexual incompatibility, poor sexual performance, declining physical appearance, homosexuality, and inability to have children); (2) abuse (verbal, physical, emotional, control); and (3) different points of view (didn't want to have children, different values or lifestyles, major age difference, religious differences, and cultural clashes). Emotional and psychological risk factors (for example, abuse, a lack of marital effort/ not being there for spouse, and substance use) are associated with long deliberations before divorce (Taylor, 2011).

Although divorce is less common in mid-life, the reverberations through a person's life can be significant. Divorce is far more than just the end of a marriage. It affects everything from each partner's self-esteem to their relationships with their children, their friends, and their relatives (Amato, 1999; Anderson, 2003; King, 2003). In addition, divorce can be an emotional roller coaster with intense moments of loneliness and anxiety (Hetherington, 2006). It also typically means major shifts in income, with alimony and child support often causing new stresses on both partners. Perhaps the most well-established and alarming of the risks associated with divorce is the increased odds of death associated with being single in mid-life, whether or not the person has been always single or was previously married (Siegler, Brummett, Martin, & Helms, 2013).

Remarriage For some, remarriage is an antidote to the stress of a divorce (Siegler et al., 2013). Remarriage has a stabilizing effect after divorce among adults over 40 (Wu & Penning, 1997). A number of factors predict who remarries after divorce or widowhood. In the Netherlands, adults who are older are less likely to remarry, and men with less education are less likely to remarry; in one study, employment at the time of divorce differentially impacted likelihood of remarriage for men and women, increasing the likelihood that a man would remarry and decreasing the likelihood that a woman would (De Jong Gierveld, 2004).

Almost 20 percent of middle-aged adults find themselves in remarriages, the majority of them following divorce and a smaller group following the death of a spouse (Hughes & Waite, 2009). Remarriages are understood to be distinctly different from first marriages. When selecting a partner educational attainment and gender play a significantly more important role in remarriages than in first marriages (Shafer, 2012). Remarriages following the death of a spouse can be affected by the memories of the deceased spouse emerging in the remarriage (Brimhall & Engblom-Deglmann, 2011).

Remarriage and repartnering in mid-life are complicated by factors that don't affect younger adults. For example, adult children's opposition, the complexity of splitting access to pension and retirement benefits, and the challenges of merging two households present unique challenges in mid-life and later adulthood (Mahay & Lewin, 2007). But like their younger counterparts, older adults find alternative ways to create and invest in intimate partnerships that fit their lives. Research suggests that more recent cohorts of middle-aged and older adults are more likely to partner without marrying (Brown, Bulanda, & Lee, 2005; Peplau & Fingerhut, 2007). One such type of relationship that is relatively new to the social demographers who study relationship statuses is **living apart together (LAT)** (Strohm, Seltzer, Cochran, & Mays, 2009). LAT describes couples who have an intimate relationship but live at different addresses. An LAT arrangement might allow older couples to maintain some independence or simplify relationships with children from a prior marriage.

> **living apart together (LAT)** When couples who have an intimate relationship maintain separate residences.

Same-sex marriages and partnerships We know very little about gay partnership and marriage in mid-life because little research has focused on the long-lasting relationships of same-sex couples (Mackey, Diemer, & O'Brien, 2004). Unsurprisingly, the research that has been conducted indicates that satisfaction and stability in long-term same-sex partnerships are associated with similar relational qualities as those associated with successful heterosexual relationships (Gottman et al., 2003; Mackey et al., 2004). In a study examining the relationships of same-sex couples that had lasted an average of 30 years, researchers found that psychological intimacy and relational stability was nurtured by minimum levels of interpersonal conflict, constructive disputing, a perception of equity within the relationship, expressions of affection, and an intimate quality of communications between partners (Mackey, Diemer, & O'Brien, 2000). Interestingly, women in same-sex relationships are more likely to report communication strategies that contribute to psychological intimacy and relational satisfaction than gay men and heterosexual couples (Connolly & Sicola, 2005; Mackey, et al., 2000). Several studies have reported that legalization of same-sex marriage has had a positive impact on the health and well-being of gay, lesbian, bisexual, and queer-identified North American citizens

Discriminatory Stress • Figure 14.6

Individuals who identify as lesbian, gay, bisexual, trans, or queer (LGBTQ) who take advantage of legal partnerships and same-sex marriage laws may experience less of the discriminatory stress associated with living in a heteronormative social environment (Buffie, 2011). Legal commitment appears to be protective for LGBTQ adults (Riggle et al., 2010).

Hill Street Studios/Blend Images/Corbis

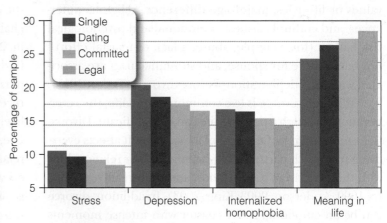

Think Critically According to the graph, in what ways do marriages and legal partnerships influence positive mental health and protect against distress?

(Gonzales, 2014; MacIntosh, Reissing, & Andruff, 2010; Riggle, Rostosky, & Horne, 2010; Wight, LeBlanc, & Lee Badgett, 2013). In mid-life, for example, same-sex marriage operates as a protective factor for mental health (**Figure 14.6**; Wight, LeBlanc, de Vries, & Detels, 2012).

Despite numerous similarities, we cannot assume that same-sex partnerships operate in exactly the same way as heterosexual partnerships. For example, women do much of the health promotion in heterosexual couples. In contrast, among gay and lesbian couples, co-operative health behaviour work is more common; that is, the partners influence each other's health behaviours (Reczek & Umberson, 2012). We also know that same-sex couples have created and adopted different commitment-making trajectories given the lack of access they have had to marriage historically (Reczek, Elliott, & Umberson, 2009). In sum, given the changing historical context of same-sex marriages and alternative pathways to union formation among same-sex partners, it is important to move forward with work that recognizes the similarities and differences that may distinguish same-sex from hetero-sex partnerships in mid-life.

Put It Together *Review the sections on personality, psychsocial development and divorce **in mid-life** to think about these questions:*
1. How might generativity be impacted by changes in marital status?
2. How might the Big Five personality traits factor into divorce and remarriage?

The sandwich generation • Figure 14.7

Mid-life parents can be an adult child's primary form of support or provide some form of partial support to an adult child. At the same time, middle-aged adults find themselves supporting their aging parents.

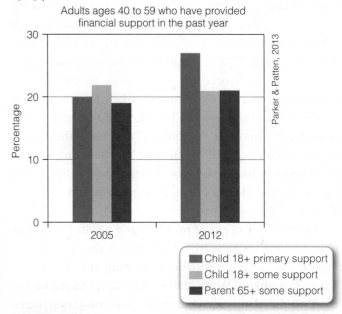

Ask Yourself
1. What type of support to adult children accounts for the largest increase from 2005 to 2012?
2. What is the percent increase in middle-aged adults providing care to adult children from 2005 to 2012?
3. What is the percent increase in middle-aged adults providing care to aging parents from 2005 to 2012?

Parental Caregiving

In many healthy families, the flow of care and support continues to transfer from parents to their children well into adulthood (Suitor, Sechrist, Gilligan, & Pillemer, 2011).

In some families, middle-aged adults continue to receive emotional and financial support from their aging parents (Kim, Zarit, Eggebeen, Birditt, & Fingerman, 2011). But middle adulthood is the time when it is most likely that an adult child will make the transition from being the recipient of care to being the care provider. Middle-aged adults are sometimes called the **sandwich generation** because they find themselves with dual caregiving roles. About half of 40- to 59-year-olds have at least one parent over the age of 65 and are actively parenting (raising a child under 18 or supporting a child over 18). Only about 15 percent of this group provides financial support to both parents and children, but this burden is rising (**Figure 14.7**;

Parker & Patten, 2013). Given the tendency for family relationships to be stronger through the wife or mother's side of the family, it's not surprising that women provide more caregiving to their aging parents than men and that more caregiving goes to mothers than to fathers (Suitor & Pillemer, 2006).

Regardless of what the parent–child relationship was like earlier in life, becoming a **caregiver** to one's parent requires adjustment to the inverted balance of power, authority, and independence between the caregiving adult child and an aging parent (Pope, Kolomer, & Glass, 2012). For some, the transition may also involve taking on the **kinkeeper,** role (Rosenthal, 1985). Caregiving for a parent stresses an individual's coping capacities and puts demands on an individual's resources,

Where Developmentalists CLICK

TheFamilyCaregiver.com

Middle-aged adult children are part of the more than 7 million Canadians caring for a loved one at home or in a care facility. We may receive medical information from doctors about parents' health issues, but often adult children lack information and resources for providing practical and emotional supports for our elders. Home care, a growing and necessary area for public services across Canada, focuses on supporting people to live in their community—in their home or with family—rather than in a hospital or institutional setting when they cannot care for themselves. Unfortunately, home care is underfunded, undervalued, and overstressed (CARP, 2011). It consists of a group of services that help people receive care at home when they are ill, disabled, recovering from illness or surgery, or dying. The variety of services varies markedly from one jurisdiction to another. On this interactive web-based resource, you can connect to practical information to find solutions to your caregiving questions and needs.

including finances and time. Despite the increased burden that caregiving represents, adult child caregivers also report feelings of joy caring for an aging parent (Igarashi, Hooker, Coehlo, & Manoogian, 2013). Supports for family caregiving vary throughout Canada and are the focus for *Where Developmentalists Click.*

Relationships with Adult Siblings and Friends

In many ways, the social support systems of mid-life adults are in flux as a result of adult children becoming increasingly independent and parents becoming increasingly dependent. In contrast, relationships with adult siblings and friends are relatively stable during mid-life,

and therefore provide an important source of support. Siblings and friends are also typically in a similar life stage, sharing many common experiences.

Adult siblings Earlier in this text, we introduced the concept of the sibling as the closest lifetime relationship a person will have in terms of shared genes and shared environment. This relatedness is often reflected in emotional closeness. In adulthood, siblings engage in specific strategies to keep their siblings close to them; for example, through the use of affectionate communications that entail more than a quick exchange of basic information (Myers, Byrnes, Frisby, & Mansson, 2011). But there is evidence that these warm communications are limited to exchanges in

Adult friendships • Figure 14.8

Different types of adult friendships meet various needs of middle-aged adults.

a. Some adult friendships provide nurturing support. Shared interests and similar backgrounds, trustworthiness, and reciprocal care are the building blocks of supportive adult friendships. These women, who have been friends for over 15 years, make time for a retreat together every year.

b. Other adult friendships provide a context for sharing and challenging one's sense of self. Adult relationships in which friends express affection and allow for problem solving when issues arise between them are likely to last over time. These men have met at this coffee shop almost every day for the past 13 years. Their frequent disagreements about everything from politics to celebrity marriages seem to stimulate their friendship rather than undermine it.

Ariel Skelley/Blend Images/Corbis

Image BROKER/Alamy

Think Critically For those middle-aged adults who report no close friendships, what feelings are likely to be associated with having and not having adult friendships?

specific types of sibling relationships, specifically those characterized as intimate, congenial, and loyal (Myers & Goodboy, 2010).

Affection is not the only facet of the sibling relationship that spills over into adulthood. Apathetic and hostile adult relationships are two additional types of relatedness that siblings may share in adulthood (Myers & Goodboy, 2010). The source of conflict appears to be the same as the source of conflict during childhood: rivalry for parental resources. Siblings get along better when they perceive their parents as being fair and equitable (Suitor, Sechrist, Plikuhn, Pardo, Gilligan, & Pillemer, 2009). When parents play favourites, jockeying for favoured status spills over into the adult years (Suitor, Sechrist, Plikuhn, Pardo, & Pillemer, 2008).

Conflict and negative exchanges between siblings may be particularly problematic when caregiving responsibilities need to be distributed. In one caregiving study, 40 percent of caregivers were experiencing serious conflict with a family member, usually a sibling (Strawbridge & Wallhagen, 1991). Conflict between adult siblings occurs in families in which one or both siblings have experienced negative life events: divorce, psychological problems, addiction, problems with the law, victimization of abuse, or financial problems (Voorpostel, van der Lippe, & Flap, 2012).

Friendships in mid-life For middle-aged adults, friendships have fewer negative qualities than relationships with partners and children (Birditt, Jackey, & Antonucci, 2009). Mid-life friendships provide a variety of different elements of social support (Adams, Blieszner, & de Vries, 2000; **Figure 14.8**). Adults who receive less support from society at large (such as minority groups) or close others (such as spouses and family of origin) may place greater value on and get more from friendships compared with adults who have other sources of social support. For example, gay men and lesbian women are more likely to report that their friendships involve a greater number of elements than friendships of heterosexual adults, including trust, loyalty, care, and compatibility (de Vries & Megathlin, 2009).

Friendships may play instrumental roles in the way adults maintain their marriages as well. Both men and women do marriage work in their friendships; that is,

they become involved in one another's marriages by seeking out and providing validation, understanding, and advice concerning their relationships with their spouses and children. Husbands do more marriage work with their wives than they do with close friends; women do more marriage work with their close friends (Helms, Crouter, & McHale, 2003). However, this does not necessarily mean that women are turning to their close friends instead of their husbands, and engaging in marriage work with friends is not associated with poor marital quality. Rather, women are equally likely to talk with husbands as they are with close friends about the majority of marital issues and conflicts (Proulx, Helms, & Payne, 2004).

Friendships play an important role in predicting the mid-life physical health of gay, lesbian, and bisexual adults after mid-life. Social support and social network size are both protective factors against poor general health, disability, and depression (Fredriksen-Goldsen et al., 2013). One study of friendship pairs looking at caregiving for chronically ill mid-life and older gay, lesbian, and bisexual couples determined that both the caregiver and care-receiver appear to benefit from the social connectedness inherent in the caregiving relationship (Muraco & Fredriksen-Goldsen, 2011).

Together, evidence of marital work and caregiving in mid-life friendships suggests that adults look for and find social support from persons other than close family members and spouses. Evidence of adults finding social support they need when they need it suggests that adults' strivings for health and well-being take many shapes—a theme we will explore more fully in the next section.

| CONCEPT CHECK |

1. **What** are the positive and negative consequences of an empty nest?

2. **Why** might a middle-aged couple choose an LAT relationship?

3. **What** are the unique challenges faced by the sandwich generation?

4. **Why** are adult siblings and friends especially important social supports during mid-life?

Emotional Development

LEARNING OBJECTIVES

1. **Describe** how emotion changes in mid-life.
2. **Compare** and contrast two types of mid-life well-being.
3. **Outline** changes to gender roles in mid-life.
4. **Characterize** career transitions that occur in mid-life.

W ith all that makes mid-life a distinct stage of the lifespan with respect to personality and social relationships, you won't be surprised to learn that it is a time of unique emotional and psychological experiences as well. In this section we will consider factors that influence the emotional and psychological health and well-being of middle-aged adults.

Emotions in Mid-life

A number of years ago, psychologist Daniel Mroczek (2001) posed an interesting question: does emotion change over the lifespan? More specifically, does emotion continue to evolve throughout adulthood? To study this question, Mroczek (2001) and his team (Mroczek & Kolarz, 1998) examined levels of **emotional expression** among individuals ranging in age from 25 to 74 years of age. The study showed that adults report increasingly positive feelings with age. Using the same sample, Mroczek and

> **emotional expression** A verbal or non-verbal behaviour that expresses emotion.
>
> **paradox of well-being** The idea that even though the aging process is characterized by significant physiological and cognitive decline, adults report feeling emotionally positive.

colleague David Almeida (2004) found that with age, adults report fewer negative feelings, less stress, and less neuroticism.

At least a few eyebrows were raised when study findings revealed that adults reported increasingly warm feelings during the same years as physical health declined. This phenomenon, known as the **paradox of well-being** (Filipp, 1996; Mroczek, 2001), remains in effect until people reach their mid-70s, when they begin to be affected by significant health issues (Smith, Fleeson, Geiselmann, Settersten, & Kunzman, 1999). A number of explanations have been put forward to account for these seemingly incompatible trends.

Cognitive development For researchers who recognize that aging involves both losses and gains, compensation in one domain (emotional) against the backdrop of change in another domain (physical) is normal and expected. That's how psychologist Laura Carstensen interprets findings

Increased positive bias with age • Figure 14.9

Charles, Mather, and Carstensen (2003) showed positive, negative, or neutral images on a computer monitor to young, middle, and older adults. The participants were then asked to recall the images. As shown in this graph, memory functioning decreased with age. The decrease, however, was not equivalent for positive and negative images. Despite the fact that younger participants had better overall memory, the older participants had better memory for positive items.

Source: Charles, S. T., Mather, M., & Carstensen, L. L. (2003). Aging and emotional memory: the forgettable nature of negative images for older adults. *Journal of Experimental Psychology: General, 132*(2), 313.

> **Think Critically** Think about attending a large family gathering to celebrate your uncle's 70th birthday. Which stories are most likely to be shared? Describe the type of feelings these stories are likely to evoke.

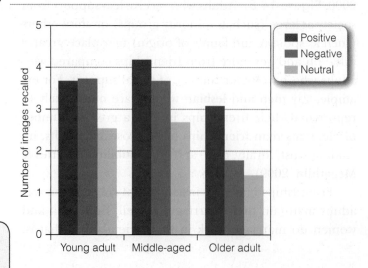

from her studies comparing young, middle-aged, and older persons on their recall of positive and negative stimuli. As adults age, they are more likely to recall images that evoke positive emotions and less likely to remember images that provoke negative feelings (Carstensen & Mikels, 2005; Charles & Carstensen, 2004; **Figure 14.9**).

socio-emotional selectivity theory (SST) The theory that people change their values as they get older, investing more socio-emotional energy in events they perceive as meaningful.

Carstensen's socio-emotional selectivity theory (SST) provides us with some insight into why aging is associated with a bias toward recall of positive stimuli (Carstensen, Isaacowitz, & Charles, 1999; Charles & Carstensen, 2004). SST draws upon our knowledge of cognitive development in adulthood, specifically knowledge that processing speed, working memory, and other attention and memory functions decline with age. SST also takes into account changes in adults' motivations. At earlier ages—for example, in young adulthood—adults perceive a great deal of time remaining in their lives. In other words, the horizon is far off in the distance. As adults age, the horizon is closer. They become less motivated to plan and more motivated to invest in the present. As a result, it makes sense that older adults become more attuned to positive experiences and less attentive to experiences that evoke negative emotions, just as Carstensen and colleagues found.

Researchers focusing on other developmental systems—for example, cognitive and brain development—have reported the same findings as Carstensen but have offered different interpretations of the findings. Psychologist Gisela Labouvie-Vief (Labouvie-Vief, Grühn, & Studer, 2010) studies cognitive aging. Through her work, she suggests that older adults may be more likely to attend to positive rather than negative information because negative information takes more effort and energy to process. Cacioppo and colleagues (2011) attribute the positivity effect to structural changes in the brain. Specifically, neural degeneration in the limbic system's amygdala is known to be associated with a person's mental and emotional state.

Emotion regulation Another reason why older adults report increasingly positive emotions is that they get better at controlling their emotions. As we discussed in earlier chapters, emotion regulation comes into play when, for instance, someone cuts you off on the highway and

you want to retaliate but do not. According to psychologist James Gross (1999, 2001), emotion regulation can be **antecedent-focused** or **response-focused**. A middle-aged woman uses antecedent-focused coping when she plans a volunteer trip the weekend that coincides with the anniversary of her father's death. By planning in advance, she can spend the anniversary differently than she did last year. Last year

antecedent-focused emotion regulation The use of emotion regulation strategies before facing a stimulus.

response-focused emotion regulation The use of emotion regulation strategies, such as self-talk, after facing a stimulus.

she used response-focused coping to smile through a training session for work. She wanted to avoid what happened last year—she spent the day trying to pay attention, sitting among strangers, while trying to control a great deal of emotional pain. As we get older, we get better at both types of emotion regulation (Gross, 2001) and more selective and specific in our use of strategies (Birditt, Fingerman, & Almeida, 2005; Blanchard-Fields, Mienaltowski, & Seay, 2007).

Emotion regulation is associated with well-being and adjustment at all stages of the lifespan. Recall from what you learned about development in toddlerhood that sometimes very young children's exposure to overwhelming stimuli far surpasses their ability to regulate their emotional response, resulting in the all-too-familiar tantrum. Older adults, on average, have better emotion regulation than younger adults. Honed emotion regulation skills pay off with respect to mid-life emotional well-being. Maintaining high levels of positive emotions in proportion to negative emotions is essential for emotional health and well-being (Campos, Frankel, & Camras, 2004); likewise, a high ratio of positive to negative affect is associated with better emotion regulation (Smith, Maas, Mayer, Helmchen, Steinhagen-Thiessen, & Baltes, 2002). Therefore, better emotion regulation is one factor contributing to middle-aged adults reporting higher overall well-being than younger adults (Charles & Carstensen, 2007; Consedine & Magai, 2006).

Well-Being in Mid-life

Although individuals become increasingly likely to feel more positive and fewer negative emotions as they age, this does not exactly mirror changes we see in well-being from the 20s through the later decades of life.

Hedonic **well-being** emphasizes happiness and life satisfaction and the absence of negative feelings in one's life. Hedonic well-being decreases to a low point in mid-life (**Figure 14.10**). However, some middle-aged adults are likely to experience an increase in hedonic well-being as happiness and enjoyment go up and stress and worry go down (Stone, Schwartz, Broderick, & Deaton, 2010). This is not surprising given what we know about the stress associated with work–family conflict from young into middle adulthood (Rantanen, Kinnunen, Pulkkinen, & Kokko, 2012).

Hedonic and **eudaimonic well-being** paint different portraits of well-being in mid-life because they are distinct but conceptually related concepts. Eudaimonic well-being reflects the positive functioning of an individual associated with engagement in meaningful goal pursuits (**Figure 14.11**; Ryff & Singer, 2008). Eudaimonic well-being is inversely associated with depression (Wood & Joseph, 2010). The absence of well-being is associated with

hedonic well-being The sense of feeling good about and satisfied with one's life while experiencing an absence of negative feelings.

eudaimonic well-being An individual's engagement in leading a productive life, associated with personal growth and fulfillment of one's potential.

mid-life crisis The psychological experience of recognizing that life is half over and making course corrections to romantic life, career, and living situation to make life more consistent with values and desires.

biological markers of poorer health and physical stress; for example, higher cortisol levels, pro-inflammatory cytokines, and cardiovascular risk, as well as shorter periods of restorative (REM) sleep (Ryff, Singer, & Love, 2004).

Given this brief review of what we know about well-being in mid-life, should you expect massive upheaval at mid-life? Elliott Jaques (1965) first used the concept of the **mid-life crisis** to summarize the experiences of 310 creative geniuses. According to Jaques, around age 35, the composers and artists he studied changed their style or experienced significant decreases in their productivity. More recently, Daniel Levinson (1978) suggested that a mid-life crisis is nothing more than a normative transition. In his book *The Seasons of a Man's Life* (1978), Levinson describes the middle adult transition (40 to 45) as a task of integration. Mid-life is no more stressful than young adulthood, but the different age groups experience different types of stress. As adults move into middle age, they are past the stage of adopting and adjusting to adult roles,

Mid-life hedonic well-being • Figure 14.10

The Canadian Community Health Survey asked people to rate their life satisfaction.

Population aged 12 and older who reported being satisfied or very satisfied with their life in general, 2014

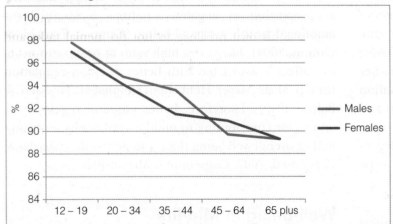

Think Critically Write a few Facebook status updates for a middle-aged woman expressing high and increasing hedonic well-being?

Source: Statistics Canada, CANSIM table 105-0501 and Catalogue no. 82-221-X. Retrieved from www.statcan.gc.ca/tables-tableaux/sum-som/l01/cst01/health87b-eng.htm.

The dimensions of eudaimonic well-being • Figure 14.11

Middle-aged adults who attain eudaimonic well-being are connected to others, feel like they have autonomy and the ability to direct their own lives, and have a sense of moving forward in life.

a. Eudaimonic well-being is multi-faceted, composed of six key factors that contribute to an individual's engagement with life and sense of purpose.

b. Mid-life adults who form hiking clubs, book clubs, or running clubs, such as this group, increase their eudaimonic well-being by staying physically healthy and socially connected.

Ann Hermes/Christian Science Monitor/The Image Works

Think Critically What indicator of mid-life personality development is conceptually related to eudaimonic well-being?

and now they are faced with integrating dominant and non-dominant parts of self (**Figure 14.12**).

Today researchers have concluded that the mid-life crisis is not a universal experience. Some people experience difficulties at mid-life, whereas others do not. One source of differences in well-being at mid-life may be linked to variation in role demands and role changes, which we explore in the next section.

Gender Roles in Mid-life

In some ways, men and women experience mid-life differently, and in other ways their life experiences become more similar. As people mature and age, they tend to identify with set cultural gender roles less and less, a phenomenon known as **gender convergence** (Gutmann, 1994; Hoare, 2002). In some instances, people may even experience **gender crossover** (**Figure 14.13**).

gender convergence The tendency for both males and females to become more similar as they mature.

gender crossover The tendency for each sex to adopt traits strongly associated with the opposite gender.

This shift in gender roles may affect a couple's heterosexual relationship positively or negatively. For example, during this phase, a husband might do more housework, which increases a wife's level of happiness but may decrease his own privilege to not do menial tasks and decrease his happiness. Women increasingly work outside the home in mid-life, resulting in a higher income, but also more stress and less time spent together (Amato, Booth, Johnson, & Rogers, 2007).

Gender differences in thinking and communication continue in middle adulthood. For example, with age, women continue to increase in verbal fluency, whereas men continue to exhibit better visual-spatial proficiency (Parsons, Rizzo, van der Zaag, McGee, & Buckwalter, 2005; Sax, 2005). These cognitive differences influence communication styles, creating gender differences well into later adulthood (Sax, 2005).

The mid-life transition • Figure 14.12

The mid-life transition is a normative challenge to the self, or identity, that comes about as a function of age and life stage. The mid-life transition is about balancing one's character and gaining strength by integrating non-dominant parts of self. Various models have been proposed to describe the primary polarities that seek integration. In the 1970s, Daniel Levinson proposed a four-dimensional model.

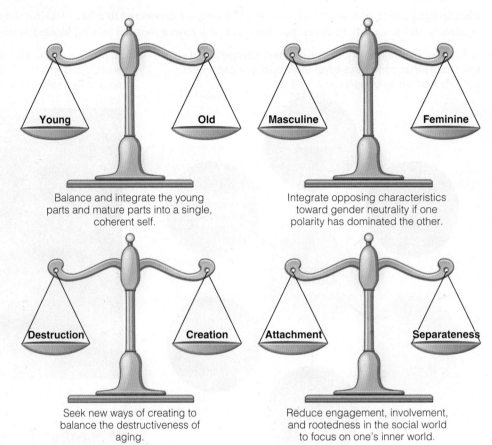

Balance and integrate the young parts and mature parts into a single, coherent self.

Integrate opposing characteristics toward gender neutrality if one polarity has dominated the other.

Seek new ways of creating to balance the destructiveness of aging.

Reduce engagement, involvement, and rootedness in the social world to focus on one's inner world.

Think Critically Thinking about a middle-aged adult in your life and using this four-dimensional model of personality, what are the specific challenges of personality integration this person faces?

Gender crossover • Figure 14.13

Jung (1933), like many others, believed that each person has both masculine and feminine aspects that are expressed strongly as young adults, but less so as people become older.

a. With age, women become more assertive and self-confident, often developing highly successful careers or moving into areas that are not stereotypically feminine, like the woman in this photo.

b. Men increasingly develop their ability to nurture and focus more on building intimate relationships with those they care about, as shown here.

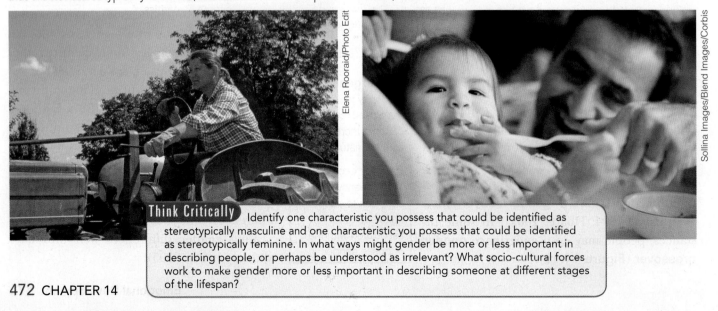

Elena Rooraid/Photo Edit

Sollina Images/Blend Images/Corbis

Think Critically Identify one characteristic you possess that could be identified as stereotypically masculine and one characteristic you possess that could be identified as stereotypically feminine. In what ways might gender be more or less important in describing people, or perhaps be understood as irrelevant? What socio-cultural forces work to make gender more or less important in describing someone at different stages of the lifespan?

Careers in Mid-life

Changing jobs is often considered another fact of life, similar to moving from one house to another or shifting from one school to the next. That factor carries on into middle age as well. Canadians will have on average approximately three careers and eight jobs over a lifetime (Human Resources and Skills Development Canada, 2004). Part of changing careers may also include returning to school. The number of Canadians aged 25 to 64 who are full-time students has more than tripled in recent years (Gower, 1997). In 2007, for example, 7 percent of university students and 9 percent of college students were between the ages of 40 and 59 (Dale, 2010). Another reason why people go back to school in mid-life is to increase their earnings. Adult education pays off the most for those who earn a post-secondary certificate, whether from a university or from a non-university institution, such as a community college or trade of vocational school. As **Figure 14.14** shows, hourly earnings of women who obtained a certificate grew at roughly double the rate of women who did not participate in adult education, taking them up to almost equivalent earnings. Women who went back to school without obtaining a certificate, on the other hand, had smaller gains than women who did not participate in adult education (Palameta & Zhang, 2006).

Mid-life is an important life stage for the accumulation of savings for retirement. Middle-aged workers (51 to 60) compose approximately one-third of the labour market.

The good news for mid-life men and women is that both are less likely to lose their jobs than younger workers (25 to 34), primarily due to seniority. But when they do lose their jobs, middle-aged men and women are less likely (39 percent for men and 18 percent for women) to be re-employed than their younger counterparts. Moreover, re-employed mid-life adults are more likely to suffer wage declines when they do become re-employed (Johnson & Mommaerts, 2011).

Canadians are living and working longer. Since the 1990s, for example, expected working life has increased, but post-retirement life expectancy has remained relatively stable because life expectancy has also increased. Today, the average age of voluntary retirement is about 66. When involuntary withdrawal from the labour market is also considered, the average of retirement drops slightly, to age 64. Although the expected working life is similar for all employed Canadians, less educated workers are expected to spend fewer years in retirement due to a shorter life expectancy (Carrière & Galarneau, 2012). Longer participation in the labour market is one reason why the traditional path of having just one career until retirement is no longer taken by most workers. The specific timing of retirement is determined by a complex process involving personal goals and circumstances, financial preparedness, and institutional forces (Carrière & Galarneau, 2012). Among those who choose to retire, retirement intentions and financial opportunity contribute to that decision (**Figure 14.15**; Damman, Henkens, & Kalmijn, 2011).

Hourly earnings of workers with a post-secondary certificate • Figure 14.14

Hourly earnings growth over a six-year period was assessed by the Survey of Labour and Income Dynamics. Obtaining a post-secondary certificate at some point in the second to fifth years resulted in the largest gains.

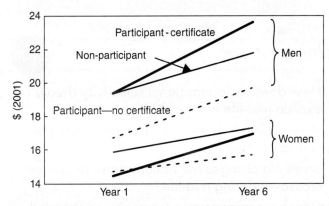

Think Critically What do you notice about the gender wage gap for each of the categories?

Source: Palameta, B., & Zhang, X. (2006). Does it pay to go back to school? *Perspectives on Labour and Income,* March 2006, Vol. 7, no. 3. Accessed at www.statcan.gc.ca/pub/75-001-x/10306/9133-eng.pdf.

Factors in retirement decision-making • Figure 14.15

In one study in the Netherlands, over 1,200 men were asked, "Do you intend to stop working before age 65?" In addition to information about their intentions to retire, data were also collected about their work and family lives and their actual retirement behaviour.

a. Older male workers who had made significant investments in attaining education, several job changes, late transitions to parenthood, and late divorces tended to have low intention to retire early.

b. Older male workers with health problems were inclined to foresee earlier retirement (Damman et al., 2011).

Chris Sattlberger/cultura/Corbis

Factors promoting later retirement

Entry into labour market at a younger age
Additional training at mid-life
Dismissal or employment change before mid-life

Think Critically What might the life stories be of two men, one who is planning to retire early and the other who is planning to retire later?

Squaredpixels/iStockphoto

Factors promoting earlier retirement

Entry into labour market at a younger age

Transition to parenthood at an earlier age

Part-time work before 50

No pension

Fewer dependent children

Low-challenge work

Poor health

Today relatively few workers over the age of 50 move directly from career to final retirement. Over 60 percent of middle-aged workers move from full-time to **bridge jobs**—less demanding full- or part-time jobs that ease the transition to retirement (Cahill, Giandrea, & Quinn, 2006). Over 40 percent of retirees move back into the labour force (Johnson, Kawachi, & Lewis, 2009). For a small minority, this means that there is time for an **encore career** (Freedman, 2007), or a career in the second half of life that combines continued income, greater personal meaning, and social impact. Among those who have not had the chance to explore other professional avenues before,

bridge jobs Less demanding full- or part-time jobs taken up in mid-life that ease the transition to retirement.

encore career A new career path developed in mid-life that combines continued income, personal meaning, and social impact.

encore careers may bring great satisfaction. New careers begun later in life have a tendency to pay less and to include fewer benefits, but they also tend to produce less stress, more flexibility, and higher levels of personal enjoyment.

CONCEPT CHECK

1. **How** does socio-emotional selectivity theory explain mid-life emotions?

2. **How** do levels of well-being change over the course of mid-life?

3. **What** life changes might contribute to gender crossover during mid-life?

4. **How** have mid-life career transitions changed since the 1950s?

Summary

1 Personality Development 452

- Personality is not fixed by mid-life but does reach peak stability. Different life stages are associated with different mechanisms of personality change. Although personality change in young adulthood occurs as a function of social maturation, personality change in mid-life is related to role transitions (such as career change, divorce, launching adult children, or major health problems). In this way, personality can change when middle-aged adults **accommodate** in response to major life events.

- Erikson defines the middle-age phase of life as a period of **generativity** or **stagnation**. During middle age, generative adults focus on finding a way to leave a legacy to future generations. Some do this through work, through volunteering or working within the community, or through raising children.

- Different psychosocial pathways lead to variation in mid-life generativity. Middle-aged adults who tell the story of the redemptive self describe one pathway to psychosocial maturity in adulthood (as shown in the figure).

The redemptive self: Pathways to generativity • Figure 14.3

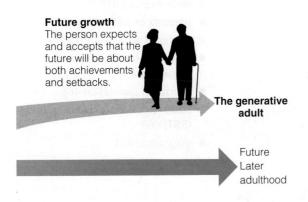

Future growth
The person expects and accepts that the future will be about both achievements and setbacks.

The generative adult

Future Later adulthood

2 Social Influences 456

- The family life stage, or the **launching phase**, intersects with mid-life adult development for the majority of Canadian parents. The **empty nest syndrome** is not universal among mid-life parents, with many adults finding greater marital satisfaction after adult children leave home.

- In recent years, more adult children have been returning home or staying home to live with their parents. Although this is more common than it was a decade or two ago, it is not a historically distinct or uncommon living arrangement. Parents sometimes feel **relational ambivalence** about adult children living at home, or about less successful adult children who do not live at home. Middle-aged adults who are voluntarily **childfree** have higher levels of well-being than those who are involuntarily childless.

- A **marital biography** provides a brief history of an adult's transitions into and out of marriages, from first marriage until a person's current status. For example, only 55 percent of middle-aged adults are continuously married through mid-life.

- Divorce is less common in mid-life than in any adult life stage prior to mid-life. Mid-life divorces are relatively rare, but they are becoming more common.

- Almost 20 percent of middle-aged adults find themselves in remarriages, as shown in the graph. But a growing movement is for more people to partner without marrying at mid-life. A new coupling trend has been described as **living apart together (LAT)**.

What a Developmentalist Sees: Mid-life Marital Biographies

% of those "married" at mid-life

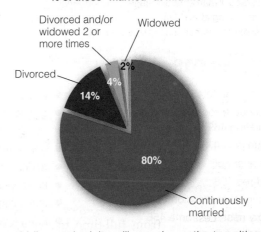

Divorced and/or widowed 2 or more times — 2%
Widowed
Divorced — 14%
4%
80%
Continuously married

- Many middle-aged adults will experience the transition to becoming a **caregiver** to one or more aging parents and the **kinkeeper** responsible for maintaining relationships between family members and organizing family celebrations. Middle-aged adults are often caught in the **sandwich generation** when they are faced with supporting children and parents simultaneously.

- Adult siblings and friends can provide strong emotional support during mid-life.

3 Emotional Development 468

- Some developmentalists use **socio-emotional selectivity theory (SST)** to explain emotional changes during mid-life (see the figure). Other developmentalists conceptualize emotional changes during mid-life as a **paradox of well-being**, wherein middle-aged adults experience increasingly positive **emotional expression** despite the physiological and cognitive decline they face as part of the aging process. The regulation of emotion is another aspect of aging that is being studied, with researchers differentiating between **antecedent-focused emotion regulation** and **response-focused emotion regulation**.

Increased positive bias with age • Figure 14.9

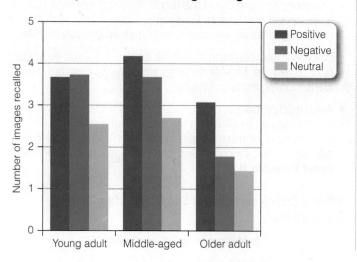

• Well-being in mid-life can be characterized as either **hedonic** or **eudaimonic**. Hedonic well-being emphasizes happiness and satisfaction and the absence of negative feelings. The stress of juggling work and family during middle age often leads to low hedonic well-being. Eudaimonic well-being is associated with personal growth and engagement in meaningful pursuits and the fulfillment of one's goals.

• The mid-life transition challenges a person's identity and sense of self as values and desires change and non-dominant parts of the self emerge. Difficulties with this transition and integration may lead to a **mid-life crisis**.

• Gender roles tend to merge and even switch in middle adulthood, called **gender convergence**. Both men and women tend to take on some of the traits of the opposite gender (called **gender crossover**) and in doing so, may change their habits and interests.

• Careers may shift in mid- to late adulthood as people's needs change. A number of people may transition to the retirement phase of life through some type of **bridge job** that is more interesting and less demanding but also tends to pay less and not have as many benefits, or move into an **encore career** that allows for the exploration of new professional avenues.

Key Terms

- accommodate 452
- antecedent-focused emotion regulation 469
- bridge jobs 474
- caregiver 465
- childfree 458
- emotional expression 468
- empty nest syndrome 456
- encore career 474

- eudaimonic well-being 470
- gender convergence 471
- gender crossover 471
- generativity 454
- hedonic well-being 470
- kinkeeper 465
- launching phase 456
- living apart together 463
- marital biography 460

- mid-life crisis 470
- paradox of well-being 468
- relational ambivalence 458
- response-focused emotion regulation 469
- sandwich generation 465
- socio-emotional selectivity theory (SST) 469
- stagnation 454

Critical and Creative Thinking Questions

1. What advice would you give to an older adult who wants to leave some kind of legacy for his or her family or future generations?

2. What type of person do you think would be more apt to suffer from some form of mid-life crisis?

3. List potential danger signs in a couple's relationship that might indicate a higher chance of divorce down the road.

4. What elements do you think create a healthy family? What factors make a difference, and which ones do not?

5. Which stage of parenting do you think would be the most demanding on the parents? Which ones do you think would result in the greatest development of maturity for the mother and father?

6. Does the empty nest syndrome seem like an authentic, realistic problem for most people? Why or why not? Make a list of at least three steps that could be taken to help lessen its impact on a family.

What is happening in this picture?

As families change, expand, and age, they may find themselves changing roles within the relationship along with discovering new elements of their personalities. This may be emphasized in families like the one shown here that has multiple generations in the same household.

Randy Olson/NG Image Collection

Think Critically 1. How are gender roles reversed in this photograph?
2. How are the generations interacting?
3. What traits do women sometimes develop in this stage of life? What traits do men develop? Why do adults tend to adopt the opposite gender's traits in middle age?
4. How might gender-typed attributes help men and women in their relationships, careers, and personal lives during middle adulthood?

REAL Development

Socio-emotional Development in Adulthood

In this video activity, you are a research assistant studying socio-emotional development in adulthood. You are collecting qualitative data for Dr. Brown, a developmental psychologist studying middle adulthood. She sends you to the Flores family to interview the parents, Eugene (age 59) and Evita (age 60). They have five children ranging in age from 20 to 33 years old. Your task is to understand their sense of identity, approach to parenting, and sense of accomplishment.

John Wiley & Sons, Inc.

WileyPLUS Go to WileyPLUS to complete the REAL Development activity.

03.01

Self-Test

(Check your answers in Appendix A.)

1. According to Erikson, what is the main crisis of middle adulthood?

   a. deciding what career pathway to follow

   b. understanding how to trust others and who to trust

   c. investing in the future vs. becoming inactive

   d. establishing family relationships and daily work routines

2. Through the twentieth century, the composition of the labour force changed, reflecting what social trend depicted in this graph?

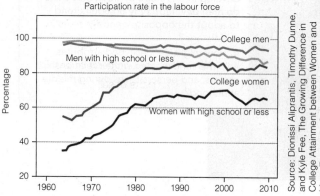

Source: Dionissi Aliprantis, Timothy Dunne, and Kyle Fee, The Growing Difference in College Attainment between Women and Men, *Economic Commentary* No. 2011-21 October 18, 2011, http://www.clevelandfed. org/research/Commentary/2011/2011-21.pdf.

   a. Colleges were required to offer as many sports for women as they did for men.

   b. Colleges stopped discriminating against minority applicants.

   c. A greater proportion of women earned college degrees.

   d. A high proportion of men left high school to go into the military.

3. The redemptive self is a story of a person who experienced all of the following on the pathway to generativity in mid-life *except*:

   a. an early, unique strength

   b. identity in adolescence

   c. a world view that serves as a moral compass

   d. balanced pursuit of investment in self and others

4. According to the graph, in 2010, adult children living at home is less common than it was _____.

   a. in the 1940s

   b. 20 years ago

   c. 40 years ago

   d. in the 1970s

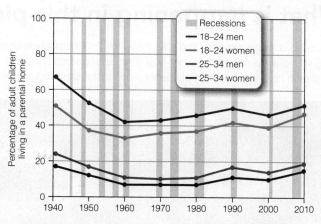

Source: Payne, Krista, "FP-12-22 Young Adults in the Parental Home, 1940-2010" (2012). National Center for Family and Marriage Research Family Profiles. Paper 16. Retrieved from: http://scholarworks.bgsu.edu/cgi/viewcontent. cgi?article=1015&context=ncfmr_family_profiles.

5. What percentage of adults are remarried at mid-life?

   a. 2 percent

   b. 20 percent

   c. 5 percent

   d. 50 percent

6. According to this graph, in which age group did divorce not increase over the past 20 years?

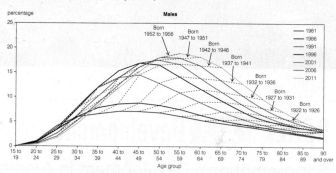

   a. emerging adulthood

   b. young adulthood

   c. mid-life

   d. older adulthood

7. Which of the following is *not* one of the top three criteria for mid-life divorce?

   a. sexual issues

   b. physical abuse

   c. stepchildren

   d. different points of view

8. What trend reveals a new family formation pattern in mid-life?

   a. divorce; remarriage to same partner in mid-life

   b. couples living apart together

   c. high rates of remaining single

   d. marriages as a consequence of online dating

9. How do middle-aged adults adjust to caregiving demands?

    a. Poor mental health is associated with caregiving in mid-life.

    b. Caregiving is both stressful and rewarding.

    c. Caregiving is stressful for men but rewarding for women.

    d. Providing care to aging mothers is stressful, but providing care to aging fathers is rewarding.

10. The sandwich generation are middle-aged parents who _____.

    a. provide care for two or more adult children

    b. care for self and care for parents

    c. care for children and care for parents

    d. care for children and a spouse

11. What does the socio-emotional selectivity theory state?

    a. People in mid-life invest positive emotions in things they value.

    b. People in mid-life invest intense emotions in memories.

    c. People in mid-life selectively remember only positive events.

    d. People in mid-life selectively remember only negative events.

12. Adult friendships are *not* known for providing _____.

    a. a context for doing marriage work

    b. nurturing support

    c. instrumental support for identity work

    d. economic support

13. All of these mid-life changes in Big Five personality traits reflect the maturity principle *except* _____.

    a. increases in conscientiousness

    b. increases in introversion

    c. increases in agreeableness

    d. decreases in neuroticism

14. Based on this graph, which statement most accurately reflects hedonic well-being in mid-life?

    a. Well-being declines steadily in mid-life.

    b. Well-being peaks in mid-life.

    c. Well-being plateaus in mid-life.

    d. Well-being is stable across adulthood, including mid-life.

Population aged 12 and older who reported being satisfied or very satisfied with their life in general, 2014

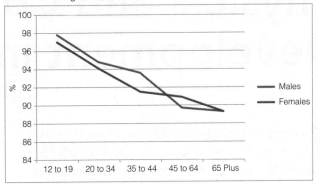

15. Middle adulthood is associated with fewer gender type expectations, which encourages men and women to _____.

    a. embrace femininity and the nurturing parts of self

    b. embrace masculinity and the aggressive parts of self

    c. balance masculine and feminine parts of self

    d. work toward a gender-neutral self

THE PLANNER ✓

Review your Chapter Planner in the chapter opener and check off your completed work.

Physical and Cognitive Development in the Later Years

Volunteering is only one way Ms. Luvia spends her time. Retired after working at the bank for 37 years, she spends three days a week mentoring young entrepreneurs in a local community program. On the other days, she meets a friend for a late lunch. Before the end of each day, she gets in at least a brief neighbourhood walk. Although she didn't think she'd find a way to put her life together again after her husband Javi unexpectedly passed away six years ago at only 66, she's happy now. Not only that, she's proud. She's the one who teaches her friends how to Facetime their grandkids.

Aging is inevitable. However, people all over the world are living healthier, longer lives. At the turn of the twenty-first century, the world population over the age of 60 was greater than the number of children below age 5.

As you might guess, now that you have followed the story of human development from birth into the seventh decade of the lifespan, there is much that is new and many opportunities for achieving one's potential in the later years. As we continue our journey through the final decades of the lifespan, be certain to pay attention to the balance of gains and losses during these important years.

Alpamayo Photo/iStockphoto

CHAPTER PLANNER ✔

- ❑ Study the picture and read the opening story.
- ❑ Scan the Learning Objectives in each section:
  p. 482 ❑   p. 488 ❑   p. 492 ❑   p. 495 ❑
- ❑ Read the text and study all visuals. Answer any questions.

Analyze key features

- ❑ Development InSight, p. 491
- ❑ What a Developmentalist Sees, p. 493
- ❑ Process Diagram, p. 499
- ❑ Challenges in Development, p. 500
- ❑ Stop: Answer the Concept Checks before you go on:
  p. 488 ❑   p. 492 ❑   p. 494 ❑   p. 501 ❑

End of chapter

- ❑ Review the Summary and Key Terms.
- ❑ Answer the Critical and Creative Thinking Questions.
- ❑ Answer *What is happening in this picture?*
- ❑ Complete the Self-Test and check your answers.

The Aging Process

LEARNING OBJECTIVES

1. **Discuss** the current trends in aging as reflected in life expectancy, median survival time, and lifespan.

2. **Outline** the various theories of physical aging.

By age 60, all people recognize signs of aging. As you have learned, when we speak about physical signs of aging that take place across adulthood and most rapidly at the end of the lifespan, we use the term "senescence" to describe this process. Like the words "senility" and "senior", senescence is derived from the Latin term *senex*, which means old.

A Statistical Picture of Aging

One of the big questions developmental researchers have been asking over time is, what factors predict healthy, long lives? One approach to this question is to study differences in the number of years people stay healthy and alive. Population studies compare different countries to identify differences between living conditions that help explain why some people who live in certain conditions live longer, healthier, happier lives (**Figure 15.1**). The most common statistic used to compare the health of older adults in various countries is average life expectancy at birth.

We can also learn a great deal about health and aging by studying life expectancy *within* a population. For example, in Canada, census data show that life expectancy varies according to gender (**Figure 15.2a**). In addition, Aboriginal Canadians have a shorter life expectancy than non-Aboriginal Canadians (**Figure 15.2b**). In 2001, for example, life expectancy was 71 years for Aboriginal men and 77 years for Aboriginal women, which is approximately 5 years lower than the life expectancy for non-Aboriginal Canadians born at the same time (Statistics Canada, 2008a). One of the more common mistakes made in discussions on aging is confusion of the terms "life expectancy" and **lifespan**. According to Guinness World Records, the

> **lifespan** The highest boundary or limit of a particular species.

oldest verified living person was Jeanne Calment, who died in 1997 at 122 (Guinness Book of Records, 2009), though there may be older persons unrecorded. Thus, the human lifespan is 122 years, although most of us cannot expect to live anywhere near as long.

In the coming years, the field of **gerontology**, the study of aging, will continue to expand. As the population lives longer, gerontologists have plenty of opportunity to learn from older people. The elderly portion of

> **gerontology** An area of social science that studies the physical, cognitive, and socio-emotional issues in later adulthood.

Life expectancy around the world • Figure 15.1

North Americans may have access to significant resources, but Canada cannot boast that its citizens have the longest life expectancy. The countries with the longest life expectancy are Monaco (89), Macau (84), Japan (84), Singapore, (84), and San Marino (83). Canada (81) ranks 14th, tied with Liechtenstein, France, Jersey, and Norway (The World Factbook, 2014).

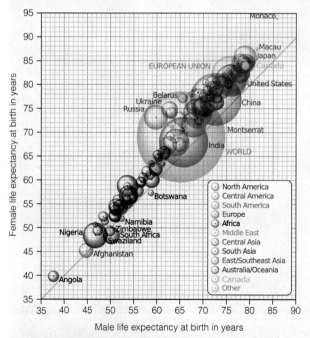

Source: *The World Factbook*, Washington, DC: Central Intelligence Agency, 2014.

Think Critically How might life expectancy shape the stages of development that a male experiences in Afghanistan? India?

Life expectancy in Canada • Figure 15.2

a. Life expectancy at birth in years, by gender
A Canadian's life expectancy at birth has been steadily climbing since 1900 and is predicted to continue to climb.

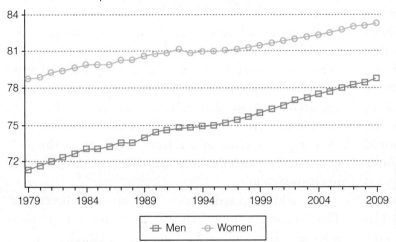

b. Life expectancy at birth in years, by sex, Registered First Nations* and Canadian population

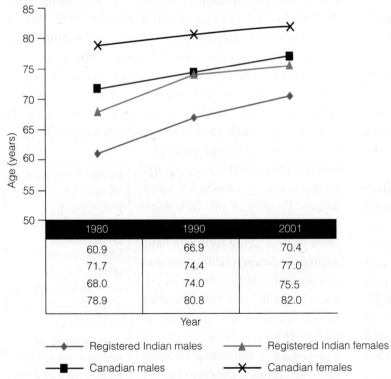

	1980	1990	2001
	60.9	66.9	70.4
	71.7	74.4	77.0
	68.0	74.0	75.5
	78.9	80.8	82.0

Year

◆ Registered Indian males   ▲ Registered Indian females
■ Canadian males   ✕ Canadian females

*Includes on- and off-reserve populations for all provinces and territories.

Think Critically **1.** In what decade was life expectancy closest for men and women? How do Registered Indian females compare to Canadian females and males? How do Registered Indian males compare to the other three groups?
2. Thinking back to the chapter opener, how might Ms. Luvia's life story have been different if she and her husband had married before 1900? What if they had been Aboriginal?

the North American population is growing quickly. Today, Canadian males and females are living to advanced ages beyond what their ancestors could imagine. If we examine the mortality that prevailed in 1931, less than 60 percent of males and 62 percent of females survived to age 65, compared to 2001 when 84 percent of males and more than 90 percent of females lived to age 65 (Statistics Canada, 2008b). According to the Centers for Disease Control and Prevention (2013), there are several trends suggesting that the U.S. population will be very grey soon. During the next 40 years, people over the age of 65 are expected to more than double in the United States. This segment is projected to grow from approximately 40 million in 2010 to 83 million by 2050 (Werner, 2011).

Canada is also greying, due mostly to longer life expectancy. Canadian life expectancy at birth has been steadily climbing since the 1920s. Note that these statistics are just expectancy at birth; the older a person gets, the higher his or her probability of living longer (Arias, 2004). By 2031, average life expectancy in Canada is projected to have risen to 81.9 for males and 86.0 for females, with the gap between the sexes continuing to narrow (Statistics Canada, 2008b).

Clarke has documented that the steady increase in life expectancy over the past centuries has been attributed to improved nutrition, better hygiene, access to safe drinking water, effective birth control and immunization, and other medical interventions. At every stage of the life cycle, males are more likely than females to die. This difference, evident since industrialization, has created a gender gap in life expectancy. Although life expectancy is increasing, not all years will necessarily be spent in full health; on average, Canadians can expect to spend 70 of 80 years in good health (Clarke, 1990).

People with lower incomes, those living in poorer neighbourhoods, and people residing in the Inuit-inhabited areas tend to have shorter life expectancies than do other Canadians (Statistics Canada, 2004; Wilkins, Uppal, Finès, Senécal, Guimond, & Dion, 2008; Berthelot, Wilkins, & Ng, 2002; Wilkins, Adams, & Brancker, 1988). Canadians who live in relatively good conditions can expect to live longer—well into their 80s. This is also true in the world population. Current global trends suggest that the number of people over 85 is projected to grow from today's 40 million to 219 million in 2050 (WHO, 2011).

centenarian
Someone who is 100 years old or older.

Even the group of society's oldest, the **centenarians**, is growing. In 2005, there were approximately 71,000 individuals 100 or older, but by 2050, thanks to an ever-increasing life expectancy, it is predicted that there will be 3.2 million celebrating triple-digit birthdays.

Global life expectancy has increased from 64 years in 1990 to 70 years in 2011. A great deal of this increase is due to a decrease in child mortality and health improvements in large countries such as China and India. During the same time period, life expectancy has decreased in countries where resources are limited: North Korea, South Africa, Lesotho, Zimbabwe, and Libya (WHO, 2013).

young-old Adults in their later years, traditionally between the ages of 60 and 75, who are still healthy, active, and independent.

old-old Adults in their later years, traditionally between the ages of 75 and 85, who are beginning to deal with declining health.

oldest-old Adults in their later years, traditionally over the age of 85, who are at risk for illness and injury and are often dependent on others for assistance with daily living activities.

The elderly are sometimes divided into three groups based on a combination of their age, health level, and well-being. The **young-old** are traditionally healthy, active, independent people between the ages of 60 and 75. The **old-old** range in age from 75 to 85 and are beginning to deal with loss of spouses and are declining in health. The **oldest-old** are those who are dependent, are at risk for illness and injury, and are often over the age of 85. This group is often living in some type of assisted living facility. As the number of elderly increases, the need to understand this stage of life and its inherent benefits and challenges becomes even more essential.

Theories of Physical Aging

Although we all agree that humans age, there is disagreement about the specific path the aging process takes. For example, the general assumption is that all physical systems decline. Although this is true overall, research suggests that various systems may begin to decline at different times. For example, the muscular system may decline at a different rate from the skeletal system, which declines at a different rate from the nervous system.

In addition, senescence may be multidirectional. That is, some systems may actually improve their functioning while others decline. For example, we see physical decline in certain areas of the brain even as cognitive functioning increases (Burgmans et al., 2009) or remains stable (Van Petten, 2004). In addition, different tissues in the same system may decline at different rates. For example, contracting muscles decline faster than do lengthening muscles (Cech & Martin, 2002). We all agree, however, that although aging may be multidirectional, it is inescapable. Given this reality, many researchers dedicate their careers to understanding aging, often turning to funding sources such as the Canadian Institutes of Health Research: Institute of Aging to support their work. (See *Where Developmentalists Click.*)

Like every developmental process we have discussed up to this point, aging is caused by many factors. In spite of this fact, some theorists still attempt to explain physiological aging with one basic approach. Semsei (2000) categorizes the varied approaches into two main branches: **program theories of aging** and **error theories of aging**. However, because physiological decline and biological aging occur as a result of the convergence of these processes, the explanatory power of the various theories lies in understanding how biological risk and environmental stress interact to affect the aging process (Ekerdt, 2002; Semsei, 2000).

program theory of aging A theory that aging occurs because of some predetermined internal or external chemical process built into cells that cause deterioration over time.

error theory of aging A theory that aging occurs because of environmental forces such as disease that affect the function of cells, causing deterioration.

The Institute of Aging: Canadian Institutes of Health Research

The Institute of Aging is one of the institutes that is part of the Canadian Institutes of Health Research (www.cihr-irsc.gc.ca), Canada's federal agency to fund health research. The Institute of Aging's mission is to advance scholarship on aging to improve not only health, but also quality of life for older Canadians.

From their homepage, you can search for Canadian research centres on aging and other associations. The Institute of Aging is a major funding source for ongoing research on aging, including several of the studies cited in this chapter.

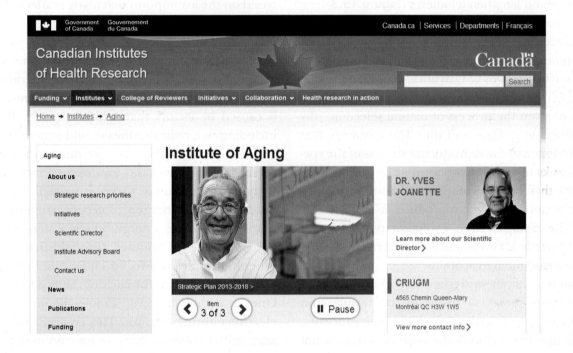

Program theories of aging One important program theory of aging focuses on the process of cell division. In an earlier chapter, we discussed the process of mitosis, in which cells divide to produce two identical cells. Bio-gerontologist Leonard Hayflick (Hayflick, 1965; 1985) suggested that with each cell division, a subtle structural change occurs. Hayflick observed that fetal cells divide normally approximately 60 times in culture. After the 60th division, the molecular structure of cells begins to decline. Thus, he proposed that cells are programmed with an internal clock that creates a finite limit of times for division or replication, a concept known as **Hayflick's limit** (Hayflick, 1965). Hayflick's theory has been associated with programmed death theories and biological clocks (Gavrilov & Gavrilova, 2002).

> **Hayflick's limit**
> The number of times a cell can divide during the lifespan based on a predetermined number of cell divisions.

Since Hayflick began his research in the early 1960s, our knowledge of the composition of cells, particularly DNA, has expanded tremendously (Berry & Watson, 2003; Dennis & Clayton, 2003). Recent support for Hayflick's theory has come from understanding a region of chromosomes called *telomeres* (Double & Thomson, 2002; de Magalhaes & Toussaint, 2004). Each time a cell divides throughout the lifespan of an organism, telomeres shorten. When telomeres reach a short enough length, they signal the cell to stop dividing (Greider, 1998; Nosek & Tomáska, 2008). For a while scientists believed that simple telomere shortening was the key factor responsible for cell death. Recent research suggests, however, that other proteins may be involved, complicating the simple explanation of telomere length (de Magalhaes & Faragher, 2008).

One of these complicating factors was the discovery of telomerase, an enzyme present in cancer cells (Collins & Mitchell, 2002). Researchers found that the telomerase present in cancer cells replaced any telomere cells lost during replication. This causes cancer cells to continue to divide (Blasco & Hahn, 2003; Hiyama, 2009). Scientists are now targeting telomerase as a potential fountain of youth, hoping to get the enzyme to target normal cells and not cancer cells (Hiyama, 2009). In just the past few years, aging research has begun to tap into methods that stimulate telomerase activity and lengthen telomeres (**Figure 15.3**).

Evolutionary theories of aging are another category of programmed theories. Just like other theories of aging, evolutionary theories are not limited to one singular approach (Gavrilov & Gavrilova, 2004; Gavrilova & Gavrilov, 2005). They all, however, begin with one simple question: given the process of natural selection, why would any person decline and die? The answer is that evolution is designed for reproductive success of the species, not one member. If members must be sacrificed so that the species survives, evolution is served. Thus, once an organism can no longer reproduce, it is no longer necessary (Le Bourg, 2001). Evolutionary theories of aging therefore look for evidence of patterns of decline during post-reproductive capability.

One evolutionary theory is the theory of programmed cell death. This theory is based on the assumption that natural selection influences biological processes, resulting in the destruction of the organisms that do not reproduce. One example is the process called *apoptosis*, in which cells are actually programmed to self-destruct (Joaquin & Gollapudi, 2001). During apoptosis, enzymes are produced to remove any damaged or deteriorating cells by breaking down their chemical structure. This process prevents any further replication. Apoptosis occurs with greater frequency as we age.

Although both of the programmed theories we discussed have some scientific support, they do not fully explain the aging process. The next group of theories is based on the assumption that aging is affected by outside forces.

Error theories of aging Unlike programmed theories, in which cells have some internal program or clock that limits replication, error theories suggest that aging is caused by factors that attack normal cell processes, including free radicals, disease, and genetic mutation.

In order to explain the free radical theory of aging, we must first understand how oxygen molecules in the body transport energy. Oxygen molecules are found in most cells. Each oxygen molecule contains mitochondria that produce energy, which is transported from one molecule to another through shared electrons. When molecules divide, an equal number of electrons are usually available for each of the two new molecules. Once in a while, however, a molecule will lose one of its electrons during division. This creates a state of imbalance called *oxidation*. Now we have an oxygen molecule

Reversing aging • Figure 15.3

Scientists study telomeres to estimate a person's disease risk and rate of aging. A recent study of 35 men with prostate cancer followed for five years showed that significant lifestyle changes resulted in an increase in telomere length.

a. The intervention involved a plant-based diet, an exercise program (30 minutes, 6 days/week), stress management (yoga), and a social support group.

Microgen/iStockphoto

b. The 10 men who participated in a significant lifestyle change program experienced an increase in telomere length, whereas non-participants experienced a decrease.

Telomere length

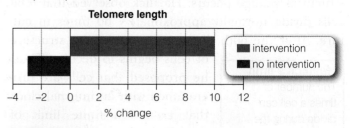

intervention
no intervention

% change

Think Critically Which of the four components of the lifestyle intervention sought to reduce biological risks, and which sought to reduce environmental risks for aging?

in search of another electron. This cell is now called a *free radical.*

Free radicals are destructive by nature: they attack molecules in their search for electrons. This search may damage DNA and other cells such as lipids and proteins that are essential for normal body function. The body typically prevents free radical damage by absorbing any extra electrons (Wilcox, 2009). However, with age, the body becomes unable to stop free radicals (Chakravarti & Chakravarti, 2007). Thus, the result of oxidative damage, according to free radical theory, is aging (Baskin & Salem, 1997; Harman, 1956; Stohs, 1995).

Research suggests that a group of chemicals called *antioxidants* can reduce the number of free radicals (Halliwell & Gutteridge, 2007). Antioxidants, such as vitamins E and C and beta-carotene, can be found in fruits and vegetables or in vitamin supplements (Kumpulainen & Salonen, 1999). There is some disagreement, however, concerning the specific damage done by free radicals and the role of antioxidants. For example, Van Raamsdonk and Hekimi (2009) removed the antioxidant molecules from worms and found that they actually lived longer in spite of having more free radicals. They concluded that perhaps free radicals are the product of aging rather than vice versa. More research needs to be conducted to provide more adequate support for a free radical theory of aging (Raha & Robinson, 2000; Valko, Leibfritz, Moncol, Cronin, Mazur, & Telser, 2007).

As we begin to consider disease theory, another type of error theory, let us recall the leading causes of death for each developmental segment. Until middle adulthood, the leading cause of death is unintentional injury and accidents. Once we reach middle adulthood, however, humans start to die in large numbers because of disease. Disease theory takes these observations into account, suggesting that how certain systems in the body cope with disease and breakdown affects the aging process.

The developing human body generally operates in a system of balances called *homeostasis.* As we age, outside forces such as bacteria and viruses meet up with a deteriorating immune system, disrupting homeostasis. As homeostasis declines, breakdowns occur in cardiovascular, muscular, skeletal, and other key systems in the body. Thus, according to disease theory, these externally created breakdowns are the cause of aging.

The final type of error theory that we will consider focuses on genetic mutations. Our genes may be a significant determinant of how we age, as can be observed in identical twins (**Figure 15.4**). When cells divide, there is a chance that some of the DNA within our cells will undergo a mutation or some type of negative process that interferes with normal recombination (Gavrilov & Gavrilova, 2002). When this happens repeatedly, cells get damaged. According to genetic mutation theories of aging, the consequence is aging (Charlesworth, 2001).

Wear and tear theory Although space limitations prevent us from covering all of the scientific theories of senescence, we end this section with one final approach that has been around for a long time. This theory suggests that the longer we live, the more likely our tissues will wear down and eventually die. Scientists call this the **wear and tear theory.**

> **wear and tear theory** A theory that suggests the human body ages as a result of use, overuse, and environmental stressors.

The wear and tear theory first became part of the scientific literature in 1882 when introduced by German biologist August Weismann. He suggested that people age because their bodies become worn down by environmental stressors such as physical trauma, environmental toxins, and overuse. Wear and tear theorists often compare the human body to a car. Just like a car, the human body decreases in efficiency over time. The body is also made up of parts. Just as in a car, there is an increase in part failure the more each part is used.

Aging in tandem • Figure 15.4 _____

These monozygotic twins illustrate how similar the aging process often is for identical twins.

Image BROKER/Alamy

Think Critically 1. What does a photo like this tell us about the role of genes in aging?
2. What other factors could explain the similarity of these women?

The car analogy falls short when it comes to repair, however. Wear and tear theory suggests that certain body parts can repair themselves over time (Gavrilov & Gavrilova, 2004; Steinsaltz & Goldwasser, 2009). One example is brain plasticity, in which neurons create new connections when others die (Tortora, 2008). With age, however, wear and tear theory predicts that the body loses its ability to engage in self-repair.

Wear and tear theory is still often discussed but is generally considered outdated. With improvements in microbiological technology, scientists were able to get a better look at the cellular structures that compose human body systems. Wear and tear theory, like theories of programmed cell death and cellular error theories, are now considered flawed. Specifically, there is circular reasoning from associating aging with wear and tear. That is, aging may cause the tear, not the wear (Gavrilov &

Gavrilova, 2004). In fact, physical use of the body seems to slow the aging process.

Although all theories of aging seem to have one or more shortcomings, taken in combination they provide a solid overview of the aging process. All in all, we know that all humans age. We also know that many things may slow it down, such as exercise and diet. Finally, we know that nothing will stop it.

CONCEPT CHECK

1. **How** does a species' life expectancy differ from its lifespan?

2. **What** is the key weakness of wear and tear theory?

Physical Development

LEARNING OBJECTIVES

1. **Describe** the key physical changes in the aging brain.

2. **Discuss** the skeletal diseases that may appear in later adulthood.

3. **Explain** how the muscular system changes during later adulthood.

A As we have established, the physical systems do decline in later adulthood. Regardless, there is great variation and individual differences in the rate and progression of that decline. First, we examine the nervous system. The brain, in particular, is a driving force of the aging process.

The Nervous System

Conventional wisdom suggests that the most important organ in the body is the brain. It is hard to argue against this idea. The brain contains the memories, commands, and programs necessary for a person to participate in daily life. Thus, an aging brain can result in many consequences.

The aging brain

Whole brain volume changes across the lifespan. Waves of growth occur in early adolescence, between ages 9 and 13 and again in young adulthood from ages 18 to 35. After age 35 there is a decrease in brain volume, which accelerates in volume loss with age, as shown in **Figure 15.5** (Hedman, van Haren, Schnack, Kahn, & Hulshoff Pol, 2012). Greater decrease in brain volume at older ages is correlated with reduced cognitive abilities (Rushton & Ankney, 2009) and slower reaction times (Deary & Der, 2005; Der & Deary, 2006).

The relationship between brain size and mental ability, however, remains unclear (Rushton & Ankney, 2009). For example, adults lose volume in the prefrontal cortex, yet they use their prefrontal cortex more than adolescents do (Burgmans et al., 2009; Grady, 2007; Greenwood, 2007; Mayr, 2008; Van Petten, 2004). These paradoxical findings suggest that older adults may be adjusting to the anatomical changes in their frontal lobes by using different strategies for everyday situations. These changes result in functional brain plasticity (Greenwood, 2007).

Brain volume with age • Figure 15.5

A review of over 50 studies of healthy brains revealed a pattern of increases and decreases in volume across the lifespan. Magnetic resonance imaging (MRI) studies showed an increase in brain volume from late childhood through early adolescence. Following this volume spurt, the brain decreases in volume until the next volume spurt, which takes place between ages 18 and 35. After age 35, the brain loses volume relatively slowly. The volume decreases accelerate until age 60, after which even more significant yearly volume loss takes place.

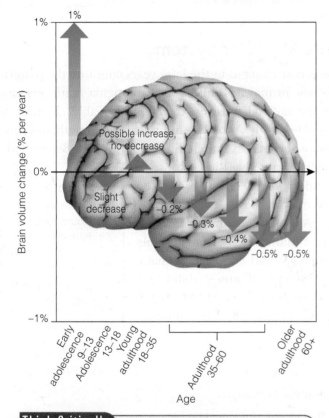

Think Critically Although these data are compelling, they are correlational, not causational. Can you think of a third variable that might influence the gains and loss in volume across the lifespan?

These findings indicate that volume loss may have little to no bearing on function.

Cardiovascular changes

As the nervous system declines, so does the cardiovascular system. This is particularly troublesome because the cardiovascular system supplies oxygen to all the other systems, including the brain. Scientists largely agree that the cardiovascular system declines with age (Ferrari, Radaelli, & Centola, 2003; Uchino, Holt-Lunstad, Bloor, & Campo, 2005). There are changes in resting blood pressure, increases in cholesterol, and diminishing lung capacity. There are also significant increases in cardiovascular diseases such as strokes, heart attacks, and atherosclerosis, or hardening of the arteries (Cheitlin & Zipes, 2001; Uchino et al., 2005).

Cardiovascular disease is a leading cause of death for older adults in Canada and other industrialized nations (Best, 2009; Kochanek, Murphy, Anderson, & Scott, 2004; Statistics Canada, 2014). This type of disease develops from a decrease in the flexibility of veins and arteries accompanied by diminishing efficiency of the heart muscle to pump (Tortora, 2008). Because aging is associated with less activity, it is not surprising that consequences to the cardiovascular system are arteriosclerosis and coronary artery disease.

Changes in the cardiovascular system also result in cognitive changes. As the heart becomes less efficient, less oxygen gets to the brain (Verhaeghen, Borchelt, & Smith, 2003; Waldstein & Elias, 2001). Alongside these key changes, the skeletal system also begins to show signs of senescence.

The Skeletal System

The most common issue in the skeletal system as people age has to do with loss of bone mass due to diminishing minerals and calcium (Davisson et al., 2009). Bone loss weakens the bones, increasing the risk of brittleness and fracture (Tortora, 2008). We will now discuss this issue, called *osteoporosis*, and another key skeletal issue, rheumatism.

Rheumatism

Rheumatism is the name given to pain in the bones, ligaments, tendons, or muscles not caused by accidents. Rheumatism, in one form or another, is the leading cause of lack of mobility in the elderly (U.S. Department of Health and Human Services, 2004). Two main types of rheumatism primarily found in aging populations are **rheumatoid arthritis** and **osteoarthritis**. It is estimated that 4.2 million Canadians are living with arthritis. Given the aging Canadian population, the prevalence of arthritis is projected to increase by nearly one percentage point every five years over the next quarter century. It is estimated that

rheumatoid arthritis A type of arthritis classified as an autoimmune disease in which the body's own immune system causes an inflammation of tissue around joints.

osteoarthritis A type of arthritis in which the skeletal joints and tissue wear down over time.

6.7 million Canadians will have arthritic symptoms by 2031 (Public Health Agency of Canada, 2011).

Rheumatoid arthritis falls into the category of auto-immune diseases. In rheumatoid arthritis, the body's immune system causes deterioration in the cartilage and the linings of the joints between the bones. This results in swelling, pain, and significant restriction of mobility, as depicted in **Figure 15.6** (Davis, Zautra, Younger, Motivala, Attrep, & Irwin, 2008).

Osteoarthritis, the most common type of arthritis, causes cartilage of the joints to gradually diminish over time. Osteoarthritis typically results from use and abuse of the skeletal system. The most common parts of the body affected by osteoarthritis are the hands, lower back, neck, knees, and hips. Currently, there is no cure for arthritis, though certain treatments may relieve some of the pain and facilitate mobility.

The most common treatment for both types of arthritis is medication. Several drugs provide satisfactory pain relief and allow sufferers to continue their daily activities such as walking or driving. The most commonly used medications are acetaminophen and ibuprofen, which are both available without prescription. Prescription medications such as narcotic painkillers and cortisone are also effective. Some arthritis sufferers choose physical therapy, working with therapists to help increase mobility and reduce pain without the use of drugs. The most drastic treatment for arthritic symptoms is surgery. Several surgical procedures exist that can help relieve pain by either realigning bones, fusing bones, or replacing joints.

Osteoporosis Osteoporosis is a degenerative disease of the skeletal system in which bone loss, or resorption (see Chapter 13), results in weakened and brittle bones. This process is depicted in **Figure 15.7**.

> **osteoporosis** A disruption in bone remodelling causing bones to become brittle and weak.

The Muscular System

Muscular changes in the later years continue the pattern we saw in middle adulthood. Sarcopenia is still present in the skeletal muscles, causing observable changes in an older adult's mobility and posture. Strength and flexibility decrease as muscle fibre deteriorates (Baum et al., 2009; Connelly, Rice, Roos, & Vandervoot, 1999). There is also loss of body mass.

Although healthy older adults can climb stairs, walk reasonable distances, and continue to maintain functional muscle abilities, at some point their **activities of daily living (ADLs)** may be affected.

> **activities of daily living (ADLs)** The necessary behavioural function of individuals in order to meet basic survival needs, including eating, dressing, and elimination, among others.

Rheumatoid arthritis • Figure 15.6

Rheumatoid arthritis affects the internal structures of the hands, resulting in visible changes.

a. The comparison of an X-ray of a normal hand and one with rheumatoid arthritis reveals changes to bone structure, including bone displacement and bone erosion.

b. The effects of rheumatoid arthritis are clearly visible. This individual also suffers from pain and restriction of movement.

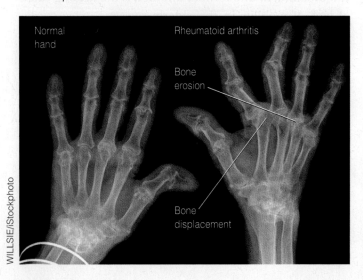

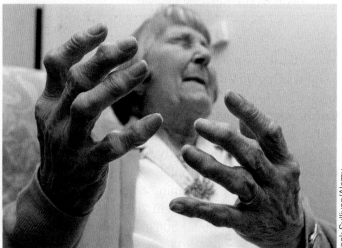

Osteoporosis is a common disease of the skeletal system. It can significantly change the appearance and mobility of older people, especially women.

a. As shown in this cross-section of a hip bone, when a person suffers from osteoporosis, bones lose minerals and calcium and become porous and brittle.

b. As a result of weakening bones in the spine and back, a person with osteoporosis may become shorter and hunched over with time.

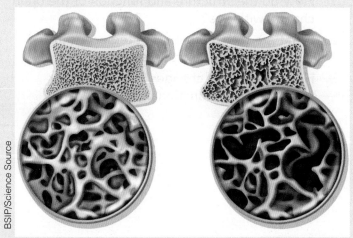

BSIP/Science Source

c. Because of their brittle bones, people with osteoporosis are at increased risk of suffering from broken bones. Hip fractures are of particular concern because up to 25 percent of elderly people die within a year of a hip fracture (Robbins, Biggs, & Cauley, 2006).

Susan H. Smith/iStockphoto

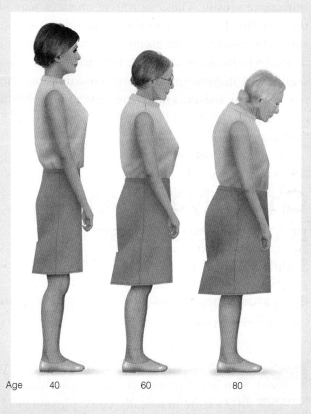

Age 40 60 80

Think Critically Given the role of physical activity in healthy aging, why are hip fractures associated with a high one-year death rate following injury?

ADLs include everyday behaviours such as dressing, eating, going to the bathroom, hygiene, and basic physical activity in the home, such as getting into and out of bed (McDowell & Newell, 1996). In order to perform these activities, muscular and skeletal systems must be strong enough to handle impact and stress. Thus, continued muscle loss and changes in the skeletal system can result in functional issues.

Healthy older adults also experience decreases in hormonal activity. These hormone changes may affect their ability to make planned sequential movements, such as getting up and going into the kitchen to grab a snack (Hajszan, Maclusky, & Leranth, 2008). Planned sequential movements require coordination among the muscular system, endocrine system, and the brain.

Scientists observe declines in this coordination in older adults, leading to slower movements. Slowing these functional declines, however, is possible through exercise. We will discuss this and other health behaviours in the next section.

CONCEPT CHECK

1. **How** do the structure and function of the brain change with age?
2. **What** are the treatment strategies for the diseases of the skeletal system?
3. **How** do physical changes in the muscular system result in functional impairment?

Cognitive Changes

LEARNING OBJECTIVES

1. **Describe** changes in attention in later adulthood.
2. **Discuss** what happens to memory during later adulthood.
3. **Explain** the concept of wisdom.

O ur discussion now turns to cognitive changes in later adulthood. Given that declines take place in practically every physiological system, it is not surprising that cognitive ability also declines (Rabbitt, 1993). Like all the other changes in later adulthood, these declines vary in timing and degree.

Information-Processing Changes

As we have discussed in earlier chapters, information-processing approaches to cognition generally focus on quantitative issues. This seems particularly relevant when discussing cognitive changes in older adults. The abilities to maintain a conversation, read a newspaper, watch a television program, or read the instructions that accompany medication all require information processing.

Attention

The visual environment contains both relevant and irrelevant information. The ability to distinguish between these two categories, a process called **selective attention**, is essential for adults to negotiate their worlds. Sometimes selectively attending is easy, such as when noticing a dark stain on a white shirt. Other situations are more difficult, such as being able to pick out a friend coming off an airplane. As visual systems decline, selective attention of these latter, more subtle situations may be affected (Madden, 2007; Salthouse, 2006).

One of the key distinctions in evaluating attention in older adults is to assess differences in **top-down processing** versus **bottom-up processing**. Although researchers have been able to separate these functions for the

selective attention The ability to attend to a particular item in the environment while inhibiting other distracting stimuli.

top-down processing Forming perceptions beginning with a more general idea and then working toward more detailed information.

bottom-up processing Forming perceptions from the smaller, finer details and then building upward into a solid, general idea.

purpose of testing, they report that attention requires both abilities (Madden, 2007).

Top-down processing involves higher-level thought processes that drive attention, such as executive function. For example, while waiting at the airport for your friend to arrive, you know she has red hair so you watch for this colour. Bottom-up processing occurs at the sensory level. For example, as your friend comes toward you, she yells out your name, to which you respond. Thus, changes in visual acuity and auditory processing mainly affect bottom-up processing.

In general, both processing types appear to decline in older adults. Top-down processing declines faster, however, than bottom-up processing. For example, researchers have observed age-related declines in prefrontal cortex regions correlated with top-down processing and with visual attention (Dennis, Hayes, Prince, Madden, Huettel, & Cabeza 2008; Madden, 2007).

All in all, cognitive decline is accompanied by changes in brain function as well as decreases in visual and perceptual sensitivity (Blake, Rizzo, & McCoy, 2008). Not surprisingly, attention declines are also correlated with changes in memory.

Memory Findings of memory changes during later adulthood vary widely (Van Dijk, Van Gerven, Van Boxtel, Van der Elst, & Jolles, 2008). Because memory is a multi-dimensional cognitive process that includes sensory memory, working memory, and long-term memory, measurement of memory declines can be difficult. In addition, longitudinal studies of memory give the same tasks over and over again (Van Dijk et al., 2008), so memory improvement may result solely from familiarity with test questions. Another issue that affects measurement of memory is the prior experiences of the subjects with the tested task (Deary, Leaper, Murray, Staff, & Whalley, 2003).

Despite these methodological difficulties, we can draw some conclusions about memory changes in later adulthood. Individuals in higher socio-economic groups appear to retain cognitive function longer than individuals who are lower in those categories. In addition, those with better quality of life and higher educational attainment also show less cognitive loss with time (Deary et al., 2003; Salthouse, 2006). Cognitive declines occur more slowly in older adults who are socially engaged. (See *What a Developmentalist Sees.*) Eventually, though, memory declines occur in all groups.

WHAT A DEVELOPMENTALIST SEES
Technology to Keep Older Adults Connected and Cognitively Sharp

Family members may not encourage older adults to learn new technology for fear it will be too difficult, even frustrating (**Figure a**). Developmentalists aren't so quick to focus on these hurdles because they know that exercising the brain and keeping the brain healthy can help delay declines in the ability to process or store and recall information. Developmentalists know that teaching older adults to use technology can push their brains to keep working, increase working memory and attention, and provide a new way to stay socially connected with their friends and family (**Figure b**).

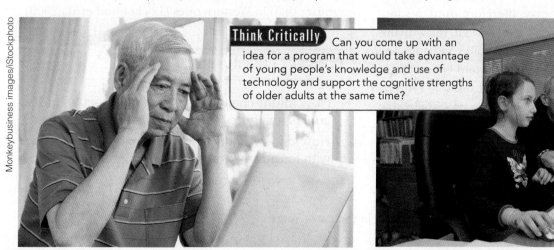

Think Critically Can you come up with an idea for a program that would take advantage of young people's knowledge and use of technology and support the cognitive strengths of older adults at the same time?

Monkeybusiness images/iStockphoto

Elizabeth Crews/Photo Edit

Working (or short-term) memory shows the most decline as we age (Laberge & Scialfa, 2005). Changes in working memory are correlated with a decrease in brain activity associated with the hippocampus. Thus, your elderly Aunt Irene cannot find her glasses, cannot find her keys, and forgets to pay her bills. She can, however, remember that day in 1976 when Uncle Herbie bought a tuxedo.

Changes in long-term memory appear to be less dramatic in older adults. Research suggests that this is because long-term memory is associated with parts of the brain that deteriorate more slowly (Raz, 2000). As a result, long-term memory changes tend to occur most rapidly when disease is present (Verhaeghen et al., 2003).

Researchers also investigate how particular types of long-term memory deteriorate. Episodic memory, a form of long-term memory for self-related events, tends to follow a distinctive forgetting curve, as shown in **Figure 15.8**. Semantic memory, or long-term memory of accumulated knowledge, declines faster than episodic memory (Bucur & Madden, 2007).

Finally, many older adults experience a particular type of forgetting in which they know they know something but just cannot think of it. This is called the **tip-of-the-tongue phenomenon**. Although everyone occasionally experiences this phenomenon, older adults experience it more frequently than adolescents or younger adults (Bucur & Madden, 2007).

tip-of-the-tongue phenomenon A feeling you know a piece of information, but you are unable to recall it.

Wisdom

Defining **wisdom** can be difficult. It is more than just knowledge and expertise, but exactly what it is can be debated. Most psychologists agree that wisdom includes some combination of common sense, experience, and personal insight along with tolerance, reason, and solid decision-making. We may therefore find wisdom somewhere between self-actualization and the ability to communicate thoughts and perceptions intelligently. Although age alone is not the sole requirement for wisdom, there is a much higher probability that we will find it in older adults than in youths.

wisdom The accumulation of knowledge and experience, along with personal insight and common sense.

Cross-cultural comparisons suggest that wisdom is perceived differently in various cultures. Industrialized and technological societies are more likely to neglect

The times we remember • Figure 15.8

This graph illustrates how many autobiographical memories middle and older adults mentioned when asked to freely recall events from their lives. As shown, they tend to not remember anything from their infancy or young childhood, and they recall a significant number of memories from their 20s compared with their 30s. They also recall memories that occurred more recently than those that occurred earlier in their lives (Rubin, Rahhal, & Poon, 1998).

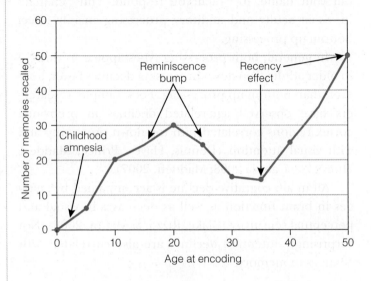

the contributions of older adults than less industrialized countries (Cowgill, 1986). In technological societies, knowledge is controlled by younger minds capable of understanding the vast new information base. As a result, Westerners tend to undervalue the contribution of older adults (Boduroglu, Yoon, Luo, & Park, 2006). The Eastern or Asian view, on the other hand, suggests an adherence to the Confucian ideal of filial piety and a reverence for ancestors. Less industrialized countries, such as Mongolia, maintain strong family contact, allowing for frequent contributions from older members of society. As a result, these cultures view older individuals as keepers of wisdom (Löckenhoff et al., 2009). All in all, researchers find a greater respect for older adults in Eastern countries than in Western ones (Löckenhoff et al., 2009).

CONCEPT CHECK STOP

1. **How** might changes in attention affect an older adult's ability to interact socially?

2. **How** does working memory change compared with long-term memory during later adulthood?

3. **How** is wisdom related to culture?

All the Systems Working Together

LEARNING OBJECTIVES

1. **Describe** the changes in sensation and perception during later adulthood.

2. **Discuss** the connection between exercise, nutrition, and aging.

3. **Differentiate** the types of dementia.

Throughout our lives, we rely on our five senses to take in information from the environment. During later adulthood, however, we lose some sensory abilities, potentially affecting our ability to enjoy food, good music, or a drive to the store. The good news is that the decline is slow and there is technology available to help us in the later years.

Sensation and Perception

Arguably, our most important sense is vision. We will start there.

Vision The visual decline that began in middle adulthood continues and becomes more significant in the later years (Lee, Gomez-Marin, Lam, Zheng, & Jane, 2004). Presbyopia, discussed in Chapter 13, continues as the eyes change their shape and become smaller. The lens hardens and becomes less flexible, causing difficulty with depth perception. The retina becomes less sensitive to light, causing difficulty seeing at night. Many activities, such as reading, going for a walk, or watching television, are affected by changing visual status as people age (Jones, Crews, Rovner, & Danielson, 2009). In addition to normal vision loss, some older adults also face diseases of the eye. Although these diseases can affect all age groups, they become more common with age.

As we age, our tear ducts become more susceptible to outside influences. They also experience structural changes. As a result, older adults may have blocked tear ducts, resulting in dry eyes or an overflow of tears that accumulate on the side of the eye. These problems can be treated by simple surgery to unblock the tear duct.

Floaters are pieces of tissue that come loose in the fluid inside the eye. Older adults experience them as spots that seem to float across the eye. They tend to be more annoying than dangerous; however, they should be checked because they can be a sign of retinal separation or tearing.

Cataracts are shaded areas on the lens of the eye, as shown in **Figure 15.9**. They can be treated surgically.

> **cataract** Shading and discoloration of the lens of the eye.

Seeing through cataracts • Figure 15.9

Cataracts are a common vision impairment in older adults. They can be treated surgically.

a. Cataracts cloud the lens of the eye, giving the pupil a cloudy look. This cloudiness blocks the light passing through the lens.

b. Blockage of light causes visual impairment. The top photo depicts normal vision, whereas the bottom photo shows the same scene through an eye affected by cataracts.

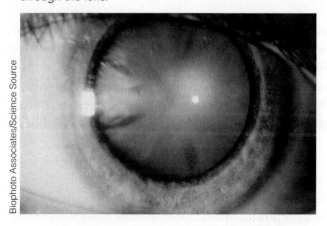

Normal Vision

Cataract

Biophoto Associates/Science Source

National Eye Institute, National Institutes of Health

National Eye Institute, National Institutes of Health

Fluid between the cornea and lens generally flows unimpeded through the eye. In some cases, however, a blockage restricts the flow of this fluid, causing an increase in pressure inside the eye. This increased pressure is called **glaucoma**. Early treatment is important because glaucoma can lead to significant vision problems.

Age-related macular degeneration (AMD) is the leading cause of vision loss for older adults (Schilling & Wahl, 2006). AMD is the deterioration of the central region in the retina, which causes significant visual difficulty. According to the Canadian National Institute for the Blind (CNIB), it affects many more people than breast cancer, prostate cancer, Parkinson's disease, and Alzheimer's disease combined and is the leading cause of vision loss in Canadians. It is estimated that more than one million Canadians have AMD (CNIB, 2015). Early treatment can be effective; however, in its mid- to late stages, treatments can only slow vision loss, not reverse it. The main approach to treating AMD is visual rehabilitation, which teaches people how to use their remaining vision more effectively, often by using a variety of visual and adaptive devices (Bambara, Wadley, Owsley, Martin, Porter, & Dreer, 2009; Owsley, McGwin, Scilley, Dreer, Bray, & Mason, 2006).

Hearing Deterioration of hearing is a prevalent debilitating chronic condition that older adults face (Tun, McCoy, & Wingfield, 2009). The anatomical causes of hearing loss that we discussed in Chapter 13 continue in later adulthood. As a result, most individuals over the age of 75 report either partial or significant hearing loss (Lethbridge-Ceijku, Schiller, & Bernadel, 2004).

Hearing loss can affect one's ability to attend to conversations and may be related to short-term memory issues (Tun et al., 2009). Hearing loss also results in safety concerns. For example, the inability to hear the high-pitched chirp of a smoke detector could have life-threatening consequences.

Taste and smell Taste and smell are related senses that both decline as we get older (Murphy & Withee, 1986). Studies of healthy older adults report declines in olfactory (smell) sensation earlier than gustatory (taste). Both impairments may affect quality of life, such as in the enjoyment of food or wine (Schiffman, 2007).

There are also safety and functional issues related to these declines. For one, taste and smell give us cues to when food has spoiled, protecting us from dangerous bouts of food poisoning. In addition, odour is important for the detection of fire or poisonous toxins. Finally, researchers are finding connections between odour receptors and memory ability (Kareken, Mosnik, Doty, Dzemidzic, & Hutchins, 2003).

Touch and pain Age appears to be associated with a diminishing ability to feel sensations (Guyton & Hall, 2005). Thus, sensations such as cold and heat have higher thresholds as we age. In general, however, older adults tend not to report concerns about touching ability (Hooper, 2009).

On the other hand, pain may be a large part of older adults' lives. The deteriorating skeletal and muscular systems can cause reports of chronic pain among elderly individuals (Herr & Garand, 2001). In fact, many seniors believe that pain is a part of life, and so they do not get proper evaluation for chronic pain. Even if pain is assessed by a doctor, treatment is difficult because there is a risk of side effects from pain medications in elderly populations (Gagliese & Melzack, 1997).

Although noticeable changes in sensation and perception are happening, older adults remain in control of their health and well-being in various ways, as we will see.

Health and Well-Being

As we have documented, people in Canada are living longer than ever. Although these extra years bring many benefits, they also introduce new challenges to the health profession. If you live to age 70, you will almost certainly be visiting health care facilities on a regular basis. When you do, the first person you will interact with might be a gerontological nurse.

Gerontological nurses Life expectancies in North America have reached record levels. As a result, the fastest growing age group is people over the age of 85 (Alliance for Aging Research, 2002). Approximately 50 percent of patients in hospitals are over the age of 65 (Centers for Disease Control and Prevention, 2002). These data provide evidence for the need for gerontological (geriatric) nursing, which focuses on the requirements of older adult populations. In addition to administering medical care to their patients, gerontological nurses serve as educators and caregivers and commonly provide emotional or spiritual care (Mion, 2003). Gerontological nurses work in a variety of settings, including hospitals, doctors' offices, nursing homes, long-term care facilities, assisted living facilities, and individuals' homes.

Nursing schools have been slow to respond to the upcoming surge of elderly adults in need of health care (Mion, 2003). Nursing education programs have been dealing with a nursing shortage for years—a shortage that is even more critical in the area of gerontological nursing (Berliner & Ginzberg, 2002; Buckwalter, 2009). In spite of this demand, less than 50 percent of nursing programs have a full-time faculty member who specializes in gerontological nursing (Mion, 2003). Furthermore, while gerontological content was found to be integrated into the majority of programs, only 8 percent of clinical hours had a focus on the nursing care of older adults and only 5.5 percent of students chose geriatrics for their final clinical practicum prior to graduation. Researchers have called for an expanded view of gerontological studies, including the potential for interdisciplinary gerontology education in the health sciences and the need to address ageism in the nursing profession (Baumbusch & Andrusyszyn, 2002).

One area that does seem to be improving is older adult exercise programs. As we will see, the research is clear: the more you exercise and the better you eat, the longer and healthier your life becomes (Cook, 2007). This effect is experienced even at the cellular level (Puterman, Lin, Blackburn, O'Donovan, Adler, & Epel, 2010).

Diet and exercise The biggest nutritional issue among older adults is overeating. Older adults have lower calorie needs than when they were younger but often continue to eat using old habits. Overeating leads to a surplus in calories that may be difficult for older adults to burn off unless they are vigilant about increasing exercise. If they don't reduce calories, older adults risk weight gain and related health burdens.

Another area of concern is mineral and vitamin deficiency. Many illnesses and diseases deplete vitamin supplies. In addition, certain medications interfere with mineral and vitamin stores. In order to combat overeating and vitamin/mineral deficiencies, nutritionists suggest that older adults eat nutrient-dense, fibre-rich foods. As an easy way to meet this goal, the U.S. Department of Agriculture suggests that all meals should contain foods of three different colours.

Healthy food choices should be combined with an active lifestyle. The role of exercise in the improvement of quality of life among older adults is well documented (Cook, 2007; Takata et al., 2008). Regular exercise in people over 65 has been correlated with increased independence (Renaud & Bherer, 2005), improvement in brain function (Colcombe & Kramer, 2003), better overall health, and a measurable slowdown of the aging process (Deary, Whalley, Batty, & Starr, 2006). People who exercise also report feeling better. In addition, research suggests that active adults live longer, have fewer chronic diseases, experience better overall functioning of motor skills, and demonstrate improved mental health. Exercise also reduces the risk of cardiovascular disease, osteoporosis, hypertension, and obesity.

Healthy activity for older adults is not restricted to exercise and nutrition. Older adults report that sexuality is an important part of their lives. In some cases, however, the aging process may interfere with normal sexual behaviour.

Sexuality Sexual behaviour in later adulthood has two barriers to overcome. The first are physiological changes that can occur as a man and woman become older. As shown in **Table 15.1**, there are a variety of treatments for

Common sexual dysfunctions of later adulthood		Table 15.1	
Sexual Dysfunction	**Primarily Affects**	**Physiological Causes**	**Treatment**
Decreased libido	Both men and women	Hormonal changes Fatigue Side effects from medications	Review medications for possible side effects Hormone replacement therapy Identify and treat any predisposing illnesses or conditions
Erectile dysfunction	Men	Decreased blood flow Chronic illness	Oral medications Penile injections Vacuum pumps Surgery
Sexual pain	Women	Hormonal changes, leading to vaginal dryness and stiffening	Lubricating cream Hormone replacement therapy Kegel exercises to increase blood flow

these physiological issues. More people are using these treatments as the stigma associated with sexual enhancement becomes less pervasive than in the past (Brotto, Heiman, & Tolman, 2009).

The second barrier to sexual satisfaction in the later years is slightly more difficult to overcome. Stereotypes and ageist attitudes toward sexual behaviour among older adults have an impact not only on how older individuals feel about themselves but also on their desire to engage in sexual behaviour (Weeks, 2002). As a result of these beliefs, some older women tend to see themselves as sexually unattractive and uninterested in sexual behaviour. In a survey of sexual behaviour among older adults (Geyer, 2008), 30 percent of men between the ages of 70 and 80 reported engaging in sexual behaviour on a regular basis, whereas only 8 percent of women said the same. Those who did not regularly engage in sexual activity reported not having a partner as the primary reason.

> **Put It Together** *Review the sections on physical changes, vision, taste and small to think about this question.* How might changes in mobility and the senses have an impact on one's nutrition?

We now turn to another issue that many older adults face: dementia.

Dementia

Approximately 5–7 percent of adults aged 60 and older live with **dementia** worldwide. Dementia is more common in Latin America, around 8.5 percent, and lower in sub-Saharan Africa, where the rate in the same age group (60+) is 2–4 percent (Prince, Bryce, Albanese, Wimo, Ribeiro, & Ferri, 2013).

dementia A loss of cognitive function, which may include language impairment, memory loss, and the inability to recognize familiar people or objects.

The word "dementia" is often confused with the word *demented*, which refers to people who are delusional or having hallucinations. Contemporary psychology uses a much broader definition of dementia. A diagnosis of dementia takes into consideration deficiencies of cognitive and intellectual ability, the inability to plan and organize, memory loss, language impairment, diminishing mobility, and difficulty recognizing familiar people (Shah, Dalvi, & Thompson, 2005).

Dementia not only affects the way a person thinks, but also interferes with behavioural and psychological function (Shah et al., 2005). These non-cognitive symptoms are called BPSD, or behavioural and psychological symptoms of dementia. BPSDs may include changes in mood, altered perceptual states, and changes in personality (Shah et al., 2005). Apathy, irritability, depression, and aggressive behaviour are other common BPSDs, especially among dementia patients who are confined to a nursing home (Cohen & Carlin, 1993).

Various forms of dementia exist. One type is **vascular dementia**, caused by problems associated with the supply of blood to the brain, typically by a series of minor strokes. It is the second most common form of dementia, accounting for approximately 20 percent of dementias. Symptoms can range from memory impairment, loss of communication skills, and gradual deterioration in the person's ability to carry out daily tasks and activities of living (Jacobsen, 2011).

vascular dementia A common dementia caused by restricted supply of blood to the brain.

Another form of dementia is Lewy body dementia. Lewy bodies are round structures that develop in the parts of the brain involved in thinking and movement. This type of dementia results in visual hallucinations, delusions, and increased rates of falling. There is no cure for Lewy body dementia.

Alzheimer's disease The most frequently diagnosed form of dementia in the world is **Alzheimer's disease (AD)** (Brookmeyer, Johnson, Ziegler-Graham, & Arrighi, 2007). The Canadian Institutes of Health Research's Institute of Aging has made funding for Alzheimer's research a priority. One in 20 Canadians over age 65 and one in four over age 85 has Alzheimer's disease. Familial autosomal dominant Alzheimer's disease, which is passed on through families, accounts for about 5–10 percent of cases; the remainder are sporadic. Nearly a quarter of a million Canadians suffer from Alzheimer's disease, and the numbers are expected to more than double by 2030, to nearly 500,000 (CIHR, 2006). The age of onset varies but usually occurs in individuals over 60 years of age, though in some cases AD will appear in younger individuals (Chaudhury, 2008). AD is irreversible and progressive, gradually destroying the brain and the ability to remember, think clearly, and perform the activities of daily living. **Figure 15.10** shows the changes in brain structure that occur when this disease takes hold.

Alzheimer's disease (AD) A progressive form of dementia in which plaques and tangles form in the brain, resulting in increasing memory loss and eventually death.

The effects of Alzheimer's disease • Figure 15.10

Plaques and tangles are culprits in cell death and tissue loss in the Alzheimer brain.

Normal

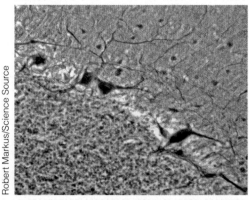

Robert Markus/Science Source

Alzheimer's

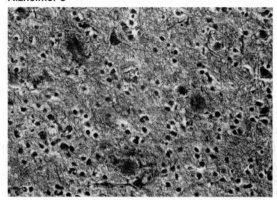

CNRI/Science Source

1 The process of AD begins much earlier than the appearance of symptoms. Tangles and plaque develop in the cortex of the brain, damaging tissue and interfering with the ability of neurotransmitters to communicate.

2 Eventually, the damage spreads through the brain and reaches the hippocampus, which is an essential part of memory storage. Grooves and ventricles in the brain are enlarged and there is an overall shrinkage of brain tissue. As short-term memory fades, the ability to perform routine tasks is impaired.

3 As the disease spreads through the cerebral cortex, the outer layer of the brain, judgement and language are impaired. Emotional outbursts become more frequent.

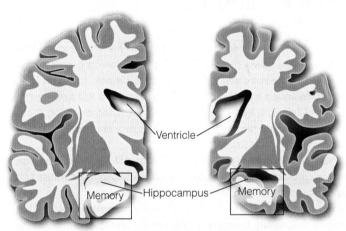

Ventricle

Memory — Hippocampus — Memory

Normal   Alzheimer's

Cortex

Severe shrinkage of cortex

Severely enlarged ventricles

Severe shrinkage of hippocampus

Normal   Alzheimer's

AlexRaths/iStockphoto

4 In the final stages of the disease, sufferers lose the ability to feed themselves or recognize faces. They typically need constant care until they finally become comatose and die (Alzheimer's Association, 2007).

Ask Yourself

1. Microscopy shows that two structures in a person's cortex, _____ and _____, are telltale signs of AD.
2. Tangles and plaques typically first result in problems with _____.
3. Eventually, _____ and language are impaired.

The specific cause of AD is still unknown. However, researchers have found correlations between AD and other physiological systems. For example, symptoms such as frequent memory problems in middle adulthood appear to be correlated with later AD. Other research has found links between mobility issues and family occurrences of AD (Alzheimer's Association, 2007; Solomon, 1994).

Unfortunately, no cure exists for AD, and it does end in death. If detected early, however, it can be treated with medications to alleviate some of the symptoms, such as memory loss and delusions. Tests to screen for AD are becoming increasingly available, helping health professionals to make accurate and early diagnoses (Kerwin,

2009). Family members are also better supported in recent years, as discussed in *Challenges in Development.*

Dementia around the world The forms of dementia are found in different rates and types around the world (**Figure 15.11**). Most of the methodology used to assess and evaluate dementia has been developed by researchers from Western cultures (Shah et al., 2005). Thus the question becomes, does dementia exist in all cultures, or is it culturally constructed? Most researchers agree that dementia is a worldwide phenomenon, although the way it is perceived may vary greatly by culture (Dein & Huline-Dickens, 1997).

CHALLENGES IN DEVELOPMENT
Families of Alzheimer's Patients

Think Critically Given that human development involves both gain and loss, can you identify some potential gains that family caregivers may experience?

BSIP/Getty Images

Caring for a person with Alzheimer's disease can be a full-time job.

There is no way to describe what it's like to live with a loved one who has Alzheimer's disease. AD begins by taking pieces of the loved one's memory away. First they lose a week, followed by a month, followed by years. At the same time, the AD sufferer becomes delusional, irritable, and aggressive, often directing these emotions at their caregivers. The toll the process takes on family members is immeasurable.

Whether accompanying a person with AD for walks because they might get lost on their own or coordinating the endless series of doctors' appointments, caring for a person with Alzheimer's can take a lot of time. As a result, the Alzheimer's Association reports that family caregivers often turn down promotions, lose job benefits, and in some cases lose their jobs (Alzheimer's Association, 2004).

Once a diagnosis has been made, family members typically begin a grieving process called *anticipatory grief* (Farran, Keane-Hagerty, Salloway, Kupferer, & Wilken, 1991). This grieving process often includes periods of denial, anger, depression, and overinvolvement in the life of the Alzheimer's sufferer (Holland, Currier, & Gallagher-Thompson, 2009). As the disease progresses, further stress-related symptoms appear in family caregivers, such as depression and anxiety.

Once the AD sufferer dies, family members are torn between feelings of grief, relief, and loss. This combination of feelings often results in significant adjustment issues. Pre-loss intervention and post-loss follow-ups have been found to help family members prepare for and process their feelings (Holland et al., 2009). Unfortunately, as our population ages, many more families will face Alzheimer's diagnoses. Although the disease itself cannot be stopped, education, family support, and intervention may help dampen its devastating consequences.

Dementia around the world • Figure 15.11

The prevalence of dementia is similar in eastern Europe, America, and Saudi Arabia. This photo shows a patient with dementia receiving care in Saudi Arabia. The breakdown varies in other countries, however. Japan reports that up to 50 percent of its dementia cases are due to vascular causes, whereas many other countries report only 10 to 20 percent from these causes (Ogunniyi et al., 1998).

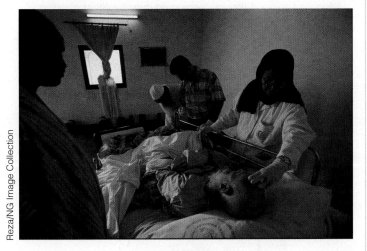

Reza/NG Image Collection

In some cultures, dementia is viewed as a normal part of the aging process (Dein & Huline-Dickens, 1997). For example, people in northern India believe that senility occurs when children fail to support their aging parents (Cohen, 1995). In China, sufferers in the early stages of dementia often fail to report their issues. They fear that they will be a burden on family members and may be perceived as losing face (Ineichen, 1996).

Assessment techniques also affect our understanding of dementia across cultures. For example, Asian countries have reported an increase in dementia cases over the recent past; however, this increase may simply reflect the availability of assessment tools (Shah et al., 2005). Assessments are becoming increasingly standardized, however. Chiu, Shyu, Liang, and Huang (2008) reported high consistency in the assessment and identification of moderate to severe dementia between Taiwan and Western, industrialized nations. They also noted accurate assessment of quality of life compared with Western evaluations. Thus, as more reliable measures of dementia are developed for use in other cultures, we will have a better idea of both its worldwide prevalence and its psychological impact.

Although dementia causes issues for many older adults, most older adults will experience only mild cognitive changes, such as issues with attention and long-term memory.

CONCEPT CHECK STOP

1. **How** do changes to the eye affect the vision of older adults?

2. **What** special role do gerontological nurses play in caring for older adults?

3. **What** are the criteria for diagnosing dementia?

✓ THE PLANNER

Summary

1 The Aging Process 482

- The term "senescence" is used to indicate the biological changes that go along with aging. Although the fact that all physical systems slow down is undisputed, there is debate as to why they do. Part of this confusion is caused by not clearly understanding what terms like "life expectancy" (the average years of life remaining) and **lifespan** (outer boundary of life for a species) actually mean. Nonetheless, life expectancy in Canada has been steadily improving, as shown in the figure, and the field of **gerontology** has been expanding as a result. Even the number of **centenarians** is growing.

- The different physical systems in humans decline but at different times. The changes are multidirectional, as some may improve while others worsen. The elderly are sometimes divided into three groups based on a combination of their age, health level, and well-being. The **young-old** are those adults in their later years who are still healthy, active, and independent. The **old-old** are generally beginning to deal with declining health and are traditionally between the ages of 75 and 85. The **oldest-old**, traditionally over 85 years of age, are at risk for illness and injury and may be dependent on others for assistance with day-to-day life.

- **Program theories** (stating that aging occurs because of predetermined internal and external chemical processes in cells) and **error theories** (stating that aging occurs because of environmental forces such as disease) are two explanations for the aging process.

- Program theories of aging include Hayflick's cellular clock theory and evolutionary theories. **Hayflick's limit** suggests that cells have an internal clock that sets a finite time for division and replication. Evolutionary theories support the concept that physical decline happens once reproductive capacity decreases. Another theory of this type is programmed cell death, where cells kill themselves in a biochemical process.

- Error theories of aging encompass the free radical theory, the disease theory, and genetic mutation theories of aging. The free radical theory is based on the concept that as bodies age, they lose the ability to stop free radicals, which are destructive and can damage DNA and other cells. The disease theory suggests that the way the body's different systems handle illness and the disruption of homeostasis is what most influences the aging process. The genetic mutation theory centres on the idea that aging is due to damaged cells.

- The **wear and tear theory** states that the longer people live, the more likely tissues are to wear down and die. This theory has been around for more than a century and is currently considered to be somewhat outdated.

Life expectancy at birth in years, by gender • Figure 15.2a

a. Life expectancy at birth in years, by gender
A Canadian's life expectancy at birth has been steadily climbing since 1900 and is predicted to continue to climb.

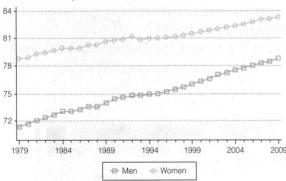

- ☐ Men - ○ Women

- as strokes, heart attacks, and atherosclerosis. Cardiovascular disease is a leading cause of death for older adults in Canada. Changes in the cardiovascular system can result in less blood getting to the brain, resulting in cognitive problems as well.

- The major change within the skeletal system is the loss of bone mass, which weakens bones and increases risk of injury. **Rheumatoid arthritis** is an autoimmune disease that causes debilitating changes to the joints, as shown in the figure, whereas **osteoarthritis** is due to the use and abuse of living and aging. Although there is no cure for either condition, physical therapy and medication can help with the pain and the loss of mobility. **Osteoporosis** is a disease in which bones lose minerals and become brittle and breakable. An exact cause has not been determined, but hormones seem to play an important role; physicians are focusing on early screening and the use of drugs that slow down resorption and even increase bone mass.

- The muscular system undergoes a number of changes as people age, including sarcopenia and loss of strength and flexibility, which negatively affects the **activities of daily living** or **ADLs** for older adults.

Rheumatoid arthritis • Figure 15.6

Jack Sullivan/Alamy

3 Cognitive Changes 492

- Cognitive changes are also a part of aging. Information-processing abilities diminish. **Selective attention** becomes more difficult, and older adults are often evaluated by how well they assess differences in **top-down processing** and **bottom-up processing**. Both skills decline with age and are related to changes in memory. Determining how much memory older people have lost is difficult because measurement is complicated. Memory declines occur in all groups, although autobiographical memories from certain periods of life are typically well remembered, as shown in the figure. Working/short-term memory declines the most. Older people experience the **tip-of-the-tongue phenomenon** more often than other age groups.

- The idea that old age often brings **wisdom** is familiar in many different cultures, especially less industrialized countries where researchers have found a greater respect for older adults.

2 Physical Development 488

- The brain is considered to be a driving force in the aging process. As people age, the brain changes size, especially between the ages of 70 and 80, although how that affects mental ability is still not determined.

- People's cardiovascular systems tend to decline with age as well, from lowered functioning to increase in diseases such

The times we remember • Figure 15.8

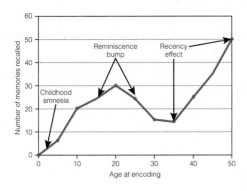

4 **All the Systems Working Together 495**

- The five senses change as people age. Eyes change shape, the lens hardens, and the retina becomes less sensitive, all of which interfere with proper vision. Some elderly people also deal with eye diseases and problems such as tear duct issues, floaters, **glaucoma**, and **cataracts**, which are shown in the figure. **Age-related macular degeneration (AMD)** is the leading cause of vision loss; although treatment can slow the loss, it can neither reverse nor prevent it. Most people over the age of 75 report partial or significant hearing loss, which can interfere with their ability to participate socially; hearing loss may also be related to short-term memory issues and safety concerns. Both taste and smell decline with age, which can interfere with the enjoyment of food. Age also seems to play a part in people's ability to detect sensation such as cold and heat, while at the same time, pain takes on a greater role.

- As overall life expectancy grows, so does the need for geriatric/gerontological nursing. These professionals not only administer medical care, but help family members to provide home care. They are commonly found in hospitals, doctors' offices, nursing homes, long-term care facilities, and assisted living facilities as well as in individuals' homes.

- For older adults, the most significant nutritional problem is overeating. Although activity levels and caloric needs have diminished, old habits—and food intake—stay in place. A secondary problem is vitamin and mineral deficiencies, due to improper diet and/or medications. Physicians and other health experts recommend that older people get regular exercise, whether in structured or unstructured settings.

- Sexuality during this period of life has to overcome physiological changes (often achieved through the use of treatments and/or medication) and stereotypes or ageist attitudes.

- **Dementia** affects an older person's thinking and behaviour. Some of the most common behavioural and psychological symptoms of dementia (BPSDs) include mood and/or personality changes, depression, apathy, and aggression. Dementia can take several pathways, including **vascular dementia** and Lewy body dementia. However, the most commonly known form is **Alzheimer's disease (AD)**, from which millions of people suffer. There is no cure, but researchers have discovered that it is largely due to tangles and plaques that develop in the brain's cortex and interfere with the ability of neurotransmitters to communicate. Eventually, the damage reaches the hippocampus and destroys memory storage. A great deal of damage is done to family relationships as family members struggle to cope with their loved one's memory loss. As they often go through a type of sadness known as *anticipatory grief*, services such as family support and education become increasingly important. Although the presentation of dementia is the same across cultures, different cultures interpret dementia symptoms in a variety of ways.

Seeing through cataracts • Figure 15.9

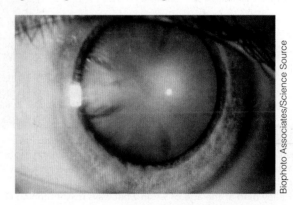

Biophoto Associates/Science Source

Key Terms

Critical and Creative Thinking Questions

1. What elements of aging can be controlled through medical treatment and drugs? Which ones cannot?

2. In what ways will medical services and professions have to change to accommodate longer and longer lifespans?

3. Which aging theories seem to make the most sense? How much of aging appears to be internal/genetic and how much is external/environmental?

4. Why has Weismann's wear and tear theory been strongly disputed over the last few decades?

5. In what ways are the activities of daily living affected by the changes of aging?

What is happening in this picture?

In his prime, John Kelley was two-time winner of the oldest annual and most prestigious marathon in the world, the Boston Marathon. Despite the inevitable changes that age brings, he continued to compete in the 26.2-mile event 58 times, stopping at the age of 84.

Think Critically

1. In what ways might Kelley's running have been affected by the aging of his muscular and respiratory system?

2. What effect did routine running most likely have on Kelley's cognitive abilities?

3. Kelley died at the age of 97. In what ways might running have increased his longevity?

4. Many older adults are nowhere near as active as John Kelley, and a large portion are completely inactive. What factors might interfere with older adults' activity?

Ted Spiegel/NG Image Collection

REAL  Development

Physical and Cognitive Development in the Later Years

In this video activity, you are a social worker observing physical and cognitive development in the later years. In particular, you are interested in what happens to memory. You work at a seniors' centre and one of your professional requirements is to interview individuals about their physical and cognitive development. You have decided to interview Arnie (70 years old) and Barbara (80 years old). Using your knowledge of cognitive development and wellness, you will help Arnie and Barbara better understand the intellectual and physical changes they are going through.

John Wiley & Sons, Inc.

WileyPLUS Go to WileyPLUS to complete the REAL Development activity.

03.01

Self-Test

(Check your answers in Appendix A.)

1. Scientists study _____ to identify cultural factors that predict healthier, longer lives.

   a. average life expectancy of men

   b. average life expectancy of women

   c. variation in life expectancy between countries

   d. variation in life expectancy at birth

2. To what do error theories attribute aging?

   a. genetics   c. demographics

   b. ethnicity   d. environment

3. What kind of cells contain the telomerase enzyme?

   a. cancer cells   c. stem cells

   b. fetal cells   d. blood cells

4. What do some professionals recommend to help treat the presence of free radicals?

   a. exercise   c. antioxidants

   b. lipids   d. minerals

5. What happens to brain size as we get older?

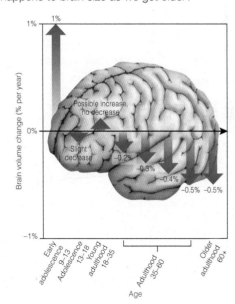

   a. It decreases.

   b. It increases.

   c. It stabilizes.

   d. It disappears.

6. Arteriosclerosis and coronary artery disease are health problems involving which system?

a. muscular

b. nervous

c. skeletal

d. cardiovascular

7. What condition is this woman most likely suffering from?

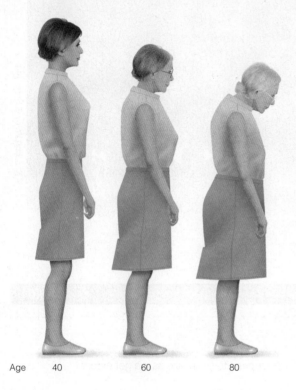

Age   40   60   80

a. arthritis

b. osteoporosis

c. arteriosclerosis

d. senescence

8. What is the most common type of treatment for arthritis?

a. medication

b. physical therapy

c. surgery

d. counselling

9. Selective attention is the _____.

a. ability to notice both internal and external stimuli

b. psychological side effect of various forms of dementia

c. process driven by directing sensation to the body's receptor sites

d. process of distinguishing between relevant and irrelevant information

10. All of the following are true about long-term memory *except* that it _____.

a. is associated with parts of the brain that deteriorate most slowly

b. shows the most overall decline with age

c. changes most slowly when disease is present

d. is where people store insignificant details

11. The tip-of-the-tongue phenomenon is the feeling that you know a fact but you cannot _____ it.

a. remember

b. memorize

c. explain

d. verify

12. Exercising in later adulthood provides many benefits including all of the following *except* _____.

a. increased lifespan   c. fewer chronic diseases

b. improved mental health   d. less risk for glaucoma

13. Which of these eye problems requires surgery to correct?

a. floaters

b. poor night vision

c. cataracts

d. macular degeneration

14. How do gerontological nurses differ from other types of nurses?

a. They work in a wide variety of settings.

b. They specialize in working with older people.

c. They focus on the spiritual needs of patients.

d. They teach family members how to provide care.

15. All of the following are true about Alzheimer's disease *except* that it is _____.

a. progressive

b. preventable

c. irreversible

d. fatal

THE PLANNER ✓

Review your Chapter Planner in the chapter opener and check off your completed work.

Socio-emotional Development in the Later Years

Frank watched the blue heron fly over the still lake. He glanced over at his granddaughter Kailey to see if she was also seeing the gentle, graceful sweep of the large bird's wings. Although some days felt long and lonely, it was moments like this when he was glad that he had retired from his job at the hospital. The lives of older adults often change pace and shape dramatically.

Lives structured by work are eventually reorganized. New hobbies are found, and older adults may take time to do the things they have been wanting to do for a long time, such as travelling or spending more time with their families.

As you know by now, with gain comes loss. In older adulthood, living arrangements often change to

accommodate decreases in independent functioning. Cultural variations in the meaning of a good life influence the way older adults feel about the lives they've lived. Culture also influences older adults' feelings about what it means to be dependent in their older years.

CHAPTER OUTLINE

CHAPTER PLANNER ✔

- ☐ Study the picture and read the opening story.
- ☐ Scan the Learning Objectives in each section:
  p. 510 ☐   p. 515 ☐   p. 524 ☐
- ☐ Read the text and study all visuals. Answer any questions.

Analyze key features

- ☐ Development InSight, p. 514
- ☐ Process Diagram, p. 517
- ☐ What a Developmentalist Sees, p. 518
- ☐ Challenges in Development, p. 522
- ☐ Stop: Answer the Concept Checks before you go on:
  p. 515 ☐   p. 523 ☐   p. 528 ☐

End of chapter

- ☐ Review the Summary and Key Terms.
- ☐ Answer *What is happening in this picture?*
- ☐ Answer the Critical and Creative Thinking Questions.
- ☐ Complete the Self-Test and check your answers.

Personality Development

LEARNING OBJECTIVES

1. **Explain** the psychosocial crisis of integrity vs. despair.

2. **Describe** personality trait changes typical in older adulthood.

3. **Compare** and **contrast** the major social theories of aging.

With age, older adults gain new perspective on life now that they can look back on the lives they have built. They make meaning of their lives by reflecting on the events that have shaped who they have become. All of the *what ifs* and *should haves* become as much a part of a person's life story as all of the *I dids*. A number of theorists help us understand how individuals change in the final decades of the lifespan.

Erikson's Stage of Integrity vs. Despair

As you have learned, Erik Erikson was one of the first theorists to outline stages of adult development in addition to stages of child and adolescent development. According to Erikson, late adulthood is the final stage of development, during which individuals face the last of eight psychosocial crises. With age, older adults gain the ability to look back and ask themselves: Did I lead a meaningful life? This question, according to Erikson, is the catalyst for resolving the eighth and final psychosocial crisis, ego integrity vs. despair. **Ego integrity**, as the words suggest, is a state of integration of the ego that has evolved over a lifetime. Having integrity means having lived a life full of complex social relationships, clear personal identity, and intimacy. Integrity is what happens when a person is generally content with how life has unfolded. In this state, a person accepts his or her life, along with the choices and social connections he or she has made (Erikson, 1985; Ryff & Heincke, 1983).

> **ego integrity** The accrued assurance of the ability to find order, meaning, and integration in one's life.

> **despair** Feeling that one's life lacks meaning and significance.

What happens when an older adult in his 60s or 70s is unable to integrate his or her life and tell a life story that conveys meaning and fulfillment? **Despair** results from both a lack of reflection and unfulfilled social interactions (Erikson, 1963). In other words, despair comes from a life full of regrets. These feelings are often complicated by fear of an uncertain future and the inevitability of approaching death (Erikson, Erikson, & Kivnick, 1986). Despair is characterized by the conflicted perception that life is full of misery and hard times, and yet it ends too quickly (Sugarman, 1986). A person who is in despair typically is bitter and blames societal institutions for creating life's problems. Erikson believed that this bitterness toward society reduces the anger one has directed toward the self (Erikson, 1985).

At times you may find yourself wondering why a grandparent or older adult is telling stories about the choices he made in his life many decades in the past. Older people recall memories and share them in order to revive, reinterpret, and reintegrate them (Kotre, 1995). What may sound like a random story may, in fact, be a glimpse of **life review**. Life review is an ongoing process of surveying, observing, and summarizing the themes that characterize one's life in retrospect (**Figure 16.1**) (Butler, 2007; Haber, 2006). According to Butler (2007), life review is a universal and normal process of aging. It is used by geropsychologists as a therapeutic technique to increase self-understanding to reduce depression and help older adults cope with feelings of loss, guilt, conflict, or defeat (Butler, 2007; Haber, 2006; King & Hicks, 2007).

> **life review** The process of telling one's life story structured around themes that make meaning of one's life.

The Aging Self

Personality is neither entirely stable nor entirely flexible across all older adults. Personality stability increases from childhood through adulthood, with moderately high stability in late adulthood (Roberts & DelVecchio, 2000). Personality stability in late adulthood is strongest for

Engaging in life review • Figure 16.1

Life review involves processing memories—including the feelings attached to the memories—in a way that allows the individual to integrate memories into his or her personal identity. Most often life review is structured around family roles such as parenting and grandparenting; work themes; and major life events such as graduations, weddings, and births.

Hill Street Studios/Age Fotostock

Masterfile

Afro American Newspapers/Gado/Getty Images

Eli Reed/Magnum Photos

Think Critically If you conducted a life review right now, what would be the themes of your life?

the Big Five personality traits compared with other traits (Ardelt, 2000). Although there is very limited change in personality traits in older adulthood, there is, of course, variation between older adults in their 60s, 70s, and 80s. For example, older adults with higher levels of agreeableness and conscientiousness are more likely to be highly engaged in social roles; in turn, engagement in social roles predicts increases in conscientiousness (Lodi-Smith & Roberts, 2012). Just like in younger adulthood and middle adulthood, individual differences influence the way people change through the lifespan.

The aging self is shaped not only by personal events and experiences, but also by society and culture. Whereas traits and goals shape personality more in earlier decades of the lifespan, adult personality is increasingly influenced by culture. Older adults evaluate the lives they lived according to their culture's notion of what it means to have lived a successful life. In this way, **life narratives**—life stories that involve images, plot, characters, and themes—are set

> **life narrative**
> An individual's life story that reflects a sense (or lack) of unity, purpose, and meaning.

Cultural influences on life narrative • Figure 16.2

Today, these grandparents celebrate the birth of a grandchild. During a traditional ceremony celebrating the baby's birth, they learned that the baby has been named in honour of both of them. They feel great pride and connection to this new life.

William Albert Allard/Getty Images

Think Critically
1. What positive evaluations about a meaningful life might an older adult living in a three-generation household have?
2. What negative evaluations might this older adult have?

in and shaped by the socio-cultural context in which an individual ages (McAdams, 2006; McAdams & Olson, 2010). Researcher Dan McAdams and others have demonstrated that life narratives are evaluated within the context of culture-specific stories that glorify good and vilify bad characters, as well as provide numerous models of characters that fall in between. In the United States, rags-to-riches stories and stories of self-fulfillment are honoured. In collectivist East Asian countries, personal narratives may reflect an individual's contributions to social harmony and integration of self in groups (**Figure 16.2**; McAdams & Olson, 2010).

Social Theories of Aging

Older adults' identities are influenced not only by evaluations of events and experiences that occurred in the past, but also by evaluations of current social roles and relationships. A number of theories provide us with frameworks for understanding how older adults continue to shape their identities and evaluations of self.

Activity theory Activity theory is one of the oldest theories of social aging (John, 1984). The basic assumption of the **activity theory of aging** is that social interaction and physical activity are indications of successful aging (Willis, 1996). This idea evolved out of the earlier work of Robert Havighurst (1971), who believed that for successful aging to occur, specific age-appropriate tasks should be accomplished throughout the lifespan. For example, learning to read and understand math are the tasks of childhood; marriage and raising a family are the tasks of emerging adulthood. According to Havighurst (1971), the task of later adulthood is maintaining contact with society through age-appropriate positive activities. Activity theory suggests that physical, cognitive, and socio-cultural activity in late adulthood leads to successful aging and positive mental health (**Figure 16.3**). Some research supports activity theory, indicating that older adults with a continued level of social interaction report positive

> **activity theory of aging** A theory of aging that suggests social interaction and physical activity are indicators of successful aging.

mental and physical health (Hinterlong & Williamson, 2007; Williamson, 2002). Other research, however, suggests that individuals must perceive the activities to be positive and enjoyable in order for them to be associated with personal satisfaction and well-being (John, 1984). Arguing against activity theory, other theorists contend that a decrease in involvement in social activity is normal in older adulthood and therefore should not be interpreted as an indicator of unsuccessful aging.

Disengagement theory

In their **disengagement theory of aging**, Cumming and Henry (1961) describe older adulthood as a life stage during which it is normal

> **disengagement theory of aging**
> A theory of aging that suggests it is normal and healthy for older individuals to disengage from their previous roles and to focus energy on personal development.

and healthy for individuals to disengage from their previous roles in society and to focus energy on personal development. From this perspective, older adults reduce their involvement with society, and, at the same time, society accepts and encourages a reduction in active social engagement. This mutual understanding allows older adults to carry on without the responsibility of societal obligations. These obligations are left for the younger members of society to assume.

As is the case with stage theories in general, activity and disengagement theory both suggest that individuals of the same relative age behave in ways similar to one another. By now, given the expertise you have gained in lifespan human development, you're already thinking that both of these theories assume that all individuals develop in the same way, whereas you know that there is a great deal of variation in normative human development. If this is what you are thinking, you will also recall lifespan development theory and its emphasis on gain and loss.

Selective optimization with compensation

In Chapter 13 you were introduced to the concept of selective optimization with compensation (SOC) and the idea that development is not all about gain or loss of ability, but involves both throughout the lifespan. SOC theory suggests that people of all ages have an inherent drive to develop and maintain abilities. In older adulthood, they have to adapt their activities in order to cope with unavoidable physical and mental losses (Baltes & Baltes, 1990). What you did not learn previously is that

Staying active in later adulthood • Figure 16.3

Activity theory suggests that older adults achieve satisfaction from staying involved in everyday life, such as through physical exercise, social interaction, cognitive pursuits like reading and discussion, or travel.

Think Critically Think of an older adult in your life. Would he or she get the same level of enjoyment from the activities you do to stay active? Why or why not?

Boomer Jerritt/All Canada Photos/Corbis

The SOC model is based on three key strategies: selection, optimization, and compensation. A 70-year-old golfer can use SOC to retain his ability to excel in the sport despite having less stamina and strength as he ages.

a. Selection

Because he has less stamina now than when he was younger, this golfer uses selection to restrict his playing to two times per week. When selection is by choice, it is called *elective selection* (Baltes, Staudinger, & Lindenberger, 1999). Sometimes selections are made because of loss, called *loss-based selection*.

b. Optimization

Optimization is the ability to maximize one's physical, economical, and socio-emotional resources. This golfer optimizes his energy for the game by taking a golf cart instead of walking the course.

c. Compensation

As he ages, the golfer has lost the strength to make long drives off the tee. Because it now takes him more strokes to get to the green, he uses compensation to reduce the number of putts it takes to make it into the hole by taking lessons to improve his putting.

Think Critically Using SOC, can you think of another compensation strategy an older golfer might use to optimize his ability to play golf and to play golf well?

Paul and Margaret Baltes introduced this theory in response to activity and disengagement theories. According to research by Baltes and colleagues, successful aging is an outcome of older adults using SOC strategies to conserve resources and deploy skills to optimize their potential to stay engaged and productive, while minimizing the loss of ability to care for themselves and engage in activities they find rewarding (**Figure 16.4**; Freund & Baltes, 1998). The SOC model is useful for understanding older adults' patterns of engagement with activities, but the same model has been useful in conceptualizing social relationships in later adulthood as well.

Socio-emotional selectivity theory Socio-emotional selectivity theory provides a framework for understanding and interpreting changes in social relationships and social networks in later adulthood (Carstensen, 1992, 1998). According to socio-emotional selectivity theory, as they draw closer to the end of life, individuals become increasingly selective about their social relationships. In other words, older individuals generally have less time and energy to devote to superficial acquaintances and want to spend their quality time with close personal friends and relatives (Carstensen, Gross, & Fung, 1998). Socio-emotional selectivity theory is a theory of motivation; generally speaking, aging is associated with increasing preference for positive over negative experiences. Thus, optimizing investment in emotionally meaningful social relationships at the expense of a larger

> **socio-emotional selectivity theory** A model of aging that focuses on diminishing social networks, leading to positive emotional regulation based on the perception that there is limited time to live.

social network is a healthy and adaptive way to regulate emotions and interact positively in social situations.

Now that we understand the developmental tasks individuals face during the final stages of the lifespan, the stage is set for thinking about how these new challenges affect the way they live their lives on a daily basis. The majority of older adults retire from work. Whether due to retirement or not, social relationships also take new shapes.

CONCEPT CHECK

1. **How** does life review relate to Erikson's eighth stage of psychosocial development?
2. **What** factors contribute to personality change in older adulthood?
3. **How** does socio-emotional selectivity theory explain changes in older adults' social networks?

Social Development

LEARNING OBJECTIVES

1. **Explain** how work and retirement influence adjustment in late adulthood.
2. **Discuss** the role of relationships with family and friends in late adulthood.
3. **Describe** the issues related to ageism.
4. **Outline** the role of religion and spirituality in late adulthood.

Throughout adulthood, relationships undergo changes. Significant shifts characterize later adulthood. As relationships to social roles and with important others are rearranged, older adults experience changes in their identities and sense of place in the world. For many, marriages and intimate relationships have to adapt to changes in physiology and physical ability. Most older adults will begin to experience illnesses and deaths of friends. Interactions between the older and younger generations are altered not only by the aging of the older adult, but also by the aging of adult children and grandchildren. Because work and family life are intimately tied together, we begin by considering how work changes for older adults and how these changes influence aging and adjustment.

Work and Retirement

Retirement at one time was mandatory in Canada, but now people can choose when to retire from most occupations. As discussed in Chapter 14, the timing of retirement is determined by a number of factors, such as personal aspirations and financial ability (Carrière & Galarneau, 2012). Structural forces can also influence retirement trends. In 2012, for example, the Canadian government announced changes to the Old Age Security program that would gradually increase the age of eligibility from 65 to 67 (Government of Canada, 2013). The average age of retirement in Canada is 64, but approximately 12 percent of Canadians over the age of 65 were employed in 2012 (Employment and Social Development Canada, 2015).

It has been shown that those with the most education tend to enjoy their work and are reluctant to be forced to leave their career. Many people want to keep working for a variety of other reasons such as a sense of purpose or routine and a sense of identity and belonging. Increasingly, it is a case of economic survival (Standard Life, 2007). Mandatory retirement requirements now need to be stated as exceptions to the jurisdiction's human rights legislation or labour standards legislation. The exceptions are presented as allowing mandatory retirement based on age if it is established that a worker's age, not necessarily 65, would significantly affect the worker's ability to perform the job duties and the employer would suffer undue hardship to accommodate the worker's limitations. Occupations such as firefighter, police officer, school bus driver, and pilot are some examples of potentially relevant careers for mandatory retirement ages (Toosi, 2012; Standard Life, 2007).

Planning for retirement is a task and challenge of middle adulthood, whereas retirement and adjustment to retirement is a task of later adulthood. Only 34 percent of the eligible American population ages 55–59 is not working, but the proportion increases to 57 percent for 60- to 64-year-olds, and 80 percent for those 65 to 69. Only 5 percent of those over age 70 remain employed. Having greater wealth is an incentive to retire earlier (Friedberg, 2000), as is poor health (Dwyer & Mitchell, 1999).

Retirement is the reward that many people spend their lives looking forward to, but, when it finally arrives, some may struggle with it (Tornstam, 2005). The relationship between retirement and well-being is unclear, however, because low levels of well-being post-retirement may be due to other factors as well (van Solinge, 2013). When individuals retire, they are forced to reorganize their lives and often have to manage additional lifestyle changes; for example, more free time and less income (**Figure 16.5**). How well a person adjusts to retirement depends on a number of factors, including overall health, income, level of education, social network, level of activity, satisfaction with life before retirement, and ability to be flexible and adjust to life changes (Baehr & Barnett, 2007; Raymo & Sweeney, 2006).

Not everyone takes the same pathway to retirement. According to Phyllis Moen, an expert on retirement, older adults can follow a number of different pathways as they approach retirement age. Some do not retire at all and continue in their jobs. Some retire but then get a new job. In fact, approximately 15 percent of older North Americans with career jobs return to work after retiring (Cahill, Giandrea, & Quinn, 2011). Some retire and get involved with volunteer work, whereas others retire and then go in and out of the job market with brief jobs. Some retire and go directly to disability status, and others decide to retire after being laid off.

Although retirement is measured on an individual basis, spouses often coordinate their retirement (Blau, 1998; Gustman & Steinmeier, 1986). Retirement affects not only income and daily routines, but also relationships. In studies examining marital quality during retirement, findings suggest that the retirement transition is associated with a decline in marital quality (Moen, Kim, & Hofmeister, 2001). In marriages in which one spouse retires and one remains working, increases in marital stress are more significant. At the same time, research suggests that the elevated stress and tension are only temporary. After an initial adjustment period, once a new routine and life rhythm have been established, marital quality increases. This is especially true after both spouses have retired (Smith & Moen, 2004).

One route that over 40 percent of those 65 and over have chosen is involvement with community volunteer work, contributing an average of 231 hours per person each year (Turcotte, 2015). It is important to recognize that volunteerism is not just an altruistic endeavour (Rozario, 2007). Even though volunteer roles do not generate income for older adults, time spent volunteering produces other benefits, including helping older adults meet their social needs.

Older adult volunteers fill a special niche in communities. According to the Administration on Aging, the need for older volunteers continues to grow (Rozario, 2007). By filling this need, volunteers can gain a personal sense of worth and public recognition for being of service to the community. Donating time to others often results in older people feeling appreciated (Tang, 2006).

The benefits of volunteering in later adulthood range from feeling personal reward to experiencing health benefits. In some positions, volunteers have an opportunity to build new and rewarding interpersonal relationships through mentoring, teaching, and guiding others (Settersten, 2002). Volunteering has also been associated with health benefits: longer lifespan (Musick, Herzog, & House, 1999), increased life satisfaction, greater well-being (George, 2006), and lower levels of anxiety and depression (Hunter & Linn, 1980).

Relationships

The social networks of older adults, like those of young and middle-aged adults, are made up primarily of

The phases of retirement • Figure 16.5

  THE PLANNER

Robert Atchley (1999) identified six distinct phases of retirement that indicate how retiring is an ongoing process instead of a singular event.

Hero Images Inc./Corbis

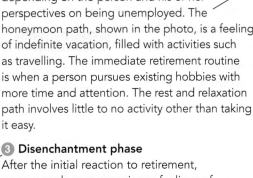

1 **Pre-retirement phase**
The person is still employed but is focusing on approaching retirement and what it may entail. During this phase, a person begins to disengage from the workplace mentally and emotionally.

2 **Retirement phase**
This phase can go in three different directions, depending on the person and his or her perspectives on being unemployed. The honeymoon path, shown in the photo, is a feeling of indefinite vacation, filled with activities such as travelling. The immediate retirement routine is when a person pursues existing hobbies with more time and attention. The rest and relaxation path involves little to no activity other than taking it easy.

3 **Disenchantment phase**
After the initial reaction to retirement, some people may experience feelings of disappointment, restlessness, or confusion. If this period is further complicated by a trauma like the death of a spouse or a move, it can be even more intense.

4 **Reorientation phase**
During this phase, people tend to look at how they are spending their time and re-evaluate what they want to do from this point forward. They typically make changes such as finding a new hobby or doing some volunteer work.

Bill Bachmann/The Image Works

A and N Photography/Shutterstock

Todd Warnock/Corbis

5 **Retirement routine**
This new focus may become the basis for the fifth phase, as the retired finally settle into a comfortable routine, which commonly lasts for many years.

6 **Termination of retirement**
This last phase of retirement comes when retirement is no longer a relevant factor, often when a person is no longer able to live independently.

Ask Yourself

1. A person tends to distance him/herself from the workplace during which phase of retirement?
   a. pre-retirement   **b.** disenchantment
2. The honeymoon path is a division of which phase in the process of retiring?
   a. reorientation   **b.** retirement
3. When a person loses the ability to live independently, the phase is usually identified as _____.
   a. retirement routine   **b.** termination of retirement

intimate partners, friends, and family. Yet older adults tend to get more satisfaction from their social networks inasmuch as they have now narrowed their networks, keeping the positive and discarding the negative in their everyday lives (English & Carstensen, 2014; Luong, Charles, & Fingerman, 2011).

Romantic relationships and sexuality Couples who stay married into later life are able to support and care for each other as they age. The children are usually gone and income has become somewhat predictable, removing two issues that often cause friction early in marriages. By the time couples have been married multiple decades,

Social Development **517**

they are so familiar with each other that they have countless shared experiences, similar values and moods, and an enduring mutual respect. They have already weathered many life-changing events together and have multiple common bonds.

Having a loving, supportive partner often acts as a buffer between the challenges of aging and an expanding life expectancy (Manzoli, Villari, Pirone, & Boccia, 2007). Among the Canadian population aged 65 and over, the majority (56.4 percent) live as part of a couple (Statistics Canada, 2012a). One of the most important demographic changes of the last 20 years in Canada has been the increasingly substantial number of men and women living in common-law unions instead of marrying. In 2011, of the nation's 4.6 million seniors over the age of 65, 166,000 lived in a common-law partnership (Milan, Wong, & Vézina, 2014). In addition, a growing number

of older couples are choosing what used to be considered a younger trend: cohabitation (Brown, Lee, & Bulanda, 2006). Statistics Canada (2007) notes that increasing numbers of Canadians are entering into common-law relationships, with people in their early 60s entering into common-law relationships at the most rapid rate of all age categories.

Across the whole age spectrum, there has been a significant increase in the percentage of individuals who are divorced. Birditt et al. (2009) discovered that couples tend to experience rising rates of negative relationship quality over time, unless they remarry in later years, in which case

Think Critically How might the increasing divorce rate be related to the rise in the percentage of common-law relationships, particularly among seniors?

WHAT A DEVELOPMENTALIST SEES
STIs in Later Adulthood

You might see this couple as a charming romantic pair, but professionals who are involved in on-site interactions in assisted living facilities see residents facing a growing risk of sexually transmitted infections. A recent study revealed that in less than 10 years, the rates of sexually transmitted infections, including chlamydia, genital herpes, gonorrhea, syphilis, and genital warts, for people

45 years old and up has more than doubled (Bodley-Tickell et al., 2008). What do developmentalists do when they see a trend like the one depicted in this graph? They work hard to immediately identify the causes. The figure highlights factors currently believed to be contributing to the rise in sexually transmitted infections among adults. Can you think of any others?

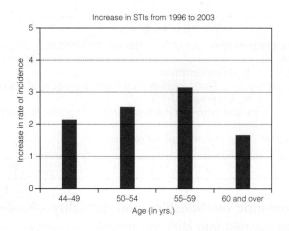

Increase in STIs from 1996 to 2003

(y-axis: Increase in rate of incidence; x-axis: Age (in yrs.) — 44–49, 50–54, 55–59, 60 and over)

Joel Sartore/NG Image Collection

Think Critically What actions could an on-site social worker in an assisted living facility take in order to educate residents about the threat of STIs?

rates decreased. Studies have found that a couple's level of overall happiness rises with the overall quality of their marriage (Proulx, Helms, & Buehler, 2007). Among seniors, the proportion of those who experienced divorce or marital separation increased from 4 percent in 1981 to 12 percent in 2011 (Milan et al., 2014).

Sexuality and senior citizens in the same sentence may seem incongruous to some, but the two are not at all paradoxical. Interest in sexual activity is maintained throughout later life. Many older people have a great need for sexual activity and affection. A survey of nursing home residents demonstrated that the elderly rated sex as moderately important, with higher levels reported among males (Aizenberg, Weizman, & Barak, 2002).

Although interest in sex remains and some research has shown that both men and women are still orgasmic well into their 70s and beyond (Hodson & Skeen, 1994), physiological factors may play a part in later-life sexuality. Both men and women experience a number of gradual physiological changes over the years. For men, testosterone levels drop, as does sperm production. Seminal fluid changes in both amount and consistency, and the force of ejaculation is often diminished. Aging of the prostate gland can also interfere with an older man's ability to achieve and maintain an erection and lengthen the period after ejaculation when a man is temporarily unresponsive to sexual stimuli (Croft, 1982).

At the same time, women experience a number of changes. The amount of pubic hair decreases along with the amount of fat on the mons pubis. Levels of estrogen and progesterone drop, as does the amount of vaginal secretions. This can make sexual intercourse painful and increase the risk of vaginitis, as well as interfere with a woman's ability to reach orgasm. Menopause can bring changes in sexual desire and cause painful intercourse. Both genders must also often deal with the complications of health problems and medications, both of which can negatively affect overall libido, ability, and self-image.

Sexually transmitted infections (STIs) have become increasingly common among older adults, as shown in *What a Developmentalist Sees.*

Friends and family: The social convoy As people age, virtually every aspect of their lives changes in one way or another, including the people they choose to spend time with, often known as the **social convoy**. A social convoy is the group of people—family, friends, and even acquaintances—that journeys through phases of life with us (**Figure 16.6**; Kahn & Antonucci, 1980). They support, encourage, and listen to us when we need them.

> **social convoy**
> A social support network to which an individual remains connected throughout the lifespan.

The social convoy • Figure 16.6

As we age, our social convoy travels through life with us. As people move, change jobs, marry, become parents, or retire, the members of the social convoy shift to reflect these changes. For example, since this man retired, "friends" remain part of his social convoy. In the past, his university friends, army buddies, and co-workers were his closest friends. Now, his closest friends are members of his chess club and his neighbours. "Family" has always been a part of his social convoy, although the family members closest to him have changed.

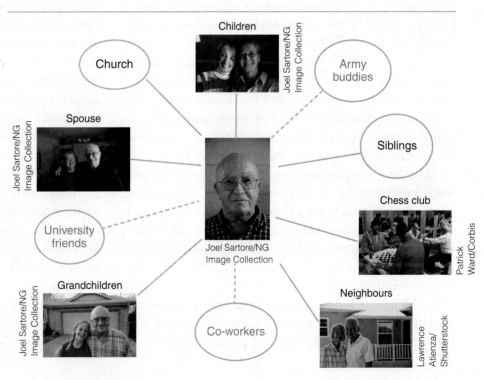

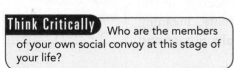
Think Critically Who are the members of your own social convoy at this stage of your life?

Social convoys begin early in adulthood and continue throughout the lifespan. Before the age of 60, marital status is of primary importance to people, but after the age of 60, ties with close friends and/or relatives gain importance (Seeman, 2000). Social convoys are organized in such a way that membership ranges; that is, some friends and family are highly involved in a person's life, whereas others in the social convoy are less involved but remain connected to the person and his or her life over time. The hierarchy is affected by several variables, such as gender, degree of intimacy, work, and shared interests (Antonucci, 1990). Even in-laws can be part of the social convoy (Santos & Levitt, 2007).

Changes in the hierarchical relationships in the social convoy vary and may be influenced by many things. For example, military experience is a known factor for keeping certain members in a social convoy. Women are more likely to maintain intergenerational connections in their social convoy because they have been traditionally assigned the roles of kinkeepers. As noted in Chapter 14, kinkeepers maintain family records and consult with older and younger family members regularly (Santos & Levitt, 2007). Social support is an integral part of successful aging, and with baby boomers moving into later adulthood in large numbers, they will be getting there with social convoys.

Most importantly, social convoys are associated with **subjective well-being** (Armstrong, 2007). As we get older, factors such as health, loss of key relationships, and socio-economic status play key parts in our perception of life satisfaction (Ajrouch, Blandon, & Antonucci, 2005). Social convoys serve to facilitate a network of support and protection from depression and loneliness. Clearly, the social convoy plays an integral role in improving an individual's subjective well-being, thus adding to an overall sense of personal happiness (Armstrong, 2007).

> **subjective well-being** A person's perception of his or her general sense of psychological satisfaction.

The family makes up a significant portion of a person's social convoy. As children grow up and become adults, their parents must adjust their roles, taking a back seat when before they were behind the wheel. This is not easy for some parents and can cause tension, especially in close relationships (van Gaalen & Dykstra, 2006). Intergenerational relationships can involve a number of problems, including conflict over who is financially supporting whom, the type of assistance needed, and the meeting of emotional needs. Like all other essential relationships, relationships between generations often have to be reconfigured and renegotiated over the lifespan (Connidis & McCullin, 2002).

Most people's social networks consist of five persons or fewer (Phillipson, 2003). For many, those people are their children and grandchildren. As people age, they tend to choose staying close to a few special friends rather than expanding to make new ones (Carstensen, 1998). The friendships of the older generation have been shown to be of more importance to them than the relationships they had when they were younger (Lawton, Winter, Kleban, & Ruckdeschel, 1999; Newsom & Schulz, 1996). A reliable social network makes coping with life's problems and losses easier (Atchley, 1999).

Grandparenting and great-grandparenting A prevalent part of older adulthood is the chance to become a grandparent or, thanks to the increased life expectancy in this country, a great-grandparent. There are more than 7 million grandparents in Canada and, not surprisingly, the likelihood of being a grandparent increases with age. In 2011, the majority (60 percent) of individuals aged 55 to 64 were grandparents. In the 65 to 74 age group, approximately 87 percent of individuals were grandparents, with another increase for those over the age of 75 (94 percent). The majority of grandparents were married (63 percent), and had, on average, 4.2 grandchildren. Approximately 8 percent of Canadian grandparents live with their grandchildren, with larger percentages among Aboriginal and Sikh families (Milan, Laflamme, & Wong, 2015). Grandparents often play an important supportive role in their grandchildren's lives. For instance, adolescents dealing with parents who are separated or divorced often receive a great deal of emotional support from their grandparents. In a recent study, students between 11 and 16 years of age demonstrated better social skills when they were able to talk to their grandparents on a regular basis (Attar-Schwartz, Tan, Buchanan, Griggs, & Flouri, 2009).

How close grandparents are to their grandchildren depends on several factors, including personalities, ethnicity, cultural background, parent–child relationship, and age. Some grandparents are considered to be **remote grandparents**, meaning they are emotionally distant and

> **remote grandparents** A grandparent–grandchild relationship in which the grandparent(s) are emotionally distant and primarily expect obedience and respect from their grandchildren.

companionate grandparents
A grandparent–grandchild relationship in which the grandparent(s) enjoy frequently entertaining their grandchildren.

involved grandparents
A grandparent–grandchild relationship in which the grandparent(s) are often involved in daily care of their grandchildren.

beanpole family
A family with members from many generations, but with few members in each generation.

primarily expect obedience and respect from their grandchildren. **Companionate grandparents** are those who typically have their grandchildren over and entertain and spoil them as much as possible. **Involved grandparents** are those who are often part of the daily care of their grandchildren, whether it is picking them up from school or providing child care during the day.

The structure and unique needs of each family situation often determine the role grandparents play. In a **beanpole family**, for example, there are often multiple generations (three, four, or even five) involved, but only a few members of each generation in each level (Bengtson, Rosenthal, & Burton, 1990). Often this family style has an only child with no immediate uncles, aunts, or cousins, so the bond between grandparents and grandchildren is quite strong. In families where there is only one parent, grandparents often play a vital role, filling in for the missing parent.

If a child is disabled, grandparents may serve an even greater role (Mitchell, 2008), especially if they are taught about the child's special needs and what needs to be done to cope with them. If grandparents are not involved with their grandchild's disability, this may create tension and conflict and end up causing parents additional stress instead of lessening their emotional burdens (Mitchell, 2008).

In some families, grandparents serve as the primary caretakers. In 2011, 30,005 Canadian children under the age of 14 (0.5 percent) were being raised by their grandparents. These families are often described as skip-generation families; children reside with one or both grandparents, but no parents are present. Across Canada, the highest rates of skip-generation families were found in Nunavut (2.2 percent), the Northwest Territories (1.8 percent), and Saskatchewan (1.4 percent). Approximately 58 percent of grandchildren in skip-generation families lived with a grandparent

couple, while the remaining 42 percent lived with only one grandparent (Statistics Canada, 2012b). Some grandparents are stepping in because their own children have died or disappeared. Others take over because their children are abusive, addicted to drugs, incarcerated, or experiencing other crises (de Toledo & Brown, 1995). These grandparents are variously known as the *silent saviours* of the youngest generation (Creighton, 1991) and the *family's safety net* (Belsky, 1990; Glass & Huneycutt, 2002).

Being surrogate parents takes a great deal of effort, dedication, time, and money. It sometimes brings an abrupt end to retirement, changes financial obligations, and creates years of hard work and sacrifice. Studies have shown that in U.S. households where grandmothers are raising their grandchildren alone, they are more likely to be poor and to be receiving public assistance and less likely to have health insurance (Cox, 2000; Glass & Huneycutt, 2002). Although some grandparents feel that it is worth the effort to know they are raising their grandchildren in a loving and safe environment, others struggle with feelings of resentment and disappointment over the direction their lives have taken.

Ageism and Its Ramifications

ageism A form of prejudice and discrimination against the elderly in the workplace, in public interactions, or at home.

Ageism, also known as *age discrimination*, is a combination of stereotypical and prejudicial attitudes and behaviours against an individual or group of individuals due to their age. In this chapter we use the term "ageism" to refer to negative beliefs and behaviours against older adults (Butler, 1975). Ageism is rooted in negative, unfounded beliefs about older adults. According to these beliefs, older adults are simply cranky individuals who add little value to society; they are frequently characterized, for example, as poor workers and bad drivers.

Ageism is experienced in everyday situations when others treat older people as if they are children or even infants. People infantilize older adults when they use baby talk to communicate. This form of ageism also appears when others assume an older person is not capable of making decisions about his or her own health care or living arrangements.

Perceptions of age across cultures Generally, Western, individualistic cultures tend to devalue age in comparison with Eastern, collectivist cultures. In fact, Western culture has been referred to as the culture of ageism (Harris & Dollinger, 2001). As one symptom of Western society's never-ending quest to maintain youth, plastic surgery has blossomed into a billion-dollar industry in North America and other industrialized regions (Loftus, 2008). In cultures where the aging process is viewed as a process of deterioration, young people actively express anxiety and fear about getting old (Sargent-Cox, Rippon, & Burns, 2014).

On the other hand, collectivist cultures are grounded in the belief that everyone in society is connected and dependent on one another, regardless of age or ability (Triandis, 1995). For example, one of the most respected words in the Chinese Mandarin language is *lao ren*, which means *old persons*. Similarly, one of the most important aspects of the philosophy of Confucianism is the idea of *filial piety*, meaning that there is a contract between parents and children. In particular, it is expected that during the early years, the parents care for the children, and during the later years, children take care of parents.

The emergence of technology in many countries may be threatening to shift some of these age-old, respectful views toward the elderly. In societies that depend on industrialized labour, individuals who lack skills, such as older adults, tend to become marginalized. In the future, then, modernization and technology may have a negative impact on how the younger generation perceives the elderly, no matter their culture.

CHALLENGES IN DEVELOPMENT
Elder Abuse

Elder abuse is an intentional act of abuse by a trusted caregiver (Cohen, Levin, Gagin, & Friedman, 2007). The caregiver may fail to satisfy basic needs or to protect an elderly person from harm (Cohen et al., 2007). This abuse can take many forms, including physical, psychological, sexual, and financial exploitation. Yelling and humiliating an elderly person is considered to be abuse. It differs from child abuse in that the abusers may also take advantage of their victims for financial gain.

It is almost impossible to determine how often elder abuse occurs because many cases go unreported; estimates range from 1.5 to 2.5 million victims suffering annually worldwide (International Council of Nurses, 2009). It occurs in all socio-economic, ethnic, and religious backgrounds, and in virtually every country of the world. In the majority of cases, the abuser is a trusted family member, usually a child of the victim (Cohen et al., 2007).

Cases of elder abuse are often associated with one of four key variables (Lee, 2009): family stress, financial resources, the relationship between the caregiver and the elder person, and family crisis. Although these factors are difficult to define operationally, all appear to play a part in elder abuse.

Researchers have been expanding efforts to develop ways to screen for potential elder abuse situations. One of the more important variables in screening is the context in which a screening process takes place. Because in many cases abused elders find themselves in hospital settings, researchers have focused their efforts on educating hospital personnel. They have also developed screening tools to evaluate things such as bruise patterns, hygiene, and signs of neglect, including dehydration and nutritional deficits (Cohen et al., 2007).

Britta Kasholm-Tengve/GettyImages

Think Critically
1. In what contexts, other than the hospital, should the caretaking staff be trained to recognize elder abuse?
2. Where might education about prevention of elder abuse be delivered?

Elder abuse An unfortunate trend related to ageism is **elder abuse**, which we discuss in *Challenges in Development*. Canada has been recognized internationally as a leader in raising public awareness of abuse of older adults and in developing innovative approaches to dealing with the issue. It is difficult to estimate the prevalence of elder abuse due to factors such as under-reporting, confusion about what constitutes abuse, and limitations in data collection. However, Canadian research indicates that between 4 and 10 percent of older adults experience one or more forms of abuse (National Seniors Council, 2007). Statistics Canada reports that, of the incidences reported to police, approximately one-third were committed by family members of the elderly person (most commonly a grown child or spouse), one-third were committed by friends or acquaintances, and one-third were committed by a stranger (Victims of Violence, 2011). Continuing research will help us evaluate causes and most importantly present ideas for the prevention of this devastating problem.

> **elder abuse** A single or repeated act, or lack of appropriate action, occurring within any relationship where there is an expectation of trust that causes harm or distress to an older person.

Religion, Spirituality, and Aging

As people approach the end of their lives, religion and spirituality often play a greater role (Atchley, 2008; Pew Forum on Religion and Public Life, 2009). Older adults are most likely to belong to a religious organization. Atchley (2008) reports that older adults purchase more religious and spiritual literature, attend more workshops, and demonstrate significantly more religious interest than younger cohorts.

Studies have shown that a stronger religious faith has a number of social benefits. Being part of a religious community can provide vital social connections with others, as well as an overall sense of belonging. Involvement in a religious community often gives senior citizens opportunities to participate in regular activities, plan get-togethers, host support groups, and plan fundraisers with others.

Religious involvement is also correlated with positive mental outcomes. People who report strong religious faith have been shown to experience fewer episodes of depression (Yoon & Lee, 2007). People espousing religious faith also report feeling fulfilled and connected to loved ones, and find their lives to be both purposeful and meaningful (McFadden & Kozberg, 2008; Zuckerman, Stanislaw, & Ostfeld, 1984). Others report that it increases the sense of well-being, especially for women (Koenig, Smiley, & Gonzales, 1988). In addition, a developed sense of a higher power seems to help people face death and accept inevitable losses (Daaleman, Perera, & Studenski, 2004). Actions such as praying and reading scripture also appear to increase with age (Ingersoll-Dayton, Krause, & Morgan, 2002).

When researchers discuss religion in later adulthood, they often clarify the difference between religious affiliation and spirituality (Lowis, Edwards, & Burton, 2009; McFadden & Kozberg, 2008). These terms are not synonymous. Atchley (2008) describes spirituality as a personal and emotional connection that transcends everyday events. In some cases, spirituality is a connection to a transcendent and omniscient being, whereas in other cases it is a sacred and comforting connection to positive energy. Spirituality typically contains some type of journey composed of insights and personal meaning. Research consistently links religion and spirituality to stress reduction and enrichment, and even identifies them as sources of strength and pain reduction in cases of severe illness (Aldwin & Gilmer, 2003; Lowis et al., 2009; McFadden, 2005).

CONCEPT CHECK STOP

1. **What** characterizes the honeymoon path of retirement?

2. **Why** do friends play such an important role in later years?

3. **What** variables are most often associated with elder abuse?

4. **What** positive outcomes are associated with religion and spirituality in late adulthood?

Emotional Development

LEARNING OBJECTIVES

1. **Discuss** factors associated with emotional well-being in later adulthood.

2. **Explain** considerations related to living situations in later adulthood.

3. **Describe** the challenges associated with loneliness and depression in later adulthood.

A At all stages of the lifespan, development and emotional well-being are complexly interconnected. In later adulthood, there is no exception to the tight connection between positive mental health and good physical health. Because aging accelerates during the final decades of the lifespan, the association between physical and emotional health takes on great significance in numerous ways.

Emotional Well-Being

In cultures where aging has more negative than positive connotations and in cultures where there is less reverence for the aging process as part of lifespan human development, it makes sense that depression and negative moods are believed to be part of the normative aging process (Clarke, Marshall, House, & Lantz, 2011; Mirowsky & Ross, 1992). However, **emotional**

> **emotional well-being** A state encompassing different dimensions of wellness, including autonomy, environmental mastery, personal growth, positive relations with others, purpose in life, and self-acceptance (Ryff & Keyes, 1999).
>
> **flourishing** A life characterized by optimal levels of goodness, generativity, growth, and resilience.
>
> **languishing** A life characterized by a lack of vitality and meaning.

well-being and mental health play an important, under-recognized role in the lives of older adults in their late 60s and 70s, as well as their 80s and 90s (Mirowsky & Ross, 1992). Emotional well-being in late adulthood protects against physical declines in old age (Diener & Chan, 2011; Luo, Hawkley, Waite, & Cacioppo, 2012), helps maintain attention and cognition (Scheibe & Carstensen, 2010), and facilitates coping with adversity (Laveretsky, 2012).

Emotional well-being is positive mental health, which is distinct from neutral mental health or poor mental health. Positive and negative mental health are often related, but they are not fully correspondent. **Flourishing** (**Figure 16.7**) is a term coined by Corey Keyes, which he introduced to reference a state of living a life within an optimal range of functioning—one that connotes goodness, generativity, growth, and resilience. The opposite of flourishing is **languishing**—living a life that

Flourishing in older adulthood • Figure 16.7 _____

Sociologist Corey Keyes coined the term "flourishing" to describe mentally healthy adults. The concept of flourishing provides us with a target for promoting well-being throughout adulthood and in older adulthood, specifically.

13/Ocean/Corbis

Think Critically 1. If you were designing an intervention to improve the mental health of older adults, given what you know about flourishing, describe three program goals.
2. How would you implement these goals?

Characteristics of adults described as flourishing	
Meaning and purpose	They routinely experience optimism, hope, and gratitude when they make a positive impact on others through their work and legacy.
Positive emotional life	When they experience challenge, adversity, or trauma, they respond with hope and optimism.
Contributing to the lives of others	Helping others leads to a sense of well-being in themselves and others.
Positive legacy	They have a sense that they have done the best work they could do with their abilities and resources.

Independent living
• Figure 16.8

Older adults often prefer to live independently for as long as possible. With age, a greater proportion of older adults require assistance doing the things they need to do each day to care for themselves.

Think Critically How might a culture's value for independence influence the feelings an older adult has about an increasing need for assistance?

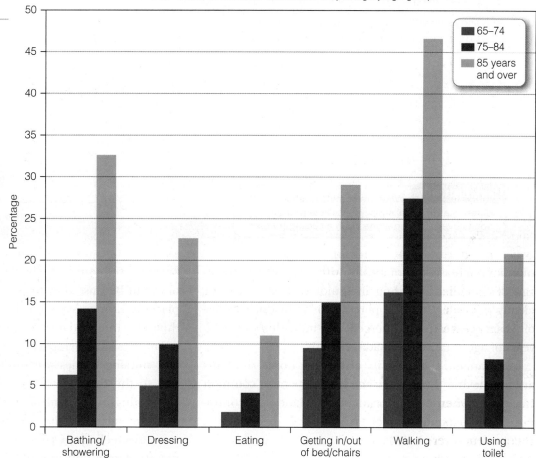

Persons with limitations in activities of daily living by age group

Legend:
- 65–74
- 75–84
- 85 years and over

is hollow and empty. Keyes contends that we are able to diagnose mentally healthy individuals in the same way we can diagnose mental illness based on the characteristics of flourishing people. Approximately 20 percent of the adult population is flourishing (Keyes, 2007), although this rate is higher for middle-aged adults than for emerging, young, and older adults. Researchers study flourishing older adults to better understand how and why some people achieve optimal mental health over the lifespan and how that optimal mental health influences health through late adulthood (Keyes & Simoes, 2012).

One way emotional well-being is protective is that it is associated with **functional independence.** An individual's ability to remain functionally able to complete the basic tasks of life has a strong impact on that person's daily activities, relationship to others, and living arrangements (**Figure 16.8**). A focus on functional independence shifts attention to an individual's abilities rather than deficits. The goal of supporting older adults and helping them

functional independence The ability to perform daily living activities safely and autonomously.

assisted living residence A long-term care residence that serves the dependent elderly/disabled and offers 24-hour protective oversight, food, shelter, and a range of medical services.

maintain their functional independence is to increase the likelihood that they will remain living in their communities and to delay or decrease the need for residential care.

Living Arrangements

When you picture older adults, what are their surroundings? What are the daily living arrangements of adults over 65? The majority live with a spouse (72 percent of men; 45 percent of women), fewer live alone (19 percent of men; 36 percent of women), and a very small minority live with an unmarried partner (2.3 percent of men; 1.3 percent of women). As age increases, the proportion of older adults living with spouses decreases, whereas the number living alone increases (Vespa, Lewis, & Kreider, 2013). **Figure 16.9** shows a typical age profile of a nursing home. It might come as a surprise to learn that only 7.1 percent of Canadians over the age of 65 live in an **assisted living residence** or a nursing home, but this

Profile of nursing home residents • Figure 16.9

This graph shows how the proportion of people in nursing homes rises dramatically during the later adult years.

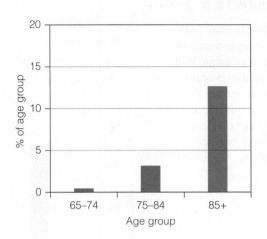

Think Critically What are some potential differences in social support available to older adults over 75 living alone vs. in a nursing home?

number increases dramatically with age. The percentage of Canadians residing in senior care facilities, for example, jumps from 0.9 percent for individuals under 69 years of age to 29.6 percent for individuals over 85 years of age (Statistics Canada, 2012b).

In Canada, the majority of nursing home residents are female and the average age is 82. The most common health issues affecting residents is bladder incontinence (70 percent), which is followed by dementia (60 percent).

Living alone Two out of three senior citizens who live alone today are women. Half of these women are single, whereas the other half are widows, due to the discrepancy between male and female lifespans. Living alone can be a positive or negative experience, depending on personality, attitudes, and health levels. It may be surprising to learn that living alone is a stronger predictor of mortality in younger adults than older adults. Older people who live alone are more likely to be lonely, but they are also more likely to be healthy and be able to function independently (Perissinotto, Cenzer, & Covinsky, 2012). Although people who live alone may experience some degree of loneliness, many are quite content with their independence and want to maintain it for as long as possible.

Around 5 percent of older adults in North America live in a multigenerational household (Vespa et al., 2013). For other older adults, the idea of going to live with family is upsetting to some not only because they would

have to relinquish their autonomy, but because they may feel it places an unnecessary burden on their children or daughters/sons-in-law. Assisted living residences and nursing homes are often considered a last resort due to the cost as well as a reluctance to leave home. Remaining in the same home, or **aging in place**, keeps an older person connected with memories of the past, increases feelings of safety and security, sustains familiarity with community and neighbours, and helps maintain independence (Senior Resource, 2009).

aging in place Growing older without having to move.

Assisted living Assisted living or community care is a relatively modern alternative to nursing home care. Many seniors pay for living in these residences out of their savings, pension plans, or other personal financial reserves, or through long-term care insurance. Also, the majority of provinces and territories offer home- and community-based programs that help low-income residents gain access to services.

In an assisted living situation, seniors retain much of their autonomy and independence while still having 24/7 access to medication management, three meals a day, housekeeping services, transportation, laundry services, full-time security, and opportunities for multiple social and recreational activities. Staff provide assistance with personal care such as bathing and dressing. In some instances, each service requested by the resident is an additional monthly fee.

Importantly, not all nursing homes are publicly run in Canada, which means they are a business venture. Approximately 44 percent of the nursing homes operating in Canada are private for-profit facilities (Canadian Institute for Health Information, 2013). The primary difference between assisted living residences and nursing homes is the level of care a person needs. Nursing homes are in a position to administer medical procedures and medications, whereas assisted living facilities are not. In assisted living, staff can transport patients who need medical care and help them manage their prescriptions, but it is illegal for assisted living staff to provide actual medical care. Sometimes the medical care that older adults need relates to their mental rather than physical health.

> **Put It Together** *Review the sections on Erikson's integrity vs. despair and living arrangments to think about this question: How might where you live influence your resolution of this stage of integrity relative to despair?*

Loneliness and Depression

Two emotions that sometimes play a large part in the lives of older adults are loneliness and depression. These emotions often manifest as constant fatigue, feeling as if there is no one to turn to for help, loss of appetite, weight gain, and even thoughts of suicide in serious cases. According to a study done at the University of Michigan, almost 60 percent of people over the age of 70 experience some level of loneliness, especially during the winter holiday season (Fiori, 2005). Major depression is a serious health risk associated with a wide range of poor health outcomes and an increased risk for early death (Arehart-Treichel, 2005).

Depression may be common in some older adults, owing to issues such as increasing physical disability and cognitive impairment, daily isolation, a sense of uselessness, lower socio-economic status, and side effects of medications (Hybels & Blazer, 2003). Sadness over loss, grief, and occasional dark or sad moods are normal responses to life. Depression is much more persistent and pervasive. Treatment usually consists of medication and/or psychotherapy (American Psychiatric Association, 2013). Common symptoms of this mood disorder include deep unhappiness that is not alleviated; unremitting boredom; lack of stamina, appetite, and motivation; sleep disturbances; loss of interest in previous pastimes; social withdrawal; and use of alcohol and/or drugs.

The type of depression experienced by the elderly is unlike that experienced in earlier years of life. In later years, it is often accompanied by anxiety, along with the slowing of thought processes and actions. It is not unusual for body symptoms to be associated with the condition as well, especially weakness, heart palpitations, or headaches (Mavandadi et al., 2007).

How depressed an older person gets depends on several factors, such as financial reserves, the social network in place, and religiosity (Schieman, van Gundy, & Taylor, 2004). Getting regular exercise is another factor that helps alleviate depression (Kostka & Praczko, 2007; Lindwall, Rennemark, Halling, Berglun, & Hassmen, 2007; Mavandadi et al., 2007). Elements that seem to predict if a person will struggle with depression include any history of earlier depression, poor health or disability, any losses, and lack of social support (Lee & Park, 2008; Wrosch, Schultz, Miller, Lupien, & Dunne, 2007).

Although depression is certainly treatable, experts believe that up to 80 percent of those who suffer from it never seek treatment because of the stigma that still is frequently attached to mental illness (Ruppel, Jenkins, Griffin, & Kizer, 2010). Older adults are beginning to search out information about stigmatized illnesses on the Internet. One organization that is encouraging such information seeking is the Canadian Coalition for Seniors' Mental Health, the topic of this chapter's *Where Developmentalists Click*.

Not all older adults who experience depression have suicidal thoughts, but a proportion do and a small number attempt suicide. Approximately 14 percent of Canadian suicides are completed by individuals aged 65 and up. In 2011, 408 men and 109 women over the age of 65 took their own lives (Statistics Canada, 2014). Unfortunately, it is likely that the extent of senior suicide is probably understated by statistics. The problem can be overlooked by health professionals and family alike, and there can be difficulties in distinguishing between self-inflicted and natural or accidental death in some cases (Monette, 2012). Although loneliness and depression are separate feelings, they often blend together, and studies

Where Developmentalists CLICK

Canadian Coalition for Seniors' Mental Health

Recognizing that seniors' mental health needs are growing and more dynamic than our health system is able to manage, the Canadian Coalition for Seniors' Mental Health (http://ccsmh.ca) is creating an active collaboration to bring people, resources, and innovative ideas together. On its website you can find the national and provincial organizations working to promote seniors' mental health, learn about advocacy activities, and use its educational tools and resources.

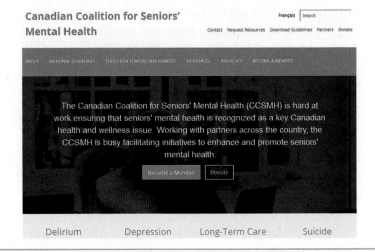

have shown that the combination can be quite serious. In a study exploring the relationship between depression, loneliness, and death in the oldest-old segment of the population, the researchers discovered that one emotion alone was not enough to negatively affect mortality. The two of them together, however, certainly was (Stek, Vinkers, Gussekloo, Beekman, van der Mast, & Westerndorp, 2003). Keep this finding in mind as we move on to our final chapter on the topics of death, dying, and grieving.

CONCEPT CHECK   STOP

1. **What** traits are associated with older adults who are characterized as flourishing?

2. **What** factors should determine whether a person chooses a nursing home or an assisted living residence?

3. **What** differentiates loneliness from depression?

 THE PLANNER

Summary

1 Personality Development 510

- The last step of Erikson's lifespan deals with the concepts of **ego integrity** and **despair**. **Life reviews** are conducted to come to terms with how the life was lived and **life narratives** reveal how socio-cultural contexts shape each person's story.

- Personality stability is the rule in older adulthood. Older adults whose personalities are more open to change are more likely to experience change. Social involvement and culture shape personality in late adulthood.

- **Activity theory** states that any disengagement is accidental and older adults want to stay connected and busy, like the people in this figure. **Disengagement theory** states that aging adults purposely distance themselves from community and family.

Staying active in later adulthood • Figure 16.3

Boomer Jerritt/All CanadaPhotos/Corbis

- Selective optimization with compensation (SOC) theory points out that people work hard to maintain and develop their abilities even if it means some level of compromise or adaptation along the way. The **socio-emotional selectivity theory**, on the other hand, focuses on the gradual reduction of social networks as people age due to less time and energy. Quantity gives way to quality as people want to spend time with the people most important to them.

2 Social Development 515

- Retirement often includes a series of six distinct phases as people adapt to the lifestyle change. Retirement affects many different elements of life beyond income, including marital satisfaction, mental health, and self-esteem.

- Volunteering in later years gives older people the chance to be social and have a purpose, and some studies have even shown that it positively affects their longevity.

- Long-term marriages can help people deal with aging, but some research has shown that the longer the couple stays together, the more the level of negative relationship quality grows. A growing trend in the aging population is cohabitation and common-law partnerships.

- Studies have shown although both men's and women's bodies go through physiological changes that can create obstacles, a healthy sexual relationship is still meaningful. Conversely, sexually transmitted infections among the elderly have also increased in recent years, as shown in this graph, partially because educational programs are usually geared for the young.

What a Developmentalist Sees: STIs in Later Adulthood

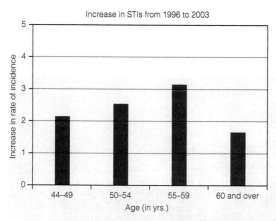

Increase in STIs from 1996 to 2003

- A person's **social convoy** tends to change over the years. Family interactions often shift throughout life, and friends tend to gain more importance with the passing of time. People's social networks typically have five persons or less, and most of these tend to be family members. The support provided by a social convoy is integral to a person's **subjective well-being**.

- Grandparenting is taking on many different faces in modern times; **remote grandparents**, **companionate grandparents**, and **involved grandparents** are categories that describe variations in the grandparent–grandchild relationship. In the **beanpole family**, there are multiple

generations that commonly form tight bonds, whereas in a family where there is a single parent and/or a disabled child, the grandparent may play an essential role in child care. For grandparents who are sitting in as surrogate parents, the involvement is extraordinarily high. Although this situation often includes a great deal of time and financial commitment as well as lifestyle changes and sacrifice, a number of grandparents see it as a blessing.

- Another aspect of later life is dealing with **ageism**, an attitude that often shows up in political issues and can be indirectly related to the problem of **elder abuse**. Although most cases go unreported, elder abuse still affects 4 to 10 percent of older Canadians.

- Toward the end of life, religion often gains in value, and studies have shown that a strong faith often has positive physical and mental influences on aging people. Time spent in church often provides essential social connection and a sense of belonging. Religious beliefs also help older adults deal with end-of-life issues.

3 Emotional Development 524

- Mental health problems and mental health are separate constructs that independently contribute to **emotional well-being** in late adulthood. Well-being is more than the absence of mental health problems. Mental health is achieved by **flourishing**—living optimally—whereas, in contrast, **languishing** is an indicator that an older adult is living a life that lacks vitality and meaning. **Functional independence** also has a strong impact on emotional well-being.

Profile of nursing home residents • Figure 16.9

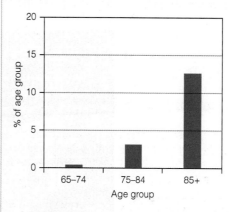

- The vast majority of Canadians over the age of 65 live independently and are often very active in work, religious organizations, school, family, and community. Most of those who live alone are women, either unmarried or widows. People who live alone often cling very hard to their independence and many prefer **aging in place**. The **assisted living residence** is a compromise between staying home and going to a nursing home. It is similar to having an apartment with the additional assistance of meals, utilities, laundry, security, and other services as part of the monthly fee. Nursing homes are designed for those who need less autonomy and more serious health care treatment and monitoring. The likelihood of residence in a nursing home increases with age, as shown in this figure.

- Loneliness and depression are two common emotions in older adults. Although both are detrimental, it is the combination of the two that poses a serious threat to senior citizens' mental health.

Key Terms

- activity theory of aging 512
- ageism 521
- aging in place 526
- assisted living residence 525
- beanpole family 521
- companionate grandparents 521
- despair 510

- disengagement theory of aging 513
- ego integrity 510
- elder abuse 523
- emotional well-being 524
- flourishing 524
- functional independence 525
- involved grandparents 521

- languishing 524
- life narrative 511
- life review 510
- remote grandparents 520
- social convoy 519
- socio-emotional selectivity theory 515
- subjective well-being 520

Critical and Creative Thinking Questions

1. What would you say to an elderly person who was clearly disengaging him/herself from the rest of the world?

2. What benefits would you point out to someone when trying to convince them to get involved in volunteering?

3. What people are in your personal social convoy? How have they changed? What do you think it will be like in 20 years?

4. What qualities make the best kind of grandparents, in your opinion? From the perspective of a parent, how active a role would you feel most comfortable with them taking and why?

5. What are some of the most important criteria to consider when choosing between an assisted living residence or a nursing home for a senior?

What is happening in this picture?

At a waterfront in Shanghai, people gather at dawn to practise the art of tai chi.

Michael Nichols/NG ImageCollection

Think Critically **1.** How might this activity benefit older adults' mental and physical health?
2. How does joining an activity like this one provide a sense of belonging?
3. What role might this kind of physical activity have on a person's self-esteem?
4. Do we have practices in Canada for older adults that fulfill needs similar to those met by tai chi?

REAL  Development

Socio-emotional Development in the Later Years

In this video activity, you are researching socio-emotional development in the later years. You are a research assistant collecting qualitative data for Dr. Wong, a developmental psychologist studying the qualities related to successful aging in late adulthood. She sends you to the Borelli family to interview Arnie (age 70) and to an art class for senior citizens at a local community centre. Arnie lives with his daughter, son-in-law, and grandchildren. Your task is to observe the living arrangement Arnie has with his family and draw some conclusions about the effect of these relationships on his psychosocial development.

At the art class, you observe two women talking about the various activities in which they engage. Your task is to recall some concepts and theories from the book and suggest which theory is reflected in the women's conversation.

WileyPLUS Go to WileyPLUS to complete the REAL Development activity.

03.01

Self-Test

(Check your answers in Appendix A.)

1. According to Erikson, what is the positive resolution of the last psychosocial task: *Did I lead a meaningful life?*

a. generativity

b. intimacy

c. ego integrity

d. immortality

2. Older adults telling their life stories can be interpreted as evidence of _____, a process they use to integrate memories and make sense of their experiences.

a. life review

b. generativity

c. goal-directed aging

d. solution-focused aging

3. Disengagement theory of aging is based on the idea that _____.

a. older adults withdraw to prepare for the end of life

b. society tends to disengage itself from older adults

c. younger members within the culture forge mutual disengagement

d. disengagement is reciprocal, involving both society and older people

4. Older adults narrow their social networks to maximize the number of positive experiences in their daily lives. This is a good example of the underlying process known as _____.

a. personality stability

b. psychosocial development

c. personality change

d. SOC

5. In the socio-emotional selectivity theory, the focus is on _____.

a. optimization

b. social networks

c. negative interaction

d. retirement plans

6. Which phase of retirement is represented by this photo?

a. reorientation

b. termination

c. disenchantment

d. preretirement

7. Which statement about volunteerism is most accurate?

a. Retirees volunteer only for altruistic reasons.

b. Retirees volunteer primarily to fill spare time.

c. Volunteering increases feelings of usefulness and appreciation in retirees.

d. Volunteering is helpful to retirees' self-esteem but has a negative effect on lifespan.

8. Which of these physiological aspects of aging affects a man's ability to have sex?

a. decrease in testosterone

b. side effects of medications

c. painful intercourse

d. gradually decreasing libido

9. The graph demonstrates which fact about STIs in adults over 60?

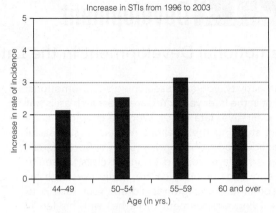

a. an increase from 1996 to 2003; lower rates compared with middle-aged adults

b. an increase from 1996 to 2003; higher rates compared with middle-aged adults

c. a decrease from 1996 to 2003; lower rates compared with middle-aged adults

d. a decrease from 1996 to 2003; higher rates compared with middle-aged adults

10. This figure illustrates this man's _____.

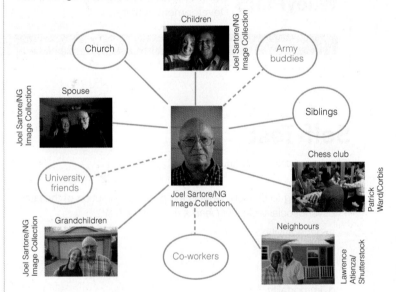

a. financial support network

b. kinship network

c. social convoy

d. emotional support network

11. How many people are in most people's social network?

   a. two or fewer

   b. five or fewer

   c. 10 or more

   d. 20 or more

12. Which type of grandparent tends to have grandchildren over and spoil them?

   a. remote

   b. involved

   c. companionate

   d. surrogate

13. In cases of elder abuse, who is most often the abuser?

   a. nursing care staff members

   b. a part-time caretaker

   c. another elderly friend

   d. a trusted family member

14. What does the term "aging in place" mean?

   a. living in a nursing home

   b. living in an assisted living residence

   c. living with one's adult children

   d. living in one's own home

15. Flourishing is characterized by all the following *except*:

   a. meaning and purpose

   b. experiencing positive emotional life

   c. contributing to the lives of others

   d. demonstrating generativity

THE PLANNER

Review your Chapter Planner in the chapter opener and check off your completed work.

17 Death, Dying, and Grieving

"**M**y friends, love is better than anger. Hope is better than fear. Optimism is better than despair. So let us be loving, hopeful and optimistic. And we'll change the world." Jack Layton's (2011) final public words, in a letter to Canadians, ignited tens of thousands of people across the country. Jack Layton's His death at the age of 61, moved a nation. Just months after leading his New Democratic party to a historic second-place finish in the federal election, where he won the hearts and minds

of many Canadians, he died of cancer. Unprecedented in the history of Canada, his state funeral, broadcast on the Canadian Broadcasting Corporation, was watched by citizens across the country and thousands came out to march in his funeral procession and to pay respects as he lay in state in the week prior. Perhaps most profound was the eulogy by Layton's friend and mentor Stephen Lewis, who drew a standing ovation when he characterized Layton's final letter to Canadians as "a manifesto of

Tara Walton/Toronto Star via Getty Images

democracy." Layton's death held the nation's attention in respect for his ideals and passions, and importantly it signalled that even in death, there is meaning.

In our final chapter, we spend time learning about death from a variety of perspectives: biological, medical, cultural, emotional, and relational. As our study of the lifespan comes to an end, it is fitting that we spend our last chapter recognizing how fascinating human development is even in the final stages.

CHAPTER PLANNER ✔

☐ Study the picture and read the opening story.

☐ Scan the Learning Objectives in each section:
   p. 536 ☐   p. 543 ☐   p. 549 ☐

☐ Read the text and study all visuals. Answer any questions.

Analyze key features

☐ Development InSight, p. 538

☐ Process Diagram, p. 546

☐ What a Developmentalist Sees, p. 548

☐ Challenges in Development, p. 550

☐ Stop: Answer the Concept Checks before you go on:
   p. 542 ☐   p. 549 ☐   p. 553 ☐

End of chapter

☐ Review the Summary and Key Terms.

☐ Answer *What is happening in this picture?*

☐ Answer the Critical and Creative Thinking Questions.

☐ Complete the Self-Test and check your answers.

What Is Death?

LEARNING OBJECTIVES

1. **Explain** the various definitions of death.
2. **Discuss** the leading causes of death in different parts of the world and at different times of life.
3. **Outline** the issues surrounding the right to die.

The vast majority of deaths occur during the later decades of the human lifespan, although death can occur at any age. As a general concept, death is an event—a specific moment when life ends. Although this definition provides a simple starting point for determining and understanding death, in fact, death is considerably more complex medically, emotionally, inter-personally, and culturally.

Defining Death

In most cases, the delineation between life and death is very clear-cut: life ends when all of a person's vital functions permanently stop. As technology has changed our ability to monitor and sustain life, however, the definition of death has become more complicated. In some cases, technology itself now mediates between life and death. Even when a person's heart is still beating, technology allows us to monitor brain activity and recognize when an individual will not regain brain function. Technology also allows us to maintain respiratory functioning for someone who is no longer able to breathe on his or her own (Tobin, 2012). Now that technology has inserted itself in a natural process, developmentalists are confronted with new challenges related to preparing for and supporting the dying process.

Advances in medical technologies have generated the need to redefine the criteria necessary for the determination of death. Historically speaking, issues concerning the definition of death arose during the examination of patients in comas (Wijdicks, 2001). In the 1950s, two French physicians introduced the term **irreversible coma** into the medical vocabulary, marking the first time that death was

Defining brain death • Table 17.1	
1. Unresponsive and lacking receptivity	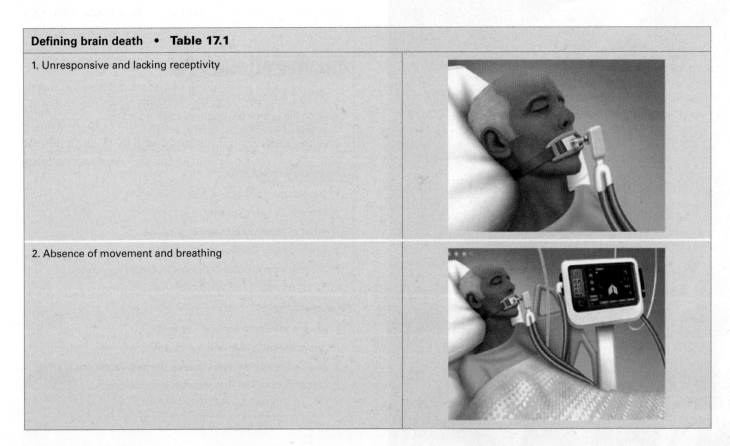
2. Absence of movement and breathing	

Defining brain death • Table 17.1 (continued)	
3. No reflexes (shown by fixed dilated blinking, no swallowing, no yawning)	
4. Absence of brain activity, demonstrated by electroencephalogram (EEG)	

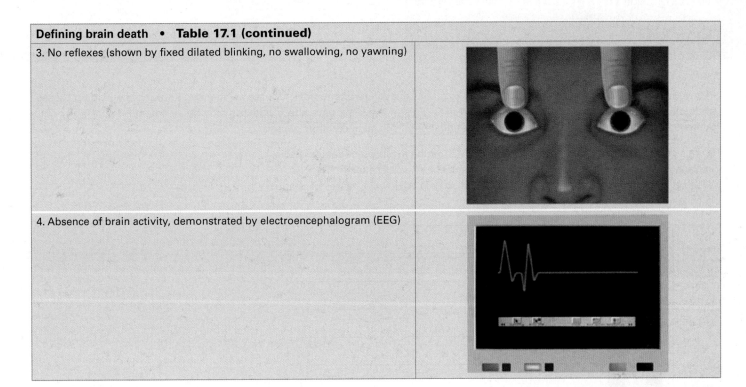

irreversible coma or **brain death** A medical condition in which there is no measurable brain activity coming from the cortex.

persistent vegetative state (PVS) A state in which a brain-damaged patient has coma-like symptoms, although a low-level arousal, such as reflexes, may be observed.

minimally conscious state A state in which a brain-damaged patient displays some deliberate behaviour or some level of self-awareness.

defined by a lack of brain activity (Mollaret & Goulon, 1959). Nine years later, an ad hoc committee of physicians and lawyers was brought together by Harvard Medical School to determine criteria for an irreversible coma, also known as **brain death** (**Table 17.1**). The report suggested that these criteria be validated again after 24 hours and that they not to be used for cases of hypothermia or narcotic-induced central nervous system dysfunction (Report of the Ad Hoc Committee of the Harvard Medical School, 1968).

A key issue in determining death is differentiating between an irreversible coma, a **persistent vegetative state (PVS)**, and a **minimally conscious state**. In a PVS, the patient has coma-like symptoms; however, low-level wakefulness may be observed, and brain activity may show slight improvement over time (Kotchoubey, Merz, et al., 2013; Kotchoubey, Veser, et al., 2013). In a minimally conscious state, the person shows some degree of deliberate behaviour. All three forms of brain damage can result from

a number of causes, including brain tumours, stroke, brain infection, trauma, or drug overdose (Andrews, 1996). Doctors differentiate among the three states through neurological examination, including EEG workups. Patients in PVS and minimally conscious states have significantly better prognoses than those in a coma, although their chances of recovery vary greatly (Rosenberg, 2009).

Neuroscientists continue to research the implications and underlying differences among irreversible coma, PVS, and minimal conscious state. Defining death based on neurological measures still leaves some family members and the public uncertain. Adding to the confusion is the fact that people diagnosed as brain dead can continue to grow, digest nutrients, and even carry a fetus to term (Joffe, 2007).

In Canada, the legal definition of brain death is "according to accepted medical practice." However, because health care is managed by the provinces and territories, such practices are largely determined regionally or even by individual hospitals. Guidelines were established by the Canadian Congress Committee on Brain Death in 1988, and in 1997 the Canadian Neurocritical Care Group clarified the criteria. Additional updates to the minimal standards for brain death diagnoses were proposed in 2005 by a national forum sponsored by the Canadian Council for Donation and Transplantation (Shemie et al., 2006). Despite ongoing amendments to medical guidelines, debate surrounding the medical definition of death, as well

In any given year, the vast majority of deaths that occur in Canada are due to heart disease and cancer. Knowing the leading causes of death in a population helps us identify prevention targets. At the same time, these statistics provide a context for thinking about differences between dying from a common cause and dying from an uncommon cause.

a. This graph depicts the top 10 causes of death in 2011 (the most recent data available) in Canada based on death certificates and the International Classification of Diseases. When all deaths are pooled, because more deaths occur in adulthood, causes of death in childhood are not represented.

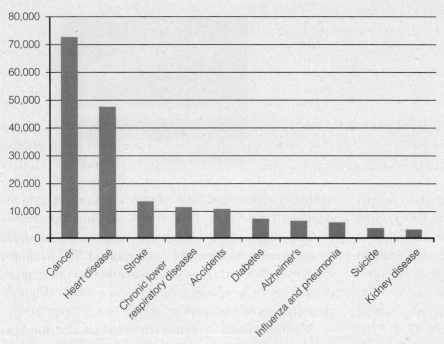

Source: Data from Statistics Canada, The 10 leading causes of death, 2011. Retrieved from www.statcan.gc.ca/pub/82-625-x/2014001/article/11896-eng.htm.

b. As we have been discussing throughout this text, particular causes of death vary greatly depending on the developmental stage. This chart provides a succinct, colour-coded summary of the three leading causes of death at all ages, enabling us to consider why the prominence of particular causes rise and fall over development. Notice, for example, that cancer appears in all four stages of the lifespan.

	Age Groups			
Rank	**1–24**	**25–44**	**45–64**	**65+**
1	Accidents	Accidents	Cancer	Cancer
2	Suicide	Cancer	Heart disease	Heart disease
3	Cancer	Suicide	Accidents	Stroke

Source: Data Statistics Canada, Chart 1, Percentage distribution for the 5 leading causes of death in Canada, 2011. Retrieved from www.statcan.gc.ca/pub/82-625-x/2014001/article/11896/c-g/c-g01-eng.htm.

Ask Yourself

1. Why does the leading cause of death change across age groups?
2. Population cause-of-death statistics reflect leading causes of death at which end of the lifespan?
3. Some causes of death are associated with the earliest years of the lifespan, such as _____.
4. One cause of death that appears later in life but not the earlier decades is _____.

as nationwide variation in diagnostic practices, persists in Canada (Sisler, 2014). However, in the broad sense, death in Canada is understood as an irreversible loss in brain functioning, which results in the absence of consciousness and an inability to breathe independently (Gardiner, Shemie, Manara, & Opdam, 2012).

Causes of Death

Cause of death is an important factor in determining whether a death is experienced as a normative or non-normative event. As we have reported in earlier chapters, the leading cause of death in Canada is cancer, followed by heart disease. However, leading causes of death vary by age and stage of the lifespan. **Figure 17.1** reviews the leading causes of death both overall and developmentally.

The World Health Organization (WHO) records the causes of death worldwide. In 2011, 55 million people died. Non-communicable diseases were responsible for two-thirds of deaths globally. The four main causes of non-communicable causes of death are heart disease, cancers, diabetes, and respiratory diseases. Leading causes of death vary around the world. The causes of death in Canada differ significantly from causes worldwide (**Figure 17.2**). The WHO makes death statistics available to anyone, as we discuss in *Where Developmentalists Click*.

The Right to Die

Another factor that blurs the line between life and death in modern societies is the ability to control the timing of death; for example, by withdrawing life support or administering lethal drugs. The right to die is a relatively modern concept. For most of history, ending one's own life was synonymous with suicide. However, in some countries governments and lawmakers have been challenged to balance the protection of vulnerable populations with citizen rights at the end of life. The Netherlands and Belgium, for example, passed legislation legalizing euthanasia and assisted suicide in 2002. In 1997, Oregon became the first American state to pass laws allowing physician-assisted suicide, and in 2009 the Death with Dignity Act went into effect in the state of Washington (CBC News, 2014).

Over the past two decades, Canada has also been confronted with this issue. In 1992, the Right to Die Society, which was founded by writer John Hofsess in 1991, partnered with amyotrophic lateral sclerosis (ALS) sufferer Sue Rodriguez to launch a well-known court challenge to the law forbidding assistance with suicide (Right to Die Society, 2013). They were unsuccessful; in a five-to-four decision, the Supreme Court of Canada dismissed Sue Rodriguez's challenge on the grounds that the ban was

Leading causes of death around the world • Figure 17.2 _____

The likelihood that individuals will die of a specific cause depends on the wealth of the country where they live, which in turn determines the country's ability to protect people from disease and death at all stages of the lifespan.

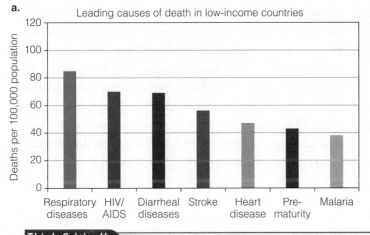

a. Leading causes of death in low-income countries

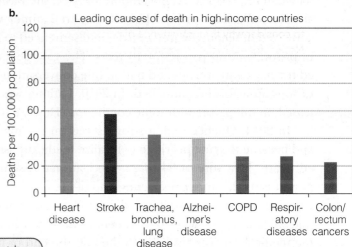

b. Leading causes of death in high-income countries

Think Critically 1. Which leading causes of death in low-income countries are not causes of death in high-income countries?
2. What differences in living conditions in high- vs. low-income countries might contribute to differences in causes of death?

WHO Global Health Observatory

The World Health Organization created the Global Health Observatory (http://www.who.int/en/), which is a gateway to health-related data and statistics from around the world. From this database, information from the WHO's 193 member countries regarding causes of death and other international indicators can be easily downloaded. Developmentalists use this interactive website to quickly gather health facts about nations around the world. The Global Health Observatory reports information related to global health goals and statistics describing variation in mortality and burden of disease across nations. Developmentalists around the world rely on WHO data to write reports and design health plans and policies to fit the needs of their respective nations.

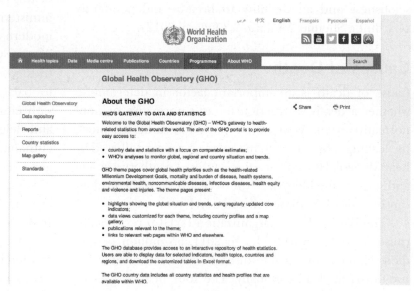

needed to uphold the sanctity of human life and protect vulnerable Canadians (Vogel, 2014). Around the same time as the Sue Rodriguez case, Robert Latimer became the focus of one of the best-known and most controversial cases of euthanasia in Canada. In 1993, Latimer killed his disabled 12-year-old daughter Tracy by placing her in the family truck and then piping exhaust fumes into it. Latimer told the police that his priority was to put her out of her pain. With a severe form of cerebral palsy, Tracy had suffered a considerable amount of pain; she was unable to walk, talk, or feed herself. Robert Latimer was convicted of second-degree murder and sentenced to life in prison with no parole for 10 years. The case generated further controversies and nationwide conversations as various appeals were launched. In 2010, Latimer was released on full parole with some conditions (Howe, 2015).

In 2014, Quebec took a strong stand on the matter and became the first province to legalize medically assisted death. In a vote of 94 to 22, the National Assembly passed Bill 52, An Act respecting end-of-life care, which allows doctors to prescribe and administer substances that will cause the death of a patient as an extension of the medical services available to those at the end of life. Under the new law, it is the responsibility of the physician to verify that the patient's informed consent is free from external pressures. Those physicians unwilling to provide medical aid with dying are able to refer requesting patients to colleagues or supervisors. Quebec was cautious when drafting the bill, attempting to navigate the issue without challenging the Criminal Code of Canada, which at the time continued to define assistance in bringing about a person's death as homicide (Dyer, 2014).

However, Canada's legal context was significantly altered in February 2015 when the Supreme Court of Canada issued the unanimous decision in Lee Carter et al. v. Attorney General of Canada et al., and extended the constitutional rights of Canadians to include autonomy over one's death in circumstances involving a permanent and grievous medical condition (Fine, 2015). The case was brought by two women who have both since died: Kathleen Carter, 89, who suffered from spinal stenosis, and Gloria Taylor, 61, who, like Sue Rodriguez, suffered from ALS. The Supreme Court relied heavily on the factual findings of Justice Lynn Smith of the B.C. Supreme Court, who conducted extensive hearings on the legal developments in other jurisdictions after the Rodriguez case (Fine, 2015).

The Supreme Court's 2015 ruling initiated a 12-month suspension period, ongoing at the time of this writing, for new rules and regulations to be drafted. The federal government did have the option to override the Court's decision using the Charter of Rights and

Freedoms' "notwithstanding clause," but had not done so at the time of writing. The federal government could also organize efforts to craft national legislation to govern assisted dying, or it could opt to leave things unregulated, in which case the provinces and territories would independently draft guidelines, or allow the medical profession to govern the practice. Importantly, the Supreme Court's ruling did not strike down laws prohibiting assisted suicide, but did invalidate the absolute prohibition that prevented physician-assisted death for competent consenting adults dealing with medical conditions causing permanent and intolerable suffering (Attaran, 2015). The federal government had invited an external panel to provide advice on physician-assisted dying, while a joint expert advisory group had been initiated by the provinces and territories (British Columbia Civil Liberties Association, 2015).

This ruling raises questions concerning who has the right to die. Should the availability of medically assisted death be limited to the terminally ill or open to those with serious disability as well? Should access be limited by age, prohibiting young adults and children from requesting death? When is someone considered "decisionally vulnerable (less able to know their own wishes and feelings and more prone to being overly influenced by others)," and who gets to make that decision? What about problems with applying this concept in the real world, such as ensuring equal access to quality end-of-life care and medically assisted death in order to give patients meaningful choice?

Vocabulary related to the right to die The lessons learned from Canadian history have informed us about the complexity involved in the right to die; often such complexities centre on the form that euthanasia takes. Euthanasia is the practice of terminating someone's life in a painless manner. The term is derived from the Greek *eu* meaning good or well and *thanatos* meaning death, together meaning "a good death." Euthanasia is either done with consent, called *voluntary euthanasia,* or in the cases where consent is not possible, without consent, called *involuntary euthanasia.*

One form of euthanasia is called **passive euthanasia**. Passive euthanasia occurs when treatment that would sustain life is withheld. For example, people who sign a **do not resuscitate (DNR) order** ask that no measures be taken to keep them alive if their heart stops beating. Other types of passive euthanasia could be the withdrawal of drugs or a respiratory technology without which the patient would die. The concept of *pulling the plug* falls within the category of passive euthanasia. This process is legal in Canada and in most countries.

Active euthanasia is the process of actively ending a person's life with some type of substance or procedure. The injection of a lethal substance by an individual would be considered active euthanasia. This procedure was recently legalized in Canada via the 2015 Supreme Court ruling discussed above, but it has been available for years in some other countries such as Switzerland (Attaran, 2015).

Physician-assisted suicide is a type of active euthanasia in which a physician provides lethal drugs to a person but does not actually administer the drugs. In this case, the euthanasia is voluntary. Patients who request physician assistance in the dying process do so because they are experiencing "unbearable suffering" (Dees, Vernooij-Dassen, Dekkers, Vissers, & van Weel, 2011).

Advance directives

Advance directives are written instructions regarding a person's medical care preferences, called upon when an individual who has a terminal illness is no longer able to make his or her own medical care decisions. One example of an advance directive is a **living will**. A living will specifically outlines the medical procedures and interventions that a person wants or doesn't want, such as mechanical breathing, tube feeding,

---

euthanasia The practice of ending a person's life to relieve pain or suffering.

passive euthanasia The practice of either withholding or withdrawing treatment from a terminally ill person, thus ending life through natural causes.

do not resuscitate (DNR) order A written request made by a person who does not want to receive any medical intervention in the event that his or her heart stops beating.

active euthanasia The practice of directly effecting death through outside sources such as lethal drugs.

physician-assisted suicide A form of active euthanasia in which lethal drugs are provided, but not administered, by a physician.

advance directive Legal instructions regarding specific health care measures to be taken in the event that an individual is rendered unconscious because of a terminal illness.

living will An example of an advance directive, which specifies what medical procedures and interventions a person wants or does not want.

Advance directives legislation • Figure 17.3

Each territory and province uses slightly different language in its advance directive legislation, and very importantly, each has different laws for making and relying on these powerful documents. The website Advance Directives (http://www.canadianelderlaw.ca/Advance%20 Directives.htm) has links for each region in Canada to research additional resources on this topic.

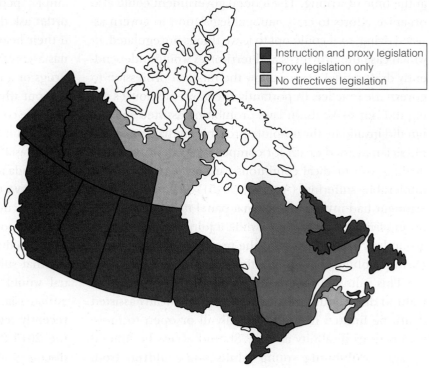

Legend:
- Instruction and proxy legislation
- Proxy legislation only
- No directives legislation

Ask Yourself

1. Which regions have no legislation?
2. How might the experiences for dying be similar and different in these two regions?

Source: http://www.canadianelderlaw.ca/Advance%20Directives.htm.

or resuscitation (Ramsaroop, Reid, & Aldeman, 2007). Advance directives can be divided into two categories: (1) an instruction directive, in which an individual sets out *what types of treatment* he or she does not want in the event that he or she becomes incompetent; and (2) a health proxy directive (health care power of attorney) in which an individual legally designates someone else to make decisions regarding treatment when the individual in question cannot. This designated person now has the power to determine or follow the wishes of the patient (Ramsaroop et al., 2007).

As **Figure 17.3** indicates, the legislation regarding advance directives varies across Canada. In light of the Supreme Court's 2015 ruling on physician-assisted death, health care and legal professionals will likely need to determine how requests for death will be incorporated into health-care directives.

Living wills can be used only for the terminally ill who can no longer make decisions about care. For example, if a person went into a coma and had created a living will in advance, that living will would enable health care providers to know the person's wishes regarding life-sustaining measures.

Living wills can be used only where there is clear agreement among physicians that the person has no chance of survival. For example, if a person has an unexpected heart attack and is unconscious, a living will would not be consulted unless there was clear agreement among physicians that the patient could not be resuscitated (Laakkonen, Pitkala, Strandberg, Berglind, & Tilvis, 2004). This person's wishes could be conveyed, however, through a loved one via a health care power of attorney or health proxy.

CONCEPT CHECK STOP

1. **What** are the physiological indicators of death?
2. **How** do the leading causes of death vary across the lifespan?
3. **What** are the critical arguments for and against the right to die?

The Process of Death and Dying

LEARNING OBJECTIVES

1. **Identify** four dimensions of cognitive understanding of death.

2. **Explain** the five stages of dying.

3. **Explain** the role of hospice.

Only from the most limited perspective is death simply a biological state or a medical process. Death is a complex, multi-dimensional experience, an active process of the living. Both the person who is dying and those witnessing and experiencing dying and death are challenged to understand death at a cognitive level. And death and dying, above all else, place demands on our ability to process emotions.

Understanding the Concept of Death

Understanding death is a matter of both attitude and cognition (Kastenbaum & Costa, 1977). By adulthood, the majority of individuals have a multi-dimensional understanding of the death experience, which involves four dimensions: **irreversibility**, **non-functionality**, **universality**, and **causality** (Orbach, Gross, Glaubman, & Berman, 1986). The concept of death tends to become better understood with age (**Table 17.2**). It is important to note, however, that an understanding of death may be non-linear, with a child gaining and

> **irreversibility**
> The concept that once something or someone dies they cannot come back to life.
>
> **non-functionality**
> The concept that death ends all functions such as talking, breathing, and social interaction.
>
> **universality**
> The concept that everything dies and that death is inevitable.
>
> **causality** The concept that everything dies due to some type of biological process.

then losing some types of understanding with age, and the ages of attainment may vary. Behavioural reactions vary based on developmental level as well (Himebauch, Arnold, & May, 2008). In fact, personal exposure to death, culture, and religion may all play a larger role in the development of death understanding than age alone (Cuddy-Casey & Orvaschel, 1997).

Attitudes about death, in contrast to the elements that compose a cognitive understanding of death, on the other hand, are less consistent among adults. There also seem to be changes in anxiety and fear related to death as one ages (Abengózar, Bueno, & Vega, 1999). Attitudes about death involve the emotions that accompany thoughts about death and dying. Two attitudes toward death are relevant in determining how a person experiences death: fear of death and death anxiety (Depaola, Griffin, Young, & Niemeyer, 2003; Kastenbaum, 1996; Kastenbaum & Costa, 1977). Fear of death is a conscious and perhaps universal emotion that can be articulated and expressed.

Developmental understanding of and reactions to death   Table 17.2

Age	Understands These Subconcepts of Death				
	Irreversibility	Non-functionality	Universality	Causality	Other Features
0–2 years	n/a	n/a	n/a	n/a	Separation anxiety is possible even though infant does not understand death.
2–6 years	n/a	n/a	n/a	n/a	Magical thinking may be demonstrated (such as "I told Daddy to go away and that made him die").
6–8 years	✓	✓	n/a	n/a	Anger, fear, and anxiety are common.
8–12 years	✓	✓	✓	✓	May experience guilt and/or become preoccupied with death rituals.
12–18 years	✓	✓	✓	✓	May isolate themselves and/or engage in high-risk activities.

death anxiety An underlying feeling of uneasiness about the possibility that death might occur.

Death anxiety, on the other hand, is not conscious and is demonstrated as denial of death. Research suggests that both fear of death and death anxiety are sources of stress and depression in adulthood (Becker, 1973), although denial is believed to be more problematic.

Childhood The research concerning a child's perception of the concept of death has taken several approaches. One predominant view is that a child's understanding of death is correlated with cognitive ability (Childers & Wimmer, 1971; Cotton & Range, 1990; Koocher, 1973). Much of the data are based on cross-sectional interviews (e.g., Nagy, 1965; Speece & Brent, 1984).

Preoperational (preschool-aged) children are unable to understand any of the subconcepts of death. They lack the logic required to transcend the present and they fall victim to egocentric thinking (Koocher, 1973). The producers of *Sesame Street* grappled with how to present the topic of death to young children in 1983 after the actor who played Mr. Hooper on the show suddenly died. When they first outlined *The Death of Mr. Hooper* episode, they planned to use video flashbacks of Mr. Hooper (Stiles, 1984). Psychologists advised against doing this because it might play into preschoolers' misconceptions about irreversibility. With the input of child developmental experts, the episode dealt with the topic of death in a way that a preschool child could understand, having Big Bird ask the typical questions a 3- to 5-year-old might ask when someone dies (**Figure 17.4**). Many preschool teachers use this episode as a way to discuss death with young children in an open and honest fashion.

Once children are school-aged, Piaget and others believe that the subconcepts of death become increasingly understood. This understanding occurs because of the increased cognitive skills inherent in the concrete operational period. Some researchers, however, question the idea that cognition and chronology are the sole factors in a child's understanding of death.

Classic studies of children's understanding of death provide some insight into how children reason about death. Developmental scientists who studied

Young children's perception of death • Figure 17.4

In this episode, Big Bird looks for Mr. Hooper to give him a picture. When told that Mr. Hooper has died, Big Bird says that he will just give him the picture later, illustrating the inability of children of preschool age to understand the irreversibility of death. Children often demonstrate the lack of ability to comprehend death by communicating their curiosity about what dead people might be doing in heaven or in other places dead people may be inhabiting (Barrett & Behne, 2005).

PBS/Courtesy: Everett Collection

Think Critically How would a 4-year-old differ from a 10-year-old in demonstrating an understanding or lack of understanding of the irreversibility of death?

6- to 11-year-olds concluded that intelligence, age, and anxiety level all affect a child's awareness of death (Orbach et al., 1986). However, those factors mattered significantly less than a personal experience with death, such as getting diagnosed with a serious illness or experiencing the death of a loved one. Social context matters, too. For example, children who grow up in war-involved countries are aware of the causes of death at younger ages than children who live in countries not at war (Nagy, 1965).

By the time a child enters the adolescent transition, a new set of factors emerges. The adolescent has the cognitive ability to understand the abstractness of the four subconcepts of death.

Adolescence Adolescents understand death in fairly abstract terms and are often adult-like in their awareness (Himebauch et al., 2008). If we separate adolescents into early (12–15) and late (16–19), however, there are clear differences that are consistent with adolescent egocentrism, idealism, and the imaginary audience.

Early adolescents are becoming independent. They often feel misunderstood and sometimes believe that no one understands them. When close friends or even strangers die, early adolescents often experience intense levels of emotion. Without mature coping resources, they may experience an inability to articulate their emotions and may, as a result, act out in frustration, taking out strong emotions on themselves. As adolescents become more socially mature, they begin to have a more realistic understanding of death. They begin to understand the consequences of their own death or that of their loved ones. They are also better able to understand and regulate their emotional reactions when a loved one dies (Bonanno, 2004).

Older adults As we get older and closer to death, the reality of death's finality becomes salient in our lives. One might expect, then, that there would be a correlated increase in fear of death and/or death anxiety, a finding supported by early research (Kastenbaum & Costa, 1977). More recent research suggests, however, that these assumptions may be incorrect. Depaola et al. (2003) reported that death anxiety was significantly lower in the elderly than in younger adults. They also reported data from several studies suggesting that older individuals tend to choose to talk about death and think about death more than younger adults do. Older individuals are also less fearful, on average, than younger adults.

Factors other than age, including socio-economic status (Rando, 1984), health, stability of family, social support, religion (Dezutter, Luyckx, & Hutsebaut, 2009), and mental health (Forsell, 2000), affect an older person's attitude about death (Fortner & Neimeyer, 1999). Many elderly adults express mixed feelings about approaching death. Interview questions such as "Are you afraid to die?" get responses such as "No, but I also want to feel good while I'm alive" (Depaola et al., 2003, p. 337). Thanatologist (one who studies death and dying) Therese Rando (1984) believes that although low death anxiety may be reported by the elderly, a realistic fear of death is a constant part of their daily lives.

We have discussed definitions and understanding of death. Now we turn to the process of dying. The work of Elisabeth Kübler-Ross is the most well-known research on the process of death and dying.

The Work of Elisabeth Kübler-Ross

Elisabeth Kübler-Ross was born as one of a set of triplets on a farm outside of Zürich, Switzerland, in 1926. It has been reported that when she was a child, one of her neighbours had an accident that left him paralyzed. During his time of paralysis and impending death, young Elisabeth became very interested in what it felt like to be dying (Worth, 2004). Thus began the illustrious career of one of the most influential persons in the field of death and dying.

Kübler-Ross's work with dying individuals led her to write *On Death and Dying*, one of the most significant books to date on the dying and grieving process (Kübler-Ross, 1969). In her book she outlined the process of dying in her now famous five stages of grief, shown in **Figure 17.5** (Kübler-Ross, 1969, 1974, 1976). She labelled individuals who do not reach acceptance of their impending death as pathological (Telford, Kralik, & Koch, 2006). Based on follow-up research, it seems that these are not stages as much as they are emotional states that may be felt in any order and may be experienced repeatedly, even over the course of a single day.

The stages of dying explain not only a terminal patient's reactions, but also the grief that others feel

PROCESS DIAGRAM

Kübler-Ross's stages of grief • Figure 17.5

From her work with dying individuals, Elisabeth Kübler-Ross theorized five stages of grief (Kübler-Ross & Kessler, 2005). The person may experience the stages in any order. A person may experience some of the stages, all of the stages, or the stages multiple times. Grief is an individual process.

1 Denial
The individual does not acknowledge the reality of the information, such as the diagnosis of a terminal illness. There is no emotion. Attempts at communication are useless.

2 Anger
The anger may be directed at a doctor, loved one, or self.

3 Bargaining
The individual tries to find a way to make the terminal disease go away, such as through religion or alternative medicines.

5 Acceptance
As the intensity of other emotions gradually fades, a comfortable understanding of what is about to happen emerges. This acceptance typically is not joyful, however; it is simply a state devoid of negative emotion.

4 Depression
The individual begins to understand the gravity of the information and feels extremely upset.

Ask Yourself

1. When a person is told he or she is going to die, typically the first reaction is _____.
   a. depression   b. denial
2. Some people may turn to religion in order to _____.
   a. make a bargain   b. get angry
3. Acceptance often brings a person _____.
   a. pathological issues   b. comfortable understanding

when they lose a loved one. The five stages can be applied to non-death scenarios as well. For example, individuals appear to go through the five stages when they perceive their job is in jeopardy or when they lose their job (Blau, 2009). Individuals going through significant medical procedures such as amputation also appear to experience the stages (Belon & Vigoda, 2014). Others report experiencing the grief cycle at the end of a relationship or a divorce (Morrow, 2009).

Although the five stages of dying have become part of North American culture, there are some who are still skeptical of its explanatory purpose and even of whether it is a valid description (Friedman & James, 2008). One major criticism is that linear—or even non-linear—stages that attempt to capture the psychological dimensions a dying person goes through may be an oversimplification (Telford et al., 2006). Similarly, some suggest that using stages to explain the grieving process is both inaccurate and harmful (Friedman & James, 2008). For example, most family members do not exhibit denial after a death, and depression is often normative and healthy. Moving away from the traditional model created by Kübler-Ross, however, has proven difficult.

Another challenge attacks the assumption that denial is a normal and healthy part of the process (Telford et al., 2006). From a medical and psychological standpoint, opportunities to educate a patient about symptoms and treatments are essential. Denial thus becomes a wall between a patient and possible support systems and is viewed by many as pathological. If health care professionals accept denial as a normal part of the process, as Kübler-Ross suggests, they may be less persistent in establishing educational communication with patients. This approach can lead to poorer health care management and misunderstandings (Kingsbury, 2000; Revenson & Felton, 1989).

Another criticism suggests that acceptance is not the normal conclusion in the process of dying or grieving. A positive acceptance of a terminal condition may lead to resistance to treatment and reduction of survival time (Reed, Kemeny, Taylor, Wang, & Visscher, 1994). Not unlike denial, acceptance becomes a barrier to motivation for improvement. In fact, having unrealistic optimism about one's prognosis may be beneficial for adjustment and actually extend life (Kingsbury, 2000). For example, HIV patients were found to engage in increased risk-taking behaviours such as drug use when they reached the stage of acceptance (Reed et al., 1994), but they exhibited positive adjustment and motivation when they were unrealistically optimistic about their condition (Taylor, Kemeny, Aspinwall, Schneider, Rodriguez, & Herbert, 1992).

Kübler-Ross's contribution to understanding the dying process is immeasurable. As we will see later in this chapter, organizations such as hospices have some connection with her early work. However, the transformative impact of losing a loved one or hearing the news that you have a terminal illness is an intimately personal event. The assumption that this experience can be the same for everyone and that it has a predictable sequence is very difficult to validate.

Palliative and Hospice Care

Health care's response to serious illness goes beyond trying to cure the disease. In cases of serious, life-threatening illness, both palliative care and hospice care provide patients with relief from pain and suffering and improve quality of life. **Palliative care** focuses on relieving pain and discomfort at any stage of a serious or chronic illness and sometimes occurs along with curative treatment. Palliative care focuses on reducing symptoms such as pain, shortness of breath, fatigue, constipation, nausea, loss of appetite, sleep difficulties, and depression. Such care can help patients both tolerate treatments and feel that they have more control over their treatment.

Palliative care may give way to hospice care when a serious illness progresses and an individual has a life expectancy of six months or less. "We do not have to cure to heal." This quote, attributed to British physician Cicely Saunders, led to what we know as the hospice movement. The main purpose of **hospice care** is to give persons with terminal illnesses care that focuses on reducing pain, suffering, and discomfort as well as on spiritual, emotional, and psychological counselling (see *What a Developmentalist Sees*). Hospice care may be provided in a hospital or nursing home, but most people receive hospice care in their own homes.

The first recognized hospice was St. Christopher's Hospice in London, England, in the early 1960s. Meanwhile, Elisabeth Kübler-Ross's landmark book opened North American culture to talking about death. Inspired by Kübler-Ross, a Canadian physician, Balfour Mount, determined to better assist terminally ill patients at Royal Victoria Hospital in Montreal. Motivated by the horrid care he had witnessed at his home hospital, he spent a week studying and working in London with Dr. Saunders at St. Christopher's, describing it thus: "It was one of the most stimulating single weeks in my life" (Duffy, 2005, p. 1). Dr. Mount modified the Saunders model for Canada, creating a specialized ward at Royal Victoria in January 1975, and thereby becoming a pioneer of the hospice movement here. He coined the term "palliative care," as the word "hospice" was already used in France to refer to nursing homes, and he wanted a more distinctive term for his native Quebec (Duffy, 2005). According to the Canadian Institute for Health Information, only 16 to 30

> **palliative care** Care focused on reducing symptoms, such as pain and discomfort, at any stage of a chronic illness or serious illness, which is sometimes provided with curative treatment.
>
> **hospice care** Care provided to persons with terminal illnesses focused on the reduction of suffering and the availability of spiritual, emotional, and psychological support.

WHAT A DEVELOPMENTALIST SEES
Hospice Care

At first glance, you might think these photos showed a patient in a typical hospital room. A developmentalist would recognize this as hospice care, with a number of features that uniquely serve the terminally ill. Generally, hospice provides support for both the dying patients and their families. Because the patients are terminal, there is no treatment of the illness, and all resources are directed toward reducing discomfort (Waldrop & Rinfrette, 2009). Hospice care has become increasingly common.

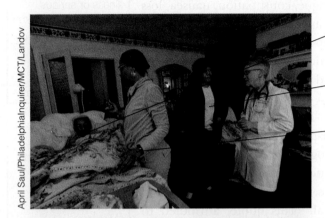

April Saul/PhiladelphiaInquirer/MCT/Landov

Morphine is often provided during hospice care to ease pain and suffering.

Hospice nurses serve as a vital member of the support team, coordinating care among physicians, families, and patients and attending to medical needs.

Hospice health aides attend to the ongoing care needs of the dying individual, including bathing and feeding.

Steve McCurry/Magnum Photos

Chaplains, such as this Buddhist chaplain in New York City, support the spiritual transition of the patient.

Monitors, including those for heart rate, typically are not present in a hospice setting. Hospice is meant to be more soothing than an ICU setting.

Social workers often work with the patient and his or her family in providing psychological and material support.

Think Critically
1. What might a hospice counsellor say to encourage the family of a terminal patient to consider using hospice care?
2. In what ways would hospice care benefit the patient and his or her family?

percent of Canadians who die currently have access to or receive hospice, palliative, and end-of-life care services, depending on where they live in Canada. Even fewer receive grief and bereavement services (CIHI, 2007). Canadians living in remote and rural areas, or those living with disabilities, have severely limited access to formal hospice palliative care services. Inadequate government support for hospice palliative care programs and a dominant health care system approach results in a significant additional burden on family and informal caregivers (Canadian Hospice Palliative Care Association, 2014).

From 2001 to 2006, the federal government funded the Secretariat on Palliative End-of-Life Care with an annual budget of approximately $1.5 million. However, in 2007 the Secretariat was disbanded and the national strategy ended (Canadian Hospice Palliative Care Association, 2014). With governments downloading care into the community, families are facing an increased burden to care for loved ones with little formal support. In 2007, the Health Care in Canada Survey (HCIC) found that 23 percent of Canadians said they had cared for a family member or close friend with a serious health problem in the last 12 months. Adverse effects on this group of people included using personal savings to survive (41 percent) and missing one or more month(s) of work (22 percent). The previous year, this group had also reported negative effects on mental health (41 percent) and negative effects on physical health (38 percent) (HCIC, 2006, 2007). Employers are required to respond fairly and in consideration of our guarantee of human rights as Canadian citizens (e.g., Ontario Human Rights Code, http://www.ohrc.on.ca/en/iv-human-rights-issues-all-stages-employment/8-meeting-accommodation-needs-employees-job).

This could mean important changes to workplaces when employers have to consider how they can support people in caring for loved ones.

CONCEPT CHECK ⬟STOP

1. **How** does understanding of death differ between children and adults?
2. **What** are the criticisms of Kübler-Ross's theory?
3. **How** is hospice care different from hospital care?

Bereavement and Grief

LEARNING OBJECTIVES

1. **Describe** the differences between normal and complicated/traumatic forms of grief.

2. **Explain** the cultural context of mourning and bereavement.

Grief is an intense emotional response to loss. People can grieve for the loss of a family member, a pet, or even a job (Agnew, Manktelow, Taylor, & Jones, 2010). The key factor in the grief response is the perception of loss of contact and interaction. This objective and intellectual definition, however, barely touches the surface of the deep emotional intensity associated with grief. Grief responses are cognitive, emotional, physiological, and evident to anyone observing a grieving person.

Much research has been done on the grieving process (Agnew et al., 2010; Parkes, 2006). There are studies examining the variables associated with grief (Stroebe, 2002), the differences between normal grief and pathological, complicated grief (Dillen, Fontaine, & Verhofstadt-Denève, 2008; Prigerson, Vanderwerker, & Maciejewski, 2007), and the differences between grief and bereavement (Kyriakopoulos, 2008). We will discuss each of these categories in turn.

Before we begin, let us note that discussing grief is never easy. While reading, you may be reminded of lost loved ones and the period when you grieved. Revisiting grief emotions can be painful and even overwhelming.

Allow yourself to reflect on these feelings while connecting with the insights researchers have gained through their objective lenses.

Normal and Complicated/Traumatic Grief

Although there are some disagreements about how long someone should grieve, counsellors and psychologists suggest that a period of about 6 months is a reasonable and normal time frame for a person to grieve (Dillen et al., 2008). During this time, a person tends to feel a sense of yearning and unfulfilled need to be with the loved one. Clear distress is experienced in any activity that might remind the person of the deceased loved one.

The grieving individual may experience many or all of the aspects of Kübler-Ross's five stages. For example, bargaining may become a way of continuing the lost relationship. This could be through personal communications with the dead loved one, rationalizations about life after death, or other creative ways to keep the loved one alive.

As the months pass, however, these negative feelings decrease. The numbness and emptiness associated with the loss gradually subside. Psychologists and counsellors suggest that this is a healthy and positive process leading to adjustment to life without the loved one (Agnew et al., 2010; Dillen et al., 2008; Stroebe, 2002).

The process we have just described is considered normal grief (NG). In some situations, the individual feels **complicated/traumatic grief (CG)**. Two key variables distinguish CG from NG: the time the grief lasts and the impairment of physical or mental health. In the case of CG, the symptoms can last several years after the death of the loved one. Individuals with CG hold on to the connection with the loved one in a pathological manner that interferes with their daily functioning. A person who has CG is also susceptible to physical illness and dysfunctional mental health (Kyriakopoulos, 2008; Stroebe & Stroebe, 1987). CG can include yearning for the deceased, depression, bitterness and anger about the death, constant distress, and a refusal to return to normalcy. Those suffering from CG report feelings of distrust and emotional disconnection from others.

A group that is at increased risk of suffering from CG is bereaved parents. Papadatu (1997) suggests that education of health professionals, particularly nurses, does not prepare them for working with families of dying children. Since the publication of her article in 1997, medical school curricula dealing with bereavement and grief of family members coping with the loss of a child have expanded (Baverstock & Finlay, 2008). The concern

> **complicated/ traumatic grief (CG)** A pathological form of grieving that tends to last longer than normal grieving and is accompanied by impaired social interaction.

CHALLENGES IN DEVELOPMENT
Coping with the Loss of a Child

If you ask parents what would be the worst thing that could ever happen to them, they would likely say the death of their child. Losing a child is contrary to the natural order. As a result, the potential for complicated grief is significantly higher for grieving parents than for those who lose other family members (Keesee, Currier, & Neimeyer, 2008).

A review of over 40 studies identified risk factors that predict the likelihood a survivor will experience CG. The risk factors with the most significant impact include (1) personally seeing or identifying the deceased in cases of violent or traumatic death, (2) having low social support, (3) insecure attachment, (4) high dependency and high neuroticism before death, and (5) spouse or parent of a deceased, especially if "mother" (Burke & Neimeyer, 2013).

Some parents report grieving for the rest of their lives over their loss (Dyregrov & Dyregrov, 1999). Because being a parent is part of one's identity, losing a child symbolizes losing a part of one's self. Therapy designed for this type of loss has shown some success in helping parents (Keesee et al., 2008). Religious and spiritual values have also helped in some cases. The challenge is to create meaning from the loss and construct personal ways of coping.

Finbarr O'Reilly/REUTERS/Landov

> **Think Critically** Based on the risk factors that predict complicated grief, can you describe a parent who is very likely to experience complicated grief?

Where is the line between normal and pathological grief? The *DSM-5* presents guidelines for distinguishing between the two.

Grief	Major depressive disorder
Feelings of emptiness and loss	Persistent depressed mood and the inability to anticipate happiness or pleasure
Decreases over time and may occur in waves associated with reminders of the deceased	More persistent and not tied to specific thoughts
May be accompanied by positive emotions and humour	Pervasive unhappiness and misery
Preoccupation with thoughts and memories of the deceased	Self-critical or pessimistic ruminations
Self-esteem generally preserved	Feelings of worthlessness and self-loathing common
Thoughts of death focus on the possibility of joining the deceased	Thoughts of death come from feeling worthless, undeserving of life, or unable to cope

Think Critically Why might some people have a more difficult time grieving a death?

for parents who lose children has arisen because CG has been demonstrated to lead to physical illness and other psychological pathologies (Rando, 1983). We explore this topic further in *Challenges in Development*.

Most people grieving the loss of a loved one do not develop depression. Officially, depression is the point at which feelings of sadness and loss of pleasure in life have grown to interfere significantly with a person's social or occupational functioning. The official name for clinical depression lasting more than two weeks along with additional symptoms and impairment in functioning is *major depressive disorder (MDD)*. Prior to the publication of the fifth edition of the *Diagnostic and Statistical Manual of Mental Disorders* (*DSM-5*; American Psychiatric Association, 2013), if an individual's major depressive episode happened within two months following the loss of a loved one, then the diagnosis of MDD was not applicable. That exclusion criterion made it difficult for people to get psychological help for depression in the months following a death. The *DSM-5*, published in May 2013, removes the exclusion

and provides guidelines for distinguishing grief from true MDD (**Figure 17.6**).

Bereavement and Mourning in a Cultural Context

Whereas grief is an emotional response, bereavement is the general process of losing a loved one (Stroebe & Stroebe, 1987). **Bereavement** involves the customs, rituals, and personal transformations that occur after a loved one dies. Thus, bereavement may vary culturally as well as at different times during the lifespan.

Within the process of bereavement, we see another reaction to loss: mourning. **Mourning** is the specific behaviours involved in bereavement. Religion and culture often influence the time

bereavement The personal process of grieving and transformation in response to the death of a loved one.

mourning The specific behaviours taken up during bereavement, including those that involve cultural or religious conventions.

Muslim funerals • Figure 17.7

Muslim funerals have a clear sequence based on the teachings of the Qur'an. Specific quotes and phrases are to be said by family members as soon as death occurs, including prayers to Allah asking for forgiveness. The body is washed by family members and then shrouded in three white wound sheets called a *kafan*. During the funeral, flowers and emotional outbursts are discouraged (Abdul-Rahman, 2003).

Think Critically How do you think this particular religious ritual came into being?

GUL RAHIM/AFP/GettyImages

of mourning. Middle Eastern and Western cultures vary significantly in the need for a continued bond with a deceased loved one (Hussein & Oyebode, 2009). China and Japan have maintained a long-term worship of ancestors. In these cultures, the deceased are believed to transition to the other world, where they continue to survey the actions of the family. Muslim religion also describes a continuing relationship with the deceased, often referring to them as role models and motivation to do well in life (Hussein & Oyebode, 2009). Western culture, however, tends to view long-term continuation of a bond with a lost loved one as pathological (Lalande & Bonnano, 2006). These different cultural views of mourning affect stress and coping. For example, Lalande and Bonnano (2006) found that maintaining connections with deceased loved ones reduced stress in a sample of Chinese individuals but not in Americans.

Culture also affects one's understanding of death. Most Eastern and Western cultures share the same four concepts we discussed earlier in the chapter: irreversibility, non-functionality, universality, and causality. What tends to vary, however, is the level of importance of each component and the way these understandings of death are ritualized. For instance, many Native American cultures believe in the finality of the physical person, but some believe that the spirit continues through a return to nature (Sullivan, 2000). Canada's Indigenous population, composed of Inuit, First Nation, and Metis cultures, has varied approaches to death and ritual. For example, some Indigenous people who are dying will need the ceremonies, medicine, and prayers that will guide their spirit back

to the spirit world. They will need their spiritual leader or a medicine person who is close to them to conduct the ceremonies, and they will need their family and clan members to be present (Anderson, n.d), In Asian culture, there is also a reconnection to the natural world. Through this reconnection, long-dead ancestors have active roles in the lives of the living (Lalande & Bonnano, 2006).

Perhaps the most obvious influence of culture and religion is seen in death rituals and practices. Islamic rituals follow the teachings of the Qur'an, as discussed in **Figure 17.7** (Hussein & Oyebode, 2009). Christian funerals are typically solemn events directed by religious leaders. Jewish ceremonies are similar; however, following the funeral there is a period called *sitting shiva*, in which family members sit on wooden benches for approximately seven days and are visited by relatives. During this time and on special holidays, a mourner's prayer called a *Kaddish* is said. On the first anniversary of the death, the tombstone is unveiled. Although these rituals appear to be unique to specific cultures, many of these practices are driven by common central beliefs.

Although culture may influence mourning, the process remains as individual as the person who is mourning. Much of the variation has to do with the timing of the death, preparedness of the survivor, and relationship with the deceased. All in all, though, mourning is a healthy form of normative grief (Bonanno & Kaltman, 2001).

The final section of this chapter and of our text has taken us to the end of our journey. It only makes sense that in a discussion of human development we concluded by discussing reactions to the lifespan's inevitable end. Development of the self and understanding of the self take place from birth through death. The final moments before death reflect the final moments of lifespan human development. In those final moments, individuals have an opportunity to look back on their lives, to identify themes, and to communicate conclusions about the meaning of the lives they lived.

Summary

1 What Is Death? 536

- The term **irreversible coma** was introduced in the 1950s, and years later, the criteria for **brain death** were established. An important determinant was the difference between a **persistent vegetative state (PVS)** and a **minimally conscious state**. In Canada, debate surrounding the medical definition of death continues to some extent, with regional differences in diagnostic practices.

- Overall, at the population level in Canada, the leading causes of death are cancer and heart disease, as shown in the figure. In childhood, adolescence, and emerging adulthood, death due to disease is relatively rare, and unintentional injury is the leading cause of death.

Leading causes of death in Canada • Figure 17.1

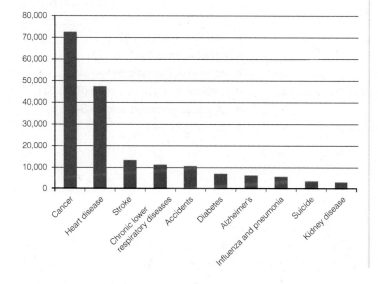

- As the medical world has developed ways to keep people alive longer, society has grappled with whether individuals should have a right to die when they are suffering with a terminal illness; for example, through **euthanasia**. **Passive euthanasia** involves withholding life-sustaining care, as is requested through a **do not resuscitate (DNR) order**, for example. It is different from **active euthanasia** (ending life with a substance/procedure) or **physician-assisted suicide** (a doctor provides lethal drugs)—issues that were being considered by the Canadian government in light of the 2015 Supreme Court of Canada ruling that decriminalized doctor-assisted death under some circumstances. All of these issues deal with **advance directives**, instructions on procedures to follow in case of a terminal illness. Examples include **living wills** and a health care power of attorney.

2 The Process of Death and Dying 543

- Understanding and accepting death depend largely on a person's age. According to psychologists, being able to accept death involves four cognitive elements: **irreversibility** (the dead person cannot return), **non-functionality** (all functions cease at death), **universality** (death is inevitable for everyone), and **causality** (everything dies for a reason). Young children cannot truly understand death, but they develop the ability as they age, although other factors can play a part. By late adolescence, young people have a stronger grasp of death and control of their emotional reactions to it. By adulthood, all four elements of death are recognized. For some, later adulthood brings along a fear of death or **death anxiety**, because of a growing awareness of death's finality.

- Elisabeth Kübler-Ross outlined stages of death, including denial, anger, bargaining, depression, and finally, acceptance, which is depicted in the figure. Although other researchers have expressed disagreement with Kübler-Ross's conclusions, her work is still considered a standard in the field of mortality.

- The **hospice** movement was created to help people with terminal conditions to have quality end-of-life care. The focus in hospice care is comfort rather than cure, and it is often provided for those who have months, or even weeks, left to live. **Palliative care** focuses on relieving pain and discomfort at any stage of a serious or chronic illness and is sometimes provided in addition to curative treatment.

Kübler-Ross's stages of grief • Figure 17.5

Taylor Kennedy-SITKA PRO/NGImage Collection

3 Bereavement and Grief 549

- Grief is a powerful emotional response to a loss, whether of a family member, friend, pet, or job. Grief affects a person in cognitive, emotional, and physiological ways. Normal grief is typically distinguished from **complicated/traumatic grief (CG)** by time or by how long a person is emotionally distressed. Six months is considered an average amount of time for normal grief, whereas complicated grief may last years, interfere with daily functioning, and cause other negative emotions like anger and depression. This type of grief is especially prevalent in parents who have lost a child, such as the man shown in this photo.

Challenges in Development: Coping with the Loss of a Child

Finbarr O'Reilly/REUTERS/Landov

- **Bereavement** is the process of losing a loved person and involves customs, rituals, and personal changes. It is strongly affected by culture. **Mourning** is involved in the bereavement process and is also influenced by religion and culture.

Key Terms

- active euthanasia 541
- advance directive 541
- bereavement 551
- causality 543
- complicated/traumatic grief (CG) 550
- death anxiety 544
- do not resuscitate (DNR) order 541

- euthanasia 541
- hospice care 547
- irreversibility 543
- irreversible coma or brain death 537
- living will 541
- minimally conscious state 537
- mourning 551

- non-functionality 543
- palliative care 547
- passive euthanasia 541
- persistent vegetative state (PVS) 537
- physician-assisted suicide 541
- universality 543

What is happening in this picture?

Funeral customs and rituals often vary dramatically from one culture to another. At this funeral in Sikkim, India, Buddhist lamas surround the body of a princess.

John Scofield/NG Image Collection

Think Critically

1. Which of Kübler-Ross's stages of grief do these people seem to be expressing?

2. How does this funeral differ from the typical funerals held in Canada?

3. Do the people at the funeral seem to be experiencing normal or complicated grief? Could you tell from a photo?

4. If you could change any cultural norms surrounding bereavement that we have in Canada, what would they be? Why?

Critical and Creative Thinking Questions

1. Why do people struggle emotionally or morally to determine when death occurs? How has technology complicated the matter?

2. How would you tell a young child about a death, compared with how you would communicate with a teenager or young adult?

3. Why do cases like Sue Rodriguez's and Robert Latimer's affect people so deeply?

4. Which one of Elisabeth Kübler-Ross's stages of grief would be the most difficult to get through? What factors would make it easier or harder to get through?

5. Why do some people fight so hard for the right to die? Why are others equally against it? What factors into the opinions?

Self-Test

(Check your answers in Appendix A.)

1. In cases of irreversible coma, what criterion is used to define death?

a. cessation of breathing

b. lack of brain activity

c. no indication of heartbeat

d. negative response to stimuli

2. In this image, which of the Harvard criteria is being directly assessed?

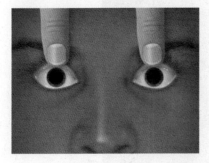

a. absence of brain activity

b. absence of breathing

c. lack of reflexes

d. heartbeat stopped

3. The right to die has more recently become an important ethical and legal topic due to _____.

a. a growing number of medical lawyers

b. advances in medical technology that allow physicians more control over death

c. laws that require each adult to draft an advanced directive

d. advances in ethical arguments in favour of parent rights over spousal rights in the case of irreversible coma

4. Health care workers following a DNR order is an example of _____.

a. active euthanasia

b. physician-assisted suicide

c. passive euthanasia

d. dual effect theory

5. In which case would an advance directive be used?

a. a patient who is recovering from surgery

b. a patient whose medical team agrees he will not survive

c. a patient who is religious

d. a patient who is non-religious

6. Which of the following is a 7-year-old likely to believe after the death of the family dog?

a. The dog died as a consequence of his barking.

b. The dog will not live again.

c. The dog will live again.

d. The dog died due to a biological reason.

7. Which stage of grief does this photo depict?

Lynn Johnson/NG Image Collection

a. denial

b. acceptance

c. anger

d. depression

8. Which of these statements about death anxiety is true?

a. It is a universal emotion.

b. It is often discussed and expressed.

c. It is a slight fear of death.

d. It is an unconscious denial of death.

9. What is the primary purpose of palliative care?

a. to cure a serious condition

b. to educate the patient's family

c. to relieve pain and discomfort

d. to determine the best course of treatment

10. Understanding that these parents are grieving the death of a child and not another family member, they are at increased risk for experiencing _____.

Finbarr O'Reilly/REUTERS/Landov

a. complicated/traumatic grief

b. Kübler-Ross's stage of denial

c. dysfunctional mental health

d. extended bereavement

11. Which statement accurately explains the difference between grief and bereavement?

a. Grief is a brief emotion, but recovery from bereavement can take years.

b. Grief is only felt for the loss of a person, but bereavement can be felt for other types of losses in addition.

c. Grief varies greatly from one culture to another, but bereavement is the same universally.

d. Grief is an emotional response, but bereavement is a process involving rituals and customs.

12. All of these statements are true *except* that _____.

a. when a child is lost, fathers tend to grieve longer and more intensely than mothers

b. violent death is often correlated with a higher risk of traumatic/complicated grief

c. parents who lose their only child have more grief than those with multiple children

d. some parents report grieving an entire lifetime over the loss of a child

13. Bereavement describes general customs, whereas _____ refers to specific behaviours.

a. mourning

b. rituals

c. ideals

d. trauma

14. The mourning process depends on all of the following factors *except* _____.

a. timing of the death

b. preparedness of the survivor

c. relationship with the deceased

d. why the person died in the first place

15. _____ involves the customs, rituals, and personal transformations that occur after a loved one dies.

a. Grief

b. Bereavement

c. Death rites

d. Faith

THE PLANNER ✓

Review your Chapter Planner in the chapter opener and check off your completed work.

References

The references are available online at the *Visualizing the Lifespan, Canadian Edition* Student and Instructor Companion Websites: www.wiley.com/go/tannercanada. The references can also be found in the e-Text of *Visualizing the Lifespan, Canadian Edition* as well as in its WileyPlus course. Instructors, would you like your students to have this material printed in their texts? Contact your Wiley representative for more details on customizing your course's content.

Appendix: Answers to Mid-chapter Questions and Self-Tests
*Please note that answers for discussion-type questions are not included in this appendix.

Chapter 1

Self-Test Answers
1. c; 2. c; 3. c; 4. a; 5. a; 6. a; 7. b; 8. d; 9. a; 10. a; 11. b; 12. c; 13. a; 14. b; 15. c

Figure Question Answers
Figure 1.3 (Ask Yourself): c
Figure 1.6 (Ask Yourself): 1. non-normative; 2. normative
Figure 1.13 (Put It Together): Early
Figure 1.15 (Ask Yourself): 1. life experience and personality maturity; 2. intelligence, personality traits; 3. age
Figure 1.19 (Ask Yourself): 1. b; 2. c; 3. a
What a Developmentalist Sees: 1. positive correlation; 2. negative correlation; 3. no correlation
Figure 1.21 (Ask Yourself): 1. cross-sectional; 2. longitudinal; 3. cross-sequential

Chapter 2

Self-Test Answers
1. b; 2. d; 3. b; 4. c; 5. d; 6. b; 7. d; 8. a; 9. c; 10. b; 11. b; 12. d; 13. a; 14. d; 15. d

Figure Question Answers
Figure 2.1 (Ask Yourself): 1. autosomes; 2. sex; 3. nucleus
Figure 2.2 (Ask Yourself): genes
Figure 2.3 (Ask Yourself): 1. brown; 2. No.
Figure 2.4 (Ask Yourself): 1. ovaries; 2. testicles; 3. vagina, cervical opening, uterus, fallopian tubes
Figure 2.6 (Ask Yourself): meiosis, mitosis
Figure 2.7 (Put It Together): mitosis
Figure 2.8 (Ask Yourself): Yes, but it is more difficult to do so.
Figure 2.10 (Put It Together): 2 weeks after conception to birth
Figure 2.12 (Put It Together): d
Figure 2.14 (Ask Yourself): The second or pushing stage of labour.
Figure 2.20 (Ask Yourself): 1. 37; 2. preterm

Chapter 3

Self-Test Answers
1. a; 2. b; 3. b; 4. b; 5. d; 6. c; 7. b; 8. c; 9. d; 10. c; 11. a; 12. a; 13. c; 14. d; 15. d

Figure Question Answers
Figure 3.1 (Ask Yourself): 1. proximodistal; 2. cephalocaudal
Figure 3.2 (Ask Yourself): PNS
Figure 3.4 (Ask Yourself): decreases; increases
Figure 3.5 (Ask Yourself): 1. sit without support; 2. hold objects
Figure 3.6 (Ask Yourself): gross motor

Figure 3.7 (Ask Yourself): substage 5
Figure 3.8 (Put It Together): 1. substage 6; 2. symbolic thought
Figure 3.10 (Ask Yourself): 1. ability to recognize a novel stimulus; 2. explicit memory of the original stimulus
Figure 3.13 (Ask Yourself): the presence of depth perception
Figure 3.15 (Ask Yourself): Canada has taken some steps to adopt the Code.
Figure 3.16 (Ask Yourself): 1. British Columbia; 2. mother with post-secondary education; 3. highest; 4. older than 35 years
What a Developmentalist Sees (Put It Together): 1. dose dependent; 2. milk production

Chapter 4

Self-Test Answers
1. c; 2. b; 3. b; 4. a; 5. c; 6. a; 7. c; 8. a; 9. d; 10. a; 11. a; 12. a; 13. d; 14. b; 15. a

Figure Question Answers
Figure 4.3 (Put It Together): extraversion/surgency
Figure 4.6 (Put It Together): stranger anxiety, clear attachment
What a Developmentalist Sees (Ask Yourself): secure

Chapter 5

Self-Test Answers
1. c; 2. b; 3. a; 4. c; 5. a; 6. c; 7. b; 8. a; 9. b; 10. d; 11. b; 12. d; 13. b; 14. d; 15. d; 16. d

Figure Question Answers
Table 5.3 (Ask Yourself): 1. height; 2. overweight; 3. obese
Figure 5.4 (Ask Yourself): No
Figure 5.11 (Put it Together): Egocentrism may help to explain why some young children do not demonstrate theory of mind; for example, in a false-belief task. When children are centred on their own frame of reference, they may be less likely to consider the thoughts and beliefs of another.
Figure 5.16 (Ask Yourself): d
Figure 5.17 (Ask Yourself): c

Chapter 6

Self-Test Answers
1. d; 2. b; 3. c; 4. d; 5. d; 6. a. authoritarian, b. authoritative, c. permissive-indulgent, d. permissive-neglectful; 7. c; 8. c; 9. b; 10. c; 11. d; 12. b; 13. c; 14. b; 15. d

Figure Question Answers
Figure 6.2 (Ask Yourself): 1. b; 2. b
Figure 6.3 (Ask Yourself): 48 percent.
Figure 6.4 (Ask Yourself): nurture

Figure 6.8 (Put It Together): **1.** authoritative, permissive-indulgent; **2.** The authoritarian parenting style is high on demandingness, while the permissive-neglectful parenting style is low on demandingness.
Figure 6.13 (Ask Yourself): c
Figure 6.18 (Ask Yourself): individualistic

Chapter 7

Self-Test Answers

1. c; **2.** d; **3.** d; **4.** a; **5.** c; **6.** a; **7.** c; **8.** b; **9.** b; **10.** a; **11.** a. Cultural standards; b. School organizations; c. Teachers' classrooms; d. Academic lessons; **12.** b; **13.** d; **14.** a; **15.** d

Figure Question Answers
Figure 7.2 (Ask Yourself): fine
Figure 7.3 (Ask Yourself): **1.** flexibility; **2.** efficiency
Figure 7.5 (Ask Yourself): seriation
Figure 7.6 (Put It Together): **2.** b. working (short-term) memory
Figure 7.7 (Ask Yourself): c. exceeds Yulan's
Figure 7.8 (Ask Yourself): 68 percent
Figure 7.9 (Ask Yourself): creative intelligence
Figure 7.10 (Put It Together): logical/mathematical
Figure 7.13 (Ask Yourself): **1.** mastery; **2.** performance

Chapter 8

Self-Test Answers

1. d; **2.** d; **3.** a; **4.** b; **5.** c; **6.** a; **7.** d; **8.** d; **9.** a; **10.** a. popular; b. controversial; c. rejected; d. neglected; e. average; **11.** a; **12.** b; **13.** c; **14.** d; **15.** a. active coping; b. ruminative coping

Figure Question Answers
Figure 8.7 (Put It Together): b. upset
Figure 8.8 (Ask Yourself): **1.** highly resilient; **2.** False

Chapter 9

Self-Test Answers

1. a. hypothalamus; b. pituitary; c. adrenals; **2.** c; **3.** b; **4.** b; **5.** d; **6.** d; **7.** d; **8.** a; **9.** b; **10.** d; **11.** b ; **12.** c; **13.** a; **14.** c; **15.** 1. Experimental stage; 2. social stage; 3. instrumental stage; 4. habitual stage; 5. compulsive stage

Figure Question Answers
Figure 9.1 (Ask Yourself): **1.** b; **2.** c
Figure 9.2 (Put It Together): **1.** testosterone; **2.** ovaries
Figure 9.8 (Put It Together): a secondary sex characteristic
Figure 9.9 (Ask Yourself): **1.** hypothetical-deductive; **2.** trial-and-error
WADS (Ask Yourself): **1.** comprehensive sexuality education; **2.** abstinence-only sex education

Chapter 10

Self-Test Answers

1. c; **2.** a; **3.** a. identity diffusion; b. identity moratorium; c. identity foreclosure; d. identity achievement; **4.** a; **5.** d; **6.** d; **7.** b; **8.** c; **9.** d; **10.** b; **11.** a; **12.** c; **13.** c; **14.** d; **15.** d

Figure Question Answers
Figure 10.1 (Ask Yourself): **1.** d. rational thought
Figure 10.3 (Ask Yourself): **1.** c. functioning of the prefrontal cortex

Chapter 11

Self-Test Answers

1. d; **2.** b; **3.** d; **4.** Male factor, Multiple factors (male and female), Unexplained cause, Diminished ovarian reserve, Multiple factors (female only); **5.** b; **6.** a; **7.** a; **8.** a; **9.** c; **10.** a ; **11.** (from the top down)

Community, School, Family, Psychological, Biological; **12.** d; **13.** a; **14.** d; **15.** c

Figure Question Answers
Figure 11.4 (Ask Yourself): **1.** a; **2.** c; **3.** Germany, Israel, Switzerland; 4. Greece
Figure 11.11 (Ask Yourself): **1.** c; **2.** a; **3.** b

Chapter 12

Self-Test Answers

1. c; **2.** b; **3.** b; **4.** a; **5.** d; **6.** a; **7.** b; **8.** c; **9.** d; **10.** a; **11.** b; **12.** c; **13.** d; **14.** b; **15.** b

Figure Question Answers
Figure 12.8 (Ask Yourself): Intimacy
Figure 12.21 (Ask Yourself): 15–24, 15–24, 25–54, 55+

Chapter 13

Self-Test Answers

1. b; **2.** c; **3.** a; **4.** c; **5.** d; **6.** c; **7.** Family, Health, Friends, Cognitive Fitness; **8.** d; **9.** b; **10.** a; **11.** b; **12.** d; **13.** 15–24 accident; 25–34 accident; 35–44 accident; 45–54 cancer; 55–64 cancer; 65+ heart disease; **14.** b; **15.** a

Figure Question Answers
Figure 13.8 (Ask Yourself): initiate, journeyman, master
Figure 13.9 (Ask Yourself): Mexico, United States, France, Australia, Japan

Chapter 14

Self-Test Answers

1. c; **2.** c; **3.** b; **4.** a; **5.** b; **6.** a; **7.** c; **8.** b; **9.** b; **10.** c; **11.** a; **12.** d; **13.** b; **14.** a; **15.** c

Figure Question Answers
Figure 14.2 (Ask Yourself): **1.** Openness, conscientiousness, extraversion, neuroticism; **2.** Conscientiousness, extraversion, agreeableness
Figure 14.7 (Ask Yourself): **1.** Primary support; **2.** 6 percent; **3.** 2 percent

Chapter 15

Self-Test Answers

1. c; **2.** d; **3.** a; **4.** c; **5.** a; **6.** d; **7.** b; **8.** a; **9.** d; **10.** c; **11.** a; **12.** d; **13.** c; **14.** b; **15.** b

Figure Question Answers
Figure 15.10 (Ask Yourself): **1.** neurons; **2.** memory; **3.** judgement

Chapter 16

Self-Test Answers

1. c; **2.** a; **3.** d; **4.** d; **5.** b; **6.** c; **7.** b; **8.** a; **9.** a; **10.** c; **11.** b; **12.** c; **13.** d; **14.** d; **15.** d

Figure Question Answers
Figure 16.5 (Ask Yourself): **1.** pre-retirement; **2.** retirement; **3.** termination of retirement

Chapter 17

Self-Test Answers

1. b; **2.** c; **3.** b; **4.** d; **5.** c; **6.** b; **7.** b; **8.** c; **9.** d; **10.** c; **11.** a; **12.** d; **13.** a; **14.** a; **15.** d

Figure Question Answers
Figure 17.1 (Ask Yourself): **1.** later years; **2.** accidents; **3.** heart disease
Figure 17.5 (Ask Yourself): **1.** b; **2.** a; **3.** b

Glossary

A-not-B error A mistake made by children in Piaget's sensorimotor stage as they search for a hidden object in a location where it has been repeatedly placed but is no longer hidden.

abstinence-only sex education Sex education programs that promote only abstinence and that do not teach safe-sex techniques.

abstract thinking The ability to think about possible situations, ideas, and objects that are not immediately present or obvious.

accommodate The adjustment of schemas in response to new experiences.

accommodation A process to create a new schema in response to information.

achievement test A measure of children's knowledge about particular academic subjects, such as reading, writing, or mathematics.

active euthanasia The practice of directly effecting death through outside sources such as lethal drugs.

activities of daily living (ADLs) The necessary behavioural function of individuals in order to meet basic survival needs, including eating, dressing, and elimination, among others.

activity theory of aging A theory of aging that suggests social interaction and physical activity are indicators of successful aging.

adolescence The transitional period in which young people move into adult cognitions, emotions, and social roles.

adolescent egocentrism Elkind's term to describe the adolescent perception that one is at the centre of the social world.

adoption agency An organization licensed by a province to prepare adoptive parents, counsel birth parents, perform home studies, complete paperwork, place children in homes, and perform other adoption-related functions.

adoption counsellor A therapeutically skilled and trained professional who is also knowledgeable about adoption issues and dynamics.

advance directive Legal instructions regarding specific health care measures to be taken in the event that an individual is rendered unconscious because of a terminal illness.

affection phase The third phase in a four-phase model of early romantic relationships in which the emphasis shifts away from the influence of peers to the development of a meaningful connection between two individuals.

affective social competence The ability to effectively communicate one's own emotions, interpret and respond to others' emotions, and successfully manage the experience of emotions.

affective support Emotionally based expressions of interest, care, and concern.

ageism A form of prejudice and discrimination against the elderly in the workplace, in public interactions, or at home.

agency The amount of control individuals perceive and assert over their life.

aging in place Growing older without having to move.

alexithymia Difficulty understanding, identifying, and describing emotions with words.

allele Normative variation between genes.

allostatic load The physiologic wear and tear on the body that is the result of repeated and long-term exposure to stress, the consequence of which is an acceleration of disease processes and health problems.

Alzheimer's disease (AD) A progressive form of dementia in which plaques and tangles form in the brain, resulting in increasing memory loss and eventually death.

amniocentesis The process of removing fluid from the amniotic sac of a pregnant woman and surveying the genome under a microscope.

amygdala The part of the brain that mediates emotion.

anal fixation A return to the anal stage in later life, shown through obsessive personality issues, as a result of too much or too little gratification during the anal stage.

analytical intelligence Abstract, verbal, mathematical, and logical types of thinking.

andropause A decrease in the male hormone testosterone resulting in physiological reproductive changes such as lower sperm count and penile responsiveness.

anecdotal evidence Non-systematic observations including personal experiences; it has the potential to inspire interesting research questions.

animism An egocentric belief that all inanimate objects have qualities associated with humans.

anorexia nervosa An eating disorder defined by excessive concern about gaining weight and restriction of food intake leading to extremely low body weight.

antecedent-focused emotion regulation The use of emotion regulation strategies before facing a stimulus.

Apgar scale A scoring system that assesses the health of newborns based on five key areas: activity and muscle tone, heart rate, reflexes, skin colour, and respiration.

applied developmental scholar Someone specializing in the study of how human development shapes and is shaped by the environment in order to describe, explain, and optimize human development.

applied research Research designed to examine specific contexts to solve a concrete problem or address policy; it has a direct and practical purpose.

arranged marriage A cultural or religious tradition in which family members and religious leaders, rather than a couple, plan matrimonial arrangements.

artificialism The belief that all objects and events are affected by human influences.

assimilation A process to expand a schema by adding information.

assisted living residence A long-term care residence that serves the dependent elderly/disabled and offers 24-hour protective oversight, food, shelter, and a range of medical services.

assisted reproductive technology (ART) A method of infertility treatment in which eggs are removed from the woman's body, are combined with sperm, and are reintroduced into the body.

associative play A form of play in which children interact and share materials but do not work together toward the same goal.

assortative mating A process throughout the animal kingdom in which species seek out similar partners as mates.

asthma A chronic illness in which the airways of the lung constrict, resulting in decreased airflow.

asynchronicity With reference to physical development during adolescence, the process of uneven growth of physical systems. The term can also describe asymmetrical changes among physical, socio-emotional, and cognitive systems.

attachment An enduring emotional bond that connects two people across time and space.

attachment behaviour A behaviour that promotes proximity or contact, such as approaching, following, and clinging in the older infant and toddler.

attachment theory The perspective that the process of social, emotional, and cognitive development occurs in the context of caregiver–infant attachment.

attention-deficit/hyperactivity disorder (ADHD) A neurobehavioural disorder characterized by inattention and/or hyperactivity-impulsivity that emerges prior to 12 years of age and causes impairment in multiple contexts.

authoritarian parenting A style of parenting that is characterized by high demands but low responsiveness. Authoritarian parents demand obedience from their children and are consequence-oriented, quick to punish disobedience.

authoritative parenting A style of parenting that is characterized by high demand and high responsiveness. Authoritative parents create rules and expectations while explaining reasons for their rules.

autism spectrum disorder (ASD) A neurodevelopmental disorder characterized by impaired social communication and interaction, and repetitive behaviours.

automatization The allocation of fewer attentional resources to perform simple, repetitive behaviours.

autonomous morality Piaget's observation that as children get older they begin to see morality as more flexible and consider the intentions of other people's behaviour.

autonomy versus shame and doubt stage Erikson's second stage of psychosocial development, during which the toddler begins to understand self-control through key accomplishments.

autosomal dominant trait A trait that requires the presence of only one parental gene for the phenotype to be expressed.

autosomal recessive trait A trait that requires the presence of both paternal and maternal genes for the phenotype to be expressed.

autosome Any one of the 22 pairs of chromosomes shared by both males and females.

average children Children who get slightly more nominations in a sociometric analysis than neglected children but not enough to rank in one of the categories.

axon A nerve fibre that typically sends electrical impulses away from the neuron's cell body.

babbling The repeated creation of meaningless sounds that typically consist of one syllable.

basic research Research designed to create fundamental knowledge about the world.

beanpole family A family with members from many generations, but with few members in each generation.

bedsharing A specific instance of co-sleeping, where infant and caregiver sleep together in the same adult bed.

behaviour genetics An area of science that studies the nature of the relationship between genes and behaviour.

behaviourism A theoretical perspective on learning that assumes human development occurs as a result of experiences shaping behaviours.

bereavement The personal process of grieving and transformation in response to the death of a loved one.

Big Five or **five-factor model of personality** A theory that there are five personality traits that combine to express personality: openness to experience, conscientiousness, extraversion, agreeableness, and neuroticism.

bilingual Able to speak two languages.

bilingual education Academic instruction in two languages: a native language and a secondary language.

birth doula A specially trained birth companion, who provides physical, emotional, and informational support during labour, birth, and the immediate postpartum.

blastocyst A collection of cells arranged as a layer surrounding a central cavity containing fluid, into which an inner cell mass protrudes.

bloody show A plug of thick, blood-tinged mucus that is discharged from the cervix shortly before labour begins.

body image A subjective, mental image of one's own physical appearance.

body mass index (BMI) A measure used to determine healthy body weight that is calculated by dividing a person's weight (in kilograms) by the square of their height (in metres); BMI = weight(kg)/height(m)^2.

bonding phase The fourth phase in a four-phase model of early romantic relationships in which relationship becomes characterized by a high level of commitment and a future orientation.

bone mineral density The amount of minerals, such as calcium, in an individual's bones as they age.

bone resorption The process of bone cells breaking down and transforming into a fluid substance that enters the blood.

bottom-up processing Forming perceptions from the smaller, finer details and then building upward into a solid, general idea.

bridge jobs Less demanding full- or part-time jobs taken up in mid-life that ease the transition to retirement.

bulimia nervosa An eating disorder that involves repeated episodes of binge eating followed by self-induced vomiting or another compensatory behaviour to prevent weight gain.

bullying Unwanted aggressive behaviour by another youth or group of youths that involves a power imbalance and is repeated multiple times.

caesarean surgery A medical intervention in which the abdomen is cut and the fetus(es) removed.

career outcome expectations The process one goes through when deciding about a future career and focusing on costs and rewards involved in career choice.

caregiver In the context of a family, an unpaid role that involves taking responsibility for someone with chronic illness or who is approaching the natural end of life.

cataract Shading and discolouration of the lens of the eye.

categorical self Self-definitions based on concrete external attributes.

categorization The process of forming a cognitive compartment, or grouping, based on specific properties.

causality The concept that everything dies due to some type of biological process.

centenarian Someone who is 100 years old or older.

centration A quality of thinking in which a person focuses on one aspect or dimension of an object while disregarding any other dimension.

centre-based child care Child care that is provided at a location away from home, generally including four or more children and a qualified child care provider.

cephalocaudal growth The tendency for growth and development to proceed from the head downward.

cephalocaudal pattern A pattern of physical growth that proceeds from the head down through the long axis of the body.

cerebral cortex The uppermost part of the brain and the centre largely responsible for complex brain functions.

cervix A powerful ring of muscles that keeps the uterus tightly shut during pregnancy but then thins and opens during labour.

childfree Never having birthed or parented a child.

chorionic villus sampling (CVS) The process of obtaining a tissue sample from the villi of the chorion, which forms the fetal part of the placenta.

ciliary muscles The small muscles of the eye that work to move each eyeball and change the shape of each eye's lens.

classical conditioning A type of learning that occurs when an original stimulus acquires a capacity to evoke a response that was originally evoked by a different stimulus.

classification The ability to create groups or classes of objects and sort them by similar properties.

clique A tight-knit group of friends who share similar values and behaviours.

cognitive domain of development The domain that includes the underlying mental functions, such as thinking, memory, attention, and perception.

cognitive flexibility An executive function that allows an individual to piece together elements of knowledge to fit the demands of a given situation.

cognitive load The total number of items that must be attended to by one's working memory, where information is temporarily stored and manipulated.

cognitive reappraisal The ability to re-evaluate the cause of an emotional state and mediate the response.

cohabit To live together and have a sexual relationship without being married.

cohort effect The unique impact a given historical era has on people living during that period as compared with people living during a different historical period.

coital sex The sexual union between a male and a female involving insertion of the penis into the vagina.

collaborative divorce A process in which a team of psychological and legal experts works with families undergoing divorce to protect the child(ren) and resolve roadblocks, facilitating an amicable divorce with minimal legal entanglements.

collective monologue Piaget's term for the egocentric private talk that sometimes occurs in a group of children.

colostrum The yellowish, sticky breast milk that is secreted during the first two to three days after birth.

coming out The process by which a homosexual person makes his or her orientation known to self, friends, and family.

commitment One of the two dimensions suggested by Marcia as determining a person's identity status at a particular time; it is a conscious choice made about a particular aspect of identity.

communion The levels of closeness and equality people want in their friendships.

companionate grandparents A grandparent–grandchild relationship in which the grandparent(s) enjoy frequently entertaining their grandchildren.

comparative psychology The scientific study of the behaviour and mental process of non-human animals.

compensation The process of revising a selected goal so that it is better suited to one's ability to reach it.

complementary feeding The process of consuming other foods and liquids, along with breast milk, to meet the nutritional requirements of infants after 6 months of age.

complicated/traumatic grief (CG) A pathological form of grieving that tends to last longer than normal grieving and is accompanied by impaired social interaction.

comprehensive sexuality education Sex education programs that present information about both abstinence and safe-sex practices.

concentric muscle movement The contraction of muscles during physical activity.

concrete operational stage Piaget's third stage of cognitive development, in which school-age children begin to think logically about concrete events.

conditioned response (CR) A response that is reliably produced by a conditioned stimulus.

conditioned stimulus (CS) A previously neutral stimulus that reliably produces a response after conditioning.

conductive hearing loss Hearing loss resulting from conduction impairments in the middle ear.

cones Neurons in the retina that respond to colour.

confidentiality The responsibility of researchers to keep private the identity and data of all research participants.

conservation The understanding that key physical properties of an object remain constant even if the appearance of the object changes.

consistency The ability to physically repeat an action in the same way with the same level of function.

constructive play A form of play that involves the creation of new objects, often by combining already existing objects.

consummate love A relationship involving both emotional and physical intimacy.

control group The group or groups that provide comparison for the experimental group and do not receive manipulation of the independent variable.

controversial children Children with high numbers of positive nominations and high negative nominations in a sociometric analysis.

conventional morality Level 2 of Kohlberg's theory of moral development, in which moral reasoning is guided by laws and social norms.

co-operative play A form of play in which children interact to work toward a common goal.

co-parenting The extent to which parents are supportive of one another's parenting.

corporal punishment The use of physical force to cause pain or discomfort in order to punish unwanted behaviour.

co-rumination The act of dwelling on negative occurrences and feelings.

co-sleeping A variety of shared sleeping arrangements, where infant and caregiver sleep within sensory range of one another (on the same or separate surfaces), thereby permitting each to detect and respond to the cues of the other.

creative intelligence Divergent, novel, and problem-solving-oriented thinking.

creativity The state or quality of being able to generate new and valuable ideas or things.

critical period A finite window of opportunity for development, outside of which environmental influences are said to have no effect.

cross-sectional design Research in which different age groups are compared simultaneously.

cross-sequential design Research in which an experimenter combines the benefits of both cross-sectional and longitudinal designs by adding a new group of subjects at progressive intervals.

crowd A group of people who may or may not be friends but who share similar attributes to one another.

crystallized intelligence The category of intelligence that contains basic information that we acquire over time, such as facts and figures.

culture The beliefs, customs, arts, and so on, of a particular society, group, and place.

cyberbullying Bullying that takes place through technology, such as email, chat rooms, text message, or social media.

death anxiety An underlying feeling of uneasiness about the possibility that death might occur.

debriefing The process of explaining the true purposes and hypotheses of a study.

deferred imitation The ability of 6- to 7-month-old infants to imitate an action after a delay and not in the presence of a model.

demandingness The level of demands parents make on their children. The number, intensity, and consistency of demands can all vary along a continuum, from very low to very high.

dementia A loss of cognitive function, which may include language impairment, memory loss, and the inability to recognize familiar people or objects.

dendrite A branching structure arising from the cell body that typically receives electrical impulses from the axons of neighbouring neurons.

dental dam Originally manufactured for use in dentist offices, a small, thin, square-shaped latex barrier that allows sensation without skin-to-skin contact; it is effective for oral-vaginal or oral-anal contact to protect from sexually transmitted infections.

dependent variable (DV) The variable measured by the experimenter to observe the effects of the independent variable.

describe A goal of developmental scholarship in which careful observations of behaviour are made and recorded.

descriptive research Research methods used to observe, record, and describe behaviour and environments; it is not for making cause–effect explanations.

despair Feeling that one's life lacks meaning and significance.

developmental assets Resources that encourage and enhance positive youth development.

developmental continuity A characteristic or feature of an individual that stays the same as a person matures through the lifespan.

developmental discontinuity A characteristic or feature of an individual that changes as a person matures through the lifespan.

developmental perspective The approach and basic set of assumptions that guide the scientific study of growth and maturation across the human lifespan.

developmental psychology The subfield of psychology concerned with studying and understanding human growth and maturation.

developmental scholar Someone specializing in the study of development in order to advance what is known about developmental processes and experiences.

developmental scholarship A multidisciplinary field of scholarship concerned with describing change and constancy in growth and maturation throughout the lifespan.

developmental systems theory A metatheory that draws from and integrates many theories, sources, and research studies related to human development.

developmentalist A scholar of development who uses their knowledge for research or applied purposes.

diathesis–stress model A model suggesting that abnormal behaviour results from a combination of genetic predispositions toward psychopathology and environmental stressors.

differentiation The ability to maintain a sense of self while in a relationship with others.

difficult temperament The temperament of a child who is generally fussy, does not respond well to new situations, and has irregular patterns of eating and sleeping.

disengagement theory of aging A theory of aging that suggests it is normal and healthy for older individuals to disengage from their previous roles and to focus energy on personal development.

dishabituation Increased responding to a stimulus, usually because it is novel.

disorganized/disoriented attachment A type of insecure attachment characterized by inconsistent behaviour upon separation and reunion that shows no clear pattern.

display rules Cultural norms that dictate socially appropriate emotional displays.

dizygotic (DZ) Twin siblings who share up to 50 percent of their genes.

DNA Deoxyribonucleic acid, the fundamental chemical of all genes that guide the construction of cells.

dominant The quality of an allele that influences the expression of a trait.

do not resuscitate (DNR) order A written request made by a person who does not want to receive any medical intervention in the event that their heart stops beating.

early maturers Adolescents who experience pubertal maturation faster than the average rate of same-age peers.

easy temperament The temperament of a child who is generally cheerful, adaptable, and has regular patterns of eating and sleeping.

eccentric muscle movement The lengthening of muscles as they return to original position after stretching.

eclectic Drawing on a broad range of ideas and perspectives from various sources.

ecological systems model A theoretical approach to the study of human development that emphasizes five environmental systems that influence individual development and assumes that individuals shape the contexts in which they develop.

efficiency The muscular and cardiovascular system energy expended to perform a physical action.

effortful control A dimension of infant temperament indicated by inhibitory control, attention control, low-intensity pleasure, and perceptual sensitivity. In an adult, the ability to regulate responses to external stimuli.

ego One of three components of the mind according to Freud; the ego is the part of the mind that deals with reality and mediates between the id instincts and superego morals.

egocentrism A cognitive quality in which one is centred in one's own frame of reference.

ego identity The goal of development in Erikson's psychosocial theory where a sense of oneself as a distinct and continuous entity is achieved.

ego integrity The accrued assurance of the ability to find order, meaning, and integration in one's life.

elder abuse A single or repeated act, or lack of appropriate action, occurring within any relationship where there is an expectation of trust that causes harm or distress to an older person.

electronic fetal monitoring (EFM) A technology for monitoring the heart rate of a fetus with electrodes attached to the mother's abdomen or placed internally on the scalp of the fetus.

emerging adulthood The developmental stage between adolescence and adulthood during which individuals are searching for a sense of identity and maturity.

emotion regulation The ability to control the behaviour one displays in response to an emotional state.

emotion vocabulary The number of words a person can use to name his or her emotional states and explain the emotional behaviour of self and others.

emotional expression A verbal or non-verbal behaviour that expresses emotion.

emotional regulation The ability to adapt to changing situations with a range of constructive emotional responses.

emotional/psychological abuse Continual verbal harassment and intimidation of a child by means of disparagement, criticism, threat, or ridicule.

emotional vocabulary The increasing ability to identify and label complex emotions.

emotional well-being A state encompassing different dimensions of wellness, including: autonomy, environmental mastery, personal growth, positive relations with others, purpose in life, and self-acceptance (Ryff & Keyes, 1999).

empathy The capacity to understand or feel what another person is feeling from their perspective.

emotion regulation The ability to control the behaviour one displays in response to an emotional state.

emotion vocabulary The number of words a person can use to name his or her emotional states and explain the emotional behaviour of self and others.

empirical study A systematic study of human behaviour and development using methodological observations, which can be analyzed quantitatively or qualitatively.

empty nest syndrome Feelings of distress and depression in mid-life as a result of losing the parental role as adult children become independent.

encore career A new career path developed in mid-life that combines continued income, personal meaning, and social impact.

English as a second language (ESL) Language education programs, in which non–English-speaking students are taught English.

epidural A local anaesthetic injected into the lower back to numb labour pain.

epiphyses The enlarged ends of a long bone, initially growing separately from the shaft.

episiotomy A surgical cut in the muscles that surround the vagina in order to enlarge the vaginal opening.

equality A reciprocal acceptance of each person's worth in the relationship.

equilibrium A state of cognitive balance.

error theory of aging A theory that aging occurs because of environmental forces such as disease that affect the function of cells, causing deterioration.

estradiol A potent form of estrogen produced by the gonads (but in much lower levels in males) that is responsible for primary and secondary sex characteristics.

ethnic identity A component of identity and self-concept that acknowledges a unique connection to a specific ethnic group and the values and beliefs associated with that group.

ethnicity A specific set of physical, cultural, regional, or national characteristics that identifies and differentiates one person or group from others.

ethological perspective A theory that assumes that human development is an outcome of individual experiences in the social environment that provide information about which behaviours should be adopted to increase chances of survival.

eudaimonic well-being An individual's engagement in leading a productive life, associated with personal growth and fulfillment of one's potential.

euthanasia The practice of ending a person's life to relieve pain or suffering.

evolutionary theory The assumption that specific human traits and behaviours develop over the lifespan and are maintained throughout history because those characteristics are adaptive for survival.

exclusive breastfeeding What occurs when infants receive only breast milk, whether from the breast or expressed, and no other liquids or solids including water.

executive function The aspect of the brain that supervises the memory process by regulating the flow of information and controlling key processes.

executive functioning Information-processing skills involved in problem solving and strategy design and execution.

executive system A set of complex and sophisticated cognitive control and management abilities that require coordination of more than one region of the brain to perform.

experience-dependent process Brain development that occurs based on unique environmental stimuli shared only by individuals in particular environmental circumstances.

experience-expectant process Brain development that occurs based on environmental experiences that all members of the species typically encounter.

experimental group The group or groups that receive the manipulation of the independent variable, which is often called the *treatment*.

explain A goal of developmental scholarship that focuses on identifying the underlying causes of behaviour.

explicit memory Repetition of a behaviour that shows a clear, observable, conscious effort to recall an event, such as when an infant imitates at a later time a behaviour seen earlier.

exploration One of the two dimensions suggested by Marcia as determining a person's identity status at a particular time; it is a positive search for identity options.

exploratory research An examination into an area in which a researcher wants to develop initial ideas and more focused research questions.

expressive language Language that an infant can produce.

expressive suppression An emotion regulation strategy that inhibits one's emotional response without reducing the level of emotion.

externalizing problems Problems that result when children undercontrol the expression of emotions, including aggression and delinquency.

extraversion/surgency A dimension of infant temperament defined by low-shyness, high-intensity pleasure, smiling and laughter, activity level, impulsivity, positive anticipation, and affiliation.

family life cycle The stages of development a family goes through as a function of the aging and maturation of individual family members.

fast mapping A process by which a child can relate unknown words to known words, thus rapidly expanding vocabulary.

fertility The natural capability to produce offspring.

fine motor skill A motor skill that relies on small muscles, such as those in the fingers.

flexibility The ability to perform a physical act in a variety of contexts with similar outcome.

flourishing A life characterized by optimal levels of goodness, generativity, growth, and resilience.

fluid intelligence The category of intelligence that drives reasoning and logic.

formal operational stage Piaget's fourth stage of cognitive development, in which adolescents and near-adolescents begin to think abstractly and to use hypothetical-deductive reasoning.

functional capacity The physiological systems of the body that maintain health and life: digestive system, endocrine system, immune system, lymphatic system, muscular system, nervous system, reproductive system, respiratory system, skeletal system, and urinary system.

functional independence The ability to perform daily living activities safely and autonomously.

functional language The idea that language acquisition is a "need-based" process in which children construct meaning out of a need to understand what others are saying and to be understood.

functional play A form of play that involves repetitive movements and simple exploratory activity, usually seen during a child's first two years.

gamete A male or female cell that contains 23 chromosomes in their singular form.

gender A social construction of expectations that a given culture associates with a person's biological sex.

gender constancy The belief that one's gender is permanent and unchanging.

gender convergence The tendency for both males and females to become more similar as they mature.

gender crossover The tendency for each sex to adopt traits strongly associated with the opposite gender.

gender differences Cognitive and behavioural differences associated with gender.

gender identity A perception of one's gender category.

gender role Specific behaviours or appearances that are expected of children, based on their culture's beliefs about gender.

gender schema theory A cognitive approach to understanding gender development that centres on children's own constructions of gender.

gender schemas Children's mental representation of gender categories.

gene A microscopic structure made of thousands of links of chemical particles that combine to construct all the parts of a living being.

general intelligence (*g*) A construct thought to underlie one's ability to adapt and determine one's competence level.

generativity The dedication and investment of self and personal resources in the promotion of the health of society and future generations.

genotype An individual's collection of genes.

gerontologist A professional who studies the social, psychological, and biological aspects of aging.

gerontology An area of social science that studies the physical, cognitive, and socio-emotional issues in later adulthood.

gifted Significantly above-average intellectual functioning as indicated by an IQ of 130 or higher.

glaucoma Increased pressure within the eye that, if left untreated, can lead to serious vision problems.

gonads Testicles in males and ovaries in females, also known as the sex glands.

goodness of fit The relationship between environmental forces and predisposed temperamental behaviour.

graduated extinction A variety of sleep-training techniques, where parents delay responding to their infants' cries for specified intervals of time, and then respond only in a limited and prescribed way.

grey matter The parts of the brain that contain neuron cell bodies and some of their connections.

gross motor skill A motor skill that relies on large muscles, such as those in the legs and arms.

growth spurt A sudden and intense increase in the rate of growth in weight and height.

guided participation A process in which a more experienced teacher becomes an interactive guide, helping a younger or less experienced person do tasks that they could not complete independently.

guilt A feeling of regret or remorse arising from perceptions of having done something wrong.

habituation Decreased responding to a stimulus that occurs because of continuous presentation of the stimulus.

handedness The preference for using one hand over the other for basic activities such as eating, throwing, and writing.

Hayflick's limit The number of times a cell can divide during the lifespan based on a predetermined number of cell divisions.

Head Start A program that seeks to promote school-readiness among disadvantaged children through the provision of educational, nutritional, and social services. Aboriginal Head Start programs include local control by First Nations and teaching in Aboriginal culture and language.

hedonic well-being The sense of feeling good about and satisfied with one's life while experiencing an absence of negative feelings.

heritability estimate A calculation used by behaviour geneticists to denote the independent contribution of genes to differences seen among people in a given trait.

heteronomous morality Piaget's description of a child's first idea of what is right and wrong and the sense that morality is an external, unchangeable set of rules with a focus on consequences of behaviour.

heteronormative Assuming that heterosexual behaviour is the norm and that men and women fall into traditional sex roles in life.

holophrase One-word utterances that express a complete thought or phrase.

hook-up A sexual encounter that involves mutual consent and mutual agreement that no relationship commitment is expected.

hormone A chemical that travels in the bloodstream to target organs, helping them regulate a variety of bodily functions such as reproduction, sleep, hunger, and stress.

hospice Care provided to persons with terminal illnesses focused on the reduction of suffering and the availability of spiritual, emotional, and psychological support.

hostile (or **reactive**) **aggression** An intentional act that harms a person or object.

hypothalamus-pituitary-adrenal (HPA) axis A communicative pathway between three endocrine glands: the hypothalamus, the pituitary gland, and the adrenal glands.

hypothetical-deductive reasoning The ability to formulate varying solutions in one's mind and to think through the effectiveness of each possible solution.

id One of three components of the mind according to Freud; the id represents instincts.

identity An individual's understanding of self in relation to his or her social context.

identity achievement As described by Marcia, an individual who has made a commitment about his or her identity following a process of exploration.

identity consolidation The challenge of refining and organizing one's personal identity in response to new adult roles, responsibilities, and contexts.

identity crisis A crisis that entails an evaluation of possible choices concerning vocation, relationships, and self-understanding.

identity diffusion As described by Marcia, an individual who has neither made a commitment about nor begun to explore his or her identity.

identity foreclosure As described by Marcia, an individual who has made a commitment about his or her identity without even exploring options.

identity moratorium As described by Marcia, an individual who has begun to explore his or her identity but has yet to make a commitment.

identity versus role confusion Erikson's fifth stage of psychosocial development, during which the adolescent must adopt a coherent and integrated sense of self.

imaginary audience Elkind's term to describe the adolescent's assumption that his or her preoccupation with personal appearance and behaviour is shared by everyone else.

implicit memory Repetition of a behaviour, such as a leg movement to make an object move, that occurs automatically and without apparent conscious effort.

imprinting Learning at a particular age or stage that is rapid and independent of the consequences of behaviour.

inclusion An approach to educating students with special educational needs based on the idea that all individuals have a right to be educated in regular classroom settings.

incorporation The final stage marking the completed transition into adulthood where new or more permanent responsibilities that signify adulthood are taken up.

independent variable (IV) The variable controlled by the experimenter to observe the impact it has on the behaviour of interest.

individualized education program A written statement that defines the individualized educational goals of a child with a disability.

individuation The extent to which individuals actualize their true selves.

induction A rational form of discipline in which adults use reasoning and explanations to help children understand the effects of their misbehaviour on others.

industry versus inferiority stage Erikson's fourth stage of psychosocial development, leading to a sense of competence or a move away from social interactions.

infant-directed speech A way of speaking to infants that is higher in pitch, simpler, and more repetitive than speech directed at adults or children. It seems to be used automatically when in the presence of an infant.

infant mortality rate (IMR) The ratio of infant deaths occurring in the first year of life per 1,000 live births.

infertility Medically defined as not conceiving a pregnancy after one year of unprotected sexual intercourse.

informed consent The process of requesting that research participants assert in writing that they understand the study, know that they can withdraw at any time, and agree to participate. In a clinical context, the process of explaining the purpose of a procedure, outlining the benefits and risks associated with it, and requesting the patient's signature to verify they understand and agree to participate.

initiation phase The first phase in a four-phase model of early romantic relationships in which adolescents begin to notice and become comfortable with others perceived as sexually attractive.

initiative versus guilt stage Erikson's third stage of psychosocial development, in which the 3- to 6-year-old child must learn to take responsibility for his or her own behaviour without feeling guilty for the outcomes of that behaviour.

insecure–avoidant attachment A type of insecure attachment in which infants show little or no distress upon separation and avoidant behaviour such as running from parent upon reunion.

insecure/dismissive An attachment category in which adolescents minimize considerations of early experiences and relationships, or downplay the importance of early attachment experiences.

insecure/preoccupied An attachment category in which adolescents display preoccupation with early experiences and attachment figures, but experience difficulty evaluating those relationships.

insecure–resistant attachment A type of insecure attachment in which infants show very high distress when separated and mixed reactions when reunited.

instrumental support The provision of tangible assistance.

intellectual disability A disorder characterized by significantly below-average intellectual functioning (an IQ of 70 or lower) and impaired adaptive functioning, with onset prior to 18 years of age.

intelligence quotient (IQ) A score calculated from results on an intelligence test originally derived from the formula of (mental age/chronological age) × 100, resulting in an average score of 100.

interactionist approach A view of language learning that stresses the role of socialization.

internal working model (IWM) A set of beliefs and expectations about attachment relationships based on the infant's experience of sensitive or insensitive caregiving.

International Code of Marketing of Breast-milk Substitutes A code adopted by the World Health Assembly to improve the health of infants and children.

interpersonal schema An expectation about whether intimate relationships satisfy or deny emotional and psychological needs.

intimacy vs. isolation stage Erikson's sixth stage of psychosocial development, leading to the capacity to share oneself with another or not.

intimate partner violence Physical, sexual, or psychological harm committed against a victim by a current or former partner or spouse.

intuitive thought The second substage of preoperational thinking, during which children want to know how and why.

in vitro fertilization (IVF) The manual combination of an egg and sperm in a laboratory dish.

involved grandparents A grandparent–grandchild relationship in which the grandparent(s) are often involved in daily care of their grandchildren.

irreversibility The belief of preoperational thinkers that objects and events, once changed, can never return to their original form. Also, the concept that once something or someone dies they cannot come back to life.

irreversible coma or **brain death** A medical condition in which there is no measurable brain activity coming from the cortex.

instrumental (or **proactive**) **aggression** A goal-oriented act through which a person or object is harmed.

internalizing problems Problems that result when children overcontrol the expression of emotions, including depression, social withdrawal, anxiety, and somatoform disorders.

joint attention The ability to direct the attention of a social partner to objects or events and, in turn, follow their attention-directing gestures, such as head-turning and pointing.

kinkeeper Within a family, the person responsible for organizing communications, maintaining relationships among family members, carrying out family traditions, and valuing family celebrations.

lactational amenorrhea Natural postpartum infertility that occurs when a woman is breastfeeding and her menstrual cycle has not yet returned.

language acquisition device (LAD) The name given by Noam Chomsky to a theoretical structure possessed by all humans that prewires us to learn language and grammar rules.

language immersion Language education programs in which students are taught academic content exclusively in a nonnative language (a language not spoken at home).

languishing A life characterized by a lack of vitality and meaning.

late maturers Adolescents who experience pubertal maturation slower than the average rate of same-age peers.

lateralization The process by which the right and left hemispheres of the brain take on specific functions.

law of effect As asserted by E. L. Thorndike, the law that behaviour that is followed by a positive outcome tends to be repeated and behaviour that is followed by a negative outcome tends not to be repeated.

lead poisoning An environmental hazard that interacts with genes to produce cognitive deficits in children.

libidinal energy The vital energy that brings life through sexual behaviour.

life course health approach A model that uses people's trajectories of health from conception through death to study and understand the development of disease and promotion of health.

life expectancy The average number of years a person can expect to live.

life narrative An individual's life story that reflects a sense (or lack) of unity, purpose, and meaning.

life review The process of telling one's life story structured around themes that make meaning of one's life.

lifespan The highest boundary or limit of a particular species.

lifespan developmental psychology The systematic study of how and why human beings change, or stay the same, over the course of their entire life.

lifespan human development The growth and maturation of the human from conception through death.

life stage A period of time with a beginning and an end within which distinct developmental changes occur.

living apart together (LAT) What happens when couples who have an intimate relationship maintain separate residences.

living will An example of an advance directive, which specifies what medical procedures and interventions a person wants or does not want.

locus The specific place on a chromosome where a gene is located.

longitudinal design Research in which one group of subjects is followed for an extended period.

long-term memory The vast and virtually limitless store of knowledge and prior events.

low birth weight (LBW) A birth weight of less than 2,500 g.

maintenance rehearsal A retention strategy in which a child repeats the thing to be remembered (words, images, actions) in order to remember them.

malnutrition A deficiency of one or more key nutrients, such as proteins, vitamins, or minerals, that has a significant impact on energy and the function of bodily systems.

marital biography Information about the number, timing, and duration of marriages in a person's life.

mastery goal An achievement goal that focuses on self-improvement and skill development, while downplaying ability level and peer comparison.

maternal mortality rate (MMR) The ratio of maternal deaths per 100,000 live births.

medical model of care A comparatively new model of maternity care guided by the belief that pregnancy and birth are potentially dangerous life processes that must be medically managed.

medical model of infant care A dominant set of assumptions that guide the provision of infant care in the Western part of the world.

meiosis The process by which cells containing 23 pairs of chromosomes divide into daughter cells containing one half of each chromosome pair.

menarche (pronounced *me-när-kē*) The first menstrual period of human females, signalling the beginning of fertility.

menopause A period of time in which a woman's production of hormones (estrogen and progesterone) begins to decline, causing changes in her reproductive capabilities.

metacognition The process of knowing about knowing.

metalinguistic awareness Understanding the complexity of language and the fact that language relies on context as well as individual word meaning.

metamemory One's understanding of one's own memory process.

metatheory A theory where the focus is the integration of multiple theories.

mid-life crisis The psychological experience of recognizing that life is half over and making course corrections to romantic life, career, and living situation to make life more consistent with values and desires.

midwifery model of care A woman-centred model of maternity care based on the idea that pregnancy and birth are normal, inherently healthy life processes.

minimally conscious state A state in which a brain-damaged patient displays some deliberate behaviour or some level of self-awareness.

miscarriage An abrupt stop in the development of the pregnancy and subsequent delivery of the embryo or nonviable fetus before the twentieth week of pregnancy.

mitosis The process by which cells create an exact copy of themselves, including all 23 pairs of chromosomes.

monozygotic (MZ) Twin siblings who share identical DNA.

moral emotions Emotions believed to play a fundamental role in morality.

moral realism The idea that there are moral facts that refer to objective, rather than subjective, features of the world.

moral relativism The idea that morality is subjectively grounded and contextually dependent.

morbidity The rate of disease in a population.

mortality The rate of death in a population.

morula A post-zygote collection of connected cells that continue to divide before forming a more complicated structure.

mourning The specific behaviours taken up during bereavement including those that involve cultural or religious conventions.

multilingual Able to speak more than two languages.

mutation An abnormality that occurs during genetic transmission and may affect the entire chromosome or specific genes.

myelination The process through which the axon of a neuron is coated with a fatty tissue, which serves as insulation and enhances speed of firing.

myopia Nearsightedness, or the ability to see close objects clearly but inability to see distant objects clearly.

natural selection The Darwinian idea that the members of a species who are best suited to their own particular environments will be the ones most likely to survive and produce offspring.

nature The hereditary influences that are passed from the genes of biological parents to their offspring.

negative affectivity A dimension of infant temperament having to do with fear, frustration, sadness, discomfort, and soothability.

neglect Failure of caretakers to provide for a child's fundamental needs, such as adequate food, housing, clothing, medical care, emotional well-being, or education.

neglected children Children with few of negative or positive nominations in a sociometric analysis.

neo-Freudian theory A theory that has been influenced by Freud's work but extends and critiques his ideas.

neural tube In the developing embryo, the precursor to the central nervous system.

neurogenesis The process of generating new neurons from stem cells.

neuron A brain or nerve cell that serves as the basic building block of the nervous system.

neutral stimulus (NS) A stimulus that does not elicit a natural reaction.

newborn reflex An inborn automatic response to stimuli, which may disappear before the end of the first year of life.

non-functionality The concept that death ends all functions such as talking, breathing, and social interaction.

non-normative event An incident that does not happen to everyone or that happens at a different time than typically experienced by others.

non-parental child care Any type of child care that is carried out by someone other than the primary child care provider.

non–rapid-eye-movement (NREM) sleep A sleep state during which rapid eye movement and dreaming do not occur, and brain-wave activity is slow and regular.

non-social play Non-interactive play in which a child focuses on either an object or a toy and appears unconnected to others, or acts as an onlooker, watching others play without joining in.

non-suicidal self-injury Deliberate self-injury with no suicidal intent for the purpose of self-punishment, managing negative emotions, or communicating personal distress.

normative event An incident that matches the sequential and historical events shared by the majority of people.

noun bias The suggested bias that children have to use nouns more frequently than other parts of speech.

nurture The environmental influences that have an impact on development, including social, geographic, and economic factors.

nutrition The process of consuming carbohydrates, fats, proteins, and other elements in the form of calories, to obtain energy and regulate body functions.

obesogenic environment The aspects of the community that create barriers for physical activity and ready access to highly nutritional food.

object permanence The understanding that an object continues to exist even when it is not immediately present or visible.

oldest-old Adults in their later years, traditionally over the age of 85, who are at risk for illness and injury and are often dependent on others for assistance with daily living activities.

old-old Adults in their later years, traditionally between the ages of 75 and 85, who are beginning to deal with declining health.

on-demand breastfeeding Nursing a baby whenever the baby shows signs of hunger during the day and night, such as by crying or rooting, rather than according to a set schedule.

on-time maturers Adolescents who experience pubertal maturation at an average rate.

openness A clear, honest, and relevant process of communication.

operant conditioning A learning process through which the likelihood of a specific behaviour is increased or decreased through positive or negative reinforcement.

operational definition A definition that uses words that are quantitative, in order to allow some form of measurement.

optimistic bias A tendency for people to underestimate their own risk and overestimate the risk to someone else engaged in the same type of behaviour.

optimization The process of investing effort and resources in a concentrated attempt to reach a selected goal.

optimize A goal of developmental scholarship that applies current information to future possibilities in the service of enhancing development.

oral fixation A return to the oral stage in later life, shown through habits such as smoking or gum chewing, as a result of too much or too little gratification during the oral stage.

organogenesis The early development and differentiation of the internal organs such as the lungs, heart, and gastrointestinal systems.

ossification The process through which cartilage becomes bone.

osteoarthritis A type of arthritis in which the skeletal joints and tissue wear down over time.

osteoporosis A disruption in bone remodelling causing bones to become brittle and weak.

otitis media Infection of the middle ear and a common cause of earaches.

overgeneralization Applying the rules of grammar to cases in which they do not apply.

overt aggression A direct and obvious harmful act, such as hitting, kicking, biting, or verbally threatening.

overweight or **obesity** A classification based on the association of various BMI cut-offs with health risks; varies in children by age and sex.

ovulation The typically monthly process that causes an ovum to ripen and be expelled by the ovaries.

ovum A mature female reproductive cell, also known as an egg, released from the ovary during ovulation. The female gamete contains 22 autosomes and 1 sex (X) chromosome.

palliative care Care focused on reducing symptoms, such as pain and discomfort, at any stage of a chronic illness or serious illness, which is sometimes provided with curative treatment.

paradox of well-being The idea that even though the aging process is characterized by significant physiological and cognitive decline, adults report feeling emotionally positive.

parallel play A form of play in which children appear to be together but are not interacting with one another.

passive euthanasia The practice of either withholding or withdrawing treatment from a terminally ill person, thus ending life through natural causes.

perception Interpretation of stimulation that occurs in the higher processing centres of the brain.

performance goal An achievement goal that emphasizes ability level and competition among peers.

permissive-indulgent parenting A style of parenting that is characterized by high responsiveness and very low demand. Indulgent parents are involved, caring, and loving but provide few rules and little guidance.

permissive-neglectful parenting A style of parenting that is low in both demand and responsiveness. Neglectful parents are uninvolved and distant, often unaware of their child's activities.

persistent vegetative state A state in which a brain-damaged patient has coma-like symptoms, although a low-level arousal, such as reflexes, may be observed.

personal fable Elkind's term to describe the adolescent belief that one is special and unique and, thus, invulnerable.

personality A combination of emotional, attitudinal, and behavioural response patterns of an individual.

personality disorder A long-term pattern of relating that causes problems in relationships and at work.

personality inventory A questionnaire used to rate a person on a set of characteristics that make up a respondent's personality.

personality profile The unique combination of personality traits that describes the more and less dominant features of an individual's personality and dominance of the Big Five traits relative to one another.

perspective taking The increasing ability to take on other people's viewpoints.

phase delay The shift to later natural sleeping and waking times that is typically seen among adolescents.

phenotype The observable characteristics of an individual.

phonics approach A form of reading instruction that emphasizes the segments of sounds in words in the learning of reading skills.

physical abuse Non-accidental physical injury as a result of caretaker acts such as shaking, slapping, punching, beating, kicking, biting, or burning.

physical domain of development The domain that includes the biological systems that make up a human being, including the nervous, skeletal, and muscular systems.

physician-assisted suicide A form of active euthanasia in which lethal drugs are provided, but not administered, by a physician.

placenta A short-lived, multifunctional organ that passes nutrients from the mother's blood to the embryo.

plasticity The potential for systematic change within a person. Also, changes in the brain resulting from our interactions with the environment; influenced by age-related change.

popular children Children with high numbers of positive nominations and low negative nominations in a sociometric analysis.

positive youth development (PYD) A positive strengths-based perspective view of adolescence as a life stage involving two overarching hypotheses: the Five Cs and youth–context alignment.

postconventional morality Level 3 of Kohlberg's theory of moral development, in which moral reasoning is guided by universal ethical principles.

postformal thought A quality of thinking beyond Piaget's formal operational stage that includes cognitive flexibility, practicality, and relativism.

postpartum depression (PPD) Clinical depressive symptoms such as apathy, sadness, and detachment associated with late pregnancy and the period of time following the birth of an infant.

postpartum doula A specially trained advisor and helper who provides physical, emotional, and informational support to women and their families during the postpartum period.

postpubescent phase When the majority of the changes associated with puberty have been experienced and are complete.

posture The way a person holds his or her body as a whole.

potential years of life lost An estimate of the average years a person would have lived if he or she had not died.

practical intelligence Common sense needed for real-world situations that require adaptation and basic knowledge.

practice play or **sensorimotor play** A type of play with repetitive actions such as shaking a rattle or clapping hands.

pragmatics The social use of communication.

preconventional morality Level 1 of Kohlberg's theory of moral development, in which moral reasoning is guided by personal rewards and punishments.

prefrontal cortex (PFC) The frontmost part of the frontal lobe that is responsible for complex thought, planning, and problem solving.

preoperational stage Piaget's second stage of cognitive development, in which the child begins to think symbolically; that is, with words.

prepubescent phase When some of the changes associated with puberty are underway, but most have yet to occur.

presbyopia The inability of the eyes to accommodate so that they can focus on objects at a normal reading distance (45–50 cm).

preterm An infant born earlier than their full gestational period, usually less than 37 weeks.

primary emotion An emotion that is present early in life and is most likely innate.

primary sex characteristic A physical characteristic, such as the internal and external genitalia, directly associated with reproduction.

private speech A language process in which children talk to themselves as they attempt to perform a task or solve a problem.

problematic Internet use An excessive preoccupation with Internet use that leads to socio-emotional maladjustment, academic difficulties, and physical health problems.

program theory of aging A theory that aging occurs because of some predetermined internal or external chemical process built into cells that cause deterioration over time.

prosocial behaviour Voluntary behaviour that is intended to benefit another person.

protective factor A positive factor in a child's life that bolsters his or her well-being and likelihood for resilience, such as high self-efficacy, authoritative parenting, and competent and caring friends.

protein-energy malnutrition (PEM) A type of malnutrition in which insufficient food intake results in a significant lack of protein and calories.

proximodistal growth The tendency for growth and development to occur from the inside of the body outward.

proximodistal pattern A pattern of physical growth that proceeds from the centre of the body through the appendages.

psychiatric disorder A mental disorder or mental illness that is a pattern of feelings, thoughts, or behaviours that cause distress or disability.

psychoanalysis A treatment method introduced by Sigmund Freud to relieve mental distress by freeing conflicts from the unconscious, bringing them into conscious awareness so they can be resolved.

psychological control Associated with authoritarian parenting, behaviours that violate and manipulate a child's feelings, thoughts, and attachments to parents.

psychosexual development A Freudian theory in which maturation of personality and sexuality occur as children experience the concentration of libidinal energy from specific body areas.

psychosocial development A set of theories that assume personality is shaped through experience and interactions with the environment throughout the lifespan.

puberty A hormonal process resulting in reproductive competence and related physical development.

pubescent phase When the majority of the changes associated with puberty are occurring.

qualitative data Information in the form of words, pictures, sounds, visual images, or objects.

qualitative interview A research method used to gain an understanding of the way others think about a topic.

quantitative data Information in the form of numbers.

quarter-life crisis The hypothesis proposing that the task of becoming adult is experienced as a personal crisis in the mid-20s.

race A way of categorizing humans that typically focuses on physical traits.

racialized People or communities that are treated poorly or experience violence because of racism or a belief that they are inferior.

rapid-eye-movement (REM) sleep A sleep state during which rapid and random eye movements, intense and irregular brain-wave activity, and dreaming occur.

reaction time The time involved in responding to a stimulus.

receptive language Language that an infant understands but may not be able to produce.

recessive An allele that can only influence the expression of a trait in the absence of a dominant allele.

recognition-primed decision-making A term used by Peter Fadde to describe a proficiency in decision-making based on the ability to quickly recognize the most relevant features of a situation.

reflex An involuntary response to a stimulus.

rejected-aggressive Children who are rejected by peers for their aggressive behaviour.

rejected children Children with high numbers of negative nominations and low positive nominations in a sociometric analysis.

rejected-withdrawn Children who are rejected by peers for their withdrawn behaviour.

relational aggression Subtle harmful acts, such as manipulating, gossiping about, or creating public humiliation for another individual.

relational ambivalence Simultaneous positive and negative feelings about a relationship.

relationship churning An on-off pattern found in some intimate relationships where partners frequently break up and reconcile.

remote grandparents A grandparent–grandchild relationship in which the grandparent(s) are emotionally distant and primarily expect obedience and respect from their grandchildren.

reproductive health A responsible, satisfying, and safe sex life, including the capability to reproduce, and the freedom to decide if, when, and how often to do so.

resilience Positive adjustment in the face of significant risk.

response-focused emotion regulation The use of emotion regulation strategies, such as self-talk, after facing a stimulus.

responsiveness The speed, sensitivity, and quality with which parents attend to the needs of their children. Like demandingness, responsiveness ranges along a continuum, from very low to very high.

reversibility The ability to understand that tangible objects can return to their original form.

rheumatoid arthritis A type of arthritis classified as an autoimmune disease in which the body's own immune system causes an inflammation of tissue around joints.

risk factor A negative factor in a child's life that endangers his or her well-being and likelihood for resilience, such as insecure attachment to a primary caregiver, parental death, and neighbourhood violence.

rite of passage A ritual that symbolizes the transition from one period of the lifespan to another.

role confusion An adolescent's inability to define an identity, resulting in a lack of direction and focus, according to Erikson.

rough-and-tumble play A form of physical play, such as wrestling, tumbling, and running.

sandwich generation A group of caregivers, commonly between ages 40 and 50, who simultaneously provide care for their children and for their parents.

sarcopenia The process of skeletal muscle loss due to aging.

scaffolding The process of assisting a less experienced individual through complex tasks by providing supports, which may be verbal or physical.

schema An organized pattern of thinking that guides our experience in the world.

schemes Mental structures that help us organize and process information.

scientific community A group of people who sustain the production of scientific knowledge through collective attitudes, rules, and conventions.

scientific method The specific procedure researchers use to ask and explore scientific questions in a way that makes connections between observations and leads to understanding.

secondary emotion An emotion that emerges with the help of certain cognitive and social developments.

secondary sex characteristic A physical characteristic associated with sex hormones but not directly associated with reproduction.

second-language learning The process of learning another, nonnative language.

secure attachment An attachment style characterized by flexible proximity between parent and infant and positive reunion behaviour.

secure/autonomous An attachment category in which adolescents display the ability to recognize both the positive and negative aspects of childhood attachment figures.

selection The process of identifying goals that are reasonable and reachable given a person's capabilities.

selective attention The ability to attend to a particular item in the environment while inhibiting other distracting stimuli.

selective optimization with compensation (SOC) A theory of successful aging that identifies three processes people use to maximize gains and minimize losses in response to aging.

self-awareness The ability to recognize oneself as a separate being.

self-concept One's multidimensional impression of one's own personality, of the attributes, abilities, and attitudes that define one's self.

self-conscious emotions Emotions that involve internal and external evaluations of the self.

self-efficacy One's perceived ability to be successful in accomplishing specific goals.

self-esteem Judgements of worth that children make about themselves and the feelings that those judgements elicit.

self-regulation The ability to deliberately change one's behaviour and emotion.

senescence A gradual age-related decline in physical systems.

sensation Physical reception of stimulation.

sensitive period An interval of heightened plasticity, when environmental influences are most efficient at affecting an organism's development.

sensorimotor stage Piaget's first stage of cognitive development, in which infants develop from reflex-driven organisms to more complex and symbolic thinkers.

sensorineural hearing loss Hearing loss resulting from loss of hair cells on the basilar membrane of the inner ear.

sensory memory The ability to briefly store sensory information so that it may be processed.

separateness A dimension of self in which individuals in a relationship maintain their boundaries.

separation The first stage marking the transition to adulthood involving the distancing of an adolescent from the earlier social context physically and/or psychologically.

separation anxiety A set of seeking and distress behaviours that occur when the primary caregiver is removed from the immediate environment of the infant/child.

seriation The ability to sort objects using a rule that determines an increasing magnitude of one or more dimensions.

sex chromosome The 23rd chromosome pair containing the genes that determine biological sex characteristics of females (XX) and males (XY).

sex differences Biologically based differences between sexes.

sex-linked gene A gene located on one of the sex chromosomes (X or Y).

sexual abuse The involvement of children and adolescents in sexual activities that they do not understand and for which they cannot give informed consent.

sexually active life expectancy The number of years remaining for a person to be sexually active.

shame A feeling that the whole self is a failure or bad, which can lead to defensiveness and social withdrawal.

sibling rivalry The competitive quality found in some sibling relationships.

slow-to-warm-up temperament The temperament of a child with low activity level who adjusts to new situations over time.

small for gestational age (SGA) A birth weight of less than 2.5 kg for an infant with a gestational age that is normal (37+ weeks).

social and emotional learning (SEL) Educational programs seeking to foster the development of five non-subject matter competencies: self-awareness, self-management, social awareness, relationship skills, and responsible decision-making.

social comparison The process of learning about one's abilities and characteristics by observing how they compare with others'.

social convoy A social support network to which an individual remains connected throughout the lifespan.

socialization The process of acquiring the skills needed to adapt behaviours and expectations to fit the norms of a given culture.

social network A group of people who identify themselves as connected because of some similar demographic such as religion, age, ethnicity, or common interest, and who interact regularly.

social networking site (SNS) An Internet-based community in which people can join and connect with others, share information, and interact socially online.

social referencing Using a caregiver's emotional cues to help understand an uncertain or ambiguous event or stimulus.

social smile In infancy, the first facial expression of pleasure, enabled by neurophysiological maturation and an increasing readiness for social interactions with caregivers.

socialization The process of acquiring the skills needed to adapt behaviours and expectations to fit the norms of a given culture.

socio-economic status (SES) The combination of a person's income, education, and occupation relative to others.

socio-emotional domain of development The domain that includes the social, cultural, and emotional components of development, such as the family, society, schools, and other social institutions.

socio-emotional selectivity theory (SST) A model of aging that focuses on diminishing social networks, leading to positive emotional regulation based on the perception that there is limited time to live.

sociometric measurement A type of measurement of interpersonal relationships through social group survey.

somatic complaints Physical problems without physiological cause.

specific learning disorder A specific difficulty with reading, writing, or math that is indicated when academic functioning is substantially below what is expected for age, IQ, and schooling.

sperm cell A male gamete containing 22 autosomes and 1 sex (X or Y) chromosome.

spermarche (pronounced *sper-mär-kē*) The first ejaculation of sperm by an adolescent male.

spermatogenesis The initial maturation of sperm into viable sperm cells with the capability of fertilization.

stage theory A theory that rests on the assumption that development is discontinuous, with new features of development emerging at each distinct stage.

stagnation Remaining focused on day-to-day self-centred activities and interests; a failure to shift one's focus and investment to future- and other-oriented goals.

status phase The second phase in a four-phase model of early romantic relationships in which crowd and status influence how an adolescent couple develops.

Strange Situation A means of categorizing attachment styles, consisting of a series of episodes in which a mother and her child are observed together, separated, and reunited in the presence of a stranger.

stranger anxiety Distressed avoidance of a novel individual.

strategy An effortful plan deliberately used to solve a specific problem.

stress response A change in the physiological functioning of the body's systems when it perceives an external threat or attack.

subjective well-being A person's perception of his or her general sense of psychological satisfaction.

substance use disorder A mental disorder that occurs when substance use interferes with a person's daily life or functioning.

sudden infant death syndrome (SIDS) The sudden and unexplained death, usually during sleep, of a seemingly healthy infant younger than 1 year of age.

suicidal ideation A continued obsession with thoughts of suicide, including the methods, time, and place of the suicide.

superego One of three components of the mind according to Freud; the superego represents the internalized rules for socially appropriate behaviour.

symbolic function The first substage of the preoperational period, during which the ability to use language gives children a new way of thinking about the world.

symbolic play A form of play that begins around 3 years of age in which children use objects as symbols to stand for something else.

sympathy Feelings of pity for another person's misfortune.

synapse The space between adjoining neurons, across which electrical impulses are sent from the axon of one neuron to the dendrite of another.

synaptic pruning The process by which the brain removes unused synapses through redirecting nutrition, cell injury, and cell death.

synchrony The reciprocal and mutually rewarding qualities of an infant–caregiver attachment relationship.

teen dating violence Physical assault by a boyfriend or girlfriend against his or her romantic partner that may include psychological and sexual violence.

telegraphic speech The creation of short phrases that convey meaning but lack some of the parts of speech that are necessary for a full and complete sentence.

temperament Biologically based individual differences in how one responds to the environment that influence emotions, physical activity level, and attention.

teratogen An environmental agent that can adversely affect prenatal development and can have long-lasting effects on subsequent development.

testosterone An androgenic sex hormone produced by the gonads (but in much lower levels in females) that is responsible for primary and secondary sex characteristics.

theory A coherent set of statements that explains an observation or set of observations in relation to one another.

theory of mind The ability to understand that others have mental states and that their thoughts and knowledge differ from one's own.

theory of multiple intelligences A theory of intelligence advanced by Howard Gardner suggesting the existence of at least eight distinct intelligences.

third variable A confounding variable influencing the correlation between variables, or a variable having an unintended impact on the relationship between the independent and dependent variables.

time outs A disciplinary measure in which the child is removed from reinforcing stimuli, events, or conditions for a short period of time.

tip-of-the-tongue phenomenon A feeling you know a piece of information, but you are unable to recall it.

top-down processing Forming perceptions beginning with a more general idea working toward more detailed information.

toxin A harmful substance that causes adverse effects.

transition The second stage marking the transition where the adolescent learns about how to be an adult.

transitivity The logical rule that says, if A is greater than B and B is greater than C, then A is greater than C.

trial-and-error A type of elementary problem solving in which the solver attempts different immediate solutions with no systematic plan.

triangular theory of love Sternberg's (1997) theory suggesting that various types of love reflect different combinations of passion, intimacy, and commitment.

triarchic theory of successful intelligence A theory of intelligence advanced by Robert Sternberg emphasizing three key components: analytical, practical, and creative.

trust versus mistrust stage Erikson's first stage of psychosocial development is resolved when the individual develops a sense of trust in the environment to meet his or her needs.

tween A term used in the popular media to describe a preadolescent, or a young person who shares characteristics of both children and teenagers.

ultrasound The use of high-frequency sound waves to visualize the embryo or fetus within the uterus.

umbilical cord A vein-filled cord that connects the embryo to the placenta.

unconditioned response (UR) A reaction that is reliably produced by an unconditioned stimulus.

unconditioned stimulus (US) Something that reliably produces a naturally occurring reaction.

unintentional injury Any type of physical trauma that is determined to have been caused by circumstances other than abuse or maltreatment.

universality The concept that everything dies and that death is inevitable.

vaccine A substance that is usually injected into a person to improve immunity against a particular disease.

vaccine hesitancy A refusal or a delay in immunization participation caused by concerns about vaccines.

vascular dementia A common dementia caused by restricted supply of blood to the brain.

very low birth weight (VLBW) A birth weight of less than 1,500 g.

visual cliff A method used to examine infant depth perception using a patterned floor and a pane of Plexiglas over a deep drop. When infants willingly crawl over the Plexiglas, it is assumed they do not perceive the depth.

vitality The capacity to live.

vocabulary spurt or **naming explosion** The rapid expansion of vocabulary that children experience during early childhood.

wear and tear theory A theory that suggests the human body ages as a result of use, overuse, and environmental stressors.

Wechsler Intelligence Scales Popular psychometric test purporting to measure the global capacity to think rationally.

white matter The spongy tissue that connects various areas of the brain to one another as well as to parts of the spinal cord.

whole-language approach A form of reading instruction that emphasizes communication over particular elements of reading and writing, such as spelling or sounds.

wisdom The accumulation of knowledge and experience, along with personal insight and common sense.

working (short-term) memory The ability to keep a small amount of information (7 ± 2 items) in an active, ready-to-use state for a short time.

world view The lens or overall perspective an individual uses to see and interpret the world; a personal philosophy of life.

young adulthood A stage of the lifespan when the adult is committed to one or more adult social roles, including employee, homeowner, committed partner, and parent.

young offender A person under the age of 18 charged with a criminal offence.

young-old Adults in their later years, traditionally between the ages of 60 and 75, who are still healthy, active, and independent.

zone of proximal development (ZPD) Vygotsky's term for the range of tasks that a person cannot accomplish independently but that can be done with the assistance of a person with more experience or more advanced cognitive ability.

zygote A fertilized ovum, in which the male and female gametes have united in one cell.

Index